Third Edition

PROJECT MANAGEMENT

ACHIEVING COMPETITIVE ADVANTAGE

Global Edition

Jeffrey K. Pinto
Pennsylvania State University

PEARSON

Boston   Columbus   Indianapolis   New York   San Francisco   Upper Saddle River
Amsterdam   Cape Town   Dubai   London   Madrid   Milan   Munich   Paris   Montreal   Toronto
Delhi   Mexico City   São Paulo   Sydney   Hong Kong   Seoul   Singapore   Taipei   Tokyo

Editor in Chief: Donna Battista
Senior Acquisitions Editor: Chuck Synovec
Senior Acquisitions Editor, Global Edition: Steven Jackson
Editorial Project Manager: Mary Kate Murray
Editorial Assistant: Ashlee Bradbury
Director of Marketing: Maggie Moylan
Senior Marketing Manager: Jami Minard
Marketing Manager, International: Dean Erasmus

Production Project Manager: Clara Bartunek
Creative Art Director: Jayne Conte
Cover Designer: Jodi Notowitz
Manager, Rights and Permissions: Michael Joyce
Cover Art: © Olena Timashova
Media Project Manager: John Cassar
Media Editor: James Bateman

Pearson Education Limited
Edinburgh Gate
Harlow
Essex CM20 2JE
England

and Associated Companies throughout the world

Visit us on the World Wide Web at:
www.pearson.com/uk

© Pearson Education Limited 2013

British Library Cataloguing-in-Publication Data
A catalogue record for this book is available from the British Library

10 9 8 7 6 5 4 3

15 14 13

Typeset in 10/12 Palatino by Integra Software Services, Ltd.

Printed and bound by Courier/Kendallville in United States of America

The publisher's policy is to use paper manufactured from sustainable forests.

ISBN-10: 0-273-76742-9
ISBN-13: 978-0-273-76742-8

To Mary Beth, my wife, with the most profound thanks and love for her unwavering support. And, to our children, Emily, AJ, and Joseph—three "projects" that are definitely over budget but that are performing far better than I could have hoped!

BRIEF CONTENTS

CONTENTS

PREFACE

Project management has become central to operations in industries as diverse as construction and information technology, architecture and hospitality, and engineering and new product development; therefore, this text simultaneously embraces the general principles of project management while addressing specific examples across the wide assortment of its applications. This text approaches each chapter from the perspective of both the material that is general to all disciplines and project types and that which is more specific to alternative forms of projects. One way this is accomplished is through the use of specific, discipline-based examples to illustrate general principles as well as the inclusion of cases and Project Profiles that focus on more specific topics (e.g., Chapter 5's treatment of IT "death march" projects).

Students in project management classes come from a wide and diverse cross section of university majors and career tracks. Schools of health, business, architecture, engineering, information systems, and hospitality are all adding project management courses to their catalogs in response to the demands from organizations and professional groups that see their value for students' future careers. Why has project management become a discipline of such tremendous interest and application? The simple truth is that we live in a "projectized" world. Everywhere we look we see people engaged in project management. In fact, project management has become an integral part of practically every firm's business model.

This text takes a holistic, integrated approach to managing projects, exploring both technical and managerial challenges. It not only emphasizes individual project execution, but also provides a strategic perspective, demonstrating the means with which to manage projects at both the program and portfolio levels.

At one time, project management was almost exclusively the property of civil and construction engineering programs where it was taught in a highly quantitative, technical manner. "Master the science of project management," we once argued, "and the 'art' of project management will be equally clear to you." Project management today is a complex, "management" challenge requiring not only technical skills but a broad-based set of people skills as well. Project management has become the management of technology, people, culture, stakeholders, and other diverse elements necessary to successfully complete a project. It requires knowledge of leadership, team building, conflict resolution, negotiation, and influence in equal measure with the traditional, technical skill set. Thus, this textbook broadens our focus beyond the traditional project management activities of planning and scheduling, project control, and termination, to a more general, inclusive, and, hence, more valuable perspective of the project management process.

WHAT'S NEW IN THE THIRD EDITION?

New Features

- Project "death marches"
- Earned Schedule
- MS Project 2010 step-by-step tutorials
- Project scheduling under uncertainty—probability of project completion
- New Project Managers in Practice profiles
- Function point IT project cost estimation
- Fast-tracking and other options for accelerating projects
- Updated problems in chapters
- New project "classic" cases
- New Project Management Research in Brief: "Delusion and Deception" Taking Place in Large Infrastructure Projects
- All MS Project examples and screen captures updated to MS Project 2010
- Quarterly updates for all book adopters on latest cases and examples in project management

Updated Project Profiles:

- *Chapter 1 Introduction: Why Project Management?*
  - Chilean Miners Rescue
  - Projects in China

OUR FOCUS

This textbook employs a managerial, business-oriented approach to the management of projects. Thus we have integrated Project Profiles into the text.

- *Project Profiles*—Each chapter contains one or more Project Profiles that highlight current examples of project management in action. Some of the profiles reflect on significant achievements; others detail famous (and not-so-famous) examples of project failures. Because they cover diverse ground (IT projects, construction, new product development, and so forth), there should be at least one profile per chapter that is meaningful to the class's focus.

The book blends project management within the context of the operations of any successful organization, whether publicly held, private, or not-for-profit. We illustrate this through the use of end-of-chapter cases.

- *Cases*—At the end of each chapter are some final cases that take specific examples of the material covered in the chapter and apply them in the alternate format of case studies. Some of the cases are fictitious, but the majority of them are based on real situations, even where aliases mask the real names of organizations. These cases include discussion questions that can be used either for homework or to facilitate classroom discussions.

Further, we explore both the challenges in the management of individual projects as well as broadening out this context to include strategic, portfolio-level concepts. To do this, we ask students to develop a project plan using MS Project 2010.

- *Integrated Project Exercises*—Many of the chapters include an end-of-chapter feature that is unique to this text: the opportunity to develop a detailed project plan. A very beneficial exercise in project management classes is to require students, either in teams or individually, to learn the mechanics of developing a detailed and comprehensive project plan, including scope, scheduling, risk assessment, budgeting and cost estimation, and so forth. The Integrated Project exercises afford students the opportunity to develop such a plan by assigning these activities and providing a detailed example of a completed example (ABCups, Inc.) in each chapter. Thus, students are assigned their project planning activities and have a template that helps them complete these exercises.

And finally, we have integrated the standards set forth by the world's largest governing body for project management. The Project Management Institute (PMI) created the Project Management Body of Knowledge (PMBOK), which is generally regarded as one of the most comprehensive frameworks for identifying the critical knowledge areas that project managers must understand if they are to master their discipline. The PMBOK has become the basis for the Project Management Professional (PMP) certification offered by PMI for professional project managers.

- *Integration with the PMBOK*—As a means to demonstrate the coverage of the critical PMBOK elements, readers will find that the chapters in this text identify and cross-list the corresponding knowledge areas from the PMBOK. Further, all terms (including the Glossary) are taken directly from the most recent edition of the PMBOK.
- *Inclusion of Sample PMP Certification Exam Questions*—The Project Management Professional (PMP) certification represents the highest standard of professional qualification for a practicing project manager and is administered by the Project Management Institute. As of the beginning of 2012, there were more than 400,000 PMPs worldwide. In order to attain PMP certification, it is necessary for candidates to undergo a comprehensive exam that tests their knowledge of all components of the PMBOK. This text includes a set of sample PMP certification exam questions at the end of most of the chapters, in order to give readers an idea of the types of questions typically asked on the exam and how those topics are treated in this book.

OTHER POINTS OF DISTINCTION

The textbook places special emphasis on blending current theory, practice, research, and case studies in such a manner that readers are given a multiple perspective exposure to the project management process. A number of in-chapter features are designed to enhance student learning, including:

- *MS Project Exercises*—An additional feature of the text is the inclusion at the end of each chapter of some sample problems or activities that require students to generate MS Project output files. For example, in the chapter on scheduling, students must create an MS Project Gantt chart and network diagram. Likewise, other reports can be assigned to help students become minimally adept at interacting with this program. It is not the purpose of this text to fully develop these skills but rather to plant the seeds for future application.
- *Research in Brief*—A unique feature of this text is to include short (usually one-page) text boxes that highlight the results of current research on the topics of interest. Students often find it useful to read about actual studies that highlight the text material and provide additional information that expands their learning. Although not every chapter includes a "Research in Brief" box, most have one and, in some cases, two examples of this feature.
- *Project Managers in Practice*—An addition to this text is the inclusion of several short profiles of real, practicing project managers from a variety of corporate and project settings. These profiles have been added to give students a sense of the types of real-world challenges project managers routinely face, the wide range of projects they are called to manage, and the satisfactions and career opportunities available to students interested in pursuing project management as a career.
- *Internet Exercises*—Each chapter contains a set of Internet exercises that require students to search the Web for key information, access course readings on the companion Web site supporting the

text, and perform other activities that lead to student learning through outside-of-class, hands-on activities. Internet exercises are a useful supplement, particularly in the area of project management, because so much is available on the World Wide Web relating to projects, including cases, news releases, and Internet-based tools for analyzing project activities.

FOR INSTRUCTORS

The following supplements are available to adopting instructors:

Instructor's Resource Center

Register.Redeem.Login, www.pearsonglobaleditions.com/pinto, is where instructors can access a variety of print, media, and presentation resources that are available with this text in downloadable, digital format.

Need Help?

Our dedicated Technical Support team is ready to assist instructors with questions about the media supplements that accompany this text. Visit http://247pearsoned.custhelp.com/ for answers to frequently asked questions and toll-free user support phone numbers. The following supplements are available to adopting instructors. Detailed descriptions of the following supplements are provided in the Instructor's Resource Center:

Instructor's Solutions Manual—Prepared by Jeffrey K. Pinto of Pennsylvania State University. The Instructor's Solutions Manual contains chapter summaries and suggested answers to all the end-of-chapter questions. It is available for download at www.pearsonglobaleditions.com/pinto.

Test Item File—Prepared by Professor Geoff Willis of the University of Central Oklahoma. The Test Item File contains true/false questions, fill-in-the-blank questions, multiple-choice questions, and short-answer/essay questions. It is available for download at www.pearsonglobaleditions.com/pinto.

TestGen— Pearson Education's test-generating software is available from www.pearsonglobaleditions.com/pinto. The software is PC/MAC compatible and preloaded with all of the Test Item File questions. You can manually or randomly view test questions and drag and drop to create a test. You can add or modify test-bank questions as needed.

Learning Management Systems—Our TestGens are converted for use in BlackBoard and WebCT. These conversions can be found in the Instructor's Resource Center. Conversions to D2L or Angel can be requested through your local Pearson Sales Representative.

PowerPoint slides—Prepared by Dana Johnson of Michigan Technological University. The PowerPoint slides provide the instructor with individual lecture outlines to accompany the text. The slides include many of the figures and tables from the text. These lecture notes can be used as is or professors can easily modify them to reflect specific presentation needs. They are available for download at www.pearsonglobaleditions.com/pinto.

Project Management Simulation Game—Created by Ken Klassen (Brock University) and Keith Willoughby (OR Consultant), is available for download at www.pearsonglobaleditions.com/pinto. It is used to provide an enjoyable and educational introduction to the topic of project management. It may also be used as a stand-alone exercise to teach about uncertainty. In addition to Student Notes and Instructor Notes (both in Word) for the game, an Excel spreadsheet is provided to track the progress of the teams. This eases administration of this in-class game and enhances the experience for the students.

CourseSmart—CourseSmart eTextbooks were developed for students looking to save on required or recommended textbooks. Students simply select their eText by title or author and purchase immediate access to the content for the duration of the course using any major credit card. With a CourseSmart eText, students can search for specific keywords or page numbers, take notes online, print out reading assignments that incorporate lecture notes, and bookmark important passages for later review. For more information or to purchase a CourseSmart eTextbook, visit www.coursesmart.co.uk.

FOR STUDENTS

The Companion Website (www.pearsonglobaleditions.com/pinto) contains valuable resources for both students and professors, including:

- *Self-Study Quizzes*—These quizzes contain a broad assortment of questions, which include multiple-choice, true/false, essay, and discussion questions. The quizzes are graded and can be transmitted to the instructor or serve as practice exams.
- *Student Survey*—This survey offers students an opportunity to voice their opinions about this book.

ACKNOWLEDGMENTS

In acknowledging the contributions of past and present colleagues to the creation of this text, I must first convey my deepest thanks and appreciation for the 30-year association with my original mentor, Dr. Dennis Slevin of the University of Pittsburgh's Katz Graduate School of Business. My collaboration with Denny on numerous projects has been fruitful and extremely gratifying, both professionally and personally. In addition, Dr. David Cleland's friendship and partnership in several ventures has been a great source of satisfaction through the years. Additional mentors and colleagues who have strongly influenced my thinking include Samuel Mantel, Jr., Peter W. G. Morris, Rodney Turner, Erik Larson, David Frame, Francis Hartman, Jonas Soderlund, Young Kwak, Rolf Lundin, Lynn Crawford, Graham Winch, Terry Williams, Francis Webster, Terry Cooke-Davies, Hans Thamhain, and Karlos Artto. Each of these individuals has had a profound impact on the manner in which I view, study, and write about project management.

Over the years, I have also been fortunate to develop friendships with some professional project managers whose work I admire enormously. They are genuine examples of the best type of project manager: one who makes it all seem effortless while consistently performing minor miracles. In particular, I wish to thank Mike Brown of Rolls-Royce for his friendship and example. I would also like to thank friends and colleagues from the Project Management Institute, including Lew Gedansky, Harry Stephanou, and Eva Goldman, for their support for and impact on this work.

I am indebted to the reviewers of this text whose numerous suggestions and critiques have been an invaluable aid in shaping its content. Among them, I would like to especially thank the following:

Ravi Behara—George Mason University

Jeffrey L. Brewer—Purdue University

Dennis Cioffi—George Washington University

David Clapp—Florida Institute of Technology

Bruce DeRuntz—Southern Illinois University at Carbondale

Ike Ehie—Kansas State University

Michael H. Ensby—Clarkson University

Lynn Fish—Canisius College

Linda Fried—University of Colorado, Denver

Mario Guimaraes—Kennesaw State University

Richard Gunther—California State University, Northridge

Kwasi-Amoako Gyampah—University of North Carolina, Greensboro

Gary Hackbarth—Iowa State University

Mamoon M. Hammad—George Washington University

Scott Robert Homan—Purdue University

John Hoxmeier—Colorado State University

Alex Hutchins—ITT Technical Institute

Robert Key—University of Phoenix

Homayoun Khamooshi—George Washington University

Dennis Krumwiede—Idaho State University

George Mechling—Western Carolina University

Julia Miyaoka—San Francisco State University

LaWanda Morant—ITT Technical Institute

Robert Morris—Florida State College at Jacksonville

Kenneth E. Murphy—Willamette University

John Nazemetz—Oklahoma State University

Patrick Penfield—Syracuse University

Ronald Price—ITT Techincal Institute

Ronny Richardson—Southern Polytechnic State University

John Sherlock—Iona College

Gregory Shreve—Kent State University

Randall G. Sleeth—Virginia Commonwealth University

Kimberlee Snyder—Winona State University

Jeff Trailer—California State University, Chico

Leo Trudel—University of Maine

Oya Tukel—Cleveland State University

Darien Unger—Howard University

Stephen Whitehead—Hilbert College

Pearson Education wishes to acknowledge and thank the following people on their work on the Global Edition:

Contributors

Asunur Cezar, Department of Business Administration, Tobb University of Economics and Technology, Turkey

Selvi Kannan, School Of Management and Information Systems, Victoria University, Australia

Saira Karim, Project Manager PMP, MCMI, Project Arab Gulf

Jon and Diane Sutherland, United Kingdom

Renosh Thomas, PreSales and Project Manager, Lightspeed Communications

Clare Walsh, Business School, Bahrain Polytechnic, Kingdom of Bahrain

Reviewers

Koh Cheng Boon, Nanyang Technological University, Nanyang Business School, Singapore

Professor Albert PC Chan, PhD, Professor of the Department of Building and Real Estate, Faculty of Construction and Environment, Hong Kong Polytechnic University, Hong Kong

T. Tolgay Kizilelma, Dokuz Eylul University, Turkey

Dr. Qing Li, Hong Kong University of Science and Technology, Hong Kong

Sa'Ed M. Salhieh, Ph.D. Industrial Engineering Department, Faculty of Engineering, Alfaisal University, Riydh, Saudi Arabia

Dr. Danielle L Talbot, Coventry University, United Kingdom

I would also like to thank my colleagues in the Samuel Black School of Business at Penn State, the Behrend College. Additionally, Christie Quick helped prepare the Instructor's Resource Manual and Student Aids, for which I thank her. Extra-special thanks go to Jeanette Case for her help in preparing the final manuscript. I am especially indebted to Ray Venkataraman, who accuracy checked the Instructor's Resource Manual. I am very grateful for his time and effort, and any errors that may remain are entirely my own.

In developing the cases for this edition of the textbook, I was truly fortunate to develop wonderful professional relationships with a number of individuals. Andrea Finger and Kathleen Prihoda of Disney were wonderfully helpful and made time in their busy schedules to assist me in developing the Expedition Everest case for this text. Stephanie Smith, Mohammed Al-Sadiq, Bill Mowery, Mike Brown, Julia Sweet, and Kevin O'Donnell provided me with invaluable information on their job responsibilities and what it takes to be a successful project manager.

Finally, I wish to extend my sincere thanks to the people at Pearson for their support for the text during its development, including Chuck Synovec, editor, and Mary Kate Murray, project manager. I reserve my deepest thanks for the efforts of Trish Nealon and Annie Puciloski, whose developmental editing and critiques were honest and right on target ("Faithful are the wounds of a friend," Proverbs 27:6). I would also like to thank other members of the Pearson editorial, production, and marketing staffs, including Jami Minard, Clara Bartunek, and Anand Natarajan.

FEEDBACK

If you have questions related to this product, please contact our customer service department online at http://247pearsoned.custhelp.com.

Finally, it is important to reflect on an additional salient issue as you begin your study of project management: *Most of you will be running a project long before you are given wider management responsibilities in your organizations.* Successful project managers are the lifeblood of organizations and bear the imprint of the fast track. I wish you great success!

Jeffrey K. Pinto, Ph.D
Andrew Morrow and Elizabeth Lee Black Chair
Management of Technology
Samuel Black School of Business
Penn State, the Behrend College
jkp4@psu.edu

1

Introduction
Why Project Management?

Chapter Outline

Chapter Objectives

After completing this chapter you should be able to:

1. Understand why project management is becoming such a powerful and popular practice in business.
2. Recognize the basic properties of projects, including their definition.
3. Understand why effective project management is such a challenge.
4. Differentiate between project management practices and more traditional, process-oriented business functions.
5. Recognize the key motivators that are pushing companies to adopt project management practices.
6. Understand and explain the project life cycle, its stages, and the activities that typically occur at each stage in the project.
7. Understand the concept of project "success," including various definitions of success, as well as the alternative models of success.

8. Understand the purpose of project management maturity models and the process of benchmarking in organizations.

9. Identify the relevant maturity stages that organizations go through to become proficient in their use of project management techniques.

PROJECT MANAGEMENT BODY OF KNOWLEDGE CORE CONCEPTS COVERED IN THIS CHAPTER

1. Definition of a Project (PMBoK sec. 1.2)

2. Definition of Project Management (PMBoK sec. 1.3)

3. Relationship to Other Management Disciplines (PMBoK sec. 1.4)

4. Project Phases and the Project Life Cycle (PMBoK sec. 2.1)

The world acquires value only through its extremes and endures only through moderation; extremists make the world great, the moderates give it stability.[1]

PROJECT PROFILE

Case—Rescue of Chilean Miners

On October 13, 2010, Foreman Luiz Urzua stepped out of the rescue capsule to thunderous applause and cries of "Viva, Chile!"; he was the last of 33 miners rescued after spending 70 days trapped beneath 2,000 feet of earth and rock. Following a catastrophic collapse, the miners were trapped in the lower shafts of the mine, initially without contact with the surface, leaving the world in suspense as to their fate. Their discovery and ultimate rescue are a story of courage, resourcefulness, and ultimately, one of the most successful projects in recent times.

The work crew of the San Jose copper and gold mine near Copiapo, in northern Chile, were in the middle of their shift when suddenly, on August 5, 2010, the earth shook and large portions of the mine tunnels collapsed, trapping 33 miners in a "workshop," in a lower gallery of the mine. Though they were temporarily safe, they were nearly a half mile below the surface, with no power and food for two days. Worse, they had no means of communicating with the surface, so their fate remained a mystery to the company and their families. Under these conditions, their main goal was simple survival, conserving and stretching out meager food supplies for 17 days, until the first drilling probe arrived, punching a hole in the ceiling of the shaft where they were trapped. Once they had established contact with the surface and provided details of their condition, a massive rescue operation was conceived and undertaken.

The first challenge was simply keeping the miners alive. The earliest supply deliveries down the narrow communication shaft included quantities of food and water, oxygen, medicine, clothing, and necessities for survival as well as materials to help the miners pass their time. While groups worked to keep up the miners' spirits, communicating daily and passing along messages from families, other project teams were formed to begin developing a plan to rescue the men.

The challenges were severe. Among the significant questions that demanded practical and immediate answers were:

1. How do we locate the miners?
2. How quickly can we drill relief shafts to their location?
3. How do we bring them up safely?

The mine tunnels had experienced such damage in the collapse that simply digging the miners out would have taken several months. A full-scale rescue operation was conceived to extract the miners as quickly as possible. The U.S.-Chilean company Geotec Boyles Brothers, a subsidiary of Layne Christensen Company, assembled the critical resources from around the world. In western Pennsylvania, two companies that were experienced in mine collapses in the South American region were brought into the project. They had UPS ship a specialty drill, capable of creating wide-diameter shafts, large enough to fit men without collapsing. The drill arrived within

48 hours, free of charge. In all, UPS shipped more than 50,000 pounds of specialty equipment to the drilling and rescue site. The design of the rescue pod was the work of a NASA engineer, Clinton Cragg, who drew on his experience as a former submarine captain in the Navy and directed a team of 20 to conceive of and develop a means to carry the miners one at a time to the surface.

Doctors from NASA and U.S. submarine experts arrived at the mine site in mid-August, to assess the psychological state of the miners. Using their expertise in the physical and mental pressures of dealing with extended isolation, they worked with local officials to develop an exercise regimen and a set of chores for the workers in order to give them a sense of structure and responsibilities. The miners knew that help was being assembled, but they had no notion of the technical challenges of making each element in the rescue succeed. Nevertheless, with contact firmly established with the surface through the original contact drill shaft, the miners now began receiving news, updates from the surface, and a variety of gifts to ease the tedium of waiting.

The United States also provided an expert driller, Jeff Hart, who was called from Afghanistan, where he was helping American forces find water at forward operating bases, to man the specialty drilling machine. The 40-year-old drilled for 33 straight days, through tough conditions, to reach the men trapped at the mine floor. A total of three drilling rigs were erected and began drilling relief shafts from different directions. By September 17, Hart's drill (referred to as "Plan B") reached the miners, though the diameter of the shaft was only 5 inches. It would take a few weeks to ream the shaft with progressively wider drill bits to the final 25-inch diameter necessary to support the rescue capsules being constructed. Nevertheless, the rescue team was exuberant over the speed with which the shaft reached the trapped miners. "This success required the extra special knowledge and skills only our team could provide," said Dave Singleton, water resource division president for Layne Christensen. "Had Layne and Geotec not been there, it probably would have taken until Christmas for 'Plan A' or 'Plan C' to break through," Singleton noted. "We cut more than two months from the original estimate."

The first rescue capsule, named Phoenix, arrived at the site on September 23, with two more under construction and due to be shipped in two weeks. The Phoenix capsule resembled a specially designed cylindrical tube. It was 13 feet long and weighed 924 pounds with an interior width of 22 inches. It was equipped with oxygen and a harness to keep occupants upright, communication equipment, and retractable wheels. The idea was for the capsule to be narrow enough to be lowered into the rescue shaft but wide enough for one person at a time to be fitted inside and brought back to the surface. To ensure that all 33 miners would fit into the Phoenix, they were put on special liquid diets and given an exercise regimen to follow while waiting for the final preparations to be made.

Hugo Infante/Chilean Government/UPI/Newscom

FIGURE 1.1   Phoenix Escape Capsule for Chilean Miner Rescue

Source: www.geekologie.com/2010/10/cramped_the_chilean_mine_rescu.php

(continued)

Finally, after extensive tests, the surface team decided that the shaft was safe enough to support the rescue efforts and lowered the first Phoenix capsule into the hole. In two successive trips, the capsule carried down a paramedic and rescue expert who volunteered to descend into the mine to coordinate the removal of the miners. The first rescued miner broke the surface just after midnight on October 13 following a 15-minute ride in the capsule. A little more than 22 hours later, the shift manager, Urzua, was brought out of the mine, ending a tense and stressful rescue project.

The rescue operation of the Chilean miners was one of the most successful emergency projects in recent memory. It highlighted the ability of people to work together, marshal resources, gather support, and use innovative technologies in a humanitarian effort that truly captured the imagination of the world. The challenges that had to be overcome were significant: first, the technical problems associated with simply finding and making contact with survivors; second, devising a means to recover the men safely; third, undertaking special steps to ensure the miners' mental and physical health remained strong; and finally, requiring all parties to develop and rely on radical technologies that had never been used before. In all these challenges, the rescue team performed wonders, recovering and restoring to their families all 33 trapped miners. On November 7, just one month after the rescue, one of the miners, Edison Pena, realized his own personal dream: running in and completing the New York City marathon. Quite an achievement for a man who had just spent more than two months buried a half mile below the surface of the earth![2]

INTRODUCTION

Projects are one of the principal means by which we change our world. Whether the goal is to split the atom, tunnel under the English Channel, introduce Windows 7, or plan the next Olympic Games in London, the means through which to achieve these challenges remains the same: project management. Project management has become one of the most popular tools for organizations, both public and private, to improve internal operations, respond rapidly to external opportunities, achieve technological breakthroughs, streamline new product development, and more robustly manage the challenges arising from the business environment. Consider what Tom Peters, best-selling author and management consultant, has to say about project management and its place in business: "Projects, rather than repetitive tasks, are now the basis for most value-added in business."[3] Project management has become a critical component of successful business operations in worldwide organizations.

One of the key features of modern business is the nature of the opportunities and threats posed by external events. As never before, companies face international competition and the need to pursue commercial opportunities rapidly. They must modify and introduce products constantly, respond to customers as fast as possible, and maintain competitive cost and operating levels. Does performing all these tasks seem impossible? At one time, it was. Conventional wisdom held that a company could compete using a low-cost strategy *or* as a product innovator *or* with a focus on customer service. In short, we had to pick our competitive niches and concede others their claim to market share. In the 1990s, however, everything turned upside down. Companies such as General Electric, Apple, Ericksson, Boeing, and Oracle became increasingly effective at realizing all of these goals rather than settling for just one. These companies seemed to be successful in every aspect of the competitive model: They were fast to market *and* efficient, cost-conscious *and* customer-focused. How were they performing the impossible?

Obviously, there is no one answer to this complex question. There is no doubt, however, that these companies shared at least one characteristic: They had developed and committed themselves to project management as a competitive tool. Old middle managers, reported *Fortune* magazine,

> are dinosaurs, [and] a new class of manager mammal is evolving to fill the niche they once ruled: project managers. Unlike his biological counterpart, the project manager is more agile and adaptable than the beast he's displacing, more likely to live by his wits than throwing his weight around.[4]

Effective project managers will remain an indispensable commodity for successful organizations in the coming years. More and more companies are coming to this conclusion and adopting project management as a way of life. Indeed, companies in such diverse industries as construction, heavy manufacturing, insurance, health care, finance, public utilities, and software are becoming project savvy and expecting their employees to do the same.

1.1 WHAT IS A PROJECT?

Although there are a number of general definitions of the term **project**, we must recognize at the outset that projects are distinct from other organizational processes. As a rule, a **process** refers to ongoing, day-to-day activities in which an organization engages while producing goods or services. Processes use existing systems, properties, and capabilities in a continuous, fairly repetitive manner.[5] Projects, on the other hand, take place outside the normal, process-oriented world of the firm. Certainly, in some organizations, such as construction, day-to-day processes center on the creation and development of projects. Nevertheless, for the majority of organizations, project management activities remain unique and separate from the manner in which more routine, process-driven work is performed. Project work is continuously evolving, establishes its own work rules, and is the antithesis of repetition in the workplace. As a result, it represents an exciting alternative to business as usual for many companies. The challenges are great, but so are the rewards of success.

First, we need a clear understanding of the properties that make projects and project management so unique. Consider the following definitions of projects:

> A project is a unique venture with a beginning and end, conducted by people to meet established goals within parameters of cost, schedule, and quality.[6]

> Projects [are] goal-oriented, involve the coordinated undertaking of interrelated activities, are of finite duration, and are all, to a degree, unique.[7]

> A project can be considered to be any series of activities and tasks that:
> - Have a specific objective to be completed within certain specifications
> - Have defined start and end dates
> - Have funding limits (if applicable)
> - Consume human and nonhuman resources (i.e., money, people, equipment)
> - Are multifunctional (i.e., cut across several functional lines)[8]

> [A project is] [o]rganized work toward a predefined goal or objective that requires resources and effort, a unique (and therefore risky) venture having a budget and schedule.[9]

Probably the simplest definition is found in the Project Management Body of Knowledge (PMBoK) guide of the Project Management Institute (PMI). PMI is the world's largest professional project management association, with more than 380,000 members worldwide as of 2012. In the PMBoK guide, a project is defined as "a temporary endeavor undertaken to create a unique product or service" (p. 4).[10]

Let us examine the various elements of projects, as identified by our set of definitions.

- *Projects are complex, one-time processes.*   A project arises for a specific purpose or to meet a stated goal. It is complex because it typically requires the coordinated inputs of numerous members of the organization. Project members may be from different departments or other organizational units or from one functional area. For example, a project to develop a new software application for a retail company may require only the output of members of the Information Systems group working with the marketing staff. On the other hand, some projects, such as new product introductions, work best with representation from many functions, including marketing, engineering, production, and design. Because a project is intended to fulfill a stated goal, it is temporary. It exists only until its goal has been met, and at that point, it is dissolved.

- *Projects are limited by budget, schedule, and resources.*   Project work requires that members work with limited financial and human resources for a specified time period. They do not run indefinitely. Once the assignment is completed, the project team disbands. Until that point, all its activities are constrained by limitations on budget and personnel availability. Projects are "resource-constrained" activities.

- *Projects are developed to resolve a clear goal or set of goals.*   There is no such thing as a project team with an ongoing, nonspecific purpose. The project's goals, or **deliverables**, define the nature of the project and that of its team. Projects are designed to yield a tangible result, either as a new product or service. Whether the goal is to build a bridge, implement a new accounts receivable system, or win a presidential election, the goal must be specific and the project organized to achieve a stated aim.

- *Projects are customer-focused.*   Whether the project is responding to the needs of an internal organizational unit (e.g., accounting) or intended to exploit a market opportunity external to the organization, the underlying purpose of any project is to satisfy customer needs. In the past, this goal was sometimes overlooked. Projects were considered successful if they attained technical, budgetary, or scheduling goals. More and more, however, companies have realized that the primary goal of a project is customer satisfaction. If that goal is neglected, a firm runs the risk of "doing the wrong things well"—pursuing projects that may be done efficiently but that ignore customer needs or fail commercially.

General Project Characteristics

Using these definitional elements, we can create a sense of the key attributes that all projects share. These characteristics are not only useful for better understanding projects, but also offer the basis for seeing how project-based work differs from other activities most organizations undertake. Projects represent a special type of undertaking by any organization. Not surprisingly, the challenges in performing them right are sometimes daunting. Nevertheless, given the manner in which business continues to evolve on a worldwide scale, becoming "project savvy" is no longer a luxury: It is rapidly becoming a necessity.

Projects are characterized by the following properties:[11]

1. *Projects are ad hoc endeavors with a clear life cycle.*   Projects are nontraditional; they are activities that are initiated as needed, operate for a specified time period over a fairly well understood development cycle, and are then disbanded. They are temporary operations.

2. *Projects are building blocks in the design and execution of organizational strategies.*   As we will see in later chapters, projects allow organizations to implement companywide strategies. They are the principal means by which companies operationalize corporate-level objectives. In effect, projects are the vehicles for realizing company goals. For example, Intel's strategy for market penetration with ever newer, smaller, and faster computer chips is realized through its commitment to a steady stream of research and development projects that allows the company to continually explore the technological boundaries of electrical and computer engineering.

3. *Projects are responsible for the newest and most improved products, services, and organizational processes.*   Projects are tools for innovation. Because they complement (and often transform) traditional process-oriented activities, many companies rely on projects as vehicles for going beyond conventional activities. Projects are the stepping-stones by which we move forward.

4. *Projects provide a philosophy and strategy for the management of change.*   "Change" is an abstract concept until we establish the means by which we can make real alterations in the things we do and produce. Sometimes called the "building blocks of strategy," projects allow organizations to go beyond simple statements of intent and to achieve actual innovation. For example, whether it is Chevrolet's Volt electric car or Apple's newest iPhone upgrade, successful organizations routinely ask for customer input and feedback to better understand their likes and dislikes. As the vehicle of change, the manner in which a company develops its projects has much to say about its ability to innovate and commitment to change.

5. *Project management entails crossing functional and organizational boundaries.*   Projects epitomize internal organizational collaboration by bringing together people from various functions across the company. A project aimed at new product development may require the combined work of engineering, finance, marketing, design, and so forth. Likewise, in the global business environment, many companies have crossed organizational boundaries by forming long-term partnerships with other firms in order to maximize opportunities while emphasizing efficiency and keeping a lid on costs. Projects are among the most common means of promoting collaboration, both across functions and across organizations.

6. *The traditional management functions of planning, organizing, motivation, directing, and control apply to project management.*   Project managers must be technically well versed, proficient at administrative functions, willing and able to assume leadership roles, and, above all, goal-oriented: The project manager is the person most responsible for keeping track of the big picture. The nature of project management responsibilities should never be underestimated because these responsibilities are both diverse and critical to project success.

7. *The principal outcomes of a project are the satisfaction of customer requirements within the constraints of technical, cost, and schedule objectives.*   Projects are defined by their limitations. They have finite budgets, definite schedules, and carefully stated specifications for completion. For example, a term paper assignment in a college class might include details regarding form, length, number of

primary and secondary sources to cite, and so forth. Likewise, in the Disney's Expedition Everest case example at the end of the chapter, the executive leading the change process established clear guidelines regarding performance expectations. All these constraints both limit and narrowly define the focus of the project and the options available to the project team. It is the very task of managing successful project development within such specific constraints that makes the field so challenging.

8. ***Projects are terminated upon successful completion of performance objectives***—or earlier in their life cycle, if results no longer promise an operational or strategic advantage. As we have seen, projects differ from conventional processes in that they are defined by limited life cycles. They are initiated, completed, and dissolved. As important alternatives to conventional organizational activities, they are sometimes called "temporary organizations."[12]

Projects, then, differ from better-known organizational activities, which often involve repetitive processes. The traditional model of most firms views organizational activities as consistently performing a discrete set of activities. For example, a retail-clothing establishment buys, stocks, and sells clothes in a continuous cycle. A steel plant orders raw materials, makes steel, and ships finished products, again in a recurring cycle. The nature of these operations focuses our attention on a "process orientation," that is, the need to perform work as efficiently as possible in an ongoing manner. When its processes are well understood, the organization always seeks better, more efficient ways of doing the same essential tasks. Projects, because they are discrete activities, violate the idea of repetition. They are temporary activities that operate outside formal channels. They may bring together a disparate collection of team members with different kinds of functional expertise. Projects function under conditions of uncertainty, and usually have the effect of "shaking up" normal corporate activities. Because of their unique characteristics, they do not conform to common standards of operations; they do things differently and often reveal new and better ways of doing things. Table 1.1 offers some other distinctions between project-based work and the more traditional, process-based activities. Note a recurring theme: Projects operate in radical ways that consistently violate the standard, process-based view of organizations.

Consider Apple's development of the iPod, a portable MP3 player that can be integrated with Apple's popular iTunes site to record and play music downloads. Apple, headed by its chairman, Steven Jobs, recognized the potential in the MP3 market, given the enormous popularity (and, some would say, notoriety) of file-sharing and downloading music through the Internet. The company hoped to capitalize on the need for a customer-friendly MP3 player, while offering a legitimate alternative to illegal music downloading. Since its introduction in 2003, consumers have bought more than 278 million iPods and purchased more than 10 billion songs through Apple's iTunes online store. In fact, Apple's iTunes division is now the largest U.S. market for music sales, accounting for 25% of all music sold in the United States.

In an interview, Jobs acknowledged that Apple's business needed some shaking up, given the steady but unspectacular growth in sales of its flagship Macintosh personal computer, still holding approximately 11% of the overall PC market. The iPod, as a unique venture within Apple, became a billion-dollar business for the company in only its second year of existence. So popular has the iPod business become for Apple

TABLE 1.1 Differences Between Process and Project Management[13]

Process	Project
Repeat process or product	New process or product
Several objectives	One objective
Ongoing	One shot—limited life
People are homogenous	More heterogeneous
Well-established systems in place to integrate efforts	Systems must be created to integrate efforts
Greater certainty of performance, cost, schedule	Greater uncertainty of performance, cost, schedule
Part of line organization	Outside of line organization
Bastions of established practice	Violates established practice
Supports status quo	Upsets status quo

Source: R. J. Graham. (1992). "A Survival Guide for the Accidental Project Manager," *Proceedings of the Annual Project Management Institute Symposium.* Drexel Hill, PA: Project Management Institute, pp. 355–61. Copyright and all rights reserved. Material from this publication has been reproduced with the permission of PMI.

that the firm created a separate business unit, moving the product and its support staff away from the Mac group. "Needless to say, iPod has become incredibly popular, even among people who aren't diehard Apple fanatics," industry analyst Paolo Pescatore told *NewsFactor,* noting that Apple recently introduced a smaller version of the product with great success. "In short, they have been very successful thus far, and I would guess they are looking at this realignment as a way to ensure that success will continue."[14]

A similar set of events are currently unfolding, centered on Apple's introduction and successive upgrades of its iPad tablet. Among the numerous features offered by the iPad is the ability to download books (including college textbooks) directly from publishers, effectively eliminating the traditional middlemen—bookstores—from the process. So radical are the implications of the iPad that competitors are rushing to introduce their own models to capture a share of this new market. Meanwhile, large bookstores are hoping to adapt their business models to the new electronic reality of book purchase by offering their own readers (Kindle for Amazon, and Nook for Barnes and Noble). Some experts are suggesting that within a decade, tablets and other electronic readers will make traditional books obsolete, capturing the majority of the publishing market. These are just some examples of the way that project-driven technological change, such as that at Apple, is reshaping the competitive landscape.

Given the enthusiasm with which **project management** is being embraced by so many organizations, we should note that the same factors that make project management a unique undertaking are also among the main reasons why successful project management is so difficult. The track record of project management is by no means one of uninterrupted success, in part because many companies encounter deep-rooted resistance to the kinds of changes needed to accommodate a "project philosophy." Indeed, recent research into the success rates for projects offers some grim conclusions:

- A study of more than 300 large companies conducted by the consulting firm Peat Marwick found that software and/or hardware development projects fail at the rate of 65%. Of companies studied, 65% reported projects that went grossly over budget, fell behind schedule, did not perform as expected, or all of the above. Half of the managers responding indicated that these findings were considered "normal."[15]
- A study by the META Group found that "more than half of all (information technology) IT projects become runaways—overshooting their budgets and timetables while failing to deliver fully on their goals."[16]
- Joe Harley, the Chief Information Officer at the Department for Work and Pensions for the UK government, stated that "only 30%" of technology-based projects and programs are a success—at a time when taxes are funding an annual budget of £14bn (over $22 billion) on public sector IT, equivalent to building 7,000 new primary schools or 75 hospitals a year.[17]
- According to the 2004 PriceWaterhouseCoopers Survey of 10,640 projects valued at $7.2 billion, across a broad range of industries, large and small, only 2.5% of global businesses achieved 100% project success, and more than 50% of global business projects failed. The Chaos Summary 2009 survey by The Standish Group reported similar findings: The majority of all projects were either "challenged" (due to late delivery, being over budget, or delivering less than required features) or "failed" and were canceled prior to completion, or the product developed was never used. Researchers have concluded that the average success rate of business-critical application development projects is 32%. Their statistics have remained remarkably steady since 1994.[18]
- The Special Inspector General for Iraq Reconstruction (SIGIR) reported that the Pentagon spent about $600 million on more than 1,200 Iraqi reconstruction projects that were eventually canceled, with 42% terminated due to mismanagement or shoddy construction.[19]

These findings underscore an important point: Although project management is becoming popular, it is not easy to assimilate into the conventional processes of most firms. For every firm discovering the benefits of projects, many more underestimate the problems involved in becoming "project savvy."

These studies also point to a core truth about project management: We should not overestimate the benefits to be gained from project management while underestimating the commitment required to make a project work. There are no magic bullets or quick fixes in the discipline. Like any other valuable activity, project management requires preparation, knowledge, training, and commitment to basic principles. Organizations wanting to make use of project-based work must recognize, as Table 1.1 demonstrates, that its very strength often causes it to operate in direct contradiction to standard, process-oriented business practices.

1.2 WHY ARE PROJECTS IMPORTANT?

There are a number of reasons why projects and project management can be crucial in helping an organization achieve its strategic goals. David Cleland, a noted project management researcher, suggests that many of these reasons arise from the very pressures that organizations find themselves facing.[20]

1. *Shortened product life cycles.*   The days when a company could offer a new product and depend on having years of competitive domination are gone. Increasingly, the life cycle of new products is measured in terms of months or even weeks, rather than years. One has only to look at new products in electronics or computer hardware and software to observe this trend. Interestingly, we are seeing similar signs in traditional service-sector firms, which also have recognized the need for agility in offering and upgrading new services at an increasingly rapid pace.

2. *Narrow product launch windows.*   Another time-related issue concerns the nature of opportunity. Organizations are aware of the dangers of missing the optimum point at which to launch a new product and must take a proactive view toward the timing of product introductions. For example, while reaping the profits from the successful sale of Product A, smart firms are already plotting the best point at which to launch Product B, either as a product upgrade or a new offering. Because of fierce competition, these optimal launch opportunities are measured in terms of months. Miss your launch window, even by a matter of weeks, and you run the risk of rolling out an also-ran.

3. *Increasingly complex and technical products.*   The world today is complex. Products are complicated, technically sophisticated, and difficult to produce efficiently. The public's appetite for "the next big thing" continues unabated and substantially unsatisfied. We want the new models of our consumer goods to be better, bigger (or smaller), faster, and more complex than the old ones. Firms constantly upgrade product and service lines to feed this demand. That causes multiple problems in design and production as we continually seek to push the technical limits. Further, in anticipating future demand, many firms embark on expensive programs of research and development while attempting to discern consumer tastes. The effect can be to erroneously create expensive and technically sophisticated projects that we assume the customer will want. For example, Rauma Corporation of Finland developed a state-of-the-art "loader" for the logging industry. Rauma's engineers loaded the product with the latest computerized gadgetry and technologies that gave the machine a space-age feel. Unfortunately, the chief customer for the product worked in remote regions of Indonesia, with logistics problems that made servicing and repairing the loaders impractical. Machines that broke down had to be airlifted more than 1,000 miles to service centers. Since the inception of this project, sales of the logging machinery have been disappointing. The project was an expensive failure for Rauma and serves to illustrate an important point: Unless companies find a way to maintain control of the process, an "engineering for engineering's sake" mentality can quickly run out of control.[21]

4. *Emergence of global markets.*   The early twenty-first century has seen the emergence of enormous new markets for almost every type of product and service. Former closed or socialist societies, as well as rapidly developing economies such as Russia, China, and India, have added huge numbers of consumers and competitors to the global business arena. The increased globalization of the economy, coupled with enhanced methods for quickly interacting with customers and suppliers, has created a new set of challenges for business. These challenges also encompass unique opportunities for those firms that can quickly adjust to this new reality. In the global setting, project management techniques provide companies with the ability to link multiple business partners, and respond quickly to market demand and supplier needs, while remaining agile enough to anticipate and respond to rapid shifts in consumer tastes. Using project management, successful organizations of the future will recognize and learn to rapidly exploit the prospects offered by a global business environment.

5. *An economic period marked by low inflation.*   One of the key indicators of economic health is the fact that inflation has been kept under control. In most of the developed Western economies, low inflation has helped to trigger a long period of economic expansion, while also helping provide the impetus for emerging economies, such as those in India and China, to expand rapidly. Unfortunately, low inflation also limits the ability of businesses to maintain profitability by passing along cost increases. Companies cannot continue to increase profit margins through simply raising prices for their products or services. Successful firms in the future will be those that enhance profits by streamlining internal processes—those that save money by "doing it better" than the competition. As a tool designed to realize goals like internal efficiency, project management is a means by which to bolster profits.

These are just some of the more obvious challenges facing business today. The key point is that the forces giving rise to these challenges are not likely to abate in the near future. In order to meet these challenges, large, successful companies like General Electric, 3M, Apple, Sony, Bechtel, and Microsoft have made project management a key aspect of their operating philosophies.

PROJECT PROFILE

Case—Projects in China: Pushing the Innovative Envelope

As one of the most vigorous economies in the world today, China is spending billions of dollars each year on upgrading its infrastructure, improving living conditions, and working to bring the benefits of economic renewal to people in all parts of the country. The sheer volume and diversity of projects being undertaken in China today are breathtaking and speak to the way that the government is seeking to move the country forward. A partial list of recent major project initiatives in China includes:

1. *Urban skyscrapers and other office/living space development*—A number of factors are pushing the Chinese government to invest heavily in new office and apartment towers throughout the country. Underlying the commitment to upgrade the quality of life in China is a genuine desire to push the edges of the architectural envelope. These projects are strongly supported because of cheaper building materials, a demand for urban density and green buildings, and pursuit of international recognition. Indeed, a recent report by the consulting firm McKinsey Group predicts that by 2025, China will have 221 cities with more than a million inhabitants, compared with 35 in Europe today. As well as the need for huge spending on infrastructure, McKinsey projects that China will build between 20,000 and 50,000 skyscrapers, many of them in less developed interior provinces far from Beijing and Shanghai.

Aurora Photos / Alamy

FIGURE 1.2 China's Tallest Building, Shanghai World Financial Center

2. ***High-speed rail projects***—China recently announced the development of a high-speed rail link between Beijing and Shanghai, the most populous and economically important corridor in the country. More than a quarter of the country's population lives close to the line, which will account for 10% of passenger transport and 7% of freight. This new high-speed line is being designed for train travel at 300 km/h (186 mph) operation and will reduce the journey time between Beijing and Shanghai from 14 hours to just 5. An estimated 220,000 passengers per day will use the trains. Based on current estimates, the project is expected to be completed by the middle of the decade and cost approximately $12 billion dollars. This line is just the latest in a series of high-speed rail links developed to connect the major population centers in the country. The Beijing-Tianjin high-speed rail line was completed three years ago and also supports a massive effort on the part of the country to better link its people and economic centers. As time progresses and rail technology continues to improve, China will consider additional opportunities to use high-speed rail.

3. ***Energy plant construction***—China's electricity-generating capacity has surged in the past five years because of a huge increase in the construction of power plants. At the same time, it is exploring all possible avenues for the production of energy. Nuclear power plants are being constructed across the country, and hydroelectric plants are being built to take advantage of major river damming projects, such as the famous Three Gorges Dam. Further, China has doubled its wind energy capacity in each of the past four years, and by the end of 2012 is expected to pass the United States as the world's largest market for wind energy and power equipment. Despite these alternative sources of energy, coal still remains the most popular choice for generating electricity, as China has the world's third largest coal reserves, behind only the United States and Russia. So committed is the Chinese government to building coal-fired power stations that such plants are being constructed at the rate of one per month across the country. China now uses more coal than the United States, Europe, and Japan combined, making it the world's largest emitter of greenhouse gases. As the same time, however, what is not as well known is that China has emerged in the past three years as the world's largest builder of more efficient, less polluting coal power plants. In fact, at a time when the technology is languishing in the United States, as governmental regulations are slowing down its development, China is rapidly increasing its construction of these plants, improving the technology and lowering costs.

China's frenetic drive toward industrialization and infrastructure improvement is not without risks: Pushing such an ambitious goal countrywide is an incredibly complex process, as it involves annual investments of hundreds of billions of dollars, the commitment of the people, and the sustained health of the economy to support these plans. Nevertheless, at a time when development has slowed across the majority of the world because of the global economic downturn, it is refreshing to see that in China the philosophy remains: full speed ahead![22]

Project management also serves as an excellent training ground for future senior executives in most organizations. One unique aspect of projects is how they blend technical and behavioral challenges. The technical side of project management requires managers to become skilled in project selection, budgeting and resource management, planning and scheduling, and tracking projects. Each of these skills will be discussed in subsequent chapters. At the same time, however, project managers face the equally strong challenge of managing the behavioral, or "people," side of projects. Projects, being temporary endeavors, require project managers to bring together individuals from across the organization, quickly mold them into an effective team, manage conflict, provide leadership, and engage in negotiation and appropriate political behavior, all in the name of project success. Again, we will address these behavioral challenges in this text. One thing we know is: Project managers who emphasize one challenge and ignore the other, whether they choose to focus on the technical or behavioral side of project management, are not nearly as successful as those who seek to become experts in both. Why is project management such a useful training ground for senior executives? Because it provides the first true test of an individual's ability to master both the technical and human challenges that characterize effective leaders in business. Project managers, and their projects, create the kind of value that companies need to survive and prosper.

1.3 PROJECT LIFE CYCLES

Imagine receiving a term paper assignment in a college class. Our first step would be to develop a sense of the assignment itself—what the professor is looking for, how long the paper should be, the number of references required, stylistic expectations, and so forth. Once we have familiarized ourselves with the assignment, our next step would be to develop a plan for how we intend to proceed with the project in order to complete it by the due date. We make a rough guess about how much time will be needed for the research, writing the first draft, proofing the paper, and completing the final draft; we use this information to create some tentative milestones for the various components of the assignment. Next, we begin to execute our

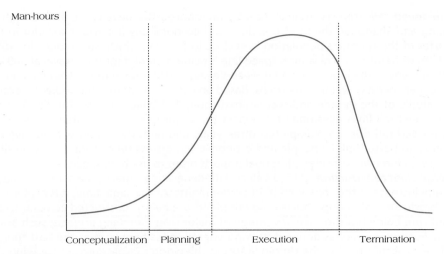

FIGURE 1.3 Project Life Cycle Stages

plan, doing the library or online research, creating an outline, writing a draft, and so forth. Our goal is to complete the assignment on time, doing the work to our best possible ability. Finally, after turning in the paper, we file or discard our reference materials, return any books to the library, breathe a sigh of relief, and wait for the grade.

This example represents a simplified but useful illustration of a project's life cycle. In this case, the project consisted of completing the term paper to the standards expected of the instructor in the time allowed. A **project life cycle** refers to the stages in a project's development. Life cycles are important because they demonstrate the logic that governs a project. They also help us develop our plans for carrying out the project. They help us decide, for example, when we should devote resources to the project, how we should evaluate its progress, and so forth. Consider the simplified model of the project life cycle shown in Figure 1.3, which divides the life cycle into four distinct phases: conceptualization, planning, execution, and termination.

- *Conceptualization* refers to the development of the initial goal and technical specifications for a project. The scope of the work is determined, necessary resources (people, money, physical plant) identified, and important organizational contributors or **stakeholders** signed on.
- *Planning* is the stage in which all detailed specifications, schematics, schedules, and other plans are developed. The individual pieces of the project, often called *work packages,* are broken down, individual assignments made, and the process for completion clearly delineated. For example, in planning our approach to complete the term paper, we determine all the necessary steps (research, drafts, editing, etc.) in the process.
- During *execution,* the actual "work" of the project is performed, the system developed, or the product created and fabricated. It is during the execution phase that the bulk of project team labor is performed. As Figure 1.3 shows, project costs (in man hours) ramp up rapidly during this stage.
- *Termination* occurs when the completed project is transferred to the customer, its resources reassigned, and the project formally closed out. As specific subactivities are completed, the project shrinks in scope and costs decline rapidly.

These stages are the waypoints at which the project team can evaluate both its performance and the project's overall status. Remember, however, that the life cycle is relevant only after the project has actually begun. The life cycle is signaled by the actual kickoff of project development, the development of plans and schedules, the performance of necessary work, and the completion of the project and reassignment of personnel. When we evaluate projects in terms of this life cycle model, we are given some clues regarding their subsequent resource requirements; that is, we begin to ask whether we have sufficient personnel, materials, and equipment to support the project. For example, when beginning to work on our term paper project, we may discover that it is necessary to purchase a PC or hire someone to help with researching the topic. Thus, as we plan the project's life cycle, we acquire important information regarding the resources that we will need. The life cycle model,

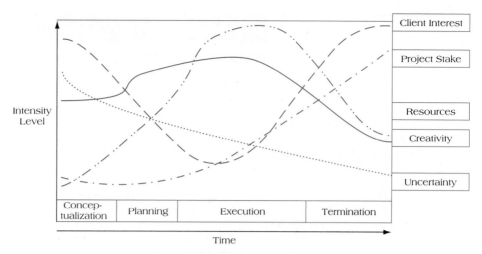

FIGURE 1.4 **Project Life Cycles and Their Effects**

Source: Victor Sohmen. (2002, July). "Project Termination: Why the Delay?" Paper presented at PMI Research Conference, Seattle, WA.

then, serves the twofold function of project timing (schedule) and project requirements (resources), allowing team members to better focus on what and when resources are needed.

The project life cycle is also a useful means of visualizing the activities required and challenges to be faced during the life of a project. Figure 1.4 indicates some of these characteristics as they evolve during the course of completing a project.[23] As you can see, five components of a project may change over the course of its life cycle:

- *Client interest:*   The level of enthusiasm or concern expressed by the project's intended customer. **Clients** can be either internal to the organization or external.
- *Project stake:*   The amount of corporate investment in the project. The longer the life of the project, the greater the investment.
- *Resources:*   The commitment of financial, human, and technical resources over the life of the project.
- *Creativity:*   The degree of innovation required by the project, especially during certain development phases.
- *Uncertainty:*   The degree of risk associated with the project. Riskiness here reflects the number of unknowns, including technical challenges that the project is likely to face. Uncertainty is highest at the beginning because many challenges have yet to be identified, let alone addressed.

Each of these factors has its own dynamic. Client interest, for example, follows a "U-shaped" curve, reflecting initial enthusiasm, lower levels of interest during development phases, and renewed interest as the project nears completion. Project stake increases dramatically as the project moves forward because an increasing commitment of resources is needed to support ongoing activities. Creativity, often viewed as innovative thought or applying a unique perspective, is high at the beginning of a project, as the team and the project's client begin developing a shared vision of the project. As the project moves forward and uncertainty remains high, creativity also continues to be an important feature. In fact, it is not until the project is well into its execution phase, with defined goals, that creativity becomes less important. To return to our example of the term paper project, in many cases, the "creativity" needed to visualize a unique or valuable approach to developing the project is needed early, as we identify our goals and plan the process of achieving them. Once identified, the execution phase, or writing the term paper, places less emphasis on creativity per se and more on the concrete steps needed to complete the project assignment.

The information simplified in Figure 1.4 is useful for developing a sense of the competing issues and challenges that a project team is likely to face over the life cycle of a project. Over time, while certain characteristics (creativity, resources, and uncertainty) begin to decrease, other elements (client interest and project stake) gain in importance. Balancing the requirements of these elements across the project life cycle is just one of the many demands placed on a project team.

PROJECT MANAGERS IN PRACTICE

Damien Baxter, Arrium Limited

Arrium Limited, a mining and mining consumables business, is listed among the top 100 companies on the Australian Securities Exchange. With a strategic focus on the growing global resources industry, Arrium is positioned as a true global partner. The company has approximately 250 locations across Australia, Asia, North and South America, and New Zealand, and revenues in excess of $7 billion Australian dollars.

Damien Baxter, General Manager (Tax, Audit & Risk), has been with Arrium, previously known as One Steel, for the last 10 years. He is a chartered accountant with a strong technical background in taxation. Although Damien's title does not include the words "project manager," he essentially functions as a program/project manager with a diverse portfolio in corporate tax, audit, and risk.

Damien believes that his project management skills complement his senior role in the organization. He takes pride in his ability to manage deadlines and to deal effectively with national and international tax authorities while simultaneously allocating appropriate resources, delegating the correct internal and external expertise, and pursuing projects that are aligned with Arrium's strategic direction. As a senior manager, he sees his role as delivering on Arrium's business strategy through his program management of the various portfolio projects.

Damien's project role involves scoping, resourcing internal and external experts, developing a stakeholders' communications plan and risk treatment plan, and setting clear milestones and goals for the project plan. He carefully delegates tasks to a project team comprised of both his internal staff and external advisory consultants. One of his major challenges is deadline changes by the regulatory authorities.

As a senior executive and program manager of projects, Damien deals with three categories of risk: legal and regulatory risk, financial risk, and strategic risk. Together with his team he develops a risk treatment plan for each project that indicates the organisation's strategic option to treat and improve each risk so that it is reduced to an acceptable level based on the organisation's risk appetite. Damien believes that various project documentations enable him to discern precisely where the work is, manage the risks, continue managing the critical path of the project, and still meet the deliverables.

Damien characterizes some of the projects as "ticking time bombs" because they involve high levels of expertise from external advisors. Some of the technical projects can be complicated by new rulings. But with his project management capabilities, together with strong negotiating and interpersonal skills, technical knowledge, and general management acumen, Damien can manage the project's costs through timely scheduling and resourcing of expertise.

Through project management, Damien has been able to motivate his team while providing training and mentoring. He has found that project team members who lack understanding of resource management or scheduling can learn from their peers. In terms of motivation, Damien has found that meeting deadlines on the various portfolios makes his teams view the work as a team effort rather than as the responsibility

FIGURE 1.5 Damien Baxter, Arrium Limited

of individuals, each overloaded with their own deadlines. He also has been able to maintain a high level of interest from his teams in projects in the pipeline.

Projects vary with different portfolios, but a typical project requires Damien to lead the project by identifying the team members for that portfolio, defining the scope of the project, and developing the necessary plans. During planning, Damien involves the team in detailing the technical outcomes of the project. He believes this technique ensures that all team members are committed to executing the work and understand the risk and costs associated with delays. This transparency in sharing project outcomes and expectations has helped him strengthen ties with his teams internally and continue good relationships with his external advisors and consultants.

In Damien's assessment, projects are successful when they are appropriately scoped and assigned realistic start and end times, and when deadlines are met. Any changes, especially those imposed by regulatory external factors, are managed without adverse impact on the project outcome. Damien has satisfactorily applied program and project management by directing and managing across his tax, audit, and risk portfolios. In addition, his project management background has enabled him to work around occasional limitations on shared resourcing within the organization, keep the costs of expertise resources within budget, meet project deadlines, and terminate projects only when it complies with the rules of the Australia Taxation Office. In particular, he has succeeded in strengthening communication with all of his stakeholders through his management of the projects.

1.4 DETERMINANTS OF PROJECT SUCCESS

Definitions of successful projects can be surprisingly elusive.[24] How do we know when a project is successful? When it is profitable? If it comes in on budget? On time? When the developed product works or sells? When we achieve our long-term payback goals? Generally speaking, any definition of **project success** *must* take into consideration the elements that define the very nature of a project: that is, time (schedule adherence), budget, functionality/quality, and customer satisfaction. At one time, managers normally applied three criteria of project success:

- *Time.*   Projects are constrained by a specified time frame during which they must be completed. They are not supposed to continue indefinitely. Thus the first constraint that governs project management involves the basic requirement: the project should come in on or before its established schedule.
- *Budget.*   A second key constraint for all projects is a limited budget. Projects must meet budgeted allowances in order to use resources as efficiently as possible. Companies do not write blank checks and hope for the best. Thus the second limit on a project raises the question: Was the project completed within budget guidelines?
- *Performance.*   All projects are developed in order to adhere to some initially determined technical specifications. We know before we begin what the project is supposed to do or how the final product is supposed to operate. Measuring performance, then, means determining whether the finished product operates according to specifications. The project's clients naturally expect that the project being developed on their behalf will work as expected. Applying this third criterion is often referred to as conducting a "quality" check.

This so-called **triple constraint** was once the standard by which project performance was routinely assessed. Today, a fourth criterion has been added to these three (see Figure 1.6):

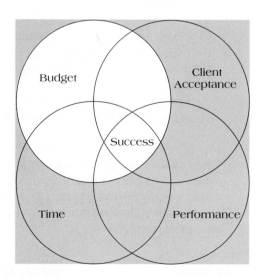

FIGURE 1.6   The New Quadruple Constraint

- *Client acceptance.*   The principle of **client acceptance** argues that projects are developed with customers, or clients, in mind, and their purpose is to satisfy customers' needs. If client acceptance is a key variable, then we must also ask whether the completed project is acceptable to the customer for whom it was intended. Companies that evaluate project success strictly according to the original "triple constraint" may fail to apply the most important test of all: the client's satisfaction with the completed project.

We can also think of the criteria for project success in terms of "internal" vs. "external" conditions. When project management was practiced primarily by construction and other heavy industries, its chief value was in maintaining internal organizational control over expenditures of money and time. The traditional triple-constraint model made perfect sense. It focused internally on efficiency and productivity measures. It provided a quantifiable measure of personnel evaluation, and it allowed accountants to control expenses.

More recently, however, the traditional triple-constraint model has come under increasing criticism as a measure of project success. The final product, for example, could be a failure, but if it has been delivered in time and on budget and satisfies its original specifications (however flawed), the project itself could still be declared a success. Adding the external criterion of client acceptance corrects such obvious shortcomings in the assessment process. First, it refocuses corporate attention outside the organization, toward the customer, who will probably be dissatisfied with a failed or flawed final product. Likewise, it recognizes that the final arbiter of project success is not the firm's accountants, but rather the marketplace. A project is successful only to the extent that it benefits the client who commissioned it. Finally, the criterion of client acceptance requires project managers and teams to create an atmosphere of openness and communication throughout the development of the project.

Consider one example. The automaker Volvo has been motivated to increase its visibility and attractiveness to female customers, a market segment that has become significantly stronger over the years. The company's market research showed that women want everything in a car that men want, "plus a lot more that male car buyers never thought to ask for," according to Hans-Olov Olsson, the former president and CEO of Volvo. In fact, Volvo discovered, in Olsson's words, "If you meet women's expectations, you exceed those for men." Volvo's solution was to allow hundreds of its female employees, including an all-female design and engineering staff, to develop a new-generation concept car. The group studied a variety of vehicle aspects, including ergonomics, styling, storage, and maintenance, keeping in mind the common theme: What do women want? Code-named the YCC (Your Concept Car), the car is designed to be nearly maintenance free, with an efficient gas-electric hybrid engine, sporty styling, and roomy storage. Volvo's efforts in developing the YCC project demonstrate a commitment to client acceptance and satisfaction as a key motivator of its project management process, supplanting the traditional triple-constraint model for project success.[25]

An additional approach to project assessment argues that another factor must always be taken into consideration: the promise that the delivered product can generate future opportunities, whether commercial or technical, for the organization.[26] In other words, it is not enough to assess a project according to its immediate success. We must also evaluate it in terms of its commercial success as well as its potential for generating new business and new opportunities. Figure 1.7 illustrates this scheme, which proposes four relevant dimensions of success:

- *Project efficiency:*   Meeting budget and schedule expectations.
- *Impact on customer:*   Meeting technical specifications, addressing customer needs, and creating a project that satisfies the client's needs.
- *Business success:*   Determining whether the project achieved significant commercial success.
- *Preparing for the future:*   Determining whether the project opened new markets or new product lines or helped to develop new technology.

This approach challenges the conventional triple-constraint principle for assessing project success. Corporations expect projects not only to be run efficiently (at the least) but also to be developed to meet customer needs, achieve commercial success, and serve as conduits to new business opportunities. Even in the case of a purely internal project (e.g., updating the software for a firm's order-entry system), project teams need to focus both on customer needs and an assessment of potential commercial or technical opportunities arising from their efforts.

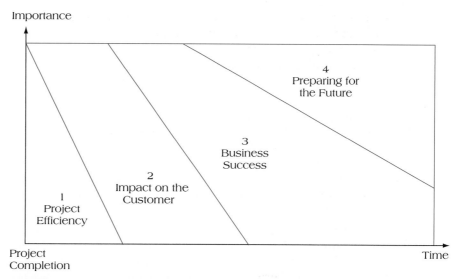

FIGURE 1.7   **Four Dimensions of Project Success Importance**

Source: A. J. Shenhar, O. Levy, and D. Dvir. (1997). "Mapping the Dimensions of Project Success," *Project Management Journal,* 28(2): 12. Copyright and all rights reserved. Material from this publication has been reproduced with the permission of PMI.

BOX 1.2

PROJECT MANAGEMENT RESEARCH IN BRIEF

Assessing Information Technology (IT) Project Success

As we noted earlier in this chapter, IT projects have a notoriously checkered history when it comes to successful implementation. Part of the problem has been an inability to define the characteristics of a successful IT project in concrete terms. The criteria for IT project success are often quite vague, and without clear guidelines for project success, it is hardly any wonder that so many of these projects do not live up to predevelopment expectations. In 1992 and again in 2003, two researchers, W. DeLone and E. McLean, analyzed several previous studies of IT projects to identify the key indicators of success. Their findings, synthesized from previous research, suggest that, at the very least, IT projects should be evaluated according to six criteria:

- *System quality.*   The project team supplying the system must be able to assure the client that the implemented system will perform as intended. All systems should satisfy certain criteria: They should, for example, be easy to use, and they should supply quality information.
- *Information quality.*   The information generated by the implemented IT must be the information required by users and be of sufficient quality that it is "actionable": In other words, generated information should not require additional efforts to sift or sort the data. System users can perceive quality in the information they generate.
- *Use.*   Once installed, the IT system must be used. Obviously, the reason for any IT system is its usefulness as a problem-solving, decision-aiding, and networking mechanism. The criterion of "use" assesses the actual utility of a system by determining the degree to which, once implemented, it is used by the customer.
- *User satisfaction.*   Once the IT system is complete, the project team must determine user satisfaction. One of the thorniest issues in assessing IT project success has to do with making an accurate determination of user satisfaction with the system. Yet, because the user is the client and is ultimately the arbiter of whether or not the project was effective, it is vital that we attain some measure of the client's satisfaction with the system and its output.
- *Individual impact.*   All systems should be easy to use and should supply quality information. But beyond satisfying these needs, is there a specific criterion for determining the usefulness of a system to the client who commissioned it? Is decision making faster or more accurate? Is information more retrievable, more affordable, or more easily assimilated? In short, does the system benefit users in the ways that are most important to those users?

(continued)

> • ***Organizational impact.***   Finally, the supplier of the system must be able to determine whether it has a positive impact throughout the client organization. Is there, for example, a collective or synergistic effect on the client corporation? Is there a sense of good feeling, or are there financial or operational metrics that demonstrate the effectiveness or quality of the system?
>
> DeLone and McLean's work provides an important framework for establishing a sense of IT project success. Companies that are designing and implementing IT systems must pay early attention to each of these criteria and take necessary steps to ensure that the systems that they deliver satisfy them.[27]

A final model, offered recently, also argues against the triple-constraint model as a measure of project success. According to Atkinson,[28] all groups that are affected by a project (stakeholders) should have a hand in assessing its success. The context and type of a project may also be relevant in specifying the criteria that will most clearly define its success or failure. Table 1.2 shows the Atkinson model, which views the traditional "iron triangle" of cost, quality, and time as merely one set of components in a comprehensive set of measures. Of course, the means by which a project is to be measured should be decided before the project is undertaken. A corporate axiom, "What gets measured, gets managed," suggests that when teams understand the standards to which a project is being held, they will place more appropriate emphases on the various aspects of project performance. Consider, for example, an information system setting. If the criteria of success are improved operating efficiency and satisfied users, and if quality is clearly identified as a key benefit of the finished product, the team will focus its efforts more strongly on these particular aspects of the project.

1.5 DEVELOPING PROJECT MANAGEMENT MATURITY

With the tremendous increase in project management practices among global organizations, a recent phenomenon has been the rise of project maturity models for project management organizations. **Project management maturity models** are used to allow organizations to benchmark the best practices of successful project management firms. Project management maturity models recognize that different organizations are currently at different levels of sophistication in their best practices for managing projects. For example, it would be reasonable to expect an organization such as Boeing (aircraft and defense systems) or Fluor-Daniel (industrial construction) to be much more advanced in how they manage projects, given the company's lengthy histories of project initiatives, than a company that has only recently developed an emphasis on project-based work.

The purpose of **benchmarking** is to systematically manage the process improvements of project delivery by a single organization over a period of time.[29] Because there are many diverse dimensions of project management practice, it is common for a new organization just introducing project management to its operations to ask, "Where do we start?" That is, which of the multiple project management processes should we investigate, model, and apply to our organization? Maturity models provide the necessary framework to first, analyze and critically evaluate current practices as they pertain to managing projects; second, compare those practices against those of chief competitors or some general industry standard; and third, define a systematic route for improving these practices.

TABLE 1.2 Understanding Success Criteria

Iron Triangle	Information System	Benefits (Organization)	Benefits (Stakeholders)
Cost	Maintainability	Improved efficiency	Satisfied users
Quality	Reliability	Improved effectiveness	Social and environmental impact
Time	Validity	Increased profits	Personal development
	Information quality	Strategic goals	Professional learning, contractors' profits
	Use	Organization learning	Capital suppliers, content
		Reduced waste	Project team, economic impact to surrounding community

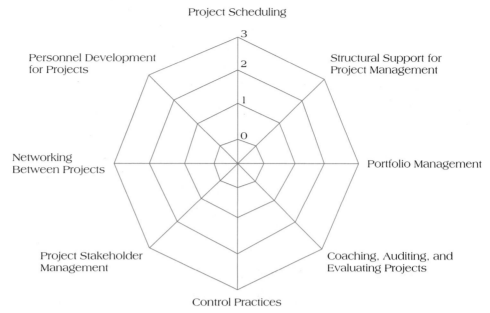

FIGURE 1.8 **Spider Web Diagram for Measuring Project Maturity**

Source: R. Gareis. (2001). "Competencies in the Project-Oriented Organization," in D. Slevin, D. Cleland, and J. Pinto, *The Frontiers of Project Management Research.* Newtown Square, PA: Project Management Institute, pp. 213–24, figure on p. 216. Copyright and all rights reserved. Material from this publication has been reproduced with the permission of PMI.

If we accept the fact that the development of better project management practices is an evolutionary process, involving not a sudden leap to top performance but rather a systematic commitment to continuous improvement, maturity models offer the template for defining and then achieving such progressive improvement.[30] As a result, most effective project maturity models chart both a set of standards that are currently accepted as state-of-the-art as well as a process for achieving significant movement toward these benchmarks. Figure 1.8 illustrates one approach to defining current project management practices a firm is using.[31] It employs a "spider web" methodology in which a set of significant project management practices have first been identified for organizations within a specific industry. In this example, a firm may identify eight components of project management practice that are key for success, based on an analysis of the firm's own needs as well as through benchmarking against competing firms in the industry. Note that each of the rings in the diagram represents a critical evaluation of the manner in which the organization matches up with industry standards. Suppose we assigned the following meanings to the different ratings:

Ring Level	Meaning
0	Not defined or poor
1	Defined but substandard
2	Standardized
3	Industry leader or cutting edge

Following this example, we may decide that in terms of project team personnel development or project control systems, our practices are poor relative to other competitors and rate those skills as 0. On the other hand, perhaps our scheduling processes are top-notch, enabling us to rate them as a 3. Figure 1.9 shows an example of the same spider web diagram with our relative skill levels assigned across the eight key elements of project management we have defined. This exercise helps us to form the basis for where we currently are in terms of project management sophistication, a key stage in any maturity model in which we seek to move to a higher level.

Once we have established a sense of our present project management abilities, as well as our shortcomings, the next step in the maturity model process is to begin charting a step-by-step, incremental path to our

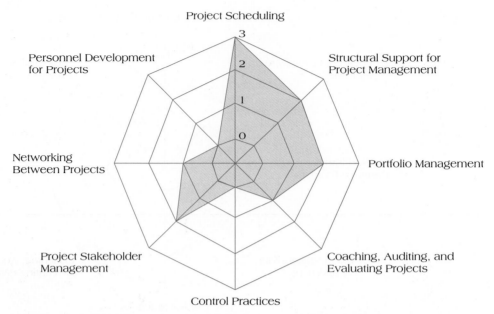

FIGURE 1.9 **Spider Web Diagram with Embedded Organizational Evaluation**

Source: R. Gareis. (2001). "Competencies in the Project-Oriented Organization," in D. Slevin, D. Cleland, and J. Pinto, *The Frontiers of Project Management Research*. Newtown Square, PA: Project Management Institute, pp. 213–24, figure on p. 216. Copyright and all rights reserved. Material from this publication has been reproduced with the permission of PMI.

desired goal. Table 1.3 highlights some of the more common project maturity models and the interim levels they have identified en route to the highest degree of organization-wide project expertise. Several of these models were developed by private project management consultancies or professional project organizations.

It is interesting to compare and contrast the four maturity models highlighted in Table 1.3. These examples of maturity models are taken from the most well-known models in the field, including Carnegie Mellon University's Software Engineering Institute's (SEI) Capability Maturity Model, Harold Kerzner's Maturity Model, ESI International's Project Framework, and the maturity model developed by the Center for Business Practices.[32] Illustrating these dimensions in pyramid form, we can see the progression toward project management maturity (Figure 1.10). Despite some differences in terminology, a clear sense of pattern exists among these models. Typically they start with the assumption that project management practices within a firm are not planned and are not collectively employed; in fact, there is likely no common language or methods for undertaking project management. As the firm grows in project maturity, it begins to adopt common practices, starts programs to train cadres of project management professionals, establishes procedures and processes for initiating and controlling its projects, and so forth. Finally, by the last stage, not only is the organization "project-savvy," but it also has progressed beyond simply applying project management to its processes and is now actively exploring ways to continuously improve its project management techniques and procedures. It is during the final stage that the organization can be truly considered "project mature"; it has internalized all necessary project management principles and is actively seeking to move beyond them in innovative ways.

Project maturity models have become very useful in recent years precisely because they reflect the growing interest in project management while highlighting one of the recurring problems: the lack of clear direction for companies in adopting, adapting, and improving these processes for optimal use. The key feature of these models is the important recognition that change typically does not occur abruptly; that is, companies that desire to become skilled in their project management approaches simply cannot progress in immediate steps from a lack of project management understanding to optimal project practices. Instead, the maturity models illustrate that "maturity" is an ongoing process, based on continuous improvement through identifiable incremental steps. Once we have an accurate picture of where we fit into the maturity process, we can begin to determine a reasonable course of action to progress to our desired level. In this manner, any organization, no matter how initially unskilled in project management, can begin to chart a course toward the type of project organization it hopes to become.

TABLE 1.3 A Comparison of Project Maturity Models and Incremental Stages

Center for Business Practices

Level 1: Initial Process	Level 2: Structure, Process, and Standards	Level 3: Institutionalized Project Management	Level 4: Managed	Level 5: Optimizing
• Ad hoc process • Management awareness	• Basic processes, not standard on all projects • Management supports use • Estimates, schedules based on expert knowledge	• All project processes are repeatable • Estimates, schedules based on industry standards	• Project management practices integrated with corporate processes • Solid analysis of project performance • Estimates, schedules based on corporate specifics	• Processes to measure project efficiency • Processes in place to improve project performance • Company focuses on continuous improvement

Kerzner's Project Management Maturity Model

Level 1: Common Language	Level 2: Common Processes	Level 3: Singular Methodology	Level 4: Benchmarking	Level 5: Continuous Improvement
• Sporadic use of project management • Small pockets of interest in the firm • No investment in PM training	• Tangible benefits made apparent • PM support throughout the firm • Development of a PM curriculum	• Integrated processes • Cultural and management support • Financial benefit from PM training	• Analysis and evaluation of practices • Project office established	• Lessons learned, files created • Knowledge transfer between teams • Mentorship program

ESI International's Project Framework

Level 1: Ad Hoc	Level 2: Consistent	Level 3: Integrated	Level 4: Comprehensive	Level 5: Optimizing
• Processes ill-defined because they are applied individually • Little support by organization	• Organization is well intentioned in its methods • No project control processes or lessons learned	• Processes are tailored to enhance all PM aspects • Common use and understanding of methods across the firm	• PM fully implemented across the firm • Information is used to evaluate processes and reduce variation • Advanced PM tools and techniques are developed	• Continual effort to improve and innovate project capability • Common failures are eliminated

SEI's Capability Maturity Model Integration

Level 1: Initial	Level 2: Managed	Level 3: Defined	Level 4: Quantitative Management	Level 5: Optimizing
• Ad hoc, chaotic processes	• Requirements management, project planning, and control occur • Process quality assurance occurs • Configuration management is used	• Requirements development and product integration occur • Verification and validation of processes • Risk management is emphasized	• Process performance is gauged • Quantitative PM highlighted	• Innovation and deployment accentuated • Causal analysis and resolution occur

FIGURE 1.10 **Project Management Maturity—A Generic Model**

1.6 PROJECT ELEMENTS AND TEXT ORGANIZATION

This text was written to provide a holistic, managerial-based approach to project management. The text is holistic in that it weaves together the wide variety of duties, responsibilities, and knowledge that successful project managers must acquire. Project management is a comprehensive and exciting undertaking. It requires us to understand aspects of management science in building schedules, assigning resources, monitoring and controlling our projects, and so forth. At the same time, successful project managers also must integrate fundamental issues of behavioral science, involving knowledge of human beings, leadership practices, motivation and team development, conflict resolution, and negotiation skills. Truly, a "science-heavy" approach to this subject will make us no more successful in our future project management responsibilities than will a focus that retains an exclusively "people-based" outlook. Project management is an exciting and challenging blend of the science and art of management.

Figure 1.11 offers a model for the organization of this text. The figure is a Gantt chart, a project scheduling and control device that we will become more familiar with in Chapter 10. For now, however, we can apply it to the structure of this book by focusing on some of its simpler features. First, note that all chapters in the book are listed down the left-hand column. Across the bottom and running from left to right is a simple time line that illustrates the point at which each of the chapters' topics will be introduced. For simplicity's sake, I have divided the X-axis time line into four distinct project phases that roughly follow the

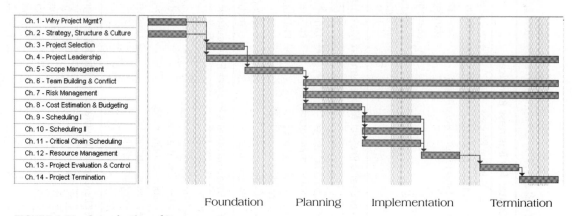

FIGURE 1.11 **Organization of Text**

project life cycle discussed earlier in this chapter: (1) Foundation, (2) Planning, (3) Implementation, and (4) Termination. Notice how some of the topics we will cover are particularly relevant only during certain phases of the project while others, such as project leadership, are significant across much of the project's life cycle. Among the benefits of setting up the text to follow this sequence are that, first, it shows the importance of blending the human-based topics (leadership and team building) directly with the more analytical or scientific elements of project management. We cannot compartmentalize our approach to project management as either exclusively technical or behavioral; the two are opposite sides of the same coin and must be appreciated jointly. Second, the structure provides a simple logic for ordering the chapters and the stage of the project at which we are most likely to concern ourselves with these topics. Some concepts, as illustrated by the figure, are more immediately concerned with project planning while others become critical at later phases in the project. Appreciating the elements of project management *and their proper sequencing* is an important learning guide. Finally, the figure offers an intuitively appealing method for visually highlighting the structure and flow we will follow across the topics in the text.

The foundation stage helps us with our fundamental understanding of what projects are and how they are typically managed in modern organizations. As part of that understanding, we must necessarily focus on the organizational setting within which projects are created, selected, and developed. Some of the critical issues that can affect the manner in which projects are successfully implemented are the contextual issues of a firm's strategy, structure, and culture. Either these elements are set to support project-based work or they are not. In the former case, it is far easier to run projects and achieve positive results for the organization. As a result, it is extremely helpful for us to clearly understand the role that organizational setting, or context, plays in project management.

In Chapter 3 we explore the process of project screening and selection. The manner in which a firm selects the projects it chooses to undertake is often critical to its chances of successful development and commercial profitability. Chapter 4 introduces the challenges of project management from the perspective of the project leader. Project management is an extremely "leader-intensive" undertaking: The project manager is the focal point of the project, often functioning as a miniature CEO. The more project managers understand about project leadership and the skills required by effective project managers, the better companies can begin training project managers within their own ranks.

The second phase is related to the up-front issues of project planning. Once a decision to proceed has been made, the organization must first select a suitable project manager to oversee the development process. Immediately, this project manager is faced with a number of responsibilities, including:

1. *Selecting a team*—Team building and conflict management are the first challenges that project managers face.
2. *Developing project objectives and a plan for execution*—Identifying project requirements and a logical plan to develop the project are crucial.
3. *Performing risk management activities*—Projects are not developed without a clear sense of the risks involved in their planning and implementation.
4. *Cost estimating and budgeting*—Because projects are resource-constrained activities, careful budgeting and cost estimation are critical.
5. *Scheduling*—The heart of project planning revolves around the process of creating clear, aggressive, yet reasonable schedules that chart the most efficient course to project completion.
6. *Managing resources*—The final step in project planning is the careful management of project resources, including project team personnel, to most efficiently perform tasks.

Chapter 5, which discusses project scope management, examines the key features in the overall plan. "Project scope management" is something of an umbrella term under which we consider a number of elements in the overall project planning process. This chapter elaborates the variety of planning techniques and steps for getting a project off on the right foot.

Chapter 6 addresses some of the behavioral challenges project managers face in terms of effective team building and conflict management. This chapter looks at another key component of effective human resource management: the need to create and maintain high-performance teams. Effectively building and nurturing team members—often people from very different backgrounds—is a constant challenge and one that requires serious consideration. Conflict occurs on a number of levels, not just among team members, but between the team and project stakeholders, including top management and customers. This chapter will identify some of the principal causes of conflict and explain various methods for resolving it.

Chapter 7 deals with project risk management. In recent years, this area of project management has become increasingly important to companies that want to ensure, as far as possible, that project selection choices are appropriate, that all the risks and downside potential have been considered, and that, where appropriate, contingency plans have been developed. Chapter 8 covers budgeting and cost estimation. Because project managers and teams are held to both standards of performance and standards of cost control, it is important to understand the key features of cost estimation and budgeting.

Chapters 9 and 10 focus on scheduling methodologies, which are a key feature of project management. These chapters offer an in-depth analysis of various project-scheduling tools, discuss critical software for project scheduling, and explain some recent breakthroughs in project scheduling. Chapter 11 covers a recent development in project scheduling, the development and application of critical chain project scheduling. Chapter 12 considers the challenges of resource allocation. Once various project activities have been identified, we must make sure they work by allocating the resources needed to support them.

The third process in project management, *implementation,* is most easily understood as the stage in which the actual "work" of the project is being performed. For example, engineers and other technical experts determine the series of tasks necessary to complete the overall project, including their individual task responsibilities, and each of the tasks is actively managed by the manager and team to ensure that there are no significant delays that can cause the project to exceed its schedule. Chapter 13 addresses the project challenges of control and evaluation. During the implementation phase, a considerable amount of ambiguity regarding the status of the project is possible unless specific, practical steps are taken to establish a clear method for tracking and controlling the project.

Finally, the processes of project termination reflect the fact that a project is a unique organizational endeavor, marked by a specified beginning and ending. The process of closing down a project, whether due to the need to "kill" it because it is no longer viable or through the steps of a planned termination, offers its own set of challenges. A number of procedures have been developed to make this process as smooth and logical as possible. Chapter 14 discusses the elements in project *closeout*—the phase in which the project is concluded and resources (both monetary and human) are reassigned.

This book was written to help create a new generation of effective project managers. By exploring the various roles of project managers and addressing the challenges and opportunities they constantly face, we will offer a comprehensive and integrative approach to better understand the task of project management—one that explores the full range of strategic, technical, and behavioral challenges and duties for project managers.

This text also includes, at the end of relevant chapters, a series of activities designed to help students develop comprehensive project plans. It is absolutely essential that persons completing a course in project management carry away with them practical knowledge about the steps involved in creating a project, planning its development, and overseeing its work. Future managers need to develop the skills to convert the theories of project management into the successful practice of the craft. With this goal in mind, the text contains a series of exercises designed to help professors and students construct overall project plans. Activities involve the development, from beginning to end, of a project plan, including narrative, risk analysis, work breakdown structure, activity estimation and network diagramming, resource leveling and project budgeting, and so forth. In order to add a sense of realism to the process, later chapters in the book also include a series of hypothetical problems. By the end of the course, students should have created a comprehensive project document that details the necessary steps in converting project plans into practical accomplishments.

As a template for providing examples, the text employs a hypothetical company called ABCups Inc., which is about to initiate an important project. Chapter-ending activities, including exercises in scheduling, budgeting, risk management, and so forth, will often include examples created from the ABCups project for students to use as a model for their own work. In this way, students will be presented both with a challenge and with an example for generating their own deliverables as they progressively build their project plans.

An additional feature of this text is the linkage between concepts that are discussed throughout and the Project Management Body of Knowledge (PMBoK), which was developed by the Project Management Institute (PMI). As the world's leading professional organization for project management, PMI has been in the forefront of efforts to standardize project management practices and codify the necessary skills to be successful in our field. The PMBoK identifies nine knowledge areas of project management skills and activities that all practitioners need to master in order to become fully trained in their profession. These knowledge areas, which are shown in Figure 1.12, encompass a broad overview of the component processes for project management. Although it is not my intention to create a text to serve as a primer for taking a professional certification exam, it is important for us to recognize that the skills we develop through reading this work are directly applicable to the professional project management knowledge areas.

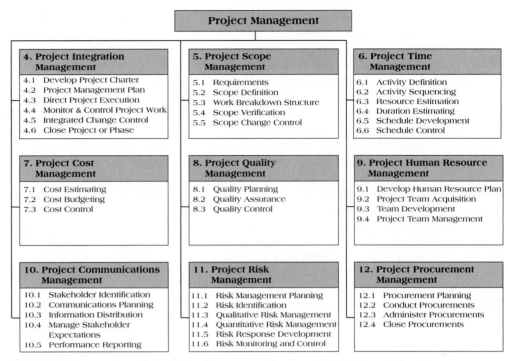

FIGURE 1.12 Overview of the Project Management Institute's PMBoK Knowledge Areas

Source: Project Management Institute. (2008). *A Guide to the Project Management Body of Knowledge (PMBoK Guide),* 4th ed. Project Management Institute, Inc. Copyright and all rights reserved. Material from this publication has been reproduced with the permission of PMI.

Students will find several direct links to the PMBoK in this text. First, the key terms and their definitions are intended to follow the PMBoK glossary (included as an appendix at the end of the text). Second, chapter introductions will also highlight references to the PMBoK as we address them in turn. We can see how each chapter not only adds to our knowledge of project management but also directly links to elements within the PMBoK. Finally, many end-of-chapter exercises and Internet references will require direct interaction with PMI through its Web site.

As an additional link to the Project Management Institute and the PMBoK, this text will include sample practice questions at the end of relevant chapters to allow students to test their in-depth knowledge of aspects of the PMBoK. Nearly 20 years ago, PMI instituted its Project Management Professional (PMP) certification as a means of awarding those with an expert knowledge of project management practice. The PMP certification is the highest professional designation for project management expertise in the world and requires in-depth knowledge in all nine areas of the PMBoK. The inclusion of questions at the end of the relevant chapters offers students a way to assess how well they have learned the important course topics, the nature of PMP certification exam questions, and to point to areas that may require additional study in order to master this material.

This text offers an opportunity for students to begin mastering a new craft—a set of skills that is becoming increasingly valued in contemporary corporations around the world. Project managers represent the new corporate elite: a corps of skilled individuals who routinely make order out of chaos, improving a firm's bottom line and burnishing their own value in the process. With these goals in mind, let us begin.[33]

Summary

1. **Understand why project management is becoming such a powerful and popular practice in business.** Project management offers organizations a number of practical competitive advantages, including the ability to be both effective in the marketplace and efficient with the use of organizational resources, and the ability to achieve technological breakthroughs, to streamline new-product

development, and to manage the challenges arising from the business environment.

2. **Recognize the basic properties of projects, including their definition.** Projects are defined as temporary endeavors undertaken to create a unique product or service. Among their key properties are that projects are complex, one-time processes; projects are limited

by budget, schedule, and resources; they are developed to resolve a clear goal or set of goals; and they are customer-focused.

3. **Understand why effective project management is such a challenge.**   Projects operate outside of normal organizational processes, typified by the work done by functional organizational units. Because they are unique, they require a different mind-set: one that is temporary and aimed at achieving a clear goal within a limited time frame. Projects are ad hoc endeavors with a clear life cycle. They are employed as the building blocks in the design and execution of organizational strategies, and they provide a philosophy and a strategy for the management of change. Other reasons why they are a challenge include the fact that project management requires the crossing of functional and organizational boundaries while trying to satisfy the multiple constraints of time, budget, functionality, and customer satisfaction.

4. **Differentiate between project management practices and more traditional, process-oriented business functions.**   Projects involve new process or product ideas, typically with one objective or a limited set of objectives. They are one-shot activities with a defined beginning and end, employing a heterogeneous group of organizational members as the project team. They operate under circumstances of change and uncertainty, outside of normal organizational channels, and are intended to upset the status quo and violate established practice, if need be, in order to achieve project goals. Process-oriented functions adhere more closely to rigid organizational rules, channels of communication, and procedures. The people within the functional departments are homogenous, engaged in ongoing activities, with well-established systems and procedures. They represent bastions of established practice designed to reinforce the organization's status quo.

5. **Recognize the key motivators that are pushing companies to adopt project management practices.**   Among the key motivators in pushing organizations to adopt project management are (1) shortened product life cycles, (2) narrow product launch windows, (3) increasingly complex and technical products, (4) the emergence of global markets, and (5) an economic period marked by low inflation.

6. **Understand and explain the project life cycle, its stages, and the activities that typically occur at each stage in the project.**   The project life cycle is a mechanism that links time to project activities and refers to the stages in a project's development. The common stages used to describe the life cycle for a project are (1) conceptualization, (2) planning, (3) execution, and (4) termination. A wide and diverse set of activities occurs during different life cycle stages; for example, during the conceptualization phase, the basic project mission and scope is developed and the key project stakeholders are signed on to support the project's development. During planning, myriad project plans and schedules are created to guide the development process. Execution requires that the principal work of the project be performed, and finally, during the termination stage, the project is completed, the work is finished, and the project is transferred to the customer.

7. **Understand the concept of project "success," including various definitions of success, as well as the alternative models of success.**   Originally, project success was predicated simply on a triple-constraint model that rewarded projects if they were completed with regard to schedule, budget, and functionality. This model ignored the emphasis that needs to be placed on project clients, however. In more accurate terms, project success involves a "quadruple constraint," linking the basic project metrics of schedule adherence, budget adherence, project quality (functionality), and customer satisfaction with the finished product. Other models of project success for IT projects employ the measures of (1) system quality, (2) information quality, (3) use, (4) user satisfaction, (5) individual impact, and (6) organizational impact.

8. **Understand the purpose of project management maturity models and the process of benchmarking in organizations.**   Project management maturity models are used to allow organizations to benchmark the best practices of successful project management firms. Project maturity models recognize that different organizations are at different levels of sophistication in their best practices for managing projects. The purpose of benchmarking is to systematically manage the process improvements of project delivery by a single organization over a period of time. As a firm commits to implementing project management practices, maturity models offer a helpful, multistage process for moving forward through increasing levels of sophistication of project expertise.

9. **Identify the relevant maturity stages that organizations go through to become proficient in their use of project management techniques.**   Although there are a number of project maturity models, several of the most common share some core features. For example, most take as their starting point the assumption that unsophisticated organizations initiate projects in an ad hoc fashion, with little overall shared knowledge or procedures. As the firm moves through intermediate steps, it will begin to initiate processes and project management procedures that diffuse a core set of project management techniques and cultural attitudes throughout the organization. Finally, the last stage in maturity models typically recognizes that by this point the firm has moved beyond simply learning the techniques of project management and is working at continuous improvement processes to further refine, improve, and solidify project management philosophies among employees and departments.

Key Terms

Benchmarking *(p. 38)*

Client acceptance *(p. 36)*

Clients *(p. 33)*

Budget *(p. 35)*

Deliverables *(p. 25)*

Performance *(p. 35)*

Process *(p. 25)*

Project *(p. 25)*

Project life cycle *(p. 32)*

Project management *(p. 28)*

Project management
  maturity models *(p. 38)*

Project success *(p. 35)*

Stakeholders *(p. 32)*

Time *(p. 35)*

Triple constraint *(p. 35)*

Discussion Questions

1. What are some of the principal reasons why project management has become such a popular business tool in recent years?
2. What do you see as being the primary challenges to introducing a project management philosophy in most organizations? That is, why is it difficult to shift to a project-based approach in many companies?
3. What are the advantages and disadvantages of using project management?
4. What key characteristics do all projects possess?
5. Describe the basic elements of a project life cycle. Why is an understanding of the life cycle relevant for our understanding of projects?
6. Think of a successful project and an unsuccessful project with which you are familiar. What distinguishes the two, both in terms of the process used to develop them and their outcomes?
7. Consider the Expedition Everest case: What elements in Disney's approach to developing its theme rides do you find particularly impressive? How can a firm like Disney balance the need for efficiency and smooth development of projects with the desire to be innovative and creative? Based on this case, what principles appear to guide its development process?
8. Consider the six criteria for successful IT projects. Why is IT project success often so difficult to assess? Make a case for some factors being more important than others.
9. As organizations seek to become better at managing projects, they often engage in benchmarking with other companies in similar industries. Discuss the concept of benchmarking. What are its goals? How does benchmarking work?
10. Explain the concept of a project management maturity model. What purpose does it serve?
11. Compare and contrast the four project management maturity models shown in Table 1.3. What strengths and weaknesses do you perceive in each of the models?

Case Study 1.1

MegaTech, Inc.

MegaTech, Inc., designs and manufactures automotive components. For years, the company enjoyed a stable marketplace, a small but loyal group of customers, and a relatively predictable environment. Though slowly, annual sales continued to grow until recently hitting $300 million. MegaTech products were popular because they required little major updating or yearly redesign. The stability of its market, coupled with the consistency of its product, allowed MegaTech to forecast annual demand accurately, to rely on production runs with long lead times, and to concentrate on internal efficiency.

Then, with the advent of the North American Free Trade Agreement (NAFTA) and other international trade agreements, MegaTech found itself competing with auto parts suppliers headquartered in countries around the world. The company was thrust into an unfamiliar position: It had to become customer-focused and quicker to market with innovative products. Facing these tremendous commercial challenges, top management at MegaTech decided to recreate the company as a project-based organization.

The transition, though not smooth, has nonetheless paid big dividends. Top managers determined, for instance, that product updates had to be much more frequent. Achieving this goal meant yearly redesigns and new technologies, which, in turn, meant making innovative changes in the firm's operations. In order to make these adjustments, special project teams were formed around each of the company's product lines and given a mandate to maintain market competitiveness.

At the same time, however, MegaTech wanted to maintain its internal operating efficiencies. Thus all project teams were given strict cost and schedule guidelines for new product introductions. Finally, the company created a sophisticated research and development team, which is responsible for locating likely new avenues for technological change 5 to 10 years down the road. Today, MegaTech operates project teams not only for managing current product lines but also for seeking longer-term payoffs through applied research.

MegaTech has found the move to project management challenging. For one thing, employees are still rethinking the ways in which they allocate their time and resources. In addition, the firm's success rate with new projects is still less than management had hoped. Nevertheless, top managers

(continued)

feel that, on balance, the shift to project management has given the company the operating advantage that it needed to maintain its lead over rivals in its globally competitive industry. "Project management," admits one MegaTech executive, "is certainly not a magic pill for success, but it has started us thinking about how we operate. As a result, we are doing smarter things in a faster way around here."

Questions

1. What is it about project management that offers MegaTech a competitive advantage in its industry?
2. What elements of the marketplace in which MegaTech operates led the firm to believe that project management would improve its operations?

Case Study 1.2

Continuing Education Center at TOBB University of Economics and Technology

TOBB University of Economics and Technology (TOBB ETU), the largest private sector institution in Turkey, was founded by the Union of Chambers and Commodity Exchanges of Turkey (TOBB) for educating entrepreneurial and qualified community leaders. In conjunction with TOBB ETU's mission of maintaining university and industry cooperation, and enhancing productivity through helping the workforce to acquire the relevant skill sets, the Continuing Education Center at TOBB ETU (ETU CEC) offers project management and consulting services. They also offer a wide range of educational programs to individuals and to organizations of all sizes, especially small and medium enterprises (SMEs), which constitute the backbone of the Turkish economy.

At the Continuing Education Center, courses are taught by TOBB ETU instructors as well as by industry professionals. Some of highly demanded courses include Project Management, Human Resources Development and Management, Performance Evaluation, Foreign Trade, Training the Trainer, and Access to EU Funding. The Continuing Education Center also utilizes the academic staff of TOBB ETU in its projects and for consulting services. Since 2006, ETU CEC has reached 13,000 people with 280 professional events including workshops, certificate courses, and customized training programs for various organizations, and has provided consulting and project management services to 40 institutions.

The administrative board of ETU CEC includes three professors, and the center employs a project manager, a business analyst, and two administrative staff

members. Also, each semester two or three TOBB ETU students join the Continuing Education Center as interns through the university's cooperative education program. Interns mainly help administrative staff; however, after they become familiar with ETU CEC activities, they are allowed to participate in projects. The project manager oversees multiple projects with full responsibility, and team members are assigned to several projects at the same time.

Dr. Ramazan Aktaş, a finance professor at TOBB ETU and the manager of ETU CEC, says that the project teams at ETU CEC achieve their missions with small teams because of their strict adherence to solid project management practices. He also states that ETU CEC places a great emphasis on customer satisfaction. By means of its project management system, ETU CEC has obtained an advantage over its competitors, formed long-term partnerships with other organizations, promoted collaboration, acquired new projects, achieved high customer satisfaction, and therefore sustained continuous increases in its customer base and profits.[34]

Questions

1. What are the benefits and drawbacks of allowing interns participate in ETU CEC projects?
2. What are the potential problems with requiring project team members to be involved in multiple projects at the same time? What are the potential advantages?
3. What benefits has ETU CEC obtained from its project management system?

Case Study 1.3

Disney's Expedition Everest

The newest thrill ride to open in the Walt Disney World Resort may just be the most impressive. As Disney approached its 50th anniversary, the company wanted to celebrate in a truly special way. What was its idea? Create a

park attraction that would, in many ways, serve as the link between Disney's amazing past and its promising future. Disney showed that it was ready to pull out all stops in order to get everything just right.

In 2006, The Walt Disney Company introduced Expedition Everest in Disney's Animal Kingdom Park at Lake Buena Vista, Florida. Expedition Everest is more than just a roller coaster. It is the embodiment of the Disney spirit: a ride that combines Disney's trademark thrills, unexpected twists and turns, incredible attention to detail, and impressive project management skills.

First, let's consider some of the technical details of Expedition Everest:

- With a peak of just under 200 feet, the ride is contained within the tallest of 18 mountains created by Disney's Imagineers at Disney parks worldwide.
- The ride contains nearly a mile of track, with twists, tight turns, and sudden drops.
- The Disney team created a Yeti: an enormous, fur-covered, Audio-Animatronics monster powered by a set of hydraulic cylinders whose combined thrust equals that of a Boeing 747 airliner. Through a series of sketches, computer-animated drawings, sculptures, and tests that took more than two years to perfect, Disney created and programmed its Abominable Snowman to stand over 10 feet tall and serve as the focal point of the ride.
- More than 900 bamboo plants, 10 species of trees, and 110 species of shrubs were planted to re-create the feeling of the Himalayan lowlands surrounding Mount Everest.
- More than 1,800 tons of steel were used to construct the mountain. The covering of the framework was done using more than 3,000 prefabricated "chips" created from 25,000 individual computer-molded pieces of steel.
- To create the proper color schemes, 2,000 gallons of stain and paint were used on rockwork and throughout the village Disney designed to serve as a backdrop for the ride.
- More than 2,000 handcrafted items from Asia are used as props, cabinetry, and architectural ornamentation.

Building an attraction does not come easily or quickly for Disney's Imagineers. Expedition Everest was several years in development as Disney sent teams, including Walt Disney Imagineering's Creative Executive Joe Rohde, on repeated trips to the Himalayas in Nepal to study the lands, architecture, colors, ecology, and culture in order to create the most authentic setting for the new attraction. Disney's efforts reflect a desire to do much more than provide a world-class ride experience; they demonstrate the Imagineers' eagerness to tell a story—a story that combines the mythology of the Yeti figure with the unique history of the Nepalese living in the shadow of the world's tallest mountain. Ultimately, the attraction, with all its background and thematic elements, took nearly five years to complete.

Riders on Expedition Everest gain a real feel for the atmosphere that Disney has worked so hard to create. The guests' adventure starts by entering the building of the "Himalayan Escape" tour company, complete with Norbu and Bob's booking office to obtain permits for their trip. Overhead flutter authentic prayer flags from monasteries in Nepal. Next, guests pass through Tashi's General Store and Bar to stock up on supplies for their journey to the peak of the mountain. Finally, guests pass through an old tea warehouse that contains a remarkable museum of artifacts reflecting Nepal's culture, a history of the Himalayas, and tales of the Yeti, which is said to inhabit the slopes of Mount Everest. It is only now that guests are permitted to board the Anandapur Rail Service for their trip to the peak. Each train is modeled after an aging, steam-engine train, seating 34 guests per train.

Over the next several minutes, guests are transported up the roller coaster track, through a series of winding turns, until their encounter with the Yeti. At this point another unique feature of the attraction emerges: The train begins rushing backward down the track, as though it were out of control. Through the balance of the ride, guests experience a landscape of sights and sounds culminating in a 50 mph final dash down the mountain and back to the safety of the Nepalese village.

Disney's approach to the management of projects such as Expedition Everest is to combine careful planning, including schedule and budget preparation, with the imagination and vision for which the company is so well known. Creativity is a critical element in the development of new projects at Disney. The company's Imagineers include some of the most skilled artists and computer-animation experts in the world. Although it is easy to be impressed by the technical knowledge of Disney's personnel, it is important to remember that each new project is approached with an understanding of the company's underlying business and attention to market projections, cost control, and careful project management discipline. New attraction proposals are carefully screened and researched. The result is the creation of some of the most innovative and enjoyable rides in the world. Disney does not add new attractions to its theme parks frequently, but when it does so, it does so with style!

Questions

1. Suppose you were a project manager for Disney. Based on the information in this case, what critical success metrics do you think the company uses when designing a new ride; that is, how would you prioritize the needs for addressing project cost, schedule, quality, and client acceptance? What evidence supports your answer?
2. Why is Disney's attention to detail in its rides unique? How does the company use the "atmosphere" discussed in the case to maximize the experience while minimizing complaints about length of wait for the ride?

Internet Exercises

1. The largest professional project management organization in the world is the Project Management Institute (PMI). Go to its Web site, www.pmi.org, and examine the links you find. Which links suggest that project management has become a sophisticated and vital element in corporate success? Select at least three of the related links and report briefly on the content of these links.

2. Go to the PMI Web site and examine the link "Global Membership and Communities." What do you discover when you begin navigating among the various chapters and cooperative organizations associated with PMI? How does this information cause you to rethink project management as a career option?

3. Go to www.pmi.org/Business-Solutions/OPM3-Case-Study-Library.aspx and examine some of the cases included on the Web page. What do they suggest about the challenges of managing projects successfully? The complexity of many of today's projects? The exciting breakthroughs or opportunities that projects allow us to exploit?

4. Using your favorite search engine (Google, Yahoo!, etc.), type in the keywords "project" and "project management." Randomly select three of the links that come up on the screen. Summarize what you find.

5. Go to the Web site for the Software Engineering Institute of Carnegie Mellon University at www.sei.cmu.edu/pub/documents/94.reports/pdf/sr07.94.pdf and access the software process maturity questionnaire. What are some of the questions that IT companies need to consider when assessing their level of project management maturity?

6. Go to the Companion Web site supporting this text, *www.pearsonglobaleditions.com/pinto*. Internet Reading: Morris, P. W. G. (1998). "Why project management doesn't always make business sense," *Project Management,* 4(1): 12–16.

7. Go to the Web site supporting this text, *www.pearsonglobaleditions.com/pinto*. Internet Reading: Cook, C. R., and Pritchard, C. L. (1998). "Why project management?" in D. I. Cleland (Ed.), *The Project Management Field Guide.* New York: Van Nostrand Reinhold, pp. 22–33.

PMP Certification Sample Questions

1. The majority of the project budget is expended upon:
   a. Project plan development.
   b. Project plan execution.
   c. Project termination.
   d. Project communication.

2. Which of the following is the most critical component of the triple constraint?
   a. Time, then cost, then quality.
   b. Quality, then budget, then time.
   c. Scope.
   d. They are all of equal importance unless otherwise stated.

3. Which of the following best describes a project stakeholder?
   a. A team member.
   b. The project manager.
   c. Someone who works in an area affected by the project.
   d. All of the above are stakeholders.

4. All of the following are elements in the definition of a project, except:
   a. A project is time-limited.
   b. A project is unique.
   c. A project is composed of unrelated activities.
   d. A project is undertaken for a purpose.

5. All of the following distinguish project management from other process activities, except:
   a. There are no fundamental differences between project and process management.
   b. Project management often involves greater certainty of performance, cost, and schedule.
   c. Process management operates outside of line organizations.
   d. None of the above correctly distinguish project from process management.

Answers: 1 b—The majority of a project budget is spent during the execution phase; 2 d—Unless otherwise stated, all elements in the triple-constraint model are equally critical; 3 d—All of the examples listed are types of project stakeholders; 4 c—A project is composed of "interrelated" activities; 5 d—None of the answers given correctly differentiates "process" from "project" management.

Notes

1. Valery, Paul, quoted in "Extreme chaos" (2001). Standish Group International.

2. www.cnn.com/2010/WORLD/americas/10/15/chile.mine.rescue.recap/index.html; www.cnn.com/2010/OPINION/10/12/gergen.miners/index.html; www.thenewamerican.com/index.php/opinion/sam-blumenfeld/5140-how-americans-engineered-the-rescue-of-the-chilean-miners.

3. Peters, Thomas. (1994). *Liberation Management: Necessary Disorganization for the Nanosecond Nineties.* New York: Fawcett Books.

4. Stewart, Thomas H. (1995). "The corporate jungle spawns a new species," *Fortune,* July 10, pp. 179–80.

5. Gilbreath, Robert D. (1988). "Working with pulses not streams: Using projects to capture opportunity," in Cleland, D., and King, W. (Eds.), *Project Management Handbook.* New York: Van Nostrand Reinhold, pp. 3–15.

6. Buchanan, D. A., and Boddy, D. (1992). *The Expertise of the Change Agent: Public Performance and Backstage Activity.* London: Prentice Hall.

7. Frame, J. D. (1995). *Managing Projects in Organizations,* 2nd ed. San Francisco, CA: Jossey-Bass. See also Frame, J. D. (2002). *The New Project Management,* 2nd ed. San Francisco, CA: Jossey-Bass.

8. Kerzner, H. (2003). *Project Management,* 8th ed. New York: Wiley.

9. Field, M., and Keller, L. (1998). *Project Management.* London: The Open University.

10. Project Management Institute. (2000). *A Guide to the Project Management Body of Knowledge.* Newtown Square, PA: PMI.

11. Cleland, D. I. (2001). "The discipline of project management," in Knutson, J. (Ed.), *Project Management for Business Professionals.* New York: Wiley, pp. 3–22.

12. Lundin, R. A., and Soderholm, A. (1995). "A theory of the temporary organization," *Scandinavian Journal of Management,* 11(4): 437–55.

13. Graham, R. J. (1992). "A survival guide for the accidental project manager." *Proceedings of the Annual Project Management Institute Symposium.* Drexel Hill, PA: Project Management Institute, pp. 355–61.

14. Sources: http://macs.about.com/b/a/087641.htm; Mossberg, W. S. (2004). "The music man," *Wall Street Journal,* June 14, p. B1.

15. Pinto, J. K., and Millet, I. (1999). *Successful Information Systems Implementation: The Human Side,* 2nd ed. Newtown Square, PA: PMI.

16. Kapur, G. K. (1998). "Don't look back to create the future." Presentation at the Frontiers of Project Management Conference, Boston, MA.

17. www.computerweekly.com/blogs/public-sector/2007/05/public-sector-it-projects-have.html.

18. "How to establish an organizational culture that promotes projects," www.bia.ca/articles/HowToEstablish aProjectManagementCulture.htm; Standish Group. (2006). *The Trends in IT Value* report; Standish Group. (2009). *Chaos Summary 2009.* Boston, MA.

19. Kelley, M. (2008). "$600M spent on canceled contracts," *USA Today,* November 18, p. 1.

20. Cleland, D. I. (1994). *Project Management: Strategic Design and Implementation.* New York: McGraw-Hill; Pinto, J. K., and Rouhiainen, P. (2001). *Building Customer-Based Project Organizations.* New York: Wiley; Gray, C. F., and Larson, E. W. (2003). *Project Management,* 2nd ed. Burr Ridge, IL: McGraw-Hill.

21. Petroski, H. (1985). *To Engineer Is Human—The Role of Failure in Successful Design.* London: St. Martin's Press.

22. http://aftermathnews.wordpress.com/2008/08/28/chinese-sky-scraper-builders-to-put-up-equivalent-of-10-new-yorks-says-rio-tinto/; www.railway-technology.com/projects/beijing/; www.nytimes.com/2009/05/11/world/asia/11coal.html.

23. Sohmen, Victor. (2002, July). "Project termination: Why the delay?" Paper presented at PMI Research Conference, Seattle, WA.

24. Freeman, M., and Beale, P. (1992). "Measuring project success," *Project Management Journal,* 23(1): 8–17.

25. Morris, P. W. G. (1997). *The Management of Projects.* Thomas Telford: London; "Women design concept car for Volvo," www.usatoday.com/money/autos/2004-03-02; "This Volvo is not a guy thing." (2004, March 15). www.businessweek.com/magazine/04_11; http://en.wikipedia.org/wiki/Volvo_YCC.

26. Shenhar, A. J., Levy, O., and Dvir, D. (1997). "Mapping the dimensions of project success," *Project Management Journal,* 28(2): 5–13.

27. DeLone, W. H., and McLean, E. R. (1992). "Information systems success: The quest for the dependent variable," *Information Systems Research,* 3(1): 60–95; Seddon, P. B. (1997). "A respecification and extension of the DeLone and McLean model of IS success," *Information Systems Research,* 8(3): 249–53; DeLone, W. H., and McLean, E. R. (2003). "The DeLone and McLean model of information system success: A ten-year update," *Journal of Management Information Systems,* 19(4): 9–30.

28. Atkinson, R. (1999). "Project management: Cost, time and quality, two best guesses and a phenomenon, it's time to accept other success criteria," *International Journal of Project Management,* 17(6): 337–42; Cooke-Davies, T. (2002). "The 'real' success factors on projects," *International Journal of Project Management,* 20(3): 185–90; Olson, D. L. (2001). *Introduction to Information Systems Project Management.* Burr Ridge, IL: Irwin/McGraw-Hill.

29. Pennypacker, J. S., and Grant, K. P. (2003). "Project management maturity: An industry benchmark," *Project Management Journal,* 34(1): 4–11; Ibbs, C. W., and Kwak, Y. H. (1998). "Benchmarking project management organizations," *PMNetwork,* 12(2): 49–53.

30. Reginato, P. E., and Ibbs, C. W. (2002). "Project management as a core competency," *Proceedings of PMI Research Conference 2002,* Slevin, D., Pinto, J., and Cleland, D. (Eds.), *The Frontiers of Project Management Research.* Newtown Square, PA: Project Management Institute, pp. 445–50.

31. Crawford, K. (2002). *Project Management Maturity Model: Providing a Proven Path to Project Management Excellence.* New York: Marcel Dekker; Foti, R. (2002). "Implementing maturity models," *PMNetwork,* 16(9): 39–43; Gareis, R. (2001). "Competencies in the project-oriented organization," in Slevin, D., Cleland, D., and Pinto, J. (Eds.), *The Frontiers of Project Management Research.* Newtown Square, PA: Project Management Institute, pp. 213–24; Gareis, R., and Huemann, M. (2000). "Project management competencies in the project-oriented organization," in Turner, J. R., and Simister, S. J. (Eds.), *The Gower Handbook of Project Management,* 3rd ed. Aldershot, UK: Gower, pp. 709–22; Ibbs, C. W., and Kwak, Y. H. (2000). "Assessing project management maturity," *Project Management Journal,* 31(1): 32–43.

32. Humphrey, W. S. (1988). "Characterizing the software process: A maturity framework," *IEEE Software,* 5(3): 73–79; Carnegie Mellon University. (1995). *The Capability Maturity Model: Guidelines for Improving the Software Process.* Boston, MA: Addison-Wesley; Kerzner, H. (2001). *Strategic Planning for Project Management Using a Project Management Maturity Model.* New York: Wiley; Crawford, J. K. (2002). *Project Management Maturity Model.* New York: Marcel Dekker; Pritchard, C. (1999). *How to Build a Work Breakdown Structure: The Cornerstone of Project Management.* Arlington, VA: ESI International.

33. Jenkins, Robert N. (2005). "A new peak for Disney," *St. Petersburg Times Online,* www.sptimes.com/2005/12/11/news_pf/travel/A_new_peak_for_Disney.

34. Information based on interviews with Dr. Ramazan Aktas, Continuing Education Center at TOBB University of Economics and Technology, www.etu.edu.tr, May 4, 2012.

The Organizational Context
Strategy, Structure, and Culture

Chapter Outline

Chapter Objectives

After completing this chapter, you should be able to:

1. Understand how effective project management contributes to achieving strategic objectives.

2. Recognize three components of the corporate strategy model: formulation, implementation, and evaluation.

3. See the importance of identifying critical project stakeholders and managing them within the context of project development.

4. Recognize the strengths and weaknesses of three basic forms of organizational structure and their implications for managing projects.

5. Understand how companies can change their structure into a "heavyweight project organization" structure to facilitate effective project management practices.

6. Identify the characteristics of three forms of project management office (PMO).

7. Understand key concepts of corporate culture and how cultures are formed.

8. Recognize the positive effects of a supportive organizational culture on project management practices versus those of a culture that works against project management.

PROJECT MANAGEMENT BODY OF KNOWLEDGE CORE CONCEPTS COVERED IN THIS CHAPTER

1. Project Scope Management Initiation (PMBoK sec. 5.1)

2. Procurement Planning (PMBoK sec. 12.1)

3. Project Stakeholders (PMBoK sec. 2.2)

4. Organizational Influences (PMBoK sec. 2.3)

5. Organizational Structure (PMBoK sec. 2.3.3)

6. Organizational Cultures and Styles (PMBoK sec. 2.3.2)

7. Socio-Economic-Environmental Influences (PMBoK sec. 2.5)

PROJECT PROFILE

Case—The U.S. Army Returns to the Era of Blimps

When we think of blimps in modern times, we usually associate the image with sporting events, where these lighter-than-air vehicles circle stadiums or golf courses to provide the occasional aerial photography to improve our enjoyment of the game. How many of us would view a blimp as the latest step forward in improving our military capability? In a case where truth is stranger than fiction, just such an advance is taking place.

Through a $517 million contract awarded by the U.S. Army to Northrop Grumman in June 2010, construction of three Long Endurance Multi-Intelligence Vehicle (LEMV) airships began with the intention of deploying them over Afghanistan by 2012. These LEMVs are a unique rethinking of the dirigible technology going back over 100 years. With the rise of global terrorism, the increasing costs of recruiting, training, and retaining professional soldiers, and the issues of overall security, two critical demands have been placed on modern armies. First, surveillance: Militaries need to be able to observe wide areas for very long periods of time—in fact, the longer the better. Scanning threat areas for several days impedes enemy opportunities to gather and move troops without detection. Second, in supporting this persistent observation capability, it is critical not to break the budget. Thus, the search for low-cost means to observe and report is of utmost importance. What is needed to solve these critical problems is the creation of a new generation of airborne capability: a very long-endurance, low-operating-cost platform such as the LEMV.

Strictly speaking, the LEMV is not really a blimp because it is heavier than air—only 80% of the LEMV's lift comes from buoyancy; the other 20% is from six thrusters powered by individual turbo-diesels for takeoff and climb. In its current configuration, the LEMV is to be remotely piloted, although it does retain the option for using an actual aircrew. A 40 × 15 foot section behind the sometimes-manned cockpit will carry an array of intelligence-gathering systems, like radar and wide-area motions sensors. Information will then be beamed back down in real time to commanders on the ground. The LEMVs are huge: They are longer than a football field, taller than a 7-story building, and can hover at 20,000 feet for 21 days at a time. In the right conditions, their thrusters will allow them to travel at speeds of up to 80 knots.

Additionally, LEMVs are a very low-cost option for extended aerial surveillance. Northrop's Director of Airship Programs, Alan Metzger, has commented:

When you do the math on that you're talking about $20,000 to keep the vehicle in the air for three weeks. It's vastly cheaper to operate than many conventional aircraft today....Some of the characteristics of our vehicle allow you to make trades between how long you'd like to stay in the air and how much cargo you'd like to carry. We have the ability to trade 23 days to go 1000 miles and carry 15, 20, 30,000 pounds....We're green, we use a quarter of the fuel as the same payload of cargo aircraft...there are fewer moving parts. There's less maintenance....

(continued)

So where do LEMVs fit in to the Army's mission? The answer is that they are intended to do what they do best. They can be deployed to operate from small forward bases, much like helicopters. Hovering over high-threat areas, they can use advanced optics and infra-red scanning to detect troop movements on the ground. They can also serve as steady communications relays, ensuring the groups of soldiers in mountainous areas never lose contact with one another, even if they don't have direct line of sight. They can track important convoys, key roadways, or other key infrastructure as semi-permanent, "eye-in-the-sky" escorts, monitor an urban area of interest to prep for major battles or enforce security, or focus on shutting down border chokepoints.

Northrop Grumman's program is not the only one the Army is currently funding. A $400 million grant to Lockheed Martin in 2009 is being used to develop an even more ambitious idea: a new prototype airship designed to stay in the stratosphere for years at a time. The airship would use 6,000 square meters of lightweight radar equipment to track everything from cruise missiles to small vehicles hidden in the undergrowth 300 kilometers away. The surface area and height of a stratospheric airship enables a very large radar aperture. As the radar aperture grows larger, the tracking performance of the radar system increases dramatically.

The LEMV program is an interesting departure from many other Department of Defense acquisition programs in that the focus here is squarely on maximizing capabilities for specific missions. In other words, the Army is not looking to buy the "newest and coolest" with airship technology but, instead, is focusing on addressing two seemingly contradictory goals: finding a means for maximum surveillance capability at an affordable price. The LEMV, which incongruously resembles the blimps from earlier decades, is an excellent example of meeting these two goals.[1]

INTRODUCTION

Within any organization, successful project management is contextual. What that means is that the *organization itself matters*—its culture, its structure, and its strategy each play an integral part, and together they create the environment in which a project will flourish or founder. For example, a project's connection to your organization's overall strategy, the care with which you staff the team, and the goals you set for the project can be critical. Similarly, your organization's policies, structure, culture, and operating systems can work to support and promote project management or work against the ability to effectively run projects. Contextual issues provide the backdrop around which project activities must operate, so understanding what is beneath these issues truly contributes to understanding how to manage projects. Issues that affect a project can vary widely from company to company.

Before beginning a project, the project manager and team must be certain about the structure of the organization as it pertains to their project and the tasks they seek to accomplish. As clearly as possible, all reporting relationships must be specified, the rules and procedures that will govern the project must be established, and any issues of staffing the project team must be identified. Prior to the start of Operation Desert Storm in 1991, the U.S. and allied countries devoted an enormous amount of time and effort to developing a working relationship among all coalition members, ensuring that each group was given its assignments, understood its job, and recognized how the overall structure and management of the coalition was expected to proceed. Desert Storm illustrated the importance of clearly establishing an organizational structure before the start of integrated operations.

For many organizations, projects and project management practices are not the operating norm. In fact, as Chapter 1 discussed, projects typically exist outside of the formal, process-oriented activities associated with many organizations. As a result, many companies are simply not structured to allow for the successful completion of projects in conjunction with other ongoing corporate activities. The key challenge is discovering how project management may best be employed, regardless of the structure the company has adopted. What are the strengths and weaknesses of various structural forms and what are their implications for our ability to manage projects? This chapter will examine the concept of organizational culture and its roots and implications for effective project management. By looking closely at three of the most important contextual issues for project management—strategy, organizational structure, and culture—you will see how the variety of structural options can affect, either positively or negatively, the firm's ability to manage projects.

2.1 PROJECTS AND ORGANIZATIONAL STRATEGY

Strategic management is the science of formulating, implementing, and evaluating cross-functional decisions that enable an organization to achieve its **objectives**.[2] In this section we will consider the relevant components of this definition as they apply to project management. Strategic management consists of the following elements:

1. *Developing vision statements and mission statements.* Vision and mission statements establish a sense of what the organization hopes to accomplish or what top managers hope it will become at some point in the future. A corporate vision serves as a focal point for members of the organization who may find themselves pulled in multiple directions by competing demands. In the face of multiple expectations and even contradictory efforts, an ultimate vision can serve as a "tie breaker," which is highly beneficial in establishing priorities. A sense of vision is also an extremely important source of motivation and purpose. As the Book of Proverbs points out: "Where there is no vision, the people perish" (Prov. 29:18). Many firms apply their vision or mission statement to evaluating new project opportunities as a first screening device. For example, Fluor-Daniel Corporation, a large construction organization, employs as its vision the goal of being "the preeminent leader in the global building and services marketplace by delivering world-class solutions." Projects that do not support this vision are not undertaken.

2. *Formulating, implementing, and evaluating.* Projects, as the key ingredients in strategy implementation, play a crucial role in the basic process model of strategic management. A firm devotes significant time and resources to evaluating its business opportunities through developing a corporate vision or mission, assessing internal strengths and weaknesses as well as external opportunities and threats, establishing long-range objectives, and generating and selecting among various strategic alternatives. All these components relate to the formulation stage of strategy. Within this context, projects serve as the vehicles that enable companies to seize opportunities, capitalize on their strengths, and implement overall corporate objectives. New product development, for example, fits neatly into this framework. New products are developed and commercially introduced as a company's response to business opportunities. Effective project management enables firms to efficiently and rapidly respond.

3. *Making cross-functional decisions.* Business strategy is a corporate-wide venture, requiring the commitment and shared resources of all functional areas to meet overall objectives. Cross-functional decision making is a critical feature of project management, as experts from various functional groups come together into a team of diverse personalities and backgrounds. Project management work is a natural environment in which to operationalize strategic plans.

4. *Achieving objectives.* Whether the organization is seeking market leadership through low-cost, innovative products, superior quality, or other means, projects are the most effective tools to allow objectives to be met. A key feature of project management is that it can potentially allow firms to be effective in the external market as well as internally efficient in operations; that is, it is a great vehicle for optimizing organizational objectives, whether they incline toward efficiency of production or product or process effectiveness.

Projects have been called the "stepping-stones" of corporate strategy.[3] This idea implies that an organization's overall strategic vision is the driving force behind its project development. For example, 3M's desire to be a leading innovator in business gives rise to the creation and management of literally hundreds of new product development projects within the multinational organization every year. Likewise, Rubbermaid Corporation is noted for its consistent pursuit of new product development and market introduction. The manner in which organizational strategies affect new project introductions will be addressed in greater detail in our chapter on project selection (Chapter 3). Projects are the building blocks of strategies; they put an action-oriented face on the strategic edifice. Some examples of how projects operate as strategic building blocks are shown in Table 2.1. Each of the examples illustrates the underlying theme that projects are the "operational reality" behind strategic vision. In other words, they serve as the building blocks to create the reality a strategy can only articulate.

Another way to visualize how projects connect to organizational strategy is shown in Figure 2.1.[4] This model envisions a hierarchy where the mission is paramount, objectives more formally define the mission, and strategy, goals, and programs underlie the objectives. The figure importantly suggests that the various strategic elements must exist in harmony with each other; that is, the mission, objectives, strategies, goals,

TABLE 2.1 Projects Reflect Strategy

Strategy	Project
Technical or operating initiatives (such as new distribution strategies or decentralized plant operations)	Construction of new plants or modernization of facilities
Redevelopment of products for greater market acceptance	Reengineering projects
New business processes for greater streamlining and efficiency	Reengineering projects
Changes in strategic direction or product portfolio reconfiguration	New product lines
Creation of new strategic alliances	Negotiation with supply chain members (including suppliers and distributors)
Matching or improving on competitors' products and services	Reverse engineering projects
Improvement of cross-organizational communication and efficiency in supply chain relationships	Enterprise IT efforts
Promotion of cross-functional interaction, streamlining of new product or service introduction, and improvement of departmental coordination	Concurrent engineering projects

and programs must remain in alignment.[5] It would make little sense, for example, to create a vision of "an environmentally aware organization" if subsequent objectives and strategies aimed at ecologically unfriendly policies.

Figure 2.2 provides concrete examples to illustrate the strategic alignment between a firm's projects and its basic vision, objectives, strategies, and goals.[6] If, for example, a manufacturer of refrigeration equipment creates a vision statement that says, in part, that the company is in "the business of supplying system components to a worldwide nonresidential air-conditioning market," this vision is clarified by specific strategic objectives: return on investment (ROI) expectation, dividend maintenance, and social responsibility. Supporting the base of the hierarchy are strategies, goals, and programs. Here the firm's strategies are stated in terms of a three-phase approach: (1) concentrate on achieving objectives through existing markets and product lines, (2) focus on new market opportunities in foreign or restricted markets, and (3) pursue new products in existing markets. The organization clearly is intent on first maintaining existing product lines and markets before pursuing new product development and innovation.

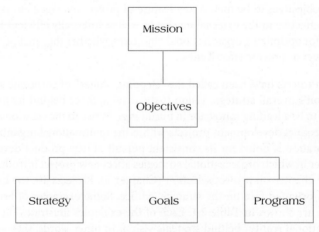

FIGURE 2.1   Relationship of Strategic Elements

Source: Adapted from W. R. King. (1988). "The Role of Projects in the Implementation of Business Strategy," in D. I. Cleland and W. R. King (Eds.), *Project Management Handbook,* 2nd ed. New York: Van Nostrand Reinhold, pp. 129–39. Reprinted with permission of John Wiley & Sons, Inc.

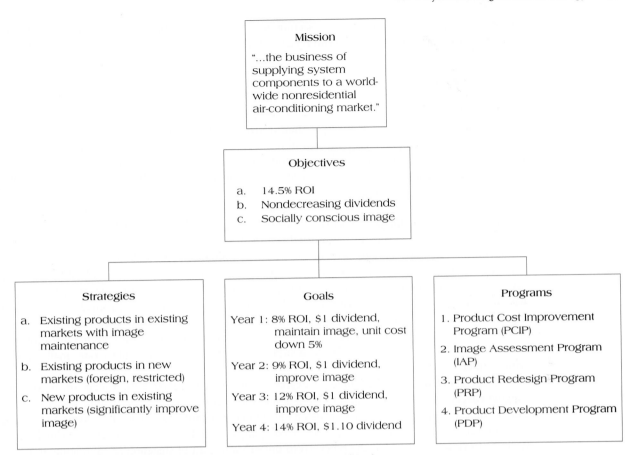

FIGURE 2.2 Illustrating Alignment Between Strategic Elements and Projects

Source: Adapted from W. R. King. (1988). "The Role of Projects in the Implementation of Business Strategy," in D. I. Cleland and W. R. King (Eds.), *Project Management Handbook,* 2nd ed. New York: Van Nostrand Reinhold, pp. 129–39. Reprinted with permission of John Wiley & Sons, Inc.

The goals, shown in the middle of the hierarchy base in Figure 2.2, reflect a four-year plan based on the aforementioned strategies. Suppose that a firm's year one goals aim for an 8% return on investment, steady dividends, decreasing unit costs of production, and solid image maintenance. Goals for years two through four are progressively more ambitious, all based on supporting the three-phase strategy. Finally, the programs indicated at the right side of the hierarchy are the sources of the company's projects. Each program is typically a collection of supporting projects; hence, even the most basic activities of the company are conducted in support of the firm's strategic elements. To demonstrate how these programs are broken down, the Image Assessment Program (IAP) is made up of several supporting projects, including:

1. Customer Survey Project
2. Corporate Philanthropy Project
3. Quality Assessment Project
4. Employee Relations Project

All of these projects promote the Image Assessment Program, which in turn is just one supporting **program** in a series designed to achieve strategic goals. In this model, it is likely that several projects actually support multiple programs. For example, the Customer Survey Project can provide valuable information to the Product Redesign Program (PRP), as customer satisfaction data are fed back to the design department. Projects, as the building blocks of strategy, are typically initiated through the corporation's strategic purposes, deriving from a clear and logical sequencing of vision, objectives, strategies, and goals.

An organization's strategic management is the first important contextual element in its project management approaches. Because projects form the building blocks that allow us to implement strategic plans, it is vital that there exist a clear sense of harmony, or complementarity, between strategy and projects that have been selected for development. In a later section, we will add to our understanding of the importance of creating the right context for projects by adding an additional variable into the mix: the organization's structure.

2.2 STAKEHOLDER MANAGEMENT

Organizational research and direct experience tell us that organizations and project teams cannot operate in ways that ignore the external effects of their decisions. One way to understand the relationship of project managers and their projects to the rest of the organization is through employing stakeholder analysis. **Stakeholder analysis** is a useful tool for demonstrating some of the seemingly irresolvable conflicts that occur through the planned creation and introduction of any new project. **Project stakeholders** are defined as all individuals or groups who have an active stake in the project and can potentially impact, either positively or negatively, its development.[7] Project stakeholder analysis, then, consists of formulating strategies to identify and, if necessary, manage for positive results the impact of stakeholders on the project.

Stakeholders can affect and are affected by organizational actions to varying degrees.[8] In some cases, a corporation must take serious heed of the potential influence some stakeholder groups are capable of wielding. In other situations, a stakeholder group may have relatively little power to influence a company's activities but its presence may still require attention. Contrast, for example, the impact that the government has on regulating the tobacco industry's activities with the relative weakness of a small subcontractor working for Oracle on new software development. In the first case, the federal government has, in recent years, strongly limited the activities and sales strategies of the tobacco companies through the threat of regulation and litigation. On the other hand, Oracle, a large organization, can easily replace one small subcontractor with another.

Stakeholder analysis is helpful to the degree that it compels firms to acknowledge the potentially wide-ranging effects, both intended and unintended, that their actions can have on various stakeholder groups.[9] For example, the strategic decision to close an unproductive manufacturing facility may make good business sense in terms of costs versus benefits that the company derives from the manufacturing site. However, the decision to close the plant has the potential to unleash a torrent of stakeholder complaints in the form of protests and challenges from local unions, workers, community leaders in the town affected by the closing, political and legal groups, environmental concerns, and so forth. Sharp managers will consider the impact of stakeholder reaction as they weigh the possible effects of their strategic decisions.

Just as stakeholder analysis is instructive for understanding the impact of major strategic decisions, project stakeholder analysis is extremely important when it comes to managing projects. The project development process itself can be directly affected by stakeholders. This relationship is essentially reciprocal in that the project team's activities can also affect external stakeholder groups.[10] Some common ways the client stakeholder group has an impact on project team operations include agitating for faster development, working closely with the team to ease project transfer problems, and influencing top management in the parent organization to continue supporting the project. The project team can reciprocate this support through actions that show willingness to closely cooperate with the client in development and transition to user groups.

The nature of these various demands can place them seemingly in direct conflict. That is, in responding to the concerns of one stakeholder, project managers often unwittingly find themselves having offended or angered another stakeholder who has an entirely different agenda and set of expectations. For example, a project team working to install a new software application across the organization may go to such levels to ensure customer satisfaction that they engage in countless revisions of the package until they have, seemingly, made their customers happy. However, in doing so, the overall project schedule may now have slipped to the point where top management is upset by the cost and schedule overruns. In managing projects, we are challenged to find ways to balance a host of demands and still maintain supportive and constructive relationships with each important stakeholder group.

Identifying Project Stakeholders

Internal stakeholders are a vital component in any stakeholder analysis, and their impact is usually felt in relatively positive ways; that is, while serving as limiting and controlling influences (in the case of the company accountant), for example, most internal stakeholders want to see the project developed successfully. On the other hand, some external stakeholder groups operate in manners that are quite challenging or even hostile to project development. Consider the case of the recent series of spikes in the price of oil. With oil prices remaining unstable but threatening to reach or even pass $100 per barrel during 2010, the impact on the global economy was severe. Many groups in the United States have advocated taking steps to lessen the country's dependence on foreign oil, including offshore exploration and the development of a new generation of nuclear power plants. Environmental groups, however, continue to oppose these steps, vowing to use litigation, political lobbying, and other measures to resist the development of these alternative energy sources. As a recent example of the danger, they cite the Deepwater Horizon disaster that leaked thousands of barrels of oil into the Gulf of Mexico. Cleland refers to these types of external stakeholders as **intervenor groups**, defined as groups external to the project but possessing the power to effectively intervene and disrupt the project's development.[11]

Among the set of project stakeholders that project managers must consider are:

Internal

- Top management
- Accounting
- Other functional managers
- Project team members

External

- Clients
- Competitors
- Suppliers
- Environmental, political, consumer, and other intervenor groups

CLIENTS   Our focus throughout this entire book will be on maintaining and enhancing client relationships. In most cases, for both external and internal clients, a project deals with an investment. Clients are concerned with receiving the project from the team as quickly as possible because the longer the project implementation, the longer the money invested sits without generating any returns. As long as costs are not passed on to them, clients seldom are overly interested in how much expense is involved in a project's development. The opposite is usually the case, however. Costs typically must be passed on, and customers are avidly interested in getting what they pay for. Also, many projects start before client needs are fully defined. Product concept screening and clarification are often made part of the project scope of work (see Chapter 5). These issues—costs and client needs—are two strong reasons why many customers seek the right to make suggestions and request alterations in the project's features and operating characteristics well into the schedule. Customers feel, with justification, that a project is only as good as it is acceptable and useful. This sets a certain flexibility requirement and requires willingness from the project team to be amenable to specification changes.

Another important fact to remember about dealing with client groups is that the term *client* does not in every case refer to the *entire* customer organization. The reality is often far more complex. A client firm consists of a number of internal interest groups, and in many cases they have different agendas. For example, a company can probably readily identify a number of distinct clients within the customer organization, including the top management team, engineering groups, sales teams, on-site teams, manufacturing or assembly groups, and so on. Under these normal circumstances, it becomes clear that the process of formulating a stakeholder analysis of a customer organization can be a complex undertaking.

The challenge is further complicated by the need to communicate, perhaps using different business language, with the various customer stakeholder groups (see Figure 2.3). Preparing a presentation to deal with the customer's engineering staff requires mastery of technical information and solid specification details. On the other hand, the finance and contractual people are looking for tightly presented numbers. Formulating stakeholder strategies requires you first to acknowledge the existence of these various client stakeholders, and then to formulate a coordinated plan for uncovering and addressing each group's specific concerns and learning how to reach them.

COMPETITORS   Competitors can be an important stakeholder element because they are affected by the successful implementation of a project. Likewise, should a rival company bring a new product to market, the project team's parent organization could be forced to alter, delay, or even abandon its project. In assessing competitors as a project stakeholder group, project managers should try to uncover any information

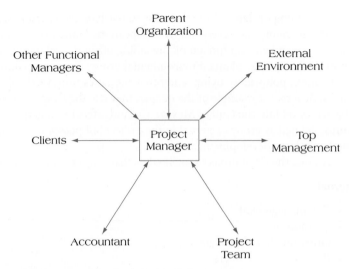

FIGURE 2.3 **Project Stakeholder Relationships**

available about the status of a competitor's projects. Further, where possible, any apparent lessons a competitor may have learned can be a source of useful information for a project manager who is initiating a similar project. If a number of severe implementation problems occurred within the competitor's project, that information could offer valuable lessons in terms of what to avoid.

SUPPLIERS   *Suppliers* are any group that provides the raw materials or other resources the project team needs in order to complete the project. When a project requires a significant supply of externally purchased components, the project manager needs to take every step possible to ensure steady deliveries. In most cases this is a two-way street. First, the project manager has to ensure that each supplier receives the input information necessary to implement its part of the project in a timely way. Second, she must monitor the deliveries so they are met according to plan. In the ideal case, the supply chain becomes a well-greased machine that automatically both draws the input information from the project team and delivers the products without excessive involvement of the project manager. For example, in large-scale construction projects, project teams daily must face and satisfy an enormous number of supplier demands. The entire discipline of supply chain management is predicated on the ability to streamline logistics processes by effectively managing the project's supply chain. When this process fails, as in the case of Boeing's 787 Dreamliner, the results can be extremely problematic for the organization, resulting in serious project delays and potential fines or penalties (see the Dreamliner case in Chapter 9).

INTERVENOR GROUPS   Any environmental, political, social, community-activist, or consumer groups that can have a positive or negative effect on the project's development and successful launch are referred to as intervenor groups.[12] That is, they have the capacity to intervene in the project development and force their concerns to be included in the equation for project implementation. There are some classic examples of intervenor groups curtailing major construction projects, particularly in the nuclear power plant construction industry. As federal, state, and even local regulators decide to involve themselves in these construction projects, intervenors have at their disposal the legal system as a method for tying up or even curtailing projects. Recently, alternative energy "wind farm" projects being proposed for sites off the coast of Cape Cod, Massachusetts, have encountered strong resistance from local groups opposed to the threat from these farms ruining the local seascape. Prudent project managers need to make a realistic assessment of the nature of their projects and the likelihood that one intervenor group or another may make an effort to impose its will on the development process.

TOP MANAGEMENT   In most organizations, top management holds a great deal of control over project managers and is in the position to regulate their freedom of action. Top management is, after all, the body that authorizes the development of the project through giving the initial "go" decision, sanctions additional resource transfers as they are needed by the project team, and supports and protects project managers and their teams from other organizational pressures. Top management requires that the project be timely (they want it out the door quickly), cost-efficient (they do not want to pay more for it than they have to), and minimally disruptive to the rest of the functional organization.

ACCOUNTING   The accountant's *raison d'être* in the organization is maintaining cost efficiency of the project teams. Accountants support and actively monitor project budgets and, as such, are sometimes perceived as the enemy by project managers. This perception is wrong minded. To be able to manage the project, to make the necessary decisions, and to communicate with the customer, the project manager has to stay on top of the cost of the project at all times. An efficient cost control and reporting mechanism is vital. Accountants perform an important administrative service for the project manager.

FUNCTIONAL MANAGERS   Functional managers who occupy line positions within the traditional chain of command are an important stakeholder group to acknowledge. Most projects are staffed by individuals who are essentially on loan from their functional departments. In fact, in many cases, project team members may only have part-time appointments to the team; their functional managers may still expect a significant amount of work out of them per week in performing their functional responsibilities. This situation can create a good deal of confusion, conflict, and the need for negotiation between project managers and functional supervisors and lead to seriously divided loyalties among team members, particularly when performance evaluations are conducted by functional managers rather than the project manager. In terms of simple self-survival, team members often maintain closer allegiance to their functional group than to the project team.

Project managers need to appreciate the power of the organization's functional managers as a stakeholder group. Functional managers are not usually out to discourage project development. Rather, they have loyalty to their functional roles, and they act and use their resources accordingly, within the limits of the company's structure. Nevertheless, as a formidable stakeholder group, functional managers need to be treated with due consideration by project managers.

PROJECT TEAM MEMBERS   The project team obviously has a tremendous stake in the project's outcome. Although some may have a divided sense of loyalty between the project and their functional group, in many companies the team members volunteer to serve on projects and, hopefully, receive the kind of challenging work assignments and opportunities for growth that motivate them to perform effectively. Project managers must understand that their project's success depends on the commitment and productivity of each member of the project team. Thus, team members' impact on the project is, in many ways, more profound than that of any other stakeholder group.

Managing Stakeholders

Project managers and their companies need to recognize the importance of stakeholder groups and proactively manage with their concerns in mind. Block offers a useful framework of the political process that has application to stakeholder management.[13] In his framework, Block suggests six steps:

1. Assess the environment.
2. Identify the goals of the principal actors.
3. Assess your own capabilities.
4. Define the problem.
5. Develop solutions.
6. Test and refine the solutions.

ASSESS THE ENVIRONMENT   Is the project relatively low-key or is it potentially so significant that it will likely excite a great deal of attention? For example, when EMC Corporation, a large computer manufacturer, began development of a new line of minicomputers and storage units with the potential for either great profits or serious losses, it took great care to first determine the need for such a product. Going directly to the consumer population with market research was the key to assessing the external environment. Likewise, one of the reasons for the popularity of Ford's Escape Hybrid is that Ford was willing to create project teams that included consumers in order to more accurately assess their needs prior to project development. Also, recognizing environmentally conscious consumers and their needs caused Ford to create an option of the SUV with a gasoline/electric hybrid engine.

IDENTIFY THE GOALS OF THE PRINCIPAL ACTORS   As a first step in fashioning a strategy to defuse negative reaction, a project manager should attempt to paint an accurate portrait of stakeholder concerns. Fisher and Ury[14] have noted that the positions various parties adopt are almost invariably based on need. What, then, are the needs of each significant stakeholder group regarding the project? A recent example will illustrate this point. A small IT firm specializing in network solutions and software development recently contracted with a larger publishing house to develop a simulation for college classroom use. The software firm was willing to negotiate a lower-than-normal price for the job because the publisher suggested that excellent performance on this project would lead to future business. The software organization, interested in follow-up business, accepted the lower fee because its more immediate needs were to gain entry into publishing and develop long-term customer contacts. The publisher needed a low price; the software developer needed new market opportunities.

Project teams must look for hidden agendas in goal assessment. It is common for departments and stakeholder groups to exert a set of overt goals that are relevant, but often illusionary.[15] In haste to satisfy these overt or espoused goals, a common mistake is to accept these goals on face value, without looking into the needs that may drive them or create more compelling goals. Consider, for example, a project in a large, project-based manufacturing company to develop a comprehensive project management scheduling system. The project manager in charge of the installation approached each department head and believed that he had secured their willingness to participate in creating a scheduling system centrally located within the project management division. Problems developed quickly, however, because IT department members, despite their public professions of support, began using every means possible to covertly sabotage the implementation of the system, delaying completion of assignments and refusing to respond to user requests. What was their concern? They believed that placing a computer-generated source of information anywhere but in the IT department threatened their position as the sole disseminator of information. In addition to probing the overt goals and concerns of various stakeholders, project managers must look for hidden agendas and other sources of constraint on implementation success.

ASSESS YOUR OWN CAPABILITIES   As Robert Burns said, "Oh wad some Power the giftie gie us/To see oursels as ithers see us!" Organizations must consider what they do well. Likewise, what are their weaknesses? Do the project manager and her team have the political savvy and a sufficiently strong bargaining position to gain support from each of the stakeholder groups? If not, do they have connections to someone who can? Each of these questions is an example of the importance of the project team understanding its own capacities and capabilities. For example, not everyone has the contacts to upper management that may be necessary for ensuring a steady flow of support and resources. If you realistically determine that political acumen is not your strong suit, then the solution may be to find someone who has these skills to help you.

DEFINE THE PROBLEM   We must seek to define problems both in terms of our own perspective and in consideration of the valid concerns of the other party. The key to developing and maintaining strong stakeholder relationships lies in recognizing that different parties can have very different but equally legitimate perspectives on a problem. When we define problems not just from our viewpoint but also by trying to understand how the same issue may be perceived by stakeholders, we are operating in a "win-win" mode. Further, we must be as precise as possible, staying focused on the specifics of the problem, not generalities. The more accurately and honestly we can define the problem, the better able we will be to create meaningful solution options.

DEVELOP SOLUTIONS   There are two important points to note about this step. First, developing solutions means precisely that: creating an action plan to address, as much as possible, the needs of the various stakeholder groups in relation to the other stakeholder groups. This step constitutes the stage in which the project manager, together with the team, seeks to manage the political process. What will work in dealing with top management? In implementing that strategy, what reaction is likely to be elicited from the accountant? The client? The project team? Asking these questions helps the project manager develop solutions that acknowledge the interrelationships of each of the relevant stakeholder groups. The topics of power, political behavior, influence, and negotiation will be discussed in greater detail in Chapter 6.

As a second point, it is necessary that we do our political homework prior to developing solutions.[16] Note the late stage at which this step is introduced. Project managers can fall into a trap if they attempt to manage a process with only fragmentary or inadequate information. The philosophy of "ready, fire, aim" is sometimes common in stakeholder management. The result is a stage of perpetual firefighting during which the project manager is a virtual pendulum, swinging from crisis to crisis. Pendulums and these project managers share one characteristic: They never reach a goal. The process of putting out one fire always seems to create a new blaze.

TEST AND REFINE THE SOLUTIONS   Implementing the solutions implies acknowledging that the project manager and team are operating under imperfect information. You may assume that stakeholders will react to certain initiatives in predictable ways, but such assumptions can be erroneous. In testing and refining solutions, the project manager and team should realize that solution implementation is an iterative process. You make your best guesses, test for stakeholder reactions, and reshape your strategies accordingly. Along the way, many of your preconceived notions about the needs and biases of various stakeholder groups must be refined as well. In some cases, you will have made accurate assessments. At other times, your suppositions may have been dangerously naive or disingenuous. Nevertheless, this final step in the stakeholder management process forces the project manager to perform a critical self-assessment. It requires the flexibility to make accurate diagnoses and appropriate midcourse corrections.

When done well, these six steps form an important method for acknowledging the role that stakeholders play in successful project implementation. They allow project managers to approach "political stakeholder management" much as they would any other form of problem solving, recognizing it as a multivariate problem as various stakeholders interact with the project and with one another. Solutions to political stakeholder management can then be richer, more comprehensive, and more accurate.

An alternative, simplified stakeholder management process consists of planning, organizing, directing, motivating, and controlling the resources necessary to deal with the various internal and external stakeholder groups. Figure 2.4 shows a model suggested by Cleland[17] that illustrates the management process within the framework of stakeholder analysis and management. Cleland notes that the various stakeholder management functions are interlocked and repetitive; that is, this cycle is recurring. As you identify and adapt to stakeholder threats, you develop plans to better manage the challenges they pose. In the process of developing and implementing these plans, you are likely to uncover new stakeholders whose demands must also be considered. Further, as the environment changes or as the project enters a new stage of its life cycle, you may

FIGURE 2.4   Project Stakeholder Management Cycle

Source: D. I. Cleland. (1988). "Project Stakeholder Management," in D. I. Cleland and W. R. King (Eds.), *Project Management Handbook,* 2nd ed. New York: Van Nostrand Reinhold, pp. 275–301. Reprinted with permission of John Wiley & Sons, Inc.

be required to cycle through the stakeholder management model again to verify that your old management strategies are still effective. If, on the other hand, you deem that new circumstances make it necessary to alter those strategies, you must work through this stakeholder management model anew to update the relevant information.

2.3 ORGANIZATIONAL STRUCTURE

The word *structure* implies organization. People who work in an organization are grouped so that their efforts can be channeled for maximum efficiency. **Organizational structure** consists of three key elements:[18]

1. *Organizational structure designates formal reporting relationships, including the number of levels in the hierarchy and the span of control of managers and supervisors.* Who reports to whom in the structural hierarchy? This is a key component of a firm's structure. A span of control determines the number of subordinates directly reporting to each supervisor. In some structures, a manager may have a wide span of control, suggesting a large number of subordinates, while other structures mandate narrow spans of control and few individuals reporting directly to any supervisor. For some companies, the reporting relationship may be rigid and bureaucratic; other firms require flexibility and informality across hierarchical levels.

2. *Organizational structure identifies the grouping together of individuals into departments and departments into the total organization.* How are individuals collected into larger groups? Starting with the smallest, units of a structure continually recombine with other units to create larger groups, or organizations of individuals. These groups, referred to as departments, may be grouped along a variety of different logical patterns. For example, among the most common reasons for creating departments are (1) *function*—grouping people performing similar activities into similar departments, (2) *product*—grouping people working on similar product lines into departments, (3) *geography*—grouping people within similar geographical regions or physical locations into departments, and (4) *project*—grouping people involved in the same project into a department. We will discuss some of these more common departmental arrangements in detail later in this chapter.

3. *Organizational structure includes the design of systems to ensure effective communication, coordination, and integration of effort across departments.* This third feature of organizational structure refers to the supporting mechanisms the firm relies on to reinforce and promote its structure. These supporting mechanisms may be simple or complex. In some firms, a method for ensuring effective communication is simply to mandate, through rules and procedures, the manner in which project team members must communicate with one another and the types of information they must routinely share. Other companies use more sophisticated or complex methods for promoting coordination, such as the creation of special project offices apart from the rest of the company where project team members work for the duration of the project. The key thrust behind this third element in organizational structure implies that simply creating a logical ordering or hierarchy of personnel for an organization is not sufficient unless it is also supported by systems that ensure clear communication and coordination across the departments.

It is also important to note that within the project management context two distinct structures operate simultaneously, and both affect the manner in which the project is accomplished. The first is the overall structure of the organization that is developing the project. This structure consists of the arrangement of all units or interest groups participating in the development of the project; it includes the project team, the client, top management, functional departments, and other relevant stakeholders. The second structure at work is the internal structure of the project team; it specifies the relationship between members of the project team, their roles and responsibilities, and their interaction with the project manager. The majority of this chapter examines the larger structure of the overall organization and how it pertains to project management. The implications of internal project team structure will be discussed here but explored more thoroughly in Chapter 6.

2.4 FORMS OF ORGANIZATIONAL STRUCTURE

Organizations can be structured in an infinite variety of ways, ranging from highly complex to extremely simple. What is important to understand is that typically the structure of an organization does not happen by chance; it is the result of a reasoned response to forces acting on the firm. A number of factors routinely affect the reasons why a company is structured the way it is. Operating environment is among the most important determinants or factors influencing an organization's structure. An organization's **external environment** consists of all forces or groups outside the organization that have the potential to affect the organization. Some elements in a company's external environment that can play a significant role in a firm's activities are competitors, customers in the marketplace, the government and other legal or regulatory bodies, general economic conditions, pools of available human or financial resources, suppliers, technological trends, and so forth. In turn, these organizational structures, often created for very sound reasons in relation to the external environment, have a strong impact on the manner in which projects are best managed within the organization. As we will see, each organizational type offers its own benefits and drawbacks as a context for creating projects.

Some common structural types classify the majority of firms. These structure types include the following:

1. *Functional organizations*—Companies are structured by grouping people performing similar activities into departments.
2. *Project organizations*—Companies are structured by grouping people into project teams on temporary assignments.
3. *Matrix organizations*—Companies are structured by creating a dual hierarchy in which functions and projects have equal prominence.

Functional Organizations

The **functional structure** is probably the most common organizational type used in business today. The logic of the functional structure is to group people and departments performing similar activities into units. In the functional structure, it is common to create departments such as accounting, marketing, or research and development. Division of labor in the functional structure is not based on the type of product or project supported, but rather according to the type of work performed. In an organization having a functional structure, members routinely work on multiple projects or support multiple product lines simultaneously.

Figure 2.5 shows an example of a functional structure. Among the clear strengths of the functional organization is efficiency; when every accountant is a member of the accounting department, it is possible to more efficiently allocate the group's services throughout the organization, account for each accountant's work assignments, and ensure that there is no duplication of effort or unused resources. Another advantage is that it is easier to maintain valuable intellectual capital when all expertise is consolidated under one functional department. When you need an expert on offshore tax implications for globally outsourced projects, you do not have to conduct a firm-wide search but can go right to the accounting department to find a resident expert.

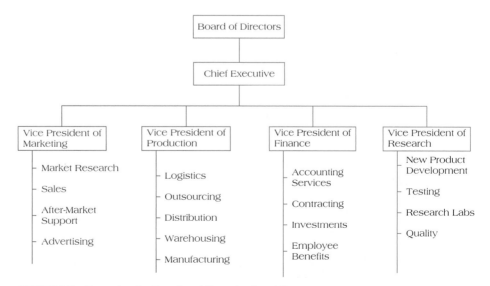

FIGURE 2.5 **Example of a Functional Organizational Structure**

The most common weakness in a functional structure from a project management perspective relates to the tendency for employees organized this way to become fixated on their concerns and work assignments to the exclusion of the needs of other departments. This idea has been labeled *functional siloing*, named for the silos found on farms (see Figure 2.6). Siloing occurs when similar people in a work group are unwilling or unable to consider alternative viewpoints, collaborate with other groups, or work in cross-functional ways. For example, within Data General Corporation, prior to its acquisition by EMC, squabbles between engineering and sales were constant. The sales department complained that its input to new product development was minimized as the engineering department routinely took the lead on innovation without meaningful consultation with other departments. Likewise, Robert Lutz, former President of Chrysler, argued that an ongoing weakness at the automobile company was the inability of the various functional departments to cooperate with and recognize the contributions of each other. Another weakness of functional structures is a generally poor responsiveness to external opportunities and threats. Communication channels tend to run up and down the hierarchy, rather than across functional boundaries. This vertical hierarchy can overload, and decision making takes time. Functional structures also may not be very innovative due to the problems inherent in the design. With siloed functional groups typically having a restricted view of the overall organization and its goals, it is difficult to achieve the cross-functional coordination necessary to innovate or respond quickly to market opportunities.

For project management, an additional weakness of the functional structure is that it provides no logical location for a central project management function. Top management may assign a project and delegate various components of that project to specialists within the different functional groups. Overall coordination of the project, including combining the efforts of the different functions assigned to perform project tasks, must then occur at a higher, top management level. A serious drawback for running projects in this operating environment is that they often must be *layered,* or applied on top of the ongoing duties of members of functional groups. The practical effect is that individuals whose main duties remain within their functional group are assigned to staff projects; when employees owe their primary allegiance to their own department, their frame of reference can remain functional. Projects can be temporary distractions in this sense, taking time away from "real work." This can explain some of the behavioral problems that occur in running projects, such as low team member motivation or the need for extended negotiations between project managers and department supervisors for personnel to staff project teams.

Another project-related problem of the functional organization is the fact that it is easy to suboptimize the project's development.[19] When the project is developed as the brainchild of one department, that group's efforts may be well considered and effective. In contrast, departments not as directly tied to or interested in the project may perform their duties to the minimum possible level. A successful project-based product or

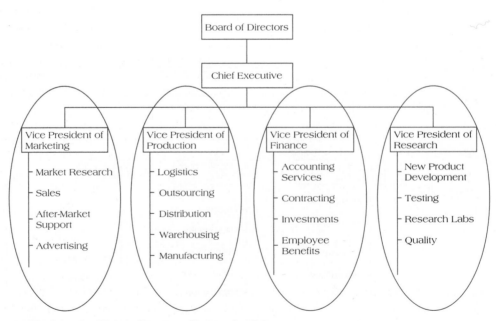

FIGURE 2.6 The Siloing Effect Found in Functional Structures

TABLE 2.2 Strengths and Weaknesses of Functional Structures

Strengths for Project Management	Weaknesses for Project Management
1. Projects are developed within the basic functional structure of the organization, requiring no disruption or change to the firm's design.	1. Functional siloing makes it difficult to achieve cross-functional cooperation.
2. Enables the development of in-depth knowledge and intellectual capital.	2. Lack of customer focus.
3. Allows for standard career paths. Project team members only perform their duties as needed while maintaining maximum connection with their functional group.	3. Projects generally take longer to complete due to structural problems, slower communication, lack of direct ownership of the project, and competing priorities among the functional departments.
	4. Projects may be suboptimized due to varying interest or commitment across functional boundaries.

service requires the fully coordinated efforts of all functional groups participating in and contributing to the project's development.

Another problem is that customers are not the primary focus of everyone within the functionally structured organization. The customer in this environment might be seen as someone else's problem, particularly among personnel whose duties tend to be supportive. Customer requirements must be met, and projects must be created with a customer in mind. Any departmental representatives on the project team who have not adopted a "customer-focused" mind-set add to the possibility of the project coming up short.

Summing up the functional structure (see Table 2.2), as it relates to the external environment, the functional structure is well suited to firms with relatively low levels of external uncertainty because their stable environments do not require rapid adaptation or responsiveness. When the environment is relatively predictable, the functional structure works well because it emphasizes efficiency. Unfortunately, project management activities within the functionally organized firm can often be problematic when they are applied in settings for which this structure's strengths are not well suited. As the above discussion indicates, although there are some ways in which the functional structure can be advantageous to managing projects, in the main, it is perhaps the poorest form of structure when it comes to getting the maximum performance out of project management assignments.[20]

Project Organizations

Project organizations are those that are set up with their exclusive focus aimed at running projects. Construction companies, large manufacturers such as Boeing or Airbus, pharmaceutical firms, and many software consulting and research and development organizations are organized as pure project organizations. Within the project organization, each project is a self-contained business unit with a dedicated project team. The firm assigns resources from functional pools directly to the project for the time period they are needed. In the project organization, the project manager has sole control over the resources the unit uses. The functional departments' chief role is to coordinate with project managers and ensure that there are sufficient resources available as they need them.

Figure 2.7 illustrates a simple form of the pure **project structure**. Projects Alpha and Beta have been formed and are staffed by project team members from the company's functional groups. The project manager is the leader of the project and the staff all report to her. The staffing decisions and duration of employees' tenure with the project are left to the discretion of the project manager, who is the chief point of authority for the project. As the figure suggests, there are several advantages to the use of a pure project structure.

- First, the project manager does not occupy a subordinate role in this structure. All major decisions and authority remain under the control of the project manager.
- Second, the functional structure and its potential for siloing or communication problems are bypassed. As a result, communication improves across the organization and within the project team. Because authority remains with the project manager and the project team, decision making is speeded up. Project decisions can occur quickly, without lengthy delays as functional groups are consulted or allowed to veto project team decisions.

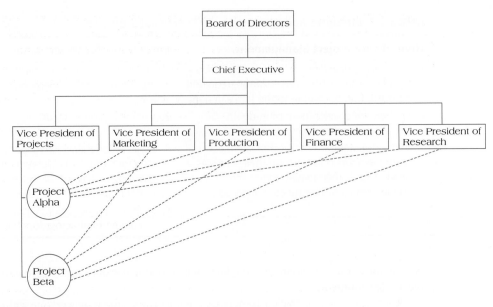

FIGURE 2.7   Example of a Project Organizational Structure

- Third, this organizational type promotes the expertise of a professional cadre of project management professionals. Because the focus for operations within the organization is project-based, everyone within the organization understands and operates with the same focus, ensuring that the organization maintains highly competent project management resources.
- Finally, the pure project structure encourages flexibility and rapid response to environmental opportunities. Projects are created, managed, and disbanded routinely; therefore, the ability to create new project teams as needed is common and team formation can be quickly undertaken.

Although there are a number of advantages in creating dedicated project teams using a project structure (see Table 2.3), this design does have some disadvantages that should be considered.

- First, the process of setting up and maintaining a number of self-contained project teams can be expensive. The different functional groups, rather than controlling their resources, must provide them on a full-time basis to the different projects being undertaken at any point. This can result in forcing the project organization to hire more project specialists (e.g., engineers) than they might need otherwise, with a resulting loss of economies of scale.
- Second, the potential for inefficient use of resources is a key disadvantage of the pure project organization. Organizational staffing may fluctuate up and down as the number of projects in the firm increases

TABLE 2.3 Strengths and Weaknesses of Project Structures

Strengths for Project Management	Weaknesses for Project Management
1. Assigns authority solely to the project manager.	1. Setting up and maintaining teams can be expensive.
2. Leads to improved communication across the organization and among functional groups.	2. Potential for project team members to develop loyalty to the project rather than to the overall organization.
3. Promotes effective and speedy decision making.	3. Difficult to maintain a pooled supply of intellectual capital.
4. Promotes the creation of cadres of project management experts.	4. Concern among project team members about their future once the project ends.
5. Encourages rapid response to market opportunities.	

or decreases. Hence, it is possible to move from a state in which many projects are running and organizational resources are fully employed to one in which only a few projects are in the pipeline, with many resources underutilized. In short, manpower requirements across the organization can increase or decrease rapidly, making staffing problems severe.

- Third, it is difficult to maintain a supply of technical or intellectual capital, which is one of the advantages of the functional structure. Because resources do not typically reside within the functional structure for long, it is common for them to shift from project to project, preventing the development of a pooled knowledge base. For example, many project organizations hire technically proficient contract employees for various project tasks. These employees may perform their work and, once finished and their contract is terminated, leave the organization, taking their expertise with them. Expertise resides not within the organization, but differentially within the functional members who are assigned to the projects. Hence, some team members may be highly knowledgeable while others are not sufficiently trained and capable.

- A fourth problem with the pure project form has to do with the legitimate concerns of project team members as they anticipate the completion of the project. What, they wonder, will be in their future once their project is completed? As noted above, staffing can be inconsistent, and often project team members finish a project only to discover that they are not needed for new assignments. Functional specialists in project organizations do not have the kind of permanent "home" that they would have in a functional organization, so their concerns are justified. In a similar manner, it is common in pure project organizations for project team members to identify with the project as their sole source of loyalty. Their emphasis is project-based and their interests reside not with the larger organization, but within their own project. When a project is completed, they may begin searching for new challenges, and may even leave the company for appealing new assignments.

Matrix Organizations

One of the more innovative organization designs to emerge in the past 30 years has been the **matrix structure**. The **matrix organization**, which is a combination of functional and project activities, seeks a balance between the functional organization and the pure project form. The way it achieves this balance is to emphasize both function and project focuses at the same time. In practical terms, the matrix structure creates a *dual hierarchy* in which there is a balance of authority between the project emphasis and the firm's functional departmentalization. Figure 2.8 illustrates how a matrix organization is set up; note that the vice president of projects occupies a unique reporting relationship in that the position is not formally part of the organization's

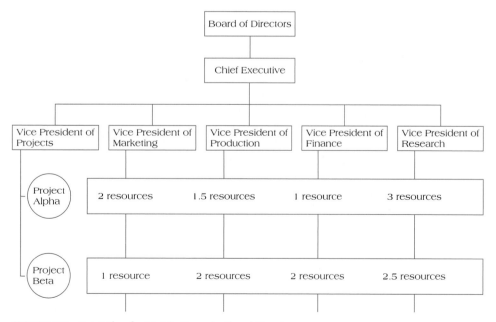

FIGURE 2.8   Example of a Matrix Organizational Structure

functional department structure. The vice president is the head of the projects division and occupies one side of the dual hierarchy, a position shared with the CEO and heads of functional departments.

Figure 2.8 also provides a look at how the firm staffs project teams. The vice president of projects controls the activities of the project managers under his authority. They, however, must work closely with functional departments to staff their project teams through loans of personnel from each functional group. Whereas in functional organizations project team personnel are still almost exclusively under the control of the functional departments and to some degree serve at the pleasure of their functional boss, in the matrix organizational structure these personnel are shared by both their departments and the project to which they are assigned. They remain under the authority of both the project manager and their functional department supervisor. Notice, for example, that the project manager for Project Alpha has negotiated the use of two **resources** (personnel) from the vice president of marketing, 1.5 resources from production, and so forth. Each project and project manager is responsible for working with the functional heads to determine the optimal staffing needs, how many people are required to perform necessary project activities, and when they will be available. Questions such as "What tasks must be accomplished on this project?" are best answered by the project manager. However, other equally important questions, such as "Who will perform the tasks?" and "How long should the tasks take?" are matters that must be jointly negotiated between the project manager and the functional department head.

It is useful to distinguish between two common forms of the matrix structure: the **weak matrix** (sometimes called the *functional matrix*) and the **strong matrix** (sometimes referred to as a *project matrix*). In a weak matrix, functional departments maintain control over their resources and are responsible for managing their components of the project. The project manager's role is to coordinate the activities of the functional departments, typically as an administrator. She is expected to prepare schedules, update project status, and serve as the link between the departments with their different project deliverables, but she does not have direct authority to control resources or make significant decisions on her own. In a strong matrix, the balance of power has shifted in favor of the project manager. She now controls most of the project activities and functions, including the assignment and control of project resources, and has key decision-making authority. Although functional managers have some input into the assignment of personnel from their departments, their role is mostly consultative. The strong matrix is probably the closest to a "project organization" mentality that we can get while working within a matrix environment.

Creating an organizational structure with two bosses may seem awkward, but there are some important advantages to this approach, provided certain conditions are met. Matrix structures are useful under circumstances in which:[21]

1. ***There is pressure to share scarce resources across product or project opportunities.*** When an organization has scarce human resources and a number of project opportunities, it faces the challenge of using its people and material resources as efficiently as possible to support the maximum number of projects. A matrix structure provides an environment in which the company can emphasize efficient use of resources for the maximum number of projects.

2. ***There is a need to emphasize two or more different types of output.*** For example, the firm may need to promote its technical competence (using a functional structure) while continually creating a series of new products (requiring a project structure). With this dual pressure for performance, there is a natural balance in a matrix organization between the functional emphasis on technical competence and efficiency and the project focus on rapid new product development.

3. ***The environment of the organization is complex and dynamic.*** When firms face the twin challenges of complexity and rapidly shifting environmental pressures, the matrix structure promotes the exchange of information and coordination across functional boundaries.

In the matrix structure, the goal is to create a simultaneous focus on the need to be quickly responsive to both external opportunities and internal operating efficiencies. In order to achieve this dual focus, equal authority must reside within both the project and the functional groups. One advantage of the matrix structure for managing projects is that it places project management parallel to functional departments in authority. This advantage highlights the enhanced status of the project manager in this structure, who is expected to hold a similar level of power and control over resources as department managers. Another advantage is that the matrix is specifically tailored to encourage the close coordination between departments, with an emphasis on producing projects quickly and efficiently while sharing resources among projects as they are needed. Unlike the functional structure, in which projects are, in effect, layered over a structure that is not necessarily supportive of their processes, the matrix structure balances the twin demands of external responsiveness and internal efficiency, creating an environment in which projects can be performed expeditiously. Finally, because resources are shared and "movable" among multiple projects, there is a greater likelihood that expertise will not be hoarded or centered on some limited set of personnel, as in the project organization, but will be diffused more widely across the firm.

Among the disadvantages of the matrix structure's dual hierarchy is the potentially negative effect that creating multiple authority points has on operations. When two parts of the organization share authority, the workers caught between them can experience great frustration when they receive mixed or conflicting messages from the head of the project group and the head of their functional departments. Suppose that the vice president of projects signaled the need for workers to concentrate their efforts on a critical project with a May 1 deadline. If, at the same time, the head of finance were to tell his staff that with tax season imminent, it was necessary for his employees to ignore projects for the time being to finish tax-related work, what might happen? From the team member's perspective, this dual hierarchy can be very frustrating. Workers daily experience a sense of being pulled in multiple directions as they receive conflicting instructions from their bosses—both on projects and in their departments. Consequently, ordinary work often becomes a balancing act based on competing demands for their time.

Another disadvantage is the amount of time and energy required by project managers in meetings, negotiations, and other coordinative functions to get decisions made across multiple groups, often with different agendas. Table 2.4 summarizes the strengths and weaknesses of the matrix structure.

Matrix structures, though they seem to be a good solution for project management, require a great deal of time to be spent coordinating the use of human resources. Many project managers comment that as part of the matrix, they devote a large proportion of their time to meetings, to resolving or negotiating resource commitments, and to finding ways to share power with department heads. The matrix structure offers some important benefits and drawbacks from the perspective of managing projects. It places project management on an equal footing with functional efficiency and promotes cross-functional coordination. At the same time, however, the dual hierarchy results in some significant behavioral challenges as authority and control within the organization are constantly in a state of flux.[22] A common complaint from project managers operating in matrix organizations is that an enormous amount of their time is taken up with "playing politics" and bargaining sessions with functional managers to get the resources and help they need. In a matrix, negotiation skills, political savvy, and networking become vital tools for project managers who want to be successful.

Moving to Heavyweight Project Organizations

The term **heavyweight project organization** refers to the belief that organizations can sometimes gain tremendous benefits from creating a fully dedicated project organization.[23] The heavyweight project organization concept is based on the notion that successful project organizations do not happen by chance or luck. Measured steps in design and operating philosophy are needed to get to the top and remain there. Taking their formulation from the "Skunkworks" model, named after the famous Lockheed Corporation programs, autonomous project teams represent the final acknowledgment by the firm of the priority of project-based work in the company. In these organizations, the project manager is given full authority, status, and responsibility to ensure project success. Functional departments are either fully subordinated to the projects or the project teams are accorded an independent resource base with which to accomplish their tasks.

TABLE 2.4 Strengths and Weaknesses of Matrix Structures

Strengths for Project Management	Weaknesses for Project Management
1. Suited to dynamic environments.	1. Dual hierarchies mean two bosses.
2. Emphasizes the dual importance of project management and functional efficiency.	2. Requires significant time to be spent negotiating the sharing of critical resources between projects and departments.
3. Promotes coordination across functional units.	3. Can be frustrating for workers caught between competing project and functional demands.
4. Maximizes scarce resources between competing project and functional responsibilities.	

In order to achieve the flexibility and responsiveness that the heavyweight organization can offer, it is important to remember some key points. First, no one goes directly to the autonomous team stage when it comes to running projects. This project organizational form represents the last transitional stage in a systematically planned shift in corporate thinking. Instead, managers gradually move to this step through making conscious decisions about how they are going to improve the way they run projects. Successful project firms work to expand the authority of the project manager, often in the face of stiff resistance from functional department heads who like the power balance the way it currently exists. Part of the process of redirecting the power balance involves giving project managers high status, authority to conduct performance evaluations of team members, authority over project resources, and direct links to the customers. Project managers who are constantly forced to rely on the good graces of functional managers for their team staffing, coordination, and financial and other resources are operating with one hand tied behind their backs.

Second, heavyweight project organizations have realigned their priorities away from functional maintenance to market opportunism, a realignment that can occur only when the resources needed to respond rapidly to market opportunities rest with the project team rather than being controlled by higher level bureaucracies within a company. Finally, as we note throughout this book, the shift in focus for many firms toward project-based work profoundly affects the manner in which the project organization, manager, and the team operate. The new focus on the external customer becomes the driving force for operations, not simply one of several competing demands that the project team must satisfy as best they can.

Ultimately, the decision of which organizational structure is appropriate to use may simply come down to one of expediency; although it may, in fact, be desirable to conduct projects within a structure that offers maximum flexibility and authority to the project manager (the pure project structure), the fact remains that for many project managers it will be impossible to significantly influence decisions to alter the overall organizational structure in support of their project. As a result, perhaps a more appropriate question to ask is: What issues should I be aware of, given the structure of the organization within which I will be managing projects? The previous discussion in this chapter has developed this focus as our primary concern. Given the nature of the structure within which we must operate and manage our projects, what are the strengths and weaknesses of that form as it pertains to our ability to do our job as best we can? In formulating a thoughtful answer to this question, we are perhaps best positioned to understand and adapt most effectively to finding the link between our organization's structure and project management success.

BOX 2.1

PROJECT MANAGEMENT RESEARCH IN BRIEF

The Impact of Organizational Structure on Project Performance

It is natural to suppose that projects may run more smoothly in some types of organizational structure than others. Increasingly, research evidence suggests that depending on the type of project being initiated, some structural forms do, in fact, offer greater advantages in promoting successful completion of the project than do others. The work of Gobeli and Larson, for example, is important in highlighting the fact that the type of structure a firm has when it runs projects will have either a beneficial or detrimental effect on the viability of the projects.

Larson and Gobeli compared projects that had been managed in a variety of structural types, including functional, matrix, and pure project. They differentiated among three subsets of matrix structure, labeled functional matrix, balanced matrix, and project matrix, based on their perception of whether the matrix structure of a firm leaned more heavily toward a functional approach, an evenly balanced style, or one more favorable toward projects. After collecting data from a sample of more than 1,600 project managers, they identified those who were conducting projects in each of the five organizational types and asked them to assess the effectiveness of that particular structure in promoting or inhibiting effective project management practices. Their findings are shown in Figure 2.9, highlighting the fact that, in general, project organizations do promote an atmosphere more supportive of successful project management.

Interestingly, when Gobeli and Larson broke their sample up into new product development projects and those related to construction, their findings were largely similar, with the exception that construction projects were marginally more effective in matrix organizations. This suggests that structure plays a significant role in the creation of successful projects.[24]

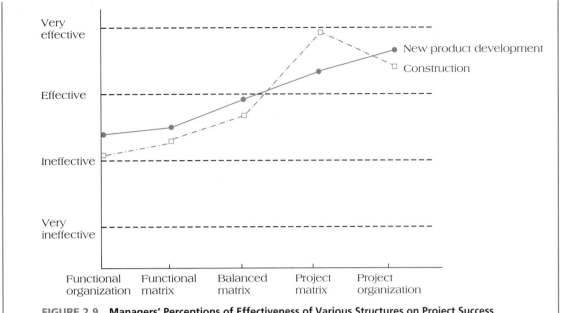

FIGURE 2.9   **Managers' Perceptions of Effectiveness of Various Structures on Project Success**

Source: D. H. Gobeli and E. W. Larson. (1987). "Relative Effectiveness of Different Project Management Structures," *Project Management Journal,* 18(2): 81–85, figure on page 83. Copyright and all rights reserved. Material from this publication has been reproduced with the permission of PMI.

2.5 PROJECT MANAGEMENT OFFICES

A **project management office** (PMO) is defined as a centralized unit within an organization or department that oversees or improves the management of projects.[25] It is seen as a center for excellence in project management in many organizations, existing as a separate organizational entity or subunit that assists the project manager in achieving project goals by providing direct expertise in vital project management duties such as scheduling, resource allocation, monitoring, and controlling the project. PMOs were originally developed in recognition of the poor track record that many organizations have demonstrated in running their projects. We cited some sobering statistics on the failure rates of IT projects, for example, in Chapter 1, indicating that the majority of such projects are likely to fail.

PMOs were created in acknowledgment of the fact that a resource center for project management within a company can offer tremendous advantages. First, as we have noted, project managers are called upon to engage in a wide range of duties, including everything from attending to the human side of project management to handling important technical details. In many cases, these individuals may not have the time or ability to handle all the myriad technical details—the activity scheduling, resource allocation, monitoring and control processes, and so forth. Using a PMO as a resource center shifts some of the burden for these activities from the project manager to a support staff that is dedicated to providing this assistance. Second, it is clear that although project management is emerging as a profession in its own right, there is still a wide gap in knowledge and expectations placed on project managers and their teams. Simply put, they may not have the skills or knowledge for handling a number of project support activities, such as resource leveling or variance reporting. Having trained project management professionals available through a PMO creates a "clearinghouse" effect that allows project teams to tap into expertise when they need it.

Another benefit of the PMO is that it can serve as a central repository of all lessons learned, project documentation, and other pertinent record keeping for ongoing projects, as well as for past projects. This function allows all project managers a central access to past project records and lessons learned materials, rather than having to engage in a haphazard search for these documents throughout the organization. A fourth benefit of the PMO is that it serves as the dedicated center for project management excellence in the company. As such, it becomes the focus for all project management process improvements that are then diffused to other organizational units. Thus, the PMO becomes the place in which new project management improvements are first identified, tested, refined, and finally, passed along to the rest of the organization

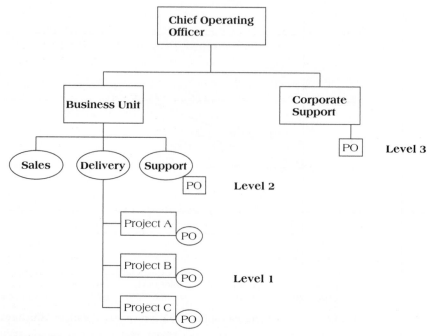

FIGURE 2.10 Alternative Levels of Project Offices

Source: W. Casey and W. Peck. (2001). "Choosing the Right PMO Setup," *PMNetwork*, 15(2): 40–47, figure on page 44. Copyright and all rights reserved. Material from this publication has been reproduced with the permission of PMI.

Each project manager can use the PMO as a resource, trusting that they will make themselves responsible for all project management innovations.

A PMO can be placed in any one of several locations within a firm.[26] As Figure 2.10 demonstrates, the PMO may be situated at a corporate level (Level 3) where it serves an overall corporate support function. It can be placed at a lower functional level (Level 2) where it serves the needs within a specific business unit. Finally, the PMO can be decentralized down to the actual project level (Level 1) where it offers direct support for each project. The key to understanding the function of the PMO is to recognize that it is designed to *support* the activities of the project manager and staff, not *replace* the manager or take responsibility for the project. Under these circumstances, we see that the PMO can take a lot of the pressure off the project manager by handling the administration duties, leaving the project manager free to focus on the equally important people issues, including leading, negotiating, customer relationship building, and so forth.

Although Figure 2.10 gives us a sense of where PMOs may be positioned in the organization and, by extension, clues to their supporting role depending on how they are structured, it is also helpful to consider some of the PMO models. PMOs have been described as operating under one of three alternative forms and purposes in companies: (1) weather station, (2) control tower, and (3) resource pool.[27] Each of these models has an alternative role for the PMO.

1. *Weather station*—Under the weather station model, the PMO is typically used only as a tracking and monitoring device. In this approach, the assumption is often one in which top management, feeling nervous about committing money to a wide range of projects, wants a weather station as a tracking device, to keep an eye on the status of the projects without directly attempting to influence or control them. The weather station PMO is intended to house independent observers who focus almost exclusively on some key questions, such as:

   • What's our progress? How is the project progressing against the original plan? What key milestones have we achieved?
   • How much have we paid for the project so far? How do our earned value projections look? Are there any budgetary warning signals?
   • What is the status of major project risks? Have we updated our contingency planning as needed?

2. *Control tower*—The control tower model treats project management as a business skill to be protected and supported. It focuses on developing methods for continually improving project management skills

by identifying what is working, where the shortcomings exist, and how to resolve ongoing problems. Most importantly, unlike the weather station model, which monitors project management activities only to report results to top management, the control tower is a model that is intended to directly work with and support the activities of the project manager and team. In doing so, it performs four functions:

- *Establishes standards for managing projects*—The control tower model of the PMO is designed to create a uniform methodology for all project management activities, including duration estimation, budgets, risk management, scope development, and so forth.
- *Consults on how to follow these standards*—In addition to determining the appropriate standards for running projects, the PMO is set up to help project managers meet those standards through providing internal consultants or project management experts throughout the development cycle as their expertise is needed.
- *Enforces the standards*—Unless there is some process that allows the organization to enforce the project management standards it has developed and disseminated, it will not be taken seriously. The control tower PMO has the authority to enforce the standards it has established, either through rewards for excellent performance or sanctions for refusal to abide by the standard project management principles. For example, the PMO for Accident Fund Insurance Co. of America has full authority to stop projects that it feels are violating accepted practices or failing to bring value to the company.
- *Improves the standards*—The PMO is always motivated to look for ways to improve the current state of project management procedures. Once a new level of project performance has been created, under a policy of continuous improvement, the PMO should already be exploring how to make good practices better.

3. *Resource pool*—The goal of the resource pool PMO is to maintain and provide a cadre of trained and skilled project professionals as they are needed. In essence, it becomes a clearinghouse for continually upgrading the skills of the firm's project managers. As the company initiates new projects, the affected departments apply to the resource pool PMO for assets to populate the project team. The resource pool PMO is responsible for supplying project managers and other skilled professionals to the company's projects. In order for this model to be implemented successfully, it is important for the resource pool to be afforded sufficiently high status within the organization that it can bargain on an equal footing with other top managers who need project managers for their projects. Referring back to Figure 2.10, the resource pool model seems to work best when the PMO is generally viewed as a Level 3 support structure, giving the head of the PMO the status to maintain control of the pool of trained project managers and the authority to assign them as deemed appropriate.

The PMO concept is rapidly being assimilated in a number of companies. However, it has some critics. For example, some critics contend that it is a mistake to "place all the eggs in one basket" with PMOs by concentrating all project professionals in one location. This argument suggests that PMOs actually inhibit the natural, unofficial dissemination of project skills across organizational units by maintaining them at one central location. Another potential pitfall is that the PMO, if its philosophy is not carefully explained, can simply become another layer of oversight and bureaucracy within the organization; in effect, rather than freeing up the project team by performing supporting functions, it actually handcuffs the project by requiring additional administrative control. Another potential danger associated with the use of PMOs is that they may serve as a bottleneck for communications flow across the organization,[28] particularly between the parent organization and the project's customer.

Although some of the criticisms of PMOs contain an element of truth, they should not be used to avoid the adoption of a project office under the right circumstances. The PMO is, at its core, recognition that project management skill development must be encouraged and reinforced, that many organizations have great need of standardized project practices, and that a central, supporting function can serve as a strong source for continuous project skill improvement. Viewed in this light, the PMO concept is likely to gain in popularity in the years to come.

2.6 ORGANIZATIONAL CULTURE

The third key contextual variable in how projects are managed effectively is that of organizational culture. So far, we have examined the manner in which a firm's strategy affects its project management, and how projects and portfolios are inextricably tied to a company's vision and serve to operationalize strategic choices.

Structure constitutes the second piece of the contextual puzzle, and we have demonstrated how various organizational designs can help or hinder the project management process. Now we turn to the third contextual variable: an organization's culture and its impact on managing projects.

One of the unique characteristics of organizations is the manner in which each develops its own outlook, operating policies and procedures, patterns of thinking, attitudes, and norms of behavior. These characteristics are often as unique as an individual's fingerprints or DNA signature; in the same way, no two organizations, no matter how similar in size, products, operating environment, or profitability, are the same. Each has developed its own unique method for indoctrinating its employees, responding to environmental threats and opportunities, and supporting or discouraging operating behaviors. In other settings, such as anthropology, a culture is seen as the collective or shared learning of a group, and it influences how that group is likely to respond in different situations. These ideas are embedded in the concept of **organizational culture**. One of the original writers on culture defined it as "the solution to external and internal problems that has worked consistently for a group and that is therefore taught to new members as the correct way to perceive, think about, and feel in relation to these problems."[29]

Travel around Europe and you will quickly become immersed in a variety of cultures. You will discern the unique cultural characteristics that distinguish nationalities, such as the Finnish and Swedish. Differences in language, social behavior, family organization, and even religious beliefs clearly demonstrate these cultural differences. Even within a country, cultural attitudes and values vary dramatically. The norms, attitudes, and common behaviors of northern and southern Italians lead to differences in dress, speech patterns, and even evening dining times. One of the key elements in courses on international business identifies cultural differences as patterns of unique behavior, so that business travelers or those living in other countries will be able to recognize "appropriate" standards of behavior and cultural attitudes, even though these cultural patterns may be very different from those of the traveler's country or origin.

For project team members who are called upon to work on projects overseas, or who are linked via the Internet and e-mail to other project team members from different countries, developing an appreciation for cross-border cultural differences is critical. The values and attitudes expressed by these various cultures are strong regulators of individual behavior; they define our belief systems and work dedication, as well as our ability to function on cross-cultural project teams.

Research has begun to actively explore the impact that workplace cultures have on the performance of projects and the manner in which individual project team members decide whether or not they will commit to its goals. Consider two contrasting examples the author has witnessed: In one *Fortune* 500 company, functional department heads for years have responded to all resource requests from project managers by assigning their worst, newest, or lowest-performing personnel to these teams. In effect, they have treated projects as dumping grounds for malcontents or poor performers. In this organization, project teams are commonly referred to as "leper colonies." It is easy to imagine the response of a member of the firm to the news that he has just been assigned to a new project! On the other hand, I have worked with an IT organization where the unspoken rule is that all departmental personnel are to make themselves available as expert resources when their help is requested by a project manager. The highest priority in the company is project delivery, and all other activities are subordinated to achieving this expectation. It is common, during particularly hectic periods, for IT members to work 12-plus hours per day, assisting on 10 or more projects at any time. As one manager put it, "When we are in crunch time, titles and job descriptions don't mean anything. If it has to get done, we are all responsible—jointly—to make sure it gets done."

The differences in managing projects at the companies illustrated in these stories are striking, as is the culture that permeates their working environment and approach to project delivery. Our definition of **culture** can be directly applied in both of these cases to refer to the unwritten rules of behavior, or norms that are used to shape and guide behavior, that are shared by some subset of organizational members, and that are taught to all new members of the company. This definition has some important elements that must be examined in more detail:

- *Unwritten*—Cultural norms guide the behavior of each member of the organization but are often not written down. In this way, there can be a great difference between the slogans or inspirational posters found on company walls and the *real,* clearly understood culture that establishes standards of behavior and enforces them for all new company members. For example, Erie Insurance, annually voted one of the best companies to work for, has a strong, supportive culture that emphasizes and rewards positive collaboration between functional groups. Although the policy is not written down, it is widely held, understood by all, and taught to new organization members. When projects require the assistance of personnel from multiple departments, the support is expected to be there.

- *Rules of behavior*—Cultural norms guide behavior by allowing us a common language for understanding, defining, or explaining phenomena and then providing us with guidelines as to how best to react to these events. These rules of behavior can be very powerful and commonly held: They apply equally to top management and workers on the shop floor. However, because they are unwritten, we may learn them the hard way. For example, if you were newly hired as a project engineer and were working considerably slower or faster than your coworkers, it is likely that one of them would quickly clue you in on an acceptable level of speed that does not make you or anyone else look bad by comparison.
- *Held by some subset of the organization*—Cultural norms may or may not be companywide. In fact, it is very common to find cultural attitudes differing widely within an organization. For example, blue-collar workers may have a highly antagonistic attitude toward top management; members of the finance department may view the marketing function with hostility and vice versa; and so forth. These "subcultures" reflect the fact that an organization may contain a number of different cultures, operating in different locations or at different levels. Pitney-Bowes, for example, is a maker of postage meters and other office equipment. Its headquarters unit reflects an image of stability, orderliness, and prestige. However, one of its divisions, Pitney-Bowes Credit Corporation (PBCC), headquartered in Shelton, Connecticut, has made a name for itself by purposely adopting an attitude of informality, openness, and fun. Its décor, featuring fake gas lamps, a French café, and Internet surfing booths, has been described as resembling an "indoor theme park." PBCC has deliberately created a subculture that reflects its own approach to business, rather than adopting the general corporate vision.[30] Another example is the Macintosh project team's approach to creating a distinct culture at Apple while they were developing this revolutionary system, to the point of being housed in different facilities from the rest of the company and flying a pirate flag from the flagpole!
- *Taught to all new members*—Cultural attitudes, because they are often unwritten, may not be taught to newcomers in formal ways. New members of an organization pick up the behaviors as they observe others engaging in them. In some organizations, however, all new hires are immersed in a formal indoctrination program to ensure that they understand and appreciate the organization's culture. The U.S. Marines, for example, take pride in the process of indoctrination and training for all recruits, which develops a collective, committed attitude toward the Marine Corps. IBM takes its new indoctrination procedures seriously, spending weeks training new employees in the IBM philosophy, work attitudes, and culture. General Electric also sends new employees away for orientation, to be "tattooed with the meatball," as members of the company refer to the GE logo.

How Do Cultures Form?

When it is possible to view two organizations producing similar products within the context of very individualistic and different cultures, the question of how cultures form gets particularly interesting. General Electric's Jet Engine Division and Rolls-Royce share many features, including product lines. Both produce jet engines for the commercial and defense aircraft industries. However, GE prides itself on its competitive, high-pressure culture that rewards aggressiveness and high commitment, but also has a high "burnout" rate among engineers and mid-level managers. Rolls-Royce, on the other hand, represents an example of a much more paternalistic culture that rewards loyalty and long job tenure.

Researchers have examined some of the powerful forces that can influence how a company's culture emerges. Among the key factors that affect the development of a culture are technology, environment, geographical location, reward systems, rules and procedures, key organizational members, and critical incidents.[31]

TECHNOLOGY   The **technology** of an organization refers to its conversion process whereby it transforms inputs into outputs. For example, the technology of many project organizations is the project development process in which projects are developed to fill a current need or anticipate a future opportunity. The technical means for creating projects can be highly complex and automated or relatively simple and straightforward. Further, the projects may be in the form of products or services. Research suggests that the type of technology used within a project organization can influence the culture that it promotes. "High-technology" organizations represent an example of how a fast-paced, technologically based culture can permeate through an organization.

ENVIRONMENT   Organizations operate under distinct environmental pressures. A firm's environment may be complex and rapidly changing, or it may remain relatively simple and stable. Some firms are global, because their competition is literally worldwide, while other companies focus on regional competition. Regardless of the specific circumstances, a company's environment affects the culture of the firm. For example, companies with simple and slow-changing environments may develop cultures that reinforce low risk taking, stability, and efficiency. Firms in highly complex environments often develop cultures aimed at promoting rapid response, external scanning for opportunities and threats, and risk taking. In this way, the firm's operating environment affects the formation of the culture and the behaviors that are considered acceptable within it. For example, a small, regional construction firm specializing in commercial real estate development is likely to have more stable environmental concerns than a Fluor-Daniel or Bechtel, competing for a variety of construction projects on a worldwide basis.

GEOGRAPHICAL LOCATION   Different geographical regions develop their own cultural mores and attitudes. The farther south in Europe one travels, for example, the later the evening meal is typically eaten; in Spain, dinner may commence after 9 PM. Likewise, in the business world, culturally based attitudes often coordinate with the geographical locations of firms or subsidiaries. It can even happen within countries: Xerox Corporation, for example, had tremendous difficulty in trying to marry the cultures of its corporate headquarters in Connecticut with the more informal and down-to-earth mentalities of its Palo Alto Research Center (PARC) personnel. Projects at one site were done much differently than those undertaken at another location. It is important not to overstate the effect that geography can play, but it certainly can result in cultural disconnects, particularly in cases where organizations have developed a number of dispersed locations, both within and outside of their country of origin.

REWARD SYSTEMS   The types of rewards that a firm offers to employees go a long way toward demonstrating the beliefs and actions its top management truly values, regardless of what official company policies might be. Reward systems support the view that, in effect, a company gets what it pays for. An organization that publicly espouses environmental awareness and customer service but routinely promotes project managers who violate these principles sends a loud message about its real interests. As a result, the culture quickly forms around acts that lead to pollution, dishonesty, or obfuscation. One has only to look at past business headlines regarding corporate malfeasance at Enron, WorldCom, or Adelphia Cable Company to see how the culture of those organizations rewarded the type of behavior that ultimately led to accounting fraud, public exposure, and millions of dollars in fines.

RULES AND PROCEDURES   One method for influencing a project management culture is to create a rule-book or system of procedures for employees to clarify acceptable behavior. The idea behind rules and procedures is to signal companywide standards of behavior to new employees. The obvious problem arises when public or formal rules conflict with informal rules of behavior. At Texas Instruments headquarters in Dallas, Texas, a formal rule is that all management staff works a standard 40-hour workweek. However, the informal rule is that each member of the company is really expected to work a 45-hour week, at a minimum, or as one senior manager explained to a newly hired employee, "Here, you work nine hours each day: eight for you and one for TI." In spite of the potential for disagreements between formal and informal rules, most programs in creating supportive project-based organizations argue that the first step toward improving patterns of behavior is to formally codify expectations in order to alter dysfunctional project cultures. Rules and procedures, thus, represent a good starting point for developing a strong project culture.

KEY ORGANIZATIONAL MEMBERS   Key organizational members, including the founder of the organization, have a tremendous impact on the culture that emerges within the company. When the founder is a traditional entrepreneur who encourages free expression or flexibility, this attitude becomes ingrained in the organization's culture in a powerful way. The founders of Ben and Jerry's Ice Cream, two proud ex-hippies, created a corporate culture that was unique and expressed their desire to develop a "fun" alternative to basic capitalism. A corporate culture in which senior executives routinely flaunt the rules or act contrary to stated policies demonstrates a culture in which there is one rule for the people at the top and another for everyone else.

CRITICAL INCIDENTS   Critical incidents express culture because they demonstrate for all workers exactly what it takes to succeed in an organization. In other words, critical incidents are a public expression of what rules *really* operate, regardless of what the company formally espouses. Critical incidents usually take the form of stories that are related to others, including new employees, illustrating the types of actions that are valued. They become part of the company's lore, either for good or ill. In a recent year, General Electric's Transportation Systems Division built up a large backlog of orders for locomotives. The company galvanized its production facilities to work overtime to complete this backlog of work. As one member of the union related, "When you see a unit vice president show up on Saturday, put on an environmental suit, and work on the line spray painting locomotives with the rest of the workers, you realize how committed the company was to getting this order completed on time."

Organizational Culture and Project Management

What are the implications of an organizational culture on the project management process? Culture can affect project management in at least four ways. First, it affects how departments are expected to interact and support each other in pursuit of project goals. Second, the culture influences the level of employee commitment to the goals of the project on balance with other, potentially competing goals. Third, the organizational culture influences project planning processes such as the way work is estimated or how resources are assigned to projects. Finally, the culture affects how managers evaluate the performance of project teams and how they view the outcomes of projects.

- *Departmental interaction*—Several of the examples cited in this chapter have focused on the importance of developing and maintaining a solid, supportive relationship between functional departments and project teams. In functional and matrix organizations, power either resides directly with department heads or is shared with project managers. In either case, the manner in which these department heads approach their willingness to support projects plays a hugely important role in the success or failure of new project initiatives. Not surprisingly, cultures that favor active cooperation between functional groups and new projects are much more successful than those that adopt a disinterested or even adversarial relationship.

- *Employee commitment to goals*—Projects depend on the commitment and motivation of the personnel assigned to their activities. A culture that promotes employee commitment and, when necessary, self-sacrifice through working extra hours or on multiple tasks is much more successful than a culture in which the unwritten rules seem to imply that, provided you don't get caught, there is nothing wrong with simply going through the motions. AMEC Corporation, for example, takes its training of employees seriously when it comes to instilling a commitment to safety. AMEC is a multinational industrial construction company, headquartered in Canada. With annual revenues of over $4 billion and 20,000 employees, AMEC is one of the largest construction firms in the world. It takes its commitment to core values extremely seriously, impressing upon all employees their responsibilities to customers, business partners, each other, the company, and the wider social environment. From the moment new people enter the organization, they are made aware of the need to commit to these guiding principles of ethical behavior, fairness, commitment to quality, and safety.[32]

- *Project planning*—We will explore the process of activity duration estimation in a later chapter; however, for now it is important just to note that the way in which employees decide to support the project planning processes is critical. Because activity estimation is often an imprecise process, it is common for some project team members to "pad" their estimates to give themselves as much time as possible. These people are often responding to a culture that reinforces the idea that it is better to engage in poor estimation and project planning than to be late with deliverables. Conversely, when there is a culture of trust among project team members, we are more inclined to give honest assessments, without fearing that, should we be wrong, we will be punished for our mistakes.

- *Performance evaluation*—Supportive cultures encourage project team members taking the initiative, even if it means taking risks to boost performance. When a culture sends the signal that the goal of the firm is to create innovative products, it reinforces a project management culture that is aggressive and offers potentially high payoffs (and the occasional significant loss!). As we noted earlier, organizations get what they pay for. If the reward systems are positive and reinforce a strong project mentality, they will reap a whirlwind of opportunities. On the other hand, if they tacitly support caution and playing it safe, the project management approaches will equally reflect this principle.

A culture can powerfully affect the manner in which departments within an organization view the process of project management. The culture also influences the manner in which employees commit themselves to the goals of their projects as opposed to other, potentially competing goals. Through symbols, stories, and other signs, companies signal their commitment to project management. This message is not lost on members of project teams, who take their cues regarding expected performance from supervisors and other cultural artifacts. Visible symbols of a culture that advocates cross-functional cooperation will create employees who are prepared and motivated to work in harmony with other groups on project goals. Likewise, when an IT department elevates some of its members to hero status because they routinely went the extra mile to handle system user complaints or problems, the company has sent the message that they are all working toward the same goals and all provide value to the organization's operations, regardless of their functional background.

To envision how culture can influence the planning and project monitoring processes, suppose that, in your organization, it was clear that those involved in late projects would be severely punished for the schedule slippage. You and your fellow project team members would quickly learn that it is critical to avoid going out on a limb to promise early task completion dates. It is much safer to grossly overestimate the amount of time necessary to complete a task in order to protect yourself. The organizational culture in this case breeds deceit. Likewise, it may be safer in some organizations to deliberately hide information in cases where a project is running off track, or mislead top management with optimistic and false estimates of project progress. Essentially, the issue is this: Does the corporate culture encourage authentic information and truthful interactions, or is it clear that the safer route is to first protect yourself, regardless of the effect this behavior may have on the success of a project?

What are some examples of an organization's culture influencing how project teams actually perform and how outcomes are perceived? One common situation is the phenomenon known as escalation of commitment. It is not uncommon to see this process at work in project organizations. **Escalation of commitment** occurs when, in spite of evidence identifying a project as failing, no longer necessary, or beset by huge technical or other difficulties, organizations continue to support it past the point an objective viewpoint would suggest that it should be terminated.[34] Although there are a number of reasons for escalation of commitment to a failed decision, one important reason is the unwillingness of the organization to acknowledge failure or its culture's working toward blinding key decision makers to the need to take corrective action.

PROJECT PROFILE

A Culture of Caring: Sanofi-Aventis and Its Commitment to Global Medical Assistance

Residents of developing countries face enormous economic and social challenges in their daily lives. One persistent problem lies in their lack of access to medicines and medical treatment for disease, many of which are treatable with prompt application of vaccines. In fact, it is estimated that 80% of the world's population has no access to medicines and so suffers from the effects of a variety of diseases, including malaria, tuberculosis, sleeping sickness, and epilepsy, among others. The challenge for organizations in the developed world is to find a commitment to resolving these problems and the means to do so.

Sanofil-Aventis, headquartered in Paris, France, is a leading research and pharmaceutical company with a commitment to addressing the challenges of global medical assistance. One department within their company, called "Access to Medicines," has the objective of providing poor patients with low-cost medicines to fight disease. This team within Sanofil has a core focus, zeroing in on medical issues where the company's product portfolio and know-how can make a difference. As part of that effort, they cover three main areas: improvement of existing drugs; preferential pricing policies to deliver drugs at a "no profit–no loss" scenario; and a program of information, education, and communication.

The culture of the Access to Medicines team within Sanofil-Aventis promotes an action orientation designed to search for opportunities where they can assist other international organizations in these ventures. The problems they face include generally poor public health infrastructures, lack of health care personnel, insufficient diagnostics, and lack of distribution structures. In these areas, the pharmaceutical industry is often limited in its role unless it can create partnerships with other "on the ground" organizations. One such alliance has formed between Access to Medicines and the Institute for OneWorld Health to promote a global malaria project. OneWorld Health is a nonprofit organization with the goal of bringing medical relief to the poor on the planet who have no other access to help.

Both organizations credit their working relationship as the key to making this project initiative successful. Kay Monroe, Director of Project Management for OneWorld Health's malaria project, notes that when it comes to finding the right partners, it's not simply a matter of picking firms with the best product portfolio or production capabilities. It also comes down to the cultural fit. "When choosing partners, you can't negate the soft stuff," she says. "The Sanofil-Aventis team is a joy to work with and that's huge. Sometimes it's not easy for people [who] are new to this kind of project to handle the stress, but Sanofil-Aventis has done it enough times not to get frustrated."[33]

The reverse is also true: In many organizations, projects are managed in an environment in which the culture strongly supports cross-functional cooperation, assigns sufficient resources to enable project managers to schedule aggressively, and creates an atmosphere that makes it possible to develop projects optimally. It is important to recognize that an organization's culture can be a strong supporter of (as well as an inhibitor to) the firm's ability to manage effective projects. Because of this impact, organizational culture must be managed, constantly assessed, and, when necessary, changed in ways that promote project management rather than discouraging its efficient practice.

The context within which we manage our projects is a key determinant in the likelihood of their success or failure. Three critical contextual factors are the organization's strategy, structure, and culture. Strategy drives projects; projects operationalize strategy. The two must work together in harmony. The key is maintaining a clear linkage between overall strategy and the firm's portfolio of projects, ensuring that some form of alignment exists among all key elements: vision, objectives, strategies, goals, and programs. Further, companies are recognizing that when they adopt a structure that supports projects, they get better results. Likewise, when the cultural ambience of the organization favors project management approaches, they are much more likely to be successful. Some of these project management approaches are the willingness to take risks, to think creatively, to work closely with other functional departments, and so forth. More and more we are seeing successful project-based organizations recognizing the simple truth that the context in which they are trying to create projects is a critical element in seeing their projects through to commercial and technical success.

Summary

1. **Understand how effective project management contributes to achieving strategic objectives.** This chapter linked projects with corporate strategy. Projects are the "building blocks" of strategy because they serve as the most basic tools by which firms can implement previously formulated objectives and strategies.

2. **Recognize three components of the corporate strategy model: formulation, implementation, and evaluation.** The chapter explored a generic model of corporate strategic management, distinguishing between the three components of strategy formulation, strategy implementation, and strategy evaluation. Each of these components incorporates a number of subdimensions. For example, strategy formulation includes the stages of:

   - Developing a vision and mission.
   - Performing an internal audit (assessing strengths and weaknesses).
   - Performing an external audit (assessing opportunities and threats).
   - Establishing long-term objectives.
   - Generating, evaluating, and selecting strategies.

   Strategy implementation requires the coordination of managerial, technological, financial, and functional assets to reinforce and support strategies. Projects often serve as the means by which strategy implementation is actually realized. Finally, strategy evaluation requires an ability to measure results and provide feedback to all concerned parties.

3. **See the importance of identifying critical project stakeholders and managing them within the context of project development.** The chapter addresses a final strategic question: the relationship between the firm and its stakeholder groups. Project stakeholders are either internal to the firm (top management, other functional departments, support personnel, internal customers) or external (suppliers, distributors, intervenors, governmental agencies and regulators, and customers). Each of these stakeholder groups must be managed in a systematic manner; the process moves from identification to needs assessment, choice of strategy, and routine evaluation and adjustment. Stakeholder management, in conjunction with strategic management, forms the context by which projects are first evaluated and then managed.

4. **Recognize the strengths and weaknesses of three basic forms of organizational structure and their implications for managing projects.** We examined the strengths and weaknesses of three major organizational structure types, including functional, project, and matrix structures. The nature of each of the three structural types and their relationship to project management were addressed. The functional structure, while the most common type of organizational form, was shown to be perhaps the least effective type for managing projects due to a variety of limitations. The project structure, in which the organization uses its projects as the primary form of grouping, has several advantages for managing projects, although it has some general disadvantages as well. Finally, the matrix structure, which seeks to balance the authority and activities between projects and functions using a dual hierarchy system, demonstrates its own unique set of strengths and weaknesses for project management practice.

5. **Understand how companies can change their structure into a "heavyweight project organization"**

structure to facilitate effective project management practices. The movements within many organizations to a stronger customer focus in their project management operations has led to the creation of a heavyweight project organization, in which the project manager is given high levels of authority in order to further the goals of the project. Because customer satisfaction is the goal of these organizations, they rely on their project managers to work toward project success within the framework of greater control of project resources and direct contact with clients.

6. **Identify the characteristics of three forms of project management office (PMO).** Project management offices (PMOs) are centralized units within an organization or department that oversee or improve the management of projects. There are three predominant types of PMO in organizations. The weather station is typically used only as a tracking and monitoring device. In this approach, the role of the PMO is to keep an eye on the status of the projects without directly attempting to influence or control them. The second form of PMO is the control tower, which treats project management as a business skill to be protected and supported. It focuses on developing methods for continually improving project management skills by identifying what is working, where the shortcomings exist, and methods for resolving ongoing problems. Most importantly, unlike the weather station model, which only monitors project management activities to report results to top management, the control tower is a model that is intended to directly work with and support the activities of the project manager and team. Finally, the resource pool is a PMO intended to maintain and provide a cadre of trained and skilled project professionals as they are needed. It serves as a clearinghouse for continually upgrading the skills of the firm's project managers. As the company initiates new projects, the affected departments apply to the resource pool PMO for assets to populate the project team.

7. **Understand key concepts of corporate culture and how cultures are formed.** Another contextual factor, organizational culture, plays an important role in influencing the attitudes and values shared by members of the organization, which, in turn, affects their commitment to project management and its practices. Culture is defined as the unwritten rules of behavior, or the norms that are used to shape and guide behavior, are shared by some subset of organizational members, and are taught to all new members of the company. When the firm has a strong culture that is supportive of project goals, members of the organization are more likely to work collaboratively, minimize departmental loyalties that could take precedence over project goals, and commit the necessary resources to achieve the objectives of the project.

    Organizational cultures are formed as the result of a variety of factors, including technology, environment, geographical location, reward systems, rules and procedures, key organizational members, and critical incidents. Each of these factors can play a role in determining whether the organization's culture is strong, collaborative, customer-focused, project-oriented, fast-paced, and so forth.

8. **Recognize the positive effects of a supportive organizational culture on project management practices versus those of a culture that works against project management.** Finally, this chapter examined the manner in which supportive cultures can work in favor of project management and ways in which the culture can inhibit project success. One common facet of a "sick" culture is the escalation of a commitment problem, in which key members of the organization continue to increase their support for clearly failing courses of action or problematic projects. The reasons for escalation are numerous, including our prestige is on the line, the conviction that we are close to succeeding, fear of ridicule if we admit to failure, and the culture of the organization in which we operate.

Key Terms

Culture *(p. 76)*

Escalation of commitment *(p. 80)*

External environment *(p. 65)*

Functional structure *(p. 65)*

Heavyweight project organization *(p. 71)*

Intervenor groups *(p. 59)*

Matrix organization *(p. 69)*

Matrix structure *(p. 69)*

Objectives *(p. 55)*

Organizational culture *(p. 76)*

Organizational structure *(p. 64)*

Program *(p. 57)*

Project management office *(p. 73)*

Project organizations *(p. 67)*

Project stakeholders *(p. 58)*

Project structure *(p. 67)*

Resources *(p. 70)*

Stakeholder analysis *(p. 58)*

Strategic management *(p. 55)*

Strong matrix *(p. 70)*

Technology *(p. 77)*

Weak matrix *(p. 70)*

Discussion Questions

1. The chapter suggests that a definition of strategic management includes four components:
   a. Developing a strategic vision and sense of mission
   b. Formulating, implementing, and evaluating
   c. Making cross-functional decisions
   d. Achieving objectives

   Discuss how each of these four elements is important in understanding the challenge of strategic project management. How do projects serve to allow an organization to realize each of these four components of strategic management?

2. Discuss the difference between organizational objectives and strategies.

3. Your company is planning to construct a nuclear power plant in Oregon. Why is stakeholder analysis important as a precondition of the decision whether or not to follow through with such a plan? Conduct a stakeholder analysis for a planned upgrade to a successful software product. Who are the key stakeholders?

4. Consider a medium-sized company that has decided to begin using project management in a wide variety of its operations. As part of its operational shift, it is going to adopt a project management office somewhere within the organization. Make an argument for the type of PMO it should be adopting (weather station, control tower, or resource pool). What are some key decision criteria that will help it determine which model makes the most sense?

5. What are some of the key organizational elements that can affect the development and maintenance of a supportive organizational culture? As a consultant, what advice would you give to a functional organization that was seeking to move from an old, adversarial culture, where the various departments actively resisted helping one another, to one that encourages "project thinking" and cross-functional cooperation?

6. You are a member of the senior management staff at XYZ Corporation. You have historically been using a functional structure setup with five departments: finance, human resources, marketing, production, and engineering.
   a. Create a drawing of your simplified functional structure, identifying the five departments.
   b. Assume you have decided to move to a project structure. What might be some of the environmental pressures that would contribute to your belief that it is necessary to alter the structure?
   c. With the project structure, you have four ongoing projects: stereo equipment, instrumentation and testing equipment, optical scanners, and defense communications. Draw the new structure that creates these four projects as part of the organizational chart.

7. Suppose you now want to convert the structure from that in Question 6 to a matrix structure, emphasizing dual commitments to function and project.
   a. Re-create the structural design to show how the matrix would look.
   b. What behavioral problems could you begin to anticipate through this design? That is, do you see any potential points of friction in the dual hierarchy setup?

Case Study 2.1

Rolls-Royce Corporation

Although the name Rolls-Royce is inextricably linked with its ultra-luxurious automobiles, the modern Rolls-Royce operates in an entirely different competitive environment. A leading manufacturer of power systems for aerospace, marine, and power companies, Rolls's market is focused on developing jet engines for a variety of uses, both commercial and defense-related. In this market, the company has two principal competitors, General Electric and Pratt & Whitney (owned by United Technologies). There are a limited number of smaller, niche players in the jet engine market, but their impact from a technical and commercial perspective is minor. Rolls, GE, and Pratt & Whitney routinely engage in fierce competition for sales to defense contractors and the commercial aviation industry. The two main airframe manufacturers, Boeing and Airbus, make continual multimillion-dollar purchase decisions that are vital for the ongoing success of the engine makers. Airbus, a private consortium of several European partner companies, has drawn level with Boeing in sales in recent years. Because the cost of a single jet engine, including spare parts, can run to several million dollars, winning large orders from either defense or commercial aircraft builders represents an ongoing challenge for each of the "big three" jet engine manufacturers.

Airlines in developing countries can often be a lucrative but risky market for these firms. Because the countries do not maintain high levels of foreign exchange, it is not unknown, for example, for Rolls (or its competitors) to take partial payment in cash with assorted commodities to pay the balance. Hence, a contract with Turkey's national airline may lead to some monetary payment for Rolls, along with several tons of pistachios or other trade goods! To maintain their sales and service targets, these jet engine makers routinely resort to creative financing, long-term contracts, or asset-based trading deals. Overall, however, the market for jet engines is projected

(continued)

to continue to expand at huge rates. Rolls-Royce projects a 20-year window with a potential market demand of 70,000 engines, valued at over $400 billion in civil aerospace alone. When defense contracts are factored in as well, the revenue projections for jet engine sales are likely to be enormous. As Rolls sees the future, the single biggest market growth opportunity is in the larger, greater thrust engines, designed to be paired with larger jet aircraft.

Rolls-Royce is currently engaged in a strategic decision that offers the potential for huge payoffs or significant losses as it couples its latest engine technology, the "Trent series," with Airbus's decision to develop an ultra-large commercial aircraft for long-distance travel. The new Airbus design, the 380 model, seats more than 550 people, flying long-distance routes (up to 8,000 miles). The Trent 900, with an engine rating of 70,000 pounds thrust per engine, has been created at great expense to see service in the large jet market. The project reflects a strategic vision shared by both Airbus and Rolls-Royce that

the commercial passenger market will triple in the next 20 years. As a result, future opportunities will involve larger, more economically viable aircraft. Since 2007, Airbus has delivered a total of 40 A380s to its customers, with 17 in 2010. Their total order book currently sits at 234 aircraft ordered. Collectively, Airbus and Rolls-Royce have taken a large financial gamble that their strategic vision of the future is the correct one.

Questions

1. Who are Rolls's principal project management stakeholders? How would you design stakeholder management strategies to address their concerns?
2. Given the financial risks inherent in developing a jet engine, make an argument, either pro or con, for Rolls to develop strategic partnerships with other jet engine manufacturers in a manner similar to Airbus's consortium arrangement. What are the benefits and drawbacks in such an arrangement?

Case Study 2.2

Classic Case: Paradise Lost: The Xerox Alto[35]

Imagine the value of cornering the technological market in personal computing. How much would a five-year window of competitive advantage be worth to a company today? It could easily mean billions in revenue, a stellar industry reputation, future earnings ensured—and the list goes on. For Xerox Corporation, however, something strange happened on the way to industry leadership. In 1970, Xerox was uniquely positioned to take advantage of the enormous leaps forward it had made in office automation technology. Yet the company stumbled badly through its own strategic myopia, lack of nerve, structural inadequacies, and poor choices. This is the story of the Xerox Alto, the world's first personal computer and one of the great "what if?" stories in business history.

The Alto was not so much a step forward as it was a quantum leap. Being in place and operating at the end of 1973, it was the first stand-alone personal computer to combine bit-mapped graphics, a mouse, menu screens, icons, an Ethernet connection, a laser printer, and word processing software. As a result of the combined efforts of an impressive collection of computer science geniuses headquartered at Xerox's Palo Alto Research Center (PARC), the Alto was breathtaking in its innovative appeal. It was PARC's answer to Xerox's top management command to "hit a home run." Xerox had profited earlier from just such a home run in the form of the Model 914 photocopier, a technological innovation that provided the impetus to turn Xerox into a billion-dollar

company in the 1960s. The Alto represented a similar achievement.

What went wrong? What forces combined to ensure that no more than 2,000 Altos were produced and that none was ever brought to market? (They were used only inside the company and at some university sites.) The answer could lie in the muddled strategic thinking that took place at Xerox while the Alto was in development.

The history of Xerox during this period shows a company that stepped back from technological leadership into a form of incrementalism, making it content to follow IBM's lead in office automation. *Incrementalism* refers to adopting a gradualist approach that plays it safe, avoiding technological leaps, large risks, and consequently the possibility of large returns. In 1974, Xerox decided to launch the Model 800 magnetic tape word processor rather than the Alto because the Model 800 was perceived as the safer bet. During the next five years, a series of ill-timed acquisitions, lawsuits, and reorganizations rendered the Alto a casualty of inattention. What division would oversee its development and launch? Whose budget would support it, and PARC in general? By leaving such tough decisions unmade, Xerox wasted valuable time and squandered its technological window of opportunity. Even when clear indications showed that competitor Wang was in line to introduce its own line of office systems, Xerox could not take the step to bring the Alto to market. By 1979, Xerox's unique opportunity was lost. No longer was the

Alto a one-of-a-kind technology, and the company quietly shelved any plans for its commercial introduction.

Perhaps the ultimate irony is this: Here was a company that had made its name through the phenomenal success of a highly innovative product, the Model 914 photocopier, but it did not know how to handle the opportunities presented by the next phenomenon. The Alto was so advanced that the company seemed unable to comprehend its possibilities. Executives did not have a strategic focus that emphasized a continual progression of innovation. Instead, they were directed toward remaining neck-and-neck with the competition in an incremental approach. When competitor IBM released a new electric typewriter, Xerox responded in the same incremental way. The organizational structure at Xerox did not allow any one division or key manager to become the champion for new technologies like the Alto.

In 1979 Steven Jobs, president of Apple Computer, was given a tour of the PARC complex and saw an Alto in use. He was so impressed with the machine's features and operating capabilities that he asked when it was due to be commercially launched. When told that much of this technology had been developed in 1973, Jobs became "physically sick," he later recounted, at the thought of the opportunity Xerox had forgone.

Questions

1. Do you see a logical contradiction in Xerox's willingness to devote millions of dollars to support pure research sites like PARC and its refusal to commercially introduce the products developed?
2. How did Xerox's strategic vision work in favor of or against the development of radical new technologies such as the Alto?
3. What other unforeseeable events contributed to making Xerox's executives unwilling to take any new risks precisely at the time the Alto was ready to be released?
4. "Radical innovation cannot be too radical if we want it to be commercially successful." Argue either in favor of or against this statement.

Case Study 2.3

Project Task Estimation and the Culture of "Gotcha!"

I recently worked with an organization that adopted a mind-set in which it was assumed that the best way to keep project team members working hard was to unilaterally trim their task duration estimates by 20%. Suppose that you were asked to estimate the length of time necessary to write computer code for a particular software product and you determined that it should take about 80 hours. Knowing you were about to present this information to your supervisor and that she was going to immediately cut the estimate by 20%, what would be your course of action? You would probably first add a "fudge factor" to the estimate in order to protect yourself. The conversation with the boss might go something like this:

Boss   "Have you had a chance to estimate that coding sequence yet?"

You   "Yes, it should take me 100 hours."

Boss   "That's too long. I can only give you 80 hours, tops."

You (Theatrical sigh)   "Well, if you say so, but I really don't know how I can pull this off."

Once you leave the office and shut the door, you turn with a smile and whisper, "Gotcha!"

Questions

1. How does the organization's culture support this sort of behavior? What pressures does the manager face? What pressures does the subordinate face?
2. Discuss the statement, "If you don't take my estimates seriously, I'm not going to give you serious estimates!" How does this statement apply to this example?

Case Study 2.4

Widgets 'R Us

Widgets 'R Us (WRU) is a medium-sized firm specializing in the design and manufacturing of quality widgets. The market for widgets has been stable. Historically, WRU has had a functional organization design with four departments: accounting, sales, production, and engineering. This design has served the company well, and it has been able to compete by being the low-priced company in the industry.

(continued)

In the past three years, the demand for widgets has exploded. New widgets are constantly being developed to feed the public's seemingly insatiable demand. The average life cycle of a newly released widget is 12–15 months. Unfortunately, WRU is finding itself unable to compete successfully in this new, dynamic market. The CEO has noted a number of problems. Products are slow to market. Many new innovations have passed right by WRU because the company was slow to pick up signs from the marketplace that they were coming. Internal communication is very poor. Lots of information gets kicked "upstairs," and no one seems to know what happens to it. Department heads constantly blame other department heads for the problems.

Questions

1. You have been called in as a consultant to analyze the operations at WRU. What would you advise?
2. What structural design changes might be undertaken to improve the operations at the company?
3. What are the strengths and weaknesses of the alternative solutions the company could employ?

Internet Exercises

1. Wegmans has been consistently voted one of the 100 best companies to work for in the United States by *Fortune* magazine. In fact, in 2005 it was ranked number 1, and in 2012 it was ranked number 4. Go to its Web site, www.wegmans.com, and click on "About Us." What messages, formal and informal, are being conveyed about Wegmans through its Web site? What does the Web site imply about the culture of the organization?

2. Go to the Web site www.projectstakeholder.com and analyze some of the case studies found on the Web site. What do these cases suggest about the importance of assessing stakeholder expectations for a project *before* it has begun its development process? In other words, what are the risks of waiting to address stakeholder concerns until after a project has begun?

3. Go to a corporate Web site of your choice and access the organizational chart. What form of organization does this chart represent: functional, project, matrix, or some other form? Based on our discussion in this chapter, what would be the likely strengths and weaknesses of this organization's project management activities?

4. Access the corporate Web site for Fluor-Daniel Corporation and examine its "Compliance and Ethics" section at www.fluor.com/sustainability/ethics_compliance/Pages/default.aspx. What does the "Fluor Code of Business Conduct and Ethics" suggest about the way the company does business? What are the strategic goals and directions that naturally flow from the ethical code? In your opinion, how would the ethics statement influence the manner in which the company manages its projects?

PMP Certification Sample Questions

1. What is the main role of the functional manager?
   a. To control resources
   b. To manage the project when the project manager isn't available
   c. To define business processes
   d. To manage the project manager

2. What is the typical role of senior management on a project?
   a. Support the project
   b. Pay for it
   c. Support the project and resolve resource and other conflicts
   d. Resolve resource and other conflicts

3. What is an organization that controls project managers, documentation, and policies called?
   a. Project Management Office
   b. Strong matrix
   c. Functional
   d. Pure project

4. A business analyst has a career path that has been very important to her throughout the 10 years of her career. She is put on a project with a strong matrix organizational structure. Which of the following is likely viewed as a negative of being on the project?
   a. Being away from the group and on a project that might make it more difficult to get promoted
   b. Working with people who have similar skills
   c. Working long hours because the project is a high priority
   d. Not being able to take her own certification tests because she is so busy

5. The functional manager is planning the billing system replacement project with the newest project manager at the company. In discussing this project, the functional manager focuses on the cost associated with running the system after it is created and the number of years the system will last before it must be replaced. What best describes what the functional manager is focusing on?
   a. Project life cycle
   b. Product life cycle
   c. Project management life cycle
   d. Program management life cycle

Answers: 1 a—The functional manager runs the day-to-day operations of his department and controls the resources; 2 c—Because senior managers usually outrank the project manager, they can help with resolving any resource or other conflicts as they arise; 3 a—The Project Management Office (PMO) typically has all of these responsibilities; 4 a—Being away from her functional group may cause her to feel that her efforts on behalf of the project are not being recognized by her functional manager, since the project employs a strong matrix structure; 5 b—The functional manager is focusing on the product life cycle, which is developed based on an example of a successful project and encompasses the range of use for the product.

INTEGRATED PROJECT

Building Your Project Plan

EXERCISE 1—DEVELOPING THE PROJECT NARRATIVE AND GOALS

You have been assigned to a project team to develop a new product or service for your organization. Your challenge is to first decide on the type of product or service you wish to develop. The project choices can be flexible, consisting of options as diverse as construction, new product development, IT implementation, and so forth.

Develop a project scope write-up on the project you have selected. Your team is expected to create a project history, complete with an overview of the project, an identifiable goal or goals (including project targets), the general project management approach to be undertaken, and significant project constraints or potential limiting effects. Additionally, if appropriate, identify any basic resource requirements (i.e., personnel or specialized equipment) needed to complete the project. What is most important at this stage is creating a history or narrative of the project you have come up with, including a specific statement of purpose or intent (i.e., why the project is being developed, what it is, what niche or opportunity it is aimed to address).

The write-up should fully explain your project concept, constraints, and expectations. It is not necessary to go into minute detail regarding the various subactivities or subcomponents of the project; it is more important to concentrate on the bigger picture for now.

SAMPLE BACKGROUND ANALYSIS AND PROJECT NARRATIVE FOR ABCUPS, INC.

Founded in 1990, ABCups, Inc., owns and operates 10 injection-molding machines that produce plastic drinkware. ABCups's product line consists of travel mugs, thermal mugs, steins, and sports tumblers. The travel mugs, thermal mugs, and steins come in two sizes: 14 and 22 ounces. The sports tumblers are offered only in the 32-ounce size. All products except the steins have lids. The travel and thermal mugs consist of a liner, body, and lid. The steins and sports tumblers have no lining. There are 15 colors offered, and any combination of colors can be used. The travel and thermal mugs have a liner that needs to be welded to the outer body; subcontractors and screen printers weld the parts together. ABCups does no welding, but it attaches the lid to the mug. ABCups's customer base consists primarily of distributors and promotional organizations. Annual sales growth has remained steady, averaging 2%–3% each year. Last year's revenues from sales were $70 million.

CURRENT PROCESS

ABCups's current method for producing its product is as follows:

1. Quote job.
2. Receive/process order.
3. Schedule order into production.
4. Mold parts.
5. Issue purchase order to screen printer with product specifications.
6. Ship parts to screen printer for welding and artwork.
7. Receive returned product from screen printer for final assembly and quality control.
8. Ship product to customer.

At current processing levels, the entire process can take from two to four weeks, depending on order size, complexity, and the nature of current production activity.

OVERVIEW OF THE PROJECT

Because of numerous complaints and quality rejects from customers, ABCups has determined to proactively resolve outstanding quality issues. The firm has determined that by bringing welding and screen printing functions "in-house," it will be able to address the current quality problems, expand its market, maintain better control over delivery and order output, and be more responsive to customers. The project consists of adding three new processes (welding, screen printing, and improved quality control) to company operations.

ABCups has no experience in or equipment for welding and screen printing. The organization needs to educate itself, investigate leasing or purchasing space and equipment, hire trained workers, and create a transition from subcontractors to in-house operators. The project needs a specified date of completion so that the transition from outsourcing to company production will be smooth and products can be delivered to customers with as little disruption to shipping as possible.

Management's strategy is to vertically integrate the organization to reduce costs, increase market share, and improve product quality. ABCups is currently experiencing problems with its vendor base, ranging from poor quality to ineffectual scheduling, causing ABCups to miss almost 20% of its customers' desired ship dates. Maintaining complete control over the product's development cycle should improve the quality and on-time delivery of ABCups's product line.

Objectives

Goals	Targets
1. Meet all project deadlines without jeopardizing customer satisfaction within a one-year project time frame.	Excellent = 0 missed deadlines Good = 1–5 missed deadlines Acceptable = <8 missed deadlines
2. Deplete dependence on subcontracted screen printing by 100% within six months without increasing customer's price or decreasing product quality.	Excellent = 100% independence Good = 80–99% independence Acceptable = 60–79% independence
3. Perform all process changes without affecting current customer delivery schedules for the one-year project time frame.	Excellent = 0% delivery delays Good = <5% delivery delays Acceptable = 5–10% delivery delays
4. Decrease customer wait time over current wait time within one year without decreasing quality or increasing price.	Excellent = 2/3 decrease in wait time Good = 1/2 decrease in wait time Acceptable = 1/3 decrease in wait time
5. Stay within 10% of capital budget without exceeding 20% within the project baseline schedule.	Excellent = 1% variance Good = 5% variance Acceptable = 10% variance
6. Decrease customer rejections by 25% within one year.	Excellent = 45% reduction Good = 35% reduction Acceptable = 25% reduction

General Approach

1. **Managerial approach**—The equipment will be purchased from outside vendors; however, ABCups's internal employees will perform the assembly work. Given the type of equipment that is required, outside contractors will not be needed because the company's facility employs the necessary maintenance staff to set up the equipment and troubleshoot as required, once the initial training has been supplied by the vendor.
2. **Technical approach**—The equipment manufacturers will utilize CAD to design the equipment. Initially, the firm will require a bank of parts to be available once the equipment arrives in order to fine-tune the machinery. Fixtures will be designed as required, but will be supplied by the machine manufacturer.

Constraints

1. **Budget constraints**—This project must ultimately increase profitability for the company. In addition, the project will have a constraining budget. It must be shown that any additional expense for both the conversion and producing finished cups on-site will result in increased profitability.
2. **Limited plant space**—ABCups is assuming this conversion does not involve building a new plant or significantly increasing facility size. Space for new machinery, new employees, and storage for dyes and inventory must be created through conversion of existing floor space. If additional floor space is required, leasing or purchasing options will need to be investigated.

3. **Time**—Since this project will require the company to break existing contracts with vendors, any missed milestones or other delays will cause an unacceptable delay to customers. A backup plan must be in place to avoid losing customers to competitors in case the time frame is not strictly met. The conversion must be undertaken with a comprehensive project scheduling system developed and adhered to.

4. **Safety regulations**—The installation and conversion activities must be in accordance with several agencies' specifications, including but not limited to guidelines from the Occupational Safety and Health Administration (OSHA), the insurance carrier, and the financing agency.

5. **Current orders must be filled on time**—All activities must be designed to avoid any delay in current orders. The transition should appear seamless to customers to avoid losing any part of the extant customer base.

Notes

1. Pearson, D. (2010). "Airships receive life from new technology," *Wall Street Journal,* http://online.wsj.com/article/SB100 014240527487039597045754533391253582542.html; Excell, J. (2010, July 12). "Meet LEMV: The first of a new generation of advanced military airship," *The Engineer,* www.theengineer. co.uk/in-depth/the-big-story/meet-lemv-the-first-of-a-new-generation-of-advanced-military-airship/1003418.article; "Rise of the blimps." (2010). www.defenseindustrydaily. com/Rise-of-the-Blimps-The-US-Armys-LEMV-06438/; "Northrop Grummans' LEMV program completes three major milestones." (2010, November 5). www.spacewar. com/reports/Northrop_Grumman_LEMV_Program_ Completes_Three_Major_Milestones_999.html.

2. David, F. R. (2001). *Strategic Management,* 8th ed. Upper Saddle River, NJ: Prentice Hall.

3. Cleland, D. I. (1998). "Strategic project management," in Pinto, J. K. (Ed.), *Project Management Handbook.* San Francisco, CA: Jossey-Bass, pp. 27–40.

4. King, W. R. (1988). "The role of projects in the implementation of business strategy," in Cleland, D. I., and King, W. R. (Eds.), *Project Management Handbook,* 2nd ed. New York: Van Nostrand Reinhold, pp. 129–39.

5. Grundy, T. (2000). "Strategic project management and strategic behavior," *International Journal of Project Management,* 18(2): 93–104; Van der Merwe, A. P. (2002). "Project management and business development: Integrating strategy, structure, processes and projects," *International Journal of Project Management,* 20: 401–11; Van der Merwe, A. P. (1997). "Multi-project management—organizational structure and control," *International Journal of Project Management,* 15: 223–33.

6. King, W. R. (1988). "The role of projects in the implementation of business strategy," in Cleland, D. I., and King, W. R. (Eds.), *Project Management Handbook,* 2nd ed. New York: Van Nostrand Reinhold, pp. 129–39.

7. Wheelen, T. L., and Hunger, J. D. (1992). *Strategic Management and Business Policy,* 4th ed. Reading, MA: Addison-Wesley.

8. Wiener, E., and Brown, A. (1986). "Stakeholder analysis for effective issues management," *Planning Review,* 36: 27–31.

9. Mendelow, A. (1986). "Stakeholder analysis for strategic planning and implementation," in King, W. R., and Cleland, D. I. (Eds.), *Strategic Planning and Management Handbook.* New York: Van Nostrand Reinhold, pp. 67–81; Winch, G. M.

(2002). *Managing Construction Projects.* Oxford: Blackwell; Winch, G. M., and Bonke, S. (2001). "Project stakeholder mapping: Analyzing the interest of project stakeholders," in Slevin, D. P., Cleland, D. I., and Pinto, J. K. (Eds.), *The Frontiers of Project Management Research.* Newtown Square, PA: PMI, pp. 385–404.

10. Wideman, R. M. (1998). "How to motivate all stakeholders to work together," in Cleland, D. I. (Ed.), *Project Management Field Guide.* New York: Van Nostrand Reinhold, pp. 212–26; Hartman, F. T. (2000). *Don't Park Your Brain Outside.* Newtown Square, PA: PMI.

11. Cleland, D. I. (1988). "Project stakeholder management," in Cleland, D. I., and King, W. R. (Eds.), *Project Management Handbook,* 2nd ed. New York: Van Nostrand Reinhold, pp. 275–301.

12. Ibid.

13. Block, R. (1983). *The Politics of Projects.* New York: Yourdon Press.

14. Fisher, R., and Ury, W. (1981). *Getting to Yes: Negotiating Agreement Without Giving In.* New York: Houghton Mifflin.

15. Frame, J. D. (1987). *Managing Projects in Organizations.* San Francisco, CA: Jossey-Bass.

16. Grundy, T. (1998). "Strategy implementation and project management," *International Journal of Project Management,* 16(1): 43–50.

17. Cleland, D. I. (1988). "Project stakeholder management," in Cleland, D. I., and King, W. R. (Eds.), *Project Management Handbook,* 2nd ed. New York: Van Nostrand Reinhold, pp. 275–301.

18. Daft, R. L. (2001). *Organization Theory and Design,* 7th ed. Mason, OH: Southwestern; Moore, D. (2002). *Project Management: Designing Effective Organizational Structures in Construction.* Oxford: Blackwell; Yourker, R. (1977). "Organizational alternatives for project management," *Project Management Quarterly,* 8(1): 24–33.

19. Meredith, J. R., and Mantel, Jr., S. J. (2003). *Project Management,* 5th ed. New York: Wiley.

20. Larson, E. W., and Gobeli, D. H. (1987). "Matrix management: Contradictions and insights," *California Management Review,* 29(4): 126–37; Larson, E. W., and Gobeli, D. H. (1988). "Organizing for product development projects," *Journal of Product Innovation Management,* 5: 180–90.

21. Daft, R. L. (2001). *Organization Theory and Design,* 7th ed. Mason, OH: Southwestern; Anderson, C. C., and Fleming, M.

M. K. (1990). "Management control in an engineering matrix organization: A project engineer's perspective," *Industrial Management,* 32(2): 8–13; Ford, R. C., and Randolph, W. A. (1992). "Cross-functional structures: A review and integration of matrix organization and project management," *Journal of Management,* 18: 267–94.

22. Larson, E. W., and Gobeli, D. H. (1987). "Matrix management: Contradictions and insights," *California Management Review,* 29(4): 126–37; Larson, E. W., and Gobeli, D. H. (1988). "Organizing for product development projects," *Journal of Product Innovation Management,* 5: 180–90; Engwall, M., and Kallqvist, A. S. (2000). "Dynamics of a multi-project matrix: Conflicts and coordination," Working paper, Chalmers University, www.fenix.chalmers.se/publications/2001/pdf/WP%202001-07.pdf.

23. Wheelwright, S. C., and Clark, K. (1992). "Creating project plans to focus product development," *Harvard Business Review,* 70(2): 70–82.

24. Gobeli, D. H., and Larson, E. W. (1987). "Relative effectiveness of different project management structures," *Project Management Journal,* 18(2): 81–85; Gray, C., Dworatschek, S., Gobeli, D. H., Knoepfel, H., and Larson, E. W. (1990). "International comparison of project organization structures," *International Journal of Project Management,* 8: 26–32.

25. Gray, C. F., and Larson, E. W. (2003). *Project Management,* 2nd ed. Burr Ridge, IL: McGraw-Hill; Dai, C. (2000). *The Role of the Project Management Office in Achieving Project Success.* PhD Dissertation, George Washington University.

26. Block, T. (1998). "The project office phenomenon," *PMNetwork,* 12(3): 25–32; Block, T. (1999). "The seven secrets of a successful project office," *PMNetwork,* 13(4): 43–48; Block, T., and Frame, J. D. (1998). *The Project Office.* Menlo Park, CA: Crisp Publications; Eidsmoe, N. (2000). "The strategic project management office," *PMNetwork,* 14(12): 39–46; Kerzner, H. (2003). "Strategic planning for the project office," *Project Management Journal,* 34(2): 13–25; Dai, C. X., and Wells, W. G. (2004). "An exploration of project management office features and their relationship to project performance," *International Journal of Project Management,*

22: 523–32; Aubry, M., Müller, R., Hobbs, B., and Blomquist, T. (2010). "Project management offices in transition," *International Journal of Project Management,* 28(8): 766–78.

27. Casey, W., and Peck, W. (2001). "Choosing the right PMO setup," *PMNetwork,* 15(2): 40–47; Gale, S. (2009). "Delivering the goods," *PMNetwork,* 23(7): 34–39.

28. Kerzner, H. (2003). *Project Management,* 8th ed. New York: Wiley; Englund, R. L., and Graham, R. J. (2001). "Implementing a project office for organizational change," *PMNetwork,* 15(2): 48–52; Fleming, Q., and Koppelman, J. (1998). "Project teams: The role of the project office," *Cost Engineering,* 40: 33–36.

29. Schein, E. (1985). *Organizational Culture and Leadership: A Dynamic View.* San Francisco, CA: Jossey-Bass, pp. 19–21; Schein, E. H. (1985). "How culture forms, develops and changes," in Kilmann, R. H., Saxton, M. J., and Serpa, R. (Eds.), *Gaining Control of the Corporate Culture.* San Francisco, CA: Jossey-Bass, pp. 17–43; Elmes, M., and Wilemon, D. (1989). "Organizational culture and project leader effectiveness," *Project Management Journal,* 19(4): 54–63.

30. Kirsner, S. (1998, November). "Designed for innovation," *Fast Company,* pp. 54, 56; Daft, R. L. (2001). *Organization Theory and Design,* 7th ed. Mason, OH: Southwestern.

31. Kilmann, R. H., Saxton, M. J., and Serpa, R. (1985). *Gaining Control of the Corporate Culture.* San Francisco, CA: Jossey-Bass.

32. "The US must do as GM has done." (1989). *Fortune,* 124(2): 70–79.

33. Gale, S. (2009). "A closer look: Sanofil-Aventis & the Institute for OneWorld Health," *PMNetwork,* 23(8): 34–37; *Access to Medicines,* http://en.sanofi-aventis.com/binaries/brochure_aam_en_tcm28-18133.pdf.

34. Staw, B. M., and Ross, J. (1987, March–April). "Knowing when to pull the plug," *Harvard Business Review,* 65: 68–74.

35. Smith, D. K., and Alexander, R. C. (1988). *Fumbling the Future: How Xerox Invented, Then Ignored, the First Personal Computer.* New York: Macmillan; Kharbanda, O. P., and Pinto, J. K. (1996). *What Made Gertie Galdop?* New York: Van Nostrand Reinhold.

Project Selection and Portfolio Management

Chapter Outline

Chapter Objectives

After completing this chapter, you should be able to:

1. Explain six criteria for a useful project selection/screening model.

2. Understand how to employ checklists and simple scoring models to select projects.

3. Use more sophisticated scoring models, such as the Analytical Hierarchy Process.

4. Learn how to use financial concepts, such as the efficient frontier and risk/return models.

5. Employ financial analyses and options analysis to evaluate the potential for new project investments.

6. Recognize the challenges that arise in maintaining an optimal project portfolio for an organization.

7. Understand the three keys to successful project portfolio management.

PROJECT PROFILE

Project Selection Procedures: A Cross-Industry Sampler

The art and science of selecting projects is one that organizations take extremely seriously. Firms in a variety of industries have developed highly sophisticated methods for project screening and selection to ensure that the projects they choose to fund offer the best promise of success. As part of this screening process, organizations often evolve their own particular methods, based on technical concerns, available data, and corporate culture and preferences. This list gives you a sense of the lengths to which some organizations go with project selection:

- Hoechst AG, a pharmaceutical firm, uses a scoring portfolio model with 19 questions in five major categories when rating project opportunities. The five categories include probability of technical success, probability of commercial success, reward to the company, business strategy fit, and strategic leverage (ability of the project to employ and elevate company resources and skills). Within each of these factors are a number of specific questions, which are scored on a 1 to 10 scale by management.
  - At German industrial giant Siemens, every business unit in each of the 190 countries in which the company operates uses a system entitled "PM@Siemens" for categorizing projects that employs a two-digit code. Each project is awarded a letter from A to F, indicating its significance to the company, and a number from 0 to 3, indicating its overall risk level. Larger or riskier projects (e.g., an "A0") require approval from Siemens's main board in Germany, but many of the lesser projects (e.g., an "F3") can be approved by local business units. Too many A0s in the portfolio can indicate mounting risks while too many F3 projects may signal a lack of economic value overall.
- The Royal Bank of Canada has developed a scoring model to rate its project opportunities. The criteria for the portfolio scoring include project importance (strategic importance, magnitude of impact, and economic benefits) and ease of doing (cost of development, project complexity, and resource availability). Expected annual expenditure and total project spending are then added to this rank-ordered list to prioritize the project options. Decision rules are used (e.g., projects of low importance that are difficult to execute get a "no-go" rating).
- The Weyerhaeuser corporate research and development (R&D) program has put processes in place to align and prioritize R&D projects. The program has three types of activities: technology assessment (changes in external environment and impact to the company), research (building knowledge bases and competencies in core technical areas), and development (development of specific commercial opportunities). Four key inputs are considered when establishing priorities: significant changes in the external environment; long-term future needs of lead customers; business strategies, priorities, and technology needs; and corporate strategic direction.
- Mobil Chemical uses six categories of projects to determine the right balance of projects that will enter its portfolio: (1) cost reductions and process improvements; (2) product improvements, product modifications, and customer satisfaction; (3) new products; (4) new platform projects and fundamental/breakthrough research projects; (5) plant support; and (6) technical support for customers. Senior management reviews all project proposals and determines the division of capital funding across these six project types. One of the key decision variables involves a comparison of "what is" with "what should be."
- At 3M's Traffic Control Materials Division, during project screening and selection, management uses a project viability chart to score project alternatives. As part of the profile and scoring exercise, personnel must address how the project accomplishes strategic project objectives and critical business issues affecting a specific group within the target market. Projected project return on investment is always counterbalanced with riskiness of the project option.
- Exxon Chemical's management begins evaluating all new project proposals in light of the business unit's strategy and strategic priorities. Target spending is decided according to the overall project mix portfolio. As the year progresses, all projects are reprioritized using a scoring model. As significant differences between projected and actual spending are uncovered, the top management group makes adjustments for the next year's portfolio.[1]

INTRODUCTION

All organizations must select the projects they decide to pursue from among numerous opportunities. What criteria determine which projects should be supported? Obviously, this is no simple decision. The consequences of poor decisions can be enormously expensive. Recent research suggests that in the realm of information technology (IT), companies squander over $50 billion a year on projects that are created but never used by their intended clients. How do we make the most reasonable choices in selecting projects? What kind of information should we collect? Should decisions be based strictly on financial analysis, or should other criteria be considered? In this chapter, we will try to answer such questions as we take a closer look at the process of project selection.

We will examine a number of different approaches for evaluating and selecting potential projects. The various methods for project selection run along a continuum from highly qualitative, or judgment-based, approaches to those that rely on quantitative analysis. Of course, each approach has benefits and drawbacks, which must be considered in turn.

We will also discuss a number of issues related to the management of a **project portfolio**—the set of projects that an organization is undertaking at any given time. For example, Rubbermaid, Inc., routinely undertakes hundreds of new product development projects simultaneously, always searching for opportunities with strong commercial prospects. When a firm is pursuing multiple projects, the challenges of strategic decision making, resource management, scheduling, and operational control are magnified.

3.1 PROJECT SELECTION

Firms are literally bombarded with opportunities, but no organization enjoys infinite resources with which to pursue every opportunity that presents itself. Choices must be made, and to best ensure that they select the most viable projects, many managers develop priority systems—guidelines for balancing the opportunities and costs entailed by each alternative. The goal is to balance the competing demands of time and advantage.[2] The pressures of time and money affect most major decisions, and decisions are usually more successful when they are made in a timely and efficient manner. For example, if your firm's sales department recognizes a commercial opportunity it can exploit, you need to generate alternative approaches to the project quickly to capitalize on the prospect. Time wasted is generally opportunity lost. On the other hand, you need to be careful: You want to be sure that, at least as far as possible, you are making the best choice among your options. Thus organizational decision makers develop guidelines—*selection models*—that permit them to save time and money while maximizing the likelihood of success.

A number of decision models are available to managers responsible for evaluating and selecting potential projects. As you will see, they run the gamut from qualitative and simple to quantitative and complex. All firms, however, try to develop a screening model (or set of models) that will allow them to make the best choices among alternatives within the usual constraints of time and money.

Suppose you were interested in developing a model that allowed you to effectively screen project alternatives. How might you ensure that the model was capable of picking potential "winners" from the large set of possible project choices? After much consideration, you decide to narrow the focus for your screening model and create one that will allow you to select only projects that have high potential payoffs. All other issues are ignored in favor of the sole criterion of commercial profitability. The question is: Would such a screening model be useful? Souder[3] identifies five important issues that managers should consider when evaluating screening models:

1. **Realism:**   An effective model must reflect organizational objectives, including a firm's strategic goals and mission. Criteria must also be reasonable in light of such constraints on resources as money and personnel. Finally, the model must take into account both commercial risks and technical risks, including performance, cost, and time. That is: Will the project work as intended? Can we keep to the original budget or is there a high potential for escalating costs? Is there a strong risk of significant schedule slippage?
2. **Capability:**   A model should be flexible enough to respond to changes in the conditions under which projects are carried out. For example, the model should allow the company to compare different types of projects (long-term versus short-term projects, projects of different technologies or capabilities, projects with different commercial objectives). It should be robust enough to accommodate new criteria and constraints, suggesting that the screening model must allow the company to use it as widely as possible in order to cover the greatest possible range of project types.
3. **Flexibility:**   The model should be easily modified if trial applications require changes. It must, for example, allow for adjustments due to changes in exchange rates, tax laws, building codes, and so forth.
4. **Ease of use:**   A model must be simple enough to be used by people in all areas of the organization, both those in specific project roles and those in related functional positions. Further, the screening model that is applied, the choices made for project selection, and the reasons for those choices should be clear and easily understood by organizational members. The model should also be timely: It should generate the screening information rapidly, and people should be able to assimilate that information without any special training or skills.
5. **Cost:**   The screening model should be cost-effective. A selection approach that is expensive to use in terms of either time or money is likely to have the worst possible effect: causing organizational members to avoid using it because of the excessive cost of employing it. The cost of obtaining selection

information and generating optimal results should be low enough to encourage use of the models rather than diminish their applicability.

Let's add a sixth criterion for a successful selection model:

6. *Comparability:* The model must be broad enough to be applied to multiple projects. If a model is too narrowly focused, it may be useless in comparing potential projects or foster biases toward some over others. A useful model must support general comparisons of project alternatives.

Project selection models come in two general classes: numeric and nonnumeric.[4] **Numeric models** seek to use numbers as inputs for the decision process involved in selecting projects. These values can be derived either objectively or subjectively; that is, we may employ objective, external values ("The bridge's construction will require 800 cubic yards of cement") or subjective, internal values ("We will need to hire two code checkers to finish the software development within eight weeks"). Neither of these two input alternatives is necessarily wrong: An expert's opinion on an issue may be subjective but very accurate. On the other hand, an incorrectly calibrated surveyor's level can give objective but wrong data. The key is to remember that most selection processes for project screening involve a combination of subjective and objective data assessment and decision making. **Nonnumeric models,** on the other hand, do not employ numbers as decision inputs, relying instead on other data.

Companies spend great amounts of time and effort trying to make the best project selection decisions possible. These decisions are typically made with regard for the overall objectives that the company's senior management staff have developed and promoted based on their strategic plan. Such objectives can be quite complex and may reflect a number of external factors that can affect a firm's operations. For example, suppose the new head of Sylvania's Lighting Division mandated that the strategic objective of the organization was to be sales growth at all costs. Any new project opportunity would be evaluated against this key strategic imperative. Thus, a project offering the potential for opening new markets might be viewed more favorably than a competing project promising a higher potential rate of return.

The list of factors that can be considered when evaluating project alternatives is enormous. Table 3.1 provides only a partial list of the various elements that a company must address, organized into the general

---

TABLE 3.1 Issues in Project Screening and Selection

1. Risk—Factors that reflect elements of unpredictability to the firm, including:
   a. Technical risk—risks due to the development of new or untested technologies
   b. Financial risk—risks from the financial exposure caused by investing in the project
   c. Safety risk—risks to the well-being of users or developers of the project
   d. Quality risk—risks to the firm's goodwill or reputation due to the quality of the completed project
   e. Legal exposure—potential for lawsuits or legal obligation
2. Commercial—Factors that reflect the market potential of the project, including:
   a. Expected return on investment
   b. Payback period
   c. Potential market share
   d. Long-term market dominance
   e. Initial cash outlay
   f. Ability to generate future business/new markets
3. Internal operating issues—Factors that have an impact on internal operations of the firm, including:
   a. Need to develop/train employees
   b. Change in workforce size or composition
   c. Change in physical environment
   d. Change in manufacturing or service operations resulting from the project
4. Additional factors, including:
   a. Patent protection
   b. Impact on company's image
   c. Strategic fit

categories of risk and commercial factors, internal operating issues, and other factors. Although such a list can be long, in reality the strategic direction emphasized by top management often highlights certain criteria over others. In fact, if we apply Pareto's 80/20 principle, which states that a few issues (20%) are vital and many (80%) are trivial, it may be fairly argued that, for many projects, less than 20% of all possible decision criteria account for over 80% of the decision about whether to pursue the project.

This being said, we should reflect on two final points regarding the use of any decision-making approach to project selection. First, the most complete model in the world is still only a partial reflection of organizational reality. The potential list of inputs into any project selection decision is literally limitless—so much so, in fact, that we must recognize this truth before exploring project selection lest we erroneously assume that it is possible, given enough time and effort, to identify all relevant issues that play a role. Second, embedded in every decision model are both objective and subjective factors. We may form opinions based on objective data; we also may derive complex decision models from subjective inputs. Acknowledging that there exists a place for both subjective and objective inputs and decisions in any useful screening model is worthwhile.

3.2 APPROACHES TO PROJECT SCREENING AND SELECTION

A **project screening model** that generates useful information for project choices in a timely and useful fashion at an acceptable cost can serve as a valuable tool in helping an organization make optimal choices among numerous alternatives.[5] With these criteria in mind, let's consider some of the more common project selection techniques.

Method One: Checklist Model

The simplest method of project screening and selection is developing a **checklist,** or a list of criteria that pertain to our choice of projects, and then applying them to different possible projects. Let's say, for example, that in our company, the key selection criteria are cost and speed to market. Because of our strategic competitive model and the industry we are in, we favor low-cost projects that can be brought to the marketplace within one year. We would screen each possible project against these two criteria and select the project that best satisfies them. But depending on the type and size of our possible projects, we may have to consider literally dozens of relevant criteria. In deciding among several new product development opportunities, a firm must weigh a variety of issues, including the following:

- *Cost of development:*   What is a reasonable cost estimate?
- *Potential return on investment:*   What kind of return can we expect? What is the likely payback period?
- *Riskiness of the new venture:*   Does the project entail the need to create new-generation technology? How risky is the venture in terms of achieving our anticipated specifications?
- *Stability of the development process:*   Are both the parent organization and the project team stable? Can we expect this project to face funding cuts or the loss of key personnel, including senior management sponsors?
- *Governmental or stakeholder interference:*   Is the project subject to levels of governmental oversight that could potentially interfere with its development? Might other stakeholders oppose the project and attempt to block completion? For example, environmental groups, one of the "intervenor" stakeholders, have a long history of opposing natural resource development projects and may work in opposition to our project objectives.[6]
- *Product durability and future market potential:*   Is this project a one-shot opportunity, or could it be the forerunner of future opportunities? A software development firm may, for example, develop an application for a client in hopes that successful performance on this project will lead to future business. On the other hand, the project may be simply a one-time opportunity with little potential for future work with the customer.

This is just a partial list of criteria that may be relevant when we are selecting among project alternatives. A checklist approach to the evaluation of project opportunities is a fairly simple device for recording opinions and encouraging discussion. Thus, checklists may be best used in a consensus-group setting, as a method for initiating conversation, stimulating discussion and the exchange of opinions, and highlighting the group's priorities.

EXAMPLE 3.1   **Checklist**

Let's assume that SAP Corporation, a leader in the business applications software industry, is interested in developing a new application package for inventory management and shipping control. It is trying to decide which project to select from a set of four potential alternatives. Based on past commercial experiences, the company feels that the most important selection criteria for its choice are *cost, profit potential, time to market,* and *development risks.* Table 3.2 shows a simple checklist model with only four project choices and the four decision criteria. In addition to developing the decision criteria, we create evaluative descriptors that reflect how well the project alternatives correspond to our key selection criteria. We evaluate each criterion (which is rated *high, medium,* or *low*) in order to see which project accumulates the highest checks—and thus may be regarded as the optimal choice.

SOLUTION

Based on this analysis, Project Gamma is the best alternative in terms of maximizing our key criteria—cost, profit potential, time to market, and development risks.

TABLE 3.2 Simplified Checklist Model for Project Selection

		Performance on Criteria		
Project	**Criteria**	**High**	**Medium**	**Low**
Project Alpha	Cost	X		
	Profit potential			X
	Time to market		X	
	Development risks			X
Project Beta	Cost		X	
	Profit potential		X	
	Time to market	X		
	Development risks		X	
Project Gamma	Cost	X		
	Profit potential	X		
	Time to market			X
	Development risks	X		
Project Delta	Cost			X
	Profit potential			X
	Time to market	X		
	Development risks		X	

The flaws in a model such as that shown in Table 3.2 include the subjective nature of the *high, medium,* and *low* ratings. These terms are inexact and subject to misinterpretation or misunderstanding. Checklist screening models also fail to resolve trade-off issues. What if our criteria are *differentially weighted*—that is, what if some criteria are more important than others? How will relative, or weighted, importance affect our final decision? Let's say, for instance, that we regard time to market as our paramount criterion. Is Project Gamma, which is rated low on this criterion, still "better" than Project Beta or Delta, both of which are rated high on time to market though lower on other, less important criteria? Are we willing to make a trade-off, accepting low time to market in order to get the highest benefits in cost, profit potential, and development risks?

Because the simple checklist model does not deal satisfactorily with such questions, let's turn next to a more complex screening model in which we distinguish more important from less important criteria by assigning each criterion a simple *weight*.

Method Two: Simplified Scoring Models

In the **simplified scoring model,** each criterion is ranked according to its relative importance. Our choice of projects will thus reflect our desire to maximize the impact of certain criteria on our decision. In order to score our simplified checklist, we assign a specific weight to each of our four criteria:

Criterion	Importance Weight
Time to market	3
Profit potential	2
Development risks	2
Cost	1

Now let's reconsider the decision that we made using the basic checklist approach illustrated in Table 3.2.

EXAMPLE 3.2 **Scoring Models**

SAP Corporation is attempting to determine the optimal project to fund using the criterion weighting values we developed above. As you can see in Table 3.3, although adding a scoring component to our simple checklist complicates our decision, it also gives us a more precise screening model—one that more closely reflects our desire to emphasize certain criteria over others.

TABLE 3.3 Simple Scoring Model

Project	Criteria	(A) Importance Weight	(B) Score	(A) × (B) Weighted Score
Project Alpha				
	Cost	1	3	3
	Profit potential	2	1	2
	Development risk	2	1	2
	Time to market	3	2	6
	Total Score			13
Project Beta				
	Cost	1	2	2
	Profit potential	2	2	4
	Development risk	2	2	4
	Time to market	3	3	9
	Total Score			19
Project Gamma				
	Cost	1	3	3
	Profit potential	2	3	6
	Development risk	2	3	6
	Time to market	3	1	3
	Total Score			18
Project Delta				
	Cost	1	1	1
	Profit potential	2	1	2
	Development risk	2	2	4
	Time to market	3	3	9
	Total Score			16

SOLUTION

In Table 3.3, the numbers in the column labeled *Importance Weight* specify the numerical values that we have assigned to each criterion: *Time to market* always receives a value of *3*, *profit potential* a value of *2*, *development risk* a value of *2*, and *cost* a value of *1*. We then assign relative values to each of our four dimensions.

The numbers in the column labeled *Score* replace the *X*s of Table 3.2 with their assigned score values:

High = 3
Medium = 2
Low = 1

In Project Alpha, for example, the *High* rating given *Cost* becomes a *3* in Table 3.3 because *High* is here valued at *3*. Likewise, the *Medium* rating given *Time to market* in Table 3.2 becomes a *2*. But notice what happens when we calculate the numbers in the column labeled *Weighted Score*. When we multiply the numerical value of *Cost* (*1*) by its rating of *High* (*3*), we get a *Weighted Score* of *3*. But when we multiply the numerical value of *Time to market* (*3*) by its rating of *Medium* (*2*), we get a *Weighted Score* of *6*. Once we add the numbers in the *Weighted Score* column for each project in Table 3.3 and examine the totals, Project Beta (with a total of *19*) is the best alternative, compared to the other options: Project Alpha (with a total of *13*), Project Gamma (with a total of *18*), and Project Delta (with a total of *16*).

Thus, the simple scoring model consists of the following steps:

- *Assign importance weights to each criterion:* The first step is to develop logic for differentiating among various levels of importance and to devise a system for assigning appropriate weights to each criterion. Relying on collective group judgment may help to validate the reasons for determining importance levels. The team may also designate some criteria as "must" items. Safety concerns, for example, may be stipulated as nonnegotiable. In other words, all projects must achieve an acceptable safety level or they will not be considered further.
- *Assign score values to each criterion in terms of its rating (High = 3, Medium = 2, Low = 1):* The logic of assigning score values is often an issue of scoring sensitivity—of making differences in scores distinct. Some teams, for example, prefer to widen the range of possible values—say, by using a 1-to-7 scale instead of a 1-to-3 scale—in order to ensure a clearer distinction among scores and, therefore, among project choices. Such decisions will vary according to the number of criteria being applied and, perhaps, the team members' experience with the accuracy of outcomes produced by a given approach to screening and selection.
- *Multiply importance weights by scores to arrive at a weighted score for each criterion:* The weighted score reflects both the value that the team assigns to each criterion and the ratings that the team gives each criterion for the project.
- *Add the weighted scores to arrive at an overall project score:* The final score for each project represents the sum of all its weighted criteria.

The pharmaceutical company Hoechst Marion Roussel uses a scoring model for selecting projects that identifies not only five main criteria—reward, business strategy fit, strategic leverage, probability of commercial success, and probability of technical success—but also a number of more specific subcriteria. Each of these 19 subcriteria is scored on a scale of 1 to 10. The score for each criterion is then calculated by averaging the scores for each criterion. The final project score is determined by adding the average score of each of the five subcategories. Hoechst has had great success with this scoring model, both in setting project priorities and in making go/no-go decisions.[7]

The simple scoring model has some useful advantages as a project selection device. First, it is easy to use in tying critical strategic goals for the company to various project alternatives. In the case of the pharmaceutical company Hoechst, the company has assigned several categories to strategic goals for its project options, including *business strategy fit* and *strategic leverage*. These strategic goals become a critical hurdle for all new project alternatives. Second, the simple scoring model is easy to comprehend and use. With a checklist of key criteria, evaluation options (high, medium, and low), and attendant scores, top managers can quickly grasp how to employ this technique.

Limitations of Scoring Models

The simple scoring model illustrated here is an abbreviated and unsophisticated version of the weighted-scoring approach. In general, scoring models try to impose some structure on the decision-making process while, at the same time, combining multiple criteria.

Most scoring models, however, share some important limitations. A scale from 1 to 3 may be intuitively appealing and easy to apply and understand, but it is not very accurate. From the perspective of mathematical scaling, it is simply wrong to treat evaluations on such a scale as real numbers that can be multiplied and summed. If *3* means *High* and *2* means *Medium,* we know that *3* is better than *2,* but we do not know by how much. Furthermore, we cannot assume that the difference between *3* and *2* is the same as the difference between *2* and *1.* Thus, in Table 3.3, if the score for Project Alpha is *13* and the score for Project Beta is *19,* may we assume that Beta is 46% better than Alpha? Unfortunately, no. Critics of scoring models argue that their ease of use may blind novice users to the false assumptions that sometimes underlie them.

From a managerial perspective, another drawback of scoring models is the fact that they depend on the relevance of the selected criteria and the accuracy of the weight given them. In other words, they do not ensure that there is a reasonable link between the selected and weighted criteria and the business objectives that prompted the project in the first place.

Here's an example. As a means of selecting projects, the Information Systems steering committee of a large bank has adopted three criteria: *contribution to quality, financial performance,* and *service.* The bank's strategy is focused on customer retention, but the criteria selected by the committee do not reflect this fact. As a result, a project aimed at improving service to potential *new* markets might score high on *service* even though it would not serve *existing* customers (the people whose business the bank wants to retain). Note, too, that the criteria of *quality* and *service* may overlap, leading managers to double-count and overestimate the value of some factors.[8] Thus, the bank has employed a project selection approach that neither achieves its desired ends nor matches its overall strategic goals.

Method Three: The Analytical Hierarchy Process

The **Analytical Hierarchy Process (AHP)** was developed by Dr. Thomas Saaty[9] to address many of the technical and managerial problems frequently associated with decision making through scoring models. An increasingly popular method for effective project selection, the AHP is a four-step process.

STRUCTURING THE HIERARCHY OF CRITERIA   The first step consists of constructing a hierarchy of criteria and subcriteria. Let's assume, for example, that a firm's IT steering committee has selected three criteria for evaluating project alternatives: (1) *financial benefits,* (2) *contribution to strategy,* and (3) *contribution to IT infrastructure.* The *financial benefits* criterion, which focuses on the tangible benefits of the project, is further subdivided into long-term and short-term benefits. *Contribution to strategy,* an intangible factor, is subdivided into three subcriteria: (a) *increasing market share for product X,* (b) *retaining existing customers for product Y,* and (c) *improving cost management.*

Table 3.4 is a representational breakdown of all these criteria. Note that subdividing relevant criteria into a meaningful hierarchy gives managers a rational method for sorting among and ordering priorities. Higher-order challenges, such as *contribution to strategy,* can be broken down into discrete sets of supporting requirements, including *market share, customer retention,* and *cost management,* thus building a hierarchy of alternatives that simplifies matters. Because the hierarchy can reflect the structure of organizational strategy and critical success factors, it also provides a way to select and justify projects according to

TABLE 3.4 Hierarchy of Selection Criteria Choices

First Level	Second Level
1. Financial benefits	1A: Short-term
	1B: Long-term
2. Contribution to strategy	2A: Increasing market share for product X;
	2B: Retaining existing customers for product Y;
	2C: Improving cost management
3. Contribution to IT infrastructure	

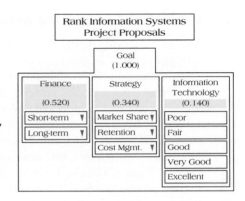

FIGURE 3.1   Sample AHP with Rankings for Salient Selection Criteria

Source: J. K. Pinto and I. Millet. (1999). *Successful Information System Implementation: The Human Side,* 2nd ed., figure on page 76. Newtown Square, PA: Project Management Institute. Copyright and all rights reserved. Material from this publication has been reproduced with the permission of PMI.

their consistency with business objectives.[10] This illustrates how we can use meaningful strategic issues and critical factors to establish logic for both the types of selection criteria and their relative weighting.

Recently, a large U.S. company used the AHP to rank more than a hundred project proposals worth millions of dollars. Because the first step in using the AHP is to establish clear criteria for selection, 10 managers from assorted disciplines, including finance, marketing, management information systems, and operations, spent a full day establishing the hierarchy of criteria. Their challenge was to determine the key success criteria that should be used to guide project selection, particularly as these diverse criteria related to each other (relative weighting). They found that, in addition to clearly defining and developing the criteria for evaluating projects, the process also produced a more coherent and unified vision of organizational strategy.

ALLOCATING WEIGHTS TO CRITERIA   The second step in applying AHP consists of allocating weights to previously developed criteria and, where necessary, splitting overall criterion weight among subcriteria. Mian and Dai[11] and others have recommended the so-called **pairwise comparison approach** to weighting, in which every criterion is compared with every other criterion. This procedure, argue the researchers, permits more accurate weighting because it allows managers to focus on a series of relatively simple exchanges—namely, two criteria at a time.

The simplified hierarchy in Figure 3.1 shows the breakdown of criterion weights across the same three major criteria that we used in Table 3.4. As Figure 3.1 shows, *Finance* (that is, *financial benefits*) received a weighting value of 52%, which was split between *Short-term benefits* (30%) and *Long-term benefits* (70%). This configuration means that *long-term financial benefits* receives an overall weighting of $(0.52) \times (0.7) = 36.4\%$.

The hierarchical allocation of criteria and splitting of weights resolves the problem of double counting in scoring models. In those models, criteria such as *service, quality,* and *customer satisfaction* may be either separate or overlapping factors, depending on the objectives of the organization. As a result, too little or too much weight may be assigned to a given criterion. With AHP, however, these factors are grouped as subcriteria and share the weight of a common higher-level criterion.

ASSIGNING NUMERICAL VALUES TO EVALUATION DIMENSIONS   For our third step, once the hierarchy is established, we can use the pairwise comparison process to assign numerical values to the dimensions of our evaluation scale. Figure 3.2 is an evaluation scale with five dimensions: *Poor, Fair, Good, Very Good,* and *Excellent.* In this figure, for purposes of illustration, we have assigned the values of *0.0, 0.10, 0.30, 0.60,* and

	Nominal	Priority	Bar Graph
Poor	0.00000	0.000	
Fair	0.10000	0.050	
Good	0.30000	0.150	
Very Good	0.60000	0.300	
Excellent	1.00000	0.500	
Total	2.00000	1.000	

FIGURE 3.2   Assigning Numerical Values to Labels

Source: J. K. Pinto and I. Millet. (1999). *Successful Information System Implementation: The Human Side,* 2nd ed., figure on page 77. Newtown Square, PA: Project Management Institute. Copyright and all rights reserved. Material from this publication has been reproduced with the permission of PMI.

1.00, respectively, to these dimensions. Naturally, we can change these values as necessary. For example, if a company wants to indicate a greater discrepancy between *Poor* and *Fair,* managers may increase the range between these two dimensions. By adjusting values to suit specific purposes, managers avoid the fallacy of assuming that the differences between numbers on a scale of, say, 1 to 5 are equal—that is, assuming that the difference between 4 and 5 is the same as the difference between 3 and 4. With the AHP approach, the "best" outcome receives a perfect score of 1.00 and all other values represent some proportion relative to that score.

When necessary, project managers are encouraged to apply different scales for each criterion. Note, for example, that Figure 3.2 uses scale points ranging from *Poor* to *Excellent.* Suppose, however, that we were interviewing a candidate for our project team and one of the criterion items was "Education level." Clearly, using a scale ranging from *Poor* to *Excellent* makes no sense, so we would adjust the scales to make them meaningful; for example, using levels such as "High School," "Some College," "College Graduate," and so forth. Allocating weights across dimensions gives us a firmer understanding of both our goals and the methods by which we are comparing opportunities to achieve them.

EVALUATING PROJECT PROPOSALS   In our final step, we multiply the numeric evaluation of the project by the weights assigned to the evaluation criteria and then add the results for all criteria. Figure 3.3 shows how five potential projects might be evaluated by an AHP program offered by Expert Choice, a maker of decision software.[12] Here's how to read the key features of the spreadsheet:

- The second row specifies the value assigned to each of five possible ratings (from *Poor = 1 = .000* to *Excellent = 5 = 1.000*).
- The fourth row specifies the five decision criteria and their relative weights (*Finance/Short-Term =* .1560, *Strategy/Cost Management =* .0816, and so forth). (Note that three criteria have been broken down into six subcriteria.)
- The second column lists the five projects (*Perfect Project, Aligned,* etc.).
- The third column labeled "Total" gives a value for each alternative. This number is found by multiplying each evaluation by the appropriate criterion weight and summing the results across all criteria evaluations.

To illustrate how the calculations are derived, let us take the *Aligned* project as an example. Remember that each rating (Excellent, Very Good, Good, etc.) carries with it a numerical score. These scores, when multiplied by the evaluation criteria and then added together, yield:

$$(.1560)(.3) + (.3640)(1.0) + (.1020)(.3) + (.1564)(1.0) + (.0816)(.3) + (.1400)(1.0) = .762$$

The *Perfect Project,* as another example, was rated *Excellent* on all six dimensions and thus received a total score of 1.000. Also, compare the evaluations of the *Aligned* and *Not Aligned* project choices. Although both projects received an equal number of *Excellent* and *Good* rankings, the *Aligned* project was clearly preferable because it was rated higher on criteria viewed as more important and thus more heavily weighted.

Finance	Short-term			
Poor 1 (.000)	Fair 2 (.100)	Good 3 (.300)	Very Good 4 (.600)	Excellent 5 (1.000)

	Alternatives	Total	Finance		Strategy			Technology
			Short-Term	Long-Term	Market Share	Retention	Cost Management	
			.1560	.3640	.1020	.1564	.0816	.1400
1	Perfect Project	1.000	Excellent	Excellent	Excellent	Excellent	Excellent	Excellent
2	Aligned	0.762	Good	Excellent	Good	Excellent	Good	Excellent
3	Not Aligned	0.538	Excellent	Good	Excellent	Good	Excellent	Good
4	All Very Good	0.600	Very Good	Very Good	Very Good	Very Good	Very Good	Very Good
5	Mixed	0.284	Poor	Fair	Good	Very Good	Excellent	Good
6								
7								
8								
9								
10								

FIGURE 3.3   The Project Rating Spreadsheet

Source: J. K. Pinto and I. Millet. (1999). *Successful Information System Implementation: The Human Side,* 2nd ed., figure on page 78. Newtown Square, PA: Project Management Institute. Copyright and all rights reserved. Material from this publication has been reproduced with the permission of PMI.

Unlike the results of typical scoring models, the AHP scores are significant. The *Aligned* project, for example, which scored 0.762, is almost three times better than the *Mixed* project, with its score of 0.284. This feature—the ability to quantify superior project alternatives—allows project managers to use AHP scores as input to other calculations. We might, for example, sort projects by the ratios of AHP scores to total their development costs. Let's say that based on this ratio, we find that the *Not Aligned* project is much cheaper to initiate than the *Aligned* project. This finding may suggest that *from a cost/benefit perspective,* the *Not Aligned* project offers a better alternative than the *Aligned* project.

The AHP methodology can dramatically improve the process of developing project proposals. In firms that have incorporated AHP analysis, new project proposals must contain, as part of their core information, a sophisticated AHP breakdown listing the proposed project, alternatives, and projected outcomes. The Analytical Hierarchy Process offers a true advantage over traditional scoring models, primarily because it reduces many of the technical and managerial problems that plague such approaches.

The AHP does have some limitations, however. First, current research suggests that the model does not adequately account for "negative utility"; that is, the fact that certain choice options do not contribute positively to the decision goals but actually lead to negative results. For example, suppose that your company identified a strong project option that carried a prohibitively expensive price tag. As a result, selecting this project is really not an option because it would be just too high an investment. However, using the AHP, you would first need to weigh all positive elements, develop your screening score, and then compare this score against negative aspects, such as cost. The result can lead to bias in the project scoring calculations.[13] A second limitation is that the AHP requires that all criteria be fully exposed and accounted for at the beginning of the selection process. Powerful members of the organization with political agendas or pet projects they wish to pursue may resist such an open selection process.

Method Four: Profile Models

Profile models allow managers to plot **risk/return** options for various alternatives and then select the project that maximizes return while staying within a certain range of minimum acceptable risk. "Risk," of course, is a subjective assessment: It may be difficult to reach overall agreement on the level of risk associated with a given project. Nevertheless, the profile model offers another way of evaluating, screening, and comparing projects.[14]

Let's return to our example of project screening at SAP Corporation. Suppose that instead of the four project alternatives for the new software project we discussed earlier, the firm had identified six candidates for development. For simplicity's sake, managers chose to focus on the two criteria of *risk* and *reward*.

In Figure 3.4, the six project alternatives are plotted on a graph showing perceived *Risk* on the y-axis and potential *Return* on the x-axis. Because of the cost of capital to the firm, we will specify some minimum

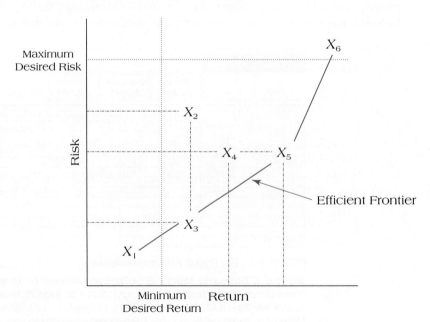

FIGURE 3.4   Profile Model

desired rate of return. All projects will be assigned some risk factor value and be plotted relative to the maximum risk that the firm is willing to assume. Figure 3.4, therefore, graphically represents each of our six alternatives on a profile model. (Risk values have been created here simply for illustrative purposes.) In our example, SAP can employ a variety of measures to assess the likely return offered by this project, including discounted cash flow analysis and internal rate of return expectations. Likewise, it is increasingly common for firms to quantify their risk assessment of various projects, enabling us to plot them along the y-axis. The key lies in employing identical evaluation criteria and quantification approaches across all projects to be profiled on the graph. Clearly, when project risks are unique or we have no way of comparing the relative risks from project to project, it is impossible to accurately plot project alternatives.

In Figure 3.4, we see that Project X_2 and Project X_3 have similar expected rates of return. Project X_3, however, represents a better selection choice. Why? Because SAP can achieve the same rate of return with Project X_3 as it can with Project X_2 but with less risk. Likewise, Project X_5 is a superior choice to X_4: Although they have similar risk levels, X_5 offers greater return as an investment. Finally, while Project X_6 offers the most potential return, it does so at the highest level of risk.

The profile model makes use of a concept most widely associated with financial management and investment analysis—the *efficient frontier*. In project management, the **efficient frontier** is the set of project portfolio options that offers either a maximum return for every given level of risk or the minimum risk for every level of return.[15] When we look at the profile model in Figure 3.4, we note that certain options (X_1, X_3, X_5, X_6) lie along an imaginary line balancing optimal risk and return combinations. Others (X_2 and X_4), however, are less desirable alternatives and would therefore be considered inferior choices. The efficient frontier serves as a decision-making guide by establishing the threshold level of risk/return options that all future project choices must be evaluated against.

One advantage of the profile model is that it offers another method by which to compare project alternatives, this time in terms of the risk/return trade-off. Sometimes it is difficult to evaluate and compare projects on the basis of scoring models or other qualitative approaches. The profile model, however, gives managers a chance to map out potential returns while considering the risk that accompanies each choice. Thus, profile models give us another method for eliminating alternatives that either threaten too much risk or promise too little return.

On the other hand, profile models also have disadvantages:

1. They limit decision criteria to just two—risk and return. Although an array of issues, including safety, quality, and reliability, can come under the heading of "risk," the approach still necessarily limits the decision maker to a small set of criteria.
2. In order to be evaluated in terms of an efficient frontier, some value must be attached to risk. Expected return is a measure that is naturally given to numerical estimate. But because risk may not be readily quantified, it may be misleading to designate "risk" artificially as a value for comparison among project choices.

EXAMPLE 3.3 **Profile Model**

Let's consider a simple example. Suppose that our company has identified two new project alternatives and we wish to use risk/return analysis to determine which of the two projects would fit best with our current project portfolio. We assess return in terms of the profit margin we expect to achieve on the projects. Risk is evaluated at our company in terms of four elements: (1) technical risk—the technical challenge of the project, (2) capital risk—the amount invested in the project, (3) safety risk—the risk of project failure, and (4) goodwill risk—the risk of losing customers or diminishing our company's image. The magnitude of each of these types of risk is determined by applying a "low, medium, high" risk scale where 1 = low, 2 = medium, and 3 = high.

After conducting a review of the likely profitability for both of the projects and evaluating their riskiness, we conclude the following:

	Risk	Return Potential
Project Saturn	10	23%
Project Mercury	6	16%

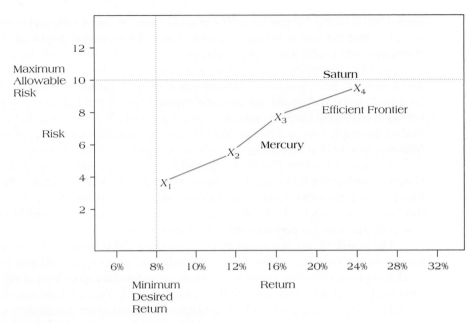

FIGURE 3.5   **Efficient Frontier for Our Firm**

Figure 3.5 shows our firm's efficient frontier for the current portfolio of projects. How would we evaluate the attractiveness of either Project Saturn or Project Mercury?

SOLUTION

When we consider the two choices, Projects Saturn and Mercury, in terms of their projected risk and return, we can chart them on our profile model relative to other projects that we are undertaking. Figure 3.5 illustrates the placement of the two new project options. Note that Project Saturn, although within our maximum risk limit, does not perform as well as the other projects in our current portfolio (it has a higher risk rating for its projected return than other comparable projects). On the other hand, Project Mercury offers us a 16% rate of return for a lower level of risk than the current efficient frontier, suggesting that this project is an attractive option and a better alternative than Project Saturn.

3.3 FINANCIAL MODELS

Another important series of models relies on financial analysis to make project selection decisions. In this section, we will examine three common financial models: *discounted cash flow analysis, net present value,* and *internal rate of return.* These are not the only financial methods for assessing project alternatives, but they are among the more popular.

Financial models are all predicated on the **time value of money** principle. The time value of money suggests that money earned today is worth more than money we expect to earn in the future. In other words, $100 that I receive four years from now is worth significantly less to me than if I were to receive that money today. In the simplest example, we can see that putting $100 in a bank account at 3% interest will grow the money at a compounded rate each year. Hence, at the end of year 1, the initial investment will be worth $103. After two years, it will have grown to $106.09, and so forth. The principle also works in reverse: To calculate the *present value* of $100 that I expect to have in the bank in four years' time, I must first discount the amount by the same interest rate. Hence, assuming an interest rate of 3%, I need only invest $88.85 today to yield $100 in four years.

We expect future money to be worth less for two reasons: (1) the impact of inflation, and (2) the inability to invest the money. Inflation, as we know, causes prices to rise and hence erodes consumers' spending power. In 1900, for example, the average house may have cost a few thousand dollars to build. Today housing costs have soared. As a result, if I am to receive $100 in four years, its value will have decreased due to the negative effects of inflation. Further, not having that $100 today means that I cannot invest it and earn a return on my money for the next four years. Money that we cannot invest is money that earns no interest. In real terms, therefore, the **present value of money** must be discounted by some factor the farther out into the future I expect to receive it. When deciding among nearly identical project alternatives, if Project A will earn our firm $50,000 in two years and Project B will earn our company $50,000 in four years, Project A is the best choice because we will receive the money sooner.

Payback Period

The project **payback period** is the estimated amount of time that will be necessary to recoup the investment in a project, that is, how long it will take for the project to pay back its initial budget and begin to generate positive cash flow for the company. In determining the payback period for a project, we must employ a discounted cash flow analysis, based on the principle of the time value of money. The goal of the **discounted cash flow (DCF) method** is to estimate cash outlays and expected cash inflows resulting from investment in a project. All potential costs of development (most of which are contained in the project budget) are assessed and projected prior to the decision to initiate the project. They are then compared with all expected sources of revenue from the project. For example, if the project is a new chemical plant, projected revenue streams will be based on expected capacity, production levels, sales volume, and so forth.

We then apply to this calculation a *discount rate* based on the firm's cost of capital. The value of that rate is weighted across each source of capital to which the firm has access (typically, debt and equity markets). In this way we weight the cost of capital, which can be calculated as follows:

$$K_{\text{firm}} = (w_d)(k_d)(1 - t) + (w_e)(k_e)$$

The weighted cost of capital is the percentage of capital derived from either debt (w_d) or equity (w_e) multiplied by the percentage costs of debt and equity (k_d and k_e, respectively). (The value t refers to the company's marginal tax rate: Because interest payments are tax deductible, we calculate the cost of debt after taxes.)

There is a standard formula for payback calculations:

$$\text{Payback period} = \text{investment/annual cash savings}$$

The reciprocal of this formula can be used to calculate the average rate of return for the project. However, note that the above formula only works in simple circumstances when cash flows (or annual cash savings) are the same for each year. So, for example, if we invested $150,000 and would receive $30,000 a year in annual savings, the payback period is straightforward:

$$\text{Payback period} = \$150,000/\$30,000 = 5 \text{ years}$$

On the other hand, when projected cash flows from annual savings are not equal, you must determine at what point the cumulative cash flow becomes positive. Thus:

$$\text{Cumulative cashflow (CF)} = (\text{Initial investment}) + \text{CF (year 1)} + \text{CF (year 2)} + \ldots$$

Once cost of capital has been calculated, we can set up a table projecting costs and revenue streams that are discounted at the calculated rate. The key is to determine how long it will take the firm to reach the breakeven point on a new project. *Breakeven point* represents the amount of time necessary to recover the initial investment of capital in the project. Shorter paybacks are more desirable than longer paybacks, primarily because the farther we have to project payback into the future, the greater the potential for additional risk.

EXAMPLE 3.4 Payback Period

Our company wants to determine which of two project alternatives is the more attractive investment opportunity by using a payback period approach. We have calculated the initial investment cost of the two projects and the expected revenues they should generate for us (see Table 3.5). Which project should we invest in?

SOLUTION

For our example, the payback for the two projects can be calculated as in Table 3.6. These results suggest that Project A is a superior choice over Project B, based on a shorter projected payback period (2.857 years versus 4.028 years) and a higher rate of return (35% versus 24.8%).

TABLE 3.5 Initial Outlay and Projected Revenues for Two Project Options

	Project A		Project B	
	Revenues	Outlays	Revenues	Outlays
Year 0		$500,000		$500,000
Year 1	$ 50,000		$ 75,000	
Year 2	150,000		100,000	
Year 3	350,000		150,000	
Year 4	600,000		150,000	
Year 5	500,000		900,000	

TABLE 3.6 Comparison of Payback for Projects A and B

Project A	Year	Cash Flow	Cum. Cash Flow
	0	($500,000)	($ 500,000)
	1	50,000	(450,000)
	2	150,000	(300,000)
	3	350,000	50,000
	4	600,000	650,000
	5	500,000	1,150,000

Payback = <u>2.857 years</u>
Rate of Return = 35%

Project B	Year	Cash Flow	Cum. Cash Flow
	0	($500,000)	($500,000)
	1	75,000	(425,000)
	2	100,000	(325,000)
	3	150,000	(175,000)
	4	150,000	(25,000)
	5	900,000	875,000

Payback = <u>4.028 years</u>
Rate of Return = 24.8%

Net Present Value

The most popular financial decision-making approach in project selection, the **net present value (NPV) method,** projects the change in the firm's value if a project is undertaken. Thus a *positive* NPV indicates that the firm will make money—and its value will rise—as a result of the project. Net present value employs discounted cash flow analysis, discounting future streams of income to estimate the present value of money.

The simplified formula for NPV is as follows:

$$NPV_{\text{(project)}} = I_0 + \sum_{n=1}^{t} F_t/(1 + r + p_t)^t$$

where

F_t = net cash flow for period t

r = required rate of return

I = initial cash investment (cash outlay at time 0)

p_t = inflation rate during period t

The optimal procedure for developing an NPV calculation consists of several steps, including the construction of a table listing the outflows, inflows, discount rate, and discounted cash flows across the relevant time periods. We construct such a table in Example 3.5 (see Table 3.7).

EXAMPLE 3.5 | **Net Present Value**

Assume that you are considering whether or not to invest in a project that will cost $100,000 in initial investment. Your company requires a rate of return of 10%, and you expect inflation to remain relatively constant at 4%. You anticipate a useful life of four years for the project and have projected future cash flows as follows:

> Year 1: $20,000
>
> Year 2: $50,000
>
> Year 3: $50,000
>
> Year 4: $25,000

SOLUTION

We know the formula for determining NPV:

$$NPV = I_0 + \sum_{n=1}^{t} F_t/(1 + r + p)^t$$

We can now construct a simple table to keep a running score on discounted cash flows (both inflows and outflows) to see if the project is worth its initial investment. We already know that we will need the following categories: *Year, Inflows, Outflows,* and *NPV.* We will also need two more categories:

> **Net flows:** *the difference between inflows and outflows*
> **Discount factor:** *the reciprocal of the discount rate* $(1/(1 + r + p)^t)$

In Table 3.7, if we fill in the *Discount Factor* column assuming that $r = 10\%$ and $p = 4\%$, we can begin work on the *NPV.* Note that *Year 0* means the present time, and *Year 1* the first year of operation.

How did we arrive at the *Discount Factor* for Year 3? Using the formula we set above, we calculated the appropriate data:

$$Discount\ factor = (1/(1 + .10 + .04)^3) = .6749$$

Now we can supply the data for the *Inflows, Outflows,* and *Net Flow* columns.

Finally, we complete the table by multiplying the *Net Flow* amount by the *Discount Factor.* The results give us the data for the *NPV* column of our table. The sum of the discounted cash flows (their net present value) shown in Table 3.8 gives us the *NPV* of the project. The total is a positive number, indicating that the investment is worthwhile and should be pursued.

TABLE 3.7 Running Score on Discounted Cash Flows

Year	Inflows	Outflows	Net Flow	Discount Factor	NPV
0		$100,000	$(100,000)	1.0000	
1	$20,000		20,000	0.8772	
2	50,000		50,000	0.7695	
3	50,000		50,000	0.6749	
4	25,000		25,000	0.5921	

TABLE 3.8 Discounted Cash Flows and NPV (I)

Year	Inflows	Outflows	Net Flow	Discount Factor	NPV
0		$100,000	$(100,000)	1.0000	$(100,000)
1	$20,000		20,000	0.8772	17,544
2	50,000		50,000	0.7695	38,475
3	50,000		50,000	0.6749	33,745
4	25,000		25,000	0.5921	14,803
Total					$4,567

Net present value is one of the most common project selection methods in use today. Its principal advantage is that it allows firms to link project alternatives to financial performance, better ensuring that the projects a company chooses to invest its resources in are likely to generate profit. Among its disadvantages is the difficulty in using NPV to make accurate long-term predictions. For example, suppose that we were considering investing in a project with an expectation that it would continue to generate returns during the next 10 years. In choosing whether or not to invest in the project today, we must make some assumptions about future interest rates, inflation, and our **required rate of return (RRR)** for the next 10 years. In uncertain financial or economic times, it can be risky to make long-term investment decisions when discount rates may fluctuate.

Discounted Payback

Now that we have considered the time value of money, as shown in the NPV method, we can apply this logic to the simple payback model to create a screening and selection model with a bit more power. Remember that with NPV we use discounted cash flow as our means to decide whether or not to invest in a project opportunity. Now, let's apply that same principle to the **discounted payback method.** With this method, the time period in which we are interested is the length of time until the sum of the discounted cash flows is equal to the initial investment.

A simple example will illustrate the difference between straight payback and discounted payback methods. Suppose we require a 12.5% return on new investments, and we have a project opportunity that will cost an initial investment of $30,000 with a promised return per year of $10,000. Under the simple payback model, the initial investment should be paid off in only three years. However, as Table 3.9 demonstrates, when we discount our cash flows at 12.5% and start adding them, it actually takes four years to pay back the initial project investment.

The advantage of the discounted payback method is that it allows us to make a more "intelligent" determination of the length of time needed to satisfy the initial project investment. That is, while simple payback is useful for accounting purposes, discounted payback is actually more representative of the financial realities that all organizations must consider when pursuing projects. The effects of inflation and future investment opportunities matter with individual investment decisions; hence, these factors should also matter when evaluating project opportunities.

TABLE 3.9 Discounted Payback Method

	Project Cash Flow[*]	
Year	Discounted	Undiscounted
1	$8,900	$10,000
2	7,900	10,000
3	7,000	10,000
4	6,200	10,000
5	5,500	10,000
Payback Period	4 Years	3 Years

[*]Cash flows rounded to the nearest $100.

Internal Rate of Return

Internal rate of return (IRR) is an alternative method for evaluating the expected outlays and income associated with a new project investment opportunity. The IRR method asks the simple question: What rate of return will this project earn? Under this model, the project must meet some required "hurdle" rate applied to all projects under consideration. Without detailing the mathematics of the process, we will say that IRR is the discount rate that equates the present values of a project's revenue and expense streams. If a project has a life of time t, the IRR is defined as:

$$IO = \sum_{n=1}^{t} \frac{ACF^t}{(1 + IRR)^t}$$

where
ACF^t = annual after-tax cash flow for time period t
IO = initial cash outlay
n = project's expected life
IRR = project's internal rate of return

The IRR is found through a straightforward process, although it requires tables representing present value of an annuity in order to determine the project's rate of return. Alternatively, many pocket calculators can determine IRR quickly. Without tables or access to a calculator, it is necessary to employ an iterative process to identify the approximate IRR for the project.

EXAMPLE 3.6 | Internal Rate of Return

Let's take a simple example. Suppose that a project required an initial cash investment of $5,000 and was expected to generate inflows of $2,500, $2,000, and $2,000 for the next three years. Further, assume that our company's required rate of return for new projects is 10%. The question is: Is this project worth funding?

SOLUTION

Answering this question requires four steps:

1. Pick an arbitrary discount rate and use it to determine the net present value of the stream of cash inflows.
2. Compare the present value of the inflows with the initial investment; if they are equal, you have found the IRR.
3. If the present value is larger (or less than) than the initial investment, select a higher (or lower) discount rate for the computation.
4. Determine the present value of the inflows and compare it with the initial investment. Continue to repeat steps 2–4 until you have determined the IRR.

Using our example, we know:

Cash investment = $5,000
Year 1 inflow = $2,500
Year 2 inflow = $2,000
Year 3 inflow = $2,000
Required rate of return = 10%

Step One: Try 12%.

Year	Inflows	Discount Factor at 12%	NPV
1	$2,500	.893	$2,233
2	2,000	.797	1,594
3	2,000	.712	1,424
Present value of inflows			5,251
Cash investment			− 5,000
Difference			$ 251

Decision: Present value difference at 12% is 250.50, which is too high. Try a higher discount rate.

Step Two: Try 15%.

		Discount Factor	
Year	Inflows	at 15%	NPV
1	$2,500	.870	$2,175
2	2,000	.756	1,512
3	2,000	.658	1,316
Present value of inflows			5,003
Cash investment			5,000
Difference			$ 3

Decision: Present value difference at 15% is $3, which suggests that 15% is a close approximation of the IRR.

If the IRR is greater than or equal to the company's required rate of return, the project is worth funding. In Example 3.6, we found that the IRR is 15% for the project, making it higher than the hurdle rate of 10% and a good candidate for investment. The advantage of using IRR analysis lies in its ability to compare alternative projects from the perspective of expected *return on investment* (ROI). Projects having higher IRR are generally superior to those having lower IRR.

The IRR method, however, does have some disadvantages. First, it is *not* the rate of return for a project. In fact, the IRR equals the project's rate of return only when project-generated cash inflows can be reinvested in new projects at similar rates of return. If the firm can reinvest revenues only on lower-return projects, the "real" return on the project is something less than the calculated IRR. Several other problems with the IRR method make NPV a more robust determinant of project viability:[16]

- IRR and NPV calculations typically agree (that is, make the same investment recommendations) only when projects are independent of each other. If projects are not mutually exclusive, IRR and NPV may rank them differently. The reason is that NPV employs a weighted average cost of capital discount rate that reflects potential reinvestment while IRR does not. Because of this distinction, NPV is generally preferred as a more realistic measure of investment opportunity.
- If cash flows are not normal, IRR may arrive at multiple solutions. For example, if net cash outflows follow a period of net cash inflows, IRR may give conflicting results. If, following the completion of plant construction, it is necessary to invest in land reclamation or other incidental but significant expenses, an IRR calculation may result in multiple return rates, only one of which is correct.

Options Models

Let's say that a firm has an opportunity to build a power plant in a developing nation. The investment is particularly risky: The company may ultimately fail to make a positive return on its investment and may fail to find a buyer for the plant if it chooses to abandon the project. Both the NPV and IRR methods fail to account for this very real possibility—namely, that a firm may not recover the money that it invests in a project. Clearly, however, many firms must consider this option when making investment decisions. An organization facing this possibility should determine two things:[17]

1. Whether it has the flexibility to postpone the project
2. Whether future information will help in making the decision

EXAMPLE 3.7 Options Model

A construction firm is considering whether or not to upgrade an existing chemical plant. The initial cost of the upgrade is $5,000,000, and the company requires a 10% return on its investment. The plant can be upgraded in one year and start earning revenue the following year. The best forecast promises cash flows of $1 million per year, but should adverse economic and political conditions prevail, the probability of realizing this amount drops to 40%, with a 60% probability that the investment will yield only $200,000 per year.

SOLUTION

We can first calculate the NPV of the proposed investment as follows:

$$\text{Cash Flows} = .4(\$1\text{million}) + .6(\$200,000) = \$520,000$$
$$\text{NPV} = -\$5,000,000 + \Sigma\,\$520,000/(1.1)^{t}$$
$$= -\$5,000,000 + (\$520,000/.1)$$
$$= -\$5,000,000 + \$5,200,000$$
$$= \$200,000$$

Because the $520,000 is a perpetuity that begins in Year 1, we divide it by the discount rate of 10% to determine the value of the perpetuity. According to this calculation, the company should undertake the project. This recommendation, however, ignores the possibility that by waiting a year, the firm may gain a better sense of the political/economic climate in the host country. Thus the firm is neglecting important information that could be useful in making its decision.

Suppose, for example, that by waiting a year, the company determines that its investment will have a 50% likelihood (up from the original projection of 40%) of paying off at the higher value of $1 million per year. However, because the firm is choosing to wait a year, the amount of the initial investment ($5,000,000) should also be discounted by 10% for one year; that is, the company is investing the money not immediately (time 0) but in Year 1. The NPV for the project would now be:

$$NPV = -\$5,000,000/1.1 + 0.5(\$1,000,000/0.1)$$
$$NPV = -\$4,545,454 + \$5,000,000$$
$$NPV = \$454,546$$

Choosing a Project Selection Approach

What can we conclude from our discussion of project selection methods? First and foremost, we have learned to focus on the *method* that we use in making selection decisions. Have we been consistent and objective in considering our alternatives? The author has worked in a consulting and training capacity with a number of firms that have experienced recurrent problems in their project selections (they kept picking losers). Why? One reason was their failure to even attempt objectivity in their selection methods. Proposed projects, often "sacred cows" or the pet ideas of senior managers, were pushed to the head of the line or, worse, financially "tweaked" until they yielded satisfactory conclusions. Team members knew in advance that such projects would fail because the projects had been massaged to the point at which they seemingly optimized the selection criteria. The key to project selection lies in being objective about the process. If you operate according to the "GIGO" principle—garbage in/garbage out—you'll soon be up to your knees in garbage.

A second conclusion we can draw is that although a wide variety of selection methods exist, certain ones may be more appropriate for specific companies and project circumstances. Some projects require sophisticated financial evidence of their viability. Others may only need to demonstrate no more than an acceptable profile when compared to other options. In other words, any of the previously discussed selection methods may be appropriate under certain situations. Some experts, for example, favor weighted scoring models on the grounds that they offer a more accurate reflection of a firm's strategic goals without sacrificing long-term effectiveness for short-term financial gains.[18] They argue that such important, nonfinancial criteria should not be excluded from the decision-making process. Perhaps the key lies in choosing a selection algorithm broad enough to encompass both financial and nonfinancial considerations. Regardless of the approach that a company selects, we can be sure of one thing: Making good project choices is a crucial step in ensuring good project management downstream.

PROJECT PROFILE

Project Selection and Screening at GE: The Tollgate Process

General Electric has developed a highly sophisticated approach to project screening and selection that the company calls the Tollgate Process. As you can see from Figure 3.6, Tollgate involves a series of seven formal procedural checkpoints (labeled *100* to *700*) established along the project development time line. Therefore, Tollgate is more than just a project selection methodology; it involves controlling the selection and development of the project as it moves through its life cycle. Each stage in this control process is carefully monitored.

(continued)

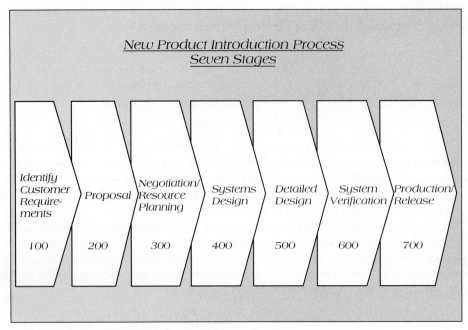

FIGURE 3.6   GE's Tollgate Process

Source: Used with permission of General Electric Company.

Each of the seven Tollgate stages can be broken down into a so-called *process map* that guides managers and teams in addressing specific necessary elements in the completion of a stage. These elements are the substeps that guide project screening in order to ensure that all projects conform to the same set of internal GE standards.

Figure 3.7 lays out the Process Flow Map that is used to evaluate the progress each project makes at the various stages to final completion. Note that teams must complete all action substeps at each Tollgate stage. Once they have completed a given stage, a cross-functional management review team provides oversight at a review conference. Approval at this stage permits the team to proceed to the next stage. Rejection means that the team must back up and deal with any issues that the review team feels it has not addressed adequately. For example, suppose that the project fails a technical conformance test during field testing at the system verification stage. The technical failure would require the team to cycle back to the appropriate point to analyze the cause for the field test failure and begin remedial steps to correct it. After a project team has received approval from the review team, it needs the approval of senior management before moving on to the next Tollgate stage. Rejection at this point by senior management often effectively kills the project.

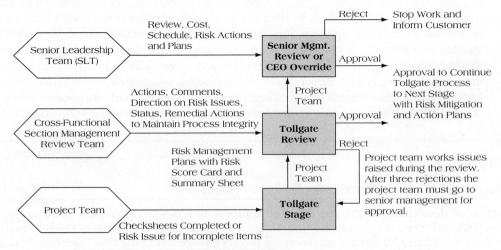

FIGURE 3.7   The GE Tollgate Review Process Flow Map

Source: Used with permission of General Electric Company.

Some critics argue that formalized and sophisticated review processes such as Tollgate add excessive layers of bureaucratic oversight to the project screening process. In fact, the sheer number of actions, steps, checklists, and managerial reviews stipulated by the Tollgate process can add significant delays to projects—a critical concern if a project is needed to address an immediate problem. On the other hand, proponents of such techniques argue that the benefits—standardization across business units, comprehensive step-by-step risk analysis, clear links to top management—more than compensate for potential problems. At GE, the company credits Tollgate with promoting significant improvements in early problem discovery and "real-time" risk management.

3.4 PROJECT PORTFOLIO MANAGEMENT

Project portfolio management is the systematic process of selecting, supporting, and managing a firm's collection of projects. Projects are managed concurrently under a single umbrella and may be either related or independent of one another. The key to portfolio management is realizing that a firm's projects share a common strategic purpose and the same scarce resources.[19] For example, Pratt & Whitney Jet Engines, a subsidiary of United Technologies Corporation, is similar to other major jet engine manufacturers in creating a wide portfolio of engine types, from those developed for helicopters to those for jet aircraft, from civilian use to military consumption. Although the products share common features, the technical challenges ensure that the product line is highly diverse. The concept of project portfolio management holds that firms should not manage projects as independent entities, but rather should regard portfolios as unified assets. There may be multiple objectives, but they are also shared objectives.[20]

Artto[21] notes that in a project-oriented company, project portfolio management poses a constant challenge between balancing long-term strategic goals and short-term needs and constraints. Managers routinely pose such questions as the following:

- What projects should the company fund?
- Does the company have the resources to support them?
- Do these projects reinforce future strategic goals?
- Does this project make good business sense?
- Is this project complementary to other company projects?

Objectives and Initiatives

Each of the questions in the previous list has both short-term and long-term implications, and, taken together, they constitute the basis for both strategic project management and effective risk management. Portfolio management, therefore, entails decision making, prioritization, review, realignment, and reprioritization of a firm's projects. Let's consider each of these tasks in more detail.

DECISION MAKING   The decision on whether or not to proceed in specific strategic directions is often influenced by market conditions, capital availability, perceived opportunity, and acceptable risk. A variety of project alternatives may be considered reasonable alternatives during portfolio development.

PRIORITIZATION   Because firms have limited resources, they typically cannot fund every project opportunity. Thus they must prioritize. For this task, several criteria may be used:

- *Cost:*   Projects with lower development costs are more favorable because they come with less upfront risk.
- *Opportunity:*   The chance for a big payout is a strong inducement for funding.
- *Top management pressure:*   Political pressure from top management (say, managers with pet projects) can influence decisions.
- *Risk:*   Project payouts must justify some level of acceptable risk; those that are too risky are scratched.
- *Strategic "fit":*   If a firm has a policy of pursuing a family of products, all opportunities are evaluated in terms of their *complementarity*—that is, either their strategic fit with existing product lines or their ability to augment the current product family.
- *Desire for portfolio balance:*   A firm may want to offset risky initiatives by funding other projects. The Boston Consulting Group's product matrix framework, for example, balances company product lines in terms of relative market share and product growth, suggesting that firms can maintain a

strategic balance within their portfolios between products with different profiles. A firm might use its profitable but low-growth products to fund investment into projects with high growth prospects. Portfolio balance supports developing a strategy that allows companies the ability to balance or offset risk, explore alternative market opportunities, and fund innovation in other product lines.

REVIEW   All project alternatives are evaluated according to the company's prioritization scheme. Projects selected for the firm's portfolio are the ones that, based on those priorities, offer maximum return. For example, at the start of the current economic downturn, DHL Express started evaluating its project portfolio through a new lens. The organization's portfolio review board decided that all ongoing projects had to meet the following criteria: deliver return on investment (ROI) in 2009, be "mission-critical" to running the business, and address government or regulatory issues required to keep the business operational. Following an extensive portfolio review, a number of projects were temporarily discontinued.

REALIGNMENT   When portfolios are altered by the addition of new projects, managers must reexamine company priorities. In the wake of new project additions, a number of important questions should be considered. Does the new project conform to strategic goals as characterized by the project portfolio, or does it represent a new strategic direction for the firm? Does a new project significantly alter the firm's strategic goals? Does the portfolio now require additional rebalancing? The decision to change a portfolio by adding new projects restarts the analysis cycle in which we must again reexamine the portfolio for signs of imbalance or updating.

REPRIORITIZATION   If strategic realignment means shifting the company's focus (i.e., creating new strategic directions), then managers must also reprioritize corporate goals and objectives. In this sense, then, portfolio management means managing overall company strategy. For example, Bayer Corporation, a global pharmaceutical giant, has found its corporate identity becoming less distinct due to the wide variety of acquisitions and other brands under which it markets its products. The company recently announced its intention to gradually eliminate many of the other brands that it owns under the "Bayer product umbrella" in order to emphasize the Bayer label. "We have thoroughly analyzed our brand portfolio and found that the diversity of brands in the Bayer Group has diluted the umbrella brand," explained Marijn Dekkers, Chairman of the Board of Management. This new branding strategy is designed to enhance the recognition and perception of Bayer products.[22]

Developing a Proactive Portfolio

Portfolio management, therefore, is an important component in strategic project management. In addition to managing specific projects, organizations routinely strategically plan for profitability, and the road to profitability often runs through the area of strategic project management. One of the most effective methods for aligning profit objectives and strategic plans is the development of a proactive project portfolio, or an integrated family of projects, usually with a common strategic goal. Such a portfolio supports overall strategic integration, rather than an approach that would simply move from project opportunity to opportunity.

Consider the example of the large pharmaceutical firm Pfizer.[23] Pfizer and its competitors routinely manage large families of projects in an integrated manner. The overall integration of project management efforts helps the company's managers deal with certain realities of the pharmaceutical industry, such as extremely high development costs and long lead times for new products. In fact, as Table 3.10 shows, the **lead time** for bringing a new drug to market can easily stretch over 15 years, and the success rate of a drug being commercially developed is estimated to be less than 0.002%.

Therefore, at any particular point in time, Pfizer has numerous projects under research and development, a smaller number of projects entering various stages of clinical trials, and finally, an even smaller line of projects already on the market. Each step in the cycle is fraught with risks and uncertainties. Will a drug work in clinical trials? Will it have minimal negative side effects? Can it be produced in a cost-effective manner? Is its release time-sensitive (is there, for instance, a limited market opportunity of which to take advantage)? Often the answers to such questions will reduce Pfizer's ongoing portfolio of development projects.

Under the risky circumstances of this industry, in which development time is lengthy, the financial repercussions of failure are huge, and success is never certain, pharmaceutical firms must practice highly sophisticated project portfolio management. Because failure rates are high and washouts constant, the need

TABLE 3.10 Phases in New Drug Development

Phase	Duration	% of Success	Contents
Discovery	4–7 yrs	1%	Research a selected pool of molecules in computer models and test tubes.
Preclinical research			Test on animals and in test tubes to research the safety, possible indications, toxicology, and metabolism of the molecule.
Phase I	1 yr	70%–75%	Small clinical studies on healthy volunteers to study the safety and ADME characteristics of the molecule.
Phase II	2 yrs	50%	Small studies on patients with the target disease to study the efficacy, dosage, and formulation of the drug.
Phase III	3 yrs	75%–85%	Large clinical studies on patients to confirm the results of phase II. The most expensive phase in the project.
Marketing Application (MA)	1.5–3 yrs	75%–80%	Compile marketing authorization application (MAA) and send to the authorities. After the authorization the drug may be sold and marketed.
Total	12–16 yrs	< 0.002%	

Source: M. Lehtonen (2001). "Resource allocation and project portfolio management in pharmaceutical R&D," in Artto, Martinsuo, and Aalto (Eds.), *Project Portfolio Management: Strategic Management Through Projects,* pp. 107–140, figure on page 112. Helsinki, Finland: Project Management Association.

to take advantage of new product opportunities is critical. Only in this way can the company ensure a steady supply of new products in the pipeline.

The pitfalls and possibilities of the pharmaceuticals development process are illustrated in Figure 3.8. Drug companies compensate for the lengthy lead times necessary to get final approval of new products by simultaneously funding and managing literally scores of development efforts. Unfortunately, only a small proportion of an R&D portfolio will show sufficient promise to be advanced to the clinical trial stage. Many projects are further weeded out during this phase, with very few projects reaching the stage of commercial rollout.

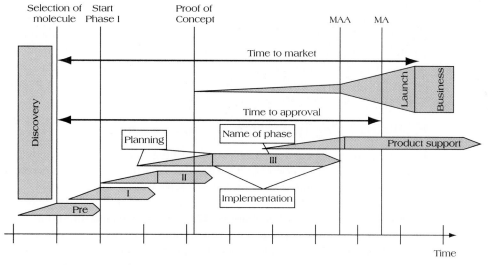

FIGURE 3.8   The Flow of New Drug Development over Time

Source: M. Lehtonen. (2001). "Resource allocation and project portfolio management in pharmaceutical R&D," in Artto, Martinsuo, and Aalto (Eds.), *Project Portfolio Management: Strategic Management through Projects,* pp. 107–140, figure on page 120. Helsinki, Finland: Project Management Association.

Pfizer uses portfolio management to manage the flow of new drug development projects, much as Nokia and Erickson use it to keep track of product pipelines that include mobile phones, baseband modems, and firewall systems. Project portfolios are necessary because a certain percentage of projects will be canceled prior to full funding, others will be eliminated during development, and still others will fail commercially. This cycle leaves only a few projects to account for a firm's return on all of its investments. In short, any company that puts all its R&D eggs in one project basket runs huge risks if that project fails during development or proves disappointing in the marketplace. As a rule, therefore, companies guarantee themselves fallback options, greater financial stability, and the chance to respond to multiple opportunities by constantly creating and updating portfolios of projects.

Keys to Successful Project Portfolio Management

Although examples of successfully managed portfolios abound, few researchers have investigated the key reasons why some companies are better at it than others. Brown and Eisenhardt[24] recently studied six firms in the computer industry; all are involved in multiple project development activities. They determined that successfully managed project portfolios usually reflect the following three factors.

FLEXIBLE STRUCTURE AND FREEDOM OF COMMUNICATION Multiple-project environments cannot operate effectively when they are constrained by restrictive layers of bureaucracy, narrow communication channels, and rigid development processes. Successful portfolios emerge from environments that foster flexibility and open communication. When project teams are allowed to improvise and experiment on existing product lines, innovative new product ideas are more likely to emerge.

LOW-COST ENVIRONMENTAL SCANNING Many firms devote a lot of time and money in efforts to hit product "home runs." They put their faith (and financing) in one promising project and aim to take the marketplace by storm, often without sufficiently analyzing alternative opportunities or future commercial trends. As a rule, successful project portfolio strategies call for launching a number of low-cost probes into the future, the idea behind environmental scanning—developing and market-testing a number of experimental product prototypes, sometimes by entering strategic alliances with potential partners. Successful firms do not rely on home runs and narrowly concentrated efforts. They are constantly building and testing new projects prior to full-scale development. Rubbermaid, for example, routinely brings dozens of new product ideas to the market, samples the commercial response, and uses the resulting information to improve potential winners and discard products that don't measure up.

TIME-PACED TRANSITION Successful portfolio management requires a sense of timing, especially as firms make transitions from one product to the next. Successful firms use project portfolio planning routinely to develop long lead times and plan ahead in order to make the smoothest possible transition from one product to another, whether the product lines are diverse or constitute creating a follow-on upgrade. Gillette, for example, has made a lucrative business out of developing and selling new models of shaving razors. Gillette's product life cycle planning is highly sophisticated, allowing it to make accurate predictions of the likely life cycle of current products and the timing necessary for beginning new product development projects to maintain a seamless flow of consumer products.

Problems in Implementing Portfolio Management

What are some of the common problems in creating an effective portfolio management system? Although numerous factors can adversely affect the practice of portfolio management, recent research seems to suggest that the following are among the most typical problem areas.[25]

CONSERVATIVE TECHNICAL COMMUNITIES In many organizations, there is a core of technical professionals—project engineers, research scientists, and other personnel—who develop project prototypes. A common phenomenon is this group's unwillingness, whether out of pride, organizational inertia, or due to arguments supporting pure research, to give up project ideas that are too risky, too costly, or out of sync with strategic goals. Often, when top management tries to trim the portfolio of ongoing projects for strategic reasons, they find engineers and scientists reluctant to accept their reasoning. Data General Corporation, a manufacturer of computers and IT products, found itself increasingly under the dominance of its hardware engineering department, a group intent on pursuing their own new product goals and fostering their own vision for the organization. By the mid-1990s, with one product after another resulting in significant losses, the company could not continue to operate independently and was acquired by EMC Corporation.

OUT-OF-SYNC PROJECTS AND PORTFOLIOS   Sometimes after a firm has begun realigning and reprioritizing its strategic outlook, it continues to develop projects or invest in a portfolio that no longer accurately reflects its new strategic focus. Strategy and portfolio management must accurately reflect a similar outlook. When strategy and portfolio management are out of alignment, one or both of two things will probably happen: either the portfolio will point the firm toward outmoded goals or the firm's strategy will revert to its old objectives.

UNPROMISING PROJECTS   The worst-case scenario finds a company pursuing poor-quality or unnecessary projects. A recent battle in consumer video electronics pitted Sony's Blu-ray high-definition Digital Video Disc (DVD) technology against Toshiba's offering, the High Definition Digital Versatile Disc (HD-DVD). Although the Sony product requires a relatively expensive machine to play the discs, the company convinced the majority of the public that its format is the superior one. Major content manufacturers and retailers had been steadily withdrawing their support for the HD-DVD technology, leaving Toshiba to continue developing it alone. After pursing HD-DVD technology for several years at high cost, Toshiba announced in early 2008 that it was abandoning its foray.

When portfolio management is geared to product lines, managers routinely rebalance the portfolio to ensure that there are a sufficient number of products of differing types to offset those with weaknesses. Revenues from "cash cows," for example, can fund innovative new products. Sometimes critical analysis of a portfolio requires hard decisions, project cancellations, and reallocated resources. But it is precisely this ongoing attention to the portfolio that prevents it from becoming weighted down with unpromising projects.

SCARCE RESOURCES   A key resource for all projects is human capital. In fact, personnel costs comprise one of the highest sources of project expense. Additional types of resources include any raw materials, financial resources, or supplies that are critical to successfully completing the project. Before spending large amounts of time creating a project portfolio, organizations thus like to ensure that the required resources will be available when needed. A principal cause of portfolio underperformance is a lack of adequate resources, especially personnel, to support required development.

Portfolio management is the process of bringing an organization's project management practices into line with its overall corporate strategy. By creating complementarity in its project portfolio, a company can ensure that its project management teams are working together rather than at cross-purposes. Portfolio management is also a visible symbol of the strategic direction and commercial goals of a firm. Taken together, the projects that a firm chooses to promote and develop send a clear signal to the rest of the company about priorities, resource commitment, and future directions. Finally, portfolio management is an alternative method for managing overall project risk by seeking a continuous balance among various families of projects, between risks and return trade-offs, and between efficiently run projects and nonperformers. As more and more organizations rely on project management to achieve these ends, it is likely that more and more firms will take the next logical step: organizing projects by means of portfolio management.

Summary

1. **Explain six criteria for a useful project selection/ screening model.**   No organization can pursue every opportunity that presents itself. Choices must be made, and to best ensure that they select the most viable projects, firms develop priority systems or guidelines— *selection/screening models* (or a set of models) that will help them make the best choices within the usual constraints of time and money—that is, help them save time and money while maximizing the likelihood of success.

A number of decision models are available to managers who are responsible for evaluating and selecting potential projects. Five important issues that managers should consider when evaluating screening models are: (1) *Realism*: An effective model must reflect organizational objectives, must be reasonable in light of constraints on resources such as money and personnel, and must take into account both commercial risks and technical risks. (2) *Capability*: A model should be flexible enough to respond to changes in the conditions under which projects are carried out and robust enough to accommodate new criteria and constraints. (3) *Flexibility:* The model should be easily modified if trial applications require changes. (4) *Ease of use:* A model must be simple enough to be used by people in all areas of the organization, and it should be timely in that it generates information rapidly and allows people to assimilate that information without any special training or skills. (5) *Cost:* The cost of gathering, storing, and arranging information in the form of useful reports or proposals should be relatively low in relation to the costs associated with implementing a project (i.e., the cost of the models must be low enough to encourage their use rather than diminish their applicability). To this list we have added one more criterion: (6) *Comparability:* The model must be broad enough that it can be applied to multiple projects and support general comparisons of project alternatives.

2. **Understand how to employ checklists and simple scoring models to select projects.** Checklists require decision makers to develop a list of the criteria that are deemed important when considering project alternatives. For example, a firm may decide that all project alternatives must be acceptable on criteria such as return on investment, safety, cost of development, commercial opportunities, and stakeholder acceptability. Once the list of criteria is created, all project alternatives are evaluated against it and assigned a rating of high, medium, or low depending on how well they satisfy each criterion in the checklist. Projects that rate highest across the relevant criteria are selected. Checklists are useful because they are simple and require the firm to make trade-off decisions among criteria to determine which issues are most important in selecting new projects. Among their disadvantages are the subjective nature of the rating process and the fact that they assume equal weighting for all criteria when some, in fact, may be much more important than others in making the final decision.

Simple scoring models are similar to checklists except that they employ criterion weights for each of the decision criteria. Hence, all project alternatives are first weighted by the importance score for the criterion, and then final scores are evaluated against one another. The advantage of this method is that it recognizes the fact that decision criteria may be weighted differently, leading to better choices among project alternatives. The disadvantages of the method arise from the difficulty in assigning meaningful values to scoring anchors such as "High = 3, Medium = 2, Low = 1." Thus, there is some uncertainty in the interpretation of the results of simple scoring models using weighted rankings. The usefulness of these models depends on the relevance of the selected criteria and the accuracy of the weight given to them.

3. **Use more sophisticated scoring models, such as the Analytical Hierarchy Process.** The Analytical Hierarchy Process (AHP) is a four-step process that allows decision makers to understand the nature of project alternatives in making selection decisions. Using the AHP, decision makers (a) structure the hierarchy of criteria to be used in the decision process, (b) allocate weights to these criteria, (c) assign numerical values to all evaluation dimensions, and (d) use the scores to evaluate project alternatives. The AHP has been shown to create more accurate decision alternatives and lead to more informed choices, provided the organization's decision makers develop accurate decision criteria and evaluate and weight them honestly.

4. **Learn how to use financial concepts, such as the efficient frontier and risk/return models.** Many projects are selected as a result of their perceived risk/return trade-off potential. That is, all projects entail risk (uncertainty), so project organizations seek to balance higher risk with comparatively higher expectations of return when considering which projects to fund. The efficient frontier concept allows projects to be evaluated against each other by assessing the potential returns for each alternative compared to the risk the firm is expected to undertake in producing the project. The efficient frontier is the set of project portfolio options that offers either a maximum return for every given level of risk or the minimum risk for every level of return.

5. **Employ financial analyses and options analysis to evaluate the potential for new project investments.** Financial analyses using discounted cash flows and internal rates of return allow us to apply the concept of the time value of money to any decision we have to make regarding the attractiveness of various project alternatives. The time value of money suggests that future streams of return from a project investment should at least offset the initial investment in the project plus provide some required rate of return imposed by the company. Options analysis takes this process one step further and considers alternatives in which an investment is either made or foregone, depending upon reasonable alternative investments the company can make in the future. Each of these financial models argues that the principal determinant of an attractive project investment must be the money it promises to return. Clearly, therefore, a reasonably accurate estimate of future streams of revenue is required for financial models to create meaningful results.

6. **Recognize the challenges that arise in maintaining an optimal project portfolio for an organization.** A number of challenges are associated with managing a portfolio of projects, including (a) conservative technical communities that refuse to support new project initiatives, (b) out-of-sync projects and portfolios in which the projects no longer align with overall strategic

portfolio plans, (c) unpromising projects that unbalance the portfolio, and (d) scarce resources that make it impossible to support new projects.

7. ***Understand the three keys to successful project portfolio management.*** There are three keys to success project portfolio management. First, firms need to create or make available a flexible structure and freedom of communication by reducing excessive bureaucracy and administrative oversight so that the portfolio management team maximum has flexibility in seeking out and

investing in projects. Second, use of successful portfolio management strategies allows for low-cost environmental scanning, which launches a series of inexpensive "probes" into the future to develop and test-market project alternatives. Finally, successful portfolio management requires a time-paced transition strategy based on a sense of the timing necessary to successfully transition from one product to the next, whether the next product is a direct offshoot of the original or an additional innovative product for the firm's portfolio.

Key Terms

Analytical Hierarchy Process (AHP) (*p. 99*)

Checklist (*p. 95*)

Discounted cash flow (DCF) method (*p. 105*)

Discounted payback method (*p. 108*)

Efficient frontier (*p. 103*)

Internal rate of return (IRR) (*p. 109*)

Lead time (*p. 114*)

Net present value (NPV) method (*p. 106*)

Nonnumeric models (*p. 94*)

Numeric models (*p. 94*)

Pairwise comparison approach (*p. 100*)

Payback period (*p. 105*)

Present value of money (*p. 104*)

Profile models (*p. 102*)

Project portfolio (*p. 93*)

Project portfolio management (*p. 113*)

Project screening model (*p. 95*)

Required rate of return (RRR) (*p. 108*)

Risk/return (*p. 102*)

Simplified scoring model (*p. 97*)

Time value of money (*p. 104*)

Solved Problems

3.1 Net Present Value

Your firm is trying to decide whether to invest in a new project opportunity based on the following information. The initial cash outlay will total $250,000 over two years. The firm expects to invest $200,000 immediately and the final $50,000 in one year's time. The company predicts that the project will generate a stream of earnings of $50,000, $100,000, $200,000, and $75,000 per year, respectively, starting in Year 2. The required rate of return is 12%, and the expected rate of inflation over the life of the project is forecast to remain steady at 3%. Should you invest in this project?

SOLUTION

In order to answer this question, we need to organize the following data in the form of a table:

Total outflow = $250,000
Total inflow = $400,000

Required rate of return $(r) = 12\%$
Inflation rate $(p) = 3\%$
Discount factor $= 1/(1 + r + p)^t$

The result is Table 3.11. Because the discounted revenue stream is positive ($11,725), the project would be a good investment and should be pursued.

3.2 Discounted Payback

Your firm has the opportunity to invest $75,000 in a new project opportunity but due to cash flow concerns, your boss wants to know when you can pay back the original investment. Using the discounted payback method, you determine that the project should generate inflows of $30,000, $30,000, $25,000, $20,000, and $20,000 respectively for an expected five years after completion of the project. Your firm's required rate of return is 10%. Calculate how long it should take to pay back the initial project investment.

TABLE 3.11 Discounted Cash Flows and NPV (II)

Year	Inflows	Outflows	Net Flow	Discount Factor	NPV
0	$ 0	$200,000	$(200,000)	1.0000	$(200,000)
1	0	50,000	(50,000)	.8696	(43,480)
2	50,000	0	50,000	.7561	37,805
3	100,000	0	100,000	.6575	65,750
4	200,000	0	200,000	.5718	114,360
5	75,000	0	75,000	.4972	37,290
Total					**$ 11,725**

SOLUTION

To answer this question, it is helpful to organize the information into a table. Remember that:

Total outflow = $75,000
Required rate of return = 10%
Discount factor = $1/(1+.10)^t$

Year	Cash Flow	Discount Factor	Net Inflows
0	($75,000)	1.00	($75,000)
1	30,000	.91	27,300
2	30,000	.83	24,900
3	25,000	.75	18,750
4	20,000	.68	13,600
5	20,000	.62	12,400

Payback = 3.3 years

3.3 Internal Rate of Return

Suppose that a project required an initial cash investment of $24,000 and was expected to generate inflows of $10,000, $10,000, and $10,000 for the next three years. Further, assume that our company's required rate of return for new projects is 12%. Is this project worth funding? Would it be a good investment if the company's required rate of return were 15%? Use the following figures to determine the answers to these questions:

Cash investment = $24,000
Year 1 inflow = $10,000
Year 2 inflow = $10,000
Year 3 inflow = $10,000
Required rate of return = 12%

SOLUTION

Step One: Try 10%.

Year	Inflows	Discount Factor at 10%	NPV
1	$10,000	.909	$ 9,090
2	10,000	.826	8,260
3	10,000	.751	7,510
Present value of inflows			24,860
Cash investment			− 24,000
Difference			$ 860

Decision: Present value difference at 10% is $860, which is too high. Try a higher discount rate.

Step Two: Try 12%.

Year	Inflows	Discount Factor at 12%	NPV
1	$10,000	.893	$ 8,930
2	10,000	.797	7,970
3	10,000	.712	7,120
Present value of inflows			24,020
Cash investment			− 24,000
Difference			$ 20

Decision: Present value difference at 12% is $20, which suggests that 12% is a close approximation of the IRR. This project would be a good investment at 12%, but it would not be acceptable if the firm's required rate of return were 15%.

Discussion Questions

1. If you were to prioritize the criteria for a successful screening model, which criteria would you rank at the top of your priority list? Why?
2. What are the benefits and drawbacks of checklists as a method for screening project alternatives?
3. How does use of the Analytical Hierarchy Process (AHP) aid in project selection? In particular, what aspects of the screening process does the AHP seem to address and improve directly?
4. What are the benefits and drawbacks of the profile model for project screening? Be specific about the problems that may arise in identifying the efficient frontier.
5. How are financial models superior to other screening models? How are they inferior?
6. How does the options model address the problem of nonrecoverable investment in a project?
7. What advantages do you see in the GE Tollgate screening approach? What disadvantages do you see? How would you alter it?
8. Why is project portfolio management particularly challenging in the pharmaceutical industry?
9. What are the keys to successful project portfolio management?
10. What are some of the key difficulties in successfully implementing project portfolio management practices?

Problems

1. **Checklist.** Suppose that you are trying to choose which of two IT projects to accept. Your company employs three primary selection criteria for evaluating all IT projects: (1) proven technology, (2) ease of transition, and (3) projected cost savings.

One option, Project Demeter, is evaluated as:

Technology	high
Ease of transition	low
Projected cost savings	high

The second option, Project Cairo, is evaluated as:

Technology	medium
Ease of transition	high
Projected cost savings	high

Construct a table identifying the projects, their evaluative criteria, and ratings. Based on your analysis, which project would you argue in favor of adopting? Why?

2. **Checklist.** Consider the following information in choosing among the four project alternatives below (labeled A, B, C, and D). Each has been assessed according to four criteria:

- Payoff potential
- Lack of risk
- Safety
- Competitive advantage

Project A is rated:

| Payoff potential | high | Safety | high |
| Lack of risk | low | Competitive advantage | medium |

Project B is rated:

| Payoff potential | low | Safety | medium |
| Lack of risk | medium | Competitive advantage | medium |

Project C is rated:

| Payoff potential | medium | Safety | low |
| Lack of risk | medium | Competitive advantage | low |

Project D is rated:

| Payoff potential | high | Safety | medium |
| Lack of risk | high | Competitive advantage | medium |

Construct a project checklist model for screening these four alternatives. Based on your model, which project is the best choice for selection? Why? Which is the worst? Why?

3. **Scoring Model.** Suppose the information in Problem 2 was supplemented by importance weights for each of the four assessment criteria, where 1 = low importance and 4 = high importance:

Assessment Criteria	Importance Weights
1. Payoff potential	4
2. Lack of risk	3
3. Safety	1
4. Competitive advantage	3

Assume, too, that evaluations of *high* receive a score of 3, *medium* 2, and *low* 1. Recreate your project scoring model and reassess the four project choices (A, B, C, and D). Now which project alternative is the best? Why?

4. **Scoring Model.** Now assume that for Problem 3, the importance weights are altered as follows:

Assessment Criteria	Importance Weights
1. Payoff potential	1
2. Lack of risk	1
3. Safety	4
4. Competitive advantage	2

How does this new information alter your decision? Which project now looks most attractive? Why?

5. **Screening Model.** Assume that the following criteria relevant to the process of screening various project opportunities are weighted in importance as follows:

Quality (7)
Cost (3)
Speed to market (5)
Visibility (1)
Reliability (7)

Our company has four project alternatives that satisfy these key features as follows:

	Alpha	Beta	Gamma	Delta
Quality	1	3	3	5
Cost	7	7	5	3
Speed	5	5	3	5
Visibility	3	1	5	1
Reliability	5	5	7	7

Construct a project screening matrix to identify among these four projects the most likely candidate to be implemented.

6. **Profile Model.** Assume the project profile model shown in Figure 3.9. Define the efficient frontier. The dotted lines represent the minimum return and the maximum risk that the company will accept. Which projects would be suitable for retaining and which should be dropped from the company's portfolio? Why?

7. **Profile Model.** Using the information from the profile model in Problem 6, construct an argument as to why project B is preferable to project C.

8. **Discounted Payback.** Your company is seriously considering investing in a new project opportunity, but cash flow is tight. Top management is concerned about how long it will take for this new project to pay back the initial investment of $50,000. You have determined that the project should generate inflows

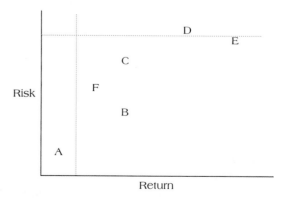

FIGURE 3.9 Project Profile Model (Problem 6)

of $30,000, $30,000, $40,000, $25,000, and $15,000 for the next five years. Your firm's required rate of return is 15%. How long will it take to pay back the initial investment?

9. **Net Present Value.** Assume that your firm wants to choose between two project options:

   - Project A: $500,000 invested today will yield an expected income stream of $150,000 per year for five years, starting in Year 1.
   - Project B: an initial investment of $400,000 is expected to produce this revenue stream: Year 1 = 0, Year 2 = $50,000, Year 3 = $200,000, Year 4 = $300,000, and Year 5 = $200,000.

   Assume that a required rate of return for your company is 10% and that inflation is expected to remain steady at 3% for the life of the project. Which is the better investment? Why?

10. **Net Present Value.** Your vice president of Management Information Systems informs you that she has researched the possibility of automating your organization's order-entry system. She has projected that the new system will reduce labor costs by $30,000 each year over the next five years. The purchase price (including installation and testing) of the new system is $110,000. What is the net present value of this investment if the discount rate is 10% per year?

11. **Net Present Value.** A company has four project investment alternatives. The required rate of return on projects is 20%, and inflation is projected to remain at 3% into the foreseeable future. The pertinent information about each alternative is listed in the following chart:

Which project should be the firm's first priority? Why? If the company could invest in more than one project, indicate the order in which it should prioritize these project alternatives.

12. **Options Model.** A heavy manufacturing company is deciding whether to initiate a new project. The success of the project depends heavily on the state of the economy, which has a 50/50 chance of being strong enough to support the venture. The project will require an initial investment of $1 million, and the company expects to earn $500,000 in annual revenues from the project—unless the economy goes into recession, in which case the project will return only $100,000 per year. The company requires a 12% return on its investments. Should it undertake the project? If the company decides to wait a year, the economy has a 75% chance of improving sufficiently to ensure $500,000 in annual returns. Does it make sense to wait for a year before making the investment? Use the options model approach to project evaluation to answer these two questions.

13. **Options Model.** Massivesoft Corporation is trying to decide whether to invest in a new software project. The initial investment will be $5 million. The project has a 40% chance of returning $1 million per year into the future and a 60% chance of generating only $100,000 in revenues. Assuming that Massivesoft requires a 15% return on capital investments, is this a viable project? If Massivesoft decides to wait one year before investing in the project, its odds of returning $1 million

Project Carol	Year	Investment	Revenue Streams
	0	$500,000	$ 0
	1		50,000
	2		250,000
	3		350,000

Project George	Year	Investment	Revenue Streams
	0	$250,000	$ 0
	1		75,000
	2		75,000
	3		75,000
	4		50,000

Project Thomas	Year	Investment	Revenue Streams
	0	$1,000,000	$ 0
	1		200,000
	2		200,000
	3		200,000
	4		200,000
	5		200,000
	6		200,000

Project Anna	Year	Investment	Revenue Streams
	0	$75,000	$ 0
	1		15,000
	2		25,000
	3		50,000
	4		50,000
	5		150,000

per year improve to 70%. Should Massivesoft wait one year to initiate the project? Use the options model approach to project evaluation to answer these two questions.

14. **Portfolio Management.** Crown Corporation is interested in expanding its project portfolio. This firm, which specializes in water conservation and land reclamation projects, anticipates a huge increase in the demand for home fuel cells as an alternative to current methods of energy generation and usage. Although fuel-cell projects involve different technologies than those in which Crown currently specializes, the profit potential is very large. Develop a list of benefits and drawbacks associated with this potential expansion of Crown's project portfolio. In your opinion, do the risks outweigh the advantages from such a move? Justify your answer.

15. **Project Screening.** Assume you are the IT manager for a large urban health care system. Lately you have been bombarded with requests for new projects, including system upgrades, support services, automated record keeping, billing, and so forth. With an average of 50 software and hardware support projects going on at any time, you have decided that you must create a system for screening new project requests from the various departments within the health care system. Develop a project selection and screening system similar to GE's Tollgate process. What elements would you include in such a system? How many steps would you recommend? At what points in the process should "gates" be installed? How might a tollgate system for a software development company differ from one used by an architectural firm specializing in the development of commercial office buildings?

Case Study 3.1

Keflavik Paper Company

In recent years, Keflavik Paper Company has been having problems with its project management process. A number of commercial projects, for example, have come in late and well over budget, and product performance has been inconsistent. A comprehensive analysis of the process has traced many of the problems back to faulty project selection methods.

Keflavik is a medium-sized corporation that manufactures a variety of paper products, including specialty papers and the coated papers used in the photography and printing industries. Despite cyclical downturns due to general economic conditions, the firm's annual sales have grown steadily though slowly. About five years ago, Keflavik embarked on a project-based approach to new product opportunities. The goal was to improve profitability and generate additional sales volume by developing new commercial products quickly, with better targeting to specific customer needs. The results so far have not been encouraging. The company's project development record is spotty. Some projects have been delivered on time, but others have been late; budgets have been routinely overrun; and product performance has been inconsistent, with some projects yielding good returns and others losing money.

Top management hired a consultant to analyze the firm's processes and determine the most efficient way to fix its project management procedures. The consultant attributed the main problems not to the project management processes themselves, but to the manner in which projects are added to the company's portfolio. The primary mechanism for new project selection focused almost exclusively on discounted cash flow models, such as net present value analysis. Essentially, if a project promised profitable revenue streams, it was approved by top management.

One result of this practice was the development of a "family" of projects that were often almost completely unrelated. No one, it seems, ever asked whether projects that were added to the portfolio fit with other ongoing projects. Keflavik attempted to expand into coated papers, photographic products, shipping and packaging materials, and other lines that strayed far from the firm's original niche. New projects were rarely measured against the firm's strategic mission, and little effort was made to evaluate them according to its technical resources. Some new projects, for example, failed to fit because they required significant organizational learning and new technical expertise and training (all of which was expensive and time-consuming). The result was a portfolio of diverse, mismatched projects that was difficult to manage.

Further, the diverse nature of the new product line and development processes decreased organizational learning and made it impossible for Keflavik's project managers to move easily from one assignment to the next. The hodgepodge of projects made it difficult for managers to apply lessons learned from one project to the next. Because the skills acquired on one project were largely nontransferable, project teams routinely had to relearn processes whenever they moved to a new project.

The consultant suggested that Keflavik rethink its project selection and screening processes. In order to lend some coherence to its portfolio, the firm needed to include alternative screening mechanisms. All new projects, for instance, had to be evaluated in terms of the company's strategic goals and were required to demonstrate complementarity with its current portfolio. He further recommended that in order to match project managers with the types of projects that the company was increasingly undertaking, it should analyze their current skill sets. Although Keflavik has begun implementing these and other recommendations, progress so far has been slow. In particular, top managers have found it hard to reject opportunities

(continued)

that offer positive cash flow. They have also had to relearn the importance of project prioritization. Nevertheless, a new prioritization scheme is in place, and it seems to be improving both the selection of new project opportunities and the company's ability to manage projects once they are funded.

Questions for Discussion

1. Keflavik Paper presents a good example of the dangers of excessive reliance on one screening technique (in this case, discounted cash flow). How might excessive or exclusive reliance on other screening methods discussed in this chapter lead to similar problems?

2. Assume that you are responsible for maintaining Keflavik's project portfolio. Name some key criteria that should be used in evaluating all new projects before they are added to the current portfolio.

3. What does this case demonstrate about the effect of poor project screening methods on a firm's ability to manage its projects effectively?

Case Study 3.2

Project Selection at Nova Western, Inc.

Phyllis Henry, vice president of new product development, sat at her desk, trying to make sense of the latest new project proposals she had just received from her staff. Nova Western, Inc., a large developer of business software and application programs, had been experiencing a downturn in operating revenues over the past three quarters. The senior management team was feeling pressure from the board of directors to take steps to correct this downward drift in revenues and profitability. The consensus opinion was that Nova Western needed some new product ideas, and fast.

The report Phyllis was reading contained the results of a project screening conducted by two independent groups within the new product development department. After several weeks of analysis, it appeared that two top contenders had emerged as the optimal new project opportunities. One project, code-named Janus, was championed by the head of software development. The other project idea, Gemini, had the support of the business applications organization. Phyllis's original charge to her staff was to prepare an evaluation of both projects in order to decide which one Nova Western should support. Because of budget restrictions, there was no way that both projects could be funded.

The first evaluation team used a scoring model, based on the key strategic categories at Nova Western, to evaluate the two projects. The categories they employed were: (1) strategic fit, (2) probability of technical success, (3) financial risk, (4) potential profit, and (5) strategic leverage (ability of the project to employ and enhance company resources and technical capabilities). Using these categories, the team evaluated the two projects as shown here. Scores were based on: 1 = low, 2 = medium, and 3 = high.

Project Janus

Category	Importance	Score	Weighted Score
1. Strategic fit	3	2	6
2. Probability of technical success	2	2	4
3. Financial risk	2	1	2
4. Potential profit	3	3	9
5. Strategic leverage	1	1	1
		Score = 22	

Project Gemini

Category	Importance	Score	Weighted Score
1. Strategic fit	3	3	9
2. Probability of technical success	2	2	4
3. Financial risk	2	2	4
4. Potential profit	3	3	9
5. Strategic leverage	1	2	2
		Score = 28	

The results obtained by this first team suggested that Project Gemini would the best choice for the next new project.

The second team of evaluators presented an NPV analysis of the two projects to Phyllis. In that analysis, the evaluators assumed a required rate of return of 15% and an anticipated inflation rate of 3% over the life of the project. The findings of this team were as follows:

Project Janus

Initial investment = $250,000

Life of the project = 5 years

Anticipated stream of future cash flows:

Year 1	= $ 50,000
Year 2	= 100,000
Year 3	= 100,000
Year 4	= 200,000
Year 5	= 75,000
Calculated NPV	= $ 60,995

Project Gemini

Initial investment = $400,000

Life of the project = 3 years

Anticipated stream of future cash flows:

Year 1	= $ 75,000
Year 2	= 250,000
Year 3	= 300,000
Calculated NPV	= $ 25,695

Thus, according to this analysis, Project Janus would be the project of choice.

The analyses of the two projects by different means yielded different findings. The scoring model indicated that Project Gemini was the best alternative, and the financial screening favored the higher projected NPV of Project Janus. Phyllis, who was due to present her recommendation to the full top management team in the afternoon, was still not sure which project to recommend. The evaluations seemed to present more questions than answers.

Questions for Discussion

1. Phyllis has called you into her office to help her make sense of the contradictions in the two project evaluations. How would you explain the reasons for the divergence of opinion from one technique to the next? What are the strengths and weaknesses of each screening method?

2. Choose the project that you think, based on the two analyses, Nova Western should select. Defend your choice.

3. What does this case suggest to you about the use of project selection methods in organizations? How would you resolve the contradictions found in this example?

Internet Exercises

1. Go to the Web sites for the following organizations:

   a. Merck & Company Pharmaceuticals: www.merck.com/about/

   b. Boeing Corporation: www.boeing.com/companyoffices/aboutus/index.html

   c. Rolls-Royce, Plc.: www.rolls-royce.com

   d. ExxonMobil, Inc.: www.exxonmobil.com/Corporate/about.aspx

   Based on your review of the companies' posted mission and strategic goals, what types of projects would you expect them to pursue? If you worked for one of these firms and sought to maintain strategic alignment with their project portfolio, what project options would you suggest?

2. Access the Web site www-01.ibm.com/software/awdtools/portfolio/. What is IBM's philosophy regarding project portfolio management as demonstrated by this software product? What do they mean by stating that their goal is to help clients "overcome the influence of the loudest voice in the room and use objective information to support decision making"?

3. Internet Reading: Pellegrinelli, S. (1997). "Programme management: Organizing project-based change," *International Journal of Project Management,* 15: 141–49. This article can be found on the Companion Web site.

Notes

1. Foti, R. (2002). "Priority decisions," *PMNetwork,* 16(4): 24–29; Crawford, J. K. (2001). "Portfolio management: Overview and best practices," in J. Knutson (Ed.), *Project Management for Business Professionals.* New York: Wiley, pp. 33–48; Wheatley, M. (2009). "Making the cut," *PMNetwork,* 23(6): 44–48.

2. Pascale, S., Carland, J. W., and Carland, J. C. (1997). "A comparative analysis of two concept evaluation methods for new product development projects," *Project Management Journal,* 28(4): 47–52; Wheelwright, S. C., and Clark, K. B. (1992, March–April). "Creating project plans to focus product development," *Harvard Business Review,* 70(2): 70–82.

3. Souder, W. E., and Sherman, J. D. (1994). *Managing New Technology Development.* New York: McGraw-Hill; Souder, W. E. (1983). *Project Selection and Economic Appraisal.* New York: Van Nostrand Reinhold.

4. Meredith, J. R., and Mantel, Jr., S. J. (2003). *Project Management,* 5th ed. New York: Wiley.

5. Khorramshahgol, R., Azani, H., and Gousty, Y. (1988). "An integrated approach to project evaluation and selection," *IEEE Transactions on Engineering Management,* EM-35(4): 265–70; Raz, T. (1997). "An iterative screening methodology for selecting project alternatives," *Project Management Journal,* 28(4): 34–39.

6. Cleland, D. I. (1988). "Project stakeholder management," in Cleland, D. I., and King, W. R. (Eds.), *Project Management Handbook,* 2nd ed. New York: Van Nostrand Reinhold, pp. 275–301.

7. Artto, K. A., Martinsuo, M., and Aalto, T. (Eds.) (2001). *Project Portfolio Management: Strategic Management Through Projects.* Helsinki: Project Management Association; Artto, K. A. (2001). "Management of project-oriented organization—Conceptual analysis," in Artto, K. A., Martinsuo, M., and Aalto, T. (Eds.), *Project Portfolio Management: Strategic Management Through Projects.* Helsinki: Project Management Association.

8. Pinto, J. K., and Millet, I. (1999). *Successful Information System Implementation: The Human Side,* 2nd ed. Newtown Square, PA: Project Management Institute.

9. Saaty, T. L. (1996). *The Analytical Hierarchy Process.* Pittsburgh, PA: RWS Publications.

10. Millet, I. (1994, February 15). "Who's on first?" *CIO Magazine,* pp. 24–27.

11. Mian, S. A., and Dai, C. X. (1999). "Decision-making over the project life cycle: An analytical hierarchy approach," *Project Management Journal,* 30(1): 40–52.

12. Foreman, E. H., Saaty, T. L., Selly, M., and Waldron, R. (1996). *Expert Choice.* McLean, VA: Decision Support Software.

13. Millet, I., and Schoner, B. (2005). "Incorporating negative values into the Analytical Hierarchy Process," *Computers and Operations Research,* 12(3): 163–73.

14. Evans, D. A., and Souder, W. E. (1998). "Methods for selecting and evaluating projects," in Pinto, J. K. (Ed.), *The Project Management Institute Project Management Handbook.* San Francisco, CA: Jossey-Bass.

15. Reilly, F. K. (1985). *Investment Analysis and Portfolio Management,* 2nd ed. Chicago, IL: The Dryden Press.

16. Keown, A. J., Scott, Jr., D. F., Martin, J. D., and Petty, J. W. (1996). *Basic Financial Management,* 7th ed. Upper Saddle River, NJ: Prentice Hall; Evans, D. A., and Souder, W. E. (1998). "Methods for selecting and evaluating projects," in Pinto, J. K. (Ed.), *The Project Management Institute Project Management Handbook.* San Francisco, CA: Jossey-Bass.

17. Dixit, A. K., and Pindyck, R. S. (1994). *Investment under Uncertainty.* Princeton, NJ: Princeton University Press; Huchzermeier, W., and Loch, C. H. (2001). "Project management under risk: Using the real options approach to evaluate flexibility in R&D," *Management Science,* 47(1): 85–101; Chan, T., Zhang, J., and Lai, K-K. (2009). "An integrated real options evaluating model for information technology projects under multiple risks," *International Journal of Project Management,* 27(8): 776–86; Yeo, K. T., and Qiu, F. (2003). "The value of management flexibility: A real option approach to investment evaluation," *International Journal of Project Management,* 21(4): 243–50.

18. Meredith, J. R., and Mantel, S. J. (2003). *Project Management,* 5th ed. New York: Wiley.

19. Dye, L. D., and Pennypacker, J. S. (Eds.) (1999). *Project Portfolio Management: Selecting and Prioritizing Projects for Competitive Advantage.* West Chester, PA: Center for Business Practices.

20. Elton, J., and Roe, J. (1998, March–April). "Bringing discipline to project management," *Harvard Business Review,* 76(2): 153–59.

21. Artto, K. A. (2001). "Management of project-oriented organization—Conceptual analysis," in Artto, K. A., Martinsuo, M., and Aalto, T. (Eds.), *Project Portfolio Management: Strategic Management Through Projects.* Helsinki: Project Management Association.

22. "Strategic realignment of brand portfolio," (2010, November 8), http://www.evaluatepharma.com/Universal/View.aspx?type=Story&id=228881.

23. Lehtonen, M. (2001). "Resource allocation and project portfolio management in pharmaceutical R&D," in Artto, K. A., Marinsuo, M., and Aalto, T. (Eds.). (2001). *Project Portfolio Management: Strategic Management Through Projects.* Helsinki: Project Management Association, pp. 107–140.

24. Brown, S. L., and Eisenhardt, K. M. (1997). "The art of continuous change: Linking complexity theory and time-paced evolution in relentlessly shifting organizations," *Administrative Science Quarterly,* 42(1): 1–34.

25. Cooper, R., and Edgett, S. (1997). "Portfolio management in new product development: Less from the leaders I," *Research Technology Management,* 40(5): 16–28; Longman, A., Sandahl, D., and Speir, W. (1999). "Preventing project proliferation," *PMNetwork,* 13(7): 39–41; Dobson, M. (1999). *The Juggler's Guide to Managing Multiple Projects.* Newtown Square, PA: Project Management Institute.

Leadership and the Project Manager

Chapter Outline

Chapter Objectives

After completing this chapter, you should be able to:

1. Understand how project management is a "leader-intensive" profession.

2. Distinguish between the role of a manager and the characteristics of a leader.

3. Understand the concept of emotional intelligence as it relates to how project managers lead.

4. Recognize traits that are strongly linked to effective project leadership.

5. Understand the implications of time orientation in project management.

6. Identify the key roles project champions play in project success.

7. Recognize the principles that typify the new project leadership.

8. Understand the development of project management professionalism in the discipline.

PROJECT MANAGEMENT BODY OF KNOWLEDGE CORE CONCEPTS COVERED IN THIS CHAPTER

1. Key General Management Skills (PMBoK sec. 2.4)
2. Team Development (PMBoK sec. 9.3)
3. Communications Planning (PMBoK sec. 10.1)

PROJECT PROFILE

Aziza Chaouni and Her Project to Save a River

Built in the ninth century, the Moroccan city of Fez is a fascinating mix of ancient palaces, narrow winding streets, bazaars, and mosques, centered on the "Medina," the ancient quarter of the city. The river for which the city is named has served for centuries as the lifeblood of the population, but unfortunately, those glory days are behind it. Since the 1950s, the river Fez has become badly polluted through unregulated dumping and its proximity to leather tanneries. In recent years, locals have renamed it the "River of Trash," and for much of its passage through the city, it is channeled into a series of concrete spillways and passages and covered to stifle the worst of the chemical smell. An eyesore and a health hazard, the River of Trash is badly in need of revitalization.

A project team headed by a former resident of Fez, Aziza Chaouni, has determined to revive the river and return it to its former glory. Chaouni's original proposal to revitalize the river and the Medina area was awarded a first prize of $300,000 in the Holcim Foundation for Sustainable Construction competition. The project authors then formed the nongovernmental organization (NGO) Sauvons Oued Fez (Save the Fez River), a network to advance the subprojects of the remediation and to encourage community involvement. Working with the Fez city officials, Chaouni and her 20-member team have proposed an ambitious plan to improve the river and living space within the Medina, a narrow and crowded quarter that houses more than 200,000 people. The Medina is also home to dozens of tanning pits for the leather industry, making the site noisy, overcrowded, and foul-smelling. The project includes a number of features: creating green spaces in the poorest areas, relocating the heavily polluting tanneries to sites outside the city and away from the river, revitalizing the heavily polluted soil beneath the tanning pits, as well as tearing down illegal construction and creating a major public space with a river walk, cafes, gardens, and markets. Additionally, the plan involves developing sewage treatment plants on the outskirts of the city to discourage direct dumping into the river.

The technical challenges are huge. The tanneries, though important to the economic life of the city, are a source of chemical-born disease and long-term illness, both for the tanners and other residents of the area. Simply

FIGURE 4.1   Tanning Pits in the Medina, Fez

removing them to alternative locations is not sufficient; the tanning systems that have been used for centuries must be brought into line with more modern approaches that can offer health benefits as well as economic incentives.

The project has not been without challenges and opponents. Chaouni notes that she and her team have had to work with numerous stakeholders, including UNESCO, who designated the city a World Heritage Site in 1981 and are suspicious of any major change efforts. "Some colleagues said I was simply naïve when I started this project," acknowledges Chaouni. Nevertheless, through her vision of what Fez and its river could become, she has worked steadily with architects, urban planners, politicians, and local business groups to ensure their support for the effort. The project will not finish quickly; in fact, it is slated to take nearly 20 years to completely revitalize and remodel the Medina. Nevertheless, it represents a worthy goal in the hands of someone with vision and the commitment to improve the lot of the local population. Chaouni notes, "[T]he driving force behind this project is a belief that the soul of Fez is its people and their liveliness, which has throughout the centuries been constantly evolving and adapting to their contexts. Thus, I believe in a process of preservation which is adaptive on one hand and on the other hand benefits the population, not freezing them into time, but projecting them into the future while still keeping the soul of the city intact."[1]

INTRODUCTION

Leadership is often recognized by its accomplishments. When Alan Mulally left Boeing in the fall of 2006 to take over a slumping and demoralized Ford Motor Company, many of his colleagues thought he was crazy. Capping a 35-year career at Boeing, Mulally had successfully supervised the development of the 777 aircraft and was considered an obvious candidate to take over the top executive position. Instead, he accepted the biggest challenge of his career: trying to turn around one of the icons of the U.S. auto business, currently in the midst of a two-year slump and hemorrhaging cash with no prospect of relief in sight.

At Ford, Mulally made a series of savvy moves early on, including reviving the Taurus model, negotiating to borrow a whopping $23.6 billion by mortgaging Ford's assets in order to finance a major overhaul, and shedding poor-performing divisions, including Jaguar, Aston Martin, Land Rover, and Volvo. His efforts to revitalize the company have paid off. During the economic crisis of 2008, Ford was the only U.S. auto firm to refuse government bail-out money and avoid bankruptcy proceedings. Many industry analysts have predicted that Ford, under Mulally's leadership, is positioned to become the leading American automaker.

The situation Jack Welch faced when he took over as CEO at General Electric was very different. He inherited a company that was considered a corporate powerhouse, had strong finances, and was a household name around the world. Within a couple of years, he stirred up the moribund bureaucracy at GE, ruthlessly selling off underperforming divisions and cutting jobs to the point where his subordinates nicknamed him "Neutron Jack," after the neutron bomb. Like the weapon, employees said, he got rid of people and left the building standing. His brisk manner, willingness to lead by personal example, and attention to detail all paid remarkable dividends as he transported GE to its highest level of corporate profitability. When he retired in 2001, Welch had overseen the transformation of GE into a firm with one of the largest market capitalizations, based on stock price, in the world.

Leadership is a difficult concept to examine because we all have our own definition of leadership, our own examples of leaders in actions, and our own beliefs about what makes leaders work. The topic of leadership has generated more than 30,000 articles and hundreds of books. Although there are many definitions of leadership, one useful definition that we will employ in this chapter is that **leadership** is the ability to inspire confidence and support among the people who are needed to achieve organizational goals.[2] For the project manager, leadership is the process by which she influences the project team to get the job done!

True leadership from the project manager has been shown time and again to be one of the most important characteristics in successful project management. The impact of good leadership is felt within the team and has an effect on other functional managers and important project stakeholders.[3] In fact, project management has been viewed as one of the most "leader-intensive" undertakings within an organization.[4]

4.1 LEADERS VERSUS MANAGERS

Most leaders are quick to reject the idea that they were, by themselves, responsible for the successes attained or the important changes undertaken within their organizations. For them, leadership involves an awareness of a partnership, an active collaboration between the leader and the team. In project management, successful team leaders are often those who were best able to create the partnership attitude between themselves and their teams. As Peter Block[5] notes, the idea of leadership as partnership is critical to project management because it highlights the important manner in which all leaders are ultimately dependent on their teams to achieve project goals. Four things are necessary to promote the partnership idea between the project manager and the team:

1. *Exchange of purpose:*   Partnerships require that every worker be responsible for defining the project's vision and goals. A steady dialogue between the project manager and team members can create a consistent and widely shared vision.

2. *A right to say no:*   It is critical that all members of the project team feel they have the ability to disagree and to offer contrary positions. Supporting people's right to voice their disagreements is a cornerstone of a partnership. Losing arguments is acceptable; losing the right to disagree is not.

3. *Joint accountability:*   In a partnership, each member of the project team is responsible for the project's outcomes and the current situation, whether it is positive or shows evidence of problems. The project is shared among multiple participants and the results of the project are also shared.

4. *Absolute honesty:*   Partnerships demand authenticity. An authentic atmosphere promotes straightforwardness and honesty among all participants. Because we respect each team member's role on the project, we make an implicit pact that all information, both good and bad, becomes community information. Just as honesty is a cornerstone of successful marriages, it is critical in project team relationships.

Leadership is distinguishable from other management roles in a number of ways. A manager is an individual who has received a title within the organization that permits her to plan, organize, direct, and control the behavior of others within her department or area of oversight. Although leadership may be part of the manager's job, the other management roles are more administrative in nature. Leadership, on the other hand, is less about administration and more about interpersonal relationships. Leadership involves inspiring, motivating, influencing, and changing behaviors of others in pursuit of a common goal. Leaders embrace change; managers support the status quo. Leaders aim for effectiveness; managers aim for efficiency. Figure 4.2 illustrates some of the distinctions between typical management behavior and the kinds of processes with which leaders are engaged. Although leaders need to recognize the importance of managerial duties, it is often difficult for managers to recognize the nonstandard, interpersonal nature of leadership. However, this is *not* to say that leadership is merely an innate characteristic that some of us have and others do not. Most research and common experience seem to indicate that leadership behaviors can be taught. That is the good news: Leadership can be learned. And a number of properties and models of leadership are quite relevant for project managers.

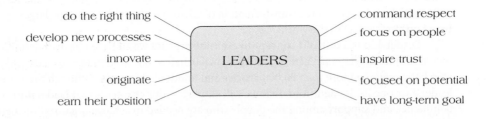

FIGURE 4.2   **Differences Between Managers and Leaders**

Although we will use the term *project manager* throughout the chapter, we do so only because it has become the common designation for the head or leader of a project team. A much better description would be "project leader." Successful project managers are successful project leaders.

This chapter will examine both the general concept of organizational leadership and the special conditions under which project managers are expected to operate. What is it about projects that make them a unique challenge to manage? Why is leadership such an integral role in successful project management? The more we are able to understand the dynamics of this concept, the better able we will be to effectively manage our implementation projects and train a future generation of managers in the tasks and skills required for them to perform their jobs.

4.2 HOW THE PROJECT MANAGER LEADS

The wide range of duties that a project manager is expected to take on covers everything from direct supervision to indirect influence, from managing "hard" technical details to controlling "soft" people issues, from developing detailed project plans and budgets to adjudicating team member quarrels and smoothing stakeholder concerns. In short, the project manager's job encapsulates, in many ways, the role of a mini-CEO, someone who is expected to manage holistically, focusing on the complete project management process from start to finish. In this section, we will examine a variety of the duties and roles that project managers must take on as they work to successfully manage their projects.

Acquiring Project Resources

Project resources refer to all personnel and material resources necessary to successfully accomplish project objectives. Many projects are underfunded in the concept stage. This lack of resource support can occur for several reasons, including:

1. *The project's goals are deliberately vague.* Sometimes a project is kicked off with its overall goals still somewhat "fluid." Perhaps the project is a pure research effort in a laboratory or an information technology project designed to explore new possibilities for chip design or computer speed. Under circumstances such as these, companies sponsor projects with a deliberately "fuzzy" mandate, in order to allow the project team maximum flexibility.

2. *The project lacks a top management sponsor.* As we will learn, having a project champion in the top management of the organization can be very helpful to project development, particularly in gaining support for the project with sufficient resources. On the other hand, when no powerful sponsor emerges for the project, it may face underfunding compared to other projects competing for scarce company resources.

3. *The project requirements were deliberately understated.* It is not uncommon for project resource needs to be purposely understated at the outset in order to get them accepted by the organization.

4. *So many projects may be under development that there is simply not enough money to go around.* A common reason for lack of resource support for a project is that the company is constantly developing so many projects that it cannot fund all of them adequately. Instead, the company adopts a "take it or leave it" attitude, presenting project managers with the option of either accepting insufficient funding or receiving none at all.

5. *An attitude of distrust between top management and project managers.* Sometimes projects receive low funding because top management is convinced that project managers are deliberately padding their estimates to gain excessive funding. We will discuss this attitude in Chapter 11, "Critical Chain Project Scheduling."

Regardless of the reasons for the lack of project resources, there is no doubt that many projects face extremely tight budgets and inadequate human resources.

Project managers, however, do have some options open to them as they seek to supplement their project's resource support. If the resource problem is a personnel issue, they may seek alternative avenues to solve the difficulty. For example, suppose that you were the project manager for an upgrade to an existing software package your company uses to control materials flow and warehousing in manufacturing. If trained programmers were simply unavailable to work on your upgrade project, you might seek to hire temporary contract employees. People with specialized skills such as programming can often be acquired on a short-term basis to fill gaps in the availability of in-house personnel to do the same assignments. The key point to remember is that recognizing and responding to resource needs is a critical function of project leadership.

Another common tactic project managers use in the face of resource shortfalls is to rely on negotiation or political tactics to influence top management to provide additional support. Because resources must often be negotiated with top management, clearly the ability to successfully negotiate and apply influence where the project manager has no direct authority is a critical skill. Again, leadership is best demonstrated by the skills a project manager uses to maintain the viability of the project, whether dealing with top management, clients, the project team, or other significant stakeholders.

Motivating and Building Teams

The process of molding a diverse group of functional experts into a cohesive and collaborative team is not a challenge to be undertaken lightly. Team building and motivation present enormously complex hurdles, and dealing comfortably with human processes is not part of every manager's background. For example, it is very common within engineering or other technical jobs for successful employees to be promoted to project manager. They typically become quickly adept at dealing with the technical challenges of project management but have a difficult time understanding and mastering the human challenges. Their background, training, education, and experiences have prepared them well for technical problems but have neglected the equally critical behavioral elements in successful project management.

In considering how to motivate individuals on our project teams, it is important to recognize that **motivation** ultimately comes from within each of us; it cannot be stimulated solely by an external presence. Each of us decides, based on the characteristics of our job, our work environment, opportunities for advancement, coworkers, and so forth, whether we will become motivated to do the work we have been assigned. Does that imply that motivation is therefore outside of the influence of project managers? Yes and no. Yes, because motivation is an individual decision: We cannot make someone become motivated. On the other hand, as one career army officer puts it, "In the army, we can't force people to do anything, but we can sure make them wish they had done it!" Underlying motivation is typically something that team members desire, whether it comes from a challenging work assignment, opportunity for recognition and advancement, or simply the desire to stay out of trouble. Successful project managers must recognize that one vital element in their job description is the ability to recognize talent, recruit it to the project team, mold a team of interactive and collaborative workers, and apply motivational techniques as necessary.

Having a Vision and Fighting Fires

Successful project managers must operate on boundaries. The boundary dividing technical and behavioral problems is one example, and project managers need to be comfortable with both tasks. Another boundary is the distinction between being a strategic visionary and a day-to-day firefighter. Project managers work with conceptual plans, develop the project scope in line with organizational directives, and understand how their project is expected to fit into the company's project portfolio. In addition, they are expected to keep their eyes firmly fixed on the ultimate prize: the completed project. In short, project managers must be able to think strategically and to consider the "big picture" for their projects. At the same time, however, crises and other project challenges that occur on a daily basis usually require project managers to make immediate, tactical decisions, to solve current problems, and to be detail-oriented. Leaders are able to make the often daily transition from keeping an eye on the big picture to dealing with immediate, smaller problems that occur on a fairly regular basis.

One executive in a project organization highlighted this distinction very well. He stated, "We seek people who can see the forest for the trees but at the same time, are intimately familiar with the species of each variety of tree we grow. If one of those trees is sick, they have to know the best formula to fix it quickly." His point was that a visionary who adopts an exclusively strategic view of the project will discover that he cannot deal with the day-to-day "fires" that keep cropping up. At the same time, someone who is too exclusively focused on dealing with the daily challenges may lose the ultimate perspective and forget the overall picture or the goals that define the project. The balance between strategic vision and firefighting represents a key boundary that successful project managers must become comfortable occupying.

Communicating

Former president Ronald Reagan was labeled "The Great Communicator." He displayed a seemingly natural and fluent ability to project his views clearly, to identify his audience and shape his messages accordingly, and to not waver or contradict his basic themes. Project managers require the same facility of communication. In

Chapter 2 we examined the role of stakeholder management in successful projects. These stakeholders can have a tremendous impact on the likelihood that a project will succeed or fail; consequently, it is absolutely critical to maintain strong contacts with all stakeholders throughout the project's development. There is a common saying in project management regarding the importance of communication with your company's top management: "If they know nothing of what you are doing, they assume you are doing nothing." The message is clear: We must take serious steps to identify relevant stakeholders and establish and maintain communications with them, not sporadically but continually, throughout the project's development.

Communicating also serves other valuable purposes. Project managers have been described as "mini billboards," the most visible evidence of the status of their project. The ways in which project managers communicate, the messages they send (intentional or unintentional), and the manner in which they discuss their projects send powerful signals to other important stakeholders about the project. Whether through developing good meeting and presentation skills, a facility for writing and speaking, or through informal networking, project managers must recognize the importance of communication and become adept at it.

One of the most critical means by which project managers can communicate is through their ability to run productive meetings. Meeting skills are important because project managers spend a large amount of time in meetings—meetings with team members, top management, clients, and other critical project stakeholders. Meetings serve a number of purposes for the project team, including these:[6]

1. They define the project and the major team players.
2. They provide an opportunity to revise, update, and add to all participants' knowledge base, including facts, perceptions, experience, judgments, and other information pertinent to the project.
3. They assist team members in understanding how their individual efforts fit into the overall whole of the project as well as how they can each contribute to project success.
4. They help all stakeholders increase their commitment to the project through participation in the management process.
5. They provide a collective opportunity to discuss the project and decide on individual work assignments.
6. They provide visibility for the project manager's role in managing the project.

As a result of the wide variety of uses meetings serve, the ability of project managers to become adept at running them in an efficient and productive manner is critical. Meetings are a key method for communicating project status, collectivizing the contributions of individual team members, developing a sense of unity and esprit de corps, and keeping all important project stakeholders up-to-date concerning the project status.[7]

Two forms of leadership behaviors are critical for effectively running project meetings. The first type of behavior is *task-oriented;* that is, it is intended to emphasize behaviors that contribute to completing project assignments, planning and scheduling activities and resources, and providing the necessary support and technical assistance. Task-oriented behavior seeks to get the job done. At the same time, effective project leaders are also concerned about *group maintenance* behavior. Group maintenance suggests that a project manager cannot act at the expense of concern for the team. Group maintenance behavior consists of supportive activities, including showing confidence and trust, acting friendly and supportive, working with subordinates to understand their problems, and recognizing their accomplishments. Group maintenance behavior increases cohesiveness, trust, and commitment, and it satisfies all team members' needs for recognition and acceptance.

Table 4.1 identifies some of the critical task and group maintenance behaviors that occur in productive project meetings. Among the important task-oriented behaviors are structuring the flow of discussion to ensure that a proper meeting agenda is followed, stimulating conversation among all meeting participants, clarifying and summarizing decisions and perceptions, and testing consensus to identify points of agreement and discord. The project manager is the key to achieving effective task behaviors, particularly through a clear sense of timing and pacing.[8] For example, pushing for consensus too quickly or stifling conversation and the free flow of ideas will be detrimental to the development of the project team and the outcomes of meetings. Likewise, continually stimulating conversation even after agreement has been achieved only serves to prolong a meeting past the point where it is productive.

Among the group maintenance behaviors that effective project leaders need to consider in running meetings are gatekeeping to ensure equal participation, harmonizing to reduce tension and promote team development, supporting by encouraging an exchange of views, regulating behavior through setting standards, and identifying and resolving any "process" problems that cause meeting participants to feel uncomfortable, hurried, or defensive. Group maintenance behaviors are just as critical as those related to task and must be addressed as part of a successful meeting strategy. Taken together, task and group maintenance

TABLE 4.1 Task and Group Maintenance Behaviors for Project Meetings[9]

Task-Oriented Behavior	Specific Outcome
1. Structuring process	Guide and sequence discussion
2. Stimulating communication	Increase information exchange
3. Clarifying communication	Increase comprehension
4. Summarizing	Check on understanding and assess progress
5. Testing consensus	Check on agreement

Group Maintenance Behavior	Specific Outcome
1. Gatekeeping	Increase and equalize participation
2. Harmonizing	Reduce tension and hostility
3. Supporting	Prevent withdrawal, encourage exchange
4. Setting standards	Regulate behavior
5. Analyzing process	Discover and resolve process problems

Source: Gary A. Yukl. *Leadership in Organizations,* 5th edition, p. 329. Copyright © 2002. Adapted by permission of Pearson Education, Inc., Upper Saddle River, NJ.

goals allow the project manager to gain the maximum benefit from meetings, which are so critical for project communication and form a constant demand on the project manager's time.

Table 4.2 paints a portrait of the roles project leaders play in project success by ranking the nine most important characteristics of effective project managers in order of importance. The data are based on a study of successful American project managers as perceived by project team members.[10] Note that the most important is the willingness of the project manager to lead by example, to highlight the project's goals, and to first commit to the challenge before calling upon other team members to make a similar commitment.

Equally interesting are findings related to the reasons why a project manager might be viewed as ineffective. These reasons include both personal quality flaws and organizational factors. Table 4.3 lists the most important personal flaws and the organizational factors that render a project manager ineffective. These factors are rank-ordered according to the percentage of respondents who identified them.

TABLE 4.2 Characteristics of Project Managers Who Lead

Rank	Characteristics of an Effective Project Manager
1	Leads by example
2	Visionary
3	Technically competent
4	Decisive
5	A good communicator
6	A good motivator
7	Stands up to top management when necessary
8	Supports team members
9	Encourages new ideas

TABLE 4.3 Characteristics of Project Managers Who Are Not Leaders

Personal Flaws	Percentage	Organizational Factors	Percentage
Sets bad example	26.3%	Lack of top management support	31.5%
Not self-assured	23.7	Resistance to change	18.4
Lacks technical expertise	19.7	Inconsistent reward system	13.2
Poor communicator	11.8	A reactive organization rather than a proactive, planning one	9.2
Poor motivator	6.6	Lack of resources	7.9

BOX 4.1

PROJECT MANAGEMENT RESEARCH IN BRIEF

Leadership and Emotional Intelligence

An interesting perspective on leadership has emerged in recent years as greater levels of research have examined the traits and abilities associated with effective project leadership. While characteristics such as technical skill, analytical ability, and intelligence are all considered important traits in project managers, an additional concept, the idea of emotional intelligence, has been suggested as a more meaningful measure of leadership effectiveness. *Emotional intelligence* refers to leaders' ability to understand that effective leadership is part of the emotional and relational transaction between subordinates and themselves. There are five elements that characterize emotional intelligence: (1) self-awareness, (2) self-regulation, (3) motivation, (4) empathy, and (5) social skill. With these traits, a project manager can develop the kind of direct, supportive relationships with the project team members that are critical to creating and guiding an effective team.

SELF-AWARENESS. Self-awareness implies having a deep understanding of one's own strengths and weaknesses, ego needs, drives, and motives. To be self-aware means to have a clear perspective of one's self; it does not mean to be excessively self-centered or self-involved. When I am self-aware, I am capable of interacting better with others because I understand how my feelings and attitudes are affecting my behavior.

SELF-REGULATION. A key ability in successful leaders is their willingness to keep themselves under control. One way each of us practices self-control is our ability to think before we act: in effect, to suspend judgment. Effective leaders are those individuals who have developed **self-regulation**; that is, the ability to reflect on events, respond to them after careful consideration, and avoid the mistake of indulging in impulsive behavior.

MOTIVATION. Effective project leaders are consistently highly motivated individuals. They are driven to achieve their maximum potential and they recognize that in order to be successful, they must also work with members of the project team to generate the maximum performance from each of them. There are two important traits of effective managers with regard to motivation: first, they are always looking for ways to keep score; that is, they like concrete or clear markers that demonstrate progress. Second, effective project managers consistently strive for greater and greater challenges.

EMPATHY. One important trait of successful project managers is their ability to recognize the differences in each of their subordinates, make allowances for those differences, and treat each team member in a manner that is designed to gain the maximum commitment from that person. **Empathy** means the willingness to consider other team members' feelings in the process of making an informed decision.

SOCIAL SKILL. The final trait of emotional intelligence, social skill, refers to a person's ability to manage relationships with others. Social skill is more than simple friendliness; it is *friendliness with a purpose*. Social skill is our ability to move people in a direction we think desirable. Among the offshoots of strong social skills are the manner in which we demonstrate persuasiveness, rapport, and building networks.

Emotional intelligence is a concept that reflects an important point: Many of the most critical project management skills that define effective leadership are not related to technical prowess, native analytical ability, or IQ. Of much greater importance are self-management skills, as reflected in self-awareness, self-regulation, and motivation and relationship management skills, shown through our empathy and social abilities. Remember: *Project management is first and foremost a people management challenge*. Once we understand the role that leadership behaviors play in effective project management, we can better identify the ways in which we can use leadership to promote our projects.[11]

4.3 TRAITS OF EFFECTIVE PROJECT LEADERS

A great deal of research on organizational leadership has been aimed at uncovering the traits that are specific to leaders. Because leaders are not the same thing as managers, they are found in all walks of life and occupying all levels of organizational hierarchies. A study that sought to uncover the traits that most managers believe leaders should possess is particularly illuminating. A large sample survey was used to ask a total of 2,615 managers within U.S. corporations what they considered to be the most important characteristics of effective leaders.[12]

The results of this survey are intriguing. A significant majority of managers felt that the most important characteristic of superior leaders was basic honesty. They sought leaders who say what they mean and live up to their promises. In addition, they sought competence and intelligence, vision, inspiration, fairness, imagination, and dependability, to list a few of the most important characteristics. These traits offer an important starting point for better understanding how leaders operate and, more importantly, how the other members of the project team or organization expect them to operate. Clearly, the most important factors we seek in leaders are the dimensions of trust, strength of character, and the intelligence and competence to succeed. The expectation of success is also important; the majority of followers do not tag along after failing project managers for very long.

Research also has been done that is specifically related to project managers and the leadership traits necessary to be successful in this more specialized arena. Three studies in particular shed some valuable light on the nature of the special demands that project managers face and the concomitant nature of the leadership characteristics they must develop. One study analyzed data from a number of sources and synthesized a set of factors that most effective project leaders shared in common.[13] It identified five important characteristics for proficient project management: oral communication skills; influencing skills; intellectual capabilities; the ability to handle stress; and diverse management skills, including planning, delegation, and decision making. These findings correlate with the fact that most project managers do not have the capacity to exercise power that derives from formal positional authority, and consequently, they are forced to develop effective influencing skills.

The second study also identified five characteristics closely associated with effective project team leaders:[14]

- *Credibility:* Is the project manager trustworthy and taken seriously by both the project team and the parent organization?
- *Creative problem-solver:* Is the project manager skilled at problem analysis and identification?
- *Tolerance for ambiguity:* Is the project manager adversely affected by complex or ambiguous (uncertain) situations?
- *Flexible management style:* Is the project manager able to handle rapidly changing situations?
- *Effective communication skills:* Is the project manager able to operate as the focal point for communication from a variety of stakeholders?

The final study of necessary abilities for effective project managers collected data from 58 firms on their project management practices and the skills most important for project managers.[15] The researchers found seven essential project manager abilities, including:

1. *Organizing under conflict:* Project managers need the abilities to delegate, manage their time, and handle conflict and criticism.
2. *Experience:* Having knowledge of project management and other organizational procedures, experience with technical challenges, and a background as a leader are helpful.
3. *Decision making:* Project managers require sound judgment, systematic analytical ability, and decision-making skills.
4. *Productive creativity:* This ability refers to the need for project managers to show creativity, develop and implement innovative ideas, and challenge the old, established order.
5. *Organizing with cooperation:* Project managers must be willing to create a positive team atmosphere, demonstrate a willingness to learn, and engage in positive interpersonal contact.
6. *Cooperative leadership:* This skill refers to the project manager's ability to motivate others, to cooperate, and to express ideas clearly.
7. *Integrative thinking:* Project managers need to be able to think analytically and to involve others in the decision-making process.

Conclusions About Project Leaders

Given the wide-ranging views, it is important to note the commonalities across these studies and to draw some general conclusions about the nature of project leadership. The specific conclusions that have practical relevance to selecting and training effective project leaders suggest several themes, including:

- Effective project managers must be good communicators.
- Project leaders must possess the flexibility to respond to uncertain or ambiguous situations with a minimum of stress.
- Strong project leaders work well with and through their project team.
- Good project leaders are skilled at various influence tactics.

Although examining the traits of successful leaders, and specifically project leaders, is valuable, it presents only part of the picture. One key to understanding leadership behavior is to focus on *what leaders do* rather than who they are.

PROJECT PROFILE

Dr. Elattuvalapil Sreedharan, India's Project Management Rock Star

The capital of India, Delhi, is a city of amazing contrasts. Home to 17 million people, many living in abject poverty, the city boasts some of the country's leading high-tech centers for industry and higher learning. Traffic snarls are notorious, and pollution levels are high as the city's 7,500 buses slowly navigate crowded streets. Like other urban centers in India, Delhi desperately needs enhanced infrastructure and a commuter rail system. Unfortunately, India's track record for large-capital projects is poor; there are many examples of projects that have run well over budget and behind schedule (refer to the Dulhasti Power cases in this text). A recent example highlights the continuing problems with managing infrastructure projects in India. Delhi launched a multiyear project to host the Commonwealth Games in the fall of 2010, a sporting event bringing together athletes from 71 territories and countries associated with the former British Empire. Unfortunately, problems with sanitation, inadequate construction, numerous delays, and poor planning left the country with a very visible black eye and reinforced the popular view that large-scale infrastructure projects in India are, at best, a chancy venture.

The good news is that all is not as bad as it seems. Delhi recently completed the first phase of a huge project, the $2.3 billion Delhi Metro. The rail line planned for this phase, covering nearly 40 miles, was finished three years *ahead* of schedule. So unexpected was this circumstance that it lead *BusinessWeek* magazine to label the project's leader, Elattuvalapil Sreedharan, "a miracle worker." So what has been the secret of Sreedharan's success, especially in a land where so many before him have failed in similar ventures?

First, he says, is the importance of accountability. "One of the biggest impediments to the timely completion of infrastructure projects in India today is a lack of focus and accountability." Poor performers are not held responsible for failure to hit their targets, so where is the incentive to be on time? According to Sreedharan, his organization took a different approach: "The organization's mission and culture include clearly defined objectives and a vision, which was to complete the project on time and within the budget without causing inconvenience to the public." Sreedharan also has almost an obsession with deadlines. Every officer in the Metro project keeps a digital board that shows the number of days left for the completion of the next target. Another critical element in his

PRAKASH SINGH/AFP/Getty Images/Newscom

FIGURE 4.3 **Dr. E. Sreedharan in One of the Delhi Metro Tunnels**

(continued)

success has been meticulous advance planning. Shreeharan said, "All tenders (bids) from contractors are decided very fast, sometimes in 18 or 19 days. [I]t is essential to lay down the criteria for settling tenders clearly in advance."

Finally, Sreedharan is adamant about transparency and constant communication with all project stakeholders. Under his watch, the project maintains open communication with all contractors, updating them about plans and holding frequent meetings and workshops. A unique feature of the Delhi Metro project is that it has held nearly a hundred "community interaction programs" (CIPs), which are open forums during which local residents are given the chance to discuss aspects of the construction that could affect them. The CIP meetings are designed to allow advocacy groups, neighborhood organizations, and other stakeholders to share ideas, air grievances, and ask questions as the project moves forward. Regarding the questions from CIP meetings, Sreedharan comments, "Most of them are resolved on the spot, while necessary action and remedial measures are taken on the rest." Sreedharan's team has used this transparency and open communication approach to allay the concerns of affected groups and spur their cooperation with the project rather than their antagonism.

The total project is designed to be rolled out in four phases, with a total coverage of 152 miles when finished. The final phase is due to be completed in 2020. The Metro project is currently in the midst of its phase two goals. Sreedharan, over 70 years old, is unsure how much longer he will personally supervise the project, but he has no doubt about the secrets to success as a project manager. "I believe that there are three basic qualities for a successful life," he notes, "punctuality, integrity and good morals, and professional competence. The future of India will be in good hands if these qualities are assiduously nurtured by the youth of our nation."[16]

Leading and Time Orientation

Recent work on the concept of time orientation has some interesting implications for project leadership behavior. **Time orientation** refers to the temporal context or space to which an individual is oriented. Specifically, researchers have long argued that each of us has a natural tendency to focus on one of three time orientations: past, present, or future. This **temporal alignment** has the effect of influencing our behaviors and causes each of us to perform some tasks well, while making others more difficult. For example, if your time orientation is future-directed, it is easier to engage in planning. On the other hand, you might find it harder to do tasks such as performance appraisals because they require you to be able to recapture past events. The ability of project managers to engage in temporal alignment with the tasks they face is an important skill that they need to develop.

Table 4.4 identifies some concepts in temporal alignment and skills that have significant implications for project managers. Temporal alignment includes five elements: time line orientation, future time perspective, time span, polychronic/monochronic preference, and time conception. The temporal skills and abilities needed to perform certain tasks include **time warping,** creating future vision, **chunking time, predicting,** and recapturing the past.

TABLE 4.4 Temporal Alignment and Temporal Skills

Temporal Alignment

- Time line orientation—The temporal context or space in time (past, present, or future) in which an individual most often sees him or herself.
- Future time perspective—The extent to which the future drives an individual's current behavior.
- Time span—The amount of future time one is capable of capturing in one's mind.
- Polychronic/monochronic preference—A desire for doing more than one thing at a time, or only one thing at a time.
- Time conception—A set of beliefs about the nature of time and life, cyclical (life repeats itself) or linear (life proceeds in a straight line, always forward).

Temporal Skills

- Time warping—Cognitively bringing the past and future closer to the present.
- Creating future vision—Creating an image of a project in the future.
- Chunking time—Creating units of future time to be used for scheduling.
- Predicting—Generating estimates of what will occur in the future.
- Recapturing the past—Remembering and using information from the past.

TABLE 4.5 Time-Related Project Leader Duties

	Project Leader Duty	Temporal Skill Needed
A. Past-oriented tasks	Project problem solving	Recapturing the past
	Team member evaluation	Recapturing the past
	Lessons-learned meetings	Recapturing the past
B. Present-oriented tasks	Scheduling	Time warping
	Managing multiple project problems	Polychromicity
C. Future-oriented tasks	Contingency planning	Time warping
		Predicting
	Creating a vision for the project	Creating future vision

Time orientation is a useful concept to consider when developing project management skills because it highlights some salient facts: (1) Each of us prefers certain time orientations, either **past, present,** or **future;** (2) these preferred orientations have some associated strengths and drawbacks when it comes to managing projects; and (3) we need to recognize that effective project management often requires us to be comfortable with other, nonpreferred time orientations. Let's consider each of these facts in turn.

1. We each have time orientation preferences, either toward the past, present, or future.

    Research in psychology has established the fact that individual personalities differ in terms of time orientation.[17] Some of us prefer to adopt a future time perspective, while others maintain a present or past time preference. Having a preference predisposes us to perform some activities well while either avoiding or doing the minimum in other areas.

2. Each time orientation has associated strengths and weaknesses for managing projects.

    Research suggests that the preferred time orientation each of us possesses naturally inclines us to perform some project management activities well and others with greater difficulty or unwillingness. Table 4.5 illustrates this notion. Note that some activities related to past time orientation, such as project problem solving or team member evaluation, directly draw on our ability to recapture the past. Think of a project lessons-learned meeting during the termination phase. It is precisely at times such as this that the ability to recapture past events, typically associated with past time orientation, is so valuable. Conversely, future time orientation, requiring skills such as time warping or predicting, is critical to our ability to handle contingency planning.

3. Effective project management requires that we develop skills in other time orientation modes.

As Table 4.5 demonstrates, while we may each have a preferred time orientation that makes certain tasks easier or harder to perform, as leaders we need to develop the full range of our skills, suggesting that we at least develop a basic expertise in all temporal skills. The first step in this process often lies in developing a clearer idea of our strengths and weaknesses with regard to temporal orientation. Then we can begin to refine our skills in the orientation that is particularly difficult for us. Successful project managers recognize the importance of operating from a perspective that includes past, present, and future time orientations.

4.4 PROJECT CHAMPIONS

Dr. Thomas Simpson (not his real name) came back from a recent medical conference enthusiastic about an innovative technique that he felt sure was just right for his hospital. He had witnessed the use of information system technology that allowed doctors to link wirelessly with patient records, retrieve documentation, and place prescription orders online. With this system, a doctor could directly input symptoms and treatment protocols on a laptop in the patient's room. The benefit of the new system was that it significantly upgraded the hospital's approach to patient record keeping while providing the doctor with more immediate flexibility in treatment options.

As chief of the medical staff, Dr. Simpson had some influence in Grace Hospital, but he could not simply order the hospital to adopt the technology. Instead, over a period of six months, he worked tirelessly to promote the system, setting up information seminars with the software designers and question-and-answer sessions with the hospital's administration and other important stakeholders. Eventually, his persistence paid off. The hospital adopted the technology and has been using it for the past two years. In spite of some start-up problems resulting from the need to transfer old paper records to the system, Grace Hospital now brags that it is "paper-record" free, and all because of Dr. Simpson's efforts.

In this example, Dr. Simpson displayed all the qualities of a project champion. Champions, sometimes referred to as project sponsors, are well known both in the organizational theory literature and within organizations themselves. A **champion** is an individual who "identifies with a new development (whether or not he made it), using all the weapons at his command, against the funded resistance of the organization. He functions as an entrepreneur within the organization, and since he does not have official authority to take unnecessary risks…he puts his job in the organization (and often his standing) on the line…. He (has) great energy and capacity to invite and withstand disapproval."[18]

Champions possess some remarkable characteristics. First, it is assumed (in fact, almost expected) that champions will operate without the officially sanctioned approval of their organizations. Often they set themselves directly at odds with the established order or popular way of thinking. Standard operating procedures are anathema to champions, and they are usually unafraid of official disapproval. Second, champions have a true entrepreneurial talent for recognizing value in innovative ideas or products; they see things the typical organizational member does not. Third, champions are risk takers in every sense of the word. Their single-minded pursuit of truth in whatever innovative form it may take often puts them at odds with entrenched bureaucrats and those who do not share their enthusiasm for a new product or idea.

Capturing the enthusiasm and fervor that champions have for their ideas is difficult. Tom Peters, bestselling author, describes champions as "fanatics" in their single-minded pursuit of their pet ideas. He states, "The people who are tenacious, committed champions are often a royal pain in the neck…. They must be fostered and nurtured—even when it hurts."[19] This statement captures the essence of the personality and impact of the champion: one who is at the same time an organizational gadfly and vitally important for project and organizational success.

Champions—Who Are They?

Champions do not consistently occupy the same positions within organizations. Although senior managers often serve as champions, many members of the organization can play the role of implementation champion, with different systems or at different times with the same system implementation project. Among the most common specific types of champions are creative originator, entrepreneur, godfather or sponsor, and project manager.[20]

CREATIVE ORIGINATOR   The **creative originator** is usually an engineer, scientist, or similar person who is the source of and driving force behind the idea. The fact that the individual who was behind the original development of the idea or technology can function as the project champion is hardly surprising. No one in the organization has more expertise or sense of vision where the new information system is concerned. Few others possess the technical or creative ability to develop the implementation effort through to fruition. Consequently, many organizations allow, and even actively encourage, the continued involvement of the scientist or engineer who originally developed the idea upon which the project is based.

ENTREPRENEUR   An **entrepreneur** is the person who adopts the idea or technology and actively works to sell the system throughout the organization, eventually pushing it to success. In many organizations, it is not possible, for a variety of reasons, for the creative originator or original project advocate to assume the role of champion. Often, scientists, technicians, and engineers are limited by their need to perform the specifically demarcated duties of their positions, and thereby precluded from becoming part of the project implementation team. In such situations, the individual who steps forward as the implementation champion is referred to as an *organizational entrepreneur*. The entrepreneur is an organizational member who recognizes the value of the original idea or technology and makes it a personal goal to gain its acceptance throughout the relevant organizational units that would be employing it. Entrepreneurial champions are usually middle- to upper-level managers who may or may not have technical backgrounds. In addition to performing their own duties within the organization, they are constantly on the lookout for innovative and useful ideas to develop.

"GODFATHER" OR SPONSOR   The project champion as **godfather** is a senior-level manager who does everything possible to promote the project, including obtaining the needed resources, coaching the project team when problems arise, calming the political waters, and protecting the project when necessary.

A **sponsor** has elected to actively support acquisition and implementation of the new technology and to do everything in his power to facilitate this process. One of the most important functions of godfathers is to make it known throughout the organization that this project is under their personal guidance or protection. In addition to supplying this "protection," the godfather engages in a variety of activities of a more substantial nature in helping the implementation effort succeed. Godfathers also use their influence to coach the team when problems arise in order to decrease the likelihood of political problems derailing the project.

PROJECT MANAGER   Another member of the organization who may play the role of champion is the project manager. At one time or another, almost every project manager has undertaken the role of champion. When one considers the definition of a project champion and the wide range of duties performed in that role, it becomes clear why the manager of the project is often in the position to engage in championing behaviors. Certainly, project managers are strongly identified with their projects, and to a degree their careers are directly tied to the successful completion of their projects. Project managers, however, may have limited effectiveness as champions if they do not possess a higher, organization-wide status that makes it possible for them to serve as project advocates at upper management levels. For example, a project manager may not have the authority to secure additional project resources or gain support throughout the larger organization.

What Do Champions Do?

What exactly do champions do to aid the implementation process? Table 4.6 lists two sets of championing activities that were identified by one study through its survey of a sample of project managers.

The first set of activities is commonly thought of as the "traditional" duties of managers. The champion can actively aid in the project development process by interpreting technical details, providing strong leadership, helping with project coordination and control, as well as supplying administrative help for the project team. It is important that the champion be familiar with the technical aspects of the project. Another important traditional activity of the project champion is the procurement of necessary resources to enable team members to perform their tasks. Champions are often in an excellent position to make available a continual supply of logistical support for the project.

The second set of activities in which champions engage is referred to as the "nontraditional" side of management, which implies that these activities are not part of the usual roles identified in traditional management literature. That does not mean, however, that these activities are in any way unnecessary or eccentric. In fact, several champions have reported that these duties are just as important for project success as the more frequently identified, well-known requirements for successful management. Performing functions such as cheerleader, visionary, politician, risk taker, and ambassador is important for most project

TABLE 4.6 Traditional and Nontraditional Roles of Project Champions

Traditional Duties	
Technical understanding	Knowledge of the technical aspects involved in developing the project
Leadership	Ability to provide leadership for the project team
Coordination and control	Managing and controlling the activities of the team
Obtaining resources	Gaining access to the necessary resources to ensure a smooth development process
Administrative	Handling the important administrative side of the project
Nontraditional Duties	
Cheerleader	Providing the needed enthusiasm (spiritual driving force) for the team
Visionary	Maintaining a clear sense of purpose and a firm idea of what is involved in creating the project
Politician	Employing the necessary political tactics and networking to ensure broad acceptance and cooperation with the project
Risk taker	Being willing to take calculated personal or career risks to support the project
Ambassador	Maintaining good relations with all project stakeholders

Source: J. K. Pinto and D. P. Slevin. (1988). "The project champion: Key to implementation success," *Project Management Journal,* 20(4): 15–20. Copyright © 1988 by Project Management Institute Publications. Copyright and all rights reserved. Material from this publication has been reproduced with the permission of PMI.

managers, and yet these roles tend to be deemphasized in literature, job specifications, and training programs. As one champion put it, "We can teach people those (traditional) skills easily enough, but experience is the best teacher for the other (nontraditional) duties. *No one prepares you for the irrational side of this job. You have to pick it up as you go.*"

In many organizations, the majority of a champion's time is not engaged in performing the traditional side of project management duties, but rather is involved in the "nontraditional" activities. The champion is often the person with the vision, the cheerleader, or the driving force behind the project. Additionally, the champion is expected to take on the key political roles in attempting to play the right kinds of games, make the right contacts, and network with the necessary people to ensure a steady supply of resources necessary for the project to succeed. Finally, because champions, by definition, strongly identify with the project, much of their time is spent in networking with other organizational units, top management, and prospective clients (users) of the project. In this task, they take on an important ambassador/advocate role throughout the organization. In many cases, champions put their careers on the line to support and gain acceptance of a new system and, as a result, become committed to aiding the project in every way possible, through both traditional and nontraditional activities.

One question often asked is whether this type of behavior really plays an important role in successful project management. The answer is an emphatic "yes." Aside from anecdotal and case study information, some compelling research studies have helped us better understand not only what champions do, but how important champions are for acquiring and gaining organizational acceptance of new projects.[21] One study, for example, examined a series of new product developments and start-ups at a variety of organizations.[22] The relationship between the presence or absence of an identifiable organizational champion and the success of the project was studied for 45 new product development efforts. Of the 17 successful new product developments, all but one, or 94%, had a readily identifiable champion. These ventures were spearheaded by an individual that the majority of those involved in the project could point to and identify as that project's sponsor or champion. On the other hand, of the 28 projects that failed, only one was coupled with an identifiable project champion. Clearly, the results of this study point to the enormously important role that a champion can play in new product development.

How to Make a Champion

All organizations differ in terms of the availability of individuals to take on the role of a project champion. Although some organizations have a supply of enthusiastic personnel at all levels willing to serve as champions, the reality for most organizations is not nearly so upbeat. The fault, in this case, is not that these organizations have inadequate or unskilled people. Very often, the problem is that the organizations have failed to recognize the benefits to be derived from champions. Champions and a climate within which they can exist must be developed and nurtured by the organization.

Some important principles and options for organizations to recognize in the development and use of project champions include identify and encourage the emergence of champions, encourage and reward risk takers, remember that champions are connected emotionally to their projects, and avoid tying champions too closely to traditional project management duties.[23]

IDENTIFY AND ENCOURAGE THE EMERGENCE OF CHAMPIONS   In many companies, there are individuals who demonstrate the enthusiasm and drive to champion new project ideas. It is important for these organizations to develop a culture that not only tolerates but actively promotes champions. In many organizations, a creative originator who continually badgered upper management with a new project idea would likely offend some of the key top management team. However, for a firm to realize the full potential of its internal champions, it must create a culture of support in which champions feel they can work without excessive criticism or oversight.

ENCOURAGE AND REWARD RISK TAKERS   Jack Welch, former CEO of General Electric, made it a personal crusade to actively encourage senior, middle, and even junior managers to take risks. His argument was that innovation does not come without risk; if one cannot bear to take risks, one cannot innovate. The corollary to encouraging risk taking is to avoid the knee-jerk response of immediately seeking culprits and punishing them for project failures. Innovations are, by definition, risky ventures. They can result in tremendous payoffs, but they also have a very real possibility of failure. Organizations have to become more aware of the positive effects of encouraging individuals to take risks and assume championing roles in innovative projects. One project success will often pay for 10 project failures.

REMEMBER THAT CHAMPIONS ARE CONNECTED EMOTIONALLY TO THEIR PROJECTS   Champions bring a great deal of energy and emotional commitment to their project ideas; however, a potential downside of the use of powerful project champions is the fact that often they refuse to give up, even in the face of a genuine project failure. As a result, many companies keep pursuing "dogs" long after any hope for successful completion or commercial success is past. For example, Microsoft introduced their "Kin" cellphone in 2010 and marketed it particularly to teens and fans of social networking. The Kin was not a "smartphone," however; it did not support apps or games, and was expensive to operate. In spite of Microsoft's best efforts, it quickly failed in the marketplace and was abandoned only two months after its introduction. Microsoft executive, Robbie Bach, mastermind behind the Kin device, left the company soon afterward.

DON'T TIE CHAMPIONS TOO TIGHTLY TO TRADITIONAL PROJECT MANAGEMENT DUTIES   Project champions and project managers may be the same people, but often they are not. Many times classic champions, as Table 4.6 demonstrated, are more comfortable supporting a project through nontraditional activities. Because they tend to be visionaries, cheerleaders, and risk takers, they approach their goal with a single-minded strength of purpose and a sense of the overall design and strategy for the new technology. Rather than supporting the more routine aspects of project management, such as planning and scheduling, allocating resources, and handling the administrative details, the champions' expertise and true value to the implementation process may be in their political connections and contributions, that is, in employing their nontraditional management skills.

BOX 4.2

PROJECT MANAGERS IN PRACTICE

Julie Slater and Kerry Anderson, CLLM

The nonprofit sector of the Australian economy is large and diverse, contributing approximately $21 billion to the Australian gross domestic product (GDP). Community Leadership Loddon Murray Inc. (CLLM) is a not-for-profit incorporated association that began operation in 1998 in North Central Victoria, Australia, to build local community leadership capacity to benefit the communities of central and northwest Victoria. The aim of CLLM is to develop leaders for vibrant and sustainable communities by engaging, encouraging, and empowering members of the community in leadership roles at regional, state, and national levels. The CEO, Julie Slater, is proud that CLLM is truly a project-based organization aimed at developing intensive leadership skills.

FIGURE 4.4   **Julie Slater and Kerry Anderson, CLLM**

(continued)

Kerry Anderson, CLLM's Projects Manager, does not just manage the organization's leadership graduate program but also regularly organizes special interest projects for the community. Some of the flagship projects have included "The Big Conversation," which encouraged irrigators to share ideas and discuss common issues faced on the Murray Darling Basin Project (details available at www.cllm.org.au/projects_2010.htm), and "LeadAbility for Women," which brought together women with a range of disabilities and successfully built on their skills, confidence, networks with similar women, and knowledge of regional issues (details available at www.cllm.org.au/LeadAbility.htm). Along with others, these successful projects have demonstrated leadership competencies by addressing fundamental community issues and simultaneously developing leadership skills through project management.

Julie Slater, CLLM's CEO, says that the involvement of key community stakeholders who play a project champion role is a secret of CLLM's project success. Of particular interest, local leaders involved with the project "Operation Next Gen" (details available at www.cllm.org.au/operationnextgen.htm) have taken on some nontraditional project champion duties, such as acting as ambassadors to inspire young people to find meaningful employment in their small towns.

Both Slater and Anderson play important leadership roles in their organization's projects. Slater focuses on project governance. CLLM projects are funded by state and federal governmental bodies, a situation which creates extra decision layers that can cause project delays. By effectively managing service delivery outcomes, Slater delivers timely project decision making. She also coordinates and controls the projects to ensure that public funds are appropriately utilized.

Anderson's role is to manage the stakeholders of each project effectively and to work with a diverse volunteer resource pool. Like most nonprofit communities, CLLM does work that is social in nature. Anderson is adept at managing the social and technical resources within CLLM, seeking funding opportunities through grant applications and forming partnerships with other organizations in the region.

The projects led by CLLM are often about change or designed to initiate change. Both Slater and Anderson see themselves as change project leaders and use their emotional competence to deal with the challenges of advocating complex changes in the community sector. Anderson believes her soft skills in building stakeholder relationships and communication helped her bring together farmers facing water irrigation issues in the "The Big Conversation" project. By understanding the sensitivity of the water issues and the tension among farmers, Anderson was able to create a steering committee of local farmers who were willing to share their knowledge and start difficult conversations. Rather than leading the project herself, she played a backstage role.

Slater's aim for the leadership program is to develop a "Skillsbank": a compendium-of-skills database of graduates. The program can boast that, apart from promoting the technical strengths of the leadership graduates, it brings out the strengths of individuals and helps them to identify their weaknesses. By helping those in the program to develop soft skills such as self-awareness, the program ensures that through project management, community leaders can exercise empathy and build trust to correlate with their vision of building sustainable communities.

Julie Slater and Kerry Anderson stand strong as leaders, with a passion for building a strong community through various projects that shine in leadership capacity.

4.5 THE NEW PROJECT LEADERSHIP

Project management requires us to harness our abilities to lead others. These skills may or (more likely) may not be innate; that is, for the majority of us, leadership is not something that we were born with. However, we know enough about the leadership challenge to recognize that leaders are as leaders do.[24] The more we begin to recognize and practice appropriate leadership roles, the more naturally these activities will come to us. An article by one of the top writers on organizational leadership, Dr. Warren Bennis, summarizes four competencies that determine our success as project leaders:[25]

1. *The new leader understands and practices the power of appreciation. These project leaders are connoisseurs of talent, more curators than creators.* Appreciation derives from our ability to recognize and reward the talent of others. Leaders may not be the best, most valuable, or most intelligent members of project teams. Their role is not to outshine others but to allow others to develop to their best potential.

2. *The new leader keeps reminding people what's important.* This simple statement carries a powerful message for project managers. We need to remember that in pursuing a project, a host of problems, difficulties, annoyances, and technical and human challenges are likely to arise. Often numerous problems are uncovered during projects that were not apparent until after serious work began. Project managers must remember that one of their most important contributions is reminding people to keep their eyes fixed on the ultimate prize, in effect, continually reminding them what is important.

3. *The new leader generates and sustains trust.* The research by Kouzes and Posner cited earlier in this chapter contains a powerful message: The most important characteristic looked for in leaders is honesty.[26] Leaders who generate trust and behave with authenticity, fairness, honesty, and caring will be

successful in creating an environment in which the project team members strive to do their best. Trust plays a critical role in developing productive leader-member relationships.[27] It is only by recognizing and applying trustworthiness that we demonstrate the loyalty and commitment to our team members as individuals that will bring out the best in them.

4. ***The new leader and the led are intimate allies.*** Earlier in this chapter we examined the concept of a partnership existing between the leader and followers. This point is important and should be emphasized in effective leadership behaviors. Project management leadership does not arise in order to control and dominate the project team, but as a natural method for supporting the team's efforts. As we work to develop leadership abilities, it is important to first recognize the reasons why leadership is necessary for project success and then take the concrete steps needed to realize the vision of the project, something we can best do when we as leaders work in close harmony with our teams.

PROJECT PROFILE

The Challenge of Managing Internationally

As project management becomes an internationalized phenomenon, it is critical for successful leaders to recognize their management style and make necessary accommodations when dealing with project team members from other countries. The current generation of project managers is discovering that international work is not a mysterious or infrequent event; in fact, it is the everyday reality for project managers in many project-based organizations. What are some of the important lessons that all project managers need to take to heart when working overseas? One list is offered by a successful project manager, Giancarlo Duranti. A native of Italy, Duranti has experience leading teams in Brazil, Cuba, and Gambia. Among his suggestions for making the right leadership choices in foreign settings are:

1. ***Develop a detailed understanding of the environment.*** Educate yourself on the setting in which you will be working by viewing documentaries and reading travel guides, tourist books, and even local newspapers. History is equally important: The better you understand the past of a particular culture, the sooner you can begin to understand team attitudes and perceptions.
2. ***Do not stereotype.*** It is easy to approach a foreign setting with preconceived notions about its people, culture, weather, and food. Without allowing ourselves to experience a setting for the "first time," it is difficult to avoid forming easy and, ultimately, useless opinions.
3. ***Be genuinely interested in cultural differences.*** People are eager to share local and national traditions and, in turn, have a curiosity about yours. Demonstrating a real interest in their culture and sharing your own helps both sides to appreciate these differences rather than be separated by them.
4. ***Do not assume there is one way (yours) to communicate.*** Communication differences among cultures are profound. Remember, for example, that use of humor and ways of giving feedback, including correction, differ greatly among cultures. Learn to appreciate alternative means of exchanging information and to recognize what is "really" being said in various exchanges.
5. ***Listen actively and empathetically.*** Suspend judgment when listening and try to view each situation with some distance and perspective.[28]

4.6 PROJECT MANAGEMENT PROFESSIONALISM

At the beginning of 2003, the U.S. Department of Energy kicked off an internal initiative to create a project management career path within its organization. The launch followed similar moves by a variety of organizations, from firms as diverse as Ernst & Young (consulting) to NASA. Bruce Carnes at the Department of Energy explained the reasoning for this move:

> Much of our work is accomplished through projects. In fact, our project managers are currently responsible for over 100 projects with a total value in excess of $20 billion, plus another $150 billion in environmental restoration work over the next several decades. It's important for us to make sure that our project managers have the best skills possible, and that each person is treated as a critical DoE asset. Therefore, we need a cohesive career management plan to develop them, match their skills with assignments, track their performance, and reward them as appropriate.[29]

Embedded in this explanation are several important points that illustrate the growing **professionalism** of the project management discipline. Let's consider them in turn.[30]

First, for more and more organizations, project work is becoming the standard. Projects are no longer simply additional and nonroutine components of organizational life; in many organizations they are becoming the principal means by which the organizations accomplish their goals. Along with the increased recognition of the importance of using project management techniques comes the concomitant need to acquire, train, and maintain a cadre of project management professionals who are dedicated to these work assignments.

Second, there is a critical need to upgrade the skills of those doing project work. It would be a mistake to continually apply organizational resources, particularly human resources, to projects without ensuring that they are learning, developing their project skills, and approaching these tasks with a solid foundation of knowledge. In short, one of the aspects of professionalism is to recognize that project management professionals are not an ad hoc feature of the organization, but a critical resource to be developed and maintained. Therefore, it is important to support these individuals as a resource that requires continual training and skill development.

Third, project management professionalism recognizes the need to create a clear career path for those who serve as project managers and support personnel. Historically, organizations "found" their project managers from among their line management staff and assigned them the responsibility to complete the project, always with the assumption that once the project was finished, the managers would return to their normal functional duties. In short, project management was a temporary assignment, and once it was completed, the manager was returned to "real" duties. In the new professionalism model, project management personnel view project work as a permanent career assignment, with managers moving from project to project, but always dedicated to this career path. Increasingly companies are officially distinguishing between their functional staff and their project management professionals, resisting the urge to move people back and forth between project assignments and functional duties.

This new professionalism mentality is typified by the experiences of NASA, particularly in the wake of the 1986 *Challenger* shuttle disaster. Following the lessons learned from that terrible event, NASA determined that there was a permanent need for a dedicated and embedded professional project management group within the organization. Ed Hoffman, who serves as the director of NASA's Academy of Program and Project Leadership, makes this point: "The NASA mind-set sees the project approach as the only way to do business. We are constantly charged with meeting cost and timeline challenges that require the cooperation of a variety of disciplines. Frankly, our folks would be confused by a functional approach."[31]

What practical steps can organizations take to begin developing a core of project management professionals? Some of the suggested strategies include the following:

- ***Begin to match personalities to project work.*** Research suggests that certain personality types may be more accepting of project work than others.[32] For example, outgoing, people-oriented individuals are felt to have a better likelihood of performing well on projects than quieter, more introverted people. Likewise, people with a greater capacity for working in an unstructured and dynamic setting are more attuned to project work than those who require structure and formal work rules. As a starting point, it may be useful to conduct some basic personality assessments of potential project resources to assess their psychological receptiveness to the work.

- ***Formalize the organization's commitment to project work with training programs.*** There is little doubt that organizational members can recognize a firm's commitment to projects by the firm's willingness to support the training and development of personnel in the skills needed for them. For training to be effective, however, several elements are necessary. First, a corporate-wide audit should be conducted to determine what critical skills are necessary for running projects. Second, the audit should determine the degree to which organizational members possess those skills. Third, where there are clear differences between the skill set needed and the skills available, project management training should first be targeted to reduce those gaps—in effect, bringing project management training into alignment with project management needs.

- ***Develop a reward system for project management that differentiates it from normal functional reward schedules.*** The types of rewards, whether promotions, bonuses, or other forms of recognition, available to project management personnel need to reflect the differences in the types of jobs they do compared to the work done by regular members of the organization. For example, in many project companies, performance bonuses are available for project team members but not for functional personnel. Likewise, raises or promotions in project firms are often based directly on the results of projects the team members have worked on. Thus, within the same organization, functional members may be promoted due to the amount of time they have been at one managerial level, while their project professional counterparts are promoted solely due to their accumulated performance on multiple projects.

- *Identify a distinct career path for project professionals.* One rather cynical project manager once noted to this author, "In our organization there are two career ladders. Unfortunately, only one of them has rungs!" His point was that excellent performance on projects did not earn individuals any rewards, particularly in terms of promotions. In his firm, projects were "a place where mediocre managers go to die." Contrast this example with that of Bechtel Corporation, in which project management is viewed as a critical resource, project management personnel are carefully evaluated, and superior performance is rewarded. Most particularly, Bechtel has a dual-track career path that allows successful project managers the same opportunities as other functional managers to move upward in the company.

Project professionalism recognizes that the enhanced interest in project management as a discipline has led to the need to create a resource pool of trained individuals for the organization to use. In short, we are seeing an example of supply and demand at work. As more and more organizations begin to apply project techniques in their operations, they will increase the need for sufficient, trained individuals to perform these tasks. One of the best sources of expertise in project management comes from inside these organizations, provided they take the necessary steps to nurture and foster an attitude of professionalism among their project management staff.

This chapter began with the proposition that project management is a "leader-intensive" undertaking; that is, few activities within organizations today depend more on the performance and commitment of a strong leader than do projects. Through exploration of the types of duties project managers must undertake, the characteristics of effective project leaders, the role of emotional intelligence in managing projects well, the concepts of project championing behavior, and the essence of the new project leadership, this chapter has painted a picture of the diverse and challenging duties that project managers are expected to undertake as they pursue project success. When we endeavor to develop our leadership skills to their highest potential, the challenge is significant but the payoffs are enormous.

Summary

1. **Understand how project management is a "leader-intensive" profession.** Project management is leader-intensive because the project manager, as the leader, plays a central role in the development of the project. The project manager is the conduit for information and communication flows, the principal planner and goal setter, the team developer, motivator, and conflict resolver, and so forth. Without the commitment of an energetic project leader, it is very unlikely the project will be successfully completed.

2. **Distinguish between the role of a manager and the characteristics of a leader.** The manager's role in an organization is characterized as one of positional authority. Managers receive titles that give them the right to exercise control over the behavior of others, they focus more on the administration and organization of the project, and they seek efficiency and maintaining the status quo. Leaders focus on interpersonal relationships, developing and inspiring others with their vision of the project and the future. They embrace change, motivate others, communicate by word and deed, and focus on the effectiveness of outcomes and long-term risk taking.

3. **Understand the concept of emotional intelligence as it relates to how project managers lead.** Five dimensions of emotional intelligence relate to project leadership: (1) self-awareness—one's understanding of strengths and weaknesses that provides perspective, (2) self-regulation—the ability to keep oneself under control by thinking before acting and suspending immediate judgment, (3) motivation—all successful leaders demonstrate first their own degree of motivation before they can inspire it in others, (4) empathy—the ability to recognize the differences in each subordinate and treat each team member in a way that is designed to gain the maximum commitment, and (5) social skill—friendliness with the purpose of moving people in a direction thought desirable.

4. **Recognize traits that are strongly linked to effective project leadership.** A number of leadership traits are strongly linked to effective project leadership, including (1) credibility or honesty, (2) problem-solving abilities, (3) tolerance for complexity and ambiguity, (4) flexibility in managing subordinates, (5) communication skills, (6) creativity, (7) decision-making

abilities, (8) experience, (9) the ability to work well through the project team, and (10) strong influence skills.

5. **Understand the implications of time orientation in project management.**   Time orientation suggests that each of us has a preferred temporal orientation, either to past, present, or future perspectives. This orientation makes some of the duties of project managers easier to pursue and others more difficult. The better we understand our own temporal perspective, including its strengths and weaknesses, the more we are capable of recognizing the roles on the project that we are likely to perform well and those that need extra attention to get them done correctly.

6. **Identify the key roles project champions play in project success.**   Champions are those individuals within an organization who identify with a new project, using all the resources at their command to support it, even in the face of organizational resistance. Champions are risk takers because they are willing to work persistently in the face of resistance or hostility to their idea from other members of the company. Research strongly supports the contention that projects with an identifiable champion are more likely to be successful than those without. Among the traditional roles that champions play are those of technical understanding, leadership, coordination and control, obtaining resources, and administration. The nontraditional nature of the champion's behavior includes engaging in activities such as being a cheerleader, project visionary, politician, risk taker, and ambassador, all in support of the project.

7. **Recognize the principles that typify the new project leadership.**   Warren Bennis's idea of the new project leadership is strongly based on relationship management through creating and maintaining a mutual commitment with each member of the project team. The four principles of the new project management include (1) understanding and practicing the power of appreciation regarding each member of the project team, (2) continually reminding people of what is important through keeping focused on the "big picture," (3) generating and sustaining trust with each member of the project team, and (4) recognizing that the leader and the led are natural allies, not opponents.

8. **Understand the development of project management professionalism in the discipline.**   As project management has become increasingly popular, its success has led to the development of a core of professional project managers within many organizations. Recognizing the law of supply and demand, we see that as the demand for project management expertise continues to grow, the supply must keep pace. Professionalism recognizes the "institutionalization" of projects and project management within organizations, both public and private. The proliferation of professional societies supporting project management is another indicator of the interest in the discipline.

Key Terms

Champion (*p. 140*)

Chunking time (*p. 138*)

Creative originator (*p. 140*)

Empathy (*p. 135*)

Entrepreneur (*p. 140*)

Future orientation (*p. 139*)

Godfather or sponsor (*p. 140*)

Leadership (*p. 129*)

Motivation (*p. 132*)

Past orientation (*p. 139*)

Predicting (*p. 138*)

Present orientation (*p. 139*)

Professionalism (*p. 145*)

Self-regulation (*p. 135*)

Temporal alignment (*p. 138*)

Time orientation (*p. 138*)

Time warping (*p. 138*)

Discussion Questions

1. The chapter stressed the idea that project management is a "leader-intensive" undertaking. Discuss in what sense this statement is true.

2. How do the duties of project managers reinforce the role of leadership?

3. What are some key differences between leaders and managers?

4. Discuss the concept of emotional intelligence as it relates to the duties of project managers. Why are the five elements of emotional intelligence so critical to successful project management?

5. Consider the studies on trait theories in leadership. Of the characteristics that emerge as critical to effective leadership, which seem most critical for project managers? Why?

6. Complete the accompanying Future Time Perspective scale. After completing it, determine whether you have a future time perspective, present time perspective, or past time perspective. What are the implications for the types of tasks you enjoy performing? How will your preferences lead to strengths and weaknesses in managing projects?

7. Why are project champions said to be better equipped to handle the "nontraditional" aspects of leadership?

8. Consider the discussion of the "new project leadership." If you were asked to formulate a principle that could be applied to project leadership, what would it be? Justify your answer.

Future Time Perspective Scale[33]

Read each statement and decide the degree to which it is true for you. For each statement, circle the number that best matches your feelings using the scale below.

1 Strongly Disagree (SD)	2 Disagree (D)	3 Neither agree nor disagree (N)		4 Agree (A)		5 Strongly Agree (SA)

	SD	D	N	A	SA
1. I never feel as if time is standing still.	1	2	3	4	5
2. Living for the future is important in my life.	1	2	3	4	5
3. I always plan things ahead.	1	2	3	4	5
4. When I try to think of events that may happen in the future, I see a clear picture.	1	2	3	4	5
5. When I think of my future, a sense of peace and tranquility comes over me.	1	2	3	4	5
6. Time is moving quickly.	1	2	3	4	5
7. There aren't enough minutes in a day to list all that I hope to do in the future.	1	2	3	4	5
8. The pace of my life is fast.	1	2	3	4	5
9. I see the future as being full of countless possibilities.	1	2	3	4	5
10. I feel that I am facing my future with confidence.	1	2	3	4	5

Scoring for Future Time Perspective Scale

Add the scores for each item and divide by 10. This will provide one measure of future time perspective. After taking the test, put an X on the scale below to indicate the level of future time perspective.

Future Time Perspective:

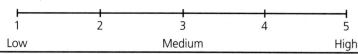

1	2	3	4	5
Low		Medium		High

Case Study 4.1

In Search of Effective Project Managers

Pureswing Golf, Inc., manufactures and sells a full line of golf equipment, including clubs, golf balls, leisurewear, and ancillary equipment (bags, rain gear, towels, etc.). The company competes in a highly competitive and fast-paced industry against better known competitors, such as Nike, Taylor Made, Titleist, PING, Calloway, and Cleveland. Among the keys to success in this industry are the continuous introduction of new club models, innovative engineering and design, and speed to market. As a smaller company trying to stay abreast of stronger competitors, Pureswing places great emphasis on the project management process in order to remain profitable. At any time, the company will have more than 35 project teams developing new ideas across the entire product range.

Pureswing prefers to find promising engineers from within the organization and promote them to project manager. It feels that these individuals, having learned the company's philosophy of competitive success, are best equipped to run new product introduction projects. For years, Pureswing relied on volunteers to move into project management, but lately it has realized that this ad hoc method for finding and encouraging project managers is not sufficient. The failure rate for these project manager volunteers is over 40%, too high for a company of Pureswing's size. With such steady turnover among the volunteers, successful managers have to pick up the slack—they often manage five or six projects simultaneously. Top management, worried about burnout among

(continued)

these high-performing project managers, has decided that the firm must develop a coordinated program for finding new project managers, including creating a career path in project management within the organization.

Questions

1. Imagine you are a human resources professional at Pureswing who has been assigned to develop a program for recruiting new project managers. Design a job description for the position.
2. What qualities and personal characteristics support a higher likelihood of success as a project manager?
3. What qualities and personal characteristics would make it difficult to be a successful project manager?

Case Study 4.2

Finding the Emotional Intelligence to Be a Real Leader

Recently, Kathy Smith, a project manager for a large industrial construction organization, was assigned to oversee a multimillion-dollar chemical plant construction project in Southeast Asia. Kathy had earned this assignment after completing a number of smaller construction assignments in North America over the past three years. This was her first overseas assignment and she was eager to make a good impression, particularly given the size and scope of the project. Successfully completing this project would increase her visibility within the organization dramatically and earmark her as a candidate for upper management. Kathy had good project management skills; in particular, she was organized and highly self-motivated. Team members at her last two project assignments used to joke that just trying to keep up with her was a full-time job.

Kathy wasted no time settling in to oversee the development of the chemical plant. Operating under her normal work approach, Kathy routinely required her staff and the senior members of the project team to work long hours, ignoring weekend breaks if important milestones were coming up, and generally adopting a round-the-clock work approach for the project. Unfortunately, in expecting her team, made up of local residents, to change their work habits to accommodate her expectations, Kathy completely misread the individuals on her team. They bitterly resented her overbearing style, unwillingness to consult them on key questions, and aloof nature. Rather than directly confront her, however, team members began a campaign of passive resistance to her leadership. They would purposely drag their feet on important assignments or cite insurmountable problems when none, in fact, existed. Kathy's standard response was to push herself and her project team harder, barraging subordinates with increasingly urgent communications demanding faster performance. To her bewilderment, nothing seemed to work.

The project quickly became bogged down due to poor team performance and ended up costing the project organization large penalties for late delivery. Although Kathy had many traits that worked in her favor, she was seriously lacking in the ability to recognize the feelings and expectations of others and take them into consideration.

Questions

1. Discuss how Kathy lacked sufficient emotional intelligence to be effective in her new project manager assignment.
2. Of the various dimensions of emotional intelligence, which dimension(s) did she appear to lack most? What evidence can you cite to support this contention?

Case Study 4.3

Problems with John

John James has worked at one of the world's largest aerospace firms for more than 15 years. He was hired into the division during the "Clinton years" when many people were being brought onto the payroll. John had not completed his engineering degree, so he was hired as a drafter. Most of the other people in his department who were hired at the time had completed their degrees and therefore began careers as associate engineers. Over the years, John has progressed through the ranks to the classification of engineer. Many of the employees hired at the same time as John have advanced more rapidly because the corporation recognized their engineering degrees as prerequisites for advancement. Years of service can be substituted, but a substantial number of years is required to offset the lack of a degree.

John began exhibiting signs of dissatisfaction with the corporation in general several years ago. He would openly vent his feelings against nearly everything the corporation was doing or trying to do. However, he did not complain about his specific situation. The complaining became progressively worse. John started to exhibit mood swings. He would be extremely productive at times (though still complaining) and then swing into periods of near zero productivity. During these times, John would openly surf the Internet for supplies for a new home repair project or for the most recent Dilbert comics. His fellow employees were hesitant to point out to management when these episodes occurred. Most of the team members had been working together for the entire 15 years and had become close friends. This is why these nonproductive episodes of John's were such a problem; no one on the team felt comfortable pointing the problem out to higher management. As time progressed and John's friends evolved into his managers, while John remained at lower salary grades, John's mood swings grew more dramatic and lasted longer.

During the most recent performance appraisal review process, John's manager (a friend of his) included a paragraph concerning his "lack of concentration at times." This was included because of numerous comments made by John's peers. The issue could no longer be swept under the rug. John became irate at the review feedback and refused to acknowledge receipt of his performance appraisal. His attitude toward his teammates became extremely negative. He demanded to know who had spoken negatively about him, and his work output diminished to virtually nothing.

Analysis of the Problem

Clearly John has not been happy. To understand why, the history of his employment at this company needs to be looked at in greater detail. The group of coworkers that started together 15 years earlier all had similar backgrounds and capabilities. A group of eight people were all about 22 years old and had just left college; John was the only exception to this pattern, as he still needed two years of schooling to finish his engineering degree. All were single and making good money at their jobs. The difference in salary levels between an associate engineer and a draftsman was quite small. Figure 4.5 shows the salary grade classifications at this corporation.

This group played softball together every Wednesday, fished together on the weekends, and hunted elk for a week every winter. Lifelong bonds and friendships were formed. One by one, the group started to get married and begin families. They even took turns standing up for each other at the weddings. The wives and the children all became great friends, and the fishing trips were replaced with family backyard barbecues.

Meanwhile, things at work were going great. All of these friends and coworkers had very strong work ethics and above-average abilities. They all liked their work and did not mind working extra hours. This combination of effort and ability meant rewards and advancement for those involved. However, since John had not yet completed his degree as he had planned, his promotions were more difficult to achieve and did not occur as rapidly as those of his friends. The differences in salary and responsibility started to expand at a rapid rate. John started to become less satisfied.

This large corporation was structured as a functional organization. All mechanical engineers reported to a functional department manager. This manager was aware of the situation and convinced John to go back

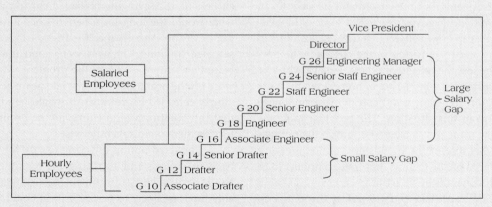

FIGURE 4.5 **Salary Grade Classifications at This Corporation**

(continued)

for his degree during the evenings. Although John had good intentions, he never stayed with it long enough to complete his degree. As John's friends advanced more quickly through the corporation, their cars and houses also became bigger and better. John's wife pressured him to keep up with the others, and they also bought a bigger house. This move meant that John was living above his means and his financial security was threatened.

Until this point, John had justified in his mind that the corporation's policies and his functional manager were the source of all of his problems. John would openly vent his anger about this manager. Then a drastic change took place in the corporation. The corporation switched over to a project team environment and eliminated the functional management. This meant that John was now reporting directly to his friends.

Even though John now worked for his friends, company policy was still restrictive and the promotions did not come as fast as he hoped. The team leader gave John frequent cash spot awards and recognition in an attempt to motivate him. John's ego would be soothed for a short time, but this did not address the real problem. John wanted money, power, and respect, and he was not satisfied because those around him had more. Although he was good at what he did, he was not great at it. He did not appear to have the innate capability to develop into a leader through expert knowledge or personality traits. Additionally, due to the lack of an engineering degree, he could not achieve power through time in grade. By now, John's attitude had deteriorated to the point where it was disruptive to the team and something had to be done. The team leader had to help John, but he also had to look after the health of the team.

This detailed history is relevant because it helps to explain how John's attitude slowly deteriorated over a period of time. At the start of his career, John was able to feel on a par with his peers. When everyone was young and basically equal, he knew that he had the respect of his friends and coworkers. This allowed John to enjoy a sense of self-esteem. As time passed and he gave up in his attempt at the college degree, he lost some of his self-esteem. As the gap grew between his friends' positions in the company and his position in the company, he perceived that he lost the esteem of others. Finally, when he became overextended with the larger home, even his basic security was threatened. It is difficult to maintain a level of satisfaction in this situation. The problem was now distracting the team and starting to diminish their efforts and results. Because of the friendships, undue pressure was being placed on the team as they tried to protect John from the consequences of his actions.

The team leader had to try to resolve this problem. The challenge was significant: The leader had to attempt to satisfy the individual's needs, the group's needs, and the task needs. When John's individual needs could not be met, the group atmosphere and task completion suffered. It was time for the team leader to act decisively and approach upper management with a solution to the problem.

Possible Courses of Action

The team leader put a lot of thought into his options. Because of the friendships and personal connections, he knew that he could not make this decision lightly. He decided to talk individually to the team members who were John's close friends and then determine the best solution to present to upper management.

After talking with the team members, the team leader decided on the following list of potential options:

1. Do nothing.
2. Bypass company policy and promote John.
3. Talk John into going back to college.
4. Relocate John to a different project team.
5. Terminate John's employment.

The option to do nothing would be the easiest way out for the team leader, but this would not solve any problems. This decision would be the equivalent of burying one's head in the sand and hoping the problem would go away by itself. Surprisingly, this was a common suggestion from the team members. There appeared to be a hope that the problem could be overlooked, as it had been in the past, and John would just accept the situation. With this option, the only person who would have to compromise was John.

The second option of bypassing company policy and promoting John to a higher level would be a very difficult sell to management. John was recently promoted to a salary grade 18 (his friends were now 24s and 26s). This promotion was achieved through the concerted efforts of his friends and the team leader. The chances of convincing management to approve another promotion so quickly were extremely low. Furthermore, if the team leader was successful at convincing management to promote John, what would the long-term benefits be? John would still not be at the same level as his friends and might not be satisfied for long. Chances were good that this would be only a temporary fix to the problem. After the shine wore off the promotion, John would again believe that his efforts exceeded his rewards. It would be nice to believe that this solution would eliminate the problem, but history seemed to indicate otherwise.

The third option of trying to talk John into going back to college and finishing his engineering degree would be the best solution to the problem, but probably the least likely to occur. If John could complete his degree, there would be no company policies that could obstruct his path. He would then be competing on an even playing field. This would allow him to justifiably receive his advancement and recapture his self-esteem. If he did not receive the rewards that he felt he deserved, he would then have to look at his performance and improve on his weaknesses, not just fall back on the same old excuse. This solution would appear to put John back on the path to job satisfaction, but the problem with it was that it had been tried unsuccessfully several times before. Why would it be different this time? Should the corporation keep trying this approach knowing that failure would again lead to dissatisfaction and produce a severe negative effect on the team? Although this third solution could produce the happy ending that everyone wants to see in a movie, it did not have a very high probability of success.

The fourth option of relocating John to a different team would be an attempt to break the ties of competition that John felt with his friends and teammates. If this option were followed, John could start with a clean slate with a completely different team, and he would be allowed to save face with his friends. He could tell them of his many accomplishments and the great job that he is doing, while complaining that his "new" boss is holding him back. Although this could be considered "smoke and mirrors," it might allow John the opportunity to look at himself in a new light. If he performed at his capabilities, he should be able to achieve the esteem of others and eventually his self-esteem. The team would consider this a victory because it would allow everyone to maintain the social relationship while washing their hands of the professional problems. This option offered the opportunity to make the situation impersonal. It should be clear, however, that this solution would do nothing to resolve the true problem. Although it would allow John to focus his dissatisfaction on someone other than his friends and give him a fresh start to impress his new coworkers, who is to say that the problem would not simply resurface?

The fifth option, termination of employment, would be distasteful to all involved. Nothing to this point had indicated that John would deserve an action this severe. Also, since this option also would sever the social relationships for all involved and cause guilt for all of the remaining team members, resulting in team output deteriorating even further, it would be exercised only if other options failed and the situation deteriorated to an unsafe condition for those involved.

Questions

1. As the team leader, you have weighed the pros and cons of the five options and prepared a presentation to management on how to address this problem. What do you suggest?
2. Consider each of the options, and develop an argument to defend your position for each option.
3. What specific leadership behaviors mentioned in this chapter are most relevant to addressing and resolving the problems with John?

Internet Exercises

1. Identify an individual you would call a business leader. Search the Web for information on this individual. What pieces of information cause you to consider this individual a leader?
2. Go to the Web site www.debian.org/devel/leader and evaluate the role of the project leader in the Debian Project. What is it about the duties and background of the project leader that lets us view him as this project's leader?
3. Knut Yrvin functions as the team leader for an initiative to replace proprietary operating systems with Linux-based technology in schools in Norway (the project is named "Skolelinux"). Read his interview at http://lwn.net/Articles/47510/. What clues do you find in this interview regarding his view of the job of project leader and how he leads projects?
4. Project champions can dramatically improve the chances of project success, but they can also have some negative effects. For example, projects championed by a well-known organizational member are very difficult to kill, even when they are failing badly. Read the article posted at www.computerworld.com/s/article/78274/Blind_Faith?taxonomyId=073 on "Blind Faith." What does the article suggest are some of the pitfalls in excessive championing by highly placed members of an organization?

PMP Certification Sample Questions

1. The project manager spends a great deal of her time communicating with project stakeholders. Which of the following represent an example of a stakeholder group for her project?
   a. Top management
   b. Customers
   c. Project team members
   d. Functional group heads
   e. All are project stakeholders

2. Effective leadership involves all of the following, except:
   a. Managing oneself through personal time management, stress management, and other activities
   b. Managing team members through motivation, delegation, supervision, and team building
   c. Maintaining tight control of all project resources and providing information to team members only as needed
   d. Employing and utilizing project champions where they can benefit the project

3. A project manager is meeting with his team for the first time and wants to create the right environment in which relationships develop positively. Which of the following guidelines should he consider employing to create an effective partnership with his team?
   a. The right to say no
   b. Joint accountability
   c. Exchange of purpose
   d. Absolute honesty
   e. All are necessary to create a partnership

4. Joan is very motivated to create a positive project experience for all her team members and is reflecting on some of the approaches she can take to employ leadership, as opposed to simply managing the process. Which of the following is an example of a leadership practice she can use?
   a. Focus on plans and budgets
   b. Seek to maintain the status quo and promote order
   c. Energize people to overcome obstacles and show personal initiative
   d. Maintain a short-term time frame and avoid unnecessary risks

5. Frank has been learning about the effect of emotional intelligence on his ability to lead his project effectively. Which of the following is *not* an example of the kind of emotional intelligence that can help him perform better?
   a. Self-awareness and self-regulation
   b. Motivation
   c. Social skills
   d. Results orientation (work to get the job done)

Answers: 1 e—Remember that stakeholders are defined as any group, either internal or external, that can affect the performance of the project; 2 c—Leadership requires allowing workers to have flexibility, providing them with all relevant information, and communicating project status and other pertinent information; 3 e—All of the above are necessary characteristics in promoting partnership between the project manager and the team; 4 c—Energizing people to overcome obstacles is a critical component of leadership, as opposed to a philosophy of management; 5 d—Although a results orientation can be a useful element in a project leader's skill set, it is not an example of emotional intelligence, which is often manifested through relationship building with others.

Notes

1. "Saving the river in Fes." (2009, May 8). http://moroccandesign.com/saving-the-river-in-fes; Danko, J. (2010). "Mystic river," *PMNetwork,* 24(7): 56–59; http://riadzany.blogspot.com/2008/12/fez-tanneries-aziza-chaouni-responds.html.

2. Kim, W. C., and Mauborgne, R. A. (1992, July–August). "Parables of leadership," *Harvard Business Review,* p. 123.

3. Posner, B. Z. (1987). "What it takes to be a good project manager," *Project Management Journal,* 18(1): 51–54; Pinto, J. K., Thoms, P., Trailer, J., Palmer, T., and Govekar, M. (1998). *Project Leadership: From Theory to Practice.* Newtown Square, PA: Project Management Institute; Slevin, D. P., and Pinto, J. K. (1988). "Leadership, motivation, and the project manager," in Cleland, D. I., and King, W. R. (Eds.), *Project Management Handbook,* 2nd ed. New York: Van Nostrand Reinhold, pp. 739–70; Geoghegan, L., and Dulewicz, V. (2008). "Do project managers' competencies contribute to project success?" *Project Management Journal,* 39(4): 58–67.

4. Pinto, J. K., and Kharbanda, O. P. (1997). *Successful Project Managers.* New York: Van Nostrand Reinhold.

5. Block, P. (1993). *Stewardship: Choosing Service over Self-Interest.* San Francisco, CA: Berrett-Koehler Publishers.

6. Verma, V. K. (1996). *Human Resource Skills for the Project Manager.* Newtown Square, PA: Project Management Institute.

7. Yukl, G. (2002). *Leadership in Organizations,* 5th ed. Upper Saddle River, NJ: Prentice Hall; Daft, R. L. (1999). *Leadership Theory and Practice.* Orlando, FL: Harcourt; Kouzes, J. M., and Posner, B. Z. (1995). *The Leadership Challenge.* San Francisco, CA: Jossey-Bass.

8. Slevin, D. P. (1989). *The Whole Manager.* New York: AMACOM.

9. Yukl, G. (2002). *Leadership in Organizations,* 5th ed. Upper Saddle River, NJ: Prentice Hall.

10. Zimmerer, T. W., and Yasin, M. M. (1998). "A leadership profile of American project managers," *Project Management Journal,* 29(1): 31–38.

11. Goleman, D. (1998). "What makes a leader?" *Harvard Business Review,* 76(6): 92–102; Clarke, N. (2010). "Emotional intelligence and its relationship to transformational leadership and key project manager competences," *Project Management Journal,* 41(2): 5–20.

12. Kouzes, J. M., and Posner, B. Z. (1995). *The Leadership Challenge.* San Francisco, CA: Jossey-Bass.

13. Pettersen, N. (1991). "What do we know about the effective project manager?" *International Journal of Project Management,* 9: 99–104. See also Javidan, M., and Dastmachian, A. (1993). "Assessing senior executives: The impact of context on their roles," *Journal of Applied Behavioral Science,* 29, 328–42; DiMarco, N., Goodson, J. R., and Houser, H. F. (1989). "Situational leadership in the project/matrix environment," *Project Management Journal,* 20(1): 11–18; Müller, R., and Turner, J. R. (2007). "Matching the project manager's leadership style to project type," *International Journal of Project Management,* 25: 21–32; Turner, J. R., and Müller, R. (2005). "The project manager's leadership style as a success factor on projects: A literature review," *Project Management Journal,* 36(2): 49–61.

14. Einsiedel, A. A. (1987). "Profile of effective project managers," *Project Management Journal,* 18(5): 51–56.

15. Medcof, J. W., Hauschildt, J., and Keim, G. (2000). "Realistic criteria for project manager selection and development," *Project Management Journal,* 31(3): 23–32.

16. Hannon, E. (2010, September 27). "Problems fuel doubts about Commonwealth Games." www.npr.org/templates/story/story.php?storyId=13014949; Swanson, S. (2008). "Worldview: New Delhi," *PMNetwork,* 22(12): 58–64;

Lakshman, N. (2007, March 14). "The miracle-worker of the Delhi Metro." www.rediff.com/money/2007/mar/14bspec.htm; www.muraleedharan.com/legends_sreedharan.html.

17. Thoms, P., and Pinto, J. K. (1999). "Project leadership: A question of timing," *Project Management Journal,* 30(1): 19–26. See also Das, T. K. (1986). *The Subjective Side of Strategy Making: Future Orientations and Perceptions of Executives.* New York: Praeger; Das, T. K. (1991). "Time: The hidden dimension in strategic planning," *Long Range Planning,* 24: 49–57; Thoms, P., and Greenberger, D. B. (1995). "The relationship between leadership and time orientation," *Journal of Management Inquiry,* 4: 272–92.

18. Schon, D. A. (1967). *Technology and Change.* New York: Delacorte; Maidique, M. A. (1980, Winter). "Entrepreneurs, champions, and technological innovation," *Sloan Management Review,* 21: 59–76.

19. Peters, T. A. (1985, May 13). "A passion for excellence," *Fortune,* pp. 47–50.

20. Meredith, J. A. (1986). "Strategic planning for factory automation by the championing process," *IEEE Transactions on Engineering Management,* EM-33(4): 229–32; Pinto, J. K., and Slevin, D. P. (1988). "The project champion: Key to implementation success," *Project Management Journal,* 20(4): 15–20; Bryde, D. (2008). "Perceptions of the impact of project sponsorship practices on project success," *International Journal of Project Management,* 26: 800–809; Wright, J. N. (1997). "Time and budget: The twin imperatives of a project sponsor," *International Journal of Project Management,* 15: 181–86.

21. Onsrud, H. J., and Pinto, J. K. (1993). "Evaluating correlates of GIS adoption success and the decision process of GIS acquisition," *Journal of the Urban and Regional Information Systems Association,* 5: 18–39.

22. Chakrabarti, A. K. (1974). "The role of champion in product innovation," *California Management Review,* XVII(2): 58–62.

23. Royer, I. (2003). "Why bad projects are so hard to kill," *Harvard Business Review,* 81(2): 48–56; Pinto, J. K., and Slevin, D. P. (1988). "The project champion: Key to implementation success," *Project Management Journal,* 20(4): 15–20.

24. Thamhain, H. J. (1991). "Developing project management skills," *Project Management Journal,* 22(3): 39–44; Pressman, R. (1998, January–February). "Fear of trying: The plight of rookie project managers," *IEEE Software,* pp. 50–54.

25. Bennis, W. (2001). "The end of leadership: Exemplary leadership is impossible without full inclusion, initiatives, and cooperation of followers," *Organizational Dynamics,* 28.

26. Kouzes, J. M., and Posner, B. Z. (1995). *The Leadership Challenge.* San Francisco, CA: Jossey-Bass.

27. Hartman, F. (2000). *Don't Park Your Brain Outside.* Newtown Square, PA: Project Management Institute.

28. Silver, D. (2009). "Abroad spectrum," *PMNetwork,* 23(1): 62–68.

29. Ayas, K. (1996). "Professional project management: A shift towards learning and a knowledge creating structure," *International Journal of Project Management,* 14: 131–36; Statement of Bruce Carnes, Chief Financial Officer, United States Department of Energy, Before the Committee on Science—U.S. House of Representatives—on the FY 2003 Budget Request for the U.S. Department of Energy. (2002, February 13). See also www.nap.edu/openbook/0309089093/html/82-91.htm.

30. Ayas, K. (1996), ibid.

31. Hoffman, E. J., Kinlaw, C. S., and Kinlaw, D. C. (2002). "Developing superior project teams: A study of the characteristics of high performance in project teams," in Slevin, D. P., Cleland, D. I., and Pinto, J. K. (Eds.), *The Frontiers of Project Management Research.* Newtown Square, PA: PMI, pp. 237–47; Kezbom, D. (1994). "Self-directed team and the changing role of the project manager." *Proceedings of the Internet 12th World Congress on Project Management,* Oslo, pp. 589–93.

32. Wideman, R. M., and Shenhar, A. J. (2001). "Professional and personal development management: A practical approach to education and training," in J. Knutson (Ed.), *Project Management for Business Professionals: A Comprehensive Guide.* New York: Wiley, pp. 353–83; Wideman, R. M. (1998). "Project teamwork, personality profiles and the population at large: Do we have enough of the right kind of people?" Presentation at the Project Management Institute's Annual Seminar/Symposium, Long Beach, CA.

33. Thoms, P. (2004). *Driven by the Future: Time Orientation in Leadership.* New York: Praeger.

5

Scope Management

Chapter Outline

Chapter Objectives

After completing this chapter, you should be able to:

1. Understand the importance of scope management for project success.

2. Understand the significance of developing a scope statement.

3. Construct a Work Breakdown Structure for a project.

4. Develop a Responsibility Assignment Matrix for a project.

5. Describe the roles of changes and configuration management in assessing project scope.

PROJECT MANAGEMENT BODY OF KNOWLEDGE CORE CONCEPTS COVERED IN THIS CHAPTER

1. Initiation (PMBoK sec. 5.1)
2. Scope Planning (PMBoK sec. 5.2)
3. Scope Definition (PMBoK sec. 5.3)
4. Scope Verification (PMBoK sec. 5.4)
5. Scope Change Control (PMBoK sec. 5.5)

PROJECT PROFILE

Case—The Expeditionary Fighting Vehicle

One of the most complex and difficult congressional budget decisions in years finally came due: the determination of the fate of the Marine Corps' Expeditionary Fighting Vehicle (EFV). Given the numerous delays, tests, conditional approvals, and retests, the EFV had been no stranger to controversy. Although the EFV was loudly defended by senior officers in the Pentagon, a growing army of critics cited the vehicle's poor test performance, and costs continued to balloon. As one reporter noted, "After 10 years and $1.7 billion, this is what the Marine Corps got for its investment in a new amphibious vehicle: A craft that breaks down about an average of once every 4½ hours, leaks, and sometimes veers off course." The biggest question is: How did things get to that point with what was viewed, for many years, as one of the Marine's highest priority acquisition programs?

The EFV program began more than 20 years ago when this armored amphibious vehicle was designed to replace the 1970s-era Amphibious Assault Vehicle. The purpose of vehicles such as the EFV is to provide armored support for the early stages of amphibious assault onto enemy shores. The EFV was designed to roll off a Navy assault ship, move under its own power at 20 mph on the water's surface for distances up to 25 miles while transporting a Marine rifle squad (up to 17 Marines), cross hostile beaches, and operate on shore. The EVF was moderately armored and carried a 30-mm cannon in a turret for offensive firepower. The EVF often was described as a Marine Corps variant of the Bradley Fighting Vehicle.

The EFV began as a state-of-the-art acquisition program for the Department of Defense (DoD). Following a concept exploration phase to determine the viability of the project that began in 1988, the project entered a program definition and risk reduction phase during which it was considered "a model defense acquisition program," winning two DoD awards for successful cost and technology management. The original contract was awarded to General Dynamics Corporation in June 1996 for full engineering and design work, and that corporation was awarded a subsequent contract for the system development and demonstration (SDD) phase of the program in July 2001. It is during this critical stage that all the complex engineering, systems development, and functionality of the program must be successfully demonstrated. Perhaps unwisely, General Dynamics budgeted only 27 months for total testing and system verification.

This far-too-ambitious schedule soon became a problem for General Dynamics and the EFV as a series of technical problems began to surface. Two additional years were added to the SDD phase as it became apparent that the EFV concept was beset with numerous unforeseen problems. In December 2004, tests of EFV prototypes demonstrated further problems. The tests showed severe failure in the vehicle's main computer system, causing the vehicle's steering to freeze. The hydraulic systems powering the vehicle's bow-flap, installed to make the EFV more seaworthy, began leaking and failing. The EFV was originally intended to operate for an average of 70 hours between mission failure breakdowns, but because of the numerous reliability problems, the Marines reduced this figure to 43.5 hours. Following these prototype tests, an additional two years were added to the program development schedule.

The year 2006 was not a good one for the Expeditionary Fighting Vehicle. The EFV was put through a critical operational assessment, which is a series of tests to demonstrate that it could meet performance requirements and was ready for production. The EFV performed abysmally, experiencing numerous system failures, breakdowns, and failure in its reliability assessment. During the tests, the vehicles were able to operate on average for only 4.5 hours between breakdowns, and it took nearly 3.5 hours of corrective maintenance for every hour of operation. Poor reliability resulted in 117 mission failures and 645 acts of unscheduled maintenance during the tests. The EFV's reliability was so poor that it successfully completed only 2 of 11 attempted amphibious tests, 1 of 10 gunnery tests, and none of the 3 land mobility tests. Other problems included the fact that the prototypes were nearly one ton overweight, suffered from limited visibility, and were so noisy that the driver was advised to wear ear

(continued)

Stocktrek Images, Inc. / Alamy

FIGURE 5.1 The Expeditionary Fighting Vehicle

plugs while in the driver's chair, despite the fact that doing so would make it nearly impossible to communicate with the EFV's commander. In fact, so poorly did the EFV fare during the operational assessment that the Marines announced they were going back to the drawing board with the design, aiming to complete a new SDD phase by 2011, eight years behind the original schedule.

Meanwhile, the program's costs just kept rising. When the EFV was first conceived, the Marines planned to purchase 1,025 of them at a total cost of $8.5 billion. Subsequently, a DoD estimate put the program's cost at upwards of $14 billion dollars, while the Marines had trimmed their order to 573 vehicles. In effect, even assuming those final figures were to hold, the cost of the EFV had risen from $8.3 million per vehicle to slightly more than $23 million. Overall, the Pentagon estimated it had spent $2.9 billion on the program in R&D and testing costs before buying a single vehicle.

Wrong Weapon for the Wrong War?

The ongoing litany of failures associated with the EFV's development gave rise to some more fundamental questions about the purpose behind developing the vehicle. Critics argued that the EFV simply did not serve a meaningful role in the modern Marine Corps' mission. Among their concerns were the following points:

- Modern warfare does not offer options for "storming the beaches," as the old Marine Corps model envisions. Low-level, regional, or urban conflicts make the need for amphibious assault an anachronism in the modern day. As Laura Peterson, a defense analyst with Taxpayers for Common Sense, suggested, "This thing isn't just fighting the last war, it's fighting last century's wars."

- The advance in cruise missile technology makes the "25 mile offshore" model obsolete. When the EFV was envisioned, it was believed that the Navy could protect its ships by remaining just over the horizon, disembarking EFVs from that distance to assault enemy shores. Critics contended that new cruise missiles have a range of over 100 miles, making the EFVs or the Navy's ships vulnerable to attack if they were to follow the original model.
- The flat bottom of the EFV, necessary for ship-to-shore transportation, makes them extremely vulnerable to the shaped charges from improvised explosive devices (IEDs), used so effectively in Iraq and Afghanistan. General Dynamics argued that redesigning the bottom of the vehicle would alter its amphibious characteristics.

A number of senior Pentagon officials, including the Commandant of the Marine Corps, stood by the EFV, arguing that the Marine's "expeditionary" mission will remain alive and in effect into the foreseeable future. The EFV, they believed, was a critical element in the deployment and striking capability of the Marines. However, other high-ranking government officials, including the Secretary of Defense, gave only tepid and qualified support for the continued development and deployment of the EFV.

Final rounds of funding began to limit additional money for the EFV and to tie continued support to the ability of General Dynamics and the Marines to demonstrate much improved reliability and overall system effectiveness. For example, in 2010 the Senate Appropriations Committee authorized $38 million for one more round of tests and set aside $184 million to shut the program down in the event the vehicle failed the tests again. The axe finally fell at the start of 2011, when Secretary Gates sent his preliminary budget to Congress. Among the casualties of the cost-cutting knife was the EFV program. The program had long been teetering on the brink, so in a world of smaller Pentagon budgets and more aggressive program oversight, perhaps it was inevitable that the EFV would finally slip over the edge.[1]

INTRODUCTION

A **project's scope** is everything about a project—work content as well as expected outcomes. Project scope consists of naming all activities to be performed, the resources consumed, and the end products that result, including quality standards.[2] Scope includes a project's goals, constraints, and limitations. **Scope management** is the function of controlling a project in terms of its goals and objectives through the processes of conceptual development, full definition, execution, and termination. It provides the foundation upon which all project work is based and is, therefore, the culmination of predevelopment planning. The process of scope management consists of several distinct activities, all based on creating a systematic set of plans for the upcoming project.

Emmitt Smith, former All-Pro running back for the Dallas Cowboys and member of the Pro Football Hall of Fame, attributes his remarkable success to his commitment to developing and working toward a series of personal goals. He likes to tell the story of his high school days and how they affected his future success. When Smith was a student at Escambia High in Pensacola, Florida, his football coach used to say, "It's a dream until you write it down. Then it's a goal."

For successful projects, comprehensive planning can make all the difference. Until a detailed set of specifications is enumerated and recorded and a control plan is developed, a project is just a dream. In the most general sense, project planning seeks to define what needs to be done, by whom, and by what date, in order to fulfill assigned responsibility.[3] Projects evolve onto an operational level, where they can begin to be developed, only after systematic planning—scope management—has occurred. The six main activities are (1) conceptual development, (2) the scope statement, (3) work authorization, (4) scope reporting, (5) control systems, and (6) project closeout.[4] Each of these steps is key to comprehensive planning and project development (see Table 5.1).

This chapter will detail the key components of project scope management. The goal of scope management is maximum efficiency through the formation and execution of plans or systems that leave as little as possible to chance.

TABLE 5.1 Elements in Project Scope Management

1. **Conceptual Development**
   Problem statement
   Information gathering
   Constraints
   Alternative analysis
   Project objectives
   Statement of Work
2. **Scope Statement**
   Goal criteria
   Management plan
   Work Breakdown Structure
   Scope baseline
   Activity responsibility matrix
3. **Work Authorization**
   Contractual requirements
   Valid consideration
   Contracted terms
4. **Scope Reporting**
   Cost, schedule, technical performance status
      S curves
      Earned value
      Variance or exception reports
5. **Control Systems**
   Configuration control
   Design control
   Trend monitoring
   Document control
   Acquisition control
   Specification control
6. **Project Closeout**
   Historical records
   Postproject analysis
   Financial closeout

5.1 CONCEPTUAL DEVELOPMENT

Conceptual development is the process that addresses project objectives by finding the best ways to meet them.[5] To create an accurate sense of conceptual development for a project, the project management team must collect data and develop several pieces of information. Key steps in information development are:

- *Problem or need statement:* Scope management for a project begins with a statement of goals: why there is a need in search of a solution, what the underlying problem is, and what the project intends to do. For example, consider the following need statement from a fictitious county:

  A 2009 report from the Maryland State Department of Health showed that the township of Freefield ranked among the worst in the state over a five-year average for infant mortality, low birth weight and premature births, late entry into prenatal care, unmarried parents, teen pregnancies, and poverty. A Clarion County health care focus group report identified patterns of poor communication between county families and doctors. There is a need for information gathering and dissemination on childbirth education opportunities, support service availability, preparation for new babies, and postpartum depression. The focus group indicated that the Freefield Public Library could be an important center for collecting this information and directing new parents to resources and materials. To adequately meet this need, the library proposes a grant program to fund expanding their collections and programs in addition to linking the library with local primary care health providers and Freefield Memorial Hospital to serve expectant and postpartum mothers and their children.

- *Information gathering:*   Research to gather all relevant data for the project is the next step. A project can be effectively initiated only when the project manager has a clear understanding of the current state of affairs—specific target dates, alternative supplier options, degree of top management support for the project, and so forth. At any step along the way, project managers should take care that they have not limited their information search. Continuing the above example, suppose that as part of our information gathering, we identify five prospective funding sources in the Maryland Department of Health that would be good sources to access for grants. Further, our information search informs us that these grants are competitive and must be submitted by the end of the current calendar year, we can count on support from local political figures including our state representative and county commissioner, and so forth. All this information must be factored into the program proposal and used to shape it.

- *Constraints:*   In light of the goal statement, project managers must understand any restrictions that may affect project development. Time constraints, budget shrinkages, and client demands can all become serious constraints on project development. Referring back to the health grant example, some important constraints that could affect our ability to develop the grant application in time could be the need to find a medical professional to serve as the grant's principal author, concern with statewide budgets and a withdrawal of support for community initiatives such as this one, and the need for a knowledgeable person within the library willing to serve as the primary collector of the prenatal and postnatal health care information.

- *Alternative analysis:*   Problems usually offer alternative methods for solution. In project management, alternative analysis consists of first clearly understanding the nature of the problem statement and then working to generate alternative solutions. This process serves two functions: It provides the team with a clearer understanding of the project's characteristics, and it offers a choice of approaches for addressing how the project should be undertaken. It may be, as a result of alternative analysis, that an innovative or novel project development alternative suggests itself. Alternative analysis prevents a firm from initiating a project without first conducting sufficient screening for more efficient or effective options.

- *Project objectives:*   Conceptual development concludes with a clear statement of the final objectives for the project in terms of outputs, required resources, and timing. All steps in the conceptual development process work together as a system to ultimately affect the outcome. When each step is well done, the project objectives will logically follow from the analysis. In our health care example above, final objectives might include specific expectations, such as receiving a $100,000 grant to support collection services, printing costs, and holding information sessions and seminars with health care providers. These seminars would begin within a 90-day window from the administration of the grant. Library collections and subscriptions would be enhanced in this area by 25%. In this way, the problem or need statement is the catalyst that triggers a series of cascading steps from motive for the project through to its intended effects.

Conceptual development begins with the process of reducing the project's overall complexity to a more basic level. Project managers must set the stage for their projects as completely as possible by forming problem statements in which goals and objectives are clearly stated and easily understood by all team members.

Many projects that are initiated with less than a clear understanding of the problem the project seeks to address far exceed their initial budgets and schedules. At base level, this problem is due to the vague understanding among team members as to exactly what the project is attempting to accomplish. For example, a recent information technology project was developed with the vague goal of "improving billing and record-keeping operations" in a large insurance firm. The IT department interpreted that goal to develop a project that provided a complex solution requiring multiple interactive screens, costly user retraining, and the generation of voluminous reports. In fact, the organization simply wanted a streamlined link between the billing function and end-of-month reporting. Because the problem was articulated vaguely, the IT department created an expensive system that was unnecessarily complex. In reality, the optimal project solution begins with creating a reasonable and complete problem statement to establish the nature of the project, its purpose, and a set of concrete goals.

A complete understanding of the problem must be generated so that the projects themselves will be successful in serving the purpose for which they were created. A key part of the problem statement is the analysis of multiple alternatives. Locking in "one best" approach for solving a problem too early in a project can lead to failure downstream.

Also, to be effective, problem statements should be kept simple and based on clearly understood needs in search of solutions. For example, a clear project goal such as "improve the processing speed of the computer by 20%" is much better than a goal that charges a project team to "significantly increase the performance of the computer." A set of simple goals provides a reference point that the team can revisit when the inevitable problems occur over the course of project development. On the other hand, project goals that are vague or excessively optimistic—such as "improve corporate profitability while maintaining quality and efficiency of resources"—may sound good, but do not provide clear reference points for problem solving.

The Statement of Work

The impetus to begin a project is often the result of a statement of work. The **Statement of Work (SOW)** is a detailed narrative description of the work required for a project.[6] Useful SOWs contain information on the key objectives for the project, a brief and general description of the work to be performed, expected project outcomes, and any funding or schedule constraints. Typically, in the case of the latter, it is difficult to present schedule requirements past some "gross" level that may only include starting and ending dates, as well as any major milestones.

An SOW can be highly descriptive, as in the case of a Department of Defense Request for Proposal (RFP) for a new Army field communication device that is "no greater than 15 inches long by 15 inches wide by 9 inches deep, can weigh no more than 12 pounds, has a transmitting and receiving range of 60 miles, must remain functional after being fully immersed in water for 30 minutes, and can sustain damage from being dropped at heights up to 25 feet." On the other hand, an SOW can be relatively general, merely specifying final performance requirements without detailed specifics. The purpose of the SOW is to give the project organization and the project manager specific guidance on both work requirements as well as the types of end results sought once the project is completed.

A Statement of Work is an important component of conceptual development, as it identifies a need within the firm or an opportunity from an outside source, for example, the commercial market. Some elements in an effective SOW include:

1. *Introduction and background*—a brief history of the organization or introduction to the root needs that identified the need to initiate a project. Part of the introduction should be a problem statement.
2. *Technical description of the project*—an analysis, in clear terms, of the envisioned technical capabilities of the project or technical challenges the project is intended to resolve.
3. *Time line and milestones*—a discussion of the anticipated time frame to completion and key project deliverables (outcomes).

A useful Statement of Work should clearly detail the expectations of the project client, the problems the project is intended to correct or address, and the work required to complete the project.

For example, the Federal Geographic Data Committee recently developed an SOW for purchasing commercial services from government or private industry as an independent contractor. The Statement of Work contained the following components:

1. *Background*—describes the project in very general terms; discusses why the project is being pursued and how it relates to other projects. It includes, as necessary, a summary of statutory authority or applicable regulations and copies of background materials in addenda or references.
2. *Objectives*—provide a concise overview of the project and how the results or end products will be used.
3. *Scope*—covers the general scope of work the contractor will be performing.
4. *Tasks or requirements*—describe detailed work and management requirements, and also spell out more precisely what is expected of the contractor in the performance of the work.
5. *Selection criteria*—identify objective standards of acceptable performance to be provided by the contractor.
6. *Deliverables or delivery schedule*—describes what the contractor shall provide; identifies the contractor's responsibilities; and identifies any specialized expertise and services, training, and documentation that is needed. In addition, it clearly states the deliverables required, the schedule for delivery, the quantities, and to whom they should be delivered. Finally, it describes the delivery schedule in calendar days from the date of the award.

7. *Security*—states the appropriate security requirement, if necessary, for the work to be done.
8. *Place of performance*—specifies whether the work is to be performed at the government site or the contractor's site.
9. *Period of performance*—specifies the performance period for completion of the contracted project.

Notice how the Statement of Work moves from the general to the specific, first articulating the project's background, including a brief history of the reasons the project is needed, and then identifying the component tasks before moving to a more detailed discussion of each task objective and the approach necessary to accomplish it.[7]

A more detailed example of a generic statement of work is shown in Table 5.2. The SOW covers the critical elements in a project proposal, including description, deliverables, resource requirements, risks,

TABLE 5.2 Elements in a Comprehensive Statement of Work

Date Submitted	
Revision Number	
Project Name	
Project Identification Number	
SOW Prepared by:	

1. Description and Scope
   a. Summary of work requested
   b. Background
   c. Description of major elements (deliverables) of the completed project
   d. Expected benefits
   e. Items not covered in scope
   f. Priorities assigned to each element in the project

2. Approach
   a. Major milestones/key events anticipated

Date	Milestone/Event

   b. Special standards or methodologies to be observed
   c. Impact on existing systems or projects
   d. Assumptions critical to the project
   e. Plans for status report updates
   f. Procedures for changes of scope or work effort

3. Resource Requirements
   a. Detailed plan/rationale for resource needs and assignments

Person	Role and Rationale

(*continued*)

TABLE 5.2 Continued

    b. Other material resource needs (hardware, software, materials, money, etc.)

    c. Expected commitments from other departments in support

    d. Concerns or alternatives related to staffing plan

4. Risks and Concerns

    a. Environmental risks

    b. Client expectation risks

    c. Competitive risks

    d. Risks in project development (technical)

    e. Project constraints

    f. Overall risk assessment

    g. Risk mitigation or abatement strategies

5. Acceptance Criteria

    a. Detailed acceptance process and criteria

    b. Testing/qualification approach

    c. Termination of project

6. Estimated Time and Costs

    a. Estimated time to complete project work

    b. Estimated costs to complete project work

    c. Anticipated ongoing costs

7. Outstanding Issues

expected outcomes, estimated time and cost constraints, and other pending issues. Table 5.2 can serve as a standard template for the construction of a reasonably detailed SOW for most projects.

The Statement of Work is important because it typically serves as the summary of the conceptual development phase of the project plan. Once armed with the SOW, the project manager can begin moving from the general to the more specific, identifying the steps necessary to adequately respond to the detailed SOW.

5.2 THE SCOPE STATEMENT

The **scope statement**, the heart of scope management, reflects a project team's best efforts at creating the documentation and approval of all important project parameters prior to proceeding to the development phase.[8] Key steps in the scope statement process include:

- *Establishing the project goal criteria.* Goal criteria include cost, schedule, performance and deliverables, and key review and approval "gates" with important project stakeholders (particularly the clients). **Deliverables** are formally defined as "any measurable, tangible, verifiable outcome, result, or item that must be produced to complete a project or part of a project." The goal criteria serve as the key project constraints and targets around which the project team must labor.
- *Developing the management plan for the project.* The management plan consists of the organizational structure for the project team, the policies and procedures under which team members will be expected to operate, their appropriate job descriptions, and a well-understood reporting structure for each member of the team. The management plan is essentially the project's bureaucratic step that creates control systems to ensure that all team members know their roles, their responsibilities, and professional relationships.
- *Establishing a Work Breakdown Structure.* One of the most vital planning mechanisms, the **Work Breakdown Structure (WBS)**, divides the project into its component substeps in order to begin

establishing critical interrelationships among activities. Until a project has gone through WBS, it is impossible to determine the relationships among the various activities (which steps must precede others, which steps are independent of previous tasks, and so on). As we will see, accurate scheduling can begin only with an accurate and meaningful Work Breakdown Structure.

- *Creating a scope baseline.*   The **scope baseline** is a document that provides a summary description of each component of the project's goal, including basic budget and schedule information for each activity. Creation of the scope baseline is the final step in the process of systematically laying out all pre-work information, in which each subroutine of the project has been identified and given its control parameters of cost and schedule.

The Work Breakdown Structure

When we are first given a project to complete, the task can seem very intimidating. How do we start? Where should we first direct our efforts? One of the best ways to begin is to recognize that any project is just a collection of a number of discrete steps, or activities, that together add up to the overall deliverable. There is no magic formula; projects get completed one step at a time, activity by activity.

According to the Project Management Body of Knowledge (PMBoK), a Work Breakdown Structure (WBS) is "a deliverable-oriented grouping of project elements which organizes and defines the total scope of the project. Each descending level represents an increasingly detailed definition of a project component. Project components may be products or services." To rephrase this PMBoK definition, the Work Breakdown Structure is a process that sets a project's scope by breaking down its overall mission into a cohesive set of synchronous, increasingly specific tasks.[9] The result is a comprehensive document reflecting this careful work.

The WBS delineates the individual building blocks that will construct the project. Visualize the WBS by imagining it as a method for breaking a project up into "bite-sized" pieces, each representing a step necessary to complete the overall project plan. It can be challenging at the project's start to envision all the elements or component tasks needed to realize the project's success, but the effort to "drill down" into the various activities at the task level actually can reinforce the overall picture of the project.

Consider the simple case of a student team working together on a term paper and final presentation for a college seminar. One of the first steps in the process of completing the assignment consists of breaking the project down into a series of tasks, each of which can be allocated to a member or members of the student team. The overall project consisting of specific products—a final paper and presentation—becomes easier to manage by reducing it to a series of simpler levels, such as:

Task One:	Refine topic
Task Two:	Assign library research responsibilities
Task Three:	Develop preliminary outline for paper and presentation
Task Four:	Assign team member to begin putting presentation together
Task Five:	Begin producing drafts of paper
Task Six:	Proofread and correct drafts
Task Seven:	Refine class presentation
Task Eight:	Turn in paper and make classroom presentation

A WBS could go much further in defining a project's steps; this example is intended only to give you a sense of the logic employed to reduce an overall project to a series of meaningful action steps. You will see, in subsequent chapters, that those same action steps are later evaluated in order to estimate the amount of time necessary to complete them.

The logic of WBS is shown visually in Figure 5.2. Rather than giving a starting date and an end goal, the diagram provides a string of checkpoints along the way. These checkpoints address the specific steps in the project that naturally lead from the start to the logical conclusion. The WBS allows you to see both the trees and the forest, so you can recognize on many levels what it will take to create the completed project.

A. Goal Setting Using WBS

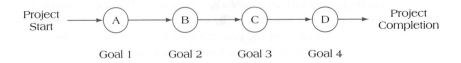

Goal 1   Goal 2   Goal 3   Goal 4

B. Goal Setting Without WBS

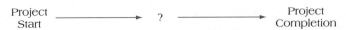

FIGURE 5.2   Goal Setting With and Without Work Breakdown Structures (WBS)

Purposes of the Work Breakdown Structure

The WBS serves six main purposes:[10]

1. *It echoes project objectives.*   Given the mission of the project, a WBS identifies the main work activities that will be necessary to accomplish this goal or set of goals. What gets mentioned in the WBS is what gets done on the project.
2. *It is the organization chart for the project.*   Organization charts typically provide a way to understand the structure of the firm (who reports to whom, how communication flows evolve, who has responsibility for which department, and so forth). A WBS offers a similar logical structure for a project, identifying the key elements (tasks) that need attention, the various subtasks, and the logical flow from activity to activity.
3. *It creates the logic for tracking costs, schedule, and performance specifications for each element in the project.*   All project activities identified in the WBS can be assigned their own budgets and performance expectations. This is the first step in establishing a comprehensive method for project control.
4. *It may be used to communicate project status.*   Once tasks have been identified and responsibilities for achieving the task goals are set, you can determine which tasks are on track, which are critical and pending, and who is responsible for their status.
5. *It may be used to improve overall project communication.*   The WBS not only dictates how to break the project into identifiable pieces, but it also shows how those pieces fit together in the overall scheme of development. As a result, team members become aware of how their component fits into the project, who is responsible for providing upstream work to them, and how their activities will affect later work. This structure improves motivation for communication within the project team, as members wish to make activity transitions as smooth as possible.
6. *It demonstrates how the project will be controlled.*   The general structure of the project demonstrates the key focus that project control will take on. For example, is the project based on creating a deliverable (new product) or improving a process or service (functional efficiency) within the firm? Either way, the WBS gives logic to the control approach and the most appropriate control methods.

Let's illustrate the WBS with a simplified example. Consider the case of a large, urban hospital that has made the decision to introduce an organization-wide information technology (IT) system for billing, accounts receivable, patient record keeping, personnel supervision, and the medical process control. The first step in launching this large installation project is to identify the important elements in introducing the technology. Here is a basic approach to identifying the deliverables in a project to install a new information system for an organization (see Figure 5.3).

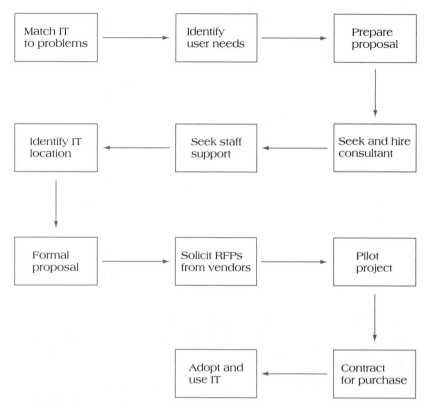

FIGURE 5.3 IT Installation Flowchart

1. Match IT to organizational tasks and problems.
2. Identify IT user needs.
3. Prepare an informal proposal to top management (or other decision makers) for IT acquisition.
4. Seek and hire an IT consultant.
5. Seek staff and departmental support for the IT.
6. Identify the most appropriate location within the organization for the IT hardware to be located.
7. Prepare a formal proposal for IT introduction.
8. Undertake a request for proposals (RFPs) from IT vendors.
9. Conduct a pilot project (or series of pilot projects using different IT options).
10. Enter a contract for purchase.
11. Adopt and use IT technology.

For simplicity's sake, this list identifies only the first-level tasks involved in completing this project. Clearly, each of the 11 steps above and in the flowchart in Figure 5.3 has various supporting subtasks associated with it. For example, step 2, identifying IT user needs, might have three subtasks:

1. Interview potential users.
2. Develop presentation of IT benefits.
3. Gain user "buy-in" to the proposed system.

Figure 5.4 illustrates a partial WBS, showing a few of the tasks and subtasks. The logic across all identified tasks that need to be accomplished for the project is similar.

We do not stop here but continue to flesh out the WBS with additional information. Figure 5.5 depicts a more complete WBS to demonstrate the logic of breaking the project up into its component pieces. The 1.0 level shown in Figure 5.5 identifies the overall project. Underneath this level are the major deliverables (e.g., 1.2, 1.3, etc.) that support the completion of the project. Underneath these deliverables are the various "work packages" that must be completed to conclude the project deliverables.

Work packages are defined as WBS elements of the project that are isolated for assignment to "work centers" for accomplishment.[11] Just as atoms are the smallest, indivisible unit of matter in physics, work packages are the smallest, indivisible components of a WBS. That is, work packages are the lowest level in

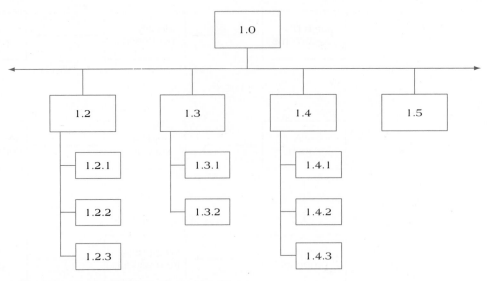

FIGURE 5.4 Partial Work Breakdown Structure

the WBS, composed of short-duration tasks that have a defined beginning and end, are assigned costs, and consume some resources. For example, in the 1.2 level of identifying IT user needs (a deliverable), we need to perform three supporting activities: (1) interviewing potential users, (2) developing a presentation of IT benefits, and (3) gaining user "buy-in" to the system. This next level down (1.2.1, 1.2.2, etc.) represents the work packages that are necessary to complete the deliverable.

Sometimes confusion arises as to the distinction made between "work package" and "task," as they relate to projects and the development of the WBS. In truth, for many organizations, the difference between the terms and their meanings is actually quite small; often they are used interchangeably by the project management organization. The key is to be consistent in applying the terminology, so that it means the same thing within different parts of the organization, in regard to both technical and managerial resources.

Overall, for a generic project, the logic of hierarchy for WBS follows this form:

Level	WBS Term	Description
Level 1 (Highest)	Project	The overall project under development
Level 2	Deliverable	The major project components
Level 3	Subdeliverable	Supporting deliverables
Level 4 (Lowest)	Work package	Individual project activities

Figure 5.5 provides an example of how project activities are broken down and identified at both the deliverable and the work package levels, as well as a brief description of each of these activities. The WBS in that figure also shows a numeric code assigned to each activity. A company's accounting function assigns **WBS codes** to each activity to allocate costs more precisely, to track the activities that are over or under budget, and to maintain financial control of the development process.

Sometimes it is necessary to differentiate between a subdeliverable, as identified in the hierarchical breakdown above, and work packages that are used to support and complete the subdeliverables. Typically, we think of subdeliverables as "rolled-up" summaries of the outcomes of two or more work packages. Unlike work packages, subdeliverables do not have a duration of their own, do not consume resources, and do not have direct assignable costs. Any resources or costs attached to a subdeliverable are simply the summary of all the work packages that support it.

Most organizations require that each deliverable (and usually each of the tasks or work packages contained within) come with descriptive documentation that supports the goals of the project and can be examined as a basis for allowing approval and scheduling resource commitments. Figure 5.6 is a sample page from a task description document, intended to support the project WBS outlined in Figure 5.5. Using work package 1.4.1, "Delegate members as search committee," a comprehensive control document can be

Breakdown	Description	WBS	Code
IT Installation Project			**1.0**
Deliverable 1	**Match IT to organizational tasks and problems**		**1.1**
WP 1	Conduct problem analysis	1.1.1	
WP 2	Develop information on IT technology	1.1.2	
Deliverable 2	**Identify IT user needs**		**1.2**
WP 1	Interview potential users	1.2.1	
WP 2	Develop presentation of IT benefits	1.2.2	
WP 3	Gain user "buy-in" to system	1.2.3	
Deliverable 3	**Prepare informal proposal**		**1.3**
WP 1	Develop cost/benefit information	1.3.1	
WP 2	Gain top management support	1.3.2	
Deliverable 4	**Seek and hire IT consultant**		**1.4**
WP 1	Delegate members as search committee	1.4.1	
WP 2	Develop selection criteria	1.4.2	
WP 3	Interview and select consultant	1.4.3	
Deliverable 5	**Seek staff and departmental support for IT**		**1.5**
Deliverable 6	**Identify the appropriate location for IT**		**1.6**
WP 1	Consult with physical plant engineers	1.6.1	
WP 2	Identify possible alternative sites	1.6.2	
WP 3	Secure site approval	1.6.3	
Deliverable 7	**Prepare a formal proposal for IT introduction**		**1.7**
Deliverable 8	**Solicit RFPs from vendors**		**1.8**
WP 1	Develop criteria for decision	1.8.1	
WP 2	Contact appropriate vendors	1.8.2	
WP 3	Select winner(s) and inform losers	1.8.3	
Deliverable 9	**Conduct a pilot project (or series of projects)**		**1.9**
Deliverable 10	**Enter a contract for purchase**		**1.10**
Deliverable 11	**Adopt and use IT technology**		**1.11**
WP 1	Initiate employee training sessions	1.11.1	
WP 2	Develop monitoring system for technical problems	1.11.2	

FIGURE 5.5 **Example of WBS for a Project**

prepared. When a supporting document functions as a project control device throughout the project's development, it is not prepared in advance and is no longer used once that project step has been completed; in other words, it is a dynamic document. This document also specifies project review meetings for the particular work package as the project moves forward; the task description document must be completed, filed, and revisited as often as necessary to ensure that all relevant information is available.

MS Project allows us to create a WBS for a project. As we input each project task, we can assign a WBS code to it by using the WBS option under the Project heading. Figure 5.7 gives a sample screen shot of some of the activities identified in the hospital IT project example. Note that we have created a partial WBS for the IT project by using the MS Project WBS option, which also allows us to distinguish between "Project Level" headings, "Deliverable" headings, and "Work Package" headings.

Project Task Description Form

Task Identification

Project Name: IT Installation   Project Code: IS02   Project Manager: Williams

WP Name: Delegate members as search committee

WP Code: 1.4.1   WP Owner: Susan Wilson

Deliverables: Assignment of personnel to IT vendor search committee

Revision no.: 3   Date: 10/22/12   Previous revision: 2 (on file)

Resources Required

Labor		Other Resources		
Type	Labor Days	Type	Quantity	Cost
Systems manager	5	Software A	1	$15,000
Senior programmer	3	Facility	N/A	
Hardware technician	2	Equipment	1	$500
Procurement manager	3	Other	N/A	
Systems engineer	5			

Required prerequisites: Deliverables 1.1, 1.2, and 1.3 (on file)

Acceptance tests: None required

Number of working days required to complete task: 5

Possible risk events, which may impair the successful completion of the task: _____
_____

TO BE COMPLETED AFTER SCHEDULING THE PROJECT:

Earliest start on the task: 1/15/13   Earliest finish on the task: 2/15/13

Review meeting according to milestones:

Name of milestone	Deliverables	Meeting date	Participants
Identify IT user needs	IT work requirements	8/31/12	Wilson, Boyd, Shaw
_____	_____	_____	_____
_____	_____	_____	_____

Design approval of the task:

Task Owner: Sue Wilson   Signature: _____   Date: _____

Customer contact: Stu Barnes   Signature: _____   Date: _____

Project Manager: Bob Williams   Signature: _____   Date: _____

FIGURE 5.6   Project Task Description

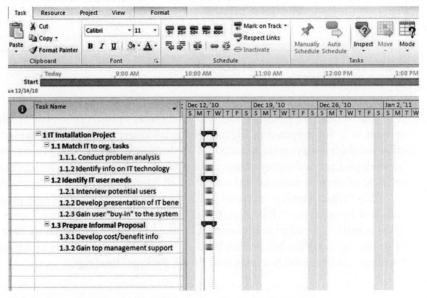

FIGURE 5.7   Sample WBS Development Using MS Project 2010

The Organization Breakdown Structure

An additional benefit of creating a comprehensive WBS for a project is the ability to organize the work needed to be performed into **cost control accounts** that are assignable to various units engaged in performing project activities within the company. The outcome of organizing this material is the **Organization Breakdown Structure (OBS)**. In short, the OBS allows companies to define the work to be accomplished and assign it to the owners of the work packages.[12] The budgets for these activities are then directly assigned to the departmental accounts responsible for the project work.

Suppose, for example, that our IT project example required the committed resources of three departments—information technology, procurement, and human resources. We want to make certain that the various work packages and their costs are correctly assigned to the person and department responsible for their completion in order to ensure that our cost control for the project can remain accurate and up-to-date. Figure 5.8 shows a visual example of the intersection of our partial WBS with an OBS for our IT installation project. The three departments within the organization are shown horizontally and the work packages underneath one of the deliverables are shown vertically. Notice that only some of the boxes used to illustrate the intersection are affected, suggesting that for some work packages multiple departments may be involved, each with its own cost accounts, while for other work packages there may be only one direct owner.

The benefit of using an OBS is that it allows for better initial linking of project activities and their budgets, either at a departmental level or, even more directly, on an individual-by-individual basis, as shown in Figure 5.9. In this case, the direct cost for each work package is assigned to a specific individual responsible for its completion. Figure 5.10 reconfigures the OBS to show the cost account rollups that can be done for each department responsible for a specific work package or project deliverable.

In managing projects, the main point to keep in mind about the scope statement is the need to spend adequate up-front time preparing schedules and budgets based on accurate and reasonable estimation. This

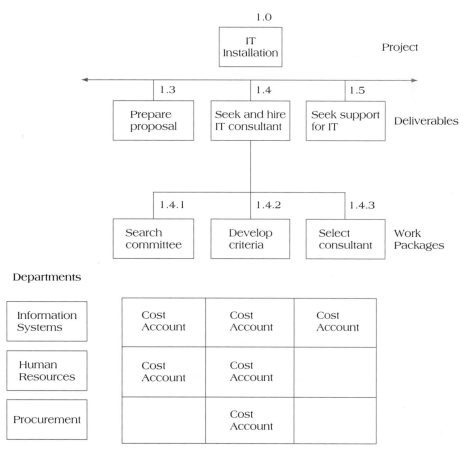

FIGURE 5.8 The Intersection of the WBS and OBS

WBS Code	Budget	Responsibility
1.0	$700,000	Bob Williams, IT Manager
1.1	5,000	Sharon Thomas
1.1.1	2,500	Sharon Thomas
1.1.2	2,500	Dave Barr
1.2	2,750	David LaCouture
1.2.1	1,000	David LaCouture
1.2.2	1,000	Kent Salfi
1.2.3	750	Ken Garrett
1.3	2,000	James Montgomery
1.3.1	2,000	James Montgomery
1.3.2	-0-	Bob Williams
1.4	2,500	Susan Wilson
1.4.1	-0-	Susan Wilson
1.4.2	1,500	Susan Wilson
1.4.3	1,000	Cynthia Thibodeau
1.5	-0-	Ralph Spence
1.6	1,500	Terry Kaplan
1.6.1	-0-	Kandra Ayotte
1.6.2	750	Terry Kaplan
1.6.3	750	Kandra Ayotte
1.7	2,000	Bob Williams
1.8	250	Beth Deppe
1.8.1	-0-	Kent Salfi
1.8.2	250	James Montgomery
1.8.3	-0-	Bob Williams
1.9	30,000	Debbie Morford
1.10	600,000	Bob Williams
1.11	54,000	David LaCouture
1.11.1	30,000	David LaCouture
1.11.2	24,000	Kandra Ayotte

FIGURE 5.9   Cost and Personnel Assignments

estimation can be adequately performed only if project managers have worked through the WBS and project goals statements thoroughly. There are fewer surefire ways to create an atmosphere for project failure than to do a cursory and incomplete WBS. When steps are left out, ignored, or underestimated during the WBS phase, they are then underbudgeted or underestimated in scheduling. The result is a project that will almost certainly have sliding schedules, rapidly inflating budgets, and confusion during the development phase. Much of this chaos can be avoided if the project manager spends enough time with her scope statement to ensure that there are no missing elements.

The Responsibility Assignment Matrix

To identify team personnel who will be directly responsible for each task in the project's development, a **Responsibility Assignment Matrix (RAM)** is developed. (The RAM is sometimes referred to as a *linear responsibility chart.*) Although it is considered a separate document, the RAM is often developed in conjunction with the WBS for a project. Figure 5.11 illustrates a Responsibility Assignment Matrix for this chapter's example project. Note that the matrix lists not only the member of the project team responsible for each activity, but also the other significant members of the team at each stage, organized according to how that activity requires their support. The RAM identifies where each person can go for task support, who should be

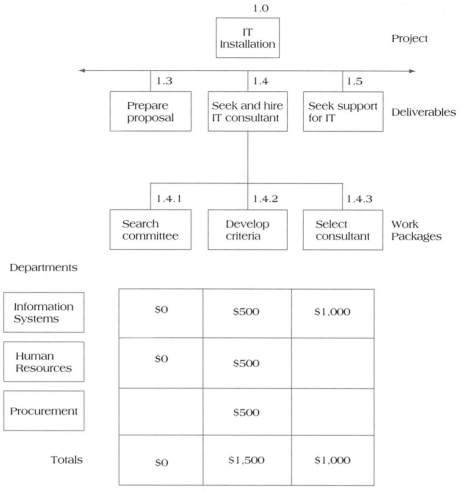

FIGURE 5.10 Cost Account Rollup Using OBS

Deliverable	Task & Code	Bob IT	David IT	Susan HR	Beth Procurement	James Engineering	Terry Legal
		Lead Project Personnel					
Match IT to Org. Tasks—1.1	Problem Analysis –1.1.1	○	■			☆	□
	Develop info on IT technology –1.1.2	☆	○	■			
Identify IT user needs—1.2	Interview potential users –1.2.1	□		○	☆		
	Develop presentation –1.2.2	○	☆			■	
	Gain user "buy-in" –1.2.3			☆	■	○	
Prepare proposal—1.3	Develop cost/benefit info –1.3.1	□			○		☆

○ Responsible   ☆ Support
■ Notification   □ Approval

FIGURE 5.11 Responsibility Assignment Matrix

PROJECT PROFILE

Defining a Project Work Package

Remember these seven important points about defining a project work package:[13]

1. The work package typically forms the lowest level in the WBS. Although some projects may employ the term *subtask,* the majority leave *work package–level* activities as the most basic WBS step.
2. A work package has a deliverable result. Each work package should have its own outcome. One work package does not summarize or modify another. Together, work packages identify all the work that must be contributed to complete the project.
3. A work package has one owner assigned—a project team member who will be most responsible for that package's completion. Although other team members can provide support as needed, only one person should be directly answerable for the work package.
4. A work package may be considered by its owner as a project in itself. If we adopt the notion that all work packages, because they are of finite length and budget and have a specific deliverable, can be considered miniature projects, each package owner can view his activities as a microproject.
5. A work package may include several milestones. A **milestone** is defined as a significant event in the project. Depending on the size and complexity of a project work package, it may contain a number of significant checkpoints or milestones that determine its progress toward completion.
6. A work package should fit organizational procedures and culture. Tasks undertaken to support project outcomes should be in accord with the overall cultural norms of the project organization. Performing a work package should never lead a team member to violate company policy (either codified or implicit); that is, assigned activities must pass both relevant legal standards for ethical behavior and also adhere to the accepted behaviors and procedures of the organization.
7. The optimal size of a work package may be expressed in terms of labor hours, calendar time, cost, report period, and risks. All work packages should be capable of being tracked, meaning that they must be structured to allow the project manager to monitor their progress. Progress is usually a measurable concept, delineated by metrics such as time and cost.

In developing a project's RAM, managers must consider the relationships between the project team and the rest of the organization as well as those within the project team. Within an organization and without it, actions of department heads and external functional managers can affect how members of a project team perform their jobs. Thus, a detailed RAM can help project managers negotiate with functional managers for resources, particularly through detailing the necessity of including various team members on the project.

---

notified of the task completion status at each stage, and any sign-off requirements. This tool provides a clear linkage among all project team members and combats the danger of a potential communication vacuum in which project team members perform their own tasks without updating others on the project team.

Working through a RAM allows the project manager to determine how best to team people for maximum efficiency. In developing the document, a project manager has a natural opportunity to assess team members' strengths, weaknesses, work commitments, and availability. Many firms spend a significant amount of money developing and using software to accurately track project activities, but not nearly as many devote time to tracking the ongoing interaction among project team members. A RAM allows project managers to establish a method for coordinating the work activities of team members, realizing the efficiencies that take place as all team members provide support, notification, and approval for each other's project responsibilities.

5.3 WORK AUTHORIZATION

This stage in scope management naturally follows the two previous steps. Once the scope definition, planning documents, management plans, and other contractual documents have been prepared and approved, the **work authorization** step gives the formal "go ahead" to commence with the project. Many times work authorization consists of the formal sign-off on all project plans, including detailed specifications for project delivery. In cases of projects developed for external clients, work authorization typically addresses contractual obligations; for internal clients, it means establishing an audit trail by linking all budget and resource requirements to the formal cost accounting system of the organization. Numerous components of contractual obligations between project organizations and clients can exist, but most contractual documentation possesses some key identifiable features:[14]

- *Contractual requirements.* All projects are promised in terms of the specific functionality, or performance criteria, they will meet. This raises the questions: What is the definition accepted by both parties of "specific performance"? Are the terms of performance clearly understood and identified by both parties?
- *Valid consideration.* What items are voluntarily promised in exchange for a reciprocal commitment by another party? Does the work authorization contract make clear the commitments agreed to by both parties?
- *Contracted terms.* What are excusable delays, allowable costs, statements of liquidated damages in the case of nonperformance? What are the criteria for inspection? Who has responsibility for correction of defects? What steps are necessary to resolve disputes? Contracted terms typically have clear legal meanings that encourage both parties to communicate efficiently.

A number of contractual arrangements can serve to codify the relationship between a project organization and a customer. It is beyond the purview of this chapter to explore the various forms of contracts and legal recourse in great detail, but some standard contractual arrangements should be considered when managing the project scope. From the perspective of the project organization, the most common contracts range from *lump-sum* or **turnkey contracts**, in which the project organization assumes all responsibility for successful performance, to **cost-plus contracts**, which fix the company's profit for a project in advance. We will discuss the latter first.

Sometimes it is nearly impossible to determine the likely cost for a project in advance. For example, the sheer technical challenges involved in putting a man on the moon, drilling a tunnel under the English Channel, or developing the Strategic Defense Initiative make the process of estimating project costs extremely difficult. In these cases, it is common for project companies to enter into a cost-plus contract that guarantees them a certain profit, regardless of the cost overruns that may occur during the project development. Cost-plus contracts can be abused; in fact, there have been notorious examples of huge overruns in governmental contracts because the lack of oversight resulted in systematic abuses. However, cost-plus contracts can minimize the risk that a company would incur if it were to undertake a highly technical project with the potential for uncertain outcomes, provided that both parties understand the terms of the agreement, the project organization acts with due diligence, and there is a final audit of the project books.

At the opposite extreme are lump-sum (sometimes referred to as turnkey) contracts in which the contractor is required to perform all work at an initially negotiated price. Lump-sum contracting works best when the parameters of the project are clearly understood by both sides (e.g., a residential construction project) and the attendant costs of the project can be estimated with some level of sophistication. In lump-sum contracts, initial cost estimation is critical; if the original estimate is too low and the contractor encounters unforeseen problems, the project's profit may be reduced or even disappear. The advantage of the lump-sum contract to the customer is that the selected project contractor has accepted the majority of the risk in the project. On the other hand, because cost estimation is so crucial, it is common for initial estimates in lump-sum contracts to be quite high, requiring negotiation and rebidding between the contractors and the customer.

The key point about work authorization is grounded in the nature of stated terms for project development. The manager must draw up contracts that clearly stipulate the work agreed to, the nature of the project development process, steps to resolve disputes, and clearly identified criteria for successfully completing the project. This specificity can be especially important when dealing with external stakeholders, including suppliers and clients. Precisely worded work authorization terminology can provide important assistance for project development downstream. On the other hand, ambiguously stated terms or incorrectly placed milestones may actually provoke the opposite results: disagreements, negotiations, and potentially legal action—all guaranteed to slow project development down to a crawl and add tremendous costs to the back end of "completed" projects.

5.4 SCOPE REPORTING

At the project's kickoff, the project team and key clients should make decisions about the need for project updates: How many will be required, and how frequently? **Scope reporting** fulfills this function by determining the types of information that will be regularly reported, who will receive copies of this information, and how this information will be acquired and disseminated.

What types of information are available and what may be appropriately reported? Clearly, a wide variety of forms of project reports can be tracked and itemized. Although the concepts will be developed in more detail in subsequent chapters, among the types of project parameter information that are most commonly included in these reports are:[15]

- Cost status: updates on budget performance

    S curves: graphical displays of costs (including labor hours and other costs) against project schedule

    Earned value: reporting project status in terms of both cost and time (the budgeted value of work performed regardless of actual costs incurred)

    Variance or exception reports: documenting any slippages in time, performance, or cost against planned measures
- Schedule status: updates on schedule adherence
- Technical performance status: updates on technical challenges and solutions

Solid communication between all concerned parties on a project is one of the most important aspects of effective scope reporting. It is necessary to avoid the temptation to limit project status information to only a handful of individuals. Often using the excuse of "need to know," many project teams keep the status of their project secretive, even past the point when it has run into serious trouble (see "Project Management Research in Brief" box). Project managers should consider who would benefit from receiving regular project updates and plan their reporting structure appropriately. Some stakeholders who could be included in regular project status reporting are:

- Members of the project team
- Project clients
- Top management
- Other groups within the organization affected by the project
- Any external stakeholders who have an interest in project development, such as suppliers and contractors

All of these groups have a stake in the development of the project or will be affected by the implementation process. Limiting information may seem to be efficient or save time in the short run, but it can fuel possible misunderstandings, rumors, and organizational resistance to the project in the long run.

BOX 5.1

PROJECT MANAGEMENT RESEARCH IN BRIEF

Information Technology (IT) Project "Death Marches": What Is Happening Here?

Every year, billions of dollars are spent on thousands of information technology (IT) projects worldwide. With the huge emphasis on IT products and advances in software and hardware systems, it is no surprise that interest in this field is exploding. Under the circumstances, we would naturally expect that, given the importance of IT projects in both our corporate and everyday lives, we are doing a reasonably good job of implementing these critical projects, right? Unfortunately, the answer is a clear "no." In fact, IT projects have a terrible track record for delivery, as numerous studies show. How bad? The average IT project is likely to be 6 to 12 months *behind* schedule and 50% to 100% *over* budget. Of course, the numbers vary with the size of the project, but the results still suggest that companies should expect their IT projects to lead to wasted effort, enormous delays, burnout, and many lost weekends while laboring for success with the cards stacked the other way.

What we are referring to here are "death march" projects. The death march project is typically one in which the project is set up for failure through the demands or expectations that the company places on it, leaving the expectation that project team will pull off a miracle. The term *death march* invokes images of team members wearily trudging along mile after mile, with no end or possibility of successful conclusion in sight. Death march projects are defined as projects "whose parameters exceed the norm by at least 50%." In practical terms, that can mean:

- The schedule has been compressed to less than half the amount estimated by a rational estimating process (e.g., the schedule suggests it should take one year to complete the project, but top management shrinks the schedule to six months).

- The project team staffing has been reduced to half the number that normally would be assigned to a project of this size and scope (e.g., a project manager needing 10 resources assigned is instead given only 5).
- The budget and other necessary resources are cut in half (e.g., as a result of downsizing and other cost-cutting exercises in the company, everyone is expected to "do more with less"; or competitive bidding to win the contract was so intense that when the smoke cleared, the company that won the project did so at such a cut-rate price it cannot possibly hire enough people to make it work).

The result of any or all of these starting conditions is a virtual guarantee that the project will fail. The prevalence of death march projects begs the question: Why are death march projects so common and why do they continue to occur? According to the research, there are a number of reasons:

1. Politics—the project may be the result of a power struggle between two ambitious senior executives, or it may have been set up to fail as a form of revenge upon some manager. In these cases, the project manager just gets caught in the blast zone.
2. Naïve promises made by marketing executives or inexperienced project managers—inexperience can result in all sorts of promises made, including those that are impossible to fulfill. In order to impress the boss, a new project manager may promise more than he can deliver. Marketing managers who are concerned with sales and how to improve them may think, "what's a little exaggerated promise if it closes the deal?"
3. Naïve optimism of youth—a technical hotshot who is ambitious and feeling particularly cocky one day may make exaggerated promises that quickly result in the project team getting in over its head. Optimism is no substitute for careful planning.
4. The "start-up" mentality of fledgling entrepreneurial companies—start-up firms come loaded with energy, enthusiasm, and an aggressive, get-it-going attitude. When that mentality translates into projects, however, problems can occur. Entrepreneurial approaches to managing projects may ignore critical planning and detailed advance preparation that no experienced project manager would sacrifice.
5. The "Marine Corps" mentality: real programmers don't need sleep—this attitude emphasizes bravado as a substitute for evaluation. The hyperoptimistic schedule or budget is not an accident; it is a deliberate manifestation of this aggressive attitude: If you can't handle it, you don't belong here.
6. Intense competition caused by globalization—the appearance of new, international competitors often comes as a rude awakening when it is first experienced. Many firms respond with radical moves that push for rapid technical advances or "catching up" behaviors, resulting in numerous new death march projects.
7. Intense competition caused by the appearance of new technologies—as new opportunities emerge through new technologies, some firms jump into them eagerly, without first understanding their capacities, scalability for larger projects, and limitations. The result is an endless game of exploiting "opportunities" without fully comprehending them or the learning curve for using new technologies.
8. Intense pressure caused by unexpected government regulations—government-mandated death march projects occur through a failure of top management to anticipate new regulations or mandates or, worse, to recognize that they are coming but put off any efforts to comply with them until deadlines have already been set. New pollution or carbon-energy controls laws, for example, may lead to huge projects with looming deadlines because the company put off until the last minute any efforts to self-regulate.
9. Unexpected and/or unplanned crises—any number of crises can be anticipated with sufficient advance planning. Examples of crises that can severely affect project delivery are the loss of key project team personnel midway through the project's development or the bankruptcy of a key supplier. Some crises, of course, are unpredictable by definition, but all too often the crisis that destroys all of the work to date on a project is one that could have been anticipated with a little foresight. The long road back from these disasters will lead to many death marches.

Death march projects are not limited to the IT industry. Indeed, as we consider the list of reasons why death marches occur, we can see similar effects in numerous projects across different industries. The end result is typically the same: massively wasted efforts spent on projects that have been set up to fail by the very conditions under which they are expected to operate. The implications are clear: To avoid setting the stage for future death march projects, we need to start with the end in mind and ask, are the goals and conditions (budget, personnel assigned, and schedule) conducive to project success, or are we just sowing the seeds of inevitable disaster?[16]

5.5 CONTROL SYSTEMS

A question we might ask is: "How does a project become one year late?" The answer is: "One day at a time." When we are not paying close attention to a project's development, anything can (and usually does) happen. At issue is that key element in scope management of project control. **Control systems** are vital to ensure that any changes to the project baseline are conducted in a systematic and thorough manner. Project managers can use a number of types of project control systems to track the status of their projects, including the following:[17]

- *Configuration control*   includes procedures that monitor emerging project scope against the original baseline scope. Is the project following its initial goals, or are they being allowed to drift as status changes or new circumstances alter the original project intent?
- *Design control*   relates to systems for monitoring the project's scope, schedule, and costs during the design stage. Chrysler developed Platform Design Teams (PDTs), composed of members from functional departments, to ensure that new automobile designs could be immediately evaluated by experts in engineering, production, and marketing. It found that this instantaneous feedback eliminated the time that had been lost when designs were deemed unworkable by the engineering organization at some later point in the car's development.
- *Trend monitoring*   is the process of tracking the estimated costs, schedules, and resources needed against those planned. Trend monitoring shows significant deviations from norms for any of these important project metrics.
- *Document control*   ensures that important documentation is compiled and disseminated in an orderly and timely fashion. Document control is a way of making sure that anything contractual or legal is documented and distributed. For example, document control would ensure that the minutes of a building committee's deliberations concerning a new construction project are reproduced and forwarded to appropriate oversight groups.
- *Acquisition control*   monitors systems used to acquire necessary project equipment, materials, or services needed for project development and implementation.
- *Specification control*   ensures that project specifications are prepared clearly, communicated to all concerned parties, and changed only with proper authorization.

One of the most important pieces of advice for project managers and teams is to establish and maintain a reasonable level of control (including clear lines of authority) *at the start of a project*. Perhaps surprisingly, *reasonable* here means avoiding the urge to overdevelop and overcontrol projects. Project managers' ability to manage day-to-day activities can be hindered by having to handle excessive control system reports—there can simply be too much paperwork. On the other hand, it is equally important not to devalue control systems as taking up too much time. Knowing the right project control systems to use and how often to employ them can eliminate much of the guesswork when dealing with project delays or cost overruns. For example, a recent large office building project brought together a project team composed of groups and contractors relating to the architectural design; the heating, ventilation, and air conditioning (HVAC); the electrical and plumbing work; concrete and steel construction; and facilities management. During meetings early in the project, the combined construction project team agreed to a clear scope for the project and a streamlined control and reporting process that had trend monitoring, configuration, and specification control as the key elements in the project review cycle. Because several of the independent contractors had a long history of working together and had built a level of mutual trust, they reasoned that the barest minimum control processes would be preferable. In this example, the team sought a balance in project control processes between the twin errors of excessive and nonexistent control.

Configuration Management

The Project Management Body of Knowledge (PMBoK) defines *configuration management* as "a system of procedures that monitors emerging project scope against the scope baseline. It requires documentation and management approval on any change to the baseline." A **baseline** is defined as the project's scope fixed at a specific point in time—for example, the project's scheduled start date. The baseline, therefore, is viewed as the project's *configuration*. Remember that the scope baseline is simply a summary description of the project's original content and end product, including budget and time constraint data. As a result, in simple terms, **configuration management** relates to the fact that projects usually consist of component parts, all contributing to the project's functionality. These parts must be individually developed and ultimately assembled, or configured, to produce the final product or service. The role of designing, making, and assembling these components belongs to configuration management. However, because this process often requires several iterations, adjustments, and corrections to get the project right, in practical terms, *configuration management is the systematic management and control of project change.*[18]

The management of project changes is most effectively accomplished at the beginning of the project when plans and project scope are first articulated. Why would you want to begin managing change at the point where you are carefully defining a project? The answer is that the need to make significant project changes is usually an acknowledged part of the planning process. Some changes are made as the result of carefully acknowledged need; others emerge almost by accident during the project's development. For example, we may discover at some point during the project's execution that certain technical specifications we designed into the original prototype may not work under specific conditions (e.g., high altitudes, humid conditions), requiring us to make midcourse alterations to the project's required functionality.

Configuration management works toward formalizing the change process as much as possible as early in the project's life as possible, rather than leaving needed downstream changes to be made in an uncoordinated manner. The need to make project changes or specification adjustments, it has been suggested, comes about for one of several reasons:[19]

- *Initial planning errors, either technological or human.*   Many projects involve technological risks. It is often impossible to accurately account for all potential problems or technological roadblocks. For example, the U.S. Navy and Marine Corps' drive to create a vertical takeoff, propeller-driven aircraft, the Osprey, resulted in a series of unexpected technical problems, including some tragic accidents during prototype testing. Initial engineering did not predict (and perhaps could not have predicted) the problems that would emerge with this new technology. Hence, many projects require midcourse changes to technical specifications as they encounter problems that are not solvable with existing resources or other unexpected difficulties. Planning errors also may be due to human mistake or lack of full knowledge of the development process. In the case of nontechnical causes for change, reconfiguration may be a simple adjustment to the original plans to accommodate new project realities.
- *Additional knowledge of project or environmental conditions.*   The project team or a key stakeholder, such as the client, may enter into a project only to discover that specific features of the project or the business, economic, or natural environment require midcourse changes to the scope. For example, the technical design of a deep-water oil-drilling rig may have to be significantly modified upon discovery of the nature of water currents or storm characteristics, underwater terrain formations, or other unanticipated environmental features.
- *Uncontrollable mandates.*   In some circumstances, events occur outside the control of the project team and must be factored into the project as it moves forward. For example, a governmental mandate for passenger safety established by the European Union in 2001 forced Boeing Corporation to redesign exit features on its new 777 aircraft, temporarily delaying the project's introduction and sale to foreign airlines.
- *Client requests.*   The situation in which a project's clients, as the project evolves, attempt to address new needs with significant alterations is a very common phenomenon. In software development, for example, a client taking the role of potential user might list several complaints, requests, new features, reworked features, and so on when first exposed to a planned software upgrade. Often IT projects run excessively behind schedule as users continue to bring forward lists of new requirements or change requests.

Configuration management can probably be traced to the change control techniques initiated by the U.S. defense community in the 1950s. Defense contractors routinely changed the configuration of various weapon systems at the request of governmental groups, especially the armed forces. In making these changes, however, little of the process would be documented or traceable; hence, when new weapon systems were introduced, the armed forces found them hard to service and maintain. Poor record keeping led to poor channels of communication to relevant contractors when problems or modification requests arose. As a result, the Defense Department routinely found it necessary to reissue general change request orders that delayed its ability to gain timely performance corrections. In the middle of the decade after much frustration (and expense), the Defense Department finally issued an order mandating that all organizations supplying systems to the government demonstrate a comprehensive change control and documentation process.[20]

Figure 5.12 presents the four stages in configuration management, including the tasks to be performed at each of the configuration management steps.[21]

Step	Action
1. Configuration identification	1. Develop a breakdown of the project to the necessary level of definition. 2. Identify the specifications of the components of the breakdown and of the total project.
2. Configuration reviews	Meet with all the project stakeholders to agree to the current project definition.
3. Configuration control	1. If agreement is achieved, repeat the first three steps, developing the breakdown and specification further, until the project is defined. 2. If agreement is not reached, either: • Cycle back to the configuration as agreed at a previous review and repeat steps 1, 2, and 3 until agreement is achieved; or • Change the specification last obtained by a process change control to match what people think it should be.
4. Status accounting	Memory of the current configurations, and all previous ones, must be maintained so that if agreement is not reached at some point, the team can cycle back to a previous configuration and restart from there. Also, memory of the configuration of all prototypes must be maintained.

FIGURE 5.12 **Four Stages of Configuration Management**

Source: © Turner, R. (2000), "Managing scope-configuration and work methods," in Turner, R. (Ed.), *Gower Handbook of Project Management,* 3rd ed. Aldershot, UK: Gower.

5.6 PROJECT CLOSEOUT

Effective scope management also includes appropriate planning for a project's termination. Although the process of effective project termination will be covered in great detail in Chapter 14, it is useful to reflect on the fact that even when planning for a project, we should be planning for the project's conclusion. The **project closeout** step requires project managers to consider the types of records and reports they and their clients will require at the completion of the project.[22] The earlier in the scope development process that these decisions are made, the more useful the information collected over the project's development can be. Closeout information can be important (1) in the case of contractual disputes after the project has been completed, since the more thorough the project records, the less likely it is that the organization will be held liable for alleged violations; (2) as a useful training tool for postproject analysis of either successes or failures; and (3) to facilitate project auditing tasks by showing the flow of expenses in and out of various project accounts.

Closeout documentation a project leader may decide to track includes the following:

- *Historical records,* or project documentation that can be used to predict trends, analyze feasibility, and highlight problem areas for similar future projects
- *Postproject analysis,* which follows a formal reporting structure, including analysis and documentation of the project's performance in terms of cost, schedule adherence, and technical specification performance
- *Financial closeout,* or the accounting analysis of how funds were dispersed on the project

One of the most important lessons for successful project managers is to "start with the end in mind." Clear goals at the beginning of a project make clear what the project's completion will require. Project closeout requires managers to consider a priori the types and amounts of information to continually collect during project development, relying on a sound project tracking and filing system. That way, when the project is in its closeout, time is not wasted scrambling for old project records and other information that is needed but missing.

A project's goals are just a dream until they are written down. Until the project's plans are laid out, its purposes specified, its constraints considered, and its results anticipated, a project is nothing more than an organization's hope for success. Scope management is the systematic process of turning these dreams into reality by formally developing project goals. Like a lighthouse, a thorough scope document illuminates the way toward project completion even while the team may be tossed on the waves of numerous crises and concerns. As long as the light continues to shine, as long as the project manager works to develop and maintain the various elements of project scope, the likelihood of passage to successful project completion is strong.

Summary

1. **Understand the importance of scope management for project success.**   This chapter examined the role of project scope management as an important planning technique. Project scope management is the detailed development of the project plan to specify the work content and outcomes of the project, the activities that must be performed, the resources consumed, and the quality standards to be maintained. The six steps in creating a project scope management procedure are conceptual development, the scope statement, work authorization, scope reporting, control systems, and project closeout.

   Conceptual development is the process of choosing the best method for achieving the project's goals. The project's conceptual development allows the project manager to begin the process of transitioning from the project as a dream to the project as a specific goal or set of objectives. Problem statements, information gathering, identified constraints, alternatives analyses, and final project objectives are all created during the conceptual development.

   The scope statement is a comprehensive definition of all parameters necessary for the project to succeed. A number of elements factor into effective scope statement development, but perhaps most key is the Work Breakdown Structure (WBS). The work breakdown process gives the project team the ability to create a hierarchy of activities-based priorities, creating work packages, tasks, and subtasks as building blocks for completing the overall project. When this is coupled with a clear Responsibility Assignment Matrix (RAM), the project manager and team are able to begin moving beyond the project as a concept and tackle the project as a set of identified activities, with responsible personnel assigned to them.

   Work authorization, the third element in project scope management, refers to the process of sanctioning all project work. This step may involve formulating contractual obligations with vendors, suppliers, and clients.

   Project scope reporting refers to any control systems and documentation that will be used to assess the project's overall status. Examples of scope reporting include the creation of control documents and budget and schedule tracking.

   Control systems, including configuration management, refer to the processes put in place to track the ongoing status of the project, compare actual with baseline projections, and offer corrective measures for bringing the project back on track.

   Finally, the project closeout phase represents the project team's best determination as to the information and transition materials necessary to ensure a smooth transfer of the project to its intended clients.

2. **Understand the significance of developing a scope statement.**   The project scope statement reflects the project team's best efforts to create the documentation and approval for all important project parameters prior to beginning the development phase. This statement is an opportunity to clearly "nail down" the elements of the project and what it is intended to accomplish, as well as to identify the project's critical features. The elements in the scope statement include (1) establishing the goal criteria—defining what will demonstrate project success and what the decision gates are for evaluating deliverables; (2) developing the management plan for the project—determining the structure for the project team, key rules and procedures that will be maintained, and the control systems to monitor effort; (3) establishing the Work Breakdown Structure (WBS)—dividing the project into component substeps in order to establish the critical interrelationships among project activities; and (4) creating a scope baseline—providing a summary description of each component of the project's goal, including budget and schedule information for each activity.

3. **Construct a Work Breakdown Structure for a project.** The Work Breakdown Structure (WBS) is a process that sets a project's scope by breaking down its overall mission into a cohesive set of synchronous, increasingly specific tasks. Defined as a "deliverable-oriented grouping of project elements which organizes and defines the total scope of the project," the WBS is the most important organizing tool project teams have in preparing their tasks.

The WBS serves six main purposes: (1) it echoes project objectives; (2) it is the organization chart for the project; (3) it creates the logic for tracking costs, schedule, and performance specifications for each element in the project; (4) it may be used to communicate project status; (5) it may be used to improve overall project communication; and (6) it demonstrates how the project will be controlled. The logic of the WBS is to subdivide project deliverables into increasingly more specific sublevels to identify all significant activities. The common terminology is to first identify the overall project, then the major deliverables for that project, and finally the work packages that must be accomplished to complete each deliverable.

Closely related to the WBS is the Organization Breakdown Structure (OBS), which allows companies to define the work to be accomplished and assign it to the owners of the work packages. The budgets for these activities are then directly assigned to the departmental accounts responsible for the project work.

4. **Develop a Responsibility Assignment Matrix for a project.** The Responsibility Assignment Matrix (RAM), sometimes referred to as a linear responsibility chart, identifies project team personnel who are directly responsible for each task in the project's development. The RAM identifies where responsible team members can go for task support, who should next be notified of the task completion status, and any sign-off requirements. The goal of the RAM is to facilitate communication between project team personnel to minimize transition disruptions as the project moves toward completion. An additional benefit of the RAM is to make the coordination between project managers and functional department heads easier as they work to make best use of personnel who may be assigned to the project for only temporary periods.

5. **Describe the roles of changes and configuration management in assessing project scope.** Significant project changes occur for a number of reasons, including (1) initial planning errors, either technological or human; (2) additional knowledge of project or environmental conditions; (3) uncontrollable mandates; and (4) client requests.

The four stages of configuration management are (1) configuration identification—breaking down the project and identifying the specifications of its components; (2) configuration reviews—meeting with stakeholders to agree to project definition; (3) configuration control—following agreement with stakeholders, developing the breakdown and specifications further; and (4) status accounting—maintaining memory of all current and previous configurations for reference.

Key Terms

Baseline (p. 178)	Cost-plus contracts (p. 175)
Conceptual development (p. 160)	Deliverables (p. 164)
Configuration management (p. 178)	Milestone (p. 174)
Control systems (p. 178)	Organization Breakdown Structure (OBS) (p. 171)
Cost control accounts (p. 171)	Project closeout (p. 180)
	Project scope (p. 159)
Responsibility Assignment Matrix (RAM) (p. 172)	Turnkey contracts (p. 175)
Scope baseline (p. 165)	WBS codes (p. 168)
Scope management (p. 159)	Work authorization (p. 174)
Scope reporting (p. 175)	Work Breakdown Structure (WBS) (p. 164)
Scope statement (p. 164)	Work packages (p. 167)
Statement of Work (SOW) (p. 162)	

Discussion Questions

1. What are the principal benefits of developing a comprehensive project scope analysis?
2. What are the key characteristics of a work package?
3. Create a Work Breakdown Structure for a term paper project or another school-related project you are working on. What are the steps in the WBS? Can you identify any substeps for each step?
4. What are the benefits of developing a Responsibility Assignment Matrix (RAM) for a project?
5. Develop an argument for scope reporting mechanisms. At a minimum, what types of reports do you consider necessary for document control of a project? Why?
6. What is the chief purpose of configuration management? In your opinion, why has it become increasingly popular in recent years as a part of the project management process?
7. What is the logic behind developing a plan for project closeout prior to even beginning the project?

Problems

1. Prepare a group project for the classroom. Use as your model one of the following:
   a. Construction project
   b. Software development project
   c. Events management project (e.g., an awards banquet)
   d. New product development project

   Develop a Statement of Work (SOW) for the project, using the format of (1) background, (2) task, (3) objectives, (4) approach, (5) input source. Next, create a Work Breakdown Structure (WBS) for the project. What are the key steps, including work packages, tasks, and any related subtasks for the project?

2. Using the project you have identified in Problem 1, create a Responsibility Assignment Matrix (RAM) for it, identifying at least six fictitious project team members.

3. Research a real project through library resources or the Internet and develop a brief scope statement for the project, a general WBS, and any other information pertaining to the scope management for that project.

Case Study 5.1

Boeing's Virtual Fence

On January 14, 2011, Secretary of Homeland Security Janet Napolitano made it official: The Virtual Fence Project was to be officially canceled. In her statement explaining the decision, Napolitano cited the difficulty in creating a unified, fully integrated security system and promised to "pursue a new path forward." What was left unsaid were the reasons that led to the final decision—principally, struggling with a too-complicated technical system that did not work but was leading to ballooning costs.

Illegal crossing into the United States along the Mexican border has reached epidemic proportions in recent years. Fear of drug smuggling, illegal aliens, and possible terrorist incursions have made the issue of homeland security one of the major "hot buttons" in the political arena, both in Washington, DC, and within states located along the southern border as well as those in proximity to Canada. The problem is compounded by the sheer sizes of the borders involved. The Mexican/U.S. border runs for nearly 2,000 miles, much of it across desert wastelands and inhospitable and remote areas. Establishing any sort of border security, in the wake of the 9/11 attacks, is a national necessity but a daunting and difficult task.

The Department of Homeland Security (DHS), organized following the attacks on the World Trade Center towers, is charged with the responsibility of securing all borders and points of illegal entry into the United States, in cooperation with Customs and Border Protection. As part of its mandate, it has developed plans for creating a more secure and stable border with Mexico to prevent the continuous flow of undocumented immigrants, drugs, and potential terrorists. For the first stage in this process, DHS proposed a project to physically and electronically seal the stretch of the desert between the United States and Mexico under a multibillion-dollar contract named the Secure Border Initiative Net (SBInet). President Bush in May 2006 called SBInet "the most technologically advanced border security initiative in American history." A 28-mile stretch of desert, centered on Nogales, Texas, was to be the pilot stage in a project that eventually would be used to monitor and control some 6,000 miles of border with both Mexico and Canada.

In late 2006, Boeing was selected as the major contractor for the SBInet project. Although better known for their military weapon systems, Boeing's Integrated Defense Systems Unit was made responsible for overall coordination of a massive system of towers as well as listening devices, motion sensors, cameras, and radar to be used to detect and help apprehend illegals crossing the border. In fact, the U.S. government chose to outsource the entire project to private firms. The government's only role was to be as the force responsible for apprehending the people first detected by the SBInet. "Virtually every detail is being outsourced from the government to private contractors," said California Democratic Congressman Henry Waxman. "The government is relying on private contractors to design the programs, build them, and even conduct oversight of them."

In a nutshell, the system used a chain of 100-foot-tall towers that each scanned a 360-degree radius for a distance of 10 miles. Ground radar sensors also attempted to detect footsteps, bicycles, and vehicles. The first $20 million pilot phase, named Project 28 after the length of the part of the desert that it was supposed to cover, was to be completed by mid-June 2007. Boeing selected more than 100 subcontractors to build various components of the system, with its project managers maintaining overall control of the development process. Unfortunately, their structure was unwieldy, and the project was further compromised by the sheer number of distinct elements and technical systems Boeing was attempting to integrate. The technical challenge of integrating systems including watch towers, sensors, radar, and specialized cameras was

(continued)

beyond anything Boeing had attempted before. As one article noted, "Successfully integrating complex components is a substantial risk in any project containing multiple, complicated subsystems. Integration risks become especially pronounced in situations where integration essentially defines the project, such as this case. The risk increases further when the subsystems themselves consist of new, or unproven, technology." So complicated was the challenge, in fact, that the virtual fence failed a series of initial tests, significantly delaying the full deployment of Project 28.

Unfortunately, these technical and coordination problems were never resolved. In the nearly three years after original testing was done on one section of the fence, SBInet had cost the government $672 million dollars, with the end nowhere in sight. Although the total project cost was anticipated at $1.1 billion, congressional watchdog groups argued that the final cost of the project could soar to over $30 billion. Costs, in fact, were a sore point with the project from the time it was bid. Originally promising to complete SBInet for $1.1 billion, Boeing's revised estimates went to $2.5 billion and then, just a few months later, to $8 billion. This rapid escalation of projected costs finally prompted a congressional oversight committee hearing, in which Congressman William Lacy Clay, a Missouri democrat, demanded information about the ballooning costs and the extension of the contract period from a Boeing executive, saying, "You bid on these contracts and then you come back and say, 'Oh we need more time. It costs more than twice as much.' Are you gaming the taxpayers here? Or gaming DHS?" In the meantime, beset by continuing problems, Boeing had also revised its estimates for the completion date to 2016, more than seven years after the date in the original plan.

A major concern was the pyramid-like management structure that critics said led to cost overruns and poor quality in other major projects. The critics noted that the multiple subcontracting tiers allowed Boeing to exact a cut at every turn, and created a conflict of interest because the company was also in charge of oversight. "The last time I saw this type of model for managing a project was 'the Big Dig' in Boston," said Massachusetts Democratic Congressman Steven Lynch, referring to the highway rerouting mega project that included a 3.5-mile-long tunnel under Boston. "This is exactly what they did. They fused the oversight function with the engineering and construction function. Everybody was in the same tent. Nobody was watching out for the owner, who in this case is the U.S. taxpayer. This is a terrible model and I see a lot of it. Generally when this model is in place, we see colossal failures and huge cost overruns."

Admittedly, the problems that sank the SBInet project were complicated and came from multiple sources. Besides the technical challenges of managing 100 subcontractors, all required to provide critical components that Boeing would integrate, the project had effectively shut out most federal agencies and oversight groups. It was difficult to get accurate project status information given the government's decision to "farm out" border security to private contractors. As a result, congressional investigators found that Homeland Security officials were simply standing by while Boeing provided information that was "replete with unexplained anomalies, thus rendering the data unfit for effective contractor management and oversight." Furthermore, many critics questioned the feasibility of the original intent of the project itself, wondering about the likelihood of ever effectively sealing a border that runs through some of the most inhospitable terrain in North America.

Senator Joe Lieberman, chair of the Senate Homeland Security and Governmental Affairs Committee, offered a scathing critique of the project during testimony by Janet Napolitano, Secretary for Homeland Security, stating: "U.S. Customs and Border Protection seems to have effectively told Boeing—the contractor—'Go ahead and do what you can do as quickly as you can.'" He added, "Without clear goals and expectations, both Customs and Border Protection and Boeing underestimated the complexity of building the system. And the Border Patrol agents themselves—the people who would be implementing and relying on the system every day—were not consulted on what their actual needs were." Lieberman concluded, "By any measure, SBInet has been a failure—a classic example of a program that was grossly oversold and has badly under-delivered."[23]

Questions

1. What problems do you see emerging from a project such as SBInet where the government allows the contractor to determine scope, manage all contractor relations, and decide how to share project status information with oversight bodies?
2. Consider the following two arguments: "The failure of SBInet was due to poor scope management" versus "SBInet failed because of poor oversight and project controls." Take one side or the other in this argument, and justify your response.

Case Study 5.2

Akbank CRM Transformation Program

With a consolidated asset size of more than $81 billion and a strong, extensive national distribution network comprising of more than 15,000 employees serving more than 8.5 million customers across nearly 950 branches, Akbank is the leading private bank in Turkey. In 2012, Akbank was named the "Most Valuable Banking Brand in Turkey" by Brand Finance in the "Brand Finance Banking 500" report. In addition, Akbank ranked 96th, globally, in the Top 500 Most Valuable Banking Brands list.

Having one of the largest customer bases in the market and a leading variety of products and channels, Akbank recognized the need to create a new technological infrastructure to maintain its high standards of innovation, and therefore implemented a new customer relationship management (CRM) solution to integrate all existing processes, data, and channels. The company's CRM program began in 2008 and was successfully completed in 2010. In 2011, it received the "CRM Excellence—Integrated Marketing" award from Gartner, specifically for its CRM system "ATOM." Candidates across Europe, the Middle East, Africa, Asia-Pacific, and China are reviewed for this award. Akbank is the first Turkish Bank to win it.

The scope of Akbank's CRM renewal program was extremely vast in contrast to other projects. There were nearly 10 business units as project stakeholders. All channels (branch, ATM, Internet banking, call center, mobile banking, POS, e-mail, and SMS servers) were integrated with the new CRM system. It would have been impossible to achieve successful results if the scope were not managed properly. So what factors led Akbank to success?

While the initial scope was being defined, the project team worked on the selection of the right software product for the project. The Akbank project team examined five different products and worked carefully to see which ones best fulfilled the requirements of the relevant business units. The feasibility and product selection phase resulted in the selection of "Chordiant" (later named "Pega Systems"). Implementing the project without the help of a system integrator involved a big risk, so Akbank employed PATNI through a fixed-price agreement. The estimated program duration was 18 months.

Since on the whole, the requests seemed more like a program than a project, the project team prioritized the projects and composed a CRM "program" in accordance with the CRM business unit needs. This step was important in managing the different projects in the right order and with the right resources. In the "scope definition" phase, the IT and business teams mutually agreed to bring the project live in various phases, rather than employing a "big bang" approach and going live on a single date. Another important decision was to first take "out of the box" product properties and to launch the customizable properties later in phases. This meant that the end users could start using some parts of the new product in a live environment about 10 months before the project termination date.

Many business units were affected by the project, including the call center, alternative delivery channels, retail banking, and credit cards. The IT and CRM business units took the project sponsorship together and managed all other business units' requests, evaluating, prioritizing, and eliminating them as necessary. Project governance was crucial for implementing measures of control across the vast scope of the program. The CRM business acted with the IT division as a real "business owner" in terms of prioritization of requests, budget control, and risk management.

To further manage the scope effectively, Akbank broke down the scope into 46 use cases. All use cases were analyzed in detail. The Akbank IT department prepared different scope statements for each case, and the CRM business unit approved each case separately. If there had been only one scope statement, it would have been very difficult to get approval and manage changes for the project scope.

Since all delivery channels had to be integrated with the new CRM application, Akbank decided to go phase by phase for the channel side to ensure efficiencies. To manage the scope effectively, the Akbank team first focused on branch integration. For Internet banking and ATMs, Akbank had already performed a "pilot production phase," enabling them to see the CRM system working on internal customers first, and then on external customers. This way, any bugs and errors that could not be specified in the integration tests and user acceptance tests were faced by Akbank staff in a real-time environment before external customers were introduced to the new system.

Business and adaptation challenges were encountered during the release process of the new CRM system, ATOM. The CRM Adaptation Program, known as CAP, was created to overcome these challenges. The CRM adaptation team, along with 24 CRM staff, created and led the program to adapt CRM users in the bank to the new-generation CRM approach. The team spent about 40,000 hours providing on-site training to more than 9,000 CRM users. Training continued with a "train the trainer" philosophy. These training sessions ensured that users

(continued)

thoroughly understood the scope of the program and the new CRM world of Akbank.

Nearly all project teams request minimum changes in project scope once the scope statement is approved, but unfortunately change at this stage is rarely possible. Usually there are some changes in scope, however, including new requests and additional functionalities to scope, during the very last stages of a project. This caused a problem with some aspects of the Akbank CRM program.

The Akbank project team's scope change control procedure was clear: to take change requests in a formal "change request form," evaluate the requests with the system integrator, and, finally, if technically possible, present an effort estimation and schedule offer to the Change Control Board (CCB), which met periodically (every three weeks) throughout the project. The CCB consisted of the CIO, CRM division head, IT project manager, CRM business project managers, and IT application development manager. After careful examination and a cost-benefit

analysis of each change request, the CCB either approved or rejected the new scope requests. This process ensured that the program had no "scope creep" and that all project stakeholders would be satisfied with the results.[24]

Questions

1. Assess the benefits and drawbacks of employing use cases in requirements gathering. In your opinion, do benefits outweigh drawbacks or vice versa? Why?
2. What are the benefits of employing a phased implementation approach and performing a pilot production?
3. Discuss the risk factors in the Akbank CRM renewal program and assess them in terms of consequences. How did Akbank's scope management strategies help the project team mitigate these risks? In your opinion, among the success factors mentioned in this case, which one was most important for the success of the program?

Case Study 5.3

Five Star Hotel ELV (Extra Low Voltage) Project

Located in Bahrain, the Five Star Hotel ELV project was completed in 2011. The purpose of this project was to install, test, and commission the IT and communication infrastructure and services for the hotel. The ELV project was part of a total program to deliver 11 subsystems, including installation of data, voice, music, wireless, and CCTV systems. The project stakeholders included the hotel owner, the consultant the hotel had employed on its behalf, and various civil, electrical, and construction teams involved in implementing the ELV project.

This case study focuses on the audiovisual (AV) subsystem, primarily installation of projectors and screens in the meeting rooms and conference facilities. Mrs. T. Reynolds, as the vendor-side project manager, was responsible for issuing to the client complete detailed drawings of the project's electrical requirements. Reynolds knew these drawings needed to be accurate, as they would be handed over to the civil and construction teams for use when building the sites. Bearing this dependency in mind, Reynolds ensured that her team completed accurate and timely drawings with the expectation that the civil and construction teams would complete the building and hand over a completed room with all the electrical requirements as planned. The final phases of the ELV project required Reynolds team to visit the sites to install and test the electrical equipment.

At initiation and during the project's planning phases, the project's AV requirements were issued and communicated via drawings between the consultant

appointed by the customer and Reynolds electrical team. The product specifications were based on lessons learned and templates from a similar project implemented in Dubai. The project scope was determined via the bill of quantities, materials, and tender documents.

Reynolds received only electrical drawings for the sites and continued to plan the installation requirements based on these drawings on the assumption that they were correct, accurate, and the most recent. Throughout planning, the electrical team was not privy to any of the civil or construction drawings from the other teams, and hence was completely unaware of structural changes being made to the original plans.

During installation of the AV system, the team encountered a major problem; the projection was faulty. The projectors and screens were not aligning, which caused the projected images to be cut off and unclear. On investigation it became apparent that structural changes had been made, causing Reynolds drawings and calculations to be inaccurate.

The customer's response to this communication oversight was to send Reynolds a full collection of civil and construction drawings that included all the latest revisions. Reynolds spent considerable time reviewing the drawings to identify the relevant adjustments. The result was delays, rework, and wasted time as he sorted through the drawings, many of which were excessive compared to his requirements.

The problem the installation team encountered was that the ceilings had been elevated higher than planned in the original design. This had been approved by the customer, who failed to communicate the new changes and approvals to Reynolds electrical team. The solution required changing the location of the projector by a meter and moving the screens forward by several centimeters. Reynolds revised the plans and issued new electrical drawings to the customer, which were subjected to the approval process again.

The site had been handed over from the civil and construction teams complete with decoration. As a result of this vital communication error regarding the electrical work, the solution required reworking of parts of the site, such as opening the ceilings to access the electrical panels, in order to make the new changes. The impact was a time delay of 8 to 10 days and rework costs of opening, adjusting, and redecorating the site.

Questions

1. What was the impact of scope changes to the project stakeholders?
2. What planning, monitoring, and control actions could the project manager have taken to avoid the situation?
3. How would you redesign the communications management processes to minimize the problems experienced by the project manager?

Case Study 5.4

London's Millennium Dome

Few major projects in the UK's capital have polarized public opinion more than the construction of the Millennium Dome. The project was conceived in the mid-1990s and extensively enlarged by the new UK government in 1997. Then Prime Minister Tony Blair described it as confident, bold, and a symbol of excellence. The idea was that the structure would be a showcase to celebrate the third millennium and would house a must-see exhibition called the Millennium Experience. In the longer term, after showcasing the exhibition over the course of the year 2000, the site would be transformed into a soccer stadium or perhaps a major arena facility for concerts, conventions, and other events.

Construction

The building was conceived as a large white marquee. Symbolically, it would have twelve 100-meter support towers that would represent the twelve months of the year and a clock face. The dome was to be 365 meters in diameter, symbolizing the days of the year. The dome was designed by the architect Richard Rogers, and the contractors were MacApline and Laing, who had created a joint venture company for the project. The engineering consultancy business Buro Happold designed the structure of the dome. The canopy itself was made from a coated glass-fiber fabric that was designed to be both durable and resistant to weather. The dome was completed on time and within budget.

Controversies

The site of the Millennium Dome was the meridian line in north Greenwich, and the structure was designed to be the largest dome in the world. The site sprawled across a vast contaminated and derelict gasworks that had been left undeveloped for two decades. In 1993, a Millennium Commission was established to raise the necessary funds to celebrate the new millennium. In the following year, the idea of a national exhibition was suggested, and in 1996, it was decided to go ahead with this concept and base it on the site in Greenwich.

The project singularly failed to attract private investment, the first clear warning sign that the long-term prospects for the site were not encouraging. The UK government undertook raising the necessary funds from the UK National Lottery. Work began on the dome in June 1997, and the majority of the construction was completed

(continued)

by June 1998. It took another year before the content, style, and purpose of the exhibition was unveiled. After a private opening of the exhibition on December 31, 1999, the dome would open to the public for the whole of 2000.

The dome was, undoubtedly, one of the most controversial publicly funded works project ever undertaken in the UK. Significant issues existed from the beginning, the first being the estimate of the number of visitors the exhibition would attract. It was originally estimated that 12 million visitors would be attracted to the dome in 2000, and broadly one million per year thereafter. In May 2000, the estimate was scaled down to about 7 million. In the end, the dome actually attracted 6.5 million.

The estimate regarding visitors was only the first of many project aspects that brought accusations that the whole project was financially mismanaged. Pressure on the project budget began to emerge as early as 1998, which was 14 months before the dome actually opened. Technically, the dome was insolvent by February 2000. Access was another major failing of the project. The London Underground was to be extended with additional stations on the Jubilee Line, and this transport network was vital in being able to bring sufficient visitors into the north Greenwich area. The extension work, however, was delayed by 14 months, and when the new station opened in May 1999, it was still unfinished and had no facilities for disabled people.

From the outset, the dome was a political project, or at least it was perceived as one by the media. The dome acquired a reputation of being a hugely expensive and financially out-of-control "white elephant." It was perceived by the media as symbolizing the prestige of Tony Blair and the government. Labelled as an expensive vanity project, the dome's reputation plummeted in the eyes of the public before the structure was even completed. When the contents of the exhibition were made public, the floodgates to criticism were opened. The public perception had been that the exhibition would focus on UK history and the country's contribution to civilization. In reality, the exhibition was modernist, thematic, and "politically correct."

On the ground, as visitors headed for the dome, the organizational frailties of the project surfaced. Thousands of people had to queue unnecessarily in cold weather because of ticketing issues. Nonetheless, opinion polls suggested an 85% satisfaction rate for visitors to the venue.

CEO Jennifer Page of the New Millennium Experience Company, which was overseeing the exhibition, was fired just a week before the dome was opened. Despite this, poor attendance figures and other setbacks, the dome became the most popular London attraction in 2000, beating the London Eye into second place.

According to the UK National Audit Office, when the New Millennium Experience Company was liquidated in 2002, the dome had cost a total of $1.24 billion. Of this total, the National Lottery had provided $988 million. The figures were disappointing, but the shortfall from ticket sales had been covered by a larger-than-estimated National Lottery grant.

After the Experience

The Millennium Experience closed at the end of 2000, and in the following year, the UK government agency English Partnerships took control of the dome, which paved the way for the liquidation of the New Millennium Experience Company. Finding a potential buyer for the dome and the site proved to be problematic. The idea of turning it into a soccer stadium had long since collapsed, as the local team, Charlton Athletic, had too small a fan base to justify the move and the expense.

Meanwhile, the dome was costing $1.6 million per month to maintain. The specially commissioned art exhibits were auctioned off at cut prices, and many of the other exhibits were dispersed to other attractions around the UK. The dome opened temporarily as a fun fair and ice rink in December 2003 and hosted some free music festivals. Over the Christmas period of 2004, the dome was used to shelter the homeless.

Finally, in 2004, the dome itself and the surrounding land were sold to Meridan Delta Ltd., which planned to create a 26,000-capacity area, providing 24,000 jobs and 10,000 homes. English Partnerships and Meridan Deltawould share the proceeds of the development, earning $786 million in the period up to 2018.

A New Lease on Life

In May 2005, the dome was renamed the O2. This was part of the rebranding of the site as a major London arena venue. The O2 opened in June 2007 and was earmarked to host the gymnastics and basketball finals for the London 2012 Olympics.

Even the deal with Meridan Delta attracted criticism. It was suggested that the financial arrangements did not represent good value for money for the UK. In the summer of 2005, Anschutz Entertainment Group (AEG), part of the Meridan Delta business consortium, announced plans to establish a super-casino in part of the dome. This was at a time when the UK government was considering giving permission to one site in the UK to become the country's first super-casino. The UK city of Manchester was given the go-ahead, but later the super-casino idea was scrapped. There would be no Las Vegas—style gambling in the UK after all.

Turning the Dome Around

There was a sense of rebirth for the dome when Meridan Delta acquired the 999-year lease in 2001. The dome had been beset with problems and criticism, and it had acquired the undeserved notoriety for cost overruns. It was also seen as a project without purpose. Government ministers, community groups, and business leaders had fought over the project and what to do with the dome after the exhibition.

From the time it opened on New Year's Eve 1999, six years elapsed before AEG announced its ambitious plans to create a multipurpose entertainment center. Undaunted by the failure to create the super-casino, AEG began a $700 million investment in the site. AEG, fronted by the U.S. billionaire Philip Anschutz, also owned the Los Angeles Staples Center. The dome would remain at the heart of the complex with a 20,000-seat stadium that would host music concerts, spectacular events from Disney, U.S. National Basketball Association games, and the ATP Tennis Masters Cup.

Transforming the dome into a multipurpose complex was not without its difficulties. AEG created an 11-screen multiplex cinema, restaurants, and a host of other attractions. The British telecommunications giant O2 had agreed to pay $12 million per year for naming rights. When the first music concert was presented in June 2007, even the sternest critics of the dome were forced to eat their words. AEG was determined to establish the venue as the prime site for events in London and announced forthcoming features including the Rolling Stones, Prince and Andrea Bocelli, and many other attractions. In the first six months, AEG was able to announce 84 events and sold a staggering 1.2 million tickets. This was an incredible turnaround from the woeful ticket sales for the Millennium Experience. The company also was able to establish a rolling program that would see as many as 150 events per year. In the first six months of the new management of the site, 70% of the retail space had been leased.

Making the Dome a Long-Term Success

The primary challenge for AEG was to ensure that the O2 (as it was now called) would be a resounding success into the future. Light years away from the bland thematic nature of the original exhibition, the new-look venue would focus on quality of product, brands, and events that had widespread appeal.

AEG had already established itself as a major force in the leisure and entertainment business. Not only was the company running the highly successful Staples Center and the Kings Hockey Club in Los Angeles, but it also was having great success with the Nokia Theater in Times Square, New York. Plans were already well advanced to create a major entertainment center in Berlin, Germany, which opened in 2008.

AEG's relaunching of the dome as a major venue for live events came at precisely the right time for the UK.

There had been a huge increase in demand for live events, and the O2 was able to deliver the very best.

From Liability to Loved

Even before the foundations were laid for the dome, the media had dubbed the site a failure—a doomed, expensive, vanity-based disaster. As the scope of the project became extended, the cost overruns reached some $400 million. The dome was a political soccer ball, bounced backward and forward from government to government, agency to agency, and finally into the hands of private investors. No one ever really knew what the dome was for or what it could become. In real terms, AEG did not have to do a great deal to improve the image of the site; in fact, the company said that the poor public image of the dome actually helped them, as any change and a clear direction for the site would be met with almost universal relief and hope.

AEG had hoped to use part of the dome to host a Las Vegas—style casino complex. The company had estimated that it could generate some $206 million in revenue per year and attract around 1.7 million customers. The UK government's change of heart about the super-casino was a blow to AEG, but the company still harbors hope that a super-casino can come to the site in the future.

In the meantime, AEG will focus on attracting overnight visitors to the site. The hope is that it can attract cruise ships and conferences and, in this way, make maximum use of the exhibition and conference space, restaurants, and hotel accommodations. The second development stage of the site was due for completion in time for the London 2012 Olympic Games.

Not the Millennium Dome

The huge naming rights deal with O2 was put under threat as a result of the Olympics. British Telecom (BT) is a "domestic tier one" sponsor of the Olympics, and to prevent a conflict of interest, for the duration of the Olympics, the O2 was rebranded as the NGA1 (North Greenwich Arena 1). The Olympic organizers had suggested a temporary return of the name Millennium Dome, but AEG was adamant that the negative connotations associated with this name were not acceptable. It would seem that although the dome could readily become the O2, reversing the name, even for a short time, was seen as the kiss of death. Obviously BT's one-off $126 million Olympic sponsorship payment far outweighed the $9.4 million AEG was receiving each year from O2 for the arena sponsorship deal. In light of this disagreement over the name of the arena for the duration of the Olympics, and given the prior name change, it became apparent that an awareness campaign would be necessary to explain to visitors that the Millennium Dome, the O2, and the NGA1 were, in fact, the same place.[25]

Questions

1. What does the story of the Millennium Dome suggest about the importance of considering both technical and commercial performance for project success?
2. In 1998, the then UK Prime Minister Tony Blair said that the Dome would be a beacon of the world. In the light of this comment, why was the Millennium Experience a comparative failure?
3. AEG as a commercial company managed to visualize the future of the dome in a way that no politician could conceive. Do you agree or disagree with this view? Why?

Internet Exercises

1. Go to www.4pm.com/articles/work_breakdown_structure. htm and view a short tutorial on developing an effective Work Breakdown Structure. Why does this site specifically warn against creating a laundry list of project activities? What are some of the dangers in creating poor work breakdown structures and the advantages of doing them effectively?
2. Go to www.oet.state.mn.us/mastercontract/statements/1863.pdf to see a process for describing and creating a Statement of Work for the Minnesota Job Bank Upgrade project. In your opinion, what are some of the critical elements in this Statement of Work? Why? The site also contains an "IT Professional Services Master Contract Work Order." Why is this work order so detailed?
3. Access www.nccommunitycolleges.edu/IT_Projects/docs/ Data%20Warehouse/Phase%20I/dw_project_scope_statement. pdf. Analyzing the comprehensive Scope Statement for the data warehousing project, what problem is this project seeking to address? What is the proposed solution?

PMP Certification Sample Questions

1. What is the lowest level of decomposition in the Work Breakdown Structure called?
   a. Work package
   b. Deliverable
   c. Subdeliverable
   d. Project

2. All of the following define a work package EXCEPT:
   a. A work package has a deliverable result
   b. It may be considered by its owner as a project in itself
   c. A work package may include several milestones
   d. A work package can be created and addressed regardless of other organizational procedures of cultural considerations

3. George has been assigned to be the new project manager for our project. He is eager to get off to a good start and wants to identify what activities he should first engage in. How would you advise him to start?
   a. Begin with the Work Breakdown Structure (WBS)
   b. Begin with a clear scope statement
   c. Begin with a problem statement and Statement of Work (SOW)
   d. Begin with clear work authorization

4. The project manager wants to make sure that he is proceeding in the right order as he moves to develop a clear scope for his project. During scope definition, what should he be doing?
   a. Involving stakeholders and verifying that they have all provided their input to the process
   b. Developing his WBS and OBS
   c. Moving as quickly as possible to the determination of scope reporting methods
   d. Identifying all necessary vendors for any outsourcing that must be done

5. A hospital expansion is being planned for a community. As part of the scope of this project, it will be necessary to close down the access routes into the emergency room for major remodeling; however, because this is the only hospital for trauma cases within 50 miles, it is not possible to completely shut down the emergency room. The project team will have to find a means to remodel the emergency room while allowing for continuous operations of the unit. This is an example of what?
   a. Negotiation points with the owner
   b. Constraints
   c. Initial assumptions
   d. Milestone development

Answers: 1. a—The work package is the lowest level in the Work Breakdown Structure (WBS); 2. d—A work package should fit organizational procedures and culture; 3. c—The project should initiate with a clear problem statement and understood SOW supporting it; 4. a—It is critical that all stakeholders have the opportunity to contribute their input to the project during the scope definition phase; 5. b—The need to keep the emergency room open during the remodeling is an example of working around existing project constraints.

MS Project Exercises

Using the information provided below, construct a simple WBS table for the project example.

Project Outline—Remodeling an Appliance

I.   Research Phase
   A.   Prepare product development proposal
      1.   Conduct competitive analysis
      2.   Review field sales reports
      3.   Conduct technological capabilities assessment
   B.   Develop focus group data
   C.   Conduct telephone surveys
   D.   Identify relevant specification improvements
II. Design and Engineering Phase
   A.   Interface with marketing staff
   B.   and so on
III. Testing Phase
IV. Manufacturing Phase
V.   Sales Phase

INTEGRATED PROJECT

Developing the Work Breakdown Structure

Develop a Work Breakdown Structure for your project based on the identified goals from the first assignment. Provide a detailed assessment of the various components of the project, going down through the work package stage to tasks and subtasks (if appropriate). Next, assess the personnel needs for the project. How many core team members will be necessary to achieve the project's goals? What are their positions within the organization? Remember to use the project scope as the basis for determining all the elements of the project, the personnel responsible for each component, and the associated budget for each task.

In addition to identifying the tasks and key personnel requirements for the project, construct a Responsibility Assignment Matrix (RAM) that demonstrates the interrelationship among project team members.

SAMPLE WORK BREAKDOWN STRUCTURE—ABCups, INC.

Personnel Table

Name	Department	Title
Carol Johnson	Safety	Safety Engineer
Bob Hoskins	Engineering	Industrial Engineer
Sheila Thomas	Management	Project Manager
Randy Egan	Management	Plant Manager
Stu Hall	Industrial	Maintenance Supervisor
Susan Berg	Accounting	Cost Accountant
Marty Green	Industrial	Shop Supervisor
John Pittman	Quality	Quality Engineer
Sally Reid	Quality	Jr. Quality Engineer
Lanny Adams	Sales	Marketing Manager
Kristin Abele	Purchasing	Purchasing Agent

WORK BREAKDOWN STRUCTURE—ABCups' PROCESS MODIFICATION

Process Modification Project			1000
Deliverable 1	**Feasibility Study**		1010
Work Package 1	Conduct feasibility study	1011	
Work Package 2	Receive technical approval	1012	
Work Package 3	Get administrative sign-off	1013	
Deliverable 2	**Vendor Selection**		1020
Work Package 1	Research equipment	1021	
Work Package 2	Qualify suppliers	1022	
Work Package 3	Solicit quotes from suppliers	1023	
Work Package 4	Negotiate price and terms	1024	
Work Package 5	Approval and contracts	1025	
Deliverable 3	**Design**		1030
Work Package 1	Factory floor redesign	1031	
Work Package 2	Drawings	1032	
Work Package 3	Process redesign approval	1033	

Deliverable 4	Engineering		1040
Work Package 1	Conduct process flow evaluation	1041	
Work Package 2	Determine site for equipment	1042	
Work Package 3	Retooling	1043	
Work Package 4	Final layout approval	1044	
Deliverable 5	**Prototype Testing**		1050
Work Package 1	Build inventory bank	1051	
Work Package 2	Set up trial run	1052	
Work Package 3	Trial run	1053	
Work Package 4	Quality assessment	1054	
Work Package 5	Process documentation	1055	
Deliverable 6	**Packaging**		1060
Work Package 1	Design new packaging	1061	
Work Package 2	Coordinate with marketing	1062	
Work Package 3	Part assembly	1063	
Work Package 4	Packaging approval	1064	
Deliverable 7	**Sales and Service**		1070
Work Package 1	Beta-test products	1071	
Work Package 2	Sales approval	1072	
Work Package 3	Customer approval	1073	
Deliverable 8	**Initiate Changeover**		1080
Work Package 1	Assemble inventory	1081	
Work Package 2	Cancel vendor contracts	1082	
Work Package 3	Close out project	1083	
Work Package 4	Develop lessons learned	1084	

Responsibility Assignment Matrix

	Sheila	Susan	Bob	Lanny
Del 1010	◯	☐		☆
Del 1020	☆	◯		☐
Del 1030	☆		☐	◯
Del 1040	⊕	☐	◯	☆
Del 1050		◯	☆	☐
Del 1060	☐		⊕	◯
Del 1070	◯	☆	☐	
Del 1080	⊕		◯	☆

◯ Responsible   ☆ Support

☐ Notification   ⊕ Approval

Notes

1. Feickert, A. (2008). "The Marines' Expeditionary Fighting Vehicle (EFV): Background and issues for Congress." Congressional Research Service, Library of Congress, www.dtic.mil/cgi-bin/GetTRDoc?Location=U2&doc=GetTRDoc.pdf&AD=ADA486513; Hodge, N. (2010, August 27). "Marines question craft needed to hit the beach," *Wall Street Journal,* p. B8; www.wired.com/dangerroom/2008/08/marines-swimmin/; Merle, R. (2007). "Problems stall Pentagon's new fighting vehicle." www.washingtonpost.com/wp-dyn/content/article/2007/02/06/AR2007020601997.html; Ackerman, S. (2010). "Senate may finally sink Marines' swimming tank." www.wired.com/dangerroom/2010/09/senate-may-finally-sink-marines-swimming-tank/; www.aviationweek.com/aw/jsp_includes/articlePrint.jsp?storyID=news/asd/2010/11/08/01.xml&headLine=null; www.aviationweek.com/aw/generic/story.jsp?id=news/asd/2010/10/12/08.xml&channel=misc.

2. Project Management Institute. (2010). "Scope Management," *Project Management Body of Knowledge* (PMBoK). Upper Darby, PA: Project Management Institute; Westney, R. E. (1993). "Paradigms for planning productive projects," in Dinsmore, P. C. (Ed.), *The AMA Handbook of Project Management.* New York: AMACOM.

3. Kerzner, H. (2001). *Project Management: A Systems Approach to Planning, Scheduling, and Controlling,* 7th ed. New York: Wiley; Mepyans-Robinson, R. (2010). "Project scope management in practice," in Dinsmore, P. C., and Cabanis-Brewin, J. (Eds.), *The AMA Handbook of Project Management,* 3rd ed. New York: AMACOM, pp. 79–87; Cleland, D. I., and Kimball, R. K. (1987). "The strategic context of projects," *Project Management Journal,* 18(3): 11–30.

4. Project Management Institute (2000), as cited in note 2.

5. Stuckenbruck, L. C. (1981). *The Implementation of Project Management: The Professional's Handbook.* Boston, MA: Addison-Wesley; Laufer, A. (1991). "Project planning: Timing issues and path of progress," *Project Management Journal,* 22(2): 39–45.

6. Martin, M. G. (1998). "Statement of work: The foundation for delivering successful service projects," *PMNetwork,* 12(10): 54–57.

7. www.fgdc.gov/geospatial-lob/smartbuy/understanding-statement-of-work.pdf/.

8. Duncan, W. R. (1994). "Scoping out a scope statement," *PMNetwork,* 8(12): 24–27; Wideman, R. M. (1983). "Scope management," *Project Management Quarterly,* 14: 31–32; Pinto, J. K. (1999). "Project scope management," in Pinto, J. K. (Ed.), *The Project Management Institute's Project Management Handbook.* San Francisco, CA: Jossey-Bass, pp. 109–18.

9. Lavold, G. D. (1988). "Developing and using the work breakdown structure," in Cleland, D. I., and King, W. R. (Eds.), *Project Management Handbook,* 2nd ed. New York: Van Nostrand Reinhold, pp. 302–23.

10. Obradovitch, M. M., and Stephanou, S. E. (1990). *Project Management: Risks & Productivity.* Bend, OR: Daniel Spencer.

11. Project Management Body of Knowledge. (2008). Project Management Institute: Newton Square, PA.

12. Meredith, J. R., and Mantel, Jr., S. J. (2003). *Project Management,* 5th ed. New York: Wiley.

13. Globerson, S. (2001). "Scope management: Do all that you need and just what you need," in Knutson, J. (Ed.), *Project Management for Business Professionals.* New York: Wiley, pp. 49–62.

14. Obradovitch, M. M., and Stephanou, S. E. (1990). *Project Management: Risks & Productivity.* Bend, OR: Daniel Spencer.

15. Project Management Institute (2010), as cited in note 2.

16. Yourdon, E. (2004). *Death March,* 2nd ed. Upper Saddle River, NJ: Prentice-Hall.

17. Kidd, C., and Burgess, T. F. (2004). "Managing configurations and data for effective project management," in Morris, P. W. G., and Pinto, J. K. (Eds.), *The Wiley Guide to Managing Projects.* New York: Wiley, pp. 498–513.

18. Meredith, J. R., and Mantel, Jr., S. J. (2003), as cited in note 12.

19. Frame, J. D. (2001). "Requirements management: Addressing customer needs and avoiding scope creep," in Knutson, J. (Ed.), *Project Management for Business Professionals.* New York: Wiley, pp. 63–80.

20. Kidd, C., and Burgess, T. F. (2004), as cited in note 17.

21. Turner, R. (2000). "Managing scope—Configuration and work methods," in Turner, R. (Ed.), *Gower Handbook of Project Management,* 3rd ed. Aldershot, UK: Gower.

22. Antonioni, D. (1997). "Post-project review prevents poor project performance," *PMNetwork,* 11(10).

23. Kouri, J. (2010, November 11). "Border 'virtual fence' project a costly failure." http://island-adv.com/2010/11/border-%E2%80%9Cvirtual-fence%E2%80%9D-project-a-costly-failure/; Krigsman, M. (2007, August 23). "Boeing virtual fence: $30 billion failure." www.zdnet.com/blog/projectfailures/boeing-virtual-fence-30-billion-failure/36; Krigsman, M. (2007, September 24). "Update: Boeing's virtual fence 'unusable.'" www.zdnet.com/blog/projectfailures/update-boeing-virtual-fence-unusable/403; Lipowicz, A. (2010, April 21). "Senate committee chairman suggests killing Boeing's virtual fence." http://washingtontechnology.com/articles/2010/04/21/lieberman-calls-sbinet-virtual-fence-a-failure.aspx; Richey, J. (2007, July 7). "Fencing the border: Boeing's high-tech plan falters." www.theinvestigativefund.org/investigations/immigrationandlabor/1243/fencing_the_border%3A_boeing%27s_high-tech_plan_falters.

24. Based on an interview with Mustafa Dönmez, Akbank, April 25, 2012, www.akbank.com.

25. "Millennium dome," www.politics.co.uk/reference/ millennium-dome; "A decade on…the Dome finally works," www.guardian.co.uk/uk/2007/jun/24/dome.architecture; "A hollow man and an empty tent," www.guardian.co.uk/ commentisfree/2006/jul/07/politics.labour; Liddell, Ian. (1999, August). "Design and construction of the Millennium Dome, UK," *Structural Engineering International*, 9(3); Ishii, Kazuo. (1999). *Membrane Designs and Structures in the World*. Tokyo, Japan: Shinkenchiku-sha Co. Ltd., pp. 114–117.

6

Project Team Building, Conflict, and Negotiation

Chapter Outline

Chapter Objectives

After completing this chapter, you will be able to:

1. Understand the steps involved in project team building.

2. Know the characteristics of effective project teams and why teams fail.

3. Know the stages in the development of groups.

4. Describe how to achieve cross-functional cooperation in teams.

5. See the advantages and challenges of virtual project teams.

6. Understand the nature of conflict and evaluate response methods.

7. Understand the importance of negotiation skills in project management.

PROJECT PROFILE

Case—Plugging a Leaking Oil Well—BP's Disaster Response

On April 20, 2010, a catastrophic explosion at BP's Deepwater Horizon oil-drilling platform 50 miles off the coast of Louisiana in the Gulf of Mexico occurred, killing 11 workers, injuring 17 others, and creating an environmental disaster, the effects of which are still being debated (see Figure 6.1). Two days later the rig sank, causing the 5,000-foot pipe that connected the wellhead to the drilling platform to bend. On April 24, robotic devices discovered two leaks in the bent pipe, nearly a mile below the ocean surface. The wellhead was equipped with a blowout preventer, a 40-foot stack of devices designed to rapidly seal the well, but the preventer failed. The results were the worst nightmare any oil company could envision; a runaway oil spill in an inhospitable and remote environment, leaving the company without any obvious means to immediately correct the disaster.

A preliminary investigation of the causes of the explosion suggested that a combination of poor maintenance, streamlined drilling procedures, and a culture of fear or reprisals led the workers to cut corners and take risks. For example, on the Deepwater Horizon rig, BP decided not to install an acoustic trigger that

FIGURE 6.1   Deepwater Horizon Explosion

US Coast Guard Photo / Alamy

(continued)

could have shut down the well if it was badly damaged. Acoustic triggers are required in most developed countries, but the United States only recommends them, leaving the choice to oil companies. However, the more immediate challenge faced by BP engineers was to find an effective means to cap the oil wellhead, located nearly one mile below the surface and leaking crude oil at a rate of 60,000 barrels a day directly into the Gulf. Their efforts to develop a creative and effective solution to the wellhead leak represent an excellent example of emergency project management, as they were forced to adapt to and overcome a number of critical constraints in order to achieve their goals.

The explosion occurred because abnormal methane gas pressure accumulated inside one of the drilling pipes (called a "marine riser") and, as it came toward the surface, it expanded rapidly and ignited. Moving up the riser column, the methane gas expanded and burst through a number of seals and barriers before it exploded—the classic example of a catastrophic blowout. In general, several procedures are to be followed when dealing with a wellhead blowout at sea, including:

- In situ burning—the key is to trap as much of the leaking oil on the surface as possible with booms and other floating devices and ignite it to burn in place.
- Dispersants—chemicals are sprayed from ships and aircraft on oil slicks to break them up before they can float to shore and harm wildlife and ecological areas.
- Booming—miles of flexible, floating barriers that contain the spread of oil can be useful in calm water or in relatively small areas.

Although BP and its partners used all of these means to contain the rapidly expanding oil slick, they were only partially successful. Too much oil was still gushing too quickly from the damaged wellhead on the ocean floor for these remedial efforts to do much good. Worse, the explosion had so severely damaged the wellhead that there were no undamaged valves at the site that could be closed. Cameras attached to remote-controlled submersible units indicated that the oil was coming out at a huge rate with virtually no way to stop it.

This was the challenge that BP emergency petroleum engineers faced when they began to plot strategies for closing the well. In past experiences, the standard response was to drill "relief wells" from other angles into the affected shaft. Relief wells would basically lower the force of the pressurized oil being forced to the surface and allow the engineers to devise a more traditional well cap. Unfortunately, in this case, it would take time—probably weeks or even months—to drill the relief wells. Meanwhile, oil would continue to gush out of the well, dispersing throughout the Gulf of Mexico and fouling beaches from Texas to Florida. Delays were simply unacceptable.

The following time frame for solutions indicates just how wide-ranging were the BP engineers' alternatives as they cast about for the most effective means to seal the well:

- April 25—First attempt to repair the blowout preventer. BP used remotely operated submersibles to try to activate the blowout preventer. Unfortunately, a critical valve had never been fully deployed and it proved impossible to activate the device following the explosion.
- April 30—Use of chemical dispersants below surface. Crews injected chemical dispersants into the oil as it flowed from the well, trying to break the oil up into small droplets before it traveled to the surface. The effects were unknown, but the flow of oil from the well did not slow down.
- May 2—BP began drilling the first of two relief wells that could later be used to inject "drilling mud" and cement into the current well.
- May 7—BP built and lowered a 40-foot-tall steel containment dome that they hoped would trap the escaping oil and channel it into valves and pipes at the top of the dome. But when crews discovered that the dome's opening was becoming clogged with an icy mix of gas and water, it was set aside on the seabed.
- May 16—BP engineers successfully inserted a mile-long tube into the broken riser pipe at the base of the wellhead to divert some of the oil to a drill ship anchored on the surface. Over nine days, the tube managed to siphon off nearly 22,000 barrels of oil, which amounted to, unfortunately, just a fraction of the total spill.
- May 26—The company tried two techniques for emergency closure of the well, the "top kill" and "junk shot." In a top kill, engineers pump heavy drilling mud directly into the well, hoping the weight of the mud will overcome the pressure of the releasing oil and plug the well. A junk shot is a procedure in which objects, including golf balls and pieces of rubber, are injected into the blowout preventer. Unfortunately, both techniques failed to plug the leak.
- May 31—In another attempt to cap the well, engineers positioned submarine robots to cut through the remainder of the collapsed riser pipe so that a more efficient cap could be placed over the blowout preventer to funnel some of the oil to a tanker on the surface. Although this effort began to capture some of the oil, more continued to flow from under the lid and through four open vents on the device (see Figure 6.2). Engineers could not close all the vents as they had originally hoped. Still, this effort began to capture nearly 15,000 barrels daily.

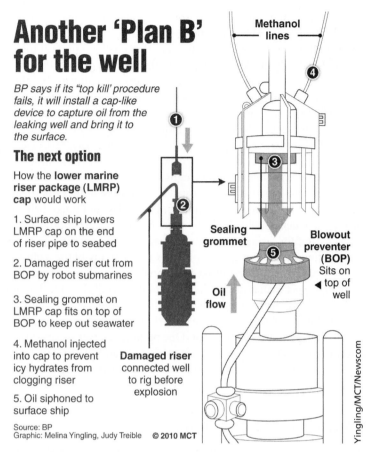

Another 'Plan B' for the well

BP says if its "top kill' procedure fails, it will install a cap-like device to capture oil from the leaking well and bring it to the surface.

The next option

How the **lower marine riser package (LMRP) cap** would work

1. Surface ship lowers LMRP cap on the end of riser pipe to seabed

2. Damaged riser cut from BOP by robot submarines

3. Sealing grommet on LMRP cap fits on top of BOP to keep out seawater

4. Methanol injected into cap to prevent icy hydrates from clogging riser

5. Oil siphoned to surface ship

Damaged riser connected well to rig before explosion

Methanol lines

Sealing grommet

Blowout preventer (BOP) Sits on ◄ top of well

Oil flow

Source: BP
Graphic: Melina Yingling, Judy Treible   © 2010 MCT

Yingling/MCT/Newscom

FIGURE 6.2   Oil Cap Fitted to the Top of Blowout Preventer Valve Stack

- June 16—A second containment system began siphoning additional oil and gas from the well. Combined with the first cap system, the two methods pumped nearly 25,000 barrels per day directly to a surface vessel. This ship did not have a storage capacity and burned the oil and gas as it reached the surface. By July 5, BP announced that its burn efforts were accounting for 25,000 barrels of oil and 57.1 million cubic feet of natural gas per day.
- July 10—BP created a better cap and placed it on top of the wellhead. By July 15, this new capping system had stopped the flow of oil from the well. Engineers continued to monitor pressure in the well to ensure its integrity.
- August 3—Engineers completed the "static kill," successfully pumping mud through a valve on the blowout preventer and into the existing well's metal casing pipe in a procedure similar to the failed top kill. They were able to pump mud slower and at lower pressure because the new cap atop the well had stemmed the flow of oil. Mud forced the oil and gas back down into the reservoir. Cement was also pumped in to seal the well.
- September 21—The federal government declared the well dead after nearly five months of failed attempts and then, finally, success in permanently plugging the well.

The Deepwater Horizon disaster was the largest oil spill in U.S. history, and its environmental and economic effects are sure to be felt for years into the future. The causes of the explosion are still under investigation and do not reflect well on the operating philosophy of BP in its drilling and maintenance procedures. However, if we can separate the *causes* of the disaster from the organization's *responses* to it, a different picture of BP emerges in its emergency reaction. There is no question that BP's team of engineers faced a unique and critical situation with the blowout. Further, because of the setting and other physical constraints, any responses had to be filtered through the realm of what was possible under the circumstances. Finally, time played an important role; every day without a solution brought more and more oil gushing from the ruptured well. Nevertheless, though undoubtedly a catastrophe, the situation would have been far worse if not for the creativity and problem-solving abilities of BP engineers, given a crucial assignment for which failure was not an option.[1]

INTRODUCTION

The difficulties involved in building and coordinating an effective team can be daunting and highly complex. Becoming technically proficient at scheduling, budgeting, and project evaluation are essential in developing the necessary project management skills; however, it is equally important to develop an appreciation for and willingness to undertake the human challenges of the job. **Team building** and conflict management are two of the most important *people skills* that project managers can cultivate, but they are also two of the most difficult undertakings. We must use our leadership skills to negotiate with department managers for access to skilled personnel for team staffing; we must recognize that no project team comes "fully assembled" and ready to go. Simply grouping a collection of diverse individuals together is not the same thing as building a team.

This chapter offers an overview of some of the key behavioral tasks facing project managers: staffing a project team, building a sense of common purpose and shared commitment, encouraging cross-functional cooperation among team members, and recognizing the causes of and resolving conflicts among all project stakeholders. The bad news is that this is not an easy process; it does not involve formulas or calculations in the same way that task duration estimation does. The "rules" of human behavior often consist of broad generalizations, at best, which should always be used only to suggest appropriate managerial actions. The good news is that when carefully evaluated and done, managing the people side of project management can be just as effective, rewarding, and important for project success as any of the technical duties.

Project staffing, team building, cross-functional cooperation, and conflict management are not supplementary topics in project management; the study of these skills is central to our ability to become proficient in a highly complex and challenging profession. This chapter will not only analyze the team building and conflict processes, but it will also offer some prescriptive advice to readers on how to improve these processes and our skills in managing human behavior. One point is clear: If we must undertake projects with a project team as our principal resource for getting the work done and the project completed, it is vital that we learn everything possible about how to mold people into a high-performing team and how to control the inevitable conflicts that are likely to emerge along the way.

6.1 BUILDING THE PROJECT TEAM

Effective project teams do not happen by accident. A great deal of careful work and preparation go into the steps necessary to first staff and then develop project team members to the point where they begin to function jointly and the project reaps positive dividends from their collective performance. The best-case scenario for project managers is to take over a project with a unified team composed of individuals who lobbied for and were awarded with membership on the team. Unfortunately, in many organizations, project teams are put together based on other criteria, most notably whoever is available. Regardless of the circumstances, the project manager is faced with the challenge of creating from a set of diverse individuals a high-performing, cohesive project team. The preferred process, however, should be as structured as possible; staffing is ideally aligned with the project manager's judgment of what is best for the project.

Figure 6.3 illustrates how project team personnel may be assigned. Within many organizations, this process emerges as the result of protracted negotiations with functional or departmental supervisors, as we discussed in Chapter 2. The flowchart in Figure 6.3 illustrates several key decision points or critical interfaces in developing a project team.[2]

Identify Necessary Skill Sets

The first stage in project team development is to conduct a realistic assessment of the types of skills the team members will need in order to complement each other and perform their project duties as effectively as possible. For example, in projects with a high technical complexity, it is imperative to ascertain the availability of skilled human resources and their capability of adding value to the project development. No one would seriously embark on a software development project without first ensuring that the technical steps in the project are clearly understood.

Identify People Who Match the Skills

Once a reasonable assessment of the required project skills has been completed, a complementary assessment of the availability of personnel with the requisite skills is necessary. We have two options: (1) hire new personnel for the project (e.g., in many cases, companies will hire contractors on a fixed-term basis for the

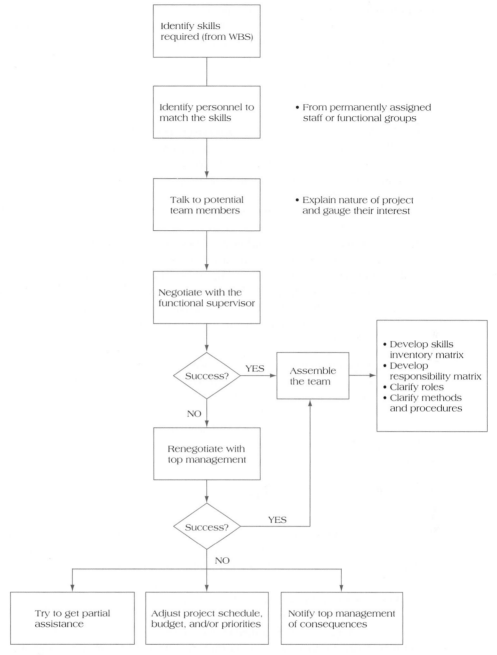

FIGURE 6.3 **Basic Steps in Assembling a Project Team**

Source: V. K. Verma. (1997). *Managing the Project Team,* p. 127. Upper Darby, PA: Project Management Institute. Copyright and all rights reserved. Material from this publication has been reproduced with the permission of PMI.

life of a project), or (2) train current personnel to become proficient in the skills they will need to perform the tasks. The final decision often comes down to a cost/benefit assessment: Who can do the work? Is the cost of hiring or training the person to do the job prohibitively expensive? Once the person has been trained/hired, will these skills be of continuing benefit to the company?

Talk to Potential Team Members and Negotiate with Functional Heads

The third step in the process of building the project team involves opening communication with likely candidates for the team and assessing their level of interest in joining the project. In some cases, personnel have a great deal of authority in assigning their own time to projects. However, in most cases (particularly within functional organizations), all functional specialists are under the authority of departmental heads. Consequently, at some point the project manager must begin to enter into negotiations with these functional heads for the services of prospective project team members. These negotiations can be complex and lengthy.

Departmental managers generally are not opposed to the use of their personnel on projects. They are, however, primarily concerned with the smooth operations of their organizations. Depriving a functional manager of key personnel to serve on a project team can be seen as threatening a smoothly operating department. Hence, negotiations are required. Among the issues to be decided are:

1. *How long are the team members services required?* Project team members can be assigned on a full-time basis (40 hours per week) or a part-time basis (less than 40 hours per week). Further, the team member may be assigned for a fixed period (e.g., six months) or for the duration of the project.
2. *Who should choose the person to be assigned to the project?* Another point of negotiation is the question of who should select the individual to serve on the project team. The functional manager may have her own ideas as to the best choice, while the project manager may employ different criteria and come up with other possible candidates.
3. *What happens when special circumstances arise?* In the event of some emergency or special circumstance, the functional department head may wish to retain control of the team member or have the option of suddenly recalling that individual back to work on departmental activities. How will "emergencies" be defined? If the team member is recalled, how will the department provide a replacement? What is the maximum amount of time a team member can be removed from his project duties? All these questions are important and should be resolved prior to the appointment of project team members.

Most project resources are negotiated with department managers. This point is critical: For the majority of project managers, their outright control over project team members may be limited, particularly early in the process when project team assignments are being made. The best strategy a project manager can engage in at this point is to have thought carefully about the types of expertise and skills that will be required for successful completion of the project and begin bargaining with these clear goals in mind. Treat functional managers as allies, not opponents. The organization supports the project; functional departments will support it as well, but their level of support must be carefully planned in advance.

Build in Fallback Positions

What are your options as the project manager when resources are not available? Suppose, for example, that you need three highly trained design engineers for the project and the head of engineering is unwilling to part with them or negotiate a compromise. As Figure 6.3 demonstrates, in the event that negotiations with functional managers and top managers are not fruitful, the project manager is faced with three basic alternatives.

TRY TO NEGOTIATE FOR PARTIAL ASSISTANCE The best alternative to an outright refusal is to seek some limited assistance. One reason for this approach is that it gets your foot in the door. Once the personnel are assigned to the project, even on limited terms, it forms the basis for your returning to the department head at a later point to ask for them again, while only slowing down the project marginally. This principle argues, in effect, that it is better to have half a loaf than none.

ADJUST PROJECT SCHEDULES AND PRIORITIES ACCORDINGLY When critical resources are not available, the project schedule must be adjusted to reflect this fact. As we will note in Chapter 12, "Resource Management," there is no point in developing a sophisticated project schedule if it is not supported by resources. Or, to put it another way, until we can match people to project tasks, we cannot make progress. With a failure to convince functional managers that their resources are needed to support the project, serious and honest adjustments must be made to all project plans, including scope documents, schedules, risk assessment, and so forth.

NOTIFY TOP MANAGEMENT OF THE CONSEQUENCES Failing to gain necessary resources must be reported to top management, the ultimate sponsors of the project. They may, in the end, become the final arbiters of the resource and staffing question. In the face of persistent resistance from a functional manager, the only recourse may be to present to top management, as candidly as possible, the implications for project success without sufficient support. The final decision then comes down to top management: They will either support the project and require that staffing be completed as requested; suggest a compromise, or support the functional manager. In the first two cases, the project will proceed; in the third, top management is effectively ending the project before it has begun.

Assemble the Team

When the project has been staffed and approved, the final step is assembling the project team. This involves developing a skills inventory matrix that identifies the skills needed for the project against the skills we have acquired and a responsibility matrix using the Responsibility Activity Matrix (RAM) methodology (discussed in Chapter 5). Also, all project team roles and responsibilities must be clarified, along with all project team methods, expectations, and standard operating procedures. Where any of these do not exist, it will be necessary to begin establishing them.

6.2 CHARACTERISTICS OF EFFECTIVE PROJECT TEAMS

A great deal of research has investigated the qualities that effective teams possess and how those same qualities are missing from less effective groups. Successful teams share common underlying features, including a clear sense of mission, an understanding of team interdependencies, cohesiveness, a high level of trust, a shared sense of enthusiasm, and a results orientation.

A Clear Sense of Mission

A key determinant of project success is a clear project mission.[3] Further, that sense of mission must be mutually understood and accepted by all team members. Research has demonstrated that a clearly understood project mission is the number one predictor of success as the project is being developed.[4] Two important issues are clear: First, project teams perform well when there is a clear sense of purpose or objectives for their project; and second, the more widely shared and understood those goals, the better the project performance. The alternative is to allow the project manager to function as the hub of a wheel, with each team member as a separate spoke, interacting only through the project manager. This arrangement is not nearly as useful or successful as one in which all project team members understand the overall project objectives and how their performance contributes to achieving those objectives.

A mistake sometimes made by project managers is to segment the team in terms of their duties, giving each member a small, well-specified task but no sense of how that activity contributes to the overall project development effort. This approach is a serious mistake for several important reasons. First, the project team is the manager's best source for troubleshooting problems, both potential and actual. If the team is kept in the dark, members who could potentially help with the smooth development of the project through participating in other aspects of the installation are not able to contribute in helpful ways. Second, team members know and resent it when they are being kept in the dark about various features of the project on which they are working. Consciously or not, when project managers keep their team isolated and involved in fragmented tasks, they are sending out the signal that they either do not trust their team or do not feel that their team has the competence to address issues related to the overall implementation effort. Finally, from a "firefighting" perspective, it simply makes good sense for team leaders to keep their people abreast of the status of the project. The more time spent defining goals and clarifying roles in the initial stages of the team's development, the less time will be needed to resolve problems and adjudicate disputes down the road.

A Productive Interdependency

Interdependency refers to the degree of joint activity among team members that is required in order to complete a project. If, for example, a project could be completed through the work of a small number of people or one department in an organization, the interdependence needed would be considered low. In most situations, however, a project manager must form a team out of members from various functional areas within the organization. For example, an IT project introduction at a large corporation could conceivably require the input or efforts of a team that included members from the Information Systems department, engineering, accounting, marketing, and administration. As the concept of **differentiation** suggests, these individuals each bring to the team their preconceived notions of the roles that they should play, the importance of their various contributions, and other parochial attitudes.

Interdependencies refer to the degree of knowledge that team members have and the importance they attach to the interrelatedness of their efforts. Developing an understanding of mutual interdependencies implies developing a mutual level of appreciation for the strengths and contributions that each team member brings to the table and is a precondition for team success. Team members must become aware not only of their own contributions but also of how their work fits into the overall scheme of the project and, further, of how it relates to the work of team members from other departments.

Cohesiveness

Cohesiveness, at its most basic level, simply refers to the degree of mutual attraction that team members hold for one another and their task. It is the strength of desire all members have to remain a team. It is safe to assume that most members of the project team need a reason or reasons to contribute their skills and time to the successful completion of a project. Although they have been assigned to the project, for many individuals, this project may compete with other duties or responsibilities pulling them in other directions. Project managers work to build a team that is cohesive as a starting point for performing their tasks. Since cohesiveness is predicated on the attraction that the group holds for each individual member, managers need to make use of all resources at their disposal, including reward systems, recognition, performance appraisals, and any other sources of organizational reward, to induce team members to devote time and energy in furthering the team's goals.

Trust

Trust means different things to different people.[5] For a project team, **trust** can best be understood as the team's comfort level with each individual member. Given that comfort level, trust is manifested in the team's ability and willingness to squarely address differences of opinion, values, and attitudes and deal with them accordingly. Trust is the common denominator without which ideas of group cohesion and appreciation become moot. The interesting point about trust is that it can actually encourage disagreement and conflict among team members. When members of a project team have developed a comfort level where they are willing to trust the opinions of others, no matter how much those opinions diverge from their own, it is possible to air opposing views, to discuss issues, and even to argue. Because we trust one another, the disagreements are never treated as personal attacks; we recognize that views different from our own are valuable and can contribute to the project. Of course, before positive results can come from disagreement, we have to develop trust.

There are a number of ways in which project team members begin to trust one another. First, it is important for the project manager to create a "What happens here, stays here" mentality in which team members are not worried that their views will be divulged or confidences betrayed. Trust must first be demonstrated by the professionalism of the project manager and the manner in which she treats all team members. Second, trust develops over time. There is no way to jump-start trust among people. We are tested continuously to ensure that we are trustworthy. Third, trust is an "all-or-nothing" issue. Either we are trustworthy or we are not. There is no such thing as being slightly trustworthy. Finally, trust occurs on several levels:[6] (1) trust as it relates to professional **interaction** and the expectation of another person's competence ("I trust you to be able to accomplish the task"), (2) trust that occurs on an integrity level ("I trust you to honor your commitments"), and (3) trust that exists on an emotional level based on intuition ("It feels right to allow you to make this decision"). Hence, it is important to recognize that trust among team members is complex, takes time to develop, is dependent on past history, and can occur on several levels, each of which is important to developing a high-performing team.

Enthusiasm

Enthusiasm is the key to creating the energy and spirit that drive effective project efforts. One method for generating team enthusiasm is to promote the idea of efficacy, the belief that if we work toward certain goals, they are attainable. Enthusiasm is the catalyst for directing positive, high energy toward the project while committing to its goals. Project managers, therefore, are best able to promote a sense of enthusiasm within the project team when they create an environment that is:

- *Challenging*—Each member of the project perceives his role to offer the opportunity for professional or personal growth, new learning, and the ability to stretch professionally.
- *Supportive*—Project team members gain a sense of team spirit and group identity that creates the feeling of uniqueness with regard to the project. All team members work collaboratively, communicate often, and treat difficulties as opportunities for sharing and joint problem solving.

- *Personally rewarding*—Project team members become more enthusiastic as they perceive personal benefits arising from successful completion of the project. Linking the opportunity for personal advancement to project team performance gives all team members a sense of ownership of the project and a vested interest in its successful completion.

The importance of enthusiasm among project team members is best illustrated by a recently witnessed example. A team leader had been charged with reengineering a manufacturing process at a large production plant in New England. Despite his initial enthusiasm and energy, he was getting increasingly frustrated with his project team, most of them having been assigned to him without any of his input on the assignments. His chief concern became how to deal with the constant litany of "We can't do that here" that he heard every time he offered a suggestion for changing a procedure or trying anything new. One Monday morning, his team members walked into the office to the vision of the words "YES WE CAN!" painted in letters three feet high across one wall of the office. (Over the weekend, the project manager had come in and done a little redecorating.) From that point on, the motto YES WE CAN! became the theme of the team and had a powerful impact on project success.

Results Orientation

Results orientation suggests that each member of the project team is committed to achieving the project's goals. The project manager can influence team performance in many ways, but it is through constantly emphasizing the importance of task performance and project **outcomes** that all team members are united toward the same **orientation**. Some have referred to this phenomenon as the "eyes on the prize" attitude, a commonly held characteristic among successful project teams. The benefit of a results orientation is that it serves to continually rally team members toward the important or significant issues, allowing them to avoid squandering time and resources on problems that may be only peripheral to the major project goals.

6.3 REASONS WHY TEAMS FAIL

Because the challenges involved in creating high-performing project teams are so profound, it is not surprising that project teams fail to perform to their potential in many circumstances. Teams operate at less than optimum performance for a number of reasons, including poorly developed or unclear goals, poorly defined project team roles and interdependencies, lack of project team motivation, poor communication or leadership, turnover among team members, and dysfunctional behavior.[7]

Poorly Developed or Unclear Goals

One of the most common causes of project team failure is the absence of clear and commonly understood project goals. When the project goals are fragmented, constantly changing, or poorly communicated, the result is a high degree of ambiguity. This ambiguity is highly frustrating for project team members for a number of reasons.

UNCLEAR GOALS PERMIT MULTIPLE INTERPRETATIONS   The most common problem with poorly developed goals is that they allow each team member to make separate and often differing interpretations of project objectives. As a result, rather than helping the team to focus on the project at hand, these goals actually serve to increase disagreements as each team member interprets the project's goals in different ways.

UNCLEAR GOALS IMPEDE THE WILLINGNESS OF TEAM MEMBERS TO WORK TOGETHER   When team members are faced with ambiguous goals, it is common for each person to interpret the goals in the most advantageous way. When goals are used to support individuals rather than team objectives, it often leads to situations in which one person's desire to satisfy the project goals *as he interprets them* actually conflicts with another team member's desire to satisfy her goals.

UNCLEAR GOALS INCREASE CONFLICT   Project team conflict is heightened by vague goals that allow for multiple, self-centered interpretations. Rather than working on completing the project, team members expend energy and time in conflict with one another sifting through project objectives.

Poorly Defined Project Team Roles and Interdependencies

Team interdependencies is a state where team members' activities coordinate with and complement other team members' work. To some degree, all team members depend on each other and must work in collaboration in order to accomplish project goals. High-performing teams are well structured in ways that leave little ambiguity about individual roles and responsibilities. When team member assignments or responsibilities are not made clear, it is natural for disagreements to occur or for time to be wasted in clarifying assignments. Another serious problem with poorly defined roles is that it allows for significant time to be lost between project activities. When team members are unaware of their roles and interdependencies in relation to other team members, it is common to lose time on the project through poor transitions, as tasks are completed and successors are expected to begin.

Lack of Project Team Motivation

A common problem with poorly performing project teams is a lack of motivation among team members. Motivation is typically a highly individualistic phenomenon, suggesting that the factors that motivate one member of the project (e.g., technical challenge, opportunities for advancement) may not be motivating for another member. When overall project team motivation is low, however, the project's performance will naturally suffer as team members work at below-optimal performance. Some of the reasons why project team motivation may be low include the following.

THE PROJECT IS PERCEIVED AS UNNECESSARY   When projects are viewed by team members as less than critical, their motivation to perform well will naturally be affected. Whether the project team members' perception of a project as "unnecessary" is correct or not, if the organization and the project manager allow this interpretation to become fixed, it is extremely difficult to achieve high motivation from the team. Consequently, project managers need to communicate to the project team, as honestly as possible, the benefits of the project, its goals, and why they are important for the organization.

THE PROJECT MAY HAVE LOW PRIORITY   Team members within organizations are often aware of which project initiatives are considered high priority and which are not. Internal company communications, including newsletters, e-mails, and other methods for highlighting activities, clearly identify the projects that top management views as critical. When project team members perceive that they are working on a project of low priority, they adopt a low level of commitment to the project and have low motivation to perform well.

Poor Communication

Poor communication comes about for a variety of reasons. For example, project team members may be uncertain about the structure of the project and the interdependencies among team members so they do not know with whom they are expected to share information. Another reason communication within the project team can break down is that some team members are unwilling to share information, viewing it as a source of power over other members of the team. Communication also may be impeded within the project team due to the different functional or professional orientations of project team members. Technical personnel, such as engineers, are comfortable employing scientific or technical jargon that is hard for nontechnical personnel to understand. Likewise, professionals with financial backgrounds may use business-related terminology that is not clear to technical team members.

The key to resolving many communication problems lies in the project manager's willingness to establish and enforce standards for information sharing among team members, creating an atmosphere within the project team that encourages frank and open exchanges. Other mechanisms for encouraging cross-functional cooperation are examined in greater detail later in this chapter.

Poor Leadership

Chapter 4 discussed the importance of the project manager's approach to leadership in great detail. Because this individual is often the linchpin holding the team together, the leadership style chosen by the project manager is a key promoter or inhibitor of project team effectiveness. Project managers who adopt a "one-style-fits-all" approach to leadership fail to recognize that different leadership styles are required in order to get the best performance out of each team member. Further, some project managers adopt a leadership approach that may be completely antithetical to the project team, browbeating, bullying, or threatening team members in the belief that the key to high project team performance is to create an atmosphere of fear and anxiety. Successful project leaders understand that leadership styles depend upon a number of relevant criteria within the project team—including makeup of the team, motivation levels, and experience and skill levels of team members—and modify their leadership style accordingly.

Turnover Among Project Team Members

A common problem in many organizations is that team members are assigned to a project and then unexpectedly pulled off the project for reassignment. The higher the turnover among project team members, the more it disrupts the project manager's ability to create project team cohesion. Further, the act of continually adding to and removing personnel from project teams causes problems with team learning and functioning. Research has found that because of learning curve effects, the act of adding team members to an ongoing project often has the effect of delaying the project. New team members need time to get caught up with the project, they are not clear on structure or team interrelationships, and they do not understand internal team dynamics.

Although the best-case scenario for project managers is to run projects in which team members do not turn over, the practical reality is that we must anticipate the potential for turnover and consider strategies that allow for minimal disruption to the project schedule when turnover does occur. One method of minimizing disruption is for the project manager to require that everyone on the team understands, as clearly as possible, not only her own role but also the roles of other team members to allow the members to support activities that could be delayed due to staff "pullaways." Another option is for the project manager to work closely with functional department heads in order to anticipate the possibility of project team members leaving the team prematurely and to begin prepping possible replacements.

Dysfunctional Behavior

Dysfunctional behavior refers to the disruptive acts of some project team members due to personality issues, hidden agendas, or interpersonal problems. Sometimes the solution simply calls for recognizing which members are engaging in these behaviors and taking steps to correct the problem. Other times, serious cases of dysfunctional behavior may require that a team member be removed from the project team.

6.4 STAGES IN GROUP DEVELOPMENT

The process of group development is a dynamic one.[8] Groups go through several maturation stages that are often readily identifiable, are generally found across a variety of organizations, and involve groups formed for a variety of different purposes. These stages are illustrated in Table 6.1 and Figure 6.4.[9]

Stage One: Forming

Forming consists of the process or approaches used to mold a collection of individuals into a coherent project team. This stage has sometimes been referred to as the "floundering" stage, because team members are unsure about the project's goals, may not know other team members, and are confused about their own assignments.[10] Team members begin to get acquainted with one another and talk about the purposes of the project, how they perceive their roles, what types of communication patterns will be used, and what will be

TABLE 6.1 Stages of Group Development

Stage	Defining Characteristics
Forming	Members get to know one another and lay the basis for project and team ground rules.
Storming	Conflict begins as team members begin to resist authority and demonstrate hidden agendas and prejudices.
Norming	Members agree on operating procedures and seek to work together, develop closer relationships, and commit to the project development process.
Performing	Group members work together to accomplish their tasks.
Adjourning	Groups may disband either following the completion of the project or through significant reassignment of team personnel.

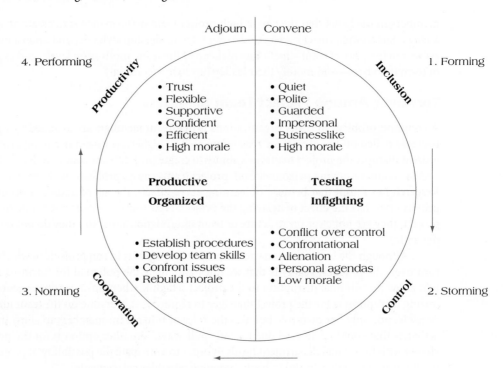

FIGURE 6.4 Stages of Team Development

Source: V. K. Verma. (1997). *Managing the Project Team,* p. 71. Upper Darby, PA: Project Management Institute. Copyright and all rights reserved. Material from this publication has been reproduced with the permission of PMI.

acceptable behaviors within the group. During the forming stage, some preliminary standards of behavior are established, including rules for interaction (who is really in charge and how members are expected to interact) and activity (how productive members are expected to be). The earlier this stage is completed, the better, so that ambiguities further along are avoided. In these early meetings, the role of the team leader is to create structure and set the tone for future cooperation and positive member attitudes.

Stage Two: Storming

Storming refers to the natural reactions members have to the initial ground rules. Members begin to test the limits and constraints placed on their behavior. Storming is a conflict-laden stage in which the preliminary leadership patterns, reporting relationships, and norms of work and interpersonal behavior are challenged and, perhaps, reestablished. During this stage, it is likely that the team leader will begin to see a number of the group members demonstrating personal agendas, attempting to defy or rewrite team rules, and exhibiting prejudices toward teammates from other functional backgrounds. For example, a team member may unilaterally decide that it is not necessary for her to attend all team meetings, proposing instead to get involved later in the project when she is "really needed." Other behaviors may involve not-so-subtle digs at members from other departments ("Gee, what are you marketing people doing here on a technical project?") or old animosities between individuals that resurface. Storming is a very natural phase through which all groups go. The second half of this chapter addresses ways to handle all types of conflict.

Stage Three: Norming

A *norm* is an unwritten rule of behavior. Norming behavior in a group implies that the team members are establishing mutually agreed-upon practices and attitudes. Norms help the team determine how it should make decisions, how often it should meet, what level of openness and trust members will have, and how conflicts will be resolved. Research has shown that it is during the **norming stage** that the cohesiveness of the group grows to its highest level. Close relationships develop, a sense of mutual concern and appreciation emerges, and feelings of camaraderie and shared responsibility become evident. The norming stage establishes the healthy basis upon which the actual work of the team will commence.

Stage Four: Performing

The actual work of the project team is done during the **performing stage**. It is only when the first three phases have been properly dealt with that the team will have reached the level of maturity and confidence needed to effectively perform their duties. During the performing stage, team relationships are characterized by high levels of trust, a mutual appreciation for one another's performance and contributions, and a willingness to actively seek to collaborate. Morale has continued to improve over the project team's development cycle to this point, at which all team members are working confidently and efficiently. As long as strong task-oriented group norms were established early in the team development and conflict was resolved, the performing stage is one of high morale and strong performance.

Stage Five: Adjourning

Adjourning recognizes the fact that projects and their teams do not last forever. At some point, the project has been completed and the team is disbanded to return to their other functional duties within the organization. In some cases, the group may downsize slowly and deliberately. For example, in the case of developing a systems engineering project, as various components of the system come online, the services of the team's design engineer may no longer be needed and he will be reassigned. In other circumstances, the team will complete its tasks and be disbanded all at once. In either case, it is important to remember that during the final stages of the implementation process, group members are likely to exhibit some concern about their future assignments and/or new duties. Project managers need to be sensitive to the real concerns felt by these team members and, where possible, help smooth the transition from the old team to the new assignments.

Punctuated Equilibrium

In the late 1980s, UCLA researcher Connie Gersick challenged the validity of the standard model of project team development.[11] Through a series of studies, she observed a dramatically different process by which project teams evolve. She referred to her model as *punctuated equilibrium,* based on a similar scientific model proposed by Stephen J. Gould to explain macroevolutionary change in the natural world. **Punctuated equilibrium** proposes that rather than evolution occurring as a steady state of gradual change, real natural change comes about through long periods of stasis, interrupted by some cataclysmic event that propels upward, evolutionary adjustment.

This phenomenon of punctuated equilibrium frequently occurs in the field of group dynamics. Gersick's work suggests that the timing of group process changes is quite consistent across teams and situations. Most teams, she discovered, develop a set of operating norms very quickly, at the time of the first team meeting and on the basis of limited interaction and knowledge of one another or the project mission. These norms, which are often less than optimal, tend to guide group behavior and performance for a substantial period of the project's life. The group will continue to operate as a result of these norms until some trigger event occurs, almost precisely at the halfway point between the initial meeting and the project deadline (see Figure 6.5). The trigger event may be general dissatisfaction with the project's progress to date, a boiling over of interpersonal antagonisms, or some other external force. Nevertheless, once this eruption has occurred, it serves as the motivation to revise group norms, develop better intragroup procedures, and promote better task performance. It is typically during this second phase of the group's life that the majority of effective work gets done and the group begins to function more as a team and less as a collection of individuals.

Punctuated equilibrium has some very important implications for project team leaders. First, it suggests that initial impressions are often lasting, as early behaviors and norms quickly solidify and become the controlling force behind the team's behavior. Project team leaders, therefore, need to take a hard look at how they run kickoff meetings and the messages they send (intentional or otherwise) regarding appropriate task and interpersonal behavior. Second, the model suggests that groups collectively experience a form of "midlife crisis" in running their project, because a lack of concrete results, coupled with escalating interpersonal tensions, tends to build to a state of dissatisfaction that finally overflows midway through the development process. Leaders need to plan for these behaviors, recognize the warning signs of their approach, and proactively chart the steps needed for more positive outcomes from the transition. Finally, Gersick's research found that group members tended to feel increased frustration because they lacked a real sense of where the project stood at any point in time. Hence, project managers who wish to avoid the more damaging effects of midlife project transitions need to recognize that the more they plan for interim milestones and other indications of progress, the more they can mitigate the adverse effects of project team blowups.

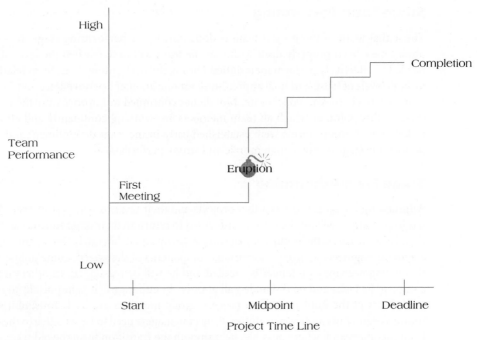

FIGURE 6.5   Model of Punctuated Equilibrium

6.5 ACHIEVING CROSS-FUNCTIONAL COOPERATION

What are some tactics that managers can use for effective team development? One research project on project teams uncovered a set of critical factors that contribute to **cross-functional cooperation.**[12] Figure 6.6 shows a two-stage model: The first set of factors influences cooperation, and the second set influences outcomes. Critical factors that influence cooperation and behavior are superordinate goals, rules and procedures, physical proximity, and accessibility. Through cross-functional cooperation, these influence both

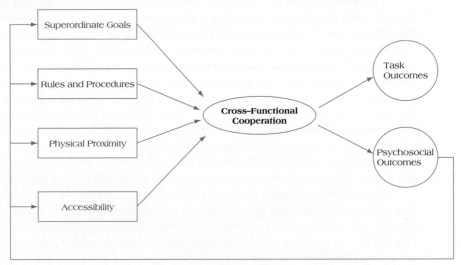

FIGURE 6.6   Project Team Cross-Functional Cooperation

Source: M. B. Pinto, J. K. Pinto, and J. E. Prescott. (1993). "Antecedents and consequences of project team cross-functional cooperation." *Management Science,* 39: 1281–97, p. 1283. Copyright 1993, the Institute for Operations Research and the Management Sciences, 7240 Parkway Drive, Suite 300, Hanover, MD 21076 USA. Reprinted by permission, Project Team Cross-Functional Cooperation.

high task outcomes (making sure the project is done right) and psychosocial outcomes (the emotional and psychological effects that strong performance will have on the project team).

Superordinate Goals

A **superordinate goal** refers to an overall goal or purpose that is important to all functional groups involved, but whose attainment requires the resources and efforts of more than one group.[13] When Apple developed its iPad tablet, that venture included a number of subprojects, including the creation of a user-friendly operating system, graphical-user interface, a number of unique features and applications for running multiple programs, 4G and wireless capabilities, and so forth. Each of these subprojects was supported by dozens of electronics engineers, IT professionals, programmers and coding specialists, graphics designers, marketing research personnel, and operations specialists, all working together collaboratively. The iPad could not have been successful if only some of the projects succeeded—they all had to be successful, requiring that their developers maintain strong, collaborative working relationships with one another.

The superordinate goal is an addition to, not a replacement for, other goals the functional groups may have set. The premise is that when project team members from different functional areas share an overall goal or common purpose, they tend to cooperate toward this end. To illustrate, let us consider an example of creating a new software project for the commercial marketplace. A superordinate goal for this project team may be "to develop a high-quality, user-friendly, and generally useful system that will enhance the operations of various departments and functions." This overall goal attempts to enhance or pull together some of the diverse function-specific goals for cost-effectiveness, schedule adherence, quality, and innovation. It provides a central objective or an overriding goal toward which the entire project team can strive.

Rules and Procedures

Rules and procedures are central to any discussion of cross-functional cooperation because they offer a means for coordinating or integrating activities that involve several functional units.[14] Organizational rules and procedures are defined as formalized processes established by the organization that mandate or control the activities of the project team in terms of team membership, task assignment, and performance evaluation. For years, organizations have relied on rules and procedures to link together the activities of organizational members. Rules and procedures have been used to assign duties, evaluate performance, solve conflicts, and so on. Rules and procedures can be used to address formalized rules and procedures established by the organization for the performance of the implementation process, as well as project-specific rules and procedures developed by the project team to facilitate its operations.

The value of rules and procedures suggests that in the absence of cooperation among team members, the company can simply mandate that it occur. In cases where project teams cannot rely on established, organization-wide rules and procedures to assist members with their tasks, they often must create their own rules and procedures to facilitate the progress of the project. For example, one such rule could be that all project team members will make themselves available to one another regarding project business.

Physical Proximity

Physical proximity refers to project team members' perceptions that they are located within physical or spatial distances that make it convenient for them to interact. Individuals are more likely to interact and communicate with others when the physical characteristics of buildings or settings encourage them to do so.[15] For example, the sheer size and spatial layout of a building can affect working relationships. In a small building or when a work group is clustered on the same floor, relationships tend to be more intimate, since people are in close physical proximity to one another. As people spread out along corridors or in different buildings, interactions may become less frequent and/or less spontaneous. In these situations, it is harder for employees to interact with members of either their own department or other departments.

Many companies seriously consider the potential effects of physical proximity on project team cooperation. In fact, some project organizations relocate personnel who are working together on a project to the same office or floor. The term "war room" is sometimes used to illustrate this deliberate regrouping of project team members into a central location. When project team members work near one another, they are more likely to communicate and, ultimately, cooperate.

Accessibility

While physical proximity is important for encouraging cross-functional cooperation, another factor, accessibility, appears to be an equally important predictor of the phenomenon. **Accessibility** is the perception by others that a person is approachable for communicating and interacting with on problems or concerns related to the success of a project. Separate from the issue of physical proximity, accessibility refers to additional factors that can inhibit the amount of interaction that occurs between organizational members (e.g., an individual's schedule, position in an organization, or out-of-office commitments). These factors often affect the accessibility among organizational members. For example, consider a public-sector organization in which a member of the engineering department is physically located near a member of the city census department. Although these individuals are in proximity to each other, they may rarely interact because of different work schedules, varied duties and priorities, and commitment to their own agendas. Such factors often create a perception of inaccessibility among the individuals involved.

Outcomes of Cooperation: Task and Psychosocial Results

As Figure 6.6 suggests, the goal of promoting cross-functional cooperation among members of a project team is not an end unto itself; it reflects a means toward better project team performance and ultimately better project outcomes. Two types of project outcomes are important to consider: task outcomes and psychosocial outcomes. **Task outcomes** refer to the factors involved in the actual implementation of the project (time, schedule, and project functionality). **Psychosocial outcomes**, on the other hand, represent the team member's assessment that the project experience was worthwhile, satisfying, and productive. It is possible, for example, to have a project "succeed" in terms of completing its task outcomes while all team members are so disheartened due to conflict and bad experiences that they have nothing but bad memories of the project. Psychosocial outcomes are important because they represent the attitudes that project team members will carry with them to subsequent projects (as shown in the feedback loop in Figure 6.6). Was the project experience satisfying and rewarding? If so, we are much more likely to start new projects with a positive attitude than in circumstances where we had bad experiences on previous projects. Regardless of how carefully we plan and execute our project team selection and development process, our efforts may take time to bear fruit.

Finally, what are some general conclusions we can draw about methods for building high-performing teams? Based on research, project managers can take three practical steps to set the stage for teamwork to emerge:[16]

1. *Make the project team as tangible as possible.* Effective teams routinely develop their own unique identity. Through publicity, promoting interaction, encouraging unique terminology and language, and emphasizing the importance of project outcomes, project managers can create a tangible sense of team identity.
2. *Reward good behavior.* There are many nonmonetary methods for rewarding good performance. The keys are (1) flexibility—recognizing that everyone views rewards differently, (2) creativity—providing alternative means to get the message across, and (3) pragmatism—recognizing what can be rewarded and being authentic with the team about how superior performance will be recognized.
3. *Develop a personal touch.* Project managers need to build one-on-one relationships with project team members. If they lead by example, provide positive feedback to team members, publicly acknowledge good performance, show interest in the team's work, and are accessible and consistent in applying work rules, project team members will come to value both the manager's efforts and his work on the project.

These suggestions are a good starting point for applying the concept of team building in the difficult setting of project management. Given the temporary nature of projects, the dynamic movement of team members on and off the team, and the fact that in many organizations team members are working on several projects simultaneously, building a cohesive project team that can work in harmony and effectively to achieve project goals is extremely valuable.[17] Using these guidelines for team building should allow project managers to more rapidly achieve a high-performing team.

6.6 VIRTUAL PROJECT TEAMS

The globalization of business has had some important effects on how projects are being run today. Imagine a multimillion-dollar project to design, construct, and install an oil-drilling platform in the North Atlantic. The project calls on the expertise of partner organizations from Russia, Finland, the United States, France, Norway, and Great Britain. Each of the partners must be fully represented on the project team, all decisions should be as consensual as possible, and the project's success will require continuous, ongoing communication between all members of the project team. Does this sound difficult? In fact, such projects are undertaken frequently. Until recently, the biggest challenge was finding a way for managers to meet and stay in close contact. Constant travel was the only option. However, now more organizations are forming virtual project teams.

Virtual teams involve the use of electronic media, including e-mail, the Internet, and teleconferencing, to link together members of a geographically dispersed project team. Virtual teams start with the assumption that physical barriers or spatial separation make it impractical for team members to meet in a regular, face-to-face manner. Hence, the virtual team involves establishing alternative communications media that enable all team members to stay in contact, make contributions to the ongoing project, and communicate all necessary project-related information with all other members of the project team. Virtual teams are using technology to solve the thorny problem of productively linking geographically dispersed project partners.

Virtual teams present two main challenges: building trust and establishing the best modes of communication.[18] Trust, as we have discussed, is a key ingredient needed to turn a disparate group of individuals into an integrated project team. Physical separation and disconnection can make trust slower to emerge. Communications media may create formal and impersonal settings, and the level of comfort that permits casual banter takes time to develop. This can slow down the process of creating trust among team members.

What are some suggestions for improving the efficiency and effectiveness of virtual team meetings? Following are some options available to project teams as they set out to use virtual technology.[19]

- *When possible, find ways to augment virtual communication with face-to-face opportunities.* Try not to rely exclusively on virtual technology. Even if it occurs only at the beginning of a project and after key milestones, create opportunities to get the team together to exchange information, socialize, and begin developing personal relationships.

- *Don't let team members disappear.* One of the problems with virtual teams is that it becomes easy for members to "sign off" for extended periods of time, particularly if regular communication schedules are not established. The best solution to this problem is to ensure that communications include both regular meetings and ad hoc get-togethers, either through videoconferencing or through e-mail and Internet connections.

- *Establish a code of conduct among team members.* While it can be relatively easy to get agreement on the types of information that need to be shared among team members, it is equally important to establish rules for when contact should be made and the length of acceptable and unacceptable delays in responding to messages.

- *Keep all team members in the communication loop.* Virtual teams require a hyperawareness by the project manager of the need to keep the communication channels open. When team members understand how they fit into the big picture, they are more willing to stay in touch.

- *Create a clear process for addressing conflict, disagreement, and group norms.* When projects are conducted in a virtual setting, the actual ability of the project manager to gauge team members' reactions and feelings about the project and one another may be minimal. It is helpful to create a set of guidelines for allowing the free expression of misgivings or disagreements among team members. For example, one virtual team composed of members of several large organizations established a Friday-afternoon complaint session, which allowed a two-hour block each week for team members to vent their feelings or disagreements. The only rule of the session was that everything said must remain within the project—no one could carry these messages outside the project team. Within two months of instituting the sessions, project team members felt that the sessions were the most productive part of project communication and looked forward to them more than to formal project meetings.

PROJECT PROFILE

Tele-Immersion Technology Eases the Use of Virtual Teams

For many users of videoconferencing technology, the benefits and drawbacks may sometimes seem about equal. Although there is no doubt that teleconferencing puts people into immediate contact with each other from great geographical distances, the current limitations on how far the technology can be applied lead to some important qualifications. As one writer noted:

> I am a frequent but reluctant user of videoconferencing. Human interaction has both verbal and nonverbal elements, and videoconferencing seems precisely configured to confound the nonverbal ones. It is impossible to make eye contact properly, for instance, in today's videoconferencing systems, because the camera and the display screen cannot be in the same spot. This usually leads to a deadened and formal affect in interactions, eye contact being a nearly ubiquitous subconscious method of affirming trust. Furthermore, participants aren't able to establish a sense of position relative to one another and therefore have no clear way to direct attention, approval or disapproval.[20]

It was to address these problems with teleconferencing that tele-immersion technology was created. Tele-immersion, a new medium for human interaction enabled by digital technologies, creates the illusion that a user is in the same physical space as other people, even though the other participants might in fact be thousands of miles away. It combines the display and interaction techniques of virtual reality with new vision technologies that transcend the traditional limitations of a camera. The result is that all the participants, however distant, can share and explore a life-sized space.

This fascinating new technology, which has emerged very recently, offers the potential to completely change the nature of how virtual project teams communicate with each other. Pioneered by Advanced Network & Services as part of the National Tele-Immersion Initiative (NTII), tele-immersion enables users at geographically distributed sites to collaborate in real time in a shared, simulated environment as if they were in the same physical room. Tele-immersion is the long-distance transmission of life-sized, three-dimensional synthesized scenes, accurately sampled and rendered in real time using advanced computer graphics and vision techniques. The use of this sophisticated representation of three-dimensional modeling has allowed teleconferencing to take on a whole new look; all members of the project literally appear in a real-time, natural setting, almost as if they were sitting across a conference table from one another.

With enhanced bandwidth and the appropriate technology, tele-immersion video conferencing offers an enormous leap forward compared to the current two-dimensional industry standards in use. In its current form, the tele-immersion technology requires the videoconference member to wear polarizing glasses and a silvery head-tracking device that can move around and see a computer-generated 3D stereoscopic image of the other teleconferencers, whereby the visual content of a block of space surrounding each participant's upper body and some adjoining workspace is essentially reproduced with computer graphics. This results in a more fully dimensional and compressible depiction of such real-world environments than is possible with existing video technology. Just how far this technology is likely to go in the years ahead is impossible to predict, but no one is betting against it becoming the basis for an entirely new manner of conducting virtual team meetings.[21]

As Figure 6.7 demonstrates, recent advances in technology have allowed tele-immersion conferencing to sometimes dispense with extra equipment link goggles or tracking devices. The ability to translate and communicate

FIGURE 6.7 Tele-Immersion Technology

sophisticated images of people, blueprints, or fully rendered three-dimensional models makes this technology unique and highly appealing as an alternative to standard telephone conferencing.

Virtual teams, though not without their limitations and challenges, offer an excellent method for employing the technical advances in the field of telecommunications to the problems encountered with global, dispersed project teams. The key to using them effectively lies in a clear recognition of what virtual technologies can and cannot do. For example, while the Internet can link team members, it cannot convey nonverbals or feelings that team members may have about the project or other members of the project. Likewise, although current videoconferencing allows for real-time, face-to-face interactions, it is not a perfect substitute for genuine "face time" among project team members. Nevertheless, the development of virtual technologies has been a huge benefit for project organizations, coming as it has at the same time that teams have become more global in their makeup and that partnering project organizations are becoming the norm for many project challenges.

6.7 CONFLICT MANAGEMENT

One study has estimated that the average manager spends over 20% of his time dealing with conflict.[22] Because so much of a project manager's time is taken up with active conflict and its residual aftermath, we need to understand this natural process within the project management context. This section of the chapter is intended to more formally explore the process of conflict, examine the nature of conflict for project teams and managers, develop a model of conflict behavior, and foster an understanding of some of the most common methods for de-escalating conflict.

What Is Conflict?

Conflict is a process that begins when you perceive that someone has frustrated or is about to frustrate a major concern of yours.[23] There are two important elements in this definition. First, it suggests that conflict is not a state, but a process. As such, it contains a dynamic aspect that is very important. Conflicts evolve.[24] Further, the one-time causes of a conflict may change over time; that is, the reasons why two individuals or groups developed a conflict initially may no longer have any validity. However, because the conflict process is dynamic and evolving, once a conflict *has* occurred, the reasons behind it may no longer matter. The process of conflict has important ramifications that we will explore in greater detail.

The second important element in the definition is that conflict is perceptual in nature. In other words, it does not ultimately matter whether or not one party has truly wronged another party. The important thing is that one party *perceives* that state or event to have occurred. That perception is enough because for that party, perception of frustration defines reality.

In general, most types of conflict fit within one of three categories,[25] although it is also common for some conflicts to involve aspects of more than one category.

Goal-oriented conflict is associated with disagreements regarding results, project scope outcomes, performance specifications and criteria, and project priorities and objectives. Goal-oriented conflicts often result from multiple perceptions of the project and are fueled by vague or incomplete goals that allow project team members to make their own interpretations.

Administrative conflict arises through management hierarchy, organizational structure, or company philosophy. These conflicts are often centered on disagreements about reporting relationships, who has authority and administrative control for functions, project tasks, and decisions. A good example of administrative conflict arises in matrix organization structures, in which each project team member is responsible to two bosses, the project manager and the functional supervisor. In effect, this structure promotes the continuance of administrative conflict.

Interpersonal conflict occurs with personality differences between project team members and important project stakeholders. Interpersonal conflict sources include different work ethics, behavioral styles, egos, and personalities of project team members.

At least three schools of thought exist about how conflicts should be perceived and addressed. These vary dramatically, depending upon the prevailing view that a person or an organization holds.[26]

The first view of conflict is the *traditional* view, which sees conflict as having a negative effect on organizations. Traditionalists, because they assume that conflict is bad, believe that conflict should be avoided and resolved as quickly and painlessly as possible when it does occur. The emphasis with traditionalists is conflict suppression and elimination.

The second view of conflict is the *behavioral* or contemporary school of thought. Behavioral theorists view conflict as a natural and inevitable part of organizational life. Differentiation across functional departments and different goals, attitudes, and beliefs are natural and permanent states among members of a company, so it is natural that conflict will result. The solution to conflict for behavioral theorists is to manage conflict effectively rather than attempt to eliminate or suppress it.

The third view of conflict, the *interactionist* view, takes behavioral attitudes toward conflict one step further. Where a behavioral view of conflict accepts it when it occurs, interactionists encourage conflict to develop. Conflict, to an interactionist, prevents an organization from becoming too stagnant and apathetic. Conflict actually introduces an element of tension that produces innovation, creativity, and higher productivity. The interactionists do not intend that conflict should continue without some controls, however; they argue that there is an optimal level of conflict that improves the organization. Beyond that point, conflict becomes too intense and severe and begins hurting the company. The trick, to an interactionist, is to find the optimal level of conflict—too little leads to inertia and too much leads to chaos.

Sources of Conflict

Potential sources of conflict in projects are numerous. Some of the most common sources include the competition for scarce resources, violations of group or organizational norms, disagreements over goals or the means to achieve those goals, personal slights and threats to job security, long-held biases and prejudices, and so forth. Many of the sources of conflict arise out of the project management situation itself. That is, the very characteristics of projects that make them unique contribute some important triggers for conflict to erupt among project stakeholders.

ORGANIZATIONAL CAUSES OF CONFLICT   Some of the most common causes of organizational conflict are reward systems, scarce resources, uncertainty, and differentiation. *Reward systems* are competitive processes some organizations have set up that pit one group or functional department against another. For example, when functional managers are evaluated on the performance of their subordinates within the department, they are loath to allow their best workers to become involved in project work for any length of time. The organization has unintentionally created a state in which managers perceive that either the project teams *or* the departments will be rewarded for superior performance. In such cases, they will naturally retain their best people for functional duties and offer their less-desirable subordinates for project teamwork. The project managers, on the other hand, will also perceive a competition between their projects and the functional departments and develop a strong sense of animosity toward functional managers whom they perceive, with some justification, are putting their own interests above the organization.

Scarce resources are a natural cause of conflict as individuals and departments compete for the resources they believe are necessary to do their jobs well. Because organizations are characterized by scarce resources sought by many different groups, the struggle to gain these resources is a prime source of organizational conflict. As long as scarce resources are the natural state within organizations, groups will be in conflict as they seek to bargain and negotiate to gain an advantage in their distribution.

Uncertainty over lines of authority essentially asks the tongue-in-cheek question, "Who's in charge around here?" In the project environment, it is easy to see how this problem can be badly exacerbated due to the ambiguity that often exists with regard to formal channels of authority. Project managers and their teams sit "outside" the formal organizational hierarchy in many organizations, particularly in functional structures. As a result, they find themselves in a uniquely fragile position of having a great deal of autonomy but also responsibility to the functional department heads who provide the personnel for the team. For example, when a project team member from R&D is given orders by her functional manager that directly contradict directives from the project manager, she is placed in the dilemma of having to find (if possible) a middle ground between two nominal authority figures. In many cases, project managers do not have the authority to conduct performance evaluations of their team members—that control is kept within the functional department. In such situations, the team member from R&D, facing role conflict brought on by this uncertainty over lines of authority, will most likely do the expedient thing and obey her functional manager because of his "power of the performance appraisal."

Differentiation reflects the fact that different functional departments develop their own mind-sets, attitudes, time frames, and value systems, which can conflict with those of other departments. Briefly, differentiation suggests that as individuals join an organization within some functional specialty, they begin to adopt the attitudes and outlook of that functional group. For example, a member of the finance department, when asked her opinion of marketing, might reply, "All they ever do is travel around and spend money. They're a bunch of cowboys who would give away the store if they had to." A marketing member's opinion of finance department personnel might be similarly unflattering: "Finance people are just a group of bean counters who don't understand that the company is only as successful as it can be at selling its products. They're so hung up on their margins that they don't know what goes on in the real world." The interesting point about these views is that, within their narrow frames of reference, they both are essentially correct: Marketing *is* interested primarily in making sales, and finance *is* devoted to maintaining high margins. However, these opinions are by no means completely true; they simply reflect the underlying attitudes and prejudices of members of the respective functional departments. The more profound the differentiation within an organization, the greater the likelihood that individuals and groups will divide into "us" versus "them" encampments, which will continue to promote and provoke conflict.

INTERPERSONAL CAUSES OF CONFLICT *Faulty attributions* refer to our misconceptions of the reasons behind another's behavior. When people perceive that their interests have been thwarted by another individual or group, they typically try to determine why the other party has acted as it did. In making attributions about another's actions, we wish to determine if their motives are based on personal malevolence, hidden agendas, and so forth. Often groups and individuals will attribute motives to another's actions that are personally most convenient. For example, when one member of a project team has his wishes frustrated, it is common to perceive the motives behind the other party's actions in terms of the most convenient causes. Rather than acknowledge the fact that reasonable people may differ in their opinions, it may be more convenient for the frustrated person to assume that the other is provoking a conflict for personal reasons: "He just doesn't like me." This attribution is convenient for an obvious and psychologically "safe" reason; if we assume that the other person disagrees with us for valid reasons, it implies a flaw in our position. Many individuals do not have the ego strength to acknowledge and accept objective disagreement, preferring to couch their **frustration** in personal terms.

Faulty communication is a second and very common interpersonal cause of conflict. Faulty communication implies the potential for two mistakes: communicating in ways that are ambiguous and lead to different interpretations, thus causing a resulting conflict, and unintentionally communicating in ways that annoy or anger other parties. Lack of clarity can send out mixed signals: the message the sender intended to communicate and that which was received and interpreted by the receiver. Consequently, the project manager may be surprised and annoyed by the work done by a subordinate who genuinely thought she was adhering to the project manager's desires. Likewise, project managers often engage in criticism in the hopes of correcting and improving project team member performance. Unfortunately, what the project manager may consider to be harmless, constructive criticism may come across as a destructive, unfair critique if the information is not communicated accurately and effectively.

Personal grudges and *prejudices* are another main cause of interpersonal conflict. Each of us brings attitudes into any work situation. These attitudes arise as the result of long-term experiences or lessons taught at some point in the past. Often these attitudes are unconsciously held; we may be unaware that we nurture them and can feel a genuine sense of affront when we are challenged or accused of holding biases. Nevertheless, these grudges or prejudices, whether they are held against another race, sex, or functional department, have a seriously debilitating effect on our ability to work with others in a purposeful team and can ruin any chance at project team cohesion and subsequent project performance.

Table 6.2 illustrates some of the findings from two studies that investigated the major sources of conflict in project teams.[27] Although the studies were conducted more than a decade apart, the findings are remarkably consistent across several dimensions. Conflicts over schedules and project priorities tend to be the most common and intense sources of disagreement. Interestingly, Posner's research found that cost and budget issues played a much larger role in triggering conflict than did the earlier work of Thamhain and Wilemon. The significant changes in the rank ordering of sources of conflict and their intensity may be due to shifts in priorities or practices of project management over time, making issues of cost of greater concern and conflict.[28] Nevertheless, Table 6.2 gives some clear indications about the chief causes of conflict within project teams and the intensity level of these conflicts.

TABLE 6.2 Sources of Conflict in Projects and Their Ranking by Intensity Level

Sources of Conflict	Conflict Intensity Ranking	
	Thamhain & Wilemon	Posner
Conflict over project priorities	2	3
Conflict over administrative procedures	5	7
Conflict over technical opinions and performance trade-offs	4	5
Conflict over human resources	3	4
Conflict over cost and budget	7	2
Conflict over schedules	1	1
Personality conflicts	6	6

Methods for Resolving Conflict

A number of methods for resolving group conflict are at the project manager's disposal. Before making a decision about which approach to follow, the project manager needs to consider several issues.[29] For example, will the project manager's siding with one party to the dispute alienate the other person? Is the conflict professional or personal in nature? Does any sort of intervention have to occur or can team members resolve the issue on their own? Does the project manager have the time and inclination to mediate the dispute? All of these questions play an important role in determining how to approach a conflict situation. Project managers must learn to develop flexibility in dealing with conflict, knowing when to intervene versus when to remain neutral. We can choose to manage conflict in terms of five alternatives.[30]

MEDIATE THE CONFLICT   In this approach, the project manager takes a direct interest in the conflict between the parties and seeks to find a solution. The project manager may employ either defusion or confrontation tactics in negotiating a solution. *Defusion* implies that the project manager is less concerned with the source of the conflict than with a mutually acceptable solution. She may use phrases such as "We are all on the same team here" to demonstrate her desire to defuse the conflict without plumbing its underlying source. Confrontation, which typically involves working with both parties to get at the root causes of the conflict, is more emotional, time-intensive, and, in the short term, may actually exacerbate the conflict as both sides air their differences. In the long run, however, confrontation can be more effective as a mediating mechanism because it seeks to determine underlying causes of the conflict so they can be corrected. Project managers mediate solutions when they are not comfortable imposing a judgment but would rather work with both parties to come to some common agreement.

ARBITRATE THE CONFLICT   In choosing to arbitrate a conflict, the project manager must be willing to impose a judgment on the warring parties. After listening to both positions, the project manager renders his decision. Much as a judge would do, it is best to minimize personalities in the decision and focus instead on the judgment itself. For example, saying, "You were wrong here, Phil, and Susan was right," is bound to lead to a negative emotional response from Phil. By imposing an impersonal judgment, however, the project manager can stick with the specifics of the case at hand rather than getting into personalities. "Company policy states that all customers must receive copies of project revision orders within three working days" is an example of an impersonal judgment that does not point the finger of guilt at either party.

CONTROL THE CONFLICT   Not all conflicts can be (nor should be) quickly resolved. In some cases, a pragmatic response to a conflict might be to wait a couple of days for the two parties to cool down. This is not a cowardly response; instead it recognizes that project managers must be selective about how they intervene and the optimal manner in which they can intervene. Another way to control conflict is through limiting the interaction between two parties. For example, if it is common knowledge that one member of the project team and the customer have a long history of animosity, good sense dictates that they should not be allowed to communicate directly except under the most controlled of circumstances.

ACCEPT THE CONFLICT   Not all conflicts are manageable. Sometimes the personalities of two project team members are simply not compatible. They disliked each other before the project and will continue to dislike each other long after the project has been completed.

ELIMINATE THE CONFLICT   We need to critically evaluate the nature and severity of conflicts that occur continually within a project. In some situations, it is necessary, for the good of the project, to transfer a team member or make other changes. If there is a clearly guilty party, a common response is to sanction that person, remove him from the project, or otherwise punish him. If two or more people share a collective guilt for the ongoing conflict, it is often useful to transfer them all—sending a signal that you intend to run the project as impartially as possible.

The important point to bear in mind is that different approaches may be appropriate in different situations. Do not assume that a problem-solving session is always beneficial or warranted, nor is ignoring conflict always "lazy" management. Project managers have to learn to understand their own preferences when it comes to handling conflict. Once we have achieved a greater sense of self-awareness, we will be in a better position first to resolve our own conflicts constructively and then to deal more effectively with subordinate conflicts. The key is flexibility. It is important not to lock into any particular conflict style nor favor one resolution tactic to the exclusion of all others. Each has its strengths and drawbacks and can be an important part of the project manager's tool chest.

Conflict often is evidence of project team progress. As we begin to assemble a group of disparate individuals with various functional backgrounds into a project team, a variety of conflicts are bound to be sparked. Team conflict is natural. Remember, however, that the approaches we choose to employ to deal with conflict say a great deal about us: Are we in tolerant, authoritarian, and intransigent, or do we really want to find mutually beneficial solutions? We can send many messages—intentional and unintentional, clear and mixed—to the rest of the project team by the manner in which we approach team building and conflict management.

6.8 NEGOTIATION

One of the central points that this chapter has made is to suggest that much of our future success will rest with our ability to appreciate and manage the variety of "people" issues that are central to life in projects. **Negotiation** is a process that is predicated on a manager's ability to use his influence productively.

Negotiation skills are so important because much of a project manager's life is taken up in bargaining sessions of one type or another. Indeed, stakeholder management can be viewed as the effective and constant mutual negotiation across multiple parties. Project managers negotiate for additional time and money, to prevent excessive interference and specification changes from clients, the loan or assignment to the team of important project team personnel with functional managers, and so forth. Negotiation represents the art of influence taken to its highest level. Because effective negotiation is an imperative for successful project management, it is vital that project managers understand the role negotiation plays in their projects, how to become better negotiators, and some of the important elements in negotiation.

Questions to Ask Prior to the Negotiation

Anyone entering a negotiation needs to consider three questions: How much power do I have? What sort of time pressures are there? Do I trust my opponent?[31]

A realistic self-assessment concerning power and any limiting constraints is absolutely vital prior to sitting down to negotiate. One important reason is that it can show the negotiators where they are strong and, most importantly, what their weaknesses are. A project manager once related this story:

> It was early in June and we were involved in the second week of pretty intense negotiations with a vendor for site considerations before starting a construction project. Unfortunately, the vendor discovered that we do our accounting books on a fiscal basis, ending June 30th, and he figured, correctly, that we were desperate to record the deal prior to the end of the month. He just sat on his hands for the next ten days. Now it's June 21st and my boss is having a heart attack about locking in the vendor. Finally, we practically crawled back to the table in late June and gave him everything he was asking for in order to record the contract.

This project manager lost out in the power *and* time departments!

How much power do you have going into the negotiation? You are not necessarily looking for a dominant position but a defensive one, that is, one from which the other party cannot dominate you. How much time do you have? The calendar can be difficult to overcome. So, too, can a domineering boss who is constantly telling you to "solve the problem with R&D, marketing, or whomever." Once word gets out that you have a time constraint, just watch your opponent slow down the pace, reasoning correctly that you will have to agree sooner rather than later, and on her terms, not yours.

Is it possible to trust the other party? Will the firm abide by its word, or does it have a reputation for changing agreements after the fact? Is it forthcoming with accurate information? Does it play negotiation hardball? Note that not all of these questions indicate someone who is untrustworthy. Indeed, it is appropriate to play hardball on occasion. On the other hand, the essential question is whether you can sit across a table from your opponent and believe that you both have a professional, vested interest in solving a mutual problem. If the answer is no, it is highly unlikely that you will negotiate with the same degree of enthusiasm or openness toward the other party.

Principled Negotiation

One of the most influential books on negotiation in recent years is *Getting to Yes,* by Roger Fisher and William Ury.[32] They offer excellent advice on **"principled" negotiation**, the art of getting agreement with the other party while maintaining a principled, win-win attitude. Among the suggestions they offer for developing an effective negotiating strategy are the following.

SEPARATE THE PEOPLE FROM THE PROBLEM   One of the most important ideas of negotiation is to remember that negotiators are people first. What this dictum means is that negotiators are no different from anyone else in terms of ego, attitudes, biases, education, experiences, and so forth. We all react negatively to direct attacks, we all become defensive at unwarranted charges and accusations, and we tend to personalize opposing viewpoints, assuming that their objections are aimed at us, rather than at the position we represent. Consequently, in observing the saliency of the notion that negotiators are people first, we must seek ways in which we can keep people (along with their personalities, defensiveness, egos, etc.) out of the problem itself. The more we can focus on the issues that separate us and pay less attention to the people behind the issues, the greater the likelihood of achieving a positive negotiated outcome.

Put yourself in their shoes. An excellent starting point in negotiations is to discuss not only our own position but also our understanding of the other party's position early in the negotiation process. When the other party hears a reasoned discussion of both positions, two important events occur: (1) it establishes a basis of trust because our opponent discovers that we are willing to openly discuss perceptions in the beginning, and (2) it reconstructs the negotiation as a win-win, rather than a winner-take-all, exercise.

Don't deduce their intentions from your fears. A common side effect of almost all negotiations, particularly early in the process, is to construct supporting stereotypes of the other side. For example, in meeting with the accountant to negotiate additional funding for our project, we may adopt a mind-set in which all accountants are penny-pinching bean counters who are only waiting for the opportunity to cancel the project. Notice that even before the negotiation takes place, we have created an image of the accounting department's members and their mind-set based on our own misperception and fears, rather than on any objective reality. When we assume that they will act in certain ways, we subconsciously begin negotiating with them as though money is their sole concern, and before we know it, we have created an opponent based on our worst fears.

Don't blame them for your problems. In negotiations, it is almost always counterproductive to initiate a finger-pointing episode as we seek to attach blame for difficulties our project has encountered. It is far more effective to move beyond the desire to assign blame and search for win-win solutions. For example, suppose that a company has just developed a software program for internal reporting and control that continually crashes in mid-operation. One approach would be for the exasperated accounting manager to call in the head of the software development project and verbally abuse him: "Your program really stinks. Every time you claim to have fixed it, it dumps on us again. If you don't get the bugs out of it within two weeks we're going to go back to the old system and make sure that everyone knows the reason why."

Although it may be satisfying for the accounting manager to react in this manner, it is unlikely to solve the problem, particularly in terms of relations with the software development project team. A far better approach would be less confrontational, seeking to frame the problem as a mutual issue that needs correction.

For example, "The reporting program crashed again in midstride. Every time it goes down, my people have to reenter data and use up time that could be spent in other ways. I need your advice on how to fix the problem with the software. Is it just not ready for beta testing, are we using it incorrectly, or what?" Note that in this case, the head of the accounting department is careful not to point fingers. He refrains from taking the easy way out through simply setting blame and demanding correction, and instead treats the problem *as a problem* that will require cooperation if it is to be resolved.

Recognize and understand emotion: theirs and yours. Although it is often easy to get emotional during the course of a negotiation, the impulse must be resisted as much as possible.[33] It is common in a difficult, protracted negotiation to see emotions begin to come to the surface, often due to anger or frustration with the tactics or attitudes of the other party. Nevertheless, it is usually not a good idea to respond in an emotional way, even when the other party becomes emotional. They may be using emotion as a tactic to get your team to respond in an equally emotional way and allow your heart to begin guiding your head— always a dangerous course. Although emotions are a natural side effect of lengthy negotiations, we need to understand precisely what is making us unhappy, stressed, tense, or angry. Further, are we astute enough to take note of the emotions emanating from our opponent? We need to be aware of what we are doing that is making the other person upset or irritable.

Listen actively. Active listening means our direct involvement in the conversation with our opponent, even when the other party is actually speaking. Most of us know from experience when people are really listening to us and when they are simply going through the motions. In the latter case, our frustration at their seeming indifference to our position can be a tremendous source of negative emotion. For example, suppose a client is negotiating with the project manager for a performance enhancement on a soon-to-be-released piece of manufacturing equipment. The project manager is equally desirous to leave the project alone because any reconfigurations at this time will simply delay the release of the final product and cost a great deal of extra money. Every time the client voices her issues, the project manager speaks up and says, "I hear what you're saying, but…." In this case, the project manager clearly is not hearing a word the client is saying but is simply paying lip service to the client's concerns.

Active listening means working hard to understand not simply the words but the underlying motivations of the other party. One effective technique involves interrupting occasionally to ask a pointed question: "As I understand it, then, you are saying…." Tactics such as this convince your opponent that you are trying to hear what is being said rather than simply adhering to your company's party line no matter what arguments or issues the other side raises. Remember that demonstrating that you clearly understand the other party's position is not the same thing as agreeing with it. There may be many points with which you take issue. Nevertheless, a constructive negotiation can only proceed from the point of complete and objective information, not from preconceived notions or entrenched and intransigent positions.

Build a working relationship. The idea of negotiating as though you are dealing with a party with whom you would like to maintain a long-term relationship is key to effective negotiations. We think of long-term relationships as those with individuals or organizations that we value and, hence, are inclined to work hard to maintain. The stronger the working relationship, the greater the level of trust that is likely to permeate its character.

FOCUS ON INTERESTS, NOT POSITIONS   There is an important difference between the positions each party adopts and the interests that underscore and mold those positions. When we refer to "interests," we mean the fundamental motivations that frame each party's positions. As Fisher and Ury note, "Interests define the problem."[34] It is not the positions taken by each party that shape the negotiation nearly as much as it is the interests that are the source of the parties' fears, needs, and desires.

Why look for underlying interests as opposed to simply focusing on the positions that are placed on the table? Certainly, it is far easier to negotiate with another party from the point of our position versus theirs. However, there are some compelling reasons why focusing on interests rather than positions can offer us an important "leg up" in successful negotiations. First, unlike positions, for every interest there are usually several alternatives that can satisfy it. For example, if my major interest is to ensure that my company will be in business over the years to come, I can look for solutions other than simply squeezing every drop of profit from the contractor in this negotiation. For example, I could enter into a long-term relationship with the contractor in which I am willing to forgo some profit on this job while locking the contractor into a sole-source agreement for the next three years. The contractor would then receive the additional profit from the job by paying me less than I desire (my position) while supplying me with long-term work (my interest).

Another reason for focusing on interests argues that negotiating from positions often leads to roadblocks as each party tries to discover their opponent's position while concealing their own. We consume valuable time and resources in making visible our various positions while hiding as long as possible our true intentions. In focusing on interests, on the other hand, we adopt a partnering mentality that acknowledges the legitimacy of both sides' interests and seeks to find solutions that will be mutually satisfying.

Invent Options for Mutual Gain

Managers sometimes put up roadblocks for themselves, making it difficult to consider win-win options when negotiating.

Managers can have premature judgment. We quickly arrive at conclusions about the other side and anything they say usually serves to solidify our impressions. Further, rather than seek to broaden our various options early in the negotiation, we typically go the other direction and put limits on how much we are willing to give up, how far we are willing to go, and so forth. Every premature judgment we make limits our freedom of action and puts us deeper into an adversarial, winners-losers exchange.

Some managers search only for the best answer. A common error made is to assume that buried underneath all the negotiating ploys and positions is one "best" answer that will eventually emerge. In reality, most negotiations, particularly if they are to result in win-win outcomes, require us to broaden our search, not limit and focus it. For example, we may erroneously define the "best" answer to typically mean the best for our side, not the other party. It is important to acknowledge that all problems lend themselves to multiple solutions. Indeed, it is through consideration of those multiple solutions that we are most likely to attain one that is mutually satisfying.

Managers assume that there's only a "fixed pie." Is there really only a fixed set of alternatives available? Maybe not. It is common to lock into a "I win, you lose" scenario that virtually guarantees hardball negotiating with little or no effort made to seek creative solutions that are mutually satisfying.

Thinking that "solving their problem is their problem" is another roadblock. Negotiation breeds egocentrism. The greater our belief that negotiation consists of simply taking care of ourselves, the greater the likelihood that we will be unwilling to engage in any win-win solutions. Our position quickly becomes one of pure self-interest.

If these are some common problems that prevent win-win outcomes, what can be done to improve the negotiation process? There are some important guidelines that we can use to strengthen the relationship between the two parties and improve the likelihood of positive outcomes. Briefly, some options to consider when searching for win-win alternatives include positive and inclusive brainstorming, broadening options, and identification of shared interests.

The use of *positive and inclusive brainstorming* implies that once a negotiation process begins, *during its earliest phase* we seek to include the other party in a problem-solving session to identify alternative outcomes. This approach is a far cry from the typical tactic of huddling to plot negotiation strategies to use against the other team. In involving the other party in a brainstorming session, we seek to convince them that we perceive the problem as a mutually solvable one that requires input and creativity from both parties. Inviting the other party to a brainstorming session of this type has a powerfully disarming effect on their initial defensiveness. It demonstrates that we are interested not in beating the other side, but in solving the problem. Further, it reinforces my earlier point about the necessity of separating the people from the problem. In this way, both parties work in cooperation to find a mutually satisfactory solution that also serves to strengthen their relationship bonds.

The concept of *broadening options* is also a direct offshoot of the notion of brainstorming. Broadening our options requires us to be open to alternative positions and can be a natural result of focusing on interests rather than positions. The more I know about the other party's interests and am willing to dissect my own, the greater the probability that together we can work to create a range of options far broader than those we may initially be tempted to lock ourselves into.

Finally, a third technique for improving chances for win-win outcomes is to *identify shared interests*. A common negotiating approach employed by experienced bargainers is to sometimes table the larger items to a later point in the negotiation, focusing instead on minor or peripheral issues that offer a greater likelihood of reaching agreement. Once the two parties begin to work together to identify their shared interests and gain some confidence from working in a collaborative way, it is possible to reintroduce the larger sticking points. By this time both sides have begun to develop a working rhythm and a level of harmony that makes it easier to look for shared interests within these larger issues.

Insist on Using Objective Criteria

One of the best methods for ensuring that a negotiation proceeds along substantive lines is to frame the discussion around objective criteria.[35] Do not get bogged down in arguing perceptions or subjective evaluations. For example, a project manager recently almost had his new product development (NPD) project canceled because of protracted negotiations with a client over delivering an "acceptable" working prototype. Obviously, the project manager had a far different interpretation of the word *acceptable* than did the client. The project manager assumed that *acceptable* included normal bugs and preliminary technical problems while the client had used the word to imply error-free. In their desire to pin the onus of responsibility on the other, neither was willing to back away from her interpretation of the nebulous "acceptable."

Objective data and other measurable criteria often form the best basis for accurate negotiations. When firms or individuals argue costs, prices, work hours, and so on, they are using established standards and concepts that both parties can understand with a minimum of interpretation error. On the other hand, the more vague the terms employed or the more subjective the language, the greater the potential to be arguing at cross-purposes, even if both parties assume that the other is using the same interpretations of these terms.

Develop fair standards and procedures. Whatever standards are used as the basis of the negotiation need to be clearly spelled out and put in terms that are equally meaningful to both parties. This point is particularly relevant in cross-cultural negotiations in that different countries and cultures often attach different meaning to terms or concepts. For example, several American heavy construction firms, including Bechtel Corporation, lodged a protest against a number of Japanese construction firms for their collusion in dividing up biddable contracts (bid rigging) prior to a major airport project in Tokyo Bay. The Japanese companies argued in turn that they were fulfilling the terms of recent free-competition agreements by simply allowing Bechtel to submit a bid. Further, in Japanese society, there is nothing inherently illegal or unethical about engaging in this form of bid rigging. Clearly, both parties had very different interpretations of the idea of fair and clear bidding practices.

Fair standards and procedures require that both parties come together and negotiate from the same basic understanding of the terms and liabilities. In project management, this concept is particularly relevant because construction contracting requires a universally understood set of terms and standards. When the two parties are engaged in negotiating from the point of appropriate standards, it effectively eliminates the source of many potential misunderstandings or misinterpretations.

In visualizing the need to become adept at team building, conflict management, and negotiation, it is important to remember that the greatest challenges project managers typically face in running their projects are the myriad "people" challenges that result from the process of forming a diverse set of project members into a unified and collaborative team, whose goal is to pursue project success. Creating a team and initiating the project development process sows the seeds for a wide variety of conflicts among all project stakeholders. These conflicts are inevitable. They should be treated not as a liability, however, but as an opportunity. Conflict can lead to positive outcomes by solidifying team member commitment and motivation, and generating the energy to complete project activities.

Nevertheless, channeling conflict in appropriate ways requires a sure touch on the part of the project manager. Our ability to sustain influence and use negotiation in skillful ways is a great advantage in ensuring that team development and conflict serve not to derail the project but to renew it. Conflict is inevitable; it is not disastrous. Indeed, the degree to which a conflict disrupts a project's development depends upon the project manager's willingness to learn enough about conflict to deal with it effectively.

Summary

1. **Understand the steps involved in project team building.** The first step in project team building is the selection of personnel to staff the project team. This process can be complicated, particularly due to the high potential for conflict and negotiation with functional managers who may retain effective control over project team members. Following an analysis of skill requirements and staff availability, the team-building process typically involves matching the best people to the identified project tasks, while at the same time understanding the need to make these staffing decisions in collaboration with other top managers or departmental heads.

2. **Know the characteristics of effective project teams and why teams fail.** High-performing teams are typically characterized by (1) a clear sense of mission, (2) an understanding of interdependencies, (3) cohesiveness, (4) trust, (5) enthusiasm, and (6) a results orientation. On the other

hand, teams that fail often do so due to poorly developed goals, poorly defined team roles, lack of motivation, poor communication, poor leadership, high project team turnover, and dysfunctional behavior.

3. **Know the stages in the development of groups.** Project teams do not begin their assignments as a unified, cohesive, and motivated body. Rather, their development is a challenge that must be effectively managed if we are to get maximum performance from the team. Teams go through some identifiable stages in their development process, and project managers need to recognize and seek to manage these developmental stages as efficiently as they can. One model of team development posits a five-stage approach—forming, storming, norming, performing, and adjourning—each with its unique challenges and group behaviors. An alternative model that has been validated through research argues that groups adopt a process of "punctuated equilibrium" as they evolve.

4. **Describe how to achieve cross-functional cooperation in teams.** Superordinate goals, rules and procedures, physical proximity, and accessibility are all important factors in motivating people to collaborate. The effects of this cross-functional cooperation are twofold: They can positively impact both project task outcomes and psychosocial project team results. Task outcomes positively affect the project at hand, while psychosocial outcomes mean that team members retain high positive attitudes toward the project experience and will enter new projects with strong motivation to succeed again.

5. **See the advantages and challenges of virtual project teams.** Virtual project teams are defined as the use of electronic media, including e-mail, the Internet, and teleconferencing, to link together members of a geographically dispersed project team, largely because of the globalization of project management. As multinational firms attempt to manage projects from geographically dispersed units, they need sophisticated technical media that support their communications and networking. The sheer physical barriers caused by globalization, coupled with the increase in multi-organizational project teams, have led to the increased use of virtual technologies to link team members. Two of the biggest challenges in effectively creating and managing virtual teams are establishing and reinforcing trust among team members and establishing effective communication patterns.

6. **Understand the nature of conflict and evaluate response methods.** Conflict is an inevitable result when team members with diverse functional backgrounds, personalities, experiences, and attitudes are brought together and expected to work collaboratively. Among the organizational causes of conflict are scarce resources, uncertainty over lines of authority, and differentiation. Interpersonal causes of conflict include faulty attributions, faulty communication, and personal grudges and prejudice. Conflict can be addressed through mediation, arbitration, control, acceptance, or elimination.

7. **Understand the importance of negotiation skills in project management.** Project managers routinely negotiate with a wide variety of organizational stakeholders for resources, contractual considerations, terms and conditions, and so forth. Effective project managers are often those individuals who approach negotiations in a systematic manner, taking the time to carefully analyze the nature of the negotiation, what they hope to achieve, and how much they are willing to offer to achieve their important goal. In principled negotiation, the primary objective is to seek win-win alternatives that allow both parties to negotiate to gain their goals.

Key Terms

Accessibility (p. 212)

Adjourning (p. 209)

Administrative conflict (p. 215)

Cohesiveness (p. 204)

Conflict (p. 215)

Cross-functional cooperation (p. 210)

Differentiation (p. 203)

Forming stage (p. 207)

Frustration (p. 217)

Goal-oriented conflict (p. 215)

Interaction (p. 204)

Interdependencies (p. 204)

Interpersonal conflict (p. 215)

Negotiation (p. 219)

Norming stage (p. 208)

Orientation (p. 205)

Outcomes (p. 205)

Performing stage (p. 209)

Physical proximity (p. 211)

Principled negotiation (p. 220)

Psychosocial outcomes (p. 212)

Punctuated equilibrium (p. 209)

Storming stage (p. 208)

Superordinate goal (p. 211)

Task outcomes (p. 212)

Team building (p. 200)

Trust (p. 204)

Virtual teams (p. 213)

Discussion Questions

1. This chapter discussed the characteristics of high-performing project teams. List the factors that characterize these teams and give examples of each one.
2. "Trust can actually encourage disagreement and conflict among team members." Explain why this could be the case.
3. Identify the stages of group development. Why is it necessary for project teams to move through these stages in order to be productive?
4. Gersick's model of punctuated equilibrium offers an alternative view of group development. Why does she suggest that some defining moment (such as an explosion of emotion) often occurs about midpoint in the project? What does this defining event accomplish for the team?
5. Explain the concepts of "task" and "psychosocial" outcomes for a project. Why are psychosocial outcomes so important for project team members?
6. Distinguish between the traditional, behavioral, and interactionist views of team conflict. How might each explain and treat a project team conflict episode?
7. Identify the five major methods for resolving conflict. Give an example of how each might be applied in a hypothetical project team conflict episode.
8. What are some of the guidelines for adopting a strategy of "principled negotiation"?
9. Explain the idea that we should "focus on interests, not positions." Can you think of an example in which you successfully negotiated with someone else using this principle?

Case Study 6.1

Columbus Instruments

Problems have been building at Columbus Instruments, Inc. (CIC) (not its real name) for several years now with the new product development process. The last six high-visibility projects were either scrapped outright after excessive cost and schedule overruns or, once released to the marketplace, were commercial disasters. The company estimates that in the past two years, it has squandered more than $15 million on poorly developed or failed projects. Every time a new project venture failed, the company conducted extensive postproject review meetings, documentation analysis, and market research to try to determine the underlying cause. To date, all CIC has been able to determine is that the problems appear to lie with the project management and development process. Something somewhere is going very wrong.

You have been called into the organization as a consultant to try to understand the source of the problems that are leading to widespread demoralization across the firm. After spending hours interviewing the senior project management staff and technical personnel, you are convinced that the problem does not lie with their processes, which are up-to-date and logical. On the other hand, you have some questions about project team productivity. It seems that every project has run late, has been over budget, and has had suboptimal functionality, regardless of the skills of the project manager in charge. This information suggests to you that there may be some problems in how the project teams are operating.

As you analyze CIC's project development process, you note several items of interest. First, the company is organized along strictly functional lines. Projects are staffed from the departments following negotiations between the project manager and the department heads. Second, the culture of CIC seems to place little status or authority on the project managers. As evidence of this fact, you note that they are not even permitted to write a performance evaluation on project team members: That right applies only to the functional department heads. Third, many projects require that team members be assigned to them on an exclusive basis; that is, once personnel have been assigned to a project, they typically remain with the project team on a full-time basis for the term of the project. The average project lasts about 14 months.

One morning, as you are walking the hallways, you notice a project team "war room" set up for the latest new product development initiative within the company. The war room concept requires that project team members be grouped together at a central location, away from their functional departments, for the life of the project. What intrigues you is a hand-lettered sign you see taped to the door of the project war room: "Leper Colony." When you ask around about the sign, some members of the firm say with a chuckle, "Oh, we like to play jokes on the folks assigned to new projects."

Further investigation of project team members suggests they are not amused by the sign. One engineer shrugs and says, "That's just their way of making sure we understand what we have been assigned to. Last week they put up another one that said 'Purgatory.'" When you ask the project manager about the signs later in the day, he

(*continued*)

confirms this story and adds some interesting information: "Around here, we use detached [meaning centralized] project teams. I get no say as to who will be assigned to the project, and lately the functional heads have been using our projects as a dumping ground for their poor performers."

When you question him further, the project manager observes, "Think about it. I have no say in who gets assigned to the team. I can't even fill out a performance review on them. Now, if you were a department head who was trying to offload a troublemaker or someone who was incompetent, what could be better than shipping them off to a project team for a year or so? Of course, you can imagine how they feel when they hear that they have been assigned to one of our project teams. It's as if you just signed their death warrant. Talk about low motivation!"

When you question various department heads about the project manager's assertions, to a person they deny that this is an adopted policy. As the head of finance puts it, "We give the project teams our best available

people when they ask." However, they also admit that they have the final say in personnel assignment and project managers cannot appeal their choices for the teams.

After these discussions, you suggest to the CEO that the method of staffing projects may be a reason for the poor performance of CIC's new product development projects. He ponders the implications of how the projects have been staffed in his organization, and then says, "Okay, what do you suggest we do about it?"

Questions

1. What are the implications of CIC's approach to staffing project teams? Is the company using project teams as training grounds for talented fast-trackers or as dumping grounds for poor performers?
2. How would you advise the CEO to correct the problem? Where would you start?
3. Discuss how issues of organizational structure and power played a role in the manner in which project management declined in effectiveness at CIC.

Case Study 6.2

The Bean Counter and the Cowboy

The morning project team meeting promised to be an interesting one. Tensions between the representative from marketing, Susan Scott, and finance, Neil Schein, have been building for several weeks now—in fact, since the project team was formed. As the project manager, you have been aware that Susan and Neil do not see eye to eye, but you figured that over time they would begin to appreciate each other's perspective and start cooperating. So far, unfortunately, that has not happened. In fact, it seems that hardly a day goes by when you do not receive a complaint from one or the other regarding the other team member's behavior, lack of commitment or cooperation, or general shoddy performance.

As the team gathers for the regular project status meeting, you start with an update on the project tasks, any problems the team members are having, and their assessment of the project's performance to date. Before you get too far into the meeting, Susan interrupts, saying, "John, I'm going to be out of town for the next 10 days visiting clients, so I can't make the status meetings either of the next two Fridays."

"That figures," Neil mutters loud enough for all to hear.

Susan whirls around. "I have another job around here, you know, and it involves selling. It may be

convenient for you to drop everything and come to these meetings, but some of us have other responsibilities."

Neil shoots back, "That's been your excuse for missing half of the meetings so far. Just out of curiosity," he continues sarcastically, "how many more do you figure on blowing off while hanging out poolside on your little out-of-towners?"

Susan turns bright red. "I don't need to put up with that from you. You bean counters have no clue how this business works or who delivers value. You're so busy analyzing every penny that you have permanent eyestrain!"

"Maybe I could pay attention if I didn't have to constantly stay on the backs of you cowboys in sales," counters Neil. "I swear you would give our products away if it would let you make your quarterly numbers, even if it does drive us into the ground!"

You sit back, amazed, as the argument between Neil and Susan flares into full-scale hostility and threatens to spin out of control. The other team members are looking at you for your response. George, from engineering, has a funny expression on his face, as if to say, "Okay, you got us to this point. Now what are you going to do about it?"

"People," you rap on the table, "that's enough. We are done for today. I want to meet with Susan and Neil in my office in a half hour."

As everyone files out, you lean back in your seat and consider how you are going to handle this problem.

Questions

1. Was the argument today between Neil and Susan the true conflict or a symptom? What evidence do you have to suggest it is merely a symptom of a larger problem?

2. Explain how differentiation plays a large role in the problems that exist between Susan and Neil.

3. Develop a conflict management procedure for your meeting in 30 minutes. Create a simple script to help you anticipate the comments you are likely to hear from both parties.

4. Which conflict resolution style is warranted in this case? Why? How might some of the other resolution approaches be inadequate in this situation?

Case Study 6.3

Johnson & Rogers Software Engineering, Inc.

Kate Thomas, a project manager with Johnson & Rogers Software Engineering, was looking forward to her first project team "meeting." She applied quotes to the term "meeting" in this case, because she would not actually be sitting down at a table with any of the other members of the project team. She had been assigned responsibility for a large software development project that would be using team members from both inside and outside the organization, none of whom were currently employed at the same Redlands, California, office where she worked. In fact, as she ticked off the names on the legal pad in front of her, she did not know whether to be impressed or apprehensive with the project she was about to kick off.

> Vignish Ramanujam (senior programmer)—New Delhi, India
> Anders Blomquist (systems designer)—Uppsala, Sweden
> Sally Dowd (systems engineer)—Atlanta, Georgia
> Penny Jones (junior programmer)—Bristol, England
> Patrick Flynn (junior programmer)—San Antonio, Texas
> Erik Westerveldt (subcontractor)—Pretoria, South Africa
> Toshiro Akame (customer representative)—Kyoto, Japan

The challenge with this team, Kate quickly realized, was going to involve figuring out how to create an integrated project team with these people, most of whom she had never dealt with before. Although Sally and Patrick worked for Johnson & Rogers at other plant locations, the rest of the "team" were strangers. Erik, from South Africa, was critical for the project because his company had developed some of the specialized processes the project required and was to be treated as an industrial partner. The other members of the team had been assembled either by Erik or through contacts with senior members of her own firm. She did not know, but would soon discover, how they felt about the project and their level of commitment to it.

The first virtual project meeting was scheduled to start promptly at 9 AM Pacific Standard Time. That led to the first problem. As Kate stared at the camera mounted above the video monitor, she kept glancing down at the screen for signs that other members of the team had logged on. Finally, at 9:15, she was joined by Sally, with Toshiro logging in shortly afterward. As they chatted and continued to wait for other members to log on, time continued to pass. When, at 9:30, no one else had signed on, Kate asked the secretary to start making phone calls to verify that other members of the team were trying to access the system. Eventually, by 10:25, the team consisted of five members: Anders, Sally, Penny, Patrick, and Toshiro. It was decided that for the sake of getting something accomplished, those who were logged on would get started. The agenda that Kate had prepared and e-mailed out the day before was produced and the meeting began. Within ten minutes, the video link to Penny was suddenly lost. The other team members waited for five minutes, shuffling in various states of impatience for Penny to rejoin the meeting. There was still no sign of Vignish or Erik.

The meeting quickly bogged down on technical details as those in attendance realized that several technical issues could not be resolved without input from the missing team members. Though he tried his best to hide it, it became apparent that Toshiro, in particular, was frustrated with the lack of progress in this meeting. Kate suggested that they adjourn until 11, while she made another attempt to contact the missing members, but Toshiro objected, saying, "That is 3 AM in my country. It is now past midnight here. I have been here today for 15 hours and I would like to get home." It was finally agreed to

(continued)

reconvene tomorrow at the same time. Toshiro agreed, but with bad grace: "Can we not find a time that is more accommodating to my schedule?" Kate promised to look into the matter.

The next day's meeting was a mixed success. Although everyone managed to log on to the system within a reasonable period, Penny's connection kept going down, to the exasperation of Vignish, the senior programmer. Although the meeting was conducted with great politeness by all parties, it was equally clear that no one was willing to offer their candid opinions of the project, the goals, and how the team was expected to execute their assignments. After asking members of the team for honest feedback and getting little response, Kate eventually dropped the point. In addition, she had a nagging feeling that there was some unspoken animosity in the manner in which Patrick and Sally interacted with each other.

After some general goal setting and a discussion of team responsibilities, Kate asked if there was a time when they could next meet. In the general silence that followed, Anders spoke up, asking, "Well, how often do you hope to meet like this? To be honest, it is inconvenient for me to attend these sessions regularly, as our telecom equipment is in Stockholm and I have to drive an hour each way."

Toshiro then spoke up as well. "I am sorry to repeat this point," he said, "but these meeting times are extremely inconvenient for me. Could we not find a time that is more generally acceptable?"

Kate replied, "Well, how about 5 PM my time. That's...," Kate paused and quickly consulted her personal planner, "9 in the morning for you."

This suggestion was met by a wave of objections, with the first from Penny who stated, "Uh, Kate, that would be 1 AM here in England."

No sooner had she spoken than Anders, Erik, and Vignish chimed in, "Kate, that's 2 AM in Stockholm and Pretoria," and "Kate, are you aware that that is 6 AM here in New Delhi?"

Back and forth the team members argued, trying to find a reasonable time they could all meet. Finally, after going around the group several times to work out a mutually agreeable time for these teleconferences, Erik spoke up: "Maybe we don't all need to meet at the same time, anyway. Kate, why don't you just schedule meetings with each of us as you need to talk?"

Kate objected by saying, "Erik, the whole point of these teleconferences is to get the team together, not to hold one-on-one meetings with each of you."

Erik responded, "Well, all I know is that this is only the first videoconference and already it is becoming a burden."

Penny spoke up, "You're lucky. At least your system works. Mine keeps going up and down at this end."

"Okay, how about just using e-mails?" suggested Erik. "That way it does not matter what the time is at our location."

The other team members agreed that this idea made sense and seemed on the verge of endorsing the use of e-mails for communications. At this point, Kate stepped back into the discussion and stated firmly, "Look, that won't do. We need the opportunity to talk together. E-mails won't do that."

More arguing ensued. Eventually, the team members signed off, agreeing that they needed to "talk further" about these issues. Kate's reaction was one of disappointment and frustration. She sensed reluctance among the other members of the team to talk about these issues and to use the videoconferencing system in the manner she had envisioned. As Kate sat down to lunch that noon, she pondered how she should proceed from here.

Questions

1. How would you advise Kate to proceed? Analyze the conversation she had this morning. What went right? What went wrong?
2. What should Kate's next steps be?
3. How can she use the technology of the Internet and teleconferencing to enhance team development and performance?

Exercise in Negotiation

The following is a negotiation scenario between two firms: Steel-Fabrik, Inc. (SFI) and Building Contractors of Toledo (BCT). You are asked to take either SFI's or BCT's side of the negotiation. How would you prepare for this negotiation? How would you attempt to create a win-win outcome for both parties?

SteelFabrik's Perspective

You are the project manager for a new steel fabrication plant construction project being built by Building Contractors of Toledo (BCT). Your client is SteelFabrik, Inc. (SFI), a multinational steel products manufacturer. Your timetable calls for completion of the project in 18 months and you have a budget of $6 million. During the last few weeks, it has been increasingly difficult to deal with on-site demands from your client. SFI has insisted on a list of change orders to suit their immediate needs for the plant layout and design. Your counterpart says that because SFI is paying millions for the plant, they are entitled to make appropriate changes to the project for as long as is necessary to "get it right." You are concerned that every day spent in processing change orders adds further delay to your targeted completion date because engineering must approve the changes, design must alter the plans, and fabrication must change the plant's structure.

BCT is already in trouble on this project. In order to win the work, they significantly underbid their local competitors, leaving very little profit margin in the best-case scenario. Unfortunately, now with the list of change requests, both the budget and the schedule are being stretched to the limit. You are under increasing pressure from upper management to complete the job with the expected profit margin. You have $50,000 to work with and still meet your profitability goals. You are personally under pressure within your organization because your track record for the past three years has not been good—several projects that came in over budget and behind schedule have given top management reason to watch your performance on this project very closely. Although no one has said it out loud, you are fully aware that another significant overrun or delay could likely cost you your job with BCT.

Because you view SFI as a potential long-term customer, you are reluctant to simply refuse their demands. You know that a win-win outcome will likely bring future SFI business to your firm and could be the source of a profitable backlog of business for at least the next five years. Your own sales department is aware that this project with SFI could lead to future business and has added to your pressure by constantly stressing the importance of keeping the customer happy. As a result, you have important elements within your own organization, as well as with the customer, all expecting you to successfully complete the project to everyone's satisfaction.

While reading your e-mails over the weekend, you have come upon the latest set of change orders from SFI for adjustments to the plant layout to accommodate enhanced rail traffic into and out of the plant. These changes will require that the current construction work be halted, your own engineers and government regulators meet to discuss these requests, and new assembly and shipping areas be designed. Based on your experience, you estimate that the changes as requested will add $150,000 to the cost of the project and push the completion date back a minimum of six weeks. Worse, as you examine the change requests, you are convinced that these alterations are unnecessarily complicated and add no value to the plant's design. The final line of the e-mail is the most troubling: SFI expects these changes to be made immediately and will not allow any schedule slippage to accommodate them; in fact, they mention that it is imperative that the steel plant become operational on schedule. The only good news is that your sales department has found out that SFI may be willing to spend some additional money for the changes, but they aren't sure how much.

You have just typed out a short note scheduling a meeting for this Wednesday to negotiate an agreement on the requested changes. You are under strong pressure to reach a settlement that preserves BCT's profit margin, but at the same time you must keep SFI happy. As you sit at your home computer this Sunday afternoon, you are already dreading a return to work tomorrow morning. What approach should you take for the upcoming negotiations?

SFI's Perspective

You are a manager with SteelFabrik, Inc. (SFI) and are responsible for overseeing the construction of their fabrication plant in the northwest Ohio region. Recently your management informed you that because of new opportunities, this plant could be extremely valuable to their company, provided the rail spur connecting it with the freight rail system could be modified and upgraded to handle high-volume traffic into and out of the facility. This facility represents a significant investment by your company in the Midwest United States, following several years of contacts with local government officials trying to bring new jobs to the region. As a result, you feel you are entitled to make any necessary adjustments to the project to get the most use out of it. These change requests are, in your opinion, reasonable, necessary, and not prohibitively expensive. However, for the past several weeks, you have been experiencing increasing "push-back" from the BCT project manager to a series of relatively minor change requests. Her approach has been to ridicule the need for the changes, try to use low-cost "quick fixes," or simply talk you out of them. As a result, you are convinced that these latest change requests will also be resisted, and your overall relationship with the BCT project manager has become increasingly strained.

You have casually informed the BCT sales representative that this is the first in what your firm anticipates will be a series of similar plants to be constructed in the Great Lakes region over the next ten years. Although you made no commitments to doing future business with BCT, you have made it clear that successful performance on this project will make them the preferred choice for future work. After all, they understand your needs and have a demonstrated history of project success behind them.

You have been getting pressure from your top management, headquartered in Brussels, to complete the project on time; in fact, finishing on schedule is your greatest concern. SFI has already been bidding construction projects in the Great Lakes region and has several contracts pending, many of substantial size. Further, local politicians are anxious to show the project as an example of a successful public/private partnership and, with local elections coming up, are asking when they can announce its completion. Failure to have the plant ready on time puts you at risk of having to void a series of important construction contracts and slow down hiring, plus it would embarrass you and the region's government. Because the company's construction contract bids are still being reviewed, you are anxious to keep this information confidential to avoid attracting the attention of your competitors.

There is $250,000 in your budget to spend on additional change order costs if necessary, though you are keen to make the best possible impression with your top management by keeping costs as low as possible. You absolutely cannot agree to schedule extensions, however, because of all the pending bids and other pressures to finish the plant on time. Sources in the industry have strongly implied that BCT is in some financial difficulty and needs as much future work as they can get.

Your plant engineers have revised the transportation capacity requirements for the new plant and recommended significant changes to the shipping area to accommodate extra rail traffic. These changes are deemed critical because of the business model projections your firm has developed for getting maximum use and profit from the new fabrication plant. You have sent an e-mail with a detailed set of needed design and construction changes to the BCT project manager late Saturday night and just got back a note requesting a formal meeting on Wednesday morning to discuss these changes and find a way to "resolve our differences." You know that means that she is already trying to decide how to respond to your requests, and you are now planning for the negotiation. As you sit and reflect on the pressures you are feeling from Brussels, you wonder what approach you should use.

Internet Exercises

1. Click on the Web page for project teams at www.projectsmart. co.uk/five-steps-to-a-winning-project-team.html/. Which of these five steps seem to be easier for a project manager to perform and which seem to be more difficult? Why? How do the ideas in this chapter compare to the advice given in a related link on "five essentials to project team success" at www.projectsmart.co.uk/5-essentials-to-project-team-success. html? What does this suggest about the importance of setting the stage for project success through team development?

2. Go to the Web site of a professional sports team and explore the site. What clues do you get regarding the importance of "teams" and "teamwork" from this site? Give two or three specific examples.

3. Go to the Web site for a pharmaceutical company. Explore the site, particularly information on new research. What kinds of project teams are used within pharmaceutical companies? Can you identify at least five functional areas within these organizations that should work together in a project team in order to develop a new drug?

4. Go to www.ebxml.org/project_teams/project_teams.htm and explore the projects and project teams listed. Notice the size and diversity of some of these project teams. What challenges would you find in attempting to bring these individuals together into a project team? How does the fact that some of the teams are made up of personnel from different organizations affect our best attempts to mold a project team?

5. Go to http://multimedia.journalism.berkeley.edu/workshops/ projects/49/show/ and explore the nature of the project working to develop tele-immersion technology. Connect to the link marked "The Mission" and observe how the technology has changed to date. What are the projected advances in tele-immersion technology by 2015?

PMP Certification Sample Questions

1. The project manager is experiencing serious, deep-rooted conflict between two key project team members. It is apparent that these differences are based on different interpretations of the project's scope. Which conflict resolution approach would be the most useful for the project manager to employ?
   a. Compromising
   b. Withdrawal
   c. Punishment
   d. Problem solving

2. Which of the following is not an example of a team development strategy?
   a. Creating a WBS for the project
   b. Performance reviews
   c. Project team outing to a sporting event
   d. Team lunches

3. Two programmers are involved in a conflict that is threatening to disrupt the development of the project. The project manager calls the two programmers into her office and reminds them that they are both "on the same side" in working to develop the software application for the company. Her conflict resolution style would best be seen as:
   a. Arbitration
   b. Defusion
   c. Controlling the conflict
   d. Eliminating the conflict

4. Carrie is from the marketing department and she has become increasingly upset with the attitude of the production member of the project team, Andrew. He seems to either ignore her opinions or make disparaging comments every time she speaks, usually referring to marketing in an unpleasant way. Which stage of group development is the project team addressing, as evidenced by the interactions of Carrie and Andrew?
   a. Norming
   b. Performing
   c. Storming
   d. Adjourning

5. Among the useful means to develop a sense of teamwork in personnel from different functional departments are all of the following EXCEPT:
   a. Colocation (physical proximity)
   b. Common goals
   c. Organizational rules governing their interaction
   d. Flexible working hours

Answers: 1. d—Problem solving would be the best alternative when the issues are not so much personal as they are perceptual (based on interpretation of the project's scope). Compromising would be a problem because it could lead to watering down the deliverables; 2. a—The other activities can all result in team development; 3. b—Because the project manager emphasizes commonalties and working together, this would be considered a method of conflict resolution through defusion; 4. c—They are clearly exhibiting behaviors that are associated with storming; 5. d—Flexible working hours have no impact on the willingness of personnel to work cooperatively with members of other departments.

Notes

1. "Methods that have been tried to stop the leaking oil well." (2010, August 17). www.nytimes.com/interactive/ 2010/05/25/us/20100525-topkill-diagram.html?ref=us; Robertson, C., and Krauss, C. (2010, August 2). "Gulf spill is the largest of its kind, scientists say," *New York Times,* www.nytimes.com/2010/08/03/us/03spill.html?_r=1&fta=y;

Brenner, N., Guegel, A., Hwee, T., and Pitt, A. (2010, April 22). "Coast Guard confirms Horizon sinks." www. upstreamonline.com/live/article212769.ece; Eley, T. (2010). "What caused the explosion on the Deepwater Horizon?" www.wsws.org/articles/2010/may2010/spil-m14.shtml; Langford, M. (2010, July 22). "Rig workers raised safety fears before blast." http://news.sky.com/skynews/Home/Business/Gulf-Of-Mexico-Oil-Disaster-Transocean-Reports-Highlight-Workers-Concerns-Over-Deepwater-Horizon/Article/201007415669165.

2. Verma, V. K. (1996). *Human Resource Skills for the Project Manager.* Upper Darby, PA: Project Management Institute; Verma, V. K. (1997). *Managing the Project Team.* Newtown Square, PA: Project Management Institute.

3. Hoegl, M., and Parboteeah, K. P. (2003). "Goal setting and team performance in innovative projects: On the moderating role of teamwork quality," *Small Group Research,* 34: 3–19; McComb, S. A., and Green, S. G. (1999). "Project goals, team performance, and shared understanding," *Engineering Management Journal,* 11(3).

4. Pinto, J. K., and Prescott, J. E. (1988). "Variations in critical success factors over the stages in the project life cycle," *Journal of Management,* 14(1): 5–18.

5. Hartman, F. T. (2000). *Don't Park Your Brain Outside: A Practical Guide to Improving Shareholder Value Through SMART Management.* Newtown Square, PA: Project Management Institute; Karlsen, J. T., Grae, K., and Massaoud, M. J. (2008). "The role of trust in project-stakeholder relationships: A study of a construction project," *International Journal of Project Organization and Management,* 1: 105–118; Lander, M. C., Purvis, R. L., McCray, G. E., and Leigh, W. (2004). "Trust-building mechanisms utilized in outsourced IS development projects: A case study," *Information and Management,* 41: 509–28; Kadefors, A. (2004). "Trust in project relationships—inside the black box," *International Journal of Project Management,* 22: 175–82; Smyth, H. J., and Thompson, N. J. (2005). "Managing conditions of trust within a framework of trust," *Journal of Construction Procurement,* 11(1): 4–18.

6. Hartman, F. T. (2002). "Update on trust: A collection of trust-based research findings," in Slevin, D. P., Pinto, J. K., and Cleland, D. I. (Eds.), *Proceedings of the PMI Research Conference 2002.* Newtown Square, PA: Project Management Institute, pp. 247–53.

7. Gido, J., and Clements, J. P. (2003). *Successful Project Management,* 2nd ed. Mason, OH: South-Western.

8. Tuchman, B. W., and Jensen, M. A. (1977). "Stages in small group development revisited." *Group and Organizational Studies,* 2: 419–27.

9. Tuchman and Jensen, ibid.

10. Verma, V. K. (1997). *Managing the Project Team,* p. 71, as cited.

11. Gersick, C. (1988). "Time and transition in work teams: Toward a new model of group development." *Academy of Management Journal,* 31: 9–41; Gersick, C. (1989). "Making time predictable transitions in task groups." *Academy of Management Journal,* 32: 274–309.

12. Pinto, M. B. (1988). *Cross-functional cooperation in the implementation of marketing decisions: The effects of superordinate goals, rules and procedures, and physical environment.* Unpublished doctoral dissertation, University of Pittsburgh, PA; Pinto, M. B., Pinto, J. K., and Prescott, J. E. (1993). "Antecedents and consequences of project team cross-functional cooperation," *Management Science,* 39: 1281–97.

13. Sherif, M. (1958). "Superordinate goals in the reduction of intergroup conflict," *American Journal of Sociology,* 63(4): 349–56.

14. Galbraith, J. R. (1977). *Organization Design.* Reading, MA: Addison-Wesley.

15. Davis, T. E. (1984). "The influence of the physical environment in offices," *Academy of Management Review,* 9(2): 271–83.

16. Frame, J. D. (2002). *The New Project Management,* 2nd ed. San Francisco, CA: Jossey-Bass.

17. Tjosvold, D. (1993). *Teamwork for Customers: Building Organizations That Take Pride in Serving.* San Francisco, CA: Jossey-Bass; Logue, A. C. (2002). "Building and keeping the dream team," *PMNetwork,* 16(3): 30–36.

18. Adams, J. R., and Adams, L. L. (1997). "The virtual projects: Management of tomorrow's team today," *PMNetwork,* 11(1): 37–41; Kostner, J. (1994). *Knights of the Tele-Round Table.* New York: Warner Books; Delisle, C. (2001). *Success and communication in virtual project teams.* Unpublished doctoral dissertation. Dept. of Civil Engineering, Project Management Specialization. University of Calgary, Calgary, Alberta; Fagerhaug, T. (2002). "Virtual project organizations—design of and challenges for," in Slevin, D. P., Pinto, J. K., and Cleland, D. I. (Eds.), *Proceedings of PMI Research Conference 2002.* Newtown Square, PA: Project Management Institute, pp. 217–23.

19. Coutu, D. L. (1998). "Organization: Trust in virtual teams," *Harvard Business Review,* 76(3): 20–21.

20. Lanier, J. (2001, April). "Virtually there: Three dimensional tele-immersion may eventually bring the world to your desk," *Scientific American,* 284(4): 66–75.

21. Ditlea, S. (2001, January). "Tele-immersion: Tomorrow's teleconferencing," *Computer Graphics World,* www.cgw.com; (2008). tele-immersion.citris-uc.org/video.

22. Posner, B. Z. (1986). "What's all the fighting about? Conflicts in project management," *IEEE Transactions on Engineering Management,* EM-33: 207–11; Thamhain, H. J., and Wilemon, D. L. (1975). "Conflict management in project life cycles," *Sloan Management Review,* 16(3): 31–50; Thamhain, H. J., and Wilemon, D. L. (1977). "Leadership, conflict, and program management effectiveness," *Sloan Management Review,* 19(1): 69–89; Chan, M. (1989). "Intergroup conflict and conflict management in the R&D divisions of four aerospace companies," *IEEE Transactions on Engineering Management,* EM-36: 95–104; Adams, J. R., and Barndt, S. E. (1988). "Behavioral implications of the project life cycle," in Cleland, D. I., and King, W. R. (Eds.), *Project Management Handbook,* 2nd ed. New York: Van Nostrand Reinhold, pp. 206–30.

23. Thomas, K. W., and Schmidt, W. H. (1976). "A survey of managerial interests with respect to conflict," *Academy of Management Journal,* 10: 315–18.

24. Thomas, K. W. (1992). "Conflict and negotiation processes in organizations," in Dunnette, M. D. (Ed.), *Handbook of Industrial and Organizational Psychology,* 2nd ed. Palo Alto, CA: Consulting Psychologists Press, pp. 889–935; Pondy, L. (1968). "Organizational conflict: Concepts and models," *Administrative Science Quarterly,* 12: 296–320.

25. Thamhain, H. J., and Wilemon, D. L. (1975), as cited in note 22.

26. Verma, V. K. (1998). "Conflict management," in Pinto, J. K. (Ed.), *The Project Management Institute's Project Management Handbook.* San Francisco, CA: Jossey-Bass.

27. Verma, V. K. (1996), as cited in note 2; Robbins, S. P. (1974). *Managing Organizational Conflict: A Nontraditional Approach.* Englewood Cliffs, NJ: Prentice-Hall.

28. Thamhain, H. J., and Wilemon, D. L. (1975), as cited in note 22; Posner, B. Z. (1986), as cited in note 22.

29. Verma, V. K. (1998), as cited in note 26.

30. Ware, J. (1983). "Some aspect of problem-solving and conflict resolution in management groups," in Schlesinger, L. A., Eccles, R. G., and Gabarro, J. L. (Eds.), *Managing Behavior in Organization: Text, Cases, Readings.* New York: McGraw-Hill, pp. 101–15.

31. Slevin, D. P. (1989). *The Whole Manager.* New York: AMACOM.

32. Fisher, R., and Ury, W. (1981). *Getting to Yes: Negotiating Agreement Without Giving In.* New York: Houghton Mifflin.

33. Fisher, R. and Ury, W. (1981), ibid.

34. Fisher, R. and Ury, W. (1981), ibid.

35. Fisher, R. and Ury, W. (1981), ibid.

Risk Management

Chapter Outline

Chapter Objectives

After completing this chapter, you should be able to:

1. Define project risk.

2. Recognize four key stages in project risk management and the steps necessary to manage risk.

3. Understand five primary causes of project risk and four major approaches to risk identification.

4. Recognize four primary risk mitigation strategies.

5. Explain the Project Risk Analysis and Management (PRAM) process.

PROJECT MANAGEMENT BODY OF KNOWLEDGE CORE CONCEPTS COVERED IN THIS CHAPTER

1. Plan Risk Management (PMBoK sec. 11.1)

2. Identify Risks (PMBoK sec. 11.2)

3. Perform Qualitative Risk Analysis (PMBoK sec. 11.3)

4. Perform Quantitative Risk Analysis (PMBoK sec. 11.4)

5. Plan Risk Responses (PMBoK sec. 11.5)

6. Monitor and Control Risks (PMBoK sec. 11.6)

PROJECT PROFILE

Case—Haitian Earthquake Relief

[O]ur goal at the moment isn't to escape poverty. It's to escape misery so we can get back to poverty.

—*Haitian Prime Minister*
Jean-Max Bellerive

Haiti, the poorest country in the Western Hemisphere, has seen its share of both misery and widespread poverty during its existence as an independent country. An unstable democracy, the country has suffered from a variety of endemic problems both before and since its overthrow of the Duvalier dictatorship in 1986. Adding to its woes, the country was struck by an earthquake with a magnitude of 7.0 on the Richter scale just before 5 PM on January 12, 2010. The earthquake caused immediate, widespread, and often catastrophic damage to buildings and critical infrastructure, centered primarily in the capital, Port-au-Prince, and outlying areas. Port-au-Prince is the most densely settled area in Haiti, with millions living in substandard housing with no building codes, and uncertain utilities and sanitary systems in the best of times. In short, an earthquake in the Western Hemisphere could not have found a more vulnerable target than the one it struck. Immediate relief efforts were hampered by two aftershocks that occurred almost immediately after the first quake, with a third aftershock at a magnitude of 6.1 occurring the following day.

The series of earthquakes is believed to have resulted in the deaths of more than 230,000 people and to have left more than 1.5 million people homeless. Estimates also suggest that more than 300,000 people were injured in the disaster, requiring immediate medical attention. The United Nations (UN) estimated that the earthquakes affected between 2.8 and 3.5 million people in the country. Regardless of the exact number of casualties from the disaster, it is plain that a country with Haiti's limited resources simply could not cope with the relief efforts needed. Just in the Port-au-Prince region, it is estimated that more than 3 million people lived in an area for which the infrastructure could support fewer than 400,000. Further, more than 250,000 private houses and 30,000 commercial buildings collapsed or were made uninhabitable. The first priority was rescue of those trapped in collapsed buildings. A full ten days were spent by portions of the Haitian army in searching for and rescuing

FIGURE 7.1   Damage in Port-au-Prince

hundreds trapped under the rubble of collapsed buildings. Meanwhile, within a short four days of the disaster, the entire region was critically low on basic survival supplies, including food, water, medicine, and shelter. It is clear that despite the frantic efforts of the army and civilian agencies, Haiti simply had no means to respond to the level of suffering the earthquake produced.

United Nations disaster relief, combined with the additional efforts of independent countries, quickly moved into action. Within hours of the first earthquakes, the United States and other countries dispatched emergency supplies of food and water, temporary shelter, and medicine to Haiti, effectively taking over the airport and surrounding facilities in order to better coordinate the relief project. It quickly became apparent that the most effective means for relief was to either bypass the Haitian authorities completely or work with them in supporting roles. The lack of developed infrastructure in the country, and especially in the Port-au-Prince region, made for severe delivery bottlenecks that initially slowed down the distribution of supplies to affected people. The list of problems requiring immediate attention was alarming:

1. The Port-au-Prince harbor was swamped by refugees and blocked by collapsed buildings, forcing relief shipping to dock on the northern coast and ship supplies to the capital.
2. Roads were closed by rubble and landslides and had to be cleared for relief transports. In some areas, the roads were still closed 10 days after the earthquake.
3. Land-line and cellular telephone communications were either totally or partially disrupted.
4. Morgue facilities in Port-au-Prince were completely overwhelmed. Thousands of the dead were simply laid out in the open for an extended time, encouraging the spread of disease, before they could be buried in mass graves.
5. Civilian government agencies, including the police, essentially shut down, encouraging looting and mob violence.

A critical "first step" in the relief efforts was providing shelter to the region's population. The earthquake had critically damaged a huge percentage of buildings, making much of the existing construction unsafe to use. Further, the UN noted that Haiti was "highly vulnerable" to a wide variety of environmental threats, including floods, landslides, storms, and hurricanes. These hazards made it critical to get temporary shelter to the people immediately. A series of refugee camps were set up around the capital and the homeless were dispersed to these sites. The American Red Cross's three-month progress report from early April claimed that the provision of shelter had been "one of the fastest shelter-relief operations in recent years" as they set up shelter for 1.3 million of Haiti's homeless. Though a commendable start, the sheltering operation had still left approximately 300,000 citizens without housing or shelter of any kind.

Though international relief efforts were rapidly organized, the Haitian disaster relief project was not a smooth operation and pointed to some clear shortcomings through poor initial planning and risk assessment. For example, while supplies and relief personnel from a number of countries quickly poured into the country, central administration of these thousands of volunteers and tons of supplies was lacking. The Port-au-Prince airport was overwhelmed by the number of daily flights in and out of the region, and the local ports simply could not accommodate the amount of shipping that was trying to offload on the docks. These bottlenecks led to delays in distributing supplies and sparked flash riots by angry mobs at different refugee camps. There was a lack of secure "supply dump" locations and looting quickly became rampant.

There also was a tendency to apply lessons learned from past disaster relief efforts even though the parameters were significantly different. As one example, aid organizations had created and sent "sophisticated, prepackaged field hospitals" to Haiti based on medical requirements anticipated from an earlier relief effort following a South Asian tsunami. Unfortunately, many of the supplies and the accompanying medical personnel in these prepackaged hospitals were not equipped to deal with the most common types of "crush injuries" sustained by the Haitian population.

Finally, the influx of medical and other relief personnel from other countries was not well coordinated. Dozens of nongovernmental organizations (NGOs) established their own efforts, often duplicating each other's work because they were not centrally controlled. The Haitian government played only a minimal role in attempting to coordinate these efforts, being paralyzed by the degree of the disaster. As one reporter observed regarding the Haitian president and his senior advisors, "the president was still conducting coordination meetings under a mango tree."

The aftermath of the Haitian earthquake disaster has left ample opportunity to second-guess and critique elements of the rescue effort. There is no denying, however, that international response to the earthquake was immediate, unselfish, and widespread. Disasters, by definition, leave relief agencies with little advance warning to prepare their responses and, instead, force them to rely on risk assessment, prior planning, and a willingness to learn all the lessons, both successes and failures, from previous efforts. The Haitian relief project did not run smoothly, but despite its flaws, it highlighted an essential altruism that prompted people to work tirelessly to relieve the suffering of millions of afflicted residents of the island nation.[1]

INTRODUCTION

More than a decade ago, a series of commercials appeared on television for FRAM oil filters. The theme of each of these commercials was essentially the same: reasonable engine maintenance, coupled with regularly changed (preferably FRAM) oil filters, could prevent serious long-term damage and much higher engine repair costs at a later date. The slogan FRAM popularized in these commercials was: "You can pay me now or pay me later." Project risk management follows a similar logic. In determining relevant risks and formulating proactive strategies for their mitigation, the project team can pay a little in terms of extra time and cost initially, or it must be prepared to pay potentially exorbitant amounts of time and money in the future.

Projects operate in an environment composed of uncertainty. There is uncertainty regarding project funding, the availability of necessary resources, potential technical problems—the list is seemingly endless. This uncertainty forms the basis for project risk and the need to engage in risk management. **Risk management**, which recognizes the capacity of any project to run into trouble, is defined as the art and science of identifying, analyzing, and responding to risk factors throughout the life of a project and in the best interests of its objectives. The difference between projects that fail and those that are ultimately successful has nothing to do with the fact that one lacks problems the other has. The key lies in the plans that have been made to deal with problems once they arise. **Project risk** can be simply defined as any possible event that can negatively affect the viability of a project. Wideman[2] defines project risk as "an estimate of the probability of loss from a large population of unwanted circumstances." Underlying these definitions is the recognition that many events, both within the organization and outside its control, can operate to thwart our best efforts to successfully complete projects.

Risk management consists of anticipating, at the beginning of the project, unexpected situations that may arise that are beyond the project manager's control. These situations have the capacity to severely undermine the success of a project. Broadly speaking, for the manager, the process of risk management includes asking the following questions:

- What is likely to happen (the probability and impact)?
- What can be done to minimize the probability or impact of these events?
- What cues will signal the need for such action (i.e., what clues should I actively look for)?
- What are the likely outcomes of these problems and my anticipated reactions?

This chapter will explore the concept of project risk management in detail. We will address some of the principal sources of uncertainty, and hence risk, in projects. The chapter also will provide information on identifying the key steps to consider in formulating project risk management processes, methods for assessing risk impact, and processes for mitigating negative effects.

Project risk is based on a simple equation:

$$\text{Risk} = (\text{Probability of Event})(\text{Consequences of Event})$$

In other words, all risks must be evaluated in terms of two distinct elements: the likelihood that the event is going to occur as well as the consequences, or effect, of its occurrence. The risk of a project manager in your company being struck by lightning on the way to work would clearly constitute a high level of consequence to the project, but the probability of such an occurrence is sufficiently low to minimize your need to worry about it. On the other hand, people do change jobs, so an event such as the loss of a key project team member midway through the development phase may have both a potentially serious impact and a high degree of probability in some organizations. Hence, in those project environments, it would be appropriate to develop mitigation strategies to address this risk, given its high likelihood of occurring and the negative consequences it would engender. For example, the project manager could develop a bonus or other incentive program to reward personnel who remain on the project team as a useful response (risk mitigation) for the potential loss of key personnel during the project.

Risk and opportunity are mirror opposites of the same coin—opportunity emerges from favorable project circumstances and risk from unfavorable events. Figure 7.2 illustrates the dynamics of risk and opportunity over the project life cycle compared to the severity of negative consequences. Early in the life of a project, both risk and opportunity are high. The concept may be thought valuable, and the opportunities are strong, as are the risks. This result is due to the basic uncertainty early in a project's life cycle. Until we move forward into the development phases, many unanswered questions remain, adding to overall project uncertainty. On the other hand, the severity of negative consequences (the "amount at stake") is minimal early in the project's life. Few resources have yet been committed to the project, so the company's exposure level is still quite low. As the project progresses and more budget money is committed, the overall potential for negative consequences ramps up dramatically. At the same time, however, risk continues to diminish.

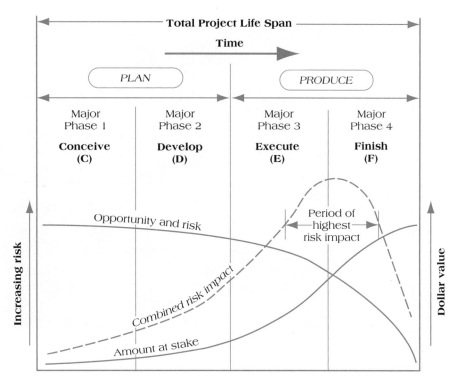

FIGURE 7.2   Risk Versus Amount at Stake: The Challenge in Risk Management

Source: R. Max Wideman. (2004). *A Management Framework for Project, Program and Portfolio Integration*. Victoria, BC, Canada, 2004. Copyright © 2004 by R. Max Wideman, AEW Services Vancouver, BC, Canada: Trafford Publishing. Figure from page 64. Reproduced with permission of R. Max Wideman.

The project takes on a more concrete form and many previously unanswered questions ("Will the technology work?" "Is the development time line feasible?") are finding answers. The result is a circumstance in which overall opportunity and risk (defined by their uncertainty) are dropping just as the amount the company has at stake in the project is rising.

The periods of greatest worry shown in Figure 7.2 are the execute and finish stages, at which point uncertainty is still relatively high and the amount at stake is rapidly increasing. The goal of a risk management strategy is to minimize the company's exposure to this unpleasant combination of uncertainty and potential for negative consequences.

BOX 7.1

PROJECT MANAGERS IN PRACTICE

Mohammed Al-Sadiq, Saudi Aramco Oil Company

For those looking for hard but unique work, problem-solving opportunities, challenges and the chance to achieve great things, consider a project management career.

—Mohammed Al-Sadiq

Mohammed Al-Sadiq is a graduate of King Fahd University of Petroleum & Minerals in Dhahran, Saudi Arabia, with a bachelor's degree in engineering. He lives and works in the Eastern Province of Saudi Arabia, where the Saudi Aramco Oil Company is located. "I'm working as a project engineer for the Offshore Projects Division of Saudi Aramco," he says, in describing his position. "As a project engineer, I'm involved in the planning stage for future projects. After an offshore project is approved, I start working on the detailed design and facilities fabrication, installation, and startup with a specialized offshore contractor." Al-Sadiq goes on to describe his company: "Our division is responsible for all oil and gas projects that take place in Saudi Arabia's waters (mainly in the Persian Gulf). Those projects vary from small control system upgrades in the offshore facilities to building new large platforms, underwater pipelines, and high voltage underwater cable systems."

(continued)

FIGURE 7.3   Mohammed Al-Sadiq of Saudi Aramco

Before graduating from the university, Al-Sadiq received a scholarship and an employment offer from Saudi Aramco. After graduation, he entered a three-year professional development program in order to prepare for his job responsibilities in engineering and project management. The company has a dedicated project management business line (headed by the vice president of project management) to execute all its projects.

Two of Al-Sadiq's most recent projects are among the largest ever in the history of Saudi Aramco. Here is what Al-Sadiq has to say about those projects and about project management itself:

> I was part of a five-member team of engineers managing this project. The project involved the installation of a "tie-in platform": a new central hub platform to gather the crude oil from a number of drilling rigs and resend it to the onshore plant. We also had to upgrade existing wellhead platforms, and install new underwater pipelines and high-voltage cables. The project life cycle took around 36 months from approval by the board to completion and had a budget of $500 million. Those 36 months are very tight in offshore projects, considering all the difficulties and weather delays expected to be faced in offshore. The project was critical because the process of upgrading and linking up to existing producing facilities means that any oil production shutdowns will be observed by the whole world. We completed this project in 2007.
>
> My current project is a similar, though much larger, one that will involve the installation of the largest tie-in platform in Saudi Aramco offshore fields, and a different installation technique will be used for the first time in Saudi Arabian waters. The project is currently in the proposal and cost estimate phase with an expected budget of $1.2 billion and completion in mid-2013.
>
> Those types of offshore projects provide the necessary infrastructure for Saudi Aramco to increase its production and hence satisfy the growing demand for oil from the industrialized and the developing world's countries. They are closely watched by the executive management of the company as well as government officials in order to make sure that the Kingdom of Saudi Arabia is capable of supplying the required oil to the world.
>
> Before joining Saudi Aramco's project management team, I barely understood the idea of project management. I always figured I would end up sitting behind a desk working on engineering drawings, specifications, or developing new solutions to problems. Now, I can confidently say that project management is a much bigger challenge. The beauty of project management is it contains all the elements and challenges of other organizational work. It involves finding engineering solutions, managing human and nonhuman resources, managing costs, developing public relations strategies, and being at hotspots 24 hours a day. It is totally nonroutine work; even if you are working on similar types of projects, I can guarantee that no two projects will ever be the same.
>
> In project management, you can see things being made out of nothing. You start the project with just an idea and then you work all the way until you achieve it. For example, here in offshore projects, we can see our platforms and facilities from the day they were only sketches and work with them until they are literally in the water producing oil. In other words, project management is what makes these ideas come true.

7.1 RISK MANAGEMENT: A FOUR-STAGE PROCESS

Systematic risk management comprises four distinct steps:

- **Risk identification**—the process of determining the specific risk factors that can reasonably be expected to affect your project.
- **Analysis of probability and consequences**—the potential impact of these risk factors, determined by how likely they are to occur and the effect they would have on the project if they did occur.
- **Risk mitigation strategies**—steps taken to minimize the potential impact of those risk factors deemed sufficiently threatening to the project.
- **Control and documentation**—creating a knowledge base for future projects based on lessons learned.

Risk Identification

A useful method for developing a risk identification strategy begins by creating a classification scheme for likely risks. Risks commonly fall into one or more of the following classification clusters:[3]

- **Financial risk**—Financial risk refers to the financial exposure a firm opens itself to when developing a project. If there is a large up-front capital investment required, as in the case of Boeing or Airbus Industries' development of a new airframe, the company is voluntarily assuming a serious financial risk in the project. Construction companies building structures "on spec" provide another example. Without a contracted buyer prior to the construction, these companies agree to accept significant financial risk in the hopes of selling office space or the building itself after it is completed.
- **Technical risk**—When new projects contain unique technical elements or unproven technology, they are being developed under significant technical risk. Naturally, there are degrees of such risk; in some cases, the technical risk is minimal (modifications to an already-developed product), while in other situations the technical risk may be substantial. For example, TRW, now part of Goodrich Corporation, recently developed a modification to its electronic hoist system, used for cable hoists in rescue helicopters. Because the company had already developed the technology and was increasing the power of the lift hoist only marginally, the technical risk was considered minimal. The greater the level of technical risk, the greater the possibility of project underperformance in meeting specification requirements.
- **Commercial risk**—For projects that have been developed for a definite commercial intent (profitability), a constant unknown is their degree of commercial success once they have been introduced into the marketplace. Commercial risk is an uncertainty that companies may willingly accept, given that it is virtually impossible to accurately predict customer acceptance of a new product or service venture.
- **Execution risk**—What are the specific unknowns related to the execution of the project plan? For example, you may question whether geographical or physical conditions could play a role. For example, developing a power plant on the slopes of Mount Pinatubo (an active volcano) in the Philippines would involve serious execution risks! Likewise, poorly trained or insufficient project team personnel might constrain project execution. Execution risk is a broad category that seeks to assess any *unique* circumstances or uncertainties that could have a negative impact on execution of the plan.
- **Contractual or legal risk**—This form of risk is often consistent with projects in which strict terms and conditions are drawn up in advance. Many forms of contracted terms (e.g., cost-plus terms, fixed cost, liquidated damages) result in a significant degree of project risk. Companies naturally seek to limit their legal exposure through legal protection, but it is sometimes impossible to pass along contractual risk to other parties. For example, most U.S. railroads will not accept penalty clauses for late deliveries of components because they have an almost monopolistic control of the market. Therefore, organizations utilizing rail transportation must accept all delivery risk themselves.

After understanding the broad categories of risk, you want to anticipate some of the more common forms of risk in projects. The following list, though not inclusive, offers a short set of some of the more common types of risk to which most projects may be exposed:

- Absenteeism
- Resignation
- Staff being pulled away by management
- Additional staff/skills not available

- Training not as effective as desired
- Initial specifications poor or incomplete
- Work or change orders multiplying due to various problems
- Enhancements taking longer than expected

Although the broad categories and common types of risk in the preceding lists are both good starting points, you also need to consider common industry-specific risks that run across different types of projects in the specific field in which you are working. A number of methods, both qualitative and quantitative, are available for conducting risk factor identification for industry-specific risks, including:

- *Brainstorming meetings*—Bringing the members of the project team, top management, and even clients together for a brainstorming meeting can generate a good list of potential risk factors. Brainstorming is a qualitative idea-creation technique, not one focused on decision making. In order to be effective, brainstorming meetings must be free of judgments, criticism of others' viewpoints, and pressure to conform. A mini-scenario of risk management is at work. Think about it: Would you be willing to place your most creative ideas on the table in front of 10 other people if you were at risk of being immediately critiqued? Or might you be tempted to hold an idea for later if your boss required that you present it in a fully developed way? In short, the brainstorming environment needs to be made safe for the risk-averse.

- *Expert opinion*—This technique can be used in two alternative ways in assessing project risks. The more quantifiable method, commonly referred to as the Delphi approach, collects and consolidates the judgments of isolated anonymous respondents. For Delphi to be used effectively, some preliminary screening of potential contributors is usually necessary. The collective "wisdom" of the set of experts is then used as the basis for decision making. The simpler, more intuitive method for using expert judgments is based on the principle that "experience counts." You simply identify and consult people within the organization who have had similar experiences in running projects in the past or who have been with the firm long enough to have a clear grasp of the mechanics of project risk analysis. As obvious as this may seem, this opportunity may not be clear to everyone, particularly if management shifts recently have taken place in a firm or if new employees are not aware of the firm's project history.

- *History*—In many cases the best source of information on future risks is history. Has a firm encountered a consistent pattern of problems while pursuing projects over time? What "storm signals," or events that have preceded past problems, have been detected? Experience can be used to identify not only risk factors but their leading indicators as well. The problem with experience is that it is no guarantee of future events. The issues or conditions that contributed to project risk in the past decade, year, or even month may not be relevant to current market conditions or the state of project work as it is now being conducted. Hence, history can be useful for identifying key project risk factors provided all parties employ a reasonable degree of caution when evaluating current projects through the portal of past events. Rauma Corporation of Finland, for example, developed state-of-the-art logging equipment that worked well in locations with good infrastructure to allow for frequent servicing. When it attempted to use the equipment in remote rain forest regions of Indonesia, however, the company found it had not anticipated the problems involved in routine servicing, including having to fly the machinery hundreds of miles out of the forests to servicing centers. Experience had not prepared the company for new risks.

- *Multiple (or team-based) assessments*—Using single-case sources to identify project risks is itself a risky proposition because of the potential bias in any one person's viewpoint.[4] It makes sense that no one individual, regardless of her perceived degree of expertise, can possibly discern all sources of threat and project risk. Although an engineer is likely to be more attuned to technical risks, a cost accountant to budgetary risks, and so forth, not even the most seasoned manager with experience in many fields is all-knowing. A team-based approach to risk factor identification encourages identification of a more comprehensive set of potential project risks. At the same time, a collaborative approach can help persuade the half-convinced or uncommitted members of the team to support project goals.[5]

Once the process of risk factor analysis is complete and the variety of circumstances or sources of risk have been uncovered, an assessment of potential risk impact can be undertaken. Table 7.1 names and describes typical risk variables.

TABLE 7.1 Typical Risk Variables[6]

Risk Variable	Description
Market risks	Probability that the forecast sales volume or actual price for the new project will not materialize or be less than the original forecast
Political risks	Expropriation; discriminatory legislative or regulatory changes covering tax codes and environmental laws; political unrest such as civil unrest, strikes, wars, terrorist activity, religious turmoil.
Technical risks	Probability that the project will not achieve the required technical standards, produce substandard products, or have excessive operating costs
Financing risks	Probability that the project revenues will not be sufficient to repay the debts and hence no financing can be organized
Environmental impact risks	Probability that the project will have adverse environmental impacts beyond acceptable limits
Cost risk	Probability that inaccurate or overly optimistic cost estimates will lead to allocating insufficient funds for completing the project
Schedule risk	Probability that the project will overrun its expected duration
Quality (functionality) risk	Probability that the project fails to deliver its expected outcomes, does not perform to its full functionality, or results in inefficient resource consumption
Managerial risk	Probability that management control systems and organizational structures put together to develop and operate the project will not perform well
Integration (stakeholder) risk	Probability that separate project stakeholders, including sponsor, developer (or client), and operator will not work in partnership
Acts of God	Probability of events beyond the control of the project team occurring

Source: Based on A. Jaafari. (2001). "Management of risks, uncertainties and opportunities on projects: time for a fundamental shift," *International Journal of Project Management,* 19(2): 89–101, figure on page 85. Copyright © 2001; reprinted with permission from Elsevier.

Analysis of Probability and Consequences

The next step in the process consists of trying to attach a reasonable estimate of the likelihood of each of these risk events occurring. We can construct a risk impact matrix similar to the one shown in Figure 7.4[7]. The matrix reflects all identified project risks, each prioritized according to the probability of its occurrence, along with the potential consequences for the project, the project team, or the sponsoring organization should the worst come to pass. Probability combined with consequences provides a sense of overall risk

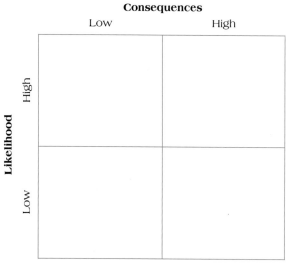

FIGURE 7.4   Risk Impact Matrix

impact. With such a prioritization scheme, the project team is better able to focus their attention where their energy can do the most good.

Figure 7.5 shows a risk impact matrix in use by several *Fortune* 500 companies. Note that instead of a high-low classification, this alternative one features three levels: high, medium, and low. This matrix is further refined by classifying risk impact as either serious, moderate, or minor. The fundamental reason for employing this more complete matrix is to develop a sense of priority in addressing the various risks.

After a project team has worked through and completed a detailed matrix, it is better equipped to recognize the sorts of risks to which the project is subject and the "criticality" of each of those risks in terms of their potential impact on project performance. Clearly, the types of risks that are most relevant to project planning are those that the team classifies as having both high likelihood of occurring (probability) and high potential for harming the project (impact). Risks that fall into this category require detailed contingency planning in order to adequately protect the project's development cycle. Figure 7.5 shows how projects might be classified on the basis of their potential risk impact. The team first identifies the risk factors and then evaluates their impact using the matrix. You can see how the high-low-moderate classification scheme plays out in this example.

Table 7.2 illustrates this quantitative method using the example of a firm developing a new software product for the retail market. The scenario considers both probability of failure and consequences of failure. In *probability of failure*, we are interested in identifying any factors that can significantly affect the probability that the new prject can be successfully completed. Think of this category as requiring us to focus on the potential *causes* of failure. For the example in this section, let us assume that the issues identified as potential contributors are (1) maturity of the software design—is it a new product or based on an existing software platform? (2) complexity of the product—is the design relatively simple or is it highly complex in structure? and (3) dependency—can the product be developed independently of any system currently in place in the company or is it tied to current operating systems or practices? A number of factors can have an impact on the probability of a new project's successful completion. Although our example identifies three (maturity, complexity, and dependency), depending upon the project, a team may identify many unique issues or factors that will increase the probability of failure.

Risk Factor	Consequence	Likelihood	Impact Potential
A. Loss of lead programmer	High	Low	Moderate
B. Technical failure	High	Medium	Serious
C. Budget cut	Medium	Low	Minor
D. Competitor first to market	High	High	Serious

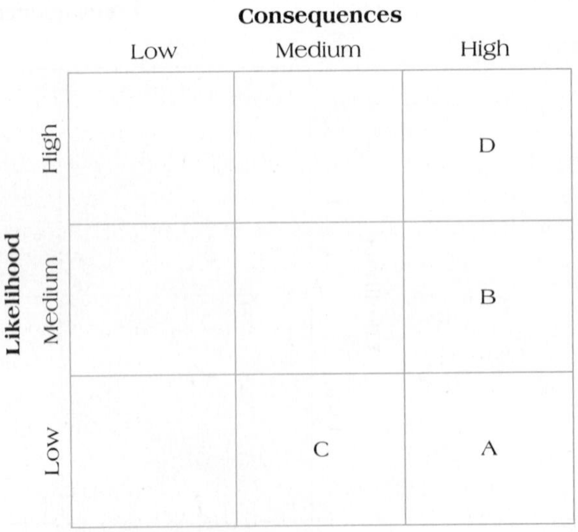

FIGURE 7.5 Classifying Project Risks

TABLE 7.2 Determining Likely Risks and Consequences

Probability of Failure (P_f)			
Score	**Maturity**	**Complexity**	**Dependency**
Low (0.1)	Existing software	Simple design	Not limited to existing system or clients. No external or uncontrollable events are likely to have an impact on the project.
Minor (0.3)	Minor redesign	Minor increase in complexity	Schedule or performance depends on an existing system. Effect on cost or schedule is minor.
Moderate (0.5)	Major change	Moderate increase	Moderate risk to schedule or performance due to dependence on existing system, facility, or processes. Effect on cost is moderate.
Significant (0.7)	Technology is available, but complex design	Significant increase	Schedule or performance depends on new system or process. Significant cost or schedule risk.
Major (0.9)	State of art, some research complete	Extremely complex	Schedule and performance depend on new system and process. Very high cost or schedule risk.

Consequence of Failure (C_f)				
Score	**Cost**	**Schedule**	**Reliability**	**Performance**
Low (0.1)	Budget estimate not exceeded	Negligible impact on program, no impact on critical path	Minimal or no reliability consequence	Minimal or no performance consequence.
Minor (0.3)	Cost estimate exceeds budget by < 5%	Minor slip in schedule (less than 5%)	Small reduction in reliability	Small reduction in system performance.
Moderate (0.5)	Cost estimate exceeds budget by < 15%	Small slip in schedule starting to impact critical path	Some reduction in reliability	Some reduction in system performance. May require moderate debugging.
Significant (0.7)	Cost estimate exceeds budget by < 30%	Development time slips in excess of 1 month, requires readjustment of critical path	Significant degradation in reliability	Significant degradation in system performance. Guarantees are at risk. Serious debugging required.
Major (0.9)	Cost estimate exceeds budget by > 50%	Large schedule slips ensure the system will miss client time frame	Reliability goals cannot be achieved under current plan	Performance goals cannot be achieved. Results may not be usable.

Under the dimension of *consequences of failure,* we are concerned with the issues that will highlight the *effects* of project failure. The consequences of failure require us to critically evaluate the results of a project's success or failure along a number of key dimensions. For this example, the organization has identified four elements that must be considered as critical effects of project failure: (1) cost—budget adherence versus overruns, (2) schedule—on time versus severe delays, (3) reliability—the usefulness and quality of the finished product, and (4) performance—how well the new software performs its designed functions. As with items shown under probability of failure, the set of issues related to the consequences of failure that should be clearly identified will be unique to each project.

Table 7.3 demonstrates the process of creating a project risk score. The scores for each individual dimension of probability and consequence are added and the sum is divided by the number of factors used to assess them. For example, under *probability of failure,* the scores of the three assessed elements (maturity, complexity, and dependency) are totaled to derive an overall score, and that number is divided by 3 to arrive at the probability score. This table shows the overall risk factor formula for the sample project, based on the quantitative assessment. A common rule of thumb assigns any project scoring below .30 as "low risk," projects scoring between .30 and .70 as "medium risk," and projects scoring over .70 as "high risk."

TABLE 7.3 Calculating a Project Risk Factor

1. Use the project team's consensus to determine the scores for each Probability of Failure category: Maturity (P_m), Complexity (P_c), Dependency (P_d).
2. Calculate P_f by adding the three categories and dividing by 3:

$$P_f = (P_m + P_c + P_d)/3$$

3. Use the project team's consensus to determine the scores for each Consequence of Failure category: Cost (C_c), Schedule (C_s), Reliability (C_r), Performance (C_p).
4. Calculate C_f by adding the four categories and dividing by 4:

$$C_f = (C_c + C_s + C_r + C_p)/4$$

5. Calculate Overall Risk Factor for the project by using the formula:

$$RF = P_f + C_f - (P_f)(C_f)$$

Rule of Thumb:

Low risk	$RF < .30$
Medium risk	$RF = .30$ to $.70$
High risk	$RF > .70$

Risk Mitigation Strategies

The next stage in risk management is the development of effective risk mitigation strategies. In a general sense, there are four possible alternatives a project organization can adopt in deciding how to address risks: (1) accept risk, (2) minimize risk, (3) share risk, or (4) transfer risk.

ACCEPT RISK   One option that a project team must always consider is whether the risk is sufficiently strong that any action is warranted. Any number of risks of a relatively minor nature may be present in a project as a matter of course. However, because the likelihood of their occurrence is so small or the consequences of their impact are so minor, they may be judged acceptable and ignored. In this case, the decision to "do nothing" is a reasoned calculation, not the result of inattention or incompetence. Likewise, for many types of projects, certain risks are simply part of the equation and must be factored in. For example, it has been estimated that the U.S. recording industry spends millions every year in developing, producing, and promoting new recording artists, knowing full well that of the thousands of albums produced every year, less than 5% are profitable.[8] Likewise, Chapter 3 detailed the extraordinary lengths that pharmaceutical manufacturers must go to and the high percentage of failures they accept in order to get a small percentage of commercially successful drugs to the marketplace. Hence, a high degree of commercial risk is embedded in the systems themselves and must be accepted in order to operate in certain industries.

MINIMIZE RISK   Strategies to minimize risk are the next option. Consider the challenges that Boeing Corporation faces in developing new airframes, such as the recently prototyped and developed 787 model. Each aircraft contains millions of individual parts, most of which must be acquired from vendors. Further, Boeing has been experimenting with the use of composite materials, instead of aluminum, throughout the airframe. The risks to Boeing in the event of faulty parts leading to a catastrophic failure are huge. Consequently, the process of selecting and ensuring quality performance from vendors is a challenge that Boeing takes extremely seriously. One method Boeing employs for minimizing risk in vendor quality is to insist that all significant vendors maintain continuous direct contact with Boeing quality assessment teams. Also, in considering a new potential vendor, Boeing insists upon the right to intervene in the vendor's production process in order to ensure that the resulting quality of all supplier parts meets its exacting standards. Because Boeing cannot produce all the myriad parts needed to fabricate an aircraft, it seeks to minimize the resultant risk by adopting strategies that allow it to directly affect the production processes of its suppliers.

SHARE RISK   Risk may be allocated proportionately among multiple members of the project. Two examples of risk sharing include the research and development done through the European Space Agency (ESA) and the Airbus consortium. Due to tremendous barriers to entry, no one country in the European Union has the capital resources and technical skills to undertake the development of the Ariane rocket for satellite delivery or the creation of a new airframe to compete with Boeing in the commercial aircraft industry. ESA and Airbus partners from a number of countries have jointly pooled their resources and, at the same time, agreed to jointly share the risk inherent in these ventures.

In addition to partnerships that pool project risk, ameliorating risk through sharing can be achieved contractually. Many project organizations create relationships with suppliers and customers that include legal requirements for risk to be shared among those involved in the project. Host countries of large industrial construction projects, such as petrochemical or power generation facilities, have begun insisting on contracts that enforce a "Build-Own-Operate-Transfer" provision for all project firms. The lead project organization is expected to build the plant and take initial ownership of it until its operating capacity has been proven and all debugging occurs before finally transferring ownership to the client. In this way, the project firm and the host country agree to jointly accept financial (risk) ownership of the project until such time as the project has been completed and its capabilities proven.

TRANSFER RISK   In some circumstances, when it is impossible to change the nature of the risk, either through elimination or minimization, it may be possible to shift the risks bound up in a project to another party. This option, transferring risk to other parties when feasible, acknowledges that even in the cases where a risk cannot be reduced, it may not have to be accepted by the project organization, provided that there is a reasonable means for passing the risk along. Companies use several methods to transfer risks, depending upon their power relative to the client organizations and the types of risks they face. For example, if our goal is to prevent excessive budget overruns, a good method for directly transferring risk lies in developing fixed-price contracts. **Fixed-price contracts** establish a firm, fixed price for the project upfront; should the project's budget begin to slip, the project organization must bear the full cost of these overruns. Alternatively, if our goal is to ensure project functionality (quality and performance), the concept of liquidated damages offers a way to transfer risk through contracts. **Liquidated damages** represent project penalty clauses that kick in at mutually agreed-on points in the project's development and implementation. A project organization installing a new information system in a large utility may, for example, agree to a liquidated damages clause should the system be inoperable after a certain date. Finally, insurance is a common option for some organizations, particularly in the construction industry. Used as a risk mitigation tool, insurance transfers the financial obligation to an insuring agency.

Use of Contingency Reserves

Contingency reserves in several forms, including financial and managerial, are among the most common methods to mitigate project risks. They are defined as the specific provision for unforeseen elements of cost within the defined project scope. Contingency reserves are viewed differently, however, depending upon the type of project undertaken and the organization that initiates it. In construction projects, it is common to set aside anywhere between 10% and 15% of the construction price in a contingency fund. A contract to construct a $5 million building will actually be built to the cost of approximately $4.5 million, with the balance retained for contingency. In other fields, however, project teams are much more reluctant to admit to the up-front need for establishing contingency reserves, fearing that customers or other project stakeholders will view this as a sign of poor planning or inadequate scope definition (see Chapter 5).

The best way to offset concerns about the use of contingency reserves is to offer documentation of past risk events—unforeseen or uncontrollable circumstances that required the need for such contingency planning. Some of the concerns that might be generated may also be offset if the project team has done its homework and demonstrated in a detailed plan how contingency funds will be released as they are needed. Since the goal of creating contingency funds is to ensure against unforeseen risks, the key to their effective use lies in proactive planning to establish reasonable triggers for their release.[9]

TASK CONTINGENCY   Perhaps the most common form of contingency reserve is **task contingency**, which is used to offset budget cutbacks, schedule overruns, or other unforeseen circumstances accruing to individual tasks or project work packages. These budget reserves can be a very valuable form of risk management because they provide the project team with a buttress in the face of task completion difficulties. It may be found, for example, that some components or work packages of the project are highly unique or innovative, suggesting that development estimates and their related costs cannot be estimated with anything less than a bound of ±20% or even greater. Hence, task contingency becomes extremely important as a method for offsetting the project team's inability to make an accurate budget estimate.

EXAMPLE 7.1 **Calculating Contingency Expected Cost**

Suppose a project task is estimated to cost $10,000 to complete, but it is viewed as a high-risk operation. A task contingency multiplier would require our budget to reflect the following:

$$(\text{Task estimated cost})(\text{Task contingency multiplier}) = \text{Expected cost}$$
$$(\$10,000)(1.2) = \$12,000$$

Naturally, as the project moves forward, it may be possible to reduce budget reserve requirements for task contingency because the project's scope will have been made clearer and its development will have progressed; that is, many of the tasks for which the contingency fund was established will have been completed. As a result, it is quite common for project organizations to assign a budget reserve to a project that is diminished across the project's development cycle.

MANAGERIAL CONTINGENCY While task contingency may involve the risk associated with the development of individual work packages or even tasks, managerial contingency is an additional safety buffer applied at the project level. **Managerial contingency** is budget safety measures that address higher-level risks. For example, suppose a project team has begun development of a new wireless communication device set to operate within guidelines established for technical performance. At some point in the midst of the development process, the primary client requests major scope changes that will dramatically alter the nature of the technology to be employed. Managerial contingency typically is used as a reserve against just such a problem. Another way managerial contingency may be used is to offset potentially disastrous "acts of God," which are natural disasters that, by definition, are unforeseeable and highly disruptive.

One final point about budget reserves at either the task or managerial level: It is extremely important that open channels of communication be maintained between top management and the project manager regarding the availability and use of contingency reserve funds. Project managers must be fully aware of the guidelines for requesting additional funding and how extra project budget is to be disbursed. If either the project manager or top management group uses contingency reserves as a political tool or method for maintaining control, the other party will quickly develop an attitude of gamesmanship toward acquiring those reserves. In this case, the atmosphere and communications between these key stakeholders will become characterized by distrust and secrecy—two factors guaranteed to ensure that a project is likely to fail.

Other Mitigation Strategies

In addition to the set of mitigation strategies already discussed, many organizations adopt practical approaches to minimizing risk through creating systems for effectively training all members of their project teams. One successful method for dealing with project risks involves **mentoring** new project managers and team members. In a mentoring program, junior or inexperienced project personnel are paired with senior managers in order to help them learn best practices. The goal of mentoring is to help ease new project personnel into their duties by giving them a formal contact who can help clarify problems, suggest solutions, and monitor them as they develop project skills. Another method for mitigating risks involves **cross-training** project team personnel so that they are capable of filling in for each other in the case of unforeseen circumstances. Cross-training requires that members of the project team learn not only their own duties but also the roles that other team members are expected to perform. Thus, in the case where a team member may be pulled from the project team for an extended period, other team members can take up the slack, thereby minimizing the time lost to the project's schedule.

Control and Documentation

Once project risk analysis has been completed, it is important to begin developing a reporting and documentation system for cataloging and future reference. Control and documentation methods help managers classify and codify the various risks the firm faces, its responses to these risks, and the outcome of its response strategies. Table 7.4 gives an example of a simplified version of the risk management report form that is used in several organizations. Managers may keep a hard-copy file of all these analyses or convert the analyses to databases for better accessibility.

TABLE 7.4 Sample Risk Management Report Form

Customer: _____ Project Name: _____

Budget Number: _____ Project Team: _____

Date of Most Recent Evaluation: _____

Risk Description: _____

_____

_____

_____

Risk Assessment: _____ Risk Factor: _____

Discussion: _____

_____

_____

Risk Reduction Plan: _____ Owner: _____

_____

Time Frame to Next Assessment: _____

Expected Outcome: _____

_____

_____

Having a repository of past risk analysis transactions is invaluable, particularly to novice project managers who may recognize the need to perform risk management duties but are not sure of the best way to do them or where to begin. The U.S. Army, for example, has invested significant budget and time in creating a comprehensive database of project risk factors and their mitigation strategies as part of project management training for their officers. Newly appointed officers to Army procurement and project management offices are required to access this information in order to begin establishing preliminary risk management strategies prior to initiating new programs. Figure 7.6 illustrates a contingency document for adjustments to the project plan.

Probable Event	Adjustment to Plans
Absenteeism	
Resignation	
Pull-aways	
Unavailable staff/skills	
Spec change	
Added work	
Need more training	
Vendors late	

FIGURE 7.6 Contingency Document for Adjustments to Project Plan

Establishing **change management** as part of risk mitigation strategies also requires a useful documentation system that all partners in the project can access. Any strategy aimed at minimizing a project risk factor, along with the member of the project team responsible for any action, must be clearly identified. The sample risk management report form shown in Table 7.4 includes the important elements in such change management. In order to be effective, the report must offer a comprehensive analysis of the problem, the plan for its minimization, a target date, and the expected outcome once the mitigation strategy has been implemented. In short, as a useful control document, a report form has to coherently identify the key information: what, who, when, why, and how.

- *What*—Identify clearly the source of risk that has been uncovered.
- *Who*—Assign a project team member direct responsibility for following this issue and maintaining ownership regarding its resolution.
- *When*—Establish a clear time frame, including milestones if necessary, that will determine when the expected mitigation is to occur. If it is impossible to identify a completion date in advance, then identify reasonable process goals en route to the final risk reduction point.
- *Why*—Pinpoint the most likely reasons for the risk; that is, identify its cause to ensure that efforts toward its minimization will correspond appropriately with the reason the risk emerged.
- *How*—Create a detailed plan for how the risk is to be abated. What steps has the project team member charted as a method for closing this particular project "risk window"? Do they seem reasonable or far-fetched? Too expensive in terms of money or time? The particular strategy for risk abatement should, preferably, be developed as a collaborative effort among team members, including those with technical and administrative expertise to ensure that the steps taken to solve the problem are technically logical and managerially possible.

Documentation of risk analysis such as is shown in Table 7.4 and Figure 7.6 represents a key final component in the overall risk management process.

PROJECT PROFILE

Case—Collapse of Shanghai Apartment Building

The science and engineering principles surrounding the construction of simple apartment blocks are well known and have been practiced for centuries. And yet, even in the most basic of construction projects, events can sometimes transpire to produce shocking results. Just such a story occurred in late June of 2009 in China, when a Shanghai high-rise, 13-story apartment building literally toppled onto its side. The nearly completed structure was part of an 11-building apartment complex in a new development known as "Lotus Riverside." Because the 629-unit apartment building was not yet completed, it was virtually empty. Although one worker was killed in the accident, the tragedy could have been far worse had the building been fully occupied.

imago stock&people/Newscom

FIGURE 7.7 **Shanghai Apartment Building Collapse**

The demand for affordable housing in Chinese cities has never been greater. With the economy humming along and a high demand for workers in economic regions such as Shanghai, there is a critical shortage of available housing. Private and governmental organizations are working to rapidly install new apartment blocks to keep up with this huge demand. Unfortunately, one of the risks with rapid building is the temptation to cut corners or use slipshod methods. When speed is paramount, the obvious concern is whether acceptable standards of building are being maintained.

In the Lotus Riverside building project, unfortunately, the construction firm opted for a procedure that is generally frowned upon (indeed, the method is outlawed in Hong Kong due to its inherent riskiness). Under this system, rather than pour a deep concrete base on which to rest the structure, a series of prestressed, precast concrete pilings were used as a set of anchors to "pin" the building into the ground. Although this system can work effectively with shorter buildings, it has long been considered unsafe for larger, higher structures.

The problem was made critical when the construction crews began digging an underground garage on the south side of the building to a depth of nearly 5 meters. The excavated dirt was piled on the north side of the building to a height of 10 meters. The underground pilings began receiving severe lateral pressure from the excavation, which was further compromised by heavy rainstorms. The storms undermined the apartment building on the south side, causing more soil erosion and putting even greater lateral pressure (estimated at 3,000 tons) on the anchor piling system (see Figure 7.8). Suddenly, the pilings began snapping and the building toppled over on its side. Local officials noted that the only lucky result of the collapse was that the building fell into an empty space. Considering that all the buildings in the complex had been constructed in a similar manner, there was a very real possibility of creating a chain reaction of toppling buildings, much like a set of dominos falling over.

The Chinese government immediately began to aggressively trace the cause of the collapse, questioning the private contractor's use of unskilled workers, questionable construction practices, and overall quality control. China's official news agency, Xinhua, said officials were taking "appropriate control measures" against nine people, including the developer, construction contractor, and supervisor of the project, after it was reported that the company's construction license had expired in 2004. Although it is certain that penalties will be imposed for the building failure, a less certain future awaits the tenants of the other buildings in the complex. After all, what more visible evidence could there be of the unsoundness of the construction in the complex than seeing a "sister building" lying on its side not far from the other structures? Hundreds of prospective tenants have besieged government offices, demanding refunds for apartments in the same complex that they purchased for upward of $60,000 but are now too frightened to live in.

Meanwhile, *China Daily*, the state-run newspaper, published an angry editorial blaming the collapse on the often corrupt relationship between Chinese property developers and local government officials who depend on property taxes and land sales for a significant proportion of their income. The paper raised fears—expressed by some construction industry insiders in China—that many buildings designed to have a 70-year life span "would not stand firm beyond 30 to 40 years" because of corner-cutting during China's rampant construction boom. "It is ironic that such an accident happened in Shanghai—one of the most advanced and international Chinese cities," the paper concluded. "The sheer fact that such a collapse occurred in the country's biggest metropolis should serve as warning to all developers and the authorities to ensure that construction projects do not cut corners and endanger people's lives."[10]

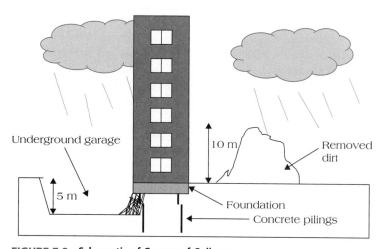

FIGURE 7.8 Schematic of Causes of Collapse

7.2 PROJECT RISK MANAGEMENT: AN INTEGRATED APPROACH

The European Association for Project Management has developed an integrated program of risk management, based on efforts to extend risk management to cover a project's entire life cycle. This program, known as **Project Risk Analysis and Management (PRAM)**, presents a generic methodology that can be applied to multiple project environments and encompasses the key components of project risk management.[11] The ultimate benefit of models such as PRAM is that they present a systematic alternative to ad hoc approaches to risk assessment, and hence can help organizations that may not have a clearly developed, comprehensive process for risk management and are instead locked into one or two aspects (e.g., risk identification or analysis of probability and consequences). The PRAM model offers a step-by-step approach to creating a comprehensive and logically sequenced method for analyzing and addressing project risk.

Among the key features of the PRAM methodology are the following:

- *The recognition that risk management follows its own life cycle, much as a project follows a life cycle.* Risk management is integrated throughout the project's entire life cycle.
- *The application of different risk management strategies at various points in the project life cycle.* The PRAM approach tailors different strategies for different project life cycle stages.
- *The integration of multiple approaches to risk management into a coherent, synthesized approach.* PRAM recommends that all relevant risk management tools be applied as they are needed, rather than in a "pick-and-choose" approach.

Each of the nine phases in the PRAM approach is based on a specific purpose and requires the completion of a comprehensive set of targets (deliverables). Completing PRAM gives the project team a template for getting the most out of risk management and helps them sharpen their efforts in the most productive manner. It also creates a document for merging risk management with overall project planning, linking them in a collaborative sense.

The nine phases of a comprehensive project risk assessment include the following steps:

1. *Define*—Make sure the project is well defined, including all deliverables, statement of work, and project scope.
2. *Focus*—Begin to plan the risk management process as a project in its own right, as well as determining the best methods for addressing project risk, given the unique nature of the project being undertaken.
3. *Identify*—Assess the specific sources of risk at the outset of the project, including the need to fashion appropriate responses. This step requires that we first search for all sources of risk and their responses and then classify these risks in some manner to prioritize or organize them.
4. *Structure*—Review and refine the manner in which we have classified risks for the project, determine if there are commonalities across the various risks we have uncovered (suggesting common causes of the risks that can be addressed at a higher level), and create a prioritization scheme for addressing these risks.
5. *Clarify ownership of risks*—Distinguish between risks that the project organization is willing to handle and those that the clients are expected to accept as well as allocate responsibility for managing risks and responses.
6. *Estimate*—Develop a reasonable estimate of the impacts on the project of both the identified risks and the proposed solutions. What are the likely scenarios and their relative potential costs?
7. *Evaluate*—Critically evaluate the results of the estimate phase to determine the most likely plan for mitigating potential risks. Begin to prioritize risks and the project team's responses.
8. *Plan*—Produce a project risk management plan that proactively offers risk mitigation strategies for the project as needed.
9. *Manage*—Monitor actual progress with the project and associated risk management plans, responding to any variances in these plans, with an eye toward developing these plans for the future.

Table 7.5 shows a generic risk management process following the PRAM methodology. At each of the risk management phases, specific project deliverables can be identified, allowing the project team to create comprehensive project risk management documentation while addressing specific steps along the way. These deliverables are important because they indicate to project managers exactly the types of information they should be collecting at different phases of the project and the materials they should make available to relevant stakeholders.

The PRAM model for risk management is extremely helpful because it offers project managers a systematic process for best employing risk assessment and mitigation strategies. Composed of nine

TABLE 7.5 A Generic Risk Management Process (RMP) Following the PRAM Methodology

Phases	Purposes	Deliverables
Define	Consolidate relevant existing information about the project.	A clear, unambiguous, shared understanding of all key aspects of the project documented, verified, and reported.
Focus	1. Identify scope and provide a strategic plan for the RMP. 2. Plan the RMP at an operational level.	A clear, unambiguous, shared understanding of all relevant key aspects of the RMP, documented, verified, and reported.
Identify	1. Identify where risk might arise. 2. Identify what we might do about this risk in proactive and reactive response terms. 3. Identify what might go wrong with our responses.	All key risks and responses identified; both threats and opportunities classified, characterized, documented, verified, and reported.
Structure	1. Test simplifying assumptions. 2. Provide more complex structure when appropriate.	A clear understanding of the implications of any important simplifying assumptions about relationships among risks, responses, and base plan activities.
Ownership	1. Client contractor allocation of ownership and management of risks and responses. 2. Allocation of client risks to named individuals. 3. Approval of contractor allocations.	Clear ownership and management allocations effectively and efficiently defined, legally enforceable in practice where appropriate.
Estimate	1. Identify areas of clear significant uncertainty. 2. Identify areas of possible significant uncertainty.	1. A basis for understanding which risks and responses are important. 2. Estimates of likelihood and impact on scenario or in numeric terms.
Evaluate	Synthesis and evaluation of the results of the estimate phase.	Diagnosis of all important difficulties and comparative analysis of the implications of responses to these difficulties, with specific deliverables like a prioritized list of risks.
Plan	Project plan ready for implementation and associated risk management plan.	1. Base plans in activity terms at the detailed level of implementation. 2. Risk assessment in terms of threats and opportunities prioritized, assessed in terms of impact. 3. Recommended proactive and reactive contingency plans in activity terms.
Manage	1. Monitoring. 2. Controlling. 3. Developing plans for immediate implementation.	1. Diagnosis of a need to revisit earlier plans and initiation of replanning as appropriate. 2. Exception reporting after significant events and associated replanning.

interconnected steps that form a logical sequence, PRAM creates a unifying structure under which effective risk management can be conducted. Because it follows the logic of the project life cycle, PRAM should be conducted not as a "one-shot" activity but as an ongoing, progressive scheme that links project development directly to accurate risk assessment and management. Finally, in identifying the key deliverables at each step in the process, the PRAM model ensures a similarity of form that allows top management to make reasonable comparisons across all projects in an organization's portfolio.

Project risk management demonstrates the value of proactive planning for projects as a way to anticipate and, hopefully, mitigate serious problems that could adversely affect the project at some point in the future.[12] The value of this troubleshooting process is that it requires us to think critically, to be devil's advocates when examining how we are planning to develop a project. Research and common sense suggest, in the words of the adage, "An ounce of prevention is worth a pound of cure." The more sophisticated and systematic we are about conducting project risk management, the more confident we can be, as the project moves through planning and into its execution phase, that we have done everything possible to prepare the way for project success.

Summary

1. **Define project risk.** Project risk is defined as any possible event that can negatively affect the viability of a project. We frequently use the equation: Risk = (Probability of event)(Consequences of event). Effective risk management goes a long way toward influencing project development. To be effective, however, project risk management needs to be done early in the project's life. To quote Shakespeare's *Macbeth:* "If it were done, when 'tis done; then 'twere well it were done quickly." As an important element in overall project planning, risk management identifies specific risks that can have a detrimental effect on project performance and quantifies the impact each risk may have. The impact of any one risk factor is defined as the product of the likelihood of the event's occurrence and the adverse consequences that would result. The tremendous number of unknowns in the early phases of a project makes this the time when risk is highest. As the project moves forward, the team continues to address risk with technical, administrative, and budgetary strategies.

2. **Recognize four key stages in project risk management and the steps necessary to manage risk.** There are four distinct phases of project risk management: (1) risk identification, (2) analysis of probability and consequences, (3) risk mitigation strategies, and (4) control and documentation. Risk identification focuses on determining a realistic set of risk factors that a project faces. In analysis of probability and consequences, the project team prioritizes its responses to these various risk factors by assessing the "impact factor" of each one. Impact factors are determined either in a qualitative manner, using a matrix approach and consensus decision making, or in more quantitative ways, in which all relevant probability and consequence parameters are laid out and used to assess overall project risk.

The project team begins the process of developing risk mitigation strategies once a clear vision of risk factors is determined. The last step in the risk management process, control and documentation, is based on the knowledge that risk management strategies are most effective when they have been codified and introduced as part of standard operating procedures. The goal is to create systematic and repeatable strategies for project risk management.

3. **Understand five primary causes of project risk and four major approaches to risk identification.** The five primary causes of project risk are (1) financial risk, (2) technical risk, (3) commercial risk, (4) execution risk, and (5) contractual or legal risk. Among the most common methods for risk identification are (1) brainstorming meetings, (2) expert opinion, (3) past history, and (4) multiple or team-based assessments.

4. **Recognize four primary risk mitigation strategies.** Risks can be mitigated through four primary approaches. First, we can simply accept the risk. We may choose to do this in a situation in which we either have no alternative or we consider the risk small enough to be acceptable. Second, we can seek to minimize risk, perhaps through entering partnerships or joint ventures in order to lower our company's exposure to the risk. Third, we can share risk with other organizations or project stakeholders. Finally, when appropriate, we may seek to transfer risk to other project stakeholders.

5. **Explain the Project Risk Analysis and Management (PRAM) process.** PRAM is a generic project risk management approach that offers a model for the life cycle steps a project team might adopt in developing a risk management methodology. Nine distinct steps in the PRAM model present each phase of the process and its associated deliverables.

Key Terms

Analysis of probability and consequences (*p. 239*)

Change management (*p. 248*)

Commercial risk (*p. 239*)

Contingency reserves (*p. 245*)

Contractual or legal risk (*p. 239*)

Control and documentation (*p. 239*)

Cross-training (*p. 246*)

Execution risk (*p. 239*)

Financial risk (*p. 239*)

Fixed-price contact (*p. 245*)

Liquidated damages (*p. 245*)

Managerial contingency (*p. 246*)

Mentoring (*p. 246*)

Project risk (*p. 236*)

Project Risk Analysis and Management (PRAM) (*p. 250*)

Risk identification (*p. 239*)

Risk management (*p. 236*)

Risk mitigation strategies (*p. 239*)

Task contingency (*p. 245*)

Technical risk (*p. 239*)

Solved Problem

7.1 Quantitative Risk Assessment

Refer to the risk factors shown in Table 7.2. Assume your project team has decided upon the following risk values:

$$P_m = .1 \quad C_c = .7$$
$$P_c = .5 \quad C_s = .5$$
$$P_d = .9 \quad C_r = .3$$
$$C_p = .1$$

You wish to determine the overall project risk using a quantitative method. Following the formulas shown in Table 7.3, we can calculate both the probability of project risk score and the consequences of project risk score, as follows:

$$P_f = (.1 + .5 + .9)/3 = .5$$
$$C_f = (.7 + .5 + .3 + .1)/4 = .4$$
$$RF = .5 + .4 - (.5)(.4) = .70$$

Conclusion: Medium risk to overall project.

Discussion Questions

1. Do you agree with the following statement: "With proper planning it is possible to eliminate most/all risks from a project"? Why or why not?
2. In evaluating projects across industries, it is sometimes possible to detect patterns in terms of the more common types of risks they routinely face. Consider the development of a new software product and compare it to coordinating an event, such as a school dance. What likely forms of risk would your project team face in either of these circumstances?
3. Analyze Figure 7.2 (degree of risk over the project life cycle). What is the practical significance of this model? What implications does it suggest for managing risk?
4. What are the benefits and drawbacks of using the various forms of risk identification mentioned in the chapter (e.g., brainstorming meetings, expert opinion, etc.)?
5. What are the benefits and drawbacks of using a qualitative risk impact matrix for classifying the types of project risk?
6. What are the benefits and drawbacks of using a quantitative risk assessment tool such as the one shown in the chapter?
7. Give some examples of projects using each of the risk mitigation strategies (accept, minimize, share, or transfer). How successful were these strategies? In hindsight, would another approach have been better?
8. Explain the difference between managerial contingency and task contingency.
9. What are the advantages of developing and using a systematic risk management approach such as the PRAM methodology? Do you perceive any disadvantages of the approach?
10. Consider the following observation: "The problem with risk analysis is that it is possible to imagine virtually anything going wrong on a project. Where do you draw the line? In other words, how far do you take risk analysis before it becomes overkill?" How would you respond?

Problems

1. **Assessing Risk Factors.** Consider the planned construction of a new office building in downtown Houston at a time when office space is in surplus demand (more office space than users). Construct a risk analysis that examines the various forms of risk (technical, commercial, financial, etc.) related to the creation of this office building. How would your analysis change if office space were in high demand?
2. **Qualitative Risk Assessment.** Imagine that you are a member of a project team that has been charged to develop a new product for the residential building industry. Using a qualitative risk analysis matrix, develop a risk assessment for a project based on the following information:

Identified Risk Factors	Likelihood
1. Key team members pulled off project	1. High
2. Chance of economic downturn	2. Low
3. Project funding cut	3. Medium
4. Project scope changes	4. High
5. Poor spec. performance	5. Low

Based on this information, how would you rate the consequences of each of the identified risk factors? Why? Construct the risk matrix and classify each of the risk factors in the matrix.

3. **Developing Risk Mitigation Strategies.** Develop a preliminary risk mitigation strategy for each of the risk factors identified in Problem 2. If you were to prioritize your efforts, which risk factors would you address first? Why?
4. **Quantitative Risk Assessment.** Assume the following information:

Probability of Failure	Consequences of Failure
Maturity = .3	Cost = .1
Complexity = .3	Schedule = .7
Dependency = .5	Performance = .5

Calculate the overall risk factor for this project. Would you assess this level of risk as low, moderate, or high? Why?

5. **Developing Risk Mitigation Strategies.** Assume that you are a project team member for a highly complex project based on a new technology that has never been directly proven in the

marketplace. Further, you require the services of a number of subcontractors to complete the design and development of this project. Because you are facing severe penalties in the event the project is late to market, your boss has asked you and your project team to develop risk mitigation strategies to minimize your company's exposure. Discuss the types of risk that you are likely to encounter. How should your company deal with them (accept them, share them, transfer them, or minimize them)? Justify your answers.

6. **Assessing Risk and Benefits.** Suppose you are a member of a project team that is evaluating the bids of potential contractors for developing some subassemblies for your project. Your boss makes it clear that any successful bid must demonstrate a balance between risk and price. Explain how this is so; specifically, why are price and risk seen as equally important but opposite issues in determining the winner of the contract? Is a low-price/high-risk bid acceptable? Is a high-price/low-risk bid acceptable? Why or why not?

Case Study 7.1

Classic Case: de Havilland's Falling Comet

The Development of the Comet

The de Havilland Aircraft Company of Great Britain had long been respected in the aircraft manufacturing industry for its innovative and high-performance designs. Coming off their performance work during World War II, the company believed that they stood poised on the brink of success in the commercial airframe industry. The de Havilland designers and executives accurately perceived that the next generation of airplane would be jet-powered. Consequently, they decreed that their newest commercial airframe, tentatively called the Comet, would employ jet power and other leading-edge technology.

Jets offered a number of advantages over propeller-driven airplanes, the most obvious of which was speed. Jets could cruise at nearly 450 miles per hour compared with the 300 miles per hour a propeller could generate. For overseas flight, in particular, this advantage was important. It could reduce the length of long flights from a mind-numbing two to three days to mere hours, encouraging more and more businesspeople and tourists to use airplanes as their primary method for travel. Further, jets tended to be quieter than propeller-driven aircraft, giving a more comfortable interior sound level and ride to passengers.

De Havilland engineers sought to create a streamlined airplane that could simultaneously carry up to 50 passengers in comfort, while maintaining aerodynamics and high speed. After working with a number of design alternatives, the Comet began to take shape. Its design was, indeed, distinctive: The four jet engines were embedded

FIGURE 7.9 **The de Havilland Comet**

in pairs in the wing roots, at the point where they joined the fuselage. From the front, the aircraft looked as though its wings were literally held in place by the engines. The result of these innovative engineering designs was an aircraft that had remarkable stability in flight, was sleek in appearance, and was very fast.

Another distinctive feature of the aircraft was the pressurized cabin, intended to maintain passenger comfort at cruising altitudes of up to 30,000 feet. In its original testing for safety, de Havilland engineers had pressurized the airframe to more than five times the recommended air density to ensure that there was a clean seal. Consequently, they were confident that the pressurization system would perform well at its lower, standardized settings. Finally, in an effort to add some flair to the design, each window in the passenger cabin was square, rather than the small, round or oval shapes so commonly used.

Knowing that they were facing competition from Boeing Corporation to be first to market with a commercial jet, de Havilland's goal was to introduce its new aircraft as quickly as possible, in order to establish the standard for the commercial airline industry. At first, it appeared that they had succeeded: BOAC (British Overseas Airways Corporation) ordered several Comets, as did Air France and the British military. De Havilland also received some queries from interested American airline companies, notably Pan American Airlines. It looked as though de Havilland's strategy was working; the company was first to market with a radical new design, using a number of state-of-the-art technologies. BOAC's first nine Comet 1s entered service with the airline on May 2, 1952. The future looked bright.

Troubles

In early May of 1953, a brand new Comet operated by BOAC left Calcutta, India, and flew off into the afternoon sky. Six minutes later and only 22 miles from Calcutta's Dum Dum Airport, the aircraft exploded and plunged to earth, killing all 43 passengers and crew on board. There had been no indication of problems and no warning from the pilots of technical difficulties. Investigators from Great Britain and India tended to believe the crash came about due to pilot error coupled with weather conditions. Evidence from the wreckage, including the tail section, seemed to indicate that the aircraft had been struck by something heavy, but without any additional information forthcoming, both the authorities and de Havilland engineers laid the blame to external causes.

January 10, 1954, was a mild, clear day in Rome as passengers boarded their BOAC aircraft for the final leg of their flight from Singapore to London. When the airplane had reached its cruising altitude and speed, it disintegrated over the Mediterranean Sea, near the island of Elba. Most of the airplane was lost at the bottom of the sea, but amid the flotsam were recovered 15 bodies of passengers and crew. A local physician who examined the remains noted: "They showed no look of terror. Death must have come without warning." As a safety precaution, BOAC instituted a ban on the use of Comets until the airplanes had been thoroughly checked over. Technicians could find nothing wrong with the new aircraft and, following recertification, the airplanes were again brought back into service.

Alas, it was too soon. On the 8th day of April, only 16 days after the Comet was reintroduced into service, a third aircraft, operated by South African Airways, departed from Rome's Ciampino airport for Cairo, one of the legs of its regular flight from London to Johannesburg. Under perfect flying weather, the airplane rapidly gained its cruising altitude of 26,000 feet and its airspeed of almost 500 miles an hour. Suddenly, the flight radio went silent and failed to answer repeated calls. A search of the ocean off the island of Stromboli, Italy, turned up an oil slick and some debris. Because of the depth of the water and the time necessary to arrive at the crash site, there was little to be found by search crews. Five bodies were all that were recovered this time, though with an eerie similarity to the victims of the second disaster: Facial expressions showed no fear, as though death had come upon them suddenly.

What Went Wrong?

Investigators swarmed over the recovered wreckage of the aircraft and reexamined the pieces of the first from the Calcutta accident while also conducting underwater searches at the sight of the second crash near the island of Elba. Guided by underwater cameras, investigators were able to collect sufficient aircraft fragments (in fact, they finally recovered nearly 70% of the airframe) to make some startling discoveries. The foremost finding, from the recovery of the entire, intact tail section, was that the fuselage of the aircraft had exploded. Second, it appeared that engine failure was not the cause of the accidents. Another finding was equally important: The wings and fuselage showed unmistakable signs of metal fatigue, later shown to be the cause of failure in all three aircraft. This point was important because it advanced the theory that the problem was one of structural design rather than simple part failure.

Britain's Civil Aviation Board immediately grounded the entire Comet fleet pending extensive reviews and airworthiness certification. For the next five months, the CAB set out on an extensive series of tests to isolate the exact causes of the mysterious crashes. Before

(continued)

testing was complete, one Comet had been tested literally to destruction, another had its fuel tanks ruptured, more than 70 complete test flights were made in a third, and between 50 and 100 test models were broken up. The results of the extensive tests indicated a number of structural and design flaws.

Although the aircraft's designers were convinced that the structure would remain sound for 10,000 flight hours before requiring major structural overhauling, simulations showed unmistakable signs of metal fatigue after the equivalent of only 3,000 flight hours. Experts argued that even when fatigue levels were revised downward to less than 3,000 hours, Comets would not be safe beyond 1,000 flying hours, a ludicrously low figure in terms of the amount of use a commercial airliner is expected to receive. In addition, testing of the fuselage offered disturbing indications of the cause of failure. Specifically, cracks began developing in the corners of the cabin windows, and these cracks were exacerbated by repeated pressurization and depressurization of the cabin. The investigators noted that this result was most pronounced along the rivet lines near the fuselage windows.

Testing also demonstrated that the wings had a low resistance to fatigue. At a number of stages in the tests, serious cracks appeared, starting at the rivet holes near the wheel wells and finally resulting in rivet heads in the top wing surface actually shearing off. Engineers and investigators were finding incontrovertible evidence in the pieces of recovered wreckage that the cause of the sudden disintegration of the aircraft could only have been due to cabin pressure blowout. Engineers suspected that the critical failure of the aircraft occurred following sudden depressurization, when one or more windows were literally blown out of the aircraft. This led to a sudden "gyroscopic moment" as the aircraft nosed down and began its plunge to earth.

Although at the time no one would admit it, the handwriting was on the wall. After two years, in which Comets carried more than 55,000 passengers over 7 million air miles, the Comet 1 was never to fly again. De Havilland had indeed won the race to be first to market with a commercial jet: a race that it would have been better to have never run at all.[13]

Questions

1. How could risk management have aided in the development of the Comet?
2. Discuss the various types of risk (technical, financial, commercial, etc.) in relation to the Comet. Develop a qualitative risk matrix for these risk factors and assess them in terms of probability and consequences.
3. Given that a modified version of the Comet (the Comet IV) was used until recently by the British government as an antisubmarine warfare aircraft, it is clear that the design flaws could have been corrected given enough time. What, then, do you see as de Havilland's critical error in the development of the Comet?
4. Comment on this statement: "Failure is the price we pay for technological advancement."

Case Study 7.2

Nicoll Highway Collapse

On April 20, 2004, part of the Nicoll Highway in Singapore collapsed. Six lanes of the highway disappeared into a 100-foot hole when a tunnel being constructed underneath the highway collapsed. Incredibly, no one was driving on the usually congested highway. The tunnel was part of the underground Circle MRT (Mass Rapid Transport) Line, and the supporting structure for the excavation work had failed.

Four workers were killed in the incident and three others were injured. Rescuers hunted in vain for survivors for three days before efforts were called off. By this stage, it was clear that the danger to the rescue teams far outweighed the likelihood of finding any survivors. The other concern was the fact that the ground around the collapse had to be stabilized in order to ensure that no further collapses would occur.

The immediate reason for the collapse was that the retaining wall holding up the evacuation work was insufficient to hold up the tunnel. Two construction cranes had fallen into the hole and there was evidence of twisted steel support beams.

Initial Response

Authorities in Singapore instituted an inquiry into the incident. They also suspended 20 other excavation projects that were ongoing at the time. These were shut down at great expense and delay as new best-practice codes were put in place. Meanwhile, experts from across the world were brought in to investigate the accident and determine exactly what had happened.

It became clear that a number of factors had contributed to the collapse. Most significant was the fact that the geological findings had been misinterpreted. The structure of the tunnel had been under-designed as a direct result of the fact that the engineers had assumed that the soil's shear strength was greater than it actually was. There were also issues with the structural bracing system being used. The collapse had taken place at a point where the bracing was overloaded, and the system lacked the capacity to redistribute the load between the other supports if this part of the bracing failed. The engineers had underestimated the strut loads.

Apportioning Blame

A Committee of Inquiry in May 2005 was told that the disaster was caused by a failure of a connection between horizontal struts and waling beams. The struts and beams supported the diaphragm walls. The general causes of the collapse had already been agreed upon by the Land Transport Authority (LTA) and Nishimatsu-Lum Chang (NLC), who were the main contractors in the joint venture; the NLC lead designer Maunsell Asia; the project engineer Paul Broome; and L&M and Kori (subcontractors).

LTA's View

It had been found that Nishimatsu-Lum Chang (NLC) was negligentful, reckless, and dishonest during design and construction, according to the LTA. LTA cited that the design errors had begun with the soil analysis at the earliest stages of the project. According to K.Shanmugam, LTA's counsel:

- Analysis of the ground conditions had been based on the use of Method A, which looked at the mechanical properties of drained soil.
- The soil encountered in the deep excavation was in fact highly plastic marine clay, and NLC should have used data for undrained soils.
- In using the wrong method, NLC under predicted the forces that would act on the works being carried out.
- This led to an under-design in the temporary works.
- As a result of this, the system being installed did not have the capacity required.
- The incorrect soil analysis also meant that as the excavations got deeper, the errors and potential failures became more acute.
- The strut connections were under-strength by a factor of two.
- NLC also substituted C channel shaped steel sections for plate stiffeners in an attempt to strengthen the connections.
- However, NLC had tried to cut costs by using scrap material to replace the stiffener plates when they had run out of supplies.

LTA went on to claim that NLC had ignored its own risk assessments. Some of the stiffener plates were already buckling, but NLC had hidden this from LTA in order to keep them from insisting on additional works. NLC was already behind schedule in April 2004 and had incurred late penalties of some $25 million. LTA would have undoubtedly ordered NLC to cease work had it known about the problems, and NLC would have had to bear the cost of the extra delays to the work schedule. Similar struts had failed on two other NLC sites, but NLC had insisted that the problem was in hand and pressured the LTA to allow works to continue. It was therefore LTA's contention that NLC had failed to reveal sufficient information for LTA to make an informed judgment.

NLC's View

NLC was certain that the reason for the collapse was unforeseen downward movement of the diaphragm walls. According to NLC:

- There was a sudden drop in the height of the wall relative to the posts that were supporting the temporary struts.
- This changed the angle at which the struts were connected.
- In turn, this caused the walls to deform and fail.

NLC called this "sway failure," which occurs when violent forces act on the diaphragm walls. The phenomenon had been seen in other parts of the Circle Line, but not at the Nicoll Highway.

NLC maintained that the collapse of the tunnel was not inevitable, but was probably caused because the forced sway mechanism accelerated the failure. NLC admitted that the struts were close to the limit of their performance, but maintained that the loads did not exceed the capacity of the temporary works they had carried out.

Furthermore, NLC expressly countered LTA's suggestion that the soil analysis was the root cause of the disaster, contending:

- It was appropriate to use drained soil data, as it provides a more conservative analysis.
- Although Method A had not been used for deeper excavations in Singapore before, LTA was aware of the method being used and generally agreed with the findings.
- LTA had been specifically briefed about the soil analysis as early as May 2002.
- At that time, LTA's own engineer had stated that other soil analysis types were too conservative.

NLC Admissions

The failure took place at the ninth-level strut connections, which was around 30 meters below the ground and just 3 meters above formation level. As the connections failed, the diaphragm wall deformed. This overloaded the struts which caused them to buckle. In turn, this triggered a gradual and progressive collapse of the tunnel walls. In the event, just one hour elapsed between the failure of the first strut connection and the complete collapse, which triggered devastating damage to the highway.

(continued)

NLC admitted that there had been a failure in the temporary works. They put this down to under-design and inappropriate detail of the connections. They also admitted that their own engineers had misinterpreted the relevant building code, which had resulted in the use of smaller steels than were actually needed for the struts.

The Greatest Engineering Disaster of the Past Decade?

Although the general causes for the collapse of the highway were agreed upon between all parties in 2005, as of May 2012, just one person had been prosecuted for their part in the disaster. Nonetheless, many lessons had been learned. Work on the MRT has commenced once more, but this time far more heavy-duty temporary works are being demanded. Additional robustness in design is now demanded of contractors.

From the outset, braced excavations were used for transport construction projects in Singapore, and each of the MRT stations were constructed using the "bottom-up" method. This meant excavating and propping up the excavations with steel struts. These were supported at their mid-span by king posts and beams across the face of the diaphragm walls. The struts were placed at 3-meter intervals.

Today, the "top-down" method is preferred. This involves constructing the station with a permanent reinforced concrete roof slab. The slab operates rather like a huge strut, which means that struts are not necessary. At a stroke, the time-consuming installation of struts has been eliminated, and the safety risks are far lower.

Government Response

In the immediate aftermath of the inquiry, the Singapore government accepted the findings in full and was quick to announce a series of new legislation that would improve safety standards in the construction industry. The Joint Review Committee (JRC), made up from various government departments, announced that there would be far stiffer penalties for professionals who had shown dereliction of duty and care. A new licensing scheme was introduced for specialist contractors; additional training and the development of a code of practice for deep excavation work were all part of a raft of new legislation.

The Singapore government was convinced that the failures that led to the collapse of the highway and the deaths had been entirely avoidable and were unacceptable. From this point, all major construction projects would be audited in terms of their safety. The government was determined to point out that small, incremental improvements would not bring about the level of safety that is expected of such projects. As a result, it was necessary for several government departments to prioritize the safety issues and bring in sweeping reforms.

Today, with the reforms in place, the pace of work to extend the MRT system is as rapid as before, but far safer. The Downtown Line is seen as the key to the development of the Marina Bay area. The Bayfront Station will be underneath the leisure and entertainment complex, the Integrated Resort. Here the excavations will be at 24 meters. In order to counter the weak soil, thick diaphragm walls have been used, and these have been stiffened by cross walls and slabs. Even the cut and cover tunnels (just like the one that caused the collapse at Nicholl Highway) have up to seven levels of strutting to support them. Lessons were learned, and legislation has been enacted to back them up.[14]

Questions

1. In what ways were the project's planning and scope management appropriate? When did the planners begin knowingly taking unnecessary risks? Discuss the issue of project constraints and other unique aspects of the tunnel in the risk management process. Were these issues taken into consideration? Why or why not?

2. Conduct either a qualitative or quantitative risk assessment on this project. Identify the risk factors that you consider most important for underground tunnel construction. How would you assess the riskiness of this project? Why?

3. What forms of risk mitigation would you consider appropriate for this project?

Internet Exercises

1. Go to http://www.informationweek.com/whitepaper/Management/ROI-TCO/managing-risk-an-integrated-approac-wp1229549889607?articleID=54000027 and access the article on "Managing Risk: An Integrated Approach." Consider the importance of proactive risk management in light of one of the cases at the end of this chapter. How were these guidelines violated by de Havilland or the Tacoma Narrows construction project organization? Support your arguments with information either from the case or from other Web sites.

2. FEMA, the Federal Emergency Management Agency, is responsible for mitigating or responding to natural disasters within the United States. Go to www.fema.gov/about/divisions/mitigation.shtm. Look around the site and scroll down to see examples of projects in which the agency is involved. How does FEMA apply the various mitigation strategies (e.g., accept, minimize, share, and transfer) in its approach to risk management?

3. Go to www.mindtools.com/pages/article/newTMC_07.htm and read the article on managing risks. What does the article say about creating a systematic methodology for managing project risks? How does this methodology compare with the qualitative risk assessment approach taken in this chapter? How does it diverge from our approach?

4. Using the keyword phrase "cases on project risk management," search the Internet to identify and report on a recent example of a project facing significant risks. What steps did the project organization take to first identify and then mitigate the risk factors in this case?

5. Access the free podcast at http://projectmanagement.ittoolbox. com/research/pm-podcast-episode-063-how-do-risk-attitudes-affect-your-project-4947?r=http%3A%2F%2Fresearch.ittoolbox.com%2Fpodcasts%2Fitmgmt%3Fpage%3D4 on risk attitudes on projects. What does the speaker, Cornelius Fichtner, PMP, suggest about the causes of project failures as they relate to issues of risk management?

PMP Certification Sample Questions

1. The project manager has just met with her team to brainstorm some of the problems that could occur on the upcoming project. Today's session was intended to generate possible issues that could arise and get everyone to start thinking in terms of what they should be looking for once the project kicks off. This meeting would be an example of what element in the risk management process?
   a. Risk mitigation
   b. Control and documentation
   c. Risk identification
   d. Analysis of probability and consequences

2. Todd is working on resource scheduling in preparation for the start of a project. There is a potential problem in the works, however, as the new collective bargaining agreement with the company's union has not been concluded. Todd decides to continue working on the resource schedule in anticipation of a satisfactory settlement. Todd's approach would be an example of which method for dealing with risk?
   a. Accept it
   b. Minimize it
   c. Transfer it
   d. Share it

3. A small manufacturer has won a major contract with the U.S. Army to develop a new generation of satellite phone for battlefield applications. Because of the significant technological challenges involved in this project and the company's own size limitations and lack of experience in dealing with the Army on these kinds of contracts, the company has decided to partner with another firm in order to collaborate on developing the technology. This decision would be an example of what kind of response to the risk?
   a. Accept it
   b. Minimize it
   c. Transfer it
   d. Share it

4. All of the following would be considered examples of significant project risks except:
   a. Financial risks
   b. Technical risks
   c. Commercial risks
   d. Legal risks
   e. All are examples of significant potential project risks

5. Suppose your organization used a qualitative risk assessment matrix with three levels each of probability and consequences (high, medium, and low). In evaluating a project's risks, you determine that commercial risks pose a low probability of occurrence but high consequences. On the other hand, legal risks are evaluated as having a high probability of occurrence and medium consequences. If you are interested in prioritizing your risks, which of these should be considered first?
   a. Commercial risk
   b. Legal risk
   c. Both should be considered equally significant
   d. Neither is really much of a threat to this project, so it doesn't matter what order you assign them

Answers: 1. c—Brainstorming meetings are usually created as an effective means to get project team members to begin identifying potential risks; 2. a—Todd is choosing to accept the risk of potential future problems by continuing to work on his resource schedule in anticipation of positive contract talks; 3. d—The firm has decided to share the risk of the new project by partnering with another company; 4. e—All are examples of significant potential project risks; 5. b—Legal risks would be of higher overall significance (high probability, medium consequence) and so should probably be considered first in a prioritization scheme.

INTEGRATED PROJECT

Project Risk Assessment

Conduct a preliminary risk analysis of your project. Use two techniques, one qualitative and one quantitative, in supporting your evaluation of project risk. In order to do this, you will need to:

- Generate a set of likely risk factors.
- Discuss them in terms of probability and consequences.
- Develop preliminary strategies for risk mitigation.

An effective risk analysis will demonstrate clear understanding of relevant project risks, their potential impact (probability and consequences), and preliminary plans for minimizing the negative effects.

SAMPLE RISK ANALYSIS—ABCᴜᴘꜱ, INC.

Among the potential threats or uncertainties contained in this project, the following have been identified:

1. Plant reorganization could take longer than anticipated. Process engineering may be more complicated or unexpected difficulties could arise while the process alterations are underway.
2. A key project team member could be reassigned or no longer able to work on the project. Due to other requirements or top management reshuffling of resources, the project could lose one of its key core team members.
3. The project budget could be cut because of budget cutbacks in other parts of the company. The project budget could be trimmed in the middle of the development cycle.
4. Suppliers might be unable to fulfill contracts. After qualifying vendors and entering into contracts with them, it might be discovered that they cannot fulfill their contractual obligations, requiring the project team and organization to rebid contracts or accept lower-quality supplies.
5. New process designs could be found not to be technically feasible. The process engineers might determine midproject that the project's technical objectives cannot be achieved in the manner planned.
6. New products might not pass QA assessment testing. The project team might discover that the equipment purchased and/or the training that plant personnel received are insufficient to allow for proper quality levels of the output.
7. Vendors could discover our intentions and cut deliveries. Current vendors might determine our intent of eliminating their work and slow down or stop deliveries in anticipation of our company canceling contracts.
8. Marketing might not approve the prototype cups produced. The sales and marketing department might determine that the quality or "presence" of the products we produce are inferior and unlikely to sell in the market.
9. The new factory design might not be approved during government safety inspections. The factory might not meet OSHA requirements.

QUALITATIVE RISK ASSESSMENT

Probability

		Low	Med	High
Consequences	**High**	5		8
	Med	3, 9	2	1
	Low	4	6, 7	

QUANTITATIVE RISK ASSESSMENT

Probability of Failure

- Maturity   (Moderate)   = .50
- Complexity   (Minor)   = .30
- Dependency   (Moderate)   = .50

Consequences of Failure

- Cost   (Significant)   = .70
- Schedule   (Moderate)   = .50
- Reliability   (Minor)   = .30
- Performance   (Moderate)   = .50

P_m	P_c	P_d		P_f
.50	.30	.50		.43
C_c	C_s	C_r	C_p	C_f
.70	.50	.30	.50	.50
Risk Factor = (.43) + (.50) − (.43)(.50) = .715 (High Risk)				

Risk Mitigation Strategies

High Risk	Mitigation Strategy
1. Plant reorganization takes longer than anticipated.	1. Develop a comprehensive project tracking program to maintain schedule.
2. Marketing does not approve the prototype cups produced.	2. Maintain close ties to sales department—keep them in the loop throughout project development and quality control cycles.

Moderate Risk	
3. New process designs are found to not be technically feasible.	3. Assign sufficient time for quality assessment during prototype stage.
4. A key project team member could be reassigned or no longer able to work on the project.	4. Develop a strategy for cross-training personnel on elements of one another's job or identify suitable replacement resources within the organization.

Low Risk	
5. The project budget could be cut.	5. Maintain close contact with top management regarding project status, including earned value and other control documentation.
6. Factory does not pass OSHA inspections.	6. Schedule preliminary inspection midway through project to defuse any concerns.
7. Suppliers are unable to fulfill contracts.	7. Qualify multiple suppliers at prototyping stage.
8. New products do not pass QA assessment testing.	8. Assign team member to work with QA department on interim inspection schedule.
9. Vendors discover our intentions and cut deliveries.	9. Maintain secrecy surrounding project development!

Notes

1. Allen, N., and Leonard, T. (2010). "Haiti earthquake: Exodus for Port-au-Prince as time runs out," www.telegraph.co.uk/news/worldnews/centralamericaandthecaribbean/haiti/7046878/Haiti-earthquake-exodus-from-Port-au-Prince-as-time-runs-out.html; OCHA Flash Appeal. (2010). *Haiti Earthquake Flash Appeal, 2010*; Padgett, T. (2010, February 22). "Haiti PM: We can rise out of our postquake squalor," *Time*, www.time.com/time/world/article/0,8599,1967003,00.html; Rencorcet, N., et al. (2010, July). "Haiti earthquake response: Context analysis, ALNAP and prevention consortium," London, www.alnap.org/pool/files/haiti-context-analysis-final.pdf; "2010 Haiti earthquake." (2010). http://en.wikipedia.org/wiki/2010_Haiti_earthquake; "Haiti devastated by massive earthquake." (2010). http://news.bbc.co.uk/2/hi/8455629.stm.

2. Wideman, M. (1998). "Project risk management," in Pinto, J. K. (Ed.), *The Project Management Institute's Project Management Handbook*. San Francisco, CA: Jossey-Bass, pp. 138–58.

3. Chapman, C. B., and Ward, S. C. (1997). *Project Risk Management: Process, Techniques, and Insights*. Chichester, UK: John Wiley; Kahkonen, K., and Artto, K. A. (1997). *Managing Risks in Projects*. London: E & FN Spon.

4. Chapman, R. J. (1998). "The effectiveness of working group risk identification and assessment techniques," *International Journal of Project Management*, 16(6): 333–44.

5. Martin, P., and Tate, K. (1998). "Team-based risk assessment: Turning naysayers and saboteurs into supporters," *PMNetwork*, 12(2): 35–38.

6. Jaafari, A. (2001). "Management of risks, uncertainties and opportunities on projects: Time for a fundamental shift," *International Journal of Project Management*, 19(2): 89–102.

7. Graves, R. (2000). "Qualitative risk assessment," *PMNetwork*, 14(10): 61–66; Pascale, S., Troilo, L., and Lorenz, C. (1998). "Risk analysis: How good are your decisions?" *PMNetwork*, 12(2): 25–28.

8. "MCA spent millions on Carly Hennessy—Haven't heard of her?" (2002, February 26). *Wall Street Journal*, pp. A1, A10.

9. Hamburger, D. H. (1990). "The project manager: Risk taker and contingency planner," *Project Management Journal*, 21(4): 11–16; Levine, H. A. (1995). "Risk management for dummies: Managing schedule, cost and technical risk, and contingency," *PMNetwork*, 9(10): 31–33.

10. http://blogs.wsj.com/chinarealtime/2009/06/29/shanghai-building-collapses-nearly-intact/; http://news.bbc.co.uk/2/hi/8123559.stm; www.telegraph.co.uk/news/worldnews/asia/china/5685963/Nine-held-over-Shanghai-building-collapse.html.

11. Chapman, C. B. (1997). "Project risk analysis and management—The PRAM generic process," *International Journal of Project Management*, 15(5): 273–81; Chapman, C. B., and Ward, S. (2003). *Project Risk Management: Processes, Techniques and Insights*, 2nd ed. Chichester, UK: John Wiley.

12. Artto, K. A. (1997). "Fifteen years of project risk management applications—Where are we going?" in Kahkonen, K., and Artto, K. A. (Eds.), *Managing Risks in Projects*. London: E & FN Spon, pp. 3–14; Williams, T. M. (1995). "A classified bibliography of recent research relating to project risk management," *European Journal of Operations Research*, 85: 18–38.

13. "Fatigue blamed in Comet crashes." (1954, October 25). *Aviation Week*, 61: 17–18; "Comet verdict upholds RAE findings." (1955, February 21). *Aviation Week*, 62: 16–17; Hull, S. (1954, November 1). "Comet findings may upset design concepts," *Aviation Week*, 61: 16–18; "Fall of a Comet." (1953, May 11). *Newsweek*, 41: 49; "A column of smoke." (1954, January 18). *Time*, 63: 35–36; "Death of the Comet I." (1954, April 19). *Time*, 63: 31–32.

14. "IAP class probes Singapore highway collapse," http://web.mit.edu/newsoffice/2008/collapse-highway-0201.html; "Nicoll highway collapse," www.channelnewsasia.com/nicoll/index.htm; "Nicoll highway collapse: Evaluation of geotechnical factors affecting design of excavation support system," http://kb.plaxis.nl/sites/kb.plaxis.nl/files/kb-publications/AJWhittle_RVDavis_2006.pdf; "The Nicoll highwaycollapse," www.hssmge.gr/HIGHT_The%20Nicoll%20Highway%20Collapse.pdf.

Cost Estimation and Budgeting

Chapter Outline

Chapter Objectives

After completing this chapter, you should be able to:

1. Understand the various types of common project costs.

2. Recognize the difference between various forms of project costs.

3. Apply common forms of cost estimation for project work, including ballpark estimates and definitive estimates.

4. Understand the advantages of parametric cost estimation and the application of learning curve models in cost estimation.

5. Discern the various reasons why project cost estimation is often done poorly.

6. Apply both top-down and bottom-up budgeting procedures for cost management.

7. Understand the uses of activity-based budgeting and time-phased budgets for cost estimation and control.

8. Recognize the appropriateness of applying contingency funds for cost estimation.

PROJECT MANAGEMENT BODY OF KNOWLEDGE CORE CONCEPTS COVERED IN THIS CHAPTER

1. Estimate Costs (PMBoK sec. 7.1)
2. Determine Budget (PMBoK sec. 7.2)
3. Control Costs (PMBoK sec. 7.3)

PROJECT PROFILE

Cost Overruns Continue to Dog Important Projects

It seems almost a routine fact of life that critical projects across diverse settings, national boundaries, and serving different purposes continue to provide a regular supply of problems, especially in the area of cost overruns. No matter how well supported projects are within their organizations and how carefully cost estimation and project budgeting attempt to plan for and track critical expenditures, many projects get into serious trouble through a seeming inability to rein in costs. As we can imagine, the end result is often projects that get canceled or are so severely affected by cost cutting that they fail to deliver their expected results, either to the sponsoring organization or in the commercial marketplace. Here is a short list of some recent projects that have suffered through poor cost control, with their current status either uncertain or at serious risk.

1. *James Webb Space Telescope*—NASA's showcase project is in trouble due to continuous cost overruns that are pointing to serious deficiencies in the agency's program oversight ability. The JWST is a large infrared space telescope with a 6.5-meter foldable mirror and a deployable sunshield about the size of a tennis court (see Figure 8.1). It was conceived in 1996 as a successor to the famous Hubble Space Telescope and is a far more sophisticated tool for modern astrophysics. The JWST is designed to be launched into deep space, to a "gravitationally stable point" approximately 1.5 million kilometers from Earth.

    Although the goals of JWST are laudable, the practical reality is that the program has been a runaway from nearly the beginning, and as it moves forward, it is in danger of wrecking NASA's overall budget. During a late 2010 news conference, NASA released the findings of an independent review that found the JWST will cost some $1.5 billion more than its current $5 billion life cycle cost estimate, and that the observatory's launch,

Photoshot/Newscom

FIGURE 8.1 James Webb Space Telescope

previously slated for June 2014, will not occur before September 2015. NASA has budgeted about $600 million to operate the JWST over the following five years. The Independent Comprehensive Review Panel attributed JWST cost growth to poor management and inadequate funding reserves needed to develop, launch, and operate the next-generation flagship astronomy mission.

The net result of poor cost control presents NASA with a serious dilemma: continue to support evelopment of the JWST, in which so much has already been invested, or use their budget to maintain their other currently operating satellite systems. More and more, it is beginning to appear that NASA cannot fulfill both goals. Alan Stern, a former associate administrator for NASA's Science Mission Directorate, said the JWST's cost growth could ravage the agency's $1.1 billion annual astrophysics budget, 40% of which is already consumed by JWST development. "Are we going to turn off all the many existing astrophysics satellites and kill the support to analyze the data from them and stop building anything else, just so JWST can continue to overrun?" Stern said. "That's the question that the astrophysics community has to ask of itself, and that NASA should be asking."

According to the review panel, Congress would need to add about $250 million to NASA's $444 million request for the JWST in 2011 alone just to maintain the newly projected 2015 launch date. Another $250 million would be needed in 2012, in addition to the agency's current projection of $380 million for the program in that year. NASA's goal of pursuing the JWST without proper oversight and cost control appears poised to have a dangerous spillover effect on their entire operating capability and, once more, calls into question governmental agencies' ability to maintain adequate budget controls for large projects.

2. *Connecting for Health,* Britain's Electronic Medical Records Failure—In 2002, England embarked on an ambitious program in support of its national health care system (NHS) toward a single, centrally mandated IT system to develop and maintain electronic medical records for patients and to connect 30,000 doctors to 300 hospitals, providing secure and audited access to these records by authorized health professionals. Originally expected to cost £2.3 billion over three years, in June 2006 the total cost of Connecting for Health was estimated by the National Audit Office to be £12.4bn over 10 years, and the British Computer Society concluded in 2006 that "the central costs incurred by NHS are such that, so far, the value for money from services deployed is poor." Officials involved in the program have been quoted in the media estimating the final cost to be as high as £20bn, indicating a cost overrun of 440% to 770%.

Among the problems the project has had to deal with are a continued failure to demonstrate any real clinical benefits from the system, resistance of local health care providers to using it, serious data security risks, and a "risk-shifting" model that includes a reimbursement scheme for the IT providers that only kicks in when all problems have been demonstrated to be fixed. Put together, these problems highlight an IT system that has not been clearly explained to the public, does not perform its role well, is resisted by doctors, is not secure, and has steadily lost credibility with both the public and the government as delays and higher costs continue to pile up. In April 2007, the Public Accounts Committee of the House of Commons issued a damning 175-page report on the program. The committee chair, Edward Leigh, claimed, "This is the biggest IT project in the world and it is turning into the biggest disaster." The report concluded that, despite a probable expenditure of £20bn (20 billion pounds), "at the present rate of progress it is unlikely that significant clinical benefits will be delivered by the end of the contract period."

Connecting for Health continues to stagger along, through huge schedule delays and budget increases. Essentially, the British government has too much invested in the project (in money and personal prestige) to cancel it, but lacks the means to move it forward any faster. A report by the King's Fund in 2007 criticized the government's "apparent reluctance to audit and evaluate the program," questioning their failure to develop a strategy where benefits are likely to outweigh costs. A later report by the Public Accounts Committee in 2009 called the risks to the successful deployment of the system "as serious as ever," adding that key deliverables at the heart of the project were "way off the pace," and concluding that "essential systems are late, or, when deployed, do not meet expectations of clinical staff."

3. The FBI's *Virtual Case File*—Originally begun in 2000, the Virtual Case File (VCF) project was supposed to automate the FBI's paper-based work environment, allow agents and intelligence analysts to share vital investigative information, and replace the obsolete Automated Case Support (ACS) system. Instead, the FBI claims, the VCF's contractor, Science Applications International Corp. (SAIC) in San Diego, delivered 700,000 lines of code so bug-ridden and functionally off-target that by mid-2005, the bureau had to scrap the $170 million project, including $105 million worth of unusable code. However, various government and independent reports show that the FBI—lacking IT management and technical expertise—shares the blame for the project's failure.

In a project audit, released in 2005, the U.S. Department of Justice's Inspector General identified eight factors that contributed to the VCF's failure, including among them poorly defined and slowly evolving design requirements; overly ambitious schedules; and the lack of a plan to guide hardware purchases, network deployments, and software development for the bureau. "The archaic Automated Case Support system— which some agents have avoided using—is cumbersome, inefficient, and limited in its capabilities, and does

(continued)

not manage, link, research, analyze, and share information as effectively or timely as needed," the report noted. "[T]he continued delays in developing the VCF affect the FBI's ability to carry out its critical missions."

Unfortunately, it seems that things have not improved much. After scrapping the VCF project, the FBI set about working on a "newer and better" case management system named Sentinel. The Sentinel project, which it was hoped would fulfill the role originally slated for the canceled VCF, was awarded to Lockheed Martin. With a budget of about $450 million, the FBI expected that it had learned from its errors in pursuing the VCF and would be able to work with Lockheed to quickly digitize its record-keeping system. Unfortunately, by late 2010, the Sentinel project was in just as poor shape as its predecessor. So bad had the project fallen behind budget and schedule that the FBI fired Lockheed Martin in September and assumed control of the project themselves. The U.S. Department of Justice's Office of the Inspector General (OIG) evaluated the new Sentinel at the end of the year and issued a highly critical report, reading in part: "Our review found that as of August 2010, after spending about $405 million of the $451 million budgeted for the Sentinel project, the FBI has delivered only two of Sentinel's four phases to its agents and analysts." The report continued: "Moreover, we believe that the most challenging development work for Sentinel still remains. By July 2010 Sentinel was intended to generate and securely process 18 paperless case-related forms through the review and approval process. Sentinel now only has the capability to generate and process 4 of the 18 forms. Moreover, even these four forms still are not fully automated."

The FBI strongly contests the OIG's assessment of Sentinel, insisting that after firing Lockheed, they would be capable of completing the project within the original budget and time frame using their own in-house expertise. Still, an independent assessment conducted in July 2010 at the FBI's request estimated that completing Sentinel under the FBI's current development approach would, at a minimum, cost an additional $351 million and take an additional 6 years.[1]

8.1 COST MANAGEMENT

Cost management is extremely important for running successful projects. The management of costs, in many ways, reflects the project organization's strategic goals, mission statement, and business plan. *Cost management* has been defined to encompass data collection, cost accounting, and cost control,[2] and it involves taking financial-report information and applying it to projects at finite levels of accountability in order to maintain a clear sense of money management for the project.[3] Cost accounting and cost control serve as the chief mechanisms for identifying and maintaining control over project costs.

Cost estimation is a natural first step in determining whether or not a project is viable; that is, can the project be done profitably? **Cost estimation** processes create a reasonable budget baseline for the project and identify project resources (human and material) as well, creating a time-phased budget for their involvement in the project. In this way, cost estimation and project budgeting are linked hand in hand: The estimates of costs for various components of the project are developed into a comprehensive project budgeting document that allows for ongoing project tracking and cost control.

During the development stage of the proposal, the project contractor begins cost estimation by identifying all possible costs associated with the project and building them into the initial proposal. While a simplified model of cost estimation might only require a bottom-line final figure, most customers will wish to see a higher level of detail in how the project has been priced out, that is, an itemization of all relevant costs. For example, a builder could simply submit to a potential home buyer a price sheet that lists only the total cost of building the house, but it is likely that the buyer will ask for some breakdown of the price to identify what costs will be incurred where. Some of the more common sources of project costs include:

1. *Labor*—Labor costs are those associated with hiring and paying the various personnel involved in developing the project. These costs can become complex, as a project requires the services of various classifications of workers (skilled, semiskilled, laborers) over time. At a minimum, a project cost estimation must consider the personnel to be employed, salary and hourly rates, and any overhead issues such as pension or health benefits. A preliminary estimate of workers' exposure to the project in terms of hours committed is also needed for a reasonable initial estimate of personnel costs.

2. *Materials*—Materials costs apply to the specific equipment and supplies the project team will require in order to complete project tasks. For building projects, materials costs are quite large and run the gamut from wood, siding, insulation, and paint to shrubbery and paving. For many other projects,

the actual materials costs may be relatively small, for example, the purchase of a software package that allows rapid compiling of computer code. Likewise, many projects in the service industries may involve little or no materials costs whatsoever. Some materials costs can be charged against general company overhead; for example, the use of the firm's mainframe computer may be charged to the project on an "as used" basis.

3. *Subcontractors*—When subcontractors provide resources (and in the case of consultants, expertise) for the project, their costs must be factored into the preliminary cost estimate for the project and be reflected in its budget. One subcontractor cost, for example, could be a charge to hire a marketing communications professional to design the project's promotional material; another might be costs for an industrial designer to create attractive product packaging.

4. *Equipment and facilities*—Projects may be developed away from the firm's home office, requiring members of the project team to work "off site." Firms commonly include rental of equipment or office facilities as a charge against the cost of the project. For example, oil companies routinely send four- or five-person site teams to work at the headquarters of major subcontractors for extended periods. The rental of any equipment or facility space becomes a cost against the project.

5. *Travel*—If necessary, expenses that are related to business travel (car rentals, airfare, hotels, and meals) can be applied to the project as an up-front charge.

Another way to examine project costs is to investigate the nature of the costs themselves. Among the various forms of project costs are those related to type (direct or indirect), frequency of occurrence (recurring or nonrecurring), opportunity to be adjusted (fixed or variable), and schedule (normal or expedited). We will examine each of these types of project costs in turn in this chapter.

Direct Versus Indirect Costs

Direct costs are those clearly assigned to the aspect of the project that generated the cost. Labor and materials may be the best examples. All labor costs associated with the workers who actually build a house are considered direct costs. Some labor costs, however, might not be viewed as direct costs for the project. For example, the costs of support personnel, such as the project's cost accountant or other project management resources, may not be allocated directly, particularly when their duties consist of servicing or overseeing multiple, simultaneous projects. In a nonproject setting such as manufacturing, it is common for workers to be assigned to specific machinery that operates on certain aspects of the fabrication or production process. In this case, labor costs are directly charged against work orders for specific parts or activities.

The formula for determining total direct labor costs for a project is straightforward:

$$(\text{Direct labor rate})\,(\text{Total labor hours}) = \text{Total direct labor costs}$$

The direct costs of materials are likewise relatively easy to calculate, as long as there is a clear understanding of what materials are necessary to complete the project. For example, the direct costs of building a bridge or hosting a conference dinner for 300 guests can be estimated with fair accuracy. These costs can be applied directly to the project in a systematic way; for example, all project purchase orders (POs) can be recorded upon receipt of bills of materials or sales and applied to the project as a direct cost.

Indirect costs, on the other hand, generally are linked to two features: overhead, and selling and general administration. Overhead costs are perhaps the most common form of indirect costs and can be one of the more complex forms in estimating. Overhead costs include all sources of indirect materials, utilities, taxes, insurance, property and repairs, depreciation on equipment, and health and retirement benefits for the labor force. Common costs that fall into the selling and general administration category include advertising, shipping, salaries, sales and secretarial support, sales commissions, and similar costs. Tracing and linking these costs to projects is not nearly as straightforward as applying direct costs, and the procedures used vary by organization. Some organizations charge a flat rate for all overhead costs, relative to the direct costs of the project. For example, some universities that conduct research projects for the federal government use a percentage multiplier to add administrative and overhead indirect costs to the proposal. The most common range for such indirect multiplier rates is from 20% to over 50% on top of direct costs. Other firms allocate indirect costs project by project, based on individual analysis. Whichever approach is preferred, it is important to emphasize that all project cost estimates include both direct and indirect cost allocations.

EXAMPLE 8.1 **Developing Direct Labor Costs**

Suppose that we are attempting to develop reasonable cost estimation for the use of a senior programmer for a software project. The programmer is paid an annual salary of $75,000, which translates to an hourly rate of approximately $37.50/hour. The programmer's involvement in the new project is expected to be 80 hours over the project's life. Remember, however, that we also need to consider overhead charges. For example, the company pays comprehensive health benefits and retirement, charges the use of plant and equipment against the project, and so forth. In order to cover these indirect costs, the firm uses an overhead multiplier of 65%. Employing an overhead multiplier is sometimes referred to as the *fully loaded* rate for direct labor costs. Thus, the most accurate calculation of the programmer's charge against the project would look like this:

Hourly rate		Hours needed		Overhead charge		Total direct labor cost
($37.50)	×	(80)	×	(1.65)	=	$4,950

Some have argued that a more realistic estimate of total direct labor costs for each person assigned to the project would reflect the fact that no one truly works a full 8-hour day as part of the job. An allowance for a reasonable degree of personal time during the workday is simply recognition of the need to make personal calls, have coffee breaks, walk the hallways to the restroom, and so forth. Meredith and Mantel (2003) have argued that if such personal time is not included in the original total labor cost estimate, a multiplier of 1.12 should be used to reflect this charge, increasing the direct labor cost of our senior programmer to:[4]

Hourly rate		Hours needed		Overhead charge		Personal Time		Total direct labor cost
($37.50)	×	(80)	×	(1.65)	×	(1.12)	=	$5,544

One other point to consider regarding the use of overhead (indirect costs) involves the manner in which overhead may be differentially applied across job categories. In some firms, for example, a distinction is made between salaried and nonsalaried employees. Thus, two or more levels of overhead percentage may be used, depending upon the category of personnel to which they are applied. Suppose that a company applied a lower overhead rate (35%) to hourly workers, reflecting the lesser need for contributions to retirement or health insurance. The calculated direct labor cost for these personnel (even assuming a charge for personal time) would resemble the following:

Hourly rate		Hours needed		Overhead charge		Personal Time		Total direct labor cost
($12.00)	×	(80)	×	(1.35)	×	(1.12)	=	$1,451.52

The decision to include personal time requires input from the project's client. Whichever approach is taken, a preliminary total labor cost budget table can be constructed when the process is completed, as shown in Table 8.1. This table assumes a small project with only five project team personnel, whose direct labor costs are to be charged against the project without a personal time charge included.

Recurring Versus Nonrecurring Costs

Costs can also be examined in terms of the frequency with which they occur; they can be recurring or nonrecurring. **Nonrecurring costs** might be those associated with charges applied once at the beginning or end of the project, such as preliminary marketing analysis, personnel training, or outplacement services. **Recurring costs** are those that typically continue to operate over the project's life cycle. Most labor, material, logistics, and sales costs are considered recurring because some budgetary charge is applied against them throughout significant portions of the project development cycle. In budget management and cost estimation, it is necessary to highlight recurring versus nonrecurring charges. As we will see, this becomes particularly important as we begin to develop time-phased budgets—those budgets that apply the project's baseline schedule to projected project expenditures.

TABLE 8.1 Preliminary Cost Estimation for Direct Labor

Personnel	Title	Salary (Hourly)	Hours Needed	Overhead Rate Applied	Total Direct Labor Cost
Linda	Lead Architect	$35/hr	250	1.60	$14,000.00
Alex	Drafter—Junior	$20/hr	100	1.60	3,200.00
Jessica	Designer—Intern	$8.50/hr	80	1.30	884.00
Todd	Engineer—Senior	$27.50/hr	160	1.60	7,040.00
Thomas	Foreman	$18.50/hr	150	1.30	3,607.50
Total					$28,731.50

Fixed Versus Variable Costs

An alternative designation for applying project costs is to identify fixed and variable costs in the project budget. **Fixed costs,** as their title suggests, do not vary with respect to their usage.[5] For example, when leasing capital equipment or other project hardware, the leasing price is likely not to go up or down with the amount of usage the equipment receives. Whether a machine is used for 5 hours or 50, the cost of its rental is the same. When entering fixed-rate contracts for equipment, a common decision point for managers is whether the equipment will be used sufficiently to justify its cost. **Variable costs** are those that accelerate or increase through usage; that is, the cost is in direct proportion to the usage level. Suppose, for example, we used an expensive piece of drilling equipment for a mining operation. The equipment degrades significantly as a result of use in a particularly difficult geographical location. In this case, the variable costs of the machinery are in direct proportion to its use. It is common, in many cases, for projects to have a number of costs that are based on fixed rates and others that are variable and subject to significant fluctuations either upward or downward.

Normal Versus Expedited Costs

Normal costs refer to those incurred in the routine process of working to complete the project according to the original, planned schedule agreed to by all project stakeholders at the beginning of the project. Certainly, this planned schedule may be very aggressive, involving extensive overtime charges in order to meet the accelerated schedule; nevertheless, these costs are based on the baseline project plan. **Expedited costs** are unplanned costs incurred when steps are taken to speed up the project's completion. For example, suppose the project has fallen behind schedule and the decision is made to "crash" certain project activities in the hopes of regaining lost time. Among the **crashing** costs could be expanded use of overtime, hiring additional temporary workers, contracting with external resources or organizations for support, and incurring higher costs for transportation or logistics in speeding up materials deliveries.

All of the above methods for classifying costs are linked together in Table 8.2.[6] Across the top rows are the various classification schemes, based on cost type, frequency, adjustment, and schedule. The left-side column indicates some examples of costs incurred in developing a project. Here we see how costs typically relate to multiple classification schemes; for example, direct labor is seen as a direct cost, which is also recurring, fixed, and normal. A building lease, on the other hand, may be classified as an indirect (or overhead) cost, which is recurring, fixed, and normal. In this way, it is possible to apply most project costs to multiple classifications.

TABLE 8.2 Cost Classifications

Costs	Type Direct	Type Indirect	Frequency Recurring	Frequency Nonrecurring	Adjustment Fixed	Adjustment Variable	Schedule Normal	Schedule Expedited
Direct Labor	X		X		X		X	
Building Lease		X	X		X		X	
Expediting Costs	X			X		X		X
Material	X		X			X	X	

8.2 COST ESTIMATION

Estimating project costs is a challenging process that can resemble an art form as much as a science. Two important project principles that can almost be called laws are at work in cost estimation. First, the more clearly you define the project's various costs in the beginning, the less chance there is of making estimating errors. Second, the more accurate your initial cost estimations, the greater the likelihood of preparing a project budget that accurately reflects reality for the project and the greater your chances of completing the project within budget estimates.

One key for developing project cost estimates is to first recognize the need to cost out the project on a disaggregated basis; that is, to break the project down by deliverable and work package as a method for estimating task-level costs. For example, rather than attempt to create a cost estimate for completing a deliverable of four work packages, it is typically more accurate to first identify the costs for completing each work package individually and then create a deliverable cost estimate, as Table 8.3 illustrates.

Companies use a number of methods to estimate project costs, ranging from the highly technical and quantitative to the more qualitative approaches. Among the more common cost estimation methods are the following:[7]

1. **Ballpark estimates**—Sometimes referred to as *order of magnitude* estimates, ballpark estimates are typically used when either information or time is scarce. Companies often use them as preliminary estimates for resource requirements or to determine if a competitive bid can be attempted for a project contract. For example, a client may file an RFQ (request for quote) for competitive bids on a project, stating a very short deadline. Managers would have little time to make a completely accurate assessment of the firm's qualifications or requirements, but they could still request ballpark estimates from their personnel to determine if they should even attempt to bid the proposal through a more detailed analysis. The unofficial rule of thumb for ballpark estimates is to aim for an accuracy of ±30%. With such a wide variance plus or minus, it should be clear that ballpark estimates are not intended to substitute for more informed and detailed cost estimation.

2. **Comparative estimates**—Comparative estimates are based on the assumption that historical data can be used as a frame of reference for current estimates on similar projects. For example, Boeing Corporation routinely employs a process known as **parametric estimation,** in which managers develop detailed estimates of current projects by taking older work and inserting a multiplier to account for the impact of inflation, labor and materials increases, and other reasonable direct costs. This parametric estimate, when carefully performed, allows Boeing to create highly accurate estimates when costing out the work and preparing detailed budgets for new aircraft development projects. Even in cases where the technology is new or represents a significant upgrade over old technologies, it is often possible to gain valuable insight into the probable costs of development, based on historical examples.

   Boeing is not the only firm that has successfully employed parametric cost estimation. Figure 8.2 shows a data graph of the parametric estimation relating to development of the Concorde aircraft in the 1960s. The Concorde represented such a unique and innovative airframe design that it was difficult to estimate the amount of design time required to complete the schematics for the airplane. However, using parametric estimation and based on experiences with other recently developed aircraft, a linear relationship was discovered between the number of fully staffed weeks (Concorde referred to this time as "manweeks") needed to design the aircraft and its projected cruising speed. That is, the figure demonstrated a direct relationship between the cruising speed of the aircraft and the amount of design time

TABLE 8.3 Disaggregating Project Activities to Create Reasonable Cost Estimates

Project Activities	Estimated Cost
Deliverable 1040—Site Preparation	
Work Package 1041—Surveying	$ 3,000
Work Package 1042—Utility line installation	15,000
Work Package 1043—Site clearing	8,000
Work Package 1044—Debris removal	3,500
Total cost for Deliverable 1040	$29,500

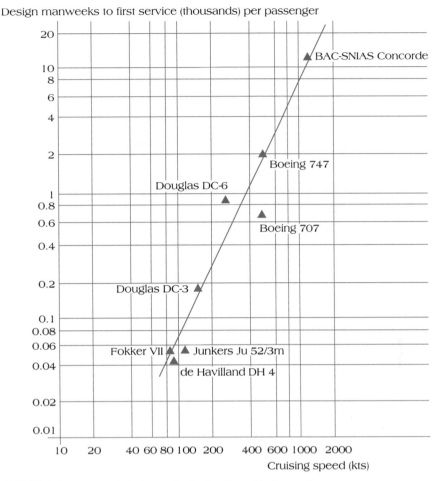

Design manweeks to first service (thousands) per passenger

Cruising speed (kts)

FIGURE 8.2   Parametric Estimate for Design Costs for Concorde

Note: Plot of design effort versus cruising speed for significant commercial aircraft types.

necessary to complete the schematics. Using these values, it was possible to make a reasonably accurate cost projection of the expected budget for design, demonstrating that in spite of significant changes in airplane design over the past decades, the relationship between cruising speed and design effort had held remarkably steady.

Effective comparative estimates depend upon some important supplementary sources including a history of similar projects and a detailed archive of project data that includes the technical, budgetary, and other cost information. Adjusting costs to account for inflation simply becomes a necessary step in the process. The key to making comparative estimates meaningful lies in the comparability to previous project work. It makes little sense to compare direct labor costs for two projects when the original was done in a foreign country with different wage rates, overhead requirements, and so forth. Although some argue that comparative cost estimation cannot achieve a degree of accuracy closer than ±15%, in some circumstances the estimate may be much more accurate and useful than that figure indicates.

3. **Feasibility estimates**—These estimates are based as a guideline on real numbers, or figures derived after the completion of the preliminary project design work. Following initial scope development, it is possible to request quotes from suppliers and other subcontractors with a greater degree of confidence, particularly as it is common to engage in some general scheduling processes to begin to determine the working project baseline. Feasibility estimates are routinely used for construction projects, where there are published materials cost tables that can give reasonably accurate cost estimates for a wide range of project activities based on an estimate of the quantities involved. Because they are developed farther down the life cycle, feasibility estimates are often expressed in terms of a degree of accuracy of ±10%.

4. **Definitive estimates**—These estimates can be given only upon the completion of most design work, at a point when the scope and capabilities of the project are quite well understood. At this point all major purchase orders have been submitted based on known prices and availabilities, there is little or no wiggle room in the project's specifications, and the steps to project completion have been identified and a comprehensive project plan is in place. Because it is understood that cost estimation should naturally improve with time, as more information becomes available and fewer project unknowns remain unresolved, definitive estimates should accurately reflect the expected cost of the project, barring unforeseen circumstances, at completion. Hence, definitive estimates can be expected to have an accuracy of ±5%. We saw in previous chapters that some projects may offer very thin profit margins; for example, in the case of fixed-cost contracts, the project organization assumes almost all risk for completing the project according to originally agreed-on contract terms. As a result, the better the job we do in estimating costs, the more likely we will be to maintain the profit margin contracted.

Which cost estimation approach should a project organization employ? The answer to this question presupposes knowledge of the firm's industry (e.g., software development vs. construction), ability to account for and manage most project cost variables, the firm's history of successful project management, the number of similar projects the firm has completed in the past, the knowledge and resourcefulness of project managers, and the company's budgeting requirements. In some instances (e.g., extremely innovative research and development projects), it may be impossible to create cost estimates with more than a ±20% degree of accuracy. On the other hand, in some projects such as events management (e.g., managing a conference and banquet), it may be reasonable to prepare definitive budgets quite early in the project.

The key to cost estimation lies in a realistic appraisal of the type of project one is undertaking, the speed with which various cost estimates must be created, and the comfort level top management has with cost estimation error. If the information is available, it is reasonable to expect the project team to provide as accurate a cost estimate as possible, as early in the project as possible. Figure 8.3 shows a sample project cost estimation form.

Learning Curves in Cost Estimation

Cost estimation, particularly for labor hours, often takes as its assumption a steady or uniform rate at which work is done. In the case of having to perform multiple activities, the amount of time necessary to complete the first activity is not significantly different from the time necessary to complete the nth activity. For example, in software development, it may be considered standard practice to estimate each activity cost independently of other, related activities with which the programmer is involved. Therefore, in the case of a programmer required to complete four work assignments, each involving similar but different coding activities, many cost estimators will simply apply a direct, multiplicative rule-of-thumb estimate:

		Number of times	
Cost of activity		activity is repeated	Total cost estimate
($8,000)	×	(4)	=	$32,000

When we calculate that each actual coding sequence is likely to take approximately 40 hours of work, we can create the more formal direct cost budget line for this resource. Assuming an overhead rate of .60 and a cost per hour for the programmer's services of $35/hour, we can come up with a direct billing charge of:

| Wage | | Unit | | Overhead Rate | | Hours/Unit | |
| ($35/hr) | × | (4 iterations) | × | (1.60) | × | (40 hours) | = | $8,960 |

Although this rule of thumb is simple, it may also be simplistic. For example, is it reasonable to suppose that in performing similar activities, the time necessary to do a coding routine the fourth time will take as long as it took to do it the first time? Or is it more reasonable to suppose that the time needed (and hence, cost) of the fourth iteration should be somewhat shorter than the earlier times?

These questions go to the heart of a discussion of how **learning curves** affect project cost estimation.[8] In short, experience and common sense teach us that repetition of activities often leads to reduction in the time necessary to complete the activity over time. Some research, in fact, supports the idea that performance improves by a fixed percentage each time production doubles.[9]

ESTIMATE AND QUOTATION SHEET				
Project No.	Description:		Type No.	
Work Package No.	Task No.		Estimate No.	
Work Package Description:		Task Description:		
Internal Labor				
Skill	Category	Rate	Hours	Cost
Senior Test Engineer	TE4	18.50	40	$ 740.00
Test Engineer	TE3	14.00	80	1,120.00
Fitter	PF4	13.30	30	399.00
Drafter	DR2	15.00	15	225.00
Drawing Checker	DR3	16.50	3	49.50
Subtotal, Hours and Costs			168	$2,533.50
Labor Contingency (10%)			17	254.00
Total Labor, Hours and Costs			185	$2,787.50
Overhead (80%)				2,230.00
Gross Labor Cost				$5,017.50
Bought-Out Costs				
Materials (Specify): Bolts plus cleating material				$ 20.00
Finished Goods (Specify): N/A				
Services and Facilities: Hire test house; instrumentation plus report				12,300.00
Subcontract Manufacture (Specify): Fixture and bolt modification				250.00
Subtotal				$12,570.00
Contingency (15%)				1,885.50
Total Bought-Out Costs				$14,455.50
Expenses				
Specify: On-site accommodation plus traveling				$ 340.00
Total Bought-Out Costs and Expenses				$14,795.50
Profit %: N/A				
Total Quoted Sum: Gross Labor plus Bought-Out Costs and Expenses				$19,813.00
Compiled by:				
Approved:			Date	

FIGURE 8.3   **Sample Project Activity Cost Estimating Sheet**

Let us assume, for example, that the time necessary to code a particular software routine is estimated at 20 hours of work for the first iteration. Doing the coding work a second time requires only 15 hours. The difference between the first and second iteration suggests a learning rate of .75 (15/20). We can now apply that figure to estimates of cost for additional coding iterations. When output is doubled from the first two routines to the required four, the time needed to complete the fourth unit is now estimated to take:

$$15 \text{ hrs. } (.75) = 11.25 \text{ hours}$$

These time and cost estimates follow a well-defined formula,[10] which is the time required to produce the steady state unit of output, and is represented as:

$$Y_x = aX^b$$

where

Y_x = the time required for the steady state, x, unit of output

a = the time required for the initial unit of output

X = the number of units to be produced to reach the steady state

b = the slope of the learning curve, represented as: log decimal learning rate/log 2

Assume the need to conduct a project cost estimation in the case of construction, where one resource will be tasked to perform multiple iterations of a similar nature (e.g., fitting, riveting, and squaring). The worker must do a total of 15 of these activities to reach the steady state. Also assume that the time estimated to perform the last iteration (the steady state) is 1 hour, and we know from past experience the learning rate for this highly repetitive activity is .60. In calculating the time necessary to complete the first activity, we would apply these values to the formula to determine the value of a, the time needed to complete the task the first time:

$$b = \log 0.60/\log 2$$
$$= -0.2219/0.301$$
$$= -0.737$$

$$1\,\text{hr.} = a(15)^{-0.737}$$
$$a = 7.358\,\text{hours}$$

Note that the difference between the first and fifteenth iteration of this activity represents a change in duration estimation (and therefore, cost) from over 7 hours for the first time the task is performed to 1 hour for the steady state. The difference this learning curve factor makes in project cost estimates can be significant, particularly when a project involves many instances of repetitive work or large "production runs" of similar activities.

EXAMPLE 8.2   Learning Curve Estimates

Let's return to the earlier example where we are trying to determine the true cost for the senior programmer's time. Recall that the first, linear estimate, in which no allowance was made for the learning curve effect, was found to be:

$$(\$35/\text{hr})\,(4\,\text{iterations})\,(1.60)\,(40\,\text{hours}) = \$8,960$$

Now we can apply some additional information to this cost estimate in the form of better knowledge of learning-rate effects. Suppose, for example, that the programmer's learning rate for coding is found to be .90. The steady state time to code the sequence is 40 hours. Our estimate of the time needed for the first coding iteration is:

$$b = \log 0.90/\log 2$$
$$= -0.0458/0.301$$
$$= -0.1521$$

$$40\,\text{hrs.} = a(4)^{-0.1521}$$
$$a = 49.39\,\text{hours}$$

Thus, for the 1st unit would take 9.39 hours longer than the steady state 40 hours. For this programming example, we can determine the appropriate unit and total time multipliers for the calculated initial unit time by consulting tables of learning curve coefficients (multipliers) derived from the formula with $a = 1$. We can also calculate unit and total time multipliers by identifying the unit time multipliers from 1 to 3 units of production (coding sequences) with a learning rate of .90. We use the units 1 to 3 because we assume that by the fourth iteration, the programmer has reached the steady state time of 40 hours. Based on

$a = 1$, the unit time learning curve coefficients are $1^{-0.5121} = 1$, $2^{-0.1521} = 0.90$, and $3^{-0.1521} = .846$, for a total time multiplier of 2.746. Therefore, the time needed to code the first three sequences is:

Total time multiplier		Time required for initial unit		Total time to program first three sequences
(2.746)	×	(49.39)	=	135.62 hours

Because the steady state time of 40 hours occurs for the final coding iteration, total coding time required for all four sequences is given as:

$$135.62 + 40 = 175.62$$

The more accurate direct labor cost for the coding activities is:

Wage ($35/hr)		Overhead Rate (1.60)		Total Hours (175.62 hours)		
($35/hr)	×	(1.60)	×	(175.62 hours)	=	$9,834.72

Compare this figure to the original value of $8,960 we had calculated the first time, which understated the programming cost by $874.72. The second figure, which includes an allowance for learning curve effects, represents a more realistic estimate of the time and cost required for the programmer to complete the project activities.

In some industries it is actually possible to chart the cost of repetitive activities to accurately adjust cost estimation for learning curves. Note the curve relating time (or cost) against activity repetition shown in Figure 8.4.[11] The learning curve effect here shows savings in time as a function of the sheer repetition of activities found in many projects. Some operations management books offer tables that show the total time multiplier, based on the learning rate values multiplied by the number of repetitive iterations of an activity.[12] Using these multipliers, the savings in revising cost estimates downward to account for learning curve effects can be significant. However, there is one important caveat: Learning curve effects may occur differentially across projects; projects with redundant work may allow for the use of learning curve multipliers while other projects with more varied work will not. Likewise, it may be more likely to see learning curve effects apply in greater proportion to projects in some industries (say, for example, construction) than in others (such as research and development). Ultimately, project budgets must be adjusted for activities in which learning curve effects are likely to occur, and these effects must be factored into activity cost estimates.

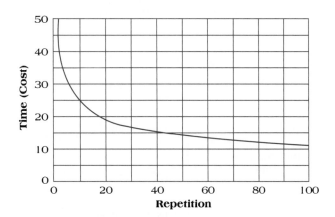

FIGURE 8.4 Unit Learning Curve Log-Linear Model

Source: J. P. Amor and C. J. Teplitz. (1998). "An efficient approximation for project composite learning curves," *Project Management Journal, 29*(3), pp. 28–42, figure on page 36. Copyright © 1998 by Project Management Institute Publications. Copyright and all rights reserved. Material from this publication has been reproduced with the permission of PMI.

Note: Graph on arithmetic coordinates.

Increasingly, project contracts are coming to reflect the impact of learning curves for repetitive operations. For example, in the automotive industry, the manufacturer of hydraulic cylinders may be given a contract for the first year to provide cylinders at a price of $24 each. Each year after, the cost of the cylinder sold to the automobile maker is priced at $1 less per year, under the assumption that learning curves will allow the cylinder manufacturer to produce the product at a steadily lower cost. Thus, learning curves are factored into the value of long-term contracts.[13]

Software Project Estimation—Function Points

Evidence from Chapter 1 and well as Box 8.1 (Software Cost Estimation) highlights the difficulties in developing realistic estimates for large-scale software projects. The track record is not encouraging: More and more software projects are overshooting their schedule and cost estimates, often by serious amounts. One of

---

BOX 8.1

PROJECT MANAGEMENT RESEARCH IN BRIEF

Software Cost Estimation

The software project industry has developed a notorious reputation when it comes to project performance. Research by the Standish Group[14] suggests that for large companies, less than 9% of IT projects are completed on schedule and at budget. Over 50% of these projects will cost 189% of their original budget, while the average schedule overrun is 202%. Clearly, from both cost and schedule estimation perspectives, the industry is frustrated by unrealistic expectations. In spite of recent improvements in software development cost, schedule, and effort estimation, using Constructive Cost Estimating models (COCOMO II), required by several branches of the federal government when bidding software contracts, our lack of ability to accurately predict software project costs remains a serious concern.[15]

A book by Steven McConnell, president of Construx Software,[16] sheds light on some of the key reasons why software projects suffer from such a poor track record. Among his findings is the common failure to budget adequate time and funding for project activities that are likely to vary dramatically, depending upon the size of the project. He distinguished among six software project activities: (1) architecture, (2) detailed design, (3) coding and debugging, (4) developer testing, (5) integration, and (6) system testing. McConnell determined that for small IT projects of 2,000 lines of code or less, 80% of the project work consisted of just three activities: detailed design, coding and debugging, and unit testing (see Figure 8.5). However, as the complexity of the software projects increased, the proportion of these activities to the

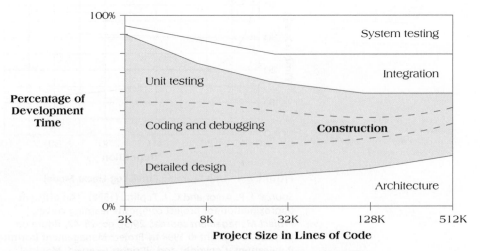

FIGURE 8.5 **Software Project Development Activities as a Function of Size**

Source: From *Code Complete,* 2d ed. (Microsoft Press, 2004), by Steve McConnell. Used with permission of the author.

overall project cost dropped dramatically. Projects of over 128,000 lines of code required significantly more attention to be paid to the other three activities: architecture, integration, and system testing (about 60% of total effort).

The implications of this research suggest that IT project budgets must consider the size of the project as they calculate the costs of each component (work package). Larger projects resulting in hundreds of thousands of lines of code require that a higher proportion of the budget be allocated to software architecture and testing, relative to the actual cost of construction (design, coding, and unit testing).

the reasons is simply due to the nature of uncertainty in these projects. We can make estimates of cost, but without a clear sense of the nature of the software, the size of the program, and its functionality, these are often just best guesses and are quickly found to be inadequate.

Function point analysis is a system for estimating the size of software projects based on what the software does. To build any system, you need time to create files that hold information and interfaces to other screens (files and interfaces). You also need to create input screens (inputs), enquiry screens (queries), and reports (outputs). If you count all the files, interfaces, inputs, queries, and outputs, you can begin estimating the amount of work to be undertaken. The measure then relates directly to the business requirements that the software is intended to address. It can therefore be readily applied across a wide range of development environments and throughout the life of a development project, from early requirements definition to full operational use.

Simply stated, **function points** are a standard unit of measure that represents the functional size of a software application. In the same way that a house is measured by the square feet it provides, the size of an application can be measured by the number of function points it delivers to the users of the application. As part of that explanation, it is critically important to recognize that the size of the application being measured is based on the *user's view* of the system. It is based on what the user asked for, not what is delivered. Further, it is based on the way the user interacts with the system, including the screens that the user accesses to enter input, and the reports the user receives as output.

We know that it takes different amounts of time to build different functions; for example, it may take twice as long to build an interface table as an input table. Once we have a general sense of the relative times for each of the functions of the system, we have to consider additional factors to weight these estimates. These factor weightings are based on "technical complexity" and "environmental complexity." Technical complexity assesses the sophistication of the application to be built. Are we developing a complex model to determine the multiple paths of geosynchronous orbiting satellites or are we simply creating a database of customer names and addresses? Environmental complexity considers the nature of the setting in which the system is designed to work. Will it support a single user on one PC or a wide-area network? What computer language will the application be written in? A relatively streamlined and commonplace language such as Visual Basic requires less work than a more complex language and, consequently, we would assume that programmers could be more productive (generate more function points). These function points are adjusted for such complexity factors and then summed to determine a reasonable cost estimate for developing the software system.

Let's take a simple example: Suppose a local restaurant commissioned our firm to develop a replenishment and ordering system to ensure that minimum levels of foods and beverages are maintained at all times. The restaurant wants the application to have a reasonable number of input screens, output screens, a small number of query options and interfaces, but large and detailed report generation capabilities. Further, we know from past experience that one programmer working for one month (a "person-month") at our firm can generate an average of 10 function points. Finally, based on our company's past history, we have a set of average system technical and environmental complexity weightings that we can apply across all functions (see Table 8.4). For example, we know that in building an input function for the application, a system with high complexity is approximately three times more complicated (and requires more effort) than one with low complexity.

With this information, we can apply the specific system requirements from the client to construct a function point estimate for the project. Suppose we determined (from our interviews with the restaurant owners) that the estimate for relative complexity was inputs (medium), outputs (high), interfaces (low), queries (medium), and files (low). Further, we know that the clients require the following number of each

TABLE 8.4 Complexity Weighting Table for Function Point Analysis

Function	Complexity Weighting			Total
	Low	**Medium**	**High**	
Number of Inputs	2 × _____ =	4 × _____ =	6 × _____ =	
Number of Outputs	4 × _____ =	6 × _____ =	10 × _____ =	
Number of Interfaces	3 × _____ =	7 × _____ =	12 × _____ =	
Number of Queries	5 × _____ =	10 × _____ =	15 × _____ =	
Number of Files	2 × _____ =	4 × _____ =	8 × _____ =	

function: input screens (15), output screens (20), interfaces (3), queries (6), and report files (40). We can combine this information with our historic weightings for complexity to create Table 8.5.

Table 8.5 shows the results of combining our estimates for complexity of various programming functions with the requirements of the client for system features, including numbers of screens and other elements for each function. The result is our estimate that the project will require approximately 409 function points. We know that our organization estimates that each resource can perform 10 function points each "person-month." Therefore, we calculate the expected number of person-months to complete this job as 409/10 = 40.1. If we assigned only four programmers to this job, it would take approximately 10 months to complete. On the other hand, by assigning our entire staff of 10 programmers, we would expect to complete the job in just over four months. Cost estimation using this information is straightforward: If our average resource cost per programmer is $5,000/month, we multiply this figure by 40.1 to determine that our estimated cost for completing the job is $200,500.

Function point analysis is not an exact science. Complexity determinations are based on historical estimates that can change over time and so must be continuously updated. Further, they may not be comparable across organizations with differing estimation procedures and standards for technical complexity. Nevertheless, function point analysis does give organizations a useful system for developing cost estimates for software projects, a historically difficult class of projects to estimate with any accuracy.[17]

Problems with Cost Estimation

In spite of project management's best efforts, a variety of issues affect the ability to conduct reasonable and accurate project cost estimates. Highly innovative projects can be notoriously difficult to estimate in terms of costs. Surprisingly, however, even projects that are traditionally viewed as highly structured, such as construction projects, can be susceptible to ruinously expensive cost overruns. Among the more common reasons for cost overruns are:[18]

1. *Low initial estimates*—Caused by misperception of the scope of the project to be undertaken, low initial estimates are a double-edged sword. In proposing the low estimates at the start of a project, management is often setting themselves up to fail to live up to the budget constraints they have

TABLE 8.5 Function Point Calculations for Restaurant Reorder System

Function	Complexity Weighting			Total
	Low	**Medium**	**High**	
Number of Inputs		4 × 15 =		60
Number of Outputs			10 × 20 =	200
Number of Interfaces	3 × 3 =			9
Number of Queries		10 × 6 =		60
Number of Files	2 × 40 =			80
Total				409

imposed. Hence, low estimates, which may be created either willingly (in the belief that top management will not fund a project that is too expensive) or unwillingly (through simple error or neglect), almost always guarantee the result of cost overrun. Part of the reason why initial estimates may be low can be the failure to consider the project in relation to other organizational activities. If we simply cost-out various project activities without considering the other surrounding organizational activities, we can be led to assume the project team member is capable of performing the activity in an unrealistic amount of time. (See Chapter 11 on critical chain project scheduling.)

Low estimates may also be the result of a corporate culture that rewards underestimation. For example, in some organizations, it is widely understood that cost overruns will not derail a project manager's career nearly as quickly as technical flaws. Therefore, it is common for project managers to drastically underestimate project costs in order to get their project funded, continually apply for supplemental funding as the project continues, and eventually turn in a product with huge cost overruns. Political considerations also can cause project teams or top management to view a project through rose-colored glasses, minimizing initial cost estimates, particularly if they run contrary to hoped-for results. The Denver International Airport represents a good example of a community ignoring warning signs of overly optimistic cost estimates in the interest of completing the project. The resulting cost overruns have been enormous.

2. *Unexpected technical difficulties*—A common problem with estimating the costs associated with many project activities is to assume that technical problems will be minimal; that is, the cost estimate is often the case of seeming to suggest that "All other things being equal, this task should cost $XX." Of course, all other things are rarely equal. An estimate, in order to be meaningful, must take a hard look at the potential for technical problems, start-up delays, and other technical risks. It is a fact that new technologies, innovative procedures, and engineering advances are routinely accompanied by failures of design, testing, and application. Sometimes the impact of these difficulties is the loss of significant money; other times the losses are more tragic, resulting in the loss of life. The Boeing V-22 Osprey transport aircraft, for example, employs a radical "tilt-rotor" technology that was developed for use by the U.S. Marines and Navy. Prototype testing identified design flaws, contributing to the deaths of test pilots in early models of these aircraft.

3. *Lack of definition*—The result of poor initial scope development is often the creation of projects with poorly defined features, goals, or even purpose (see Chapter 5 on scope management). This lack of a clear view of the project can quickly spill over into poorly realized cost estimates and inevitable cost overruns. It is important to recognize that the process of cost estimation and project budgeting must follow a comprehensive scope statement and work breakdown structure. When the first steps are done poorly, they effectively render futile any attempt at reasonable estimation of project costs.

4. *Specification changes*—One of the banes of project management cost estimation and control is the midcourse specifications changes (sometimes referred to as "scope creep") that many projects are so prone to. Information technology projects, for example, are often riddled with requests for additional features, serious modifications, and updated processes—all while the project's activities are still in development. In the face of serious changes to project scope or specification, it is no wonder that many projects routinely overrun their initial cost estimates. In fact, with many firms, initial cost estimates may be essentially meaningless, particularly when the company has a well-earned reputation for making midcourse adjustments to scope.

5. *External factors*—Inflation and other economic impacts can cause a project to overrun its estimates, many times seriously. For example, in the face of a financial crisis or an unexpected worldwide shortage of a raw material, cost estimates that were made without taking such concerns into account are quickly moot. To cite one recent example, China and India's aggressive modernization and industrialization efforts, coupled with a weak American dollar, have been driving the price of crude oil to near-record highs. Because crude oil is benchmarked against the U.S. dollar, which is currently being kept weak by the Federal Reserve, it now takes more dollars to purchase oil. Further, Chinese and Indian demand for oil has led to higher international prices. A project that requires significant supplies of crude oil will have to be recalculated upward due to the significant increase in the cost of this critical resource. Other common external effects can occur in the case of political considerations shaping the course that a project is expected to follow. This phenomenon is often found in government projects, particularly military acquisition contracts, which have a history of cost overruns, governmental intervention in the form of oversight committees, multiple constituents, and numerous midcourse change requests.

BOX 8.2

PROJECT MANAGEMENT RESEARCH IN BRIEF

"Delusion and Deception" Taking Place in Large Infrastructure Projects

This should be the golden age of infrastructure projects. A recent issue of *The Economist* reported that an estimated $22 trillion is to be invested in these projects over the next 10 years, making spending on infrastructure "the biggest investment boom in history." Because of this long-term commitment to large infrastructure improvements, coupled with the enormous costs of successfully completing these projects, it is critical that the governments and their agents responsible for designing and managing them get things right. In other words, too much is at stake to mismanage these projects.

Unfortunately, as previous examples in this chapter make clear, private organizations as well as the public sector have terrible performance records when it comes to successfully managing and delivering on their large infrastructure cost and performance targets. Examples such as the Sydney Opera House (original projected cost of 7 million Australian dollars; final cost of 102 million), the Eurotunnel (final costs more than double the original projections), and the Boston "Big Dig" (original estimated cost of $2.5 billion; final cost of nearly $15 billion) continue to be the rule rather than the exception when it comes to infrastructure project performance. The long list of incredibly overrun projects begs some simple questions: What is going on here? Why are we routinely so bad at cost estimation? What factors are causing us to continually miss our targets when it comes to estimating project costs?

Professor Bent Flyvbjerg, a project management researcher at Oxford University, and several colleagues have studied the track records of large infrastructure projects over the years and have arrived at some startling conclusions about the causes of their runaway costs: In most cases, the causes come from one of three sources—over-optimism bias, deliberate deception, or simple bad luck.

1. *Optimism bias*—Flyvbjerg's work showed that executives commonly fall victim to delusions when it comes to projects, something he refers to as the "planning fallacy." Under the planning fallacy, managers routinely minimize problems and make their decisions on the basis of delusional optimism— underestimating costs and obstacles, involuntarily spinning scenarios for success, and assuming best- case options and outcomes. Optimism bias leads project managers and top executives to err on the side of underestimation of costs and time for project activities even in the face of previous evidence or past experiences. In short, we tend to develop overly positive scenarios of schedule and cost for projects and make forecasts that reflect these delusions.

2. *Deliberate deception*—Large capital investment projects often require complex layers of decision making in order to get them approved. For example, governments have to work with private contractors and other agents who are responsible for making initial cost projections. Flyvbjerg found that some opportunities to inappropriately bias the project (deception) occur when a project's stakeholders all hold different incentives for the project. For example, the construction consortium wants the project, the government wants to provide for taxpayers and voters, bankers want to secure long-term investments, and so on. Under this situation, contractors may feel an incentive to provide estimates that are deliber- ately undervalued in order to secure the contract. They know that "true" cost estimates could scare off the public partners so they adopt a policy of deliberate deception to first win the contract, knowing that once the government is committed, it is extremely difficult for them to change their minds, even in the face of a series of expanding cost estimates. In short, the goal here is to get the project contracts signed; once the project is "on the books," it tends to stay there.

3. *Bad luck*—A final reason for escalating project costs is simple bad luck. Bad luck implies that in spite of sound estimates, due diligence from all parties involved in the project, and the best intentions of both the contractors and project clients, there are always going to be cases where circumstances, environ- mental impacts, and sheer misfortune can conspire to derail a project or severely cripple its delivery. Though there is no doubt that bad luck does sometimes occur, Flyvbjerg warns that it is usually a handy excuse to attribute project problems to "bad luck," when the reality is that overruns and schedule slip- page are typically caused by much more foreseeable reasons, as suggested above.

The research on serious project overruns and their causes offers some important insight into reasons why we keep missing our targets for critical projects. It also suggests additional effects that are equally important: underestimating costs and overestimating benefits from any project leads to two problems. First, we opt to begin many projects that are not (and never were) economically viable. Second, starting these projects means we are effectively ignoring alternatives that actually may have yielded higher returns had we made a better ini- tial analysis. Ultimately, the common complaint about large infrastructure projects ("Over budget, over time, over and over again") is one for which most organizations have no one to blame but themselves.[19]

8.3 CREATING A PROJECT BUDGET

The process of developing a project budget is an interesting mix of estimation, analysis, intuition, and repetitive work. The central goal of a budget is the need to support rather than conflict with the project's and the organization's goals. The **project budget** is a plan that identifies the allocated resources, the project's goals, and the schedule that allows an organization to achieve those goals. Effective budgeting always seeks to integrate corporate-level goals with department-specific objectives; short-term requirements with long-term plans; and broader, strategic missions with concise, needs-based issues. Useful budgets evolve through intensive communication with all concerned parties and are compiled from multiple data sources. Perhaps most importantly, the project budget and project schedule must be created in tandem; the budget effectively determines whether or not project milestones can be achieved.

As one of the cornerstones of project planning, the project budget must be coordinated with project activities defined in the Work Breakdown Structure (see Chapter 5). As Figure 8.6 suggests, the WBS sets the stage for creating the project schedule; the project budget subsequently assigns the necessary resources to support that schedule.

A number of important issues go into the creation of the project budget, including the process by which the project team and the organization gather data for cost estimates, budget projections, cash flow income and expenses, and expected revenue streams. The methods for data gathering and allocation can vary widely across organizations; some project firms rely on the straight, linear allocation of income and expenses, without allowing for time, while others use more sophisticated systems. The ways in which cost data are collected and interpreted mainly depend upon whether the firm employs a top-down or a bottom-up budgeting procedure. These approaches involve radically different methods for collecting relevant project budget information and can potentially lead to very different results.

Top-Down Budgeting

Top-down budgeting requires the direct input from the organization's top management; in essence, this approach seeks to first ascertain the opinions and experiences of top management regarding estimated project costs. The assumption is that senior management is experienced with past projects and is in a position to provide accurate feedback and estimates of costs for future project ventures. They take the first stab at estimating both the overall costs of a project and its major work packages. These projections are then passed down the hierarchy to the next functional department levels where additional, more specific information is collected. At each step down the hierarchy, the project is broken into more detailed pieces, until project personnel who actually will be performing the work ultimately provide input on specific costs on a task-by-task basis.

This approach can create a certain amount of friction within the organization, both between top and lower levels and also between lower-level managers competing for budget money. When top management establishes an overall budget at the start, they are, in essence, driving a stake into the ground and saying, "This is all we are willing to spend." As a result, all successive levels of the budgeting process must make their estimates fit within the context of the overall budget that was established at the outset. This process naturally leads to jockeying among different functions as they seek to divide up the budget pie in what has become a zero-sum game—the more budget money engineering receives, the less there is for procurement to use.

On the positive side, research suggests that top management estimates of project costs are often quite accurate, at least in the aggregate.[20] Using this figure as a basis for drilling down to assign costs to work packages and individual tasks brings an important sense of budgetary discipline and cost control. For example, a building contractor about to enter into a contract to develop a convention center is often knowledgeable enough to judge the construction costs with reasonable accuracy, given sufficient information about the building's features, its location, and any known building impediments or worksite constraints. All subcontractors and project team members must then develop their own budgets based on the overall, top-down contract.

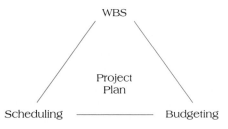

FIGURE 8.6 The Relationship Among WBS, Scheduling, and Budgeting

Bottom-Up Budgeting

Bottom-up budgeting takes a completely different approach than that pursued by top-down methods. The **bottom-up budgeting** approach begins inductively from the work breakdown structure to apply direct and indirect costs to project activities. The sum of the total costs associated with each activity are then aggregated, first to the work package level, then at the deliverable level, at which point all task budgets are combined, and then higher up the chain where the sum of the work package budgets are aggregated to create the overall project budget.

In this budgeting approach, each project manager is required to prepare a project budget that identifies project activities and specifies funds requested to support these tasks. Using these first-level budget requests, functional managers develop their own carefully documented budgets, taking into consideration both the requirements of the firms' projects and their own departmental needs. This information is finally passed along to top managers, who merge and streamline to eliminate overlap or double counting. They are then responsible for creating the final master budget for the organization.

Bottom-up budgeting emphasizes the need to create detailed project plans, particularly Work Breakdown Structures, as a first step for budget allocations. It also facilitates coordination between the project managers and functional department heads and, because it emphasizes the unique creation of budgets for each project, it allows top managers a clear view for prioritization among projects competing for resources. On the other hand, a disadvantage of bottom-up budgeting is that it reduces top management's control of the budget process to one of oversight, rather than direct initiation, which may lead to significant differences between their strategic concerns and the operational-level activities in the organization. Also, the fine-tuning that often accompanies bottom-up budgeting can be time-consuming as top managers make adjustments and lower-level managers resubmit their numbers until an acceptable budget is achieved.

Activity-Based Costing

Most project budgets use some form of activity-based costing. **Activity-based costing (ABC)** is a budgeting method that assigns costs first to activities and then to the projects based on each project's use of resources. Remember that project activities are any discrete task that the project team undertakes to make or deliver the project. Activity-based costing, therefore, is based on the notion that projects consume activities and activities consume resources.[21]

Activity-based costing consists of four steps:

1. Identify the activities that consume resources and assign costs to them, as is done in a bottom-up budgeting process.
2. Identify the cost drivers associated with the activity. Resources, in the form of project personnel, and materials are key cost drivers.
3. Compute a cost rate per cost driver unit or transaction. Labor, for example, is commonly simply the cost of labor per hour, given as:

$$\text{Cost rate/unit} \longrightarrow \text{\$Cost/hour}$$

4. Assign costs to projects by multiplying the cost driver rate times the volume of cost driver units consumed by the project. For example, assume the cost of a senior software programmer is \$40/hour and that she is to work on the project for a total of 80 hours. The cost to the project would be:

$$(\$40/\text{hr})(80\,\text{hours}) = \$3,200.00$$

As we discussed earlier in this chapter, numerous sources of project costs (cost drivers) apply to both the direct and the indirect costs of a project. Activity-based costing, a technique employed within most project budgets, requires the early identification of these variables in order to create a meaningful control document.

Table 8.6 demonstrates part of a project budget. The purpose of the preliminary budget is to identify the direct costs and those that apply to overhead expenses. It is sometimes necessary to further break down overhead costs to account for separate budget lines. The overhead figure of \$500 for *Survey*, for example, may include expenses covering health insurance, retirement contributions, and other forms of overhead, which would be broken out in a more detailed project budget.

TABLE 8.6 Sample Project Budget

Activity	Direct Costs	Budget Overhead	Total Cost
Survey	3,500	500	4,000
Design	7,000	1,000	8,000
Clear Site	3,500	500	4,000
Foundation	6,750	750	7,500
Framing	8,000	2,000	10,000
Plumb and Wire	3,750	1,250	5,000

Table 8.7 shows a budget in which the total planned expenses given in Table 8.6 are compared against actual accrued project expenses. With periodic updating, this budget can be used for variance reporting to show differences, both positive and negative, between the baseline budget assigned to each activity and the actual cost of completing those tasks. This method offers a central location for the tabulation of all relevant project cost data and allows for the preliminary development of variance reports. On the other hand, this type of budget is a static budget document that does not reflect the project schedule and the fact that activities are phased in following the network's sequencing.

TABLE 8.7 Sample Budget Tracking Planned and Actual Activity Costs

Activity	Planned	Budget Actual	Variance
Survey	4,000	4,250	250
Design	8,000	8,000	- 0 -
Clear Site	4,000	3,500	(500)
Foundation	7,500	8,500	1,000
Framing	10,000	11,250	1,250
Plumb and Wire	5,000	5,150	150
Total	38,500	40,650	2,150

Table 8.8 shows a sample from a time-phased budget, in which the total budget for each project activity is disaggregated across the schedule when its work is planned. The **time-phased budget** allocates costs across both project activities and the anticipated time in which the budget is to be expended. It allows the project team to match its schedule baseline with a budget baseline, identifying milestones for both schedule performance and project expense. As we will see in Chapter 13, the creation of a time-phased budget works in tandem with more sophisticated project control techniques, such as earned value management.

We can produce a tracking chart that illustrates the expected budget expenditures for this project by plotting the cumulative budgeted cost of the project against the baseline schedule. Figure 8.7 is a simple

TABLE 8.8 Example of a Time-Phased Budget

Activity	Months January	February	March	April	May	Total by Activity
Survey	4,000					4,000
Design		5,000	3,000			8,000
Clear Site		4,000				4,000
Foundation			7,500			7,500
Framing				8,000	2,000	10,000
Plumb and Wire				1,000	4,000	5,000
Monthly Planned	4,000	9,000	10,500	9,000	6,000	
Cumulative	4,000	13,000	23,500	32,500	38,500	38,500

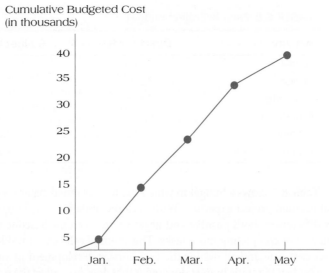

Cumulative Budgeted Cost
(in thousands)

FIGURE 8.7 Cumulative Budgeted Cost of the Project

graphic of the plot and is another method for identifying the project baseline for schedule and budget over the anticipated life of the project.

8.4 DEVELOPING BUDGET CONTINGENCIES

Budget contingencies symbolize the recognition that project cost estimates are just that: estimates. Unforeseen events often conspire to render initial project budgets inaccurate, or even useless. (Suppose a construction project that had budgeted a fixed amount for digging a building's foundation accidentally discovered serious subsidence problems or groundwater.) Even in circumstances in which project unknowns are kept to a minimum, there is simply no such thing as a project developed with the luxury of full knowledge of events. A **budget contingency** is the allocation of extra funds to cover these uncertainties and improve the chances that the project can be completed within the time frame originally specified. Contingency money is typically added to the project's budget following the identification of all project costs; that is, the project budget does not include contingency as part of the activity-based costing process. Rather, the contingency is calculated as an extra cushion on top of the calculated cost of the project.

There are several reasons why it may make good sense to include contingency funding in project cost estimates. Many of these reasons point to the underlying uncertainty that accompanies most project cost estimation:[22]

1. *Project scope is subject to changes.* Many projects aim at moving targets; that is, the project scope may seem well articulated and locked in. However, as the project moves through its development cycle, external events or environmental changes can often force us to modify or upgrade a project's goals. For example, suppose that our organization set out to develop an electronics product for the commercial music market only to discover, halfway through the development, that technological advances had rendered our original product obsolete. One option, other than abandoning the project, might be to engineer a product design upgrade midstream in the project's development. Those scope changes will cause potentially expensive cost readjustments.

2. *Murphy's Law is always present.* Murphy's Law suggests that if something can go wrong, it often will. Budget contingency represents one important method for anticipating the likelihood of problems occurring during the project life cycle. Thus, contingency planning just makes prudent sense.

3. *Cost estimation must anticipate interaction costs.* It is common to budget project activities as independent operations. Thus, in a product development project, we develop a discrete budget for each work package under product design, engineering, machining, and so forth. However, this approach fails to recognize the often "interactive" nature of these activities. For example, suppose that the engineering phase requires a series of iterative cycles to occur between the designers and the engineers. As a series of designs are created, they are forwarded to the engineering section for proofing and quality

assessment. When problems are encountered, they must be shipped back to design to be corrected. Coordinating the several cycles of design and rework as a product moves through these two phases is often not accounted for in a standard project budget. Hence, contingency budgets allow for the likely rework cycles that link project activities interactively.

4. ***Normal conditions are rarely encountered.*** Project cost estimates usually anticipate "normal conditions." However, many projects are conducted under anything but normal working conditions. Some of the ways in which the normal conditions assumption is routinely violated include the availability of resources and the nature of environmental effects. Cost estimators assume that resources required for the project will be available when needed; however, personnel may be missing, raw materials may be of poor quality, promised funding may not materialize, and so forth. When resources are missing or limited, the activities that depend upon their availability are often delayed, leading to extra costs. Likewise, the geography and environmental effects on some projects demonstrate the difficulty in creating a "normal" project situation. For example, a project manager was assigned to develop a power plant in the West Bengal province of India only to discover, upon arrival, that the project was set to begin at the same time that the annual torrential monsoon rains were due to arrive! His first project activity, after reaching the construction site, was to spend three weeks erecting a five-foot retaining wall and coffer dam around the site to ensure it would not flood. Of course, the cost of this necessary construction had not been factored into his initial budget.

While project teams naturally favor contingencies as a buffer for project cost control, their acceptance by project stakeholders, particularly clients, is less assured. Some clients may feel that they are being asked to cover poor budget control on the part of the project firm. Other clients object to what seems an arbitrary process for calculating contingency. For example, it is common in the building industry to apply a contingency rate of 10%–15% to any structure prior to architectural design. As a result, a building budgeted for $10 million would be designed to cost $9 million. The additional million dollars is held in escrow as contingency against unforeseen difficulties during the construction and is not applied to the operating budget. Finally, does the contingency fund apply equally across all project work packages or should it be held in reserve to support critical activities as needed? Where or across what project activities contingency funds should be applied is the final point of contention. Despite these drawbacks, there are several benefits to the use of contingency funding for projects, including:

1. It recognizes that the future contains unknowns, and the problems that do arise are likely to have a direct effect on the project budget. In providing contingency, the project allows for the negative effects of both time and money variance.

2. Provision is made in the company plans for an increase in project cost. Contingency has sometimes been called the first project fire alarm. Allowing contingency funds to be applied to a project is a preliminary step in gaining approval for budget increases, should they become necessary.

3. Application to the contingency fund gives an early warning signal of a potential overdrawn budget. In the event of such signals, the organization's top management needs to take a serious look at the project and the reasons for its budget variance, and begin formulating fallback plans should the contingency prove to be insufficient to cover the project overspend. In large defense-industry contracts, for example, project organizations facing budget overruns often first apply any contingency money they possess to the project before approaching the governmental agency for additional funding. An Army project contract manager will understandably demand full accounting of project expenditures, including contingency funds, before considering additional funding.

Project cost estimation and budgeting are two important components of project control. Because a significant constraint on any project is its budget, the manner in which we estimate project costs and create realistic budgets is critical to effective project planning. Further, the best defense against overrunning our budgets is to prepare project cost estimates as carefully as possible. Although we cannot possibly anticipate every eventuality, the more care that is used in initial estimation, the greater the likelihood that we can create a budget that is a reasonably accurate reflection of the true project cost. Cost estimation challenges us to develop reasonable assumptions and expectations for project costs through clearly articulating the manner in which we arrive at our estimates. Budgeting is the best method for applying project expenditures systematically, with an eye toward keeping project costs in line with initial estimates. Taken together, cost estimation and budgeting require every project manager to become comfortable with not only the technical challenges of the project, but its monetary constraints as well.

Summary

1. **Understand the various types of common project costs.** Project budgeting comprises two distinct elements: cost estimation and the budgeting process itself. Among the well-known expenses in most projects are:
   a. *Cost of labor*—the charge against the human resources needed to complete the project.
   b. *Cost of materials*—costs relating to any specific equipment or supplies needed for project development.
   c. *Subcontractors*—charges against the project budget for the use of consultants or other subcontracted work.
   d. *Cost of equipment and facilities*—the costs of any plant and equipment, either at the project's location or off-site.
   e. *Travel*—a sometimes necessary charge for the expense of having project team members in the field or at other sites.

2. **Recognize the difference between various forms of project costs.** The types of costs that a project can incur can be identified in a number of ways. Among the more common types of costs are:
   - *Direct versus indirect*—Direct costs are those that can be directly assigned to specific project activities performed to create the project. Indirect costs relate to general company overhead expenses or administration. For example, overhead expenses charged to a project may include health benefits or retirement contributions. General administration includes shipping costs, secretarial or computer support, sales commissions, and so on.
   - *Recurring versus nonrecurring*—Recurring costs are ongoing expenses, such as labor or material costs. They appear across the project's life cycle. Nonrecurring costs are typically one-time expenses related to some special expense or purchase, such as training or purchase of a building.
   - *Fixed versus variable*—Fixed costs do not vary with respect to their usage. Variable costs generally increase in proportion to the degree they are used.
   - *Normal versus expedited*—Normal costs are the normally scheduled costs of the project, set in relation to the schedule baseline. Expedited costs are sometimes referred to as "crashing costs" and increase due to the extra resources assigned to speed the completion of a specific project activity.

3. **Apply common forms of cost estimation for project work, including ballpark estimates and definitive estimates.** Cost estimating may follow one of several approaches, usually increasing in accuracy as estimates coincide more closely with the completion of project design work. Preliminary estimates for task completion, sometimes called "ballpark estimates," may be accurate only to ±30%. On the other hand, as the project gets closer to the completion of the design phase, it is more realistic to expect more accurate, definitive estimates (±5%). One method for cost estimation is through the use of parametric techniques, which compare current project activities to the cost of past, similar activities and then assign a multiplier that considers inflation or other additional cost increases.

4. **Understand the advantages of parametric cost estimation and the application of learning curve models in cost estimation.** Parametric cost estimation allows project managers to develop detailed estimates of current project costs by taking older work and inserting a multiplier to account for the impact of inflation, labor and materials increases, and other reasonable direct costs. Parametric estimation allows project managers to begin formulating cost estimates from a position of past historical record, which can be very helpful in complex projects for which it is difficult to formulate reasonable estimates.

   One element in project cost estimation that cannot be ignored is the effect of learning rates on an individual's ability to perform a project task. Learning curve effects typically are relevant only in cases where a project team member is required to perform multiple iterations of a task. When these situations occur, it is usually easier and faster to complete the nth iteration than it was to complete the first, due to the effect of learning on repetitive activities. Using available formulas, we can readjust cost estimates for some project activities to reflect the effect of the learning curve on the cost of an activity.

5. **Discern the various reasons why project cost estimation is often done poorly.** Cost estimation may be poorly done for several reasons, including:
   a. *Low initial estimates*—These are caused by poor knowledge of the project's scope or due to an organizational atmosphere that rewards low initial estimates and does not sanction subsequent cost or schedule overruns.
   b. *Unexpected technical difficulties*—This is a common problem for many projects when technical performance is cutting-edge and unexpected problems emerge.
   c. *Lack of definition*—Poorly specified projects usually lead to poorly budgeted and controlled projects.
   d. *Specification changes*—The continuing distraction of specification change requests can quickly lead to cost overruns.
   e. *External factors*—The uncontrollable effects of inflation or economic or political interference in a project can render initial cost estimates invalid.

6. **Apply both top-down and bottom-up budgeting procedures for cost management.** Project budgeting involves the process of taking the individual activity cost estimates and creating a working document for planned project expenditures. Two approaches to budgeting involve the use of top-down and bottom-up efforts to better identify costs and allocate project

budget money. Using activity-based budgeting techniques, project teams typically identify the activities that consume resources and assign costs to them. Second, they determine the cost drivers associated with the activities (usually human resources and materials costs), and third, a cost rate per cost driver is then computed. Activity-based budgeting allows for the creation of project budgets with specific budget lines for each task necessary to complete the project.

7. **Understand the uses of activity-based budgeting and time-phased budgets for cost estimation and control.** Taking activity-based budgeting one step further, we can create time-phased budgets when the specific activity costs are then allocated across the project schedule baseline to reflect the points on the project time line when the budget will be consumed. Using a time-phased budget approach allows the project team to link time and cost into a unified baseline that can be set to serve as the project plan. Project cost control, as the project moves forward, is predicated on creating the time-phased budget.

8. **Recognize the appropriateness of applying contingency funds for cost estimation.** In some projects, it is necessary, for a variety of reasons, to set aside a certain amount of the project budget into an account to handle any uncertainties or unexpected events that could not have been anticipated in the initial cost estimation and budgeting sequence. This account is referred to as a project contingency fund. In many types of projects, particularly construction projects, a contingency fund is a normal part of the project budget. Contingency is not assigned to any specific project activities; rather, it is used as a general project-level emergency fund to handle the costs associated with problems, should any arise.

Key Terms

Activity-based costing (ABC) *(p. 282)*
Ballpark estimates *(p. 270)*
Bottom-up budgeting *(p. 282)*
Budget contingency *(p. 284)*
Comparative estimates *(p. 270)*
Cost estimation *(p. 266)*

Crashing *(p. 269)*
Definitive estimates *(p. 272)*
Direct costs *(p. 267)*
Expedited costs *(p. 269)*
Feasibility estimates *(p. 271)*
Fixed costs *(p. 269)*
Function point analysis *(p. 277)*

Function points *(p. 277)*
Indirect costs *(p. 267)*
Learning curves *(p. 272)*
Nonrecurring costs *(p. 268)*
Normal costs *(p. 269)*
Parametric estimation *(p. 270)*
Project budget *(p. 281)*

Recurring costs *(p. 268)*
Time-phased budget *(p. 283)*
Top-down budgeting *(p. 281)*
Variable costs *(p. 269)*

Solved Problems

1. **Calculating Direct Labor Costs** Calculate the direct cost of labor for the project team using the following data. What are the costs for the individual project team members? What is the overall direct cost of labor?

Name	Hours Needed	Overhead Charge	Personal Time Rate	Hourly Rate	Total Direct Labor Cost
John	40	1.80	1.12	$21/hr	
Bill	40	1.80	1.12	$40/hr	
J.P.	60	1.35	1.05	$10/hr	
Sonny	25	1.80	1.12	$32/hr	
Total Direct Labor Cost =					

SOLUTION

We use the formula for calculating direct costs, given as:

Hourly rate × Hours needed ×
    Overhead charge × Personal time = Total direct labor cost

Applying each rate given above in turn, we fill in the direct cost table as follows:

Name	Hours Needed	Overhead Charge	Personal Time Rate	Hourly Rate	Total Direct Labor Cost
John	40	1.80	1.12	$21/hr	$1,693.44
Bill	40	1.80	1.12	$40/hr	3,225.60
J.P.	60	1.35	1.05	$10/hr	850.50
Sonny	25	1.80	1.12	$32/hr	1,612.80
Total Direct Labor Cost =					$7,382.34

2. **Estimating Software Costs with Function Points** Suppose you were required to create a reasonably detailed estimate for developing a new student information and admissions system at a local college. Your firm's programmers average 6 function points on a person-month basis. After speaking with representatives from the college, you know that their request is based on the following screen requirements: inputs (4), outputs (7), interfaces (12), queries (20), and files (16). Further, we have determined that the relative complexity of each of these functions is as follows: inputs (low), outputs (medium), interfaces (high), queries (medium), and files (medium). Using this information and the following table, calculate the number of function points for this project.

| | Complexity Weighting | | | |
Function	Low	Medium	High	Total
Number of Inputs	$3 \times$ ____ =	$6 \times$ ____ =	$9 \times$ ____ =	
Number of Outputs	$2 \times$ ____ =	$6 \times$ ____ =	$10 \times$ ____ =	
Number of Interfaces	$1 \times$ ____ =	$3 \times$ ____ =	$5 \times$ ____ =	
Number of Queries	$4 \times$ ____ =	$8 \times$ ____ =	$12 \times$ ____ =	
Number of Files	$4 \times$ ____ =	$6 \times$ ____ =	$8 \times$ ____ =	

SOLUTION

Once we know the number of requirements for each of the five programmer functions and the complexity weighting for the activities, the calculation of total function points requires that we create a table as shown below, in which the relative complexity of the five programming functions is multiplied by the number of screen requirements. The table shows that the total number of function points for this project is 370.

| | Complexity Weighting | | | |
Function	Low	Medium	High	Total
Number of Inputs	$3 \times 4 =$			12
Number of Outputs		$6 \times 7 =$		42
Number of Interfaces			$5 \times 12 =$	60
Number of Queries		$8 \times 20 =$		160
Number of Files		$6 \times 16 =$		96

3. **Calculating Budget Estimates Using the Learning Curve**
Assume you have a software project that will require the coding services of a senior programmer to complete 14 coding sequences that are relatively similar. We know that the programmer's learning rate is .90 and that the first coding sequence is likely to take her 15 hours to complete. Using the learning curve formula, calculate the steady state time to code these sequences.

SOLUTION

Recall that the learning curve formula for calculating the time required to produce the steady state unit of output is represented as:

$$Y_x = aX^b$$

where

Y_x = the time required for the steady state, x, unit of output
a = the time required for the initial unit of output
X = the number of units to be produced to reach the steady state
b = the slope of the learning curve, represented as: log decimal learning rate/log 2

$$b = \log 0.90/\log 2$$
$$= -0.4576/0.301$$
$$= -0.1521$$
$$Y_x = 15(14)^{-0.1521}$$
$$Y_x = 10.04 \, \text{hours}$$

Discussion Questions

1. Describe an environment in which it would be common to bid for contracts with low profit margins. What does this environment suggest about the competition levels?
2. How has the global economy affected the importance of cost estimation and cost control for many project organizations?
3. Why is cost estimation such an important component of project planning? Discuss how it links together with the Work Breakdown Structure and the project schedule.
4. Imagine you are developing a software package for your company's intranet. Give examples of the various types of costs (labor, materials, equipment and facilities, subcontractors, etc.) and how they would apply to your project.
5. Give reasons both in favor of and against the use of a personal time charge as a cost estimate for a project activity.
6. Think of an example of parametric estimating in your personal experience, such as the use of a cost multiplier based on a similar, past cost. Did parametric estimating work or not? Discuss the reasons why.
7. Suppose your organization used function point analysis to estimate costs for software projects. How would the expertise level of a recently hired programmer affect your calculation of their function points on a monthly basis when compared to an older, more experienced programmer?
8. Put yourself in the position of a project customer. Would you insist on the cost adjustments associated with learning curve effects or not? Under what circumstances would learning curve costs be appropriately budgeted into a project?

9. Consider the common problems with project cost estimation and recall a project with which you have been involved. Which of these common problems did you encounter most often? Why?

10. Would you prefer the use of bottom-up or top-down budgeting for project cost control? What are the advantages and disadvantages associated with each approach?

11. Why do project teams create time-phased budgets? What are their principal strengths?

12. Project contingency can be applied to projects for a variety of reasons. List three of the key reasons why a project organization should consider the application of budget contingency.

Problems

1. Calculate the direct cost of labor for a project team member using the following data:

Hourly rate:	$35/hr
Hours needed:	150
Overhead rate:	55%

2. Calculate the direct cost of labor for the project team using the following data. What are the costs for the individual project team members? What is the overall direct cost of labor?

Name	Hours Needed	Overhead Charge	Personal Time Rate	Hourly Rate	Total Direct Labor Cost
Sandy	60	1.35	1.12	$18/hr	
Chuck	80	1.75	1.12	$31/hr	
Bob	80	1.35	- 0 -	$9/hr	
Penny	40	1.75	1.12	$30/hr	
	Total Direct Labor Cost =				

3. Assume that overhead is charged on a flat-rate basis. Each member of the project is assigned an overhead charge of $150/week. What would the direct cost of labor be for an employee, given that she is assigned to the project for 200 hours at $10.50/hour?

For Problems 4 through 6, refer to the chart of learning curve coefficients (unit and total time multipliers) shown at the bottom of this page.

The simplified formula for calculating learning rate time using the table coefficients is given as:

$$T_N = T_1 C$$

where

T_N = Time needed to produce the nth unit
T_1 = Time needed to produce the first unit
C = Learning curve coefficient

4. It took MegaTech, Inc., 100,000 labor-hours to produce the first of several oil-drilling rigs for Antarctic exploration. Your company, Natural Resources, Inc., has agreed to purchase the fifth (steady state) oil-drilling rig from MegaTech's manufacturing yard. Assume that MegaTech experiences a learning rate of 80%. At a labor rate of $35 per hour, what should you, as the purchasing agent, expect to pay for the fifth unit?

5. Problem 4 identified how long it should take to complete the fifth oil-drilling platform that Natural Resources plans to purchase. How long should all five oil-drilling rigs take to complete?

6. Suppose that you are assigning costs to a major project to be undertaken this year by your firm, DynoSoft Applications. One particular coding process involves many labor-hours, but highly redundant work. You anticipate a total of 200,000 labor-hours to complete the first iteration of the coding and a learning curve rate of 70%. You are attempting to estimate the cost of the twentieth (steady state) iteration of this coding sequence. Based on this information and a $60 per hour labor rate, what would you expect to budget as the cost of the twentieth iteration? The fortieth iteration?

	70%		75%		80%		85%	
Steady State Unit	Unit Time	Total Time	Unit Time	Total Time	Unit Time	Total Time	Unit Time	Total Time
5	.437	3.195	.513	3.459	.596	3.738	.686	4.031
10	.306	4.932	.385	5.589	.477	6.315	.583	7.116
15	.248	6.274	.325	7.319	.418	8.511	.530	9.861
20	.214	7.407	.288	8.828	.381	10.485	.495	12.402
25	.191	8.404	.263	10.191	.355	12.309	.470	14.801
30	.174	9.305	.244	11.446	.335	14.020	.450	17.091
35	.160	10.133	.229	12.618	.318	15.643	.434	19.294
40	.150	10.902	.216	13.723	.305	17.193	.421	21.425

Learning Curve Coefficients (Unit Time and Total Time Multipliers)

Based on $a = 1$.

7. Assume you are a project cost engineer calculating the cost of a repetitive activity for your project. There are a total of 20 iterations of this activity required for the project. The project activity takes 2.5 hours at its steady state rate and the learning rate is 75%. Calculate the initial output time for the first unit produced, using the learning curve formula:

$$Y_x = aX^b$$

where

Y_x = the time required for the steady state, x, unit of output

a = the time required for the initial unit of output

X = the number of units to be produced to reach the steady state

b = the slope of the learning curve, represented as: log decimal learning rate/log 2

8. You work at a regional health care center and have been asked to calculate the expected cost for a software project in your organization. You know that historically your programmers can handle 5 function points each person-month and that the cost per programmer in your company is $4,000 per month. The project whose costs you are estimating is based on the following requirements:

Function	Number of Screens	Complexity
Input	8	Low
Output	6	Low
Interfaces	15	High
Queries	5	High
Files	25	Medium

Further, you know that the complexity weighting for these functions follows a standard internal formula, shown as:

a. Calculate the total estimated number of function points for this project.

b. Calculate the total expected cost of the project.

Function	Complexity Weighting			Total
	Low	Medium	High	
Number of Inputs	2 × ____ =	4 × ____ =	6 × ____ =	
Number of Outputs	3 × ____ =	6 × ____ =	12 × ____ =	
Number of Interfaces	6 × ____ =	12 × ____ =	18 × ____ =	
Number of Queries	4 × ____ =	6 × ____ =	8 × ____ =	
Number of Files	2 × ____ =	4 × ____ =	8 × ____ =	

Case Study 8.1

The Dulhasti Power Plant

Begun in 1983, the Dulhasti Power project, set in the northern Indian provinces of Jammu and Kashmir, represents an example of a disaster in project cost estimation and delivery. As initially conceived, the project's cost was estimated at 1.6 billion rupees (about $40 million). By the time the contract was let, the cost estimates had risen to 4.5 billion rupees and later to 8, 11, 16, and 24 billion rupees (nearly $750 million). In April 2008, when the project was finally dedicated by Indian Prime Minister Manmohan Singh, the final estimated cost of the project was put at just under $1.1 billion.

The project was based on a straightforward concept: Dulhasti was designed as a 390-megawatt hydroelectric power plant to be built on the swift Chenab River in the Doda region, a rugged section of the Himalayas, and several hundred kilometers from larger cities. The project sought to build a dam, erect a hydroelectric generating station, and string hundreds of miles of transmission lines starting near the headwaters of a system of rivers flowing onto the plains south of the mountain region. When the contract was awarded at a price of $50 million, the contracting organizations anticipated that the project could be completed in a reasonable time frame.

The contract for the power generation project was first awarded to a French consortium, who almost immediately asked for an upward price revision. The Indian government refused, suspecting that the French consortium had known all along that its initial bid was too low and was hoping to simply "buy" the project prior to renegotiating. The government's refusal to revise its price resulted in a second bidding process. Because of wider competition from other European countries now in the field, the second, accepted French offer was even lower than the earlier one. Although this process initially appeared to save the Indian government money, it was not a good beginning to the partnership between the government and the French consortium.

Situated in the mountainous Jammu and Kashmir provinces, the site was intended to capitalize on the proximity to large river systems capable of providing the water capacity needed to run a hydroelectric plant of Dulhasti's dimensions. Unfortunately, the site selected for the project came with some serious drawbacks as well. First, it was situated in the disputed border region between Pakistan and India. Jammu and Kashmir have been the center of numerous and serious clashes between separatist forces supported by the Pakistani government and Indian army units stationed in the region to keep the peace. Constructing such an obvious target as a power plant in the disputed area was sure to provoke reaction by nationalist groups, using terrorism as their chief means of opposition. Thus, the additional costs of providing security to the site quickly become prohibitively expensive. A second problem concerned the sheer geographical challenge of creating a large plant in a region almost totally devoid of supporting infrastructure, including an adequate logistics network (roads and rail lines). The foothills of the Himalayas may be scenic, but building a plant there is not cost-effective, particularly as almost all supplies had to be brought in with air transportation, at exorbitant costs. All raw materials, including cement, wood, stone, and steel, had to be hauled by helicopter for miles over snowbound areas.

The work on the plant continued in fits and starts for more than 20 years. By the turn of the century, nearly $1 billion had been spent on the Dulhasti project and the plant was still not operational. Further, in order to offset the expense of the project, the cost of power to be generated by the plant had risen by over 500%, making the plant an inefficient producer of electrical power for the countryside. The original French-led consortium that contracted to develop the plant had pulled out, forcing the Indian government to rebid it, at which time they awarded the contract to a Norwegian firm.

The project was finally completed in mid-2008 after a 24-year, checkered history. There is no doubt that the finished project will help alleviate electricity needs for the northern part of the country. In fact, the Jammu and Kashmir state governments have requested that the control of the plant and its revenues be transferred to their local oversight, as a means to boost regional economies. On the other hand, one is left to wonder about a project originally budgeted for $40 million that ended up taking more than 20 years and costing more than 25 times its initial target. Was it bad estimation, bad luck, or bad project control? Perhaps the answer is: all three![23]

Questions

1. Explain the challenge of producing accurate cost estimation when working in harsh geographical conditions.
2. The original bidding process favored the lowest project construction bids using a fixed-price contract. What are the advantages and disadvantages to the Indian government when using this type of bidding process? How did this process contribute to gross underbids and successive cost escalations?

Case Study 8.2

After the Oil

In 2008, 33 companies assembled 41 different solar panel systems on a site close to the planned site of Masdar City in Abu Dhabi. For 10 months, the different systems had been tested against one another, the first time a test had ever been carried out on this scale. The testing would continue for another eight months.

This was no scientific research project, but a real field test to determine which system to buy for the zero-carbon Masdar City. The panels would be placed on every roof in the city, and would generate 230 megawatts and 80% of the entire energy demands of the 50,000 population. The winner of the field testing would be awarded a vast contract worth billions.

The location of the testing and the site of Masdar City were remarkable given the fact that the states on the Persian Gulf are the largest exporter of oil in the world and expect their valuable resource to not run out for at least 50 years.

Masdar City is now a carbon-neutral site that is designed to illustrate the United Arab Emirates' commitment to renewable energy. The UAE sees Masdar as being the blueprint for the cities of the virtually oil-free future. The narrow streets of Masdar are shaded by huge black solar panels; there is even a large wind tower that funnels cool air through the central plaza area. Water is carefully collected, filtered, and reused. Although Masdar is small,

(continued)

© Masdar

FIGURE 8.8 Proposed Masterplan of Masdar City

rather like a university campus, the project has already cost billions; however, the excess energy is fed back into Abu Dhabi's power grid.

So why does the UAE, so oil rich, feel the need to investigate and invest in renewable energy and create the ambitious Masdar City? The UAE is of the opinion that global oil production has already reached a peak. Inevitably, the output will soon decline and, by investing in renewable energy now, countries like the UAE can dominate the next phase of energy for the world.

Across the Persian Gulf there is a drive to use less oil and to export more. This is why there is a trend for government-funded solar, wind, and nuclear programs. Government-backed energy investments across the Persian Gulf are huge. Abu Dhabi has already spent $20 billion on nuclear plants and aims to be able to create 7% of its energy from renewable sources by 2030. In Dubai, the plan is to create renewable energy sources capable of supplying 5% of their energy needs by 2030. Dubai is in the process of building a massive 1-gigawatt, $3.7 billion solar array to help achieve this goal. In Saudi Arabia, which is the largest oil producer in the region, the renewable plan is even more ambitious, with a goal of 20% contribution by 2030 driven by an $80 billion investment in 16 nuclear plants.

Compared to the approach of the biggest net buyer of oil, the United States, the Persian Gulf approach could not be more different. Incredibly, Dubai, for example, with a population of around 2 million, actually spends more on renewable energy than the United States with a population of 350 million. According to the U.S. Department of Energy budget, only $3 billion was allocated to efficiency and renewable energy in 2013.

Who Is Burying Their Heads in the Sand?

According to the chair of the U.S. House Energy and Power Subcommittee, the United States has 250 years of coal and oil reserves and probably more in natural gas. On this basis, the chair is not alone in not being concerned about running out of fossil fuels. It would seem that many members of U.S. Congress agree with the chair, which is the reason for their resistance to President Obama's 2008 declaration that he intended to support the domestic renewable industry with billions of dollars of subsidies. It was Obama's vision that by 2025, renewable sources would account for 25% of the United States' energy needs. By 2012, Obama had failed to push through a climate change bill (2010), but automobile fuel economy measures had been approved.

In 2009, the U.S. Department of Energy had received $35.2 billion for a range of clean-energy programs. Grants and tax credits to the value of $13 billion were available through the U.S. Treasury Department. Many of the U.S.-based renewable energy businesses would have floundered without this kind of support. During the past 60 years, fossil fuel businesses in the United States have received $594 billion in various government payments including subsidies, tax breaks, and incentives. With this kind of continuing support, the differences between the United States and the UAE could not be more marked.

Political Will or Economic Muscle?

The UAE and other Gulf States rely on oil revenues and can afford to make huge investments in renewable energy sources. However, the other dimension is the fact that the majority of the projects are state owned and sponsored. In the United States, there are competing demands for government investment and the culture is very different, with government ownership unpopular and government intervention frowned upon.

Practicalities drive the UAE initiatives. The CEO of the Masdar project, Sultan al-Jaber, acknowledges the fact that the oil will not run out in the near future. He also acknowledges the truism that oil is running out and will at some point be exhausted. He counters this by stating that renewable energy, by its very nature, will never run out. Indeed, by investing in ways to capture that energy, it can only increase. Hence, the UAE is determined to prepare for both eventualities. One day, there will be no more oil to sell, and long before that the country will have established a renewable energy economy that will not only supply its own energy needs, but provide the replacement income for the oil.

Renewable Exports

A logical part of the grand strategy to switch to a "renewable economy" is to export that technology, know-how, and experience around the globe. The Abu Dhabi government funds Masdar and in turn funds projects in markets that are still hungry for the oil they sell. Just outside London, the UAE has a 20% stake in a huge wind farm. Other projects have seen investments exceeding $540 million in the United States and Europe. These funds are delivered via a series of Abu Dhabi backed private equity groups. The lessons being learned at Masdar can be directly transposed to sites and opportunities around the world.

Save at Home, Sell Abroad

The vast range and scope of the projects cut across the whole of the Persian Gulf. In Saudi Arabia, there is recognition of the fact that if they were to cut their own use of their own oil, there would be huge benefits. On the one hand, they would save oil and prepare for the future with renewable sources. On the other hand, the oil saved from domestic use would be available for export

and generate billions in revenue. To put things into perspective, per capita, Saudi Arabia consumes double the amount of energy compared to the United States, and 50% of all electricity is generated from burning oil. Would a shift, perhaps, mean that the oil will last longer?

As proof that the UAE is at the cutting-edge of renewable technologies, it is now home to the prestigious International Renewable Energy Agency (IREA). Their new energy-efficient headquarters is being built in Abu Dhabi, and the country will host their annual summit.

Meanwhile, the private equity funds of Masdar are still looking for new partners in the United States and Europe as part of their continuing drive to find workable renewable energy technologies. Each investment strengthens the UAE's future, post oil, whether that is 50 years away or 200. State-sponsored projects like Masdar serve as a touchstone for the future of energy, and the investment trend is likely not only to continue, but to accelerate.

The UAE has fast become a hub for international trade and tourism; these are other prime examples of the desire to diversify and no longer be entirely reliant on oil exports. It is not surprising that renewable energies have become a prime focus of the UAE. Solar energy may prove to be the primary source for the region during the peak demand periods. Today, the energy-demanding air-conditioning systems run on electricity generated from diesel or crude oil plants. Tomorrow, at peak demand periods, the solar panels will be providing that electricity.

With government-funded projects, the UAE is in a win-win situation, both at home and abroad. At home, the UAE anticipates lower oil consumption and a shift to renewable sources, and abroad the country expects to have more oil to sell and new markets and opportunities for renewable initiatives.[24]

Questions

1. Consider the following statement: "Government-funded projects intended to serve as 'prestige projects,' such as Masdar, should not be judged on the basis of cost." Do you agree or disagree with this statement? Why?

2. Project success is defined as adherence to: budget, schedule, functionality (performance), and client satisfaction. Under these criteria, when might the UAE be able to judge the success or failure of Masdar-style initiatives and overseas investments?

3. What are the lessons to be learned from the Masdar project? How might a similar project work in other countries?

Internet Exercises

1. Go to the Internet and search using the phrase "cost analysis tools." What are some of the links and examples of cost analysis as it applies to projects? Consider www.galorath.com/tools_sem.shtm. What approaches to project cost analysis are taken by Galorath, Inc.?

2. Go to http://pmworldtoday.net/ and type "case studies" in the search window. Select a project and report on it from the perspective of its cost estimation, budgeting, and (if applicable) expediting perspectives. Was the project a success or failure? Why?

3. Go to www.seattlearch.org/NR/rdonlyres/BBDEC5EC-8DD6-4A4D-8AB7-3DE63476E8C3/0/ABCBudgetWorksheet.pdf and reproduce the summary project budget worksheet. After examining the various elements in the budget, what are the main cost drivers for construction projects of this sort?

4. Go to www.stickyminds.com/articles.asp and click on "Stickyminds.com Original Articles." Search for and click on the article by Karl Wiegers, "Estimation Safety Tips." In the article (found as a pdf link to the site), the author offers tips on making estimates that are accurate and defensible by avoiding common mistakes. Which of these points makes the most sense to you personally? Why does it seem a plausible suggestion?

PMP Certification Sample Questions

1. The project administrator is preparing a preliminary budget for a project and adds in the cost of a new computer for the project team to use. What type of cost would this computer purchase represent?
   a. Variable
   b. Direct
   c. Indirect
   d. Variable direct

2. The project manager for a large project being developed in northern Ontario recognizes that it will be necessary for her to maintain a close presence at the construction site during its development and has negotiated the use of a building for her team near the construction project. The cost of the building must be factored into the project cost and will increase with use; that is, the cost of heating and other utilities is subject to change depending upon weather and team use. What type of cost would this building represent?
   a. Variable direct
   b. Indirect

   c. Nonrecurring
   d. None of the above

3. A project budget identifies $5,000 budgeted for programming costs. The actual amount for programming costs is $5,450. Which of the following statements is correct?
   a. The $450 represents a negative variance to the budget
   b. There is no variance to the budget
   c. The $450 represents a positive variance to the budget
   d. The entire $5,450 represents a positive variance to the budget

4. The project planning phase is moving forward. The project team has solicited the opinions of some senior project managers with experience in similar types of projects to try and develop a cost estimate for the project. This process is an example of:
   a. Activity-based budgeting
   b. Contingency planning
   c. Top-down budgeting
   d. Cost estimation

5. John is putting together his budget for the project and as part of this process, he is actively discussing and soliciting estimates from each member of the project team for the overall budget. He presents his budget to senior management and Susan rejects it, stating, "Team members are always going to pad their estimates. I will give you the figure I want you to shoot for." Susan is employing what method for project cost budgeting?
   a. Bottom-up
   b. Top-down
   c. Parametric
   d. Comparative

Answers: 1. b—A computer purchase would be an example of a direct cost for the project; 2. a—The cost of using a site building varies to the degree it is used and is charged as a direct cost to the project; 3. c—The overrun of $450 would be referred to as a positive variance to the budget; 4. d—The process of asking senior project managers for their best estimates of project costs is part of the cost estimation process; 5. b—Susan is using a top-down method in which she, as the senior manager, is providing the project budget estimate.

INTEGRATED PROJECT

Developing the Cost Estimates and Budget

Develop an in-depth cost estimate to support your initial project proposal narrative and scope statement, including the Work Breakdown Structure. Create a detailed justification of personnel costs, materials costs, overhead, and other forms of costs that are likely to accrue to your project. Be specific, particularly as regards personnel costs and commitment of time. For example, your cost table could look something like the following:

Personnel	Level	Rate	Loaded Rate	Labor-Weeks Needed	Total Cost
Programmer	Senior	$35	$49/hr	20	$39,200
Sys. Analyst	Junior	$22	$31/hr	10	$12,400

*40-hour work week

Remember that the "loaded rate" assumes that you include the organization's overhead expenses for each employee. A typical multiplier for this figure could run anywhere up to and over 100% of the employee's wage rate. Make sure the course instructor indicates the overhead rate you should apply for your project. So, using the senior programmer example above with a fully loaded rate and assuming an overhead multiplier of 1.40, we get:

$$(\$49)\,(40\,\text{hrs})\,(20\,\text{weeks})\,(1.40) \;=\; \$54,880$$

Sample Project Plan: ABCups, Inc.

Name	Resource Type	Title	Salary (incl. Benefits)	Hour Rate ($)	Fully Loaded Rate (Overhead = .40)	Time Needed (Hours/ week)	Duration (in weeks)	Total
Carol Johnson	Safety	Safety Engineer	64,600	32.30	45.22	10 hrs/wk	15	$ 6,783
Bob Hoskins	Engineering	Industrial Engineer	35,000	17.50	24.50	20 hrs/wk	35	17,150
Sheila Thomas	Management	Project Manager	55,000	27.50	38.50	40 hrs/wk	50	77,000
Randy Egan	Management	Plant Manager	74,000	37.00	51.80	10 hrs/wk	6	3,108
Stu Hall	Industrial	Maintenance Supervisor	32,000	16.00	22.40	15 hrs/wk	8	2,688
Susan Berg	Accounting	Cost Accountant	45,000	22.50	31.50	10 hrs/wk	12	3,780
Marty Green	Industrial	Shop Supervisor	24,000	12.00	16.80	10 hrs/wk	3	504
John Pittman	Quality	Quality Engineer	33,000	16.50	23.10	20 hrs/wk	25	11,550
Sally Reid	Quality	Jr. Quality Engineer	27,000	13.50	18.90	20 hrs/wk	18	6,804
Lanny Adams	Sales	Marketing Manager	70,000	35.00	49.00	10 hrs/wk	16	7,840
Kristin Abele	Purchasing	Purchasing Agent	47,000	23.50	32.90	15 hrs/wk	20	9,870
							Total	$147,077

Time-Phased Budget for ABCups, Inc.

Work Packages	June	July	Aug.	Sept.	Oct.	Nov.	Dec.	Jan.	Feb.	Mar.	April	May	Totals
Feasibility	2,500												2,500
Vendor Selection	7,678	3,934	1,960	3,934									17,506
Design			12,563	8,400	5,300								26,263
Engineering					9,992	14,790	15,600						40,382
Prototype Testing						3,250	12,745	7,250					23,245
Sales and Service							1,467	4,467	1,908				7,842
Packaging								2,434	8,101	650			11,185
Assembly									1,676	9,234	890		11,800
Close-out											1,198	5,156	6,354
Monthly Planned	10,178	3,934	14,523	12,334	15,292	18,040	29,812	14,151	11,685	9,884	2,088	5,156	147,077
Monthly Cumulative	10,178	14,112	28,635	40,969	56,261	74,301	104,113	118,264	129,949	139,833	141,921	147,077	147,077

Notes

1. Klamper, A. (2010, November 15). "NASA's space telescope cost overruns may imperil other projects," www.space.com/9530-nasa-space-telescope-cost-overruns-imperil-projects.html; Moulds, J. (2006, September 28). "IT providers left in the debris of NHS's 'big bang,'" *The Telegraph*, www.telegraph.co.uk/finance/2948063/IT-providers-left-in-the-debris-of-NHSs-big-bang.html; http://en.wikipedia.org/wiki/NHS_Connecting_for_Health; Doward, J. (2008, August 10). "Chaos as £13bn computer system falters," *The Guardian*, www.guardian.co.uk/society/2008/aug/10/nhs.computersystem; Goldstein, H. (2005, September). "Who killed the Virtual Case File?" *IEEE Spectrum*, http://spectrum.ieee.org/computing/software/who-killed-the-virtual-case-file; Charette, R. (2010, October 21). "FBI's Sentinel project: In bad shape as IG claims, or now okay, as FBI management claims?" *IEEE Spectrum*, http://spectrum.ieee.org/riskfactor/computing/it/fbis-sentinel-project-in-bad-shape-as-ig-claims-or-now-okay-as-fbi-management-claims.

2. Needy, K. S., and Petri, K. L. (1998). "Keeping the lid on project costs," in Cleland, D. I. (Ed.), *Field Guide to Project Management*. New York: Van Nostrand Reinhold, pp. 106–20.

3. Miller, G. J., and Louk, P. (1988). "Strategic manufacturing cost management," APICS 31st International Conference Proceedings, Falls Church, VA: APICS; Kerzner, H. (1988). "Pricing out the work," in Cleland, D. I., and King, W. R. (Eds.), *Project Management Handbook,* 2nd ed. New York: Van Nostrand Reinhold, pp. 394–410.

4. Meredith, J. R., and Mantel, Jr., S. J. (2003). *Project Management*, 5th ed. New York: Wiley.

5. Needy, K. S., and Petri, K. L. (1998). "Keeping the lid on project costs," in Cleland, D. I. (Ed.), *Field Guide to Project Management*. New York: Van Nostrand Reinhold, pp. 106–20.

6. Source for Table 8.2: Needy, K. S., and Petri, K. L. (1998). "Keeping the lid on project costs," in Cleland, D. I. (Ed.), *Field Guide to Project Management*. New York: Van Nostrand Reinhold, p. 110.

7. Lock, D. (2000). "Managing cost," in Turner, J. R., and Simister, S. J. (Eds.), *Gower Handbook of Project Management,* 3rd ed. Aldershot, UK: Gower, pp. 293–322.

8. Amor, J. P., and Teplitz, C. J. (1998). "An efficient approximation for project composite learning curves," *Project Management Journal*, 29(3): 28–42; Badiru, A. B. (1995). "Incorporating learning curve effects into critical resource diagramming," *Project Management Journal*, 26(2): 38–46; Camm, J. D., Evans, J. R., and Womer, N. K. (1987). "The unit learning curve approximation of total cost," *Computers in Industrial Engineering*, 12: 205–13; Fields, M. A. (1991). "Effect of the learning curve on the capital budgeting process," *Managerial Finance*, 17(2–3): 29–41; Teplitz, C. J., and Amor, J. P. (1993). "Improving CPM's accuracy using learning curves," *Project Management Journal*, 24(4): 15–19.

9. Meredith, J. R., and Mantel, Jr., S. J. (2003). *Project Management,* 5th ed. New York: Wiley.

10. Amor, J. P., and Teplitz, C. J. (1998). "An efficient approximation for project composite learning curves," *Project Management Journal*, 29(3): 28–42.

11. Crawford, J. R. (n.d.), *Learning curve, ship curve, rations, related data*. Burbank, CA: Lockheed Aircraft Corp.

12. Heiser, J., and Render, B. (2001). *Operation Management,* 6th ed. Upper Saddle River, NJ: Prentice Hall.

13. Hackbarth, G. (2005), personal communication.

14. "Extreme chaos." (2001). Standish Group International.

15. For a discussion of COCOMO II standards, see http://sunset.usc.edu/csse/research/COCOMOII/cocomo_main.html.

16. McConnell, S. (2004). *Code Complete*. Redmond, WA: Microsoft.

17. Turbit, N. "Function points overview," www.project-perfect.com.au/downloads/Info/info_fp_overview.pdf; International Functional Points Users Group, www.ifpug.org; Dillibabu, R., and Krishnaiah, K. (2005). "Cost estimation of a software product using COCOMO II.2000 model—a case study," *International Journal of Project Management*, 23(4): 297–307; Jeffery, R., Low, G. C., and Barnes, M. (1993). "A comparison of function point counting techniques," *IEEE Transactions on Software Engineering*, 19(5): 529–32.

18. Hamburger, D. (1986). "Three perceptions of project cost—Cost is more than a four-letter word," *Project Management Journal*, 17(3): 51–58; Sigurdsen, A. (1996). "Principal errors in capital cost estimating work, part 1: Appreciate the relevance of the quantity-dependent estimating norms," *Project Management Journal*, 27(3): 27–34; Toney, F. (2001). "Accounting and financial management: Finding the project's bottom line," in J. Knutson (Ed.), *Project Management for Business Professionals*. New York: John Wiley, pp. 101–27; Shtub, A., Bard, J. F., and Globerson, S. (1994). *Project Management: Engineering, Technology, and Implementation*. Englewood Cliffs, NJ: Prentice-Hall; Smith, N. J. (Ed.). (1995). *Project Cost Estimating*. London: Thomas Telford; Sweeting, J. (1997). *Project Cost Estimating: Principles and Practices*. Rugby, UK: Institution of Chemical Engineers; Goyal, S. K. (1975). "A note of a simple CPM time-cost tradeoff algorithm," *Management Science*, 21(6): 718–22; Venkataraman, R., and Pinto, J. K. (2008). *Cost and Value Management in Projects*. New York: Wiley.

19. Flyvbjerg, B., Garbuio, M., and Lavallo, D. (2009). "Delusion and deception in large infrastructure projects: Two models for explaining and preventing executive disaster," *California Management Review*, 51(2): 170–93; "Building BRICs of growth." (2008, June 7). *The Economist*, www.economist.com/node/11488749; Lovallo, D., and Kahneman, D. (2003). "Delusions of success: How optimism undermines executives' decisions," *Harvard Business Review*, 81(7): 56–63; Flyvbjerg, B., Holm, M. S., and Buhl, S. (2002). "Underestimating costs in public works projects: Error or lie?" *Journal of the American Planning Association*, 68(3): 279–95.

20. Meredith, J. R., and Mantel, Jr., S. J. (2003). *Project Management,* 5th ed. New York: Wiley; see also Christensen, D. S., and Gordon, J. A. (1998). "Does a rubber baseline

guarantee cost overruns on defense acquisition contracts?" *Project Management Journal,* 29(3): 43–51.

21. Maher, M. (1997). *Cost Accounting: Creating Value for Management,* 5th ed. Chicago: Irwin.

22. Gray, C. F., and Larson, E. W. (2003). *Project Management,* 2nd ed. Burr Ridge, IL: McGraw-Hill.

23. Kharbanda, O. P., and Pinto, J. K. (1996). *What Made Gertie Gallop?* New York: Van Nostrand Reinhold; www.jammu-kashmir.com/archives/archives2007/kashmir20070508a.html; www.india-server.com/news/pm-dedicates-dulhasti-project-to-nation-589.html.

24. "Cloudy skies for Masdar's solar project," www.thenational.ae/business/energy/cloudy-skies-for-masdars-solar-project; "UAE: Powering down," http://pulitzercenter.org/reporting/masdar-carbon-neutral-uae-emirates-renewable-energy; "United Arab Emirates—Economy," www.qfinance.com/country-profiles/united-arab-emirates; "MassoudBarzani gets briefing on Abu Dhabi's renewable energy sector," www.chicagotribune.com/business/sns-mct-massoud-barzani-gets-briefing-on-abu-dhabis-20120502,0,6549833.story; "Dubai seeks renewable power sources for the future," www.thenational.ae/thenationalconversation/industry-insights/energy/dubai-seeks-renewable-power-sources-for-the-future.

CHAPTER

9

Project Scheduling
Networks, Duration Estimation, and Critical Path

Chapter Outline

Chapter Objectives

After completing this chapter, you should be able to:

1. Understand and apply key scheduling terminology.

2. Apply the logic used to create activity networks, including predecessor and successor tasks.

3. Develop an activity network using Activity-on-Node (AON) techniques.

4. Perform activity duration estimation based on the use of probabilistic estimating techniques.

5. Construct the critical path for a project schedule network using forward and backward passes.

6. Identify activity float and the manner in which it is determined.

7. Calculate the probability of a project finishing on time under PERT estimates.

8. Understand the steps that can be employed to reduce the critical path.

PROJECT MANAGEMENT BODY OF KNOWLEDGE CORE CONCEPTS COVERED IN THIS CHAPTER

1. Define Activities (PMBoK sec. 6.1)
2. Sequence Activities (PMBoK sec. 6.2)
3. Estimate Activity Resources (PMBoK sec. 6.3)
4. Estimate Activity Durations (PMBoK sec. 6.4)
5. Develop Schedule (PMBoK sec. 6.5)
6. Control Schedule (PMBoK sec. 6.6)

PROJECT PROFILE

South Africa Gets Stadiums Ready for 2010 World Cup

Sport has the power to change the world. It has the power to unite in a way that little else does.

—Nelson Mandela, the first democratically elected president of South Africa

The World Cup, international soccer's most visible and enduring event, occurs once every four years at venues selected nearly a decade in advance. Nations bid for the right to host the World Cup and after months of intense competition, when the winners are announced, the event sets off jubilant celebrations in the winning country and depression in others worldwide. An enormously important issue in the decision to bid for the World Cup is whether your country's infrastructure is set up to support the bid and, ultimately, to allow the event to be held in a positive atmosphere of excitement and competition.

The winner of the World Cup bid for 2010 was South Africa, the first African nation to host the tournament in its 80-year history. Although possessing the strongest economy in the southern hemisphere of the African continent, with a vibrant culture and a natural enthusiasm as it emerged from its Apartheid era, South Africa was by no means a rich nation, nor one that could easily absorb the costs of committing to hosting the games. The challenges were huge. Over the course of a relatively short time period, South Africa spent more than $6 billion dollars and engaged in a number of significant projects to support the World Cup, including:

- Building stadiums—A total of 10 soccer venues around the country had to be developed for the tournament. Five existing stadiums were given extensive face-lifts or other refurbishment, and five others had to be constructed.
- Airport upgrades—A number of airports throughout the country had to be reconstructed, to support the events, allowing for tourist flow and passenger travel from event to event.
- Road and infrastructure repair and development—Coupled with the construction work on the stadiums and the airports, hundreds of miles of roadways had to be widened, reconstructed, or heavily repaired to support traffic flows. The South African government invested over $2 billion in transportation and infrastructure projects, which were expected to be the lasting legacy to the country of the World Cup event.
- A high-speed train—Africa's first high-speed rail link, the "Gautrain," running between Johannesburg's financial center Sandton and the O.R. Tambo International Airport, was put in place. Work on the railway was approved even before the World Cup was awarded to South Africa, and its construction was brought forward to help the country cope with the hordes of tourists during the month-long event. The train was expected to provide efficient and affordable transport for the general population for many years after the World Cup and help to alleviate road traffic problems.
- Development of public spaces and urban parks—Although the World Cup attracts guests from around the globe, the poorest within South Africa would be effectively precluded from attending any games. Recognizing that actually getting to Johannesburg's stadium could be difficult for the poorest of this city's 3.5 million people; officials also took advantage of the World Cup as an economic engine to build a series of public spaces in some of the less advantaged parts of the city. Just in Johannesburg, officials created 23 new public parks and community facilities with large screens to allow residents to see the games. Similar building took place throughout the country, creating huge new green-space areas.

The stadium construction was a particularly impressive feature of South Africa's road to hosting the World Cup. Constructed at 10 sites around the country, the stadiums were models for artistic impressionism and function. For example, the most extensive renovation involved the 700,000-square-foot Soccer City Stadium in Johannesburg. Originally opened in 1987, Soccer City was South Africa's first international soccer venue; citizens also rallied there when Nelson Mandela was released from prison in 1990. The construction firms stripped the building and "re-skinned"

Allstar Picture Library / Alamy

FIGURE 9.1 Johannesburg Soccer City Stadium

it in a colorful mosaic of glass-fiber-reinforced concrete tiles, meant to resemble the round, gourd-like fruit of a traditional African calabash tree, interspersed with windows. The stadium held 94,000 spectators for the final match.

Troubles Along the Way

With the enormous undertaking, expenditures of national resources, and nationwide commitment to host this event, the lead-up to the World Cup was not an entirely smooth process. Projects went vastly over budget, past deadlines, and beyond feasibility. The cost of Cape Town's Bus Rapid Transit (BRT) system ballooned from an estimated $171 million in 2008 to more than $600 million, and it was announced that one section of the Johannesburg Rea Vaya BRT system would not be ready in time for the tournament as had previously been planned. Earlier, optimistic expectations for Johannesburg's Gautrain system had been scaled back. Planned BRT systems had been delayed or called off in Durban, Bloemfontein, and Tshwane.

Many of the stadiums were hampered by serious schedule delays or protests regarding construction bidding practices. In fact, charges of "bid rigging" were leveled at government officials in some cases while funding was first approved and then temporarily denied at any number of sites, halting construction or disrupting schedules. A number of venues, including Cape Town's Green Point Stadium, Mbombela Stadium in Nelspruit, and King's Park Soccer Stadium in Durban, were all adversely affected by disruptions in funding or bid protests.

On July 9, 2009, 70,000 construction workers went on strike nationwide, demanding increases of 13% to continue work on the various projects associated with the World Cup. Workers threatened to slow down or stop construction until their pay levels were brought up to acceptable levels. Their strikes came at a particularly vulnerable time for event planners, as numerous stadiums were still under construction and much of the infrastructure work was ongoing; the FIFA threatened to begin leveling fines on the country if nothing was done to resume construction. The South African government negotiated with the lead union in the strike and swiftly ended the stoppage, after agreeing to substantially increase pay and other benefits for construction workers.

More controversially, the 2009 documentary *Fahrenheit 2010* accused South Africa of diverting scarce resources from the HIV/AIDS epidemic and other urgent social causes. The film took special aim at Mbombela Stadium for lacking effective uses after its World Cup occupancy.

In spite of these problems and distractions, the World Cup, which saw Spain win its first championship, was a remarkably well-run and prosperous event. Some 400,000 fans and tourists visited South Africa during the month of the World Cup, coming away with lasting memories of modern facilities, bustling infrastructure, and superbly managed events. A June 3 editorial in *The Economist* stated that South Africa—a country rife with problems—was to be commended for its World Cup preparations. "Skeptics said South Africa would never make it," the article noted. "But, billions of dollars and much heartache later, it is ready. With ten spectacular new or upgraded stadiums, as many new or revamped airports, hundreds of kilometers of expanded highways and city streets, and the continent's first high-speed train up and running (just), South Africa is rightly proud of its achievement."[1]

INTRODUCTION

Project scheduling is a complex undertaking that involves a number of related steps. When we think about scheduling, it helps if we picture a giant jigsaw puzzle. At first, we lay out the border and start creating a mental picture in our heads of how the pieces are designed to fit together. As the border starts to take shape, we can add more and more pieces, gradually giving the puzzle shape and image. Each step in building the puzzle depends on having done the previous work correctly. In this way, the methodologies in project scheduling build upon each other. *Project scheduling requires us to follow some carefully laid-out steps, in order, for the schedule to take shape.* Just as a jigsaw puzzle will eventually yield a finished picture if we have followed the process correctly, the shape of the project's schedule will also come into direct focus when we learn the steps needed to bring it about.

9.1 PROJECT SCHEDULING

Project scheduling techniques lie at the heart of project planning and subsequent monitoring and control. Previous chapters have examined the development of vision and goals for the project, project screening activities, risk management practices, and project scope (including the Work Breakdown Structure). Project scheduling represents the conversion of project goals into an achievable methodology for their completion; it creates a timetable and reveals the network logic that relates project activities to each other in a coherent fashion. Because project management is predicated on completing a finite set of goals under a specified time frame, exactly how we develop the project's schedule is vitally important to success.

This chapter will examine a number of elements in project scheduling and demonstrate how to build the project plan from a simple set of identified project activities into a graphical set of sequential relationships between those tasks which, when performed, result in the completion of the project goals. **Project planning**, as it relates to the scheduling process, has been defined by the Project Management Body of Knowledge as "the identification of the project objectives and the ordered activity necessary to complete the project [including t]he identification of resource types and quantities required to carry out each activity or task."[2] The term **ordered activity** is important because it illustrates the scheduling goal. Project scheduling defines network logic for all **activities**; that is, **tasks** must either precede or follow other tasks from the beginning of the project to its completion.

Suppose you and your classroom team were given an assignment on leadership and were expected to turn in a paper and give a presentation at the end of the semester. It would first be necessary to break up the assignment into the discrete set of individual activities (Work Breakdown Structure) that would allow your team to finish the project. Perhaps you identified the following tasks needed to complete the assignment:

1. Identify topic
2. Research topic
3. Write first draft of paper
4. Edit and rewrite paper
5. Prepare class presentation
6. Complete final draft
7. Complete presentation
8. Hand in paper and present topic in class

Carefully defining all the steps necessary to complete the assignment is an important first step in project scheduling, as it adds a sequential logic to the tasks and goes further in that it allows you to create a coherent project plan from start to finish. Suppose, to ensure the best use of your time and availability, you were to create a network of the activities listed above, that is, the most likely order in which they must occur to be done correctly. First, it would be necessary to determine a reasonable sequence. *Preceding activities* are those that must occur before others can be done. For example, it would be necessary to first identify the term paper topic before beginning to conduct research on it. Therefore, activity 1, *Identify topic,* is a preceding activity; and activity 2, *Research topic,* is referred to as a subsequent, or *successor, activity.*

Once you have identified a reasonable sequential logic for the network, you can construct a **network diagram**, which is a schematic display of the project's sequential activities and the logical relationships between them. Figure 9.2 shows two examples of a network diagram for your project. Note that in Option A, the easiest method for constructing a network diagram is to simply lay out all activities in serial order, starting with the first task and concluding with the final activity. This option, however, is usually not the most

Option A: Serial Sequential Logic

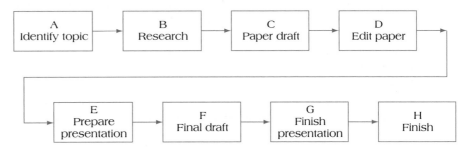

Option B: Nonserial Sequential Logic

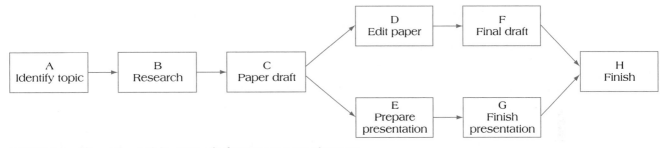

FIGURE 9.2 **Alternative Activity Networks for Term Paper Assignment**

efficient one. It could be argued, for example, that it is not necessary that the whole project team be involved in each of the activities, requiring you to delay the start of activity 6, *Complete final draft* (F in Figure 9.2), until after activity 5, *Prepare class presentation*. Another choice might be to use the time better by having some members of the team begin work on the presentation while others are still completing the paper. Any of these options mean that you are now constructing a project network with two paths, or parallel streams of activities, some of which are going on simultaneously. This alternative network can be seen in Option B of Figure 9.2.

This simplified example illustrates the process of applying sequential logic to project tasks in order to construct an activity network. In creating a sense of timing for activities in addition to their functions, the activity network allows project teams to use a method for planning and scheduling. There are several reasons why it is so important that project networks and scheduling be done well. Among the reasons are the following:[3]

- A network clearly illustrates the interdependence of all tasks and work packages. Doing something wrong earlier in the project has severe implications for downstream activities.
- Because a network illustrates this interrelationship among activities and project personnel, it facilitates communication flows. People are much more attuned to the work that went on before their involvement, and they develop a keener appreciation of the concerns of those who will take over at later points.
- A network helps with master scheduling of organizational resources because it shows times when various personnel must be fully committed to project activities. Without some sense of where the project fits into the overall organizational scheme, personnel may be assigned to multiple activities at a time when they are most needed on the project.
- A network identifies the critical activities and distinguishes them from the less critical. The network reveals the activities that absolutely must be completed on time to ensure that the overall project is delivered on time; in the process, activities that have some "wiggle room" are identified as well.
- Networks determine when you can expect projects to be completed.
- Dates on which various project activities must start and end in order to keep to the overall schedule are identified in a network.
- A network demonstrates which activities are dependent on which other activities. You then know the activities that need to be highly coordinated in order to ensure the smooth development of the project.

These are just some of the advantages of using activity networks for project scheduling.

9.2 KEY SCHEDULING TERMINOLOGY

Every profession has its unique jargon and terminology. In project scheduling, a number of specific terms are commonly employed and so need specific definitions. In many cases, their definitions are taken from the Project Management Institute's Body of Knowledge. Some concepts that you will see again and again throughout this chapter (and subsequent chapters) are listed here. You have already run across some of these terms in previous chapters.

Scope—The work content and products of a project or component of a project. Scope is fully described by naming all activities performed, the resources consumed, and the end products that result, including quality standards.

Work Breakdown Structure (WBS)—A task-oriented "family tree" of activities that organizes, defines, and graphically displays the total work to be accomplished in order to achieve the final objectives of a project. Each descending level represents an increasingly detailed definition of the project objective.

Work package—A deliverable at the lowest level of the Work Breakdown Structure; it is an element of work performed during the course of a project. A work package normally has an expected duration plus an expected cost. Other generic terms for project work include *task* or *activity*.

Project network diagram (PND)—Any schematic display of the logical relationships of project activities.

Path—A sequence of activities defined by the project network logic.

Event—A point when an activity is either started or completed. Often used in conjunction with AOA networks, events consume no resources and have no time to completion associated with them.

Node—One of the defining points of a network; a junction point joined to some or all of the others by dependency lines (paths).

Predecessors—Those activities that must be completed prior to initiation of a later activity in the network.

Successors—Activities that cannot be started until previous activities have been completed. These activities follow predecessor tasks.

Early start (ES) date—The earliest possible date on which the uncompleted portions of an activity (or the project) can start, based on the network logic and any schedule constraints. Early start dates can change as the project progresses and changes are made to the project plan.

Late start (LS) date—The latest possible date that an activity may begin without delaying a specified milestone (usually the project finish date).

Forward pass—Network calculations that determine the earliest start/earliest finish time (date) for each activity. The earliest start and finish dates are determined by working forward through each activity in the network.

Backward pass—Calculation of late finish times (dates) for all uncompleted network activities. The latest finish dates are determined by working backward through each activity.

Merge activity—An activity with two or more immediate predecessors (tasks flowing into it). Merge activities can be located by doing a forward pass through the network.

Burst activity—An activity with two or more immediate successor activities (tasks flowing out from it). Burst activities can be located by doing a backward pass through the network.

Float—The amount of time an activity may be delayed from its early start without delaying the finish of the project. Float is a mathematical calculation and can change as the project progresses and changes are made in the project plan. Also called *slack, total float,* and *path float.* In general, float is the difference between the late start date and the early start date (LS – ES) or between the late finish date and early finish date (LF – EF).

Critical path—The path through the project network with the longest duration. The critical path may change from time to time as activities are completed ahead of or behind schedule. Critical path activities are identified as having zero float in the project.

Critical Path Method (CPM)—A *network analysis* technique used to determine the amount of scheduling flexibility (the amount of float) on various logical network paths in the project schedule network, and to determine the minimum total project duration. It involves the calculation of early (forward scheduling) and late (backward scheduling) start and finish dates for each activity. Implicit in this technique is the assumption that whatever resources are required in any given time period will be available.

Resource-limited schedule—A project schedule whose start and finish dates reflect expected resource availability. The final project schedule should always be resource-limited.

Program Evaluation and Review Technique (PERT)—An event- and probability-based network analysis system generally used in projects where activities and their durations are difficult to define. PERT is often used in large programs where the projects involve numerous organizations at widely different locations.

The two most common methods for constructing activity networks involve **Activity-on-Arrow (AOA)** and **Activity-on-Node (AON)** logic. In the AOA method, the **arrow** represents the task, or activity, and the node signifies an event marker that suggests the completion of one activity and the potential to start the next. In AON methodology, the node represents an activity and the path arrows demonstrate the logical sequencing from node to node through the network. AOA approaches were most popular several decades ago and are still used to some extent in the construction industry, but with the rapid rise in computer-based scheduling programs, there is now a strong emphasis on AON methodology. Hence, in this chapter, we use AON examples and diagrams exclusively. Chapter 10 will discuss the rudiments of AOA network modeling.

9.3 DEVELOPING A NETWORK

Network diagramming is a logical, sequential process that requires you to consider the order in which activities should occur to schedule projects as efficiently as possible. There are two primary methods for developing activity networks, PERT and CPM. PERT, which stands for Program Evaluation and Review Technique, was developed in the late 1950s in collaboration between the U.S. Navy, Booz-Allen Hamilton, and Lockheed Corporation for the creation of the Polaris missile program. PERT originally was used in research and development (R&D), a field in which activity duration estimates can be difficult to make, and resulted from probability analysis. CPM, or Critical Path Method, was developed independently at the same time as PERT by DuPont, Inc. CPM, used commonly in the construction industry, differs from PERT primarily in the assumptions it makes about estimating activity durations. CPM assumes that durations are more deterministic; that is, they are easier to ascertain and can be assigned to activities with greater confidence. Further, CPM was designed to better link (and therefore control) project activity time and costs, particularly the time/cost trade-offs that lead to **crashing** decisions (speeding up the project). Crashing the project will be explained in more detail in Chapter 10. In practice, however, over the years the differences between PERT and CPM have blurred to the point where it is now common to simply refer to these networking techniques as PERT/CPM.[4]

Prior to constructing an activity network, there are some simple rules of thumb you need to become familiar with as you develop the network diagram. These rules are very helpful in understanding the logic of activity networks.[5]

1. Some determination of activity precedence ordering must be done prior to creating the network. That is, all activities must be logically linked to each other—those that precede others, as well as successor activities (those that must follow others).
2. Network diagrams usually flow from left to right.
3. An activity cannot begin until all preceding connected activities have been completed.
4. Arrows on networks indicate precedence and logical flow. Arrows can cross over each other, although it is helpful for clarity's sake to limit this effect when possible.
5. Each activity should have a unique identifier associated with it (number, letter, code, etc.). For simplicity, these identifiers should occur in ascending order; each one should be larger than the identifiers of preceding activities.
6. Looping, or recycling through activities, is not permitted.
7. Although not required, it is common to start a project from a single beginning node, even in the case when multiple start points are possible. A single node point also is typically used as a project end indicator.

With these simple rules of thumb firmly in mind, you can begin to uncover some of the basic principles of establishing a network diagram. Remember that AON methodology represents all activities within the network as nodes. Arrows are used only to indicate the sequential flow of activities from the start of the project to its conclusion.

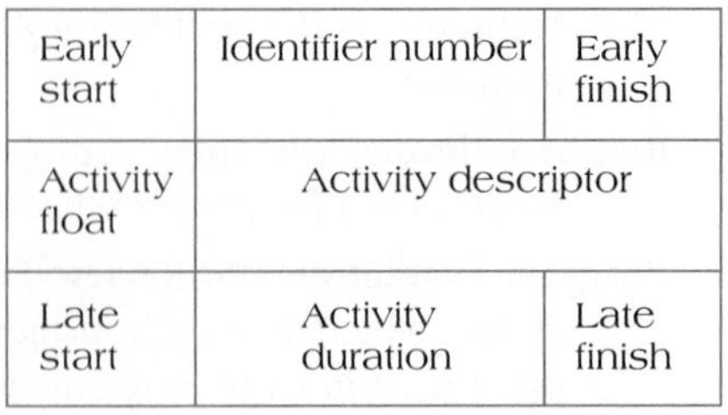

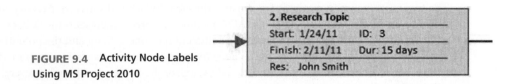

FIGURE 9.3 **Labels for Activity Node**

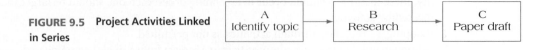

FIGURE 9.4 **Activity Node Labels Using MS Project 2010**

Labeling Nodes

Nodes representing project activities should be clearly labeled with a number of different pieces of information. It is helpful if the nodes at least contain the following data: (1) identifier, (2) descriptive label, (3) activity duration, (4) early start time, (5) early finish time, (6) late start time, (7) late finish time, and (8) activity float. Figure 9.3 shows the labeling for a node with each piece of information assigned to a location within the activity box. The arrangement selected for this node was arbitrary; there is no accepted standard for labeling activity nodes. For example, the node shown in Figure 9.4 was derived from a standard Microsoft Project 2010 output file. Note that in this example, the activity start and finish dates are shown, as well as the resource person responsible for the activity's completion.

Complete labels on activity nodes make it easier to use the network to perform additional calculations such as identifying critical path, activity float (or slack), total project duration, and so on. When constructing network diagrams during the early development of the project, all necessary information about the activity can be retrieved quickly as long as nodes are fully labeled.

Serial Activities

Serial activities are those that flow from one to the next, in sequence. Following the logic of Figure 9.5, we cannot begin work on activity B until activity A has been completed. Activity C cannot begin until both activities A and B are finished. Serial activity networks are the simplest in that they create only linkages of activity sequencing. In many cases, serial networks are appropriate representations of the project activities. Figure 9.5 demonstrates how, in the earlier example of preparing for a term paper and presentation, several activities must necessarily be linked serially. Identifying the topic, conducting research, and writing the first draft are activities that must link in series, because subsequent activities cannot begin until the previous (predecessor) ones have been completed.

Network logic suggests that:

Activity A can begin immediately.

Activity B cannot begin until activity A is completed.

Activity C cannot begin until both activities A and B are completed.

FIGURE 9.5 **Project Activities Linked in Series**

Concurrent Activities

In many circumstances, it is possible to begin work on more than one activity simultaneously, assuming that we have the resources available for both. Figure 9.6 provides an example of how concurrent or parallel project paths are represented in an activity network. When the nature of the work allows for more than

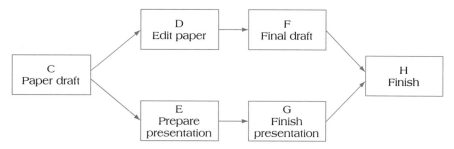

FIGURE 9.6   **Activities Linked in Parallel (Concurrent)**

one activity to be accomplished at the same time, these activities are called **concurrent**, and parallel project activity paths are constructed through the network. In order to successfully operate concurrent activities, the project must be staffed with sufficient human resources to support all simultaneous activities. This is a critical issue, because a network cannot be created without giving thought to the resource requirements needed to support it.

Network logic suggests that:

Activities D and E can begin following the completion of activity C.

Activity F can begin following the completion of activity D and is independent of activity E.

Activity G can begin following the completion of activity E and is independent of activity D.

Activity H can begin following the completion of both activities F and G.

Merge Activities

Merge activities are those with two or more immediate predecessors. Figure 9.7 is a partial network diagram that shows how merge activities are expressed graphically. Merge activities often are critical junction points, places where two or more parallel project paths converge within the overall network. Figure 9.7 demonstrates the logic of merge activity: You cannot begin activity D until all predecessor activities, A, B and C, have been completed. The start of the merge activity is subject to the completion of the longest prior activity. For example, suppose that activities A, B, and C all start on the same day. Activity A has a duration of 3 days, activity B's duration is 5 days, and activity C has a duration of 7 days. The earliest day activity D, the merge point, can start is on day 7, following completion of all three predecessor activities.

Network logic suggests that:

Activity D can only begin following the completion of activities A, B, and C.

Burst Activities

Burst activities are those with two or more immediate successor activities. Figure 9.8 graphically depicts a burst task, with activities B, C, and D scheduled to follow the completion of activity A. All three successors can only be undertaken upon the completion of activity A. Unlike merge activities, in which the successor is

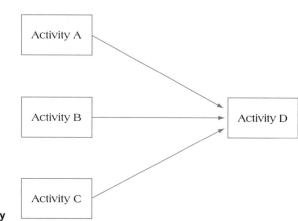

FIGURE 9.7   **Merge Activity**

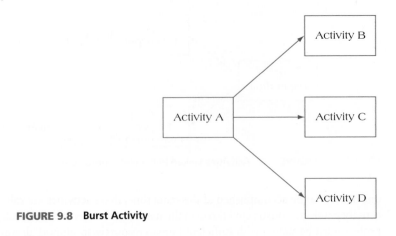

FIGURE 9.8   Burst Activity

dependent upon completion of the longest predecessor activity before it can begin, all immediate successors can begin simultaneously upon completion of the burst activity.

Network logic suggests that:

Activities B, C, and D can only begin following the completion of activity A.

EXAMPLE 9.1

Let's begin constructing a basic activity network. Table 9.1 identifies eight activities and their predecessors in a simple example project. Once we have determined the tasks necessary to accomplish the project, it is important to begin linking those tasks to each other. In effect, we are taking the project tasks in the Work Breakdown Structure and adding a project chronology.

Once the network activity table has been developed and the predecessors identified, we can begin the process of network construction. The first activity (A) shows no predecessors; it is the starting point in the network and placed to the far left of our diagram. Next, activities B and C both identify activity A as their predecessor. We can place them on the network as well. Activity D lists both activities B and C as predecessors. Figure 9.9 gives a partial network diagram based on the information we have compiled to this point. Note that, based on our definitions, activity A is a burst activity and activity D is a merge activity.

We can continue to create the network iteratively as we add additional activity nodes to the diagram. Figure 9.10 shows the final activity network. Referring back to an earlier point, note that this network begins with a single node point (activity A) and concludes with a single point (activity H). The merge activities associated with this network include activities D (with activities B and C merging at this node) and H (with activities E, F, and G merging at this node). Activities A, B, and C are burst activities. Recall that burst activities are defined as those with two or more immediate successors in the network. Activity A has the successor tasks B and C, activity B has tasks D and E following it, and activity C has two successors (D and G).

TABLE 9.1 Information for Network Construction

Name: Project Delta

Activity	Description	Predecessors
A	Contract signing	None
B	Questionnaire design	A
C	Target market ID	A
D	Survey sample	B, C
E	Develop presentation	B
F	Analyze results	D
G	Demographic analysis	C
H	Presentation to client	E, F, G

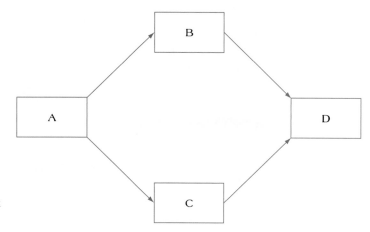

FIGURE 9.9 Partial Activity Network Based on Project Delta

If we employed Microsoft Project 2010 to create the network diagram, we would first enter each of the activities into the template shown in Figure 9.11. Note that for this example, we are not assigning any durations to the activities, so the default is set at 1 day for each activity.

The next step in using MS Project to create a network is to identify the predecessor activities at each step in the project. In Figure 9.12, we begin to build the network by specifying each predecessor and successor

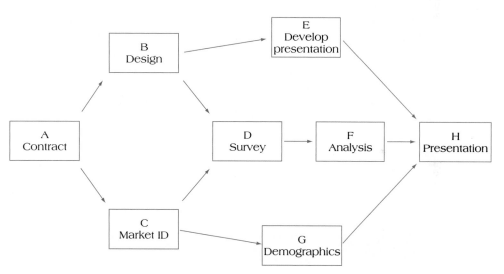

FIGURE 9.10 Complete Activity Network for Project Delta

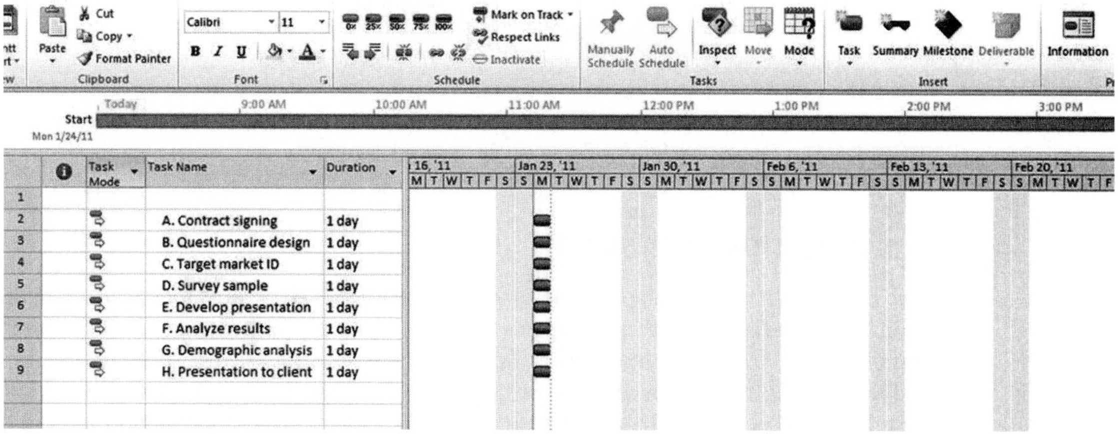

		Task Mode	Task Name	Duration
1				
2			A. Contract signing	1 day
3			B. Questionnaire design	1 day
4			C. Target market ID	1 day
5			D. Survey sample	1 day
6			E. Develop presentation	1 day
7			F. Analyze results	1 day
8			G. Demographic analysis	1 day
9			H. Presentation to client	1 day

FIGURE 9.11 Developing the Activity Network Using MS Project 2010

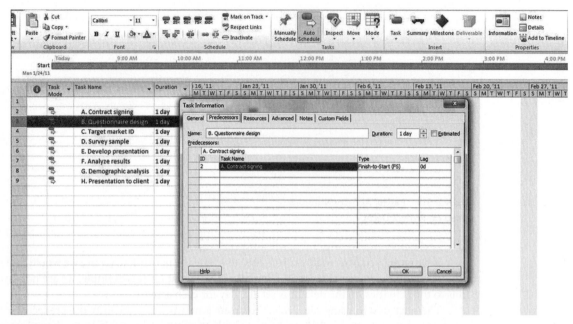

FIGURE 9.12 **Task Information Window Used to Specify Predecessors for Activity Networks**

in the network. Double-clicking the mouse on an activity will bring up a Task Information window (shown in Figure 9.12). In that window, we can specify the task or tasks that are predecessors of our current activity. For activity B (questionnaire design), we have specified a single predecessor (contract signing).

Once we have added each task in turn, the project network is completed. MS Project can be used to generate the final network, as shown in Figure 9.13. Note that each activity is still labeled as needing only 1 day for completion. In the next section of this chapter, we begin to consider the manner in which individual activity durations can be determined.

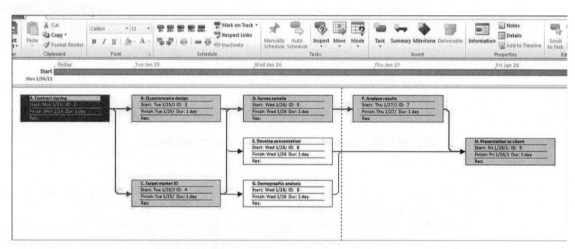

FIGURE 9.13 **The Completed MS Project 2010 Network Diagram**

9.4 DURATION ESTIMATION

The next step in building the network is to estimate activity **durations** for each step in the project. The first point to remember is that these estimates are based on what is assumed to be normal working methods during normal business or working hours. Second, although factors such as past experience or familiarity with the work will influence the accuracy of these estimates, activity durations are always somewhat uncertain. Third, time frames for task estimates can vary from several hours for short projects to days and weeks for longer projects.

Activity durations can be estimated in a number of different ways, including:[6]

- ***Experience.*** In cases where the organization has previously done similar work, we can use history as a guide. This approach is relatively easy; we simply call upon past examples of similar projects and use them as a baseline. The main drawback to this approach is that it assumes what worked in the past will continue to work today. Projects are affected by external events that are unique to their own time. Therefore, in using experience, we must be aware of the potential for using distorted or outdated information.
- ***Expert opinion.*** At times we may be told to contact a past project manager or expert in a particular area to get accurate information on activity estimates. Intuitively this approach would seem to be useful—if you want to know something, go to an expert. Yet "experts" are considered experts precisely because they know the easiest avenues, best contacts, and fastest processes to complete tasks. Would an expert's estimate of completion time be valid for nonexperts doing the same activity? The answer is not absolute, but the question suggests that we use caution in our application of expert opinion.
- ***Mathematical derivation.*** Another approach offers a more objective alternative to activity duration estimation and sidesteps many of the problems that can be found in more subjective methods. This method consists of developing duration probability based on a reasoned analysis of best-case, most likely case, and worst-case scenarios.

In order to understand how to use mathematical derivation to determine expected activity times, we need to consider the basics of probability distributions. Probability suggests that the amount of time an activity is likely to take can rarely be positively determined; rather, it is found as the result of sampling a range of likelihoods, or probabilities, of the event occurring. These likelihoods range from 0 (no probability) to 1 (complete probability). In order to derive a reasonable probabilistic estimate for an activity's duration, we need to identify three values: (1) the activity's most likely duration, (2) the activity's most pessimistic duration, and (3) the activity's most optimistic duration. The most likely duration is determined to be the length of time expected to complete an activity assuming the development of that activity proceeds normally. Pessimistic duration is the expected length of time needed to develop the activity under the assumption that everything will go badly (Murphy's Law). Finally, optimistic duration is estimated under the assumption that the development process will proceed extremely well.

For these time estimates, we can use probability distributions that are either symmetrical (the normal distribution) or asymmetrical (the beta distribution). A normal distribution implies that the probability of an event taking the most likely time is one that is centered on the mean of the distribution (see Figure 9.14). Because pessimistic and optimistic values are estimated at the 95% confidence level from either end of the distribution, they will cancel each other out, leaving the mean value as the expected duration time for the activity.

In real life it is extremely rare to find examples in which optimistic and pessimistic durations are symmetrical to each other about the mean. In project management, it is more common to see probability distributions that are asymmetrical; these are referred to as **beta distributions**. The asymmetry of the probability distribution suggests we recognize that certain events are less likely to occur than others. An activity's optimistic time may lie within one standard deviation from the mean while its pessimistic time may be as much as three or four standard deviations away. To illustrate, suppose that we began construction on a highway

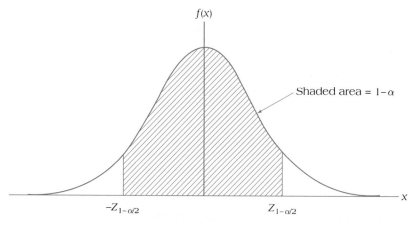

FIGURE 9.14 **Symmetrical (Normal) Distribution for Activity Duration Estimation**

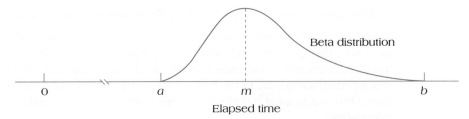

FIGURE 9.15   Asymmetrical (Beta) Distribution for Activity Duration Estimation

bridge and wished to estimate the length of time (duration) it would take to place the steel girders needed to frame the bridge. We expect that the duration for the framing task will take six days; however, a number of factors could change that duration estimate. We could, for example, experience uncommonly good weather and have no technical delays, allowing us to finish the framing work in only four days. On the other hand, we could have terrible weather, experience delivery delays for needed materials, and lose time in labor disputes, all leading to a pessimistic estimate of 14 days. This example demonstrates the asymmetrical nature of duration estimates; while our most likely duration is 6 days, the range can vary from 4 to 14 days to complete the task.

The optimistic and pessimistic duration values essentially serve as upper and lower bounds for the distribution range. Figure 9.15 illustrates a beta distribution with the values *m* (most likely duration), *a* (most optimistic duration), and *b* (most pessimistic duration) identified.

Two assumptions are used to convert the values of *m, a,* and *b* into estimates of the expected time (TE) and variance (s^2) of the duration for the activity. One important assumption is that *s*, the standard deviation of the duration required to complete the task, equals one-sixth of the range for reasonably possible time requirements. The **variance** for an activity duration estimate is given by the formula:

$$s^2 = [(b - a)/6]^2$$

The logic for this assumption is based on the understanding that to achieve a probability distribution with a 99% confidence interval, observations should lie within three standard deviations of the mean in either direction. A spread of six standard deviations from tail to tail in the probability distribution, then, accounts for 99.7% of the possible activity duration alternatives.

Because optimistic and pessimistic times are not symmetrical about the mean, the second assumption refers to the shape of the probability distribution. Again, the beta, or asymmetrical, distribution better represents the distribution of possible alternative expected duration times (TE) for estimating activities. The beta distribution suggests that the calculation for deriving TE is shown as:

$$\text{TE} = (a + 4m + b)/6$$

where

    TE = estimated time for activity

     a = most optimistic time to complete the activity

    m = most likely time to complete the activity, the mode of the distribution

    b = most pessimistic time to complete the activity

In this calculation, the midpoint between the pessimistic and optimistic values is the weighted arithmetic mean of the mode and midrange, representing two-thirds of the overall weighting for the calculated expected time. The additional weighting is intended to highlight the clustering of expected values around the distribution mean, regardless of the length of both pessimistic and optimistic tails (total distribution standard deviation).

How do we put together all of these assumptions to perform an accurate activity duration estimation? The next step is to construct an activity duration estimate table (see Table 9.2). For simplicity, all numbers shown are in weeks.

Table 9.2 demonstrates the most likely times for each activity based on a reasonably accurate assessment of how long a task *should* take, *could* take if everything went well, and *would* take if everything went poorly. If we assign the value *a* to the most optimistic duration estimate, the project manager must assign a

TABLE 9.2 Activity Duration Estimates for Project Delta

Name: Project Delta

Durations are listed in weeks

Activity	Description	Optimistic	Likely	Pessimistic
A	Contract signing	3	4	11
B	Questionnaire design	2	5	8
C	Target market ID	3	6	9
D	Survey sample	8	12	20
E	Develop presentation	3	5	12
F	Analyze results	2	4	7
G	Demographic analysis	6	9	14
H	Presentation to client	1	2	4

value to this activity such that the actual amount of time needed to complete the activity will be *a* or greater 99% of the time. Conversely, in assigning a value for the most pessimistic duration, *b,* the project manager should estimate the duration of the activity to have a 99% likelihood that it will take *b* or less amount of time.

The standard formula for estimating expected activity duration times is based on the weighting ratio of 1 × optimistic, 4 × likely, and 1 × pessimistic. Researchers and practitioners alike, however, have found that this ratio is best viewed as a heuristic whose basic assumptions are affected by a project's unique circumstances. One argument holds that the above ratio is far too optimistic and does not take into consideration the negative impact created when the worst-case or pessimistic estimate proves accurate. Further, given the inherent uncertainty in many projects, significant levels of risk must be accounted for in all probabilistic estimates of duration.

Extensive research into the topic of improving the accuracy of activity duration estimation has not led to definitive results. Modeling techniques such as Monte Carlo simulation and linear and nonlinear programming algorithms generally have demonstrated that the degree of uncertainty in task durations can have a significant impact on the optimum method for duration estimation. Because uncertainty is so common in activity estimation, more than one activity estimate may be reasonably held. The goal is to achieve a **confidence interval** that provides the highest reasonable probability of being accurate. Probability estimation using 99% confidence intervals represents a degree of confidence few project managers would be willing to demonstrate, according to Meredith and Mantel.[7] Consequently, when the confidence interval level assumption is relaxed to, for example, 90%, the variance calculations and estimates of duration must be modified accordingly. Although the debate is likely to continue, an estimation formula of 1:4:1 (optimistic : likely : pessimistic)/6 is commonly accepted.

Using this ratio as a tool, it is now possible to calculate expected activity duration times for each of the tasks identified in Table 9.2. Table 9.3 shows the calculated times for each activity, based on the assumption of a beta distribution.

TABLE 9.3 Estimated Project Activity Times Using Beta Distribution

Name: Project Delta

Durations are listed in weeks

Activity	Description	Beta (1:4:1 ratio)/6
A	Contract signing	5
B	Questionnaire design	5
C	Target market ID	6
D	Survey sample	12.7
E	Develop presentation	5.8
F	Analyze results	4.2
G	Demographic analysis	9.3
H	Presentation to client	2.2

Creating the project network and calculating activity durations are the first two key steps in developing the project schedule. The next stage is to combine these two pieces of information in order to create the project's critical path diagram.

9.5 CONSTRUCTING THE CRITICAL PATH

The next step is to link activity duration estimates and begin construction of the critical path. Critical path calculations link activity durations to the preconstructed project activity network. This point is important: The project network is first developed using activity precedence logic, *then,* following task duration estimates, these values are applied in a structured process to each activity to determine overall project length. In addition to allowing us to determine how long the project is going to take, applying time estimates to the network lets us discover activity float (which activities can be delayed and which cannot), the latest and earliest times each activity can be started or must be completed, and the latest and earliest times each activity can be completed.

Calculating the Network

The process for developing the network with time estimates is fairly straightforward. Once the activity network and duration estimates are in place, the actual network calculation computations can proceed. Look again at the network in Figure 9.10 and the duration estimates given in Table 9.3 that assume a beta distribution. In this example, the time estimates are rounded to the nearest whole integer. The activity information is summarized in Table 9.4.

The methodology for using this information to create a critical path requires two steps: a *forward pass* through the network from the first activity to the last and a *backward pass* through the network from the final activity to the beginning. The forward pass is an additive process that calculates the earliest times an activity can begin and end. Once we have completed the forward pass, we will know how long the overall project is expected to take. The backward pass is a subtractive process that gives us information on when the latest activities can begin and end. Once both the forward and backward passes have been completed, we will also be able to determine individual activity float and, finally, the project's critical path.

After labeling the network with the activity durations, we begin to determine the various paths through the network. Figure 9.16 shows a partial activity network with durations labeled for each of the eight project activities. Each path is discovered by assessing all possible sequences of precedence activities from the beginning node to the end. Here, we can identify four separate paths, labeled:

Path One:	A − B − E − H
Path Two:	A − B − D − F − H
Path Three:	A − C − D − F − H
Path Four:	A − C − G − H

Since we now know the activity times for each task, we can also identify the critical path. The *critical path* is defined as the "series of interdependent activities of a project, connected end-to-end, which determines

TABLE 9.4 Project Information

Project Delta

Activity	Description	Predecessors	Estimated Duration
A	Contract signing	None	5
B	Questionnaire design	A	5
C	Target market ID	A	6
D	Survey sample	B, C	13
E	Develop presentation	B	6
F	Analyze results	D	4
G	Demographic analysis	C	9
H	Presentation to client	E, F, G	2

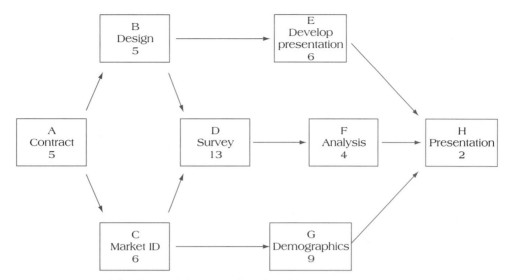

FIGURE 9.16 **Partial Project Activity Network with Task Durations**

the shortest total length of the project."[8] The shortest total length of time needed to complete a project is determined by the *longest path* through the network. The length of the four paths listed above can be derived simply by adding their individual activity durations together. Hence,

Path One: A − B − E − H = 18 weeks

Path Two: A − B − D − F − H = 29 weeks

Path Three: A − C − D − F − H = 30 weeks

Path Four: A − C − G − H = 22 weeks

Path Three, which links the activities A – C – D – F – H, is scheduled for duration of 30 weeks and is the critical path for this activity. In practical terms, this path has no float, or slack time, associated with it.

The Forward Pass

We can now begin adding more information to the network by conducting the forward pass to determine the earliest times each activity can begin and the earliest it can be completed. The process is iterative; each step builds on the information contained in the node immediately preceding it in the network. The beginning activity, contract signing, can be started at time 0 (immediately). Therefore, the earliest that activity A can be completed is on day 5. Early finish for any activity (EF) is found by taking its early start (ES) time and adding its activity duration (ES + Dur = EF). Therefore, activity B (questionnaire design) has an activity early start time of 5. This value corresponds to the early finish of the activity immediately preceding it in the network. Likewise, activity C, which is also dependent upon the completion of activity A to start, has an early start of 5. The early finish for activity B, calculated by (ES + Dur = EF), is 5 + 5, or 10. The early finish for activity C is found by 5 + 6 = 11. Figure 9.17 shows the process for developing the forward pass through the activity network.

The first challenge occurs at activity D, the merge point for activities B and C. Activity B has an early finish (EF) time of 10 weeks; however, activity C has an EF of 11 weeks. What should be the activity early start (ES) for activity D?

In order to answer this question, it is helpful to review the rules that govern the use of forward pass methodology. Principally, there are three steps for applying the forward pass:

1. Add all activity times along each path as we move through the network (ES + Dur = EF).
2. Carry the EF time to the activity nodes immediately succeeding the recently completed node. That EF becomes the ES of the next node, unless the succeeding node is a merge point.
3. At a merge point, the largest preceding EF becomes the ES for that node.

Applying these rules, at activity D, a merge point, we have the option of applying either an EF of 10 (activity B) or of 11 (activity C) as our new ES. Because activity C's early finish is larger, we would select the ES value of 11 for this node. The logic for this rule regarding merge points is important: Remember that early

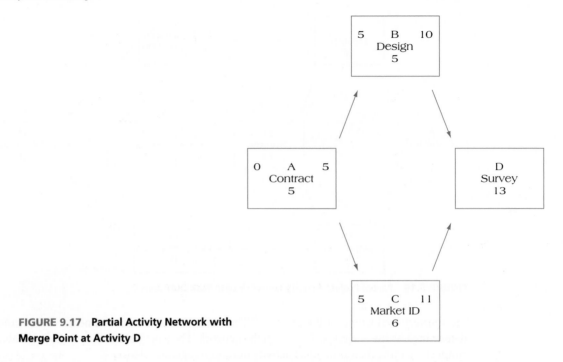

FIGURE 9.17 Partial Activity Network with Merge Point at Activity D

start is defined as the earliest an activity can begin. When two or more immediate predecessors have varying EF times, *the earliest the successor can begin is when all preceding activities have been completed.* Thus, we can determine that it would be impossible for activity D to begin at week 10 because one of its predecessors (activity C) would not have been finished by that point.

If we continue applying the forward pass to the network, we can work in a straightforward manner until we reach the final node, activity H, which is also a merge point. Activity H has three immediate predecessors, activities E, F, and G. The EF for activity E is 16, the EF for activity F is 28, and the EF for activity G is 20. Therefore, the ES for activity H must be the largest EF, or 28. The final length of the project is 30 weeks. Figure 9.18 illustrates the overall network with all early start and early finish dates indicated.

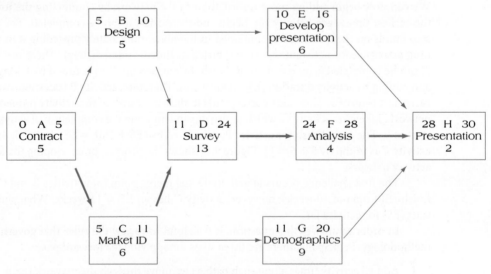

FIGURE 9.18 Activity Network with Forward Pass

The Backward Pass

We now are able to determine the overall length of the project, as well as each activity's early start and early finish times. When we take the next step of performing the backward pass through the network, we will be able to ascertain the project's critical path and the total float time of each project activity. The backward pass

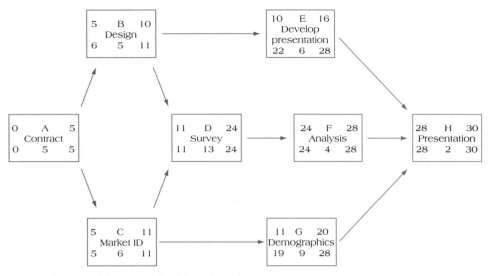

FIGURE 9.19 Activity Network with Backward Pass

is an iterative process, just as the forward pass is. The difference here is that we begin at the end of the network, with the final node. The goal of the backward pass is to determine each activity's late start (LS) and late finish (LF) times. LS and LF are determined through a subtractive methodology.

In Figure 9.19, we begin the backward pass with the node representing activity H (presentation). The first value we can fill out in the node is the late finish (LF) value for the project. This value is the same as the early finish (30 weeks). For the final node in a project network, the EF = LF. Once we have identified the LF of 30 weeks, the LS for activity H is the difference between the LF and the activity's duration; in this case, 30 – 2 = 28. The formula for determining LS is LF – Dur = LS. Thus, the LS for activity H is 28 and the LF is 30. These values are shown in the bottom of the node, with the LS in the bottom left corner and the LF in the bottom right corner. In order to determine the LF for the next three activities that are linked to activity H (activities E, F, and G), we carry the LS value of activity H backward to these nodes. Therefore, activities E, F, and G will each have 28 as their LF value.

Again, we subtract the durations from the LF values of each of the activities. The process continues to proceed backward, from right to left, through the network. However, just as in the forward pass we came upon a problem at merge points (activities D and H), we find ourselves in similar difficulty at the burst points—activities A, B, and C. At these three nodes, more than one preceding activity arrow converges, suggesting that there are multiple options for choosing the correct LF value. Burst activities, as we defined them, are those with two or more immediate successor activities. With activity B, both activities D and E are successors. For activity D, the LS = 11, and for activity E, the LS = 22. Which LS value should be selected as the LF for these burst activities?

To answer this question, we need to review the rules for the backward pass.

1. Subtract activity times along each path as you move through the network (LF – Dur = LS).
2. Carry back the LS time to the activity nodes immediately preceding the successor node. That LS becomes the LF of the next node, unless the preceding node is a burst point.
3. In the case of a burst point, the smallest succeeding LS becomes the LF for that node.

The correct choice for LF for activity B is 11 weeks, based on activity D. The correct choice for activity C, either 11 or 19 weeks from the network diagram, is 11 weeks. Finally, the LS for activity B is 6 weeks and it is 5 weeks for activity C; therefore, the LF for activity A is 5 weeks. Once we have labeled each node with its LS and LF values, the backward pass through the network is completed.

We can now determine the float, or **slack**, for each activity as well as the overall critical path. Again, float informs us of the amount of time an activity can be delayed and still not delay the overall project. Activity float is found through using one of two equations: LF – EF = Float or LS – ES = Float. Consider activity E with 12 weeks of float. Assume the worst-case scenario, in which the activity is unexpectedly delayed 10 weeks, starting on week 20 instead of the planned week 10. What are the implications of this delay on the overall project? None. With 12 weeks of float for activity E, a delay of 10 weeks will not affect the overall

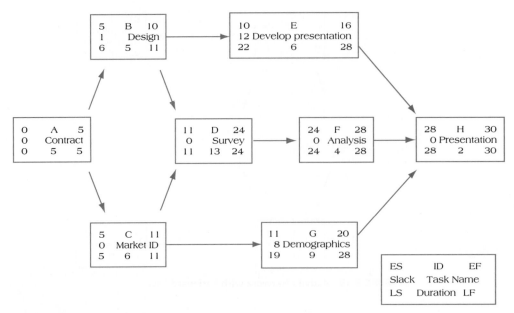

FIGURE 9.20 Project Network with Activity Slack and Critical Path

Note: Critical path is indicated with bold arrows.

length of the project or delay its completion. What would happen if the activity were delayed by 14 weeks? The ES, instead of 10, is now 24. Adding activity duration (6 weeks), the new EF is 30. Take a look at the network shown in Figure 9.20 to see the impact of this delay. Because activity H is a merge point for activities E, F, and G, the largest EF value is the ES for the final node. The new largest EF is 30 in activity E. Therefore, the new node EF = ES + Dur, or 30 + 2 = 32. The effect of overusing available slack delays the project by 2 weeks.

One other important point to remember about activity float is that *it is determined as a result of performing the forward and backward passes through the network.* Until we have done the calculations for ES, EF, LS, and LF, we cannot be certain which activities have float associated with them and which do not. Using this information to determine the project critical path suggests that *the critical path is the network path with no activity slack associated with it.* In our project, we can determine the critical path by linking the nodes with no float: A – C – D – F – H. The only time this rule is violated is when an arbitrary value has been used for the project LF; for example, suppose that a critical deadline date is inserted at the end of the network as the LF. Regardless of how many days the project is calculated to take based on the forward pass calculation, if a deadline is substituted for the latest possible date to complete the project (LF), there is going to be some negative float associated with the project. *Negative float* refers to delays in which we have used up all available safety, or float, and are now facing project delays. For example, if top management unilaterally sets a date that allows the project only 28 weeks to the LF, the project critical path will start with 2 weeks of negative slack. It is often better to resolve problems of imposed completion dates by paring down activity estimates rather than beginning the project with some stored negative float.

We can also determine path float; that is, the linkage of each node within a noncritical path. The path A – B – E – H has a total of 13 weeks of float; however, it may be impossible to "borrow" against the float of later activities if the result is to conflict with the critical path. Although there are 13 weeks of float for the path, activity B cannot consume more than one week of the total float before becoming part of the critical path. This is because B is a predecessor activity to activity D, which is on the critical path. Using more than one week of extra float time to complete activity B will result in delaying the ES for critical activity D and thereby lengthening the project's critical path.

Probability of Project Completion

Calculating the critical path in our example shows us that the expected completion of Project Delta was 30 weeks, but remember that our original time estimates for each activity were probabilistic, based on the beta distribution. This implies that there is the potential for variance (perhaps *serious* variance) in the overall estimate for project duration. Variations in activities on the critical path can affect the overall project completion time and possibly delay it significantly. As a result, it is important to consider the manner in

TABLE 9.5 Expected Activity Durations and Variances for Project Delta

Activity	Optimistic (a)	Most Likely (m)	Pessimistic (b)	Expected Time	Variance $[(b-a)/6]^2$
A	3	4	11	5	$[(11-3)/6]^2 = 64/36 = 1.78$
B	2	5	8	5	$[(8-2)/6]^2 = 36/36 = 1.00$
C	3	6	9	6	$[(9-3)/6]^2 = 36/36 = 1.00$
D	8	12	20	12.7	$[(20-8)/6]^2 = 144/36 = 4.00$
E	3	5	12	5.8	$[(12-3)/6]^2 = 81/36 = 2.25$
F	2	4	7	4.2	$[(7-2)/6]^2 = 25/36 = 0.69$
G	6	9	14	9.3	$[(14-6)/6]^2 = 64/36 = 1.78$
H	1	2	4	2.2	$[(4-1)/6]^2 = 9/36 = 0.25$

which we calculate and make use of activity duration variances. Recall that the formula for variance in activity durations is:

$$s^2 = [(b-a)/6]^2, \text{ where } b \text{ is the most pessimistic time and } a \text{ is the most optimistic}$$

Determining the individual activity variances is straightforward. As an example, let's refer back to Table 9.3 to find the variance for activity A (contract signing). Since we know the most optimistic and pessimistic times for this task (3 and 11 days, respectively), we calculate its variance as:

$$\text{Activity A: } [(11-3)/6]^2 = (8/6)^2 = 64/36, \text{ or } 1.78 \text{ weeks}$$

This information is important for project managers because we want to know not just likely times for activities but also how much confidence we can place in these estimates; thus, for our project's activity A, we can see that although it is most likely that it will finish in 5 weeks, there is a considerable amount of variance in that estimate (nearly 2 weeks). It is also possible to use this information to calculate the expected variance and standard deviation for all activities in our Project Delta, as Table 9.5 demonstrates.

We can use the information in Table 9.5 to calculate the overall project variance as well. Project variance is found by summing the variances of all *critical* activities and can be represented as the following equation:

$$\sigma_p^2 = \text{Project variance} = \sum(\text{variances of activities on critical path})$$

Thus, using our example, we can calculate the overall project variance and standard deviation for Project Delta. Recall that the critical activities for this project were A – C – D – F – H. For the overall project variance, the calculation is:

$$\text{Project variance } (\sigma_p^2) = 1.78 + 1.00 + 4.00 + .69 + .25 = 7.72$$

The project standard deviation (σ_p) is found as: $\sqrt{\text{Project variance}} = \sqrt{7.72} = 2.78$ weeks.

This project variance information is useful for assessing the probability of on-time project completion because PERT estimates make two more helpful assumptions: (1) total project completion times use a normal probability distribution, and (2) the activity times are statistically independent. As a result, the normal bell curve shown in Figure 9.21 can be used to represent project completion dates. Normal distribution here implies that there is 50% likelihood that Project Delta's completion time will be less than 30 weeks and a 50% chance that it will be greater than 30 weeks. With this information we are able to determine the probability that our project will be finished on or before a particular time.

Suppose, for example, that it is critical to our company that Project Delta finishes before 32 weeks. Although the schedule calls for a 30-week completion date, remember that our estimates are based on probabilities. Therefore, if we wanted to determine the probability that the project would finish no later than

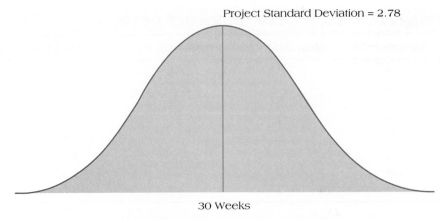

FIGURE 9.21 **Probability Distribution for Project Delta Completion Times**

32 week, we would need to determine the appropriate area under the normal curve from Figure 9.22 that corresponds to a completion date on or before week 32. We can use a standard normal equation to determine this probability. The standard normal equation is represented as:

$$Z = (\text{Due date} - \text{Expected date of completion})/\sigma_p$$

$$= (32 - 30)/2.78, \text{ or } 0.72$$

where Z is the number of standard deviations the target date (32 weeks) lies from the mean or expected date to completion (30 weeks). We can now use a normal distribution table (see Appendix A) to determine that a Z value of 0.72 indicates a probability of 0.7642. Thus, there is a 76.42% chance that Project Delta will finish on or before the critical date of 32 weeks. Visually, this calculation would resemble the picture in Figure 9.22, showing the additional two weeks represented as part of the shaded normal curve to the left of the mean.

Remember from this example that the 32-week deadline is critical for the company to meet. How confident would we be in working on this project if the likelihood of meeting that deadline was only 76.42%? Odds are that the project team (and the organization) might find a 76% chance of success in meeting the deadline unacceptable, which naturally leads to the question: How much time will the project team need in order to guarantee delivery with a high degree of confidence?

The first question that needs to be answered is: What is the minimal acceptable likelihood percentage that an organization needs when making this decision? For example, there is a big difference is requiring a 99% confidence of completion versus a 90% likelihood. Let's suppose that the organization developing Project Delta requires a 95% likelihood of on-time delivery. Under this circumstance, how much additional time should the project require to ensure a 95% likelihood of on-time completion?

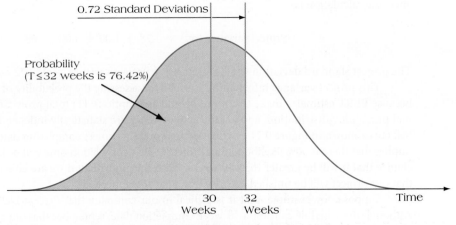

FIGURE 9.22 **Probability of Completing Project Delta by Week 32**

We are able to determine this value, again, with the aid of Z-score normal distribution tables. The tables indicate that for 95% probability, a Z-score of 1.65 most closely represents this likelihood. We can rewrite the previous standard normal equation and solve for the due date as follows:

$$\text{Due Date} = \text{Expected date of completion} + (Z \times \sigma_p)$$
$$= 30\,\text{weeks} + (1.65)(2.78)$$
$$= 34.59\,\text{weeks}$$

If the project team can negotiate for an additional 4.59 weeks, they have a very strong (95%) likelihood of ensuring that Project Delta will be completed on time.

It is important to consider one final point regarding estimating probabilities of project completion. So far, we have only addressed activities on the critical path because, logically, they define the overall length of a project. However, there are some circumstances where it may also be necessary to consider noncritical activities and their effect on overall project duration, especially if those activities have little individual slack time and a high variance. For example, in our Project Delta example, activity B has only 1 day of slack and there is sufficient variance of 1.00. In fact, the pessimistic time for activity B is 8 weeks, which would cause the project to miss its target deadline of 30 weeks, even though activity B is not on the critical path. For this reason, it may be necessary to calculate the individual task variances not only for critical activities, but for all project activities, especially those with higher variances. We can then calculate the likelihood of meeting our projected completion dates for all paths, both critical and noncritical.

FIGURE 9.23   AON Network for Programming Sequence Without Laddering

Laddering Activities

The typical PERT/CPM network operates on the assumption that a preceding activity must be completely finished before the start of the successor task. In many circumstances, however, it may be possible to begin a portion of one activity while work continues on other elements of the task, particularly in lengthy or complex projects. Consider a software development project for a new order-entry system. One task in the overall project network could be to create the Visual Basic code composed of several subroutines to cover the systems of multiple departments. A standard PERT chart would diagram the network logic from coding through debugging as a straightforward logical sequence in which system design precedes coding, which precedes debugging (see Figure 9.23). Under severe time pressure to use our resources efficiently, however, we might want to find a method for streamlining, or making the development sequence more efficient.

Laddering is a technique that allows us to redraw the activity network to more closely sequence project subtasks to make the overall network sequence more efficient. Figure 9.24 shows our software development

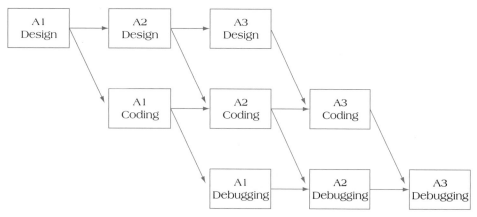

FIGURE 9.24   AON Network with Laddering Effect

path with laddering. Note that for simplicity's sake, we have divided the steps of design, coding, and debugging into three subtasks. The number of ladders constructed is typically a function of the number of identified break points of logical substeps available. If we assume that the software design and coding project has three significant subroutines, we can create a laddering effect that allows the project team to first complete design phase 1, then move to design phase 2 while coding of design phase 1 has already started. As we move through the laddering process, by the time our designers are ready to initiate design phase 3 in the project, the coders have started on the second subroutine and the debugging staff are ready to begin debugging subroutine 1. The overall effect of laddering activities is to streamline the linkage and sequencing between activities and keep our project resources fully employed.

Hammock Activities

Hammock activities can be used as summaries for some subsets of the activities identified in the overall project network. If the firm needed an outside consultant to handle the coding activities for a software upgrade to its inventory system, a hammock activity within the network can be used to summarize the tasks, duration, and cost. The hammock is so named because it hangs below the network path for consultant tasks and serves as an aggregation of task durations for the activities it "rolls up." Duration for a hammock is found by first identifying all tasks to be included and then subtracting the ES of the first task from the EF of the latest successor. In Figure 9.25, we can see that the hammock's total duration is 26 days, representing a combination of activities D, E, and F with their individual activity durations of 6, 14, and 6 days respectively.

Hammocks allow the project team to better disaggregate the overall project network into logical summaries. This process is particularly helpful when the project network is extremely complex or consists of a large number of individual activities. It is also useful when the project budget is actually shared among a number of cost centers or departments. Hammocking the activities that are assignable to each cost center makes the job of cost accounting for the project much easier.

Options for Reducing the Critical Path

It is common, when constructing an activity network and discovering the expected duration of the project, to look for ways in which the project can be shortened. To do this, start with an open mind to critically evaluate how activity durations were estimated, how the network was originally constructed, and to recognize any assumptions that guided the creation of the network. Reducing the critical path may require several initiatives or steps, but they need to be internally consistent (e.g., their combined effects do not cancel each other out) and logically prioritized.

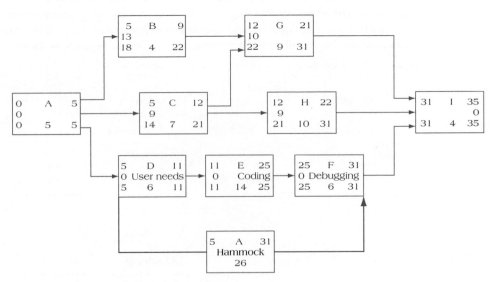

FIGURE 9.25 Example of a Hammock Activity

TABLE 9.6 Steps to Reduce the Critical Path

1. Eliminate tasks on the critical path.
2. Replan serial paths to be in parallel.
3. Overlap sequential tasks.
4. Shorten the duration of critical path tasks.
5. Shorten early tasks.
6. Shorten longest tasks.
7. Shorten easiest tasks.
8. Shorten tasks that cost the least to speed up.

Table 9.6 shows some of the more common methods for reducing the critical path for a project. The options include not only those aimed at adjusting the overall project network, but also options that address the individual tasks in the network themselves. Among the alternatives for shrinking the critical path are:[9]

1. *Eliminate tasks on the critical path.*   It may be the case that some of the tasks that are found on the critical path can be eliminated if they are not necessary or can be moved to noncritical paths with extra slack that will accommodate them.
2. *Replan serial paths to be in parallel.*   In some circumstances, a project may be excessively loaded with serial activities that could just as easily be moved to parallel or concurrent paths in the network. Group brainstorming can help determine alternative methods for pulling serial activities off the critical path and moving them to concurrent, noncritical paths.
3. *Overlap sequential tasks.*   Laddering is a good method for overlapping sequential activities. Rather than developing a long string of serial tasks, laddering identifies subpoints within the activities where project team members can begin to perform concurrent operations.
4. *Shorten the duration of critical path tasks.*   This option must be explored carefully. The underlying issue here must be to first examine the assumptions that guided the original activity duration estimates for the project. Was beta distribution used reasonably? Were the duration estimates for tasks excessively padded by the project manager or team? Depending upon the answers to these questions, it may indeed be possible to shorten the duration of critical path activities. Sometimes, however, the options of simply shrinking duration estimates by some set amount (e.g., 10% off all duration estimates) all but guarantees that the project will come in behind schedule.
5. *Shorten early tasks.*   Early tasks in a project are sometimes shortened before later tasks because usually they are more precise than later ones. There is greater uncertainty in a schedule for activities set to occur at some point in the future. Many project managers see that there is likely to be little risk in shortening early tasks, because any lags in the schedule can be made up downstream. Again, however, any time we purposely shorten project activities, we need to be aware of possible ripple effects through the network as these adjustments are felt later.
6. *Shorten longest tasks.*   The argument for shortening long tasks has to do with relative shrinkage; it is less likely that shortening longer activities will lead to any schedule problems for the overall project network because longer duration tasks can more easily absorb cuts without having an impact on the overall project. For example, shortening a task with 5 days' duration by 1 day represents a 20% cut in the duration estimate. On the other hand, shortening a task of 20 days' duration by 1 day results in only a 5% impact on that activity.
7. *Shorten easiest tasks.*   The logic here is that the learning curve for a project activity can make it easier to adjust an activity's duration downward. From a cost and budgeting perspective, we saw in Chapter 8 that learning curve methodology does result in lower costs for project activities. Duration estimates for easiest tasks can be overly inflated and can reasonably be lowered without having an adverse impact on the project team's ability to accomplish the task in the shortened time span.
8. *Shorten tasks that cost the least to speed up.*   "Speeding up" tasks in a project is another way of saying the activities are being crashed. We will cover the process of crashing project activities in more detail in Chapter 10. The option of crashing project activities is one that must be carefully considered against the time/cost trade-off so that the least expensive activities are speeded up.

BOX 9.1

PROJECT MANAGEMENT RESEARCH IN BRIEF

Software Development Delays and Solutions

One of the most common problems in IT project management involves the schedule delays found in software development projects. Time and cost overruns in excess of 100% on initial schedules are the industry average. A study by Callahan and Moretton sought to examine how these delays could be reduced. Analyzing the results of 44 companies involved in software development projects, they found that the level of experience firms had with IT project management had a significant impact on the speed with which they brought new products to market. When companies had little experience, the most important action they could take to speed up development times was to interact with customer groups and their own sales organizations early and often throughout the development cycle. The more information they were able to collect on the needs of the customers, the faster they could develop their software products. Also, frequent testing and multiple design iterations were found to speed up the delivery time.

For firms with strong experience in developing software projects, the most important determinants of shorter development cycles were found to be developing relationships with external suppliers, particularly during the product requirements, system design, and beta testing phases of the project. Supplier involvement in all phases of the development cycle proved to be key to maintaining aggressive development schedules.[10]

This chapter has introduced the essential elements in beginning a project schedule, including the logic behind constructing a project network, calculating activity duration estimates, and converting this information into a critical path diagram. These three activities form the core of project scheduling and give us the impetus to begin to consider some of the additional, advanced topics that are important if we are to become expert in the process of project scheduling. These topics will be covered in subsequent chapters.

Summary

1. **Understand and apply key scheduling terminology.** Key processes in project scheduling include how activity networks are constructed, task durations are estimated, the critical path and activity float are calculated, and lag relationships are built into activities.

2. **Apply the logic used to create activity networks, including predecessor and successor tasks.** The chapter discussed the manner in which network logic is employed. Following the creation of project tasks, through use of Work Breakdown Structures, it is necessary to apply logic to these tasks in order to identify those activities that are considered predecessors (coming earlier in the network) and those that are successors (coming later, or after the predecessor activities have been completed).

3. **Develop an activity network using Activity-on-Node (AON) techniques.** The chapter examined the process for creating an AON network through identification of predecessor relationships among project activities. Once these relationships are known, it is possible to begin linking the activities together to create the project network. Activity-on-Node (AON) applies the logic of assigning all tasks as specific "nodes" in the network and linking them with arrows to identify the predecessor-successor relationships.

4. **Perform activity duration estimation based on the use of probabilistic estimating techniques.** Activity duration estimation is accomplished through first identifying the various tasks in a project and then applying a method for estimating the duration of each of these activities. Among the methods that can aid us in estimating activity durations are (1) noncomputational techniques, for example, examining past records for similar tasks that were performed at other times in the organization and obtaining expert opinion; (2) deriving duration estimates through computational, or mathematical, analysis; and (3) using the Program Evaluation and Review Technique (PERT), which uses probabilities to estimate a task's duration. In applying PERT, the formula for employing a beta probability distribution is to first determine optimistic, most likely, and pessimistic estimates for the duration of each activity and then assign them in a ratio of:

$$[(1 \times \text{optimistic}) + (4 \times \text{most likely}) + (1 \times \text{pessimistic})]/6$$

5. **Construct the critical path for a project schedule network using forward and backward passes.** Conducting the forward pass allows us to determine the overall expected duration for the project by using the decision rules, adding early start plus activity duration to determine early finish, and then applying this early finish value to the next node in the network, where it becomes that activity's early start. We then use our decision rules for the backward pass to identify all activities and paths with slack and the project's critical path (the project path with no slack time).

6. **Identify activity float and the manner in which it is determined.** Once the network linking all project activities has been constructed, it is possible to begin determining the estimated duration of each activity. Duration estimation is most often performed using probabilistic estimates based on Program Evaluation and Review Technique (PERT) processes, in which optimistic, most likely, and pessimistic duration estimates for each activity are collected. Using a standard formula based on the statistically derived beta distribution, project activity durations for each task are determined and used to label the activity nodes in the network.

   Using activity durations and the network, we can identify the individual paths through the network, their lengths, and the critical path. The project's critical path is defined as the activities of a project which, when linked, define its shortest total length. The critical path identifies how quickly we can complete the project. All other paths contain activities that have, to some degree, float or slack time associated with them.

The identification of the critical path and activity float times is done through using a forward and backward pass process in which each activity's early start (ES), early finish (EF), late start (LS), and late finish (LF) times are calculated.

7. **Calculate the probability of a project finishing on time under PERT estimates.** Because PERT estimates are based on a range of estimated times (optimistic, most likely, pessimistic), there will be some variance associated with these values and expected task duration. Determining the variance of all activities on the critical (and noncritical) paths allows us to more accurately forecast the probability of completing the project on or before the expected finish date. We can also use the standard normal equation (and associated Z score) to forecast the additional time needed to complete a project under different levels of overall confidence.

8. **Understand the steps that can be employed to reduce the critical path.** Project duration can be reduced through a number of different means. Among the options project managers have to shorten the project critical path are the following: (1) Eliminate tasks on the critical path, (2) replan serial paths to be in parallel, (3) overlap sequential tasks, (4) shorten the duration of critical path tasks, (5) shorten early tasks, (6) shorten longest tasks, (7) shorten easiest tasks, and (8) shorten tasks that cost the least to speed up. The efficacy of applying one of these approaches over another will vary depending on a number of issues related both to the project constraints, client expectations, and the project manager's own organization.

Key Terms

Activity (also called task) (p. 302)
Activity-on-Arrow (AOA) (p. 305)
Activity-on-Node (AON) (p. 305)
Arrow (p. 305)
Backward pass (p. 304)
Beta distribution (p. 311)
Burst activity (p. 304)
Concurrent activities (p. 307)
Confidence interval (p. 313)
Crashing (p. 305)
Critical path (p. 304)

Critical Path Method (CPM) (p. 304)
Duration estimation (p. 310)
Early start (ES) date (p. 304)
Event (p. 304)
Float (also called slack) (p. 304)
Forward pass (p. 304)
Hammock activities (p. 322)
Laddering activities (p. 321)
Late start (LS) date (p. 304)

Network diagram (p. 302)
Node (p. 304)
Ordered activity (p. 302)
Path (p. 304)
Predecessors (p. 304)
Program Evaluation and Review Technique (PERT) (p. 305)
Project network diagram (PND) (p. 304)
Project planning (p. 302)
Resource-limited schedule (p. 305)
Scope (p. 304)

Serial activities (p. 306)
Slack (also called float) (p. 317)
Successors (p. 304)
Task (see activity) (p. 302)
Variance (activity and project) (p. 312)
Work Breakdown Structure (WBS) (p. 304)
Work package (p. 304)

Solved Problems

9.1 Creating an Activity Network

Assume the following information:

Activity	Predecessors
A	—
B	A
C	B
D	B
E	C, D
F	C
G	E, F
H	D, G

Create an activity network that shows the sequential logic between the project tasks. Can you identify merge activities? Burst activities?

SOLUTION

This activity network can be solved as shown in Figure 9.26. The merge points in the network are activities E, G, and H. The burst activities are activities B, C, and D.

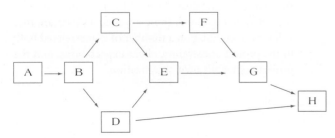

FIGURE 9.26   Solution to Solved Problem 9.1

9.2 Calculating Activity Durations and Variances

Assume that you have the following pessimistic, likely, and optimistic estimates for how long activities are estimated to take. Using the beta distribution, estimate the activity durations and variances for each task.

	Duration Estimates		
Activity	Pessimistic	Likely	Optimistic
A	7	5	2
B	5	3	2
C	14	8	6
D	20	10	6
E	8	3	3
F	10	5	3
G	12	6	4
H	16	6	5

SOLUTION

Remember that the beta distribution calculates expected activity duration (TE) as:

$$TE = (a + 4m + b)/6$$

Where

TE = estimated time for activity
a = most optimistic time to complete the activity
m = most likely time to complete the activity, the mode of the distribution
b = most pessimistic time to complete the activity

The formula for activity variance is:

$$s^2 = [(b - a)/6]^2$$

Therefore, in calculating expected activity duration (TE) and variance for each task we find the value as shown in the table below:

	Duration Estimates				
Activity	Pessimistic	Likely	Optimistic	TE (Beta)	Variance
A	7	5	2	4.8	$[(7 - 2)/6]^2 = 25/36 = 0.69$
B	5	3	2	3.2	$[(5 - 2)/6]^2 = 9/36 = 0.25$
C	14	8	6	8.7	$[(14 - 6)/6]^2 = 64/36 = 1.78$
D	20	10	6	11.0	$[(20 - 6)/6]^2 = 196/36 = 5.44$
E	8	3	3	3.8	$[(8 - 3)/6]^2 = 25/36 = 0.69$
F	10	5	3	5.5	$[(10 - 3)/6]^2 = 49/36 = 1.36$
G	12	6	4	6.7	$[(12 - 4)/6]^2 = 64/36 = 1.78$
H	16	6	5	7.5	$[(16 - 5)/6]^2 = 121/36 = 3.36$

9.3 Determining Critical Path and Activity Slack

Assume we have a set of activities, their expected durations, and immediate predecessors. Construct an activity network; identify the critical path and all activity slack times.

Activity	Predecessors	Expected Duration
A	—	6
B	A	7
C	A	5
D	B	3
E	C	4
F	C	5
G	D, E	8
H	F, G	3

SOLUTION

We follow an iterative process of creating the network and labeling the nodes as completely as possible. Then, following Figure 9.27, we first conduct a forward pass through the network to determine that the expected duration of the project is 27 days. Using a backward pass, we can determine the individual activity slack times as well as the critical path. The critical path for this example is as follows: A – B – D – G – H. Activity slack times are:

$$C = 1 \text{ day}$$
$$E = 1 \text{ day}$$
$$F = 8 \text{ days}$$

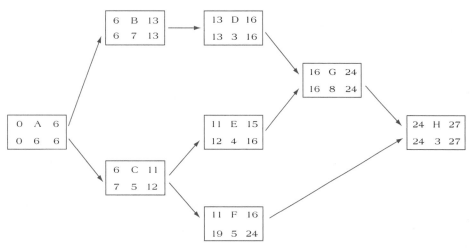

FIGURE 9.27 Solution to Solved Problem 9.3

Discussion Questions

1. Define the following terms:
   a. Path
   b. Activity
   c. Early start
   d. Early finish
   e. Late start
   f. Late finish
   g. Forward pass
   h. Backward pass
   i. Node
   j. AON
   k. Float
   l. Critical path
   m. PERT

2. Distinguish between serial activities and concurrent activities. Why do we seek to use concurrent activities as a way to shorten the project's length?

3. List three methods for deriving duration estimates for project activities. What are the strengths and weaknesses associated with each method?

4. In your opinion, what are the chief benefits and drawbacks of using beta distribution calculations (based on PERT techniques) to derive activity duration estimates?

5. "The shortest total length of a project is determined by the longest path through the network." Explain the concept behind this statement. Why does the longest path determine the shortest project length?

6. The float associated with each project task can only be derived following the completion of the forward and backward passes. Explain why this is true.

Problems

1. Consider a project, such as moving to a new neighborhood, completing a long-term school assignment, or even cleaning your bedroom. Develop a set of activities necessary to accomplish that project and then order them in a precedence manner to create sequential logic. Explain and defend the number of steps you identified and the order in which you placed those steps for best completion of the project.

2. What is the time estimate of the following activity in which the optimistic estimate is 4 days, pessimistic is 12 days, and most likely 5 days? Show your work.

3. Consider the following project tasks and their identified best, likely, and worst-case estimates of task duration. Assume the organization you work for computes TE based on the standard beta distribution formula. Calculate the TE for each of the following tasks (round to the nearest integer):

Activity	Best	Likely	Worst	TE
A	5	5	20	
B	3	5	9	
C	7	21	26	
D	4	4	4	
E	10	20	44	
F	3	15	15	
G	6	9	11	
H	32	44	75	
I	12	17	31	
J	2	8	10	

4. Construct a network activity diagram based on the following information:

Activity	Preceding Activities
A	—
B	—
C	A
D	B, C
E	B
F	C, D
G	E
H	F
I	G, H

5. Using the following information, create an AON network activity diagram. Calculate each activity TE (rounding to the nearest integer); the total duration of the project; its early start, early finish, late start, and late finish times; and the slack for each activity. Finally, show the project's critical path.

Activity	Preceding Activities	Best	Likely	Worst
A	—	12	15	25
B	A	4	6	11
C	—	12	12	30
D	B, C	8	15	20
E	A	7	12	15
F	E	9	9	42
G	D, E	13	17	19
H	F	5	10	15
I	G	11	13	20
J	G, H	2	3	6
K	J, I	8	12	22

   a. Now, assume that activity E has taken 10 days past its anticipated duration to complete. What happens to the project's schedule? Has the duration changed? Is there a new critical path? Show your conclusions.

6. An advertising project manager has developed a program for a new advertising campaign. In addition, the manager has gathered the time information for each activity, as shown in the table below.

	Time Estimates (week)			
Activity	Optimistic	Most Likely	Pessimistic	Immediate Predecessor(s)
A	1	4	7	—
B	2	6	10	—
C	3	3	9	B
D	6	13	14	A
E	4	6	14	A, C
F	6	8	16	B
G	2	5	8	D, E, F

   a. Calculate the expected activity times (round to nearest integer).
   b. Calculate the activity slacks. What is the total project length? Make sure you fully label all nodes in the network.
   c. Identify the critical path. What are the alternative paths and how much slack time is associated with each feeder path?
   d. Identify the burst activities and the merge activities.
   e. Given the activity variances, what is the likelihood of the project finishing on week 24?
   f. Suppose you wanted to have a 99% confidence in the project finishing on time. How many additional weeks would your project team need to negotiate for in order to gain this 99% likelihood?

7. Consider a project with the following information:

Activity	Duration	Predecessors
A	3	—
B	5	A
C	7	A
D	3	B, C
E	5	B
F	4	D
G	2	C
H	5	E, F, G

Activity	Duration	ES	EF	LS	LF	Slack
A	3	0	3	0	3	—
B	5	3	8	8	13	5
C	7	3	10	3	10	—
D	3	10	13	10	13	—
E	5	8	12	13	17	5
F	4	13	17	13	17	—
G	2	10	12	15	17	5
H	5	17	22	17	22	—

a. Construct the project activity network using AON methodology and label each node.
b. Identify the critical path and other paths through the network.

8. Use the following information to determine the probability of this project finishing within 34 weeks of its scheduled completion date. Assume activities A – B – D – F – G are the project's critical path.

Activity	Optimistic	Likely	Pessimistic	Expected Time	Variance
A	1	4	8		
B	3	5	9		
C	4	6	10		
D	3	7	15		
E	5	10	16		
F	3	6	15		
G	4	7	12		

a. Calculate the expected durations for each activity.
b. Calculate individual task variances and overall project variance.
c. The company must file a permit request with the local government within a narrow time frame after the project is expected to be completed. What is the likelihood that the project will be finished by week 34?
d. If we wanted to be 99% confident of on-time delivery of the project, how much additional time would we need to add to the project's expected delivery time?

Internet Exercises

1. Go to www.gamedev.net/page/resources/_/business/business-and-law/critical-path-analysis-and-scheduling-for-game-r1440 and click around the site. There are several articles on how to run your own computer game company. Click on articles related to project management and critical path scheduling for game design. Why is project scheduling so important for developing computer games?
2. Click on http://management.about.com/lr/project_time_management/174690/1/ and consider several of the articles on time management in projects. What sense do you get that project scheduling is as much about personal time management as it is about effective scheduling? Cite some articles or information to support or disagree with this position.
3. Go to www.infogoal.com/pmc/pmcart.htm and examine some of the archived articles and white papers on project planning

and scheduling. Select one article and synthesize the main points. What are the messages the article is intending to convey?
4. Key in "project scheduling" for a search of the Web. Hundreds of thousands of hits are generated from such a search. Examine a cross section of the hits. What are some of the common themes found on these Web sites?
5. Key in a search with the prompt "projects in _____" in which you select a country of interest (e.g., "projects in Finland"). Many of the projects generated by such a search are government-sponsored initiatives. Discuss the role of proper scheduling and planning for one such project you find on the Internet. Share your findings and the reasons you believe planning was so critical to the project.

MS Project Exercises

Please note that a step-by-step primer on using MS Project 2010 to create project schedules is available in Appendix B. For those considering the following exercises, it would first be helpful to refer to Appendix B for tips on getting started.

Exercise 9.1

Consider the following information that you have compiled regarding the steps needed to complete a project. You have identified all relevant steps and have made some determinations regarding predecessor/successor relationships. Using MS Project, develop a simple network diagram for this project, showing the links among the project activities.

Activity	Predecessors
A – Survey site	—
B – Install sewer and storm drainage	A
C – Install gas and electric power lines	A
D – Excavate site for spec house	B, C
E – Pour foundation	D

Exercise 9.2

Suppose we have a complete activity predecessor table (shown here) and we wish to create a network diagram highlighting the activity sequence for this project. Using MS Project, enter the activities and their predecessors and create a complete activity network diagram for this project.

Project—Remodeling an Appliance

Activity		Predecessors
A	Conduct competitive analysis	—
B	Review field sales reports	—
C	Conduct tech capabilities assessment	—
D	Develop focus group data	A, B, C
E	Conduct telephone surveys	D
F	Identify relevant specification improvements	E
G	Interface with marketing staff	F
H	Develop engineering specifications	G
I	Check and debug designs	H
J	Develop testing protocol	G
K	Identify critical performance levels	J
L	Assess and modify product components	I, K
M	Conduct capabilities assessment	L
N	Identify selection criteria	M
O	Develop RFQ	M
P	Develop production master schedule	N, O
Q	Liaise with sales staff	P
R	Prepare product launch	Q

Exercise 9.3

Suppose that we add some duration estimates to each of the activities from exercise 9.1. A portion of the revised table is shown here. Recreate the network diagram for this project and note how MS Project uses nodes to identify activity durations, start and finish dates, and predecessors. What is the critical path for this network diagram? How do we know?

Activity	Duration	Predecessors
A – Survey site	5 days	—
B – Install sewer and storm drainage	9 days	A
C – Install gas and electric power lines	4 days	A
D – Excavate site for spec house	2 days	B, C
E – Pour foundation	2 days	D

PMP Certification Sample Questions

1. A building contractor is working on a vacation home and is looking over his schedule. He notices that the schedule calls for the foundation footers to be poured and then the rough floor decking to be installed. In this plan, the decking would be an example of what type of activity?
   a. Successor task
   b. Predecessor task
   c. Lag activity
   d. Crashed activity

2. Your project team is working on a brand-new project with leading-edge technology. As a result, it is very difficult for your team to give reasonable accurate estimates for how long their activities are going to take in order to be completed. Because of this uncertainty, it would be appropriate for you to require team members to use what kind of logic when estimating durations?
   a. Normal distribution
   b. Beta distribution
   c. Deterministic estimates
   d. Experience

3. Suppose a project plan had three distinct paths through the network. The first path consisted of activities A (3 days), B (4 days), and C (2 days). The second path consisted of activities D (4 days), E (5 days), and F (5 days). The third path consisted of activities G (2 days), H (3 days), and I (10 days). Which is the critical path?
   a. ABC
   b. DEF
   c. GHI
   d. ADG

4. Activity slack (also known as float) can be calculated through which of the following means?
   a. Early finish (EF) – late finish (LF)
   b. Early finish (EF) – early start (ES)
   c. Late finish (LF) – late start (LS)
   d. Late start (LS) – early start (ES)

5. Your project team is working from a network diagram. This type of tool will show the team:
   a. Activity precedence
   b. Duration estimates for the activities and overall schedule
   c. The dates activities are expected to begin
   d. The network diagram will show none of the above

Answers: 1. a—The decking is a successor task, as it is scheduled to occur after completion of the footers; 2. b—The beta distribution would work best because it takes into consideration best-case, most likely, and worst-case estimates; 3. c—GHI has a path duration of 15 days; 4. d—One way to calculate float is LS – ES, and the other way is LF – EF; 5. a—The primary advantage of activity networks is precedence ordering of all project activities.

Notes

1. www.sa-venues.com/2010/2010-stadium.htm; www.exploresouthafrica.net/2010soccerworldcup/stadiums.htm; Bearak, B. (2010, March 12). "Cost of stadium reveals tensions in South Africa," www.nytimes.com/2010/03/13/world/africa/13stadium.html; Berg, N. (2010, May 10). "The infrastructural benefit of South Africa's World Cup," www.planetizen.com/node/44124; Clayton, J. (2009, July 8). "Construction workers strike threatens 2010 World Cup preparations," www.timesonline.co.uk/tol/news/world/africa/article6660910.ece; Sokol, D. (2010, June 7). "South Africa, host of 2010 World Cup, is ready for its big debut," http://archrecord.construction.com/news/daily/archives/2010/100607south_africa_world_cup.asp; "When the whistle blows." (2010, June 3). www.economist.com/node/16274395.

2. Project Management Institute. (2000). *Project Management Body of Knowledge.* Newtown Square, PA: PMI.

3. There are a number of citations for the development of project networks. Among the more important are Callahan, J., and Moretton, B. (2001). "Reducing software product development time," *International Journal of Project Management,* 19: 59–70; Elmaghraby, S. E., and Kamburowski, J. (1992). "The analysis of activity networks under generalized precedence relations," *Management Science,* 38: 1245–63; Kidd, J. B. (1991). "Do today's projects need powerful network planning tools?" *International Journal of Production Research,* 29: 1969–78; Malcolm, D. G., Roseboom, J. H., Clark, C. E., and Fazar, W. (1959). "Application of a technique for research and development program evaluation," *Operations Research,* 7: 646–70; Smith-Daniels, D. E., and Smith-Daniels, V. (1984). "Constrained resource project scheduling," *Journal of Operations Management,* 4: 369–87; Badiru, A. B. (1993). "Activity-resource assignments using critical resource diagramming," *Project Management Journal,* 24(3): 15–22; Gong, D., and Hugsted, R. (1993). "Time-uncertainty analysis in project networks with a new merge event time-estimation technique," *International Journal of Project Management,* 11: 165–74.

4. The literature on PERT/CPM is voluminous. Among the citations readers may find helpful are the following: Gallagher, C. (1987). "A note on PERT assumptions," *Management Science,* 33: 1350; Gong, D., and Rowlings, J. E. (1995). "Calculation of safe float use in risk-analysis-oriented network scheduling," *International Journal of Project Management,* 13: 187–94; Hulett, D. (2000). "Project schedule risk analysis: Monte Carlo simulation or PERT?" *PMNetwork,* 14(2): 43–47; Kamburowski, J. (1997). "New validations of PERT times," *Omega: International Journal of Management Science,* 25(3): 189–96; Keefer, D. L., and Verdini, W. A. (1993). "Better estimation of PERT activity time parameters," *Management Science,* 39: 1086–91; Mummolo, G. (1994). "PERT-path network technique: A new approach to project planning," *International Journal of Project Management,* 12: 89–99; Mummolo, G. (1997). "Measuring uncertainty and criticality in network planning by PERT-path technique," *International Journal of Project Management,* 15: 377–87; Moder, J. J., and Phillips, C. R. (1970). *Project Management with CPM and PERT.* New York: Van Nostrand Reinhold; Mongalo, M. A., and Lee, J. (1990). "A comparative study of methods for probabilistic project scheduling," *Computers in Industrial Engineering,* 19: 505–9; Wiest, J. D., and Levy, F. K. (1977). *A Management Guide to PERT/CPM,* 2nd ed. Englewood Cliffs, NJ: Prentice-Hall; Sasieni, M. W. (1986). "A note on PERT times," *Management Science,* 32: 942–44; Williams, T. M. (1995). "What are PERT estimates?" *Journal of the Operational Research Society,* 46(12): 1498–1504; Chae, K. C., and Kim, S. (1990). "Estimating the mean and variance of PERT activity time using likelihood-ratio of the mode and the mid-point," *IIE Transactions,* 3: 198–203.

5. Gray, C. F., and Larson, E. W. (2003). *Project Management,* 2nd ed. Burr Ridge, IL: McGraw-Hill.

6. Hill, J., Thomas, L. C., and Allen, D. C. (2000). "Experts' estimates of task durations in software development projects," *International Journal of Project Management,* 18: 13–21; Campanis, N. A. (1997). "Delphi: Not a Greek oracle, but close," *PMNetwork,* 11(2): 33–36; DeYoung-Currey, J. (1998). "Want better estimates? Let's get to work," *PMNetwork,* 12(12): 12–15; Lederer, A. L., and Prasad, J. (1995). "Causes of inaccurate software-development cost estimates," *Journal of Systems and Software,* 31: 125–34; Libertore, M. J. (2002). "Project schedule uncertainty analysis using fuzzy logic," *Project Management Journal,* 33(4): 15–22.

7. Meredith, J. R., and Mantel, Jr., S. J. (2003). *Project Management,* 5th ed. New York: Wiley.

8. Project Management Institute. (2000). *Project Management Body of Knowledge.* Newtown Square, PA: PMI.

9. DeMarco, T. (1982). *Controlling Software Projects: Management, Measurement and Estimate.* New York: Yourdon; Horner, R. M. W., and Talhouni, B. T. (n.d.). *Effects of Accelerated Working, Delays and Disruptions on Labour Productivity.* London: Chartered Institute of Building; Emsley, M. (2000). *Planning and Resource Management—Module 3.* Manchester, UK: UMIST.

10. Callahan, J., and Moretton, B. (2001). "Reducing software product development time," *International Journal of Project Management,* 19: 59–70.

C H A P T E R

10

Project Scheduling
Lagging, Crashing, and Activity Networks

Chapter Outline

Chapter Objectives

After completing this chapter, you should be able to:

1. Apply lag relationships to project activities.

2. Construct and comprehend Gantt charts.

3. Recognize alternative means to accelerate projects, including their benefits and drawbacks.

4. Understand the trade-offs required in the decision to crash project activities.

5. Develop activity networks using Activity-on-Arrow techniques.

6. Understand the differences in AON and AOA and recognize the advantages and disadvantages of each technique.

**PROJECT MANAGEMENT BODY OF KNOWLEDGE CORE CONCEPTS COVERED
IN THIS CHAPTER**

1. Define Activities (PMBoK sec. 6.1)
2. Sequence Activities (PMBoK sec. 6.2)
3. Lead and Lag Activities (PMBoK sec 6.2.3)
4. Estimate Activity Resources (PMBoK sec. 6.3)
5. Estimate Activity Durations (PMBoK sec. 6.4)
6. Develop Schedule (PMBoK sec. 6.5)
7. Schedule Compression (PMBoK sec. 6.5.2.7)
8. Control Schedule (PMBoK sec. 6.6)

PROJECT PROFILE

Boeing's 787 Dreamliner: Failure to Launch

It was never supposed to be this difficult. When Boeing announced the development of its newest and most high-tech aircraft, the 787 Dreamliner, it seemed that they had made all the right decisions. By focusing on building a more fuel-efficient aircraft, using lighter composite materials that saved on overall weight and resulted in a 20% lower fuel consumption, outsourcing development work to a global network of suppliers, and pioneering new assembly techniques, it appeared that Boeing had taken a clear-eyed glimpse into the future of commercial air travel and designed the equivalent of a "home run"—a new aircraft that ticked all the boxes.

Airline customers seemed to agree. When Boeing announced the development of the 787 and opened its order book, it quickly became the best-selling aircraft in history, booking 847 advance orders for the airplane. With list prices varying from $161 to $205 million each, depending on the model, the Dreamliner was worth billions in long-term revenue streams for the company. The aircraft was designed for long-range flight and could seat up to 330 passengers. Most industry analysts agreed: With the introduction of the Dreamliner, the future had never seemed brighter for Boeing.

But when the first delivery dates slipped, yet again, into 2012, four years behind schedule, and the company's stock price was battered in the marketplace, Boeing and its industry backers began trying to unravel a maze of technical and supply chain problems that were threatening not just the good name of Boeing, but the viability

FIGURE 10.1 Boeing's 787 Dreamliner

(continued)

of the Dreamliner. Derisively nicknamed the "7-L-7" for "late," the project had fallen victim to extensive cost overruns and continuous schedule slippages, and had recently encountered a number of worrisome structural and electrical faults that were alarming airlines awaiting delivery of their aircraft. These events combined to put Boeing squarely on the hot seat, as they sought to find a means to correct these problems and salvage both their reputation and the viability of their high-profile aircraft.

The time frame for the development of the Dreamliner offers some important milestones in its path to commercialization, including the following:

- 2003—Boeing officially announced the development of the "7E7," its newest aircraft.
- 2004—First orders were received for 55 of the aircraft from All Nippon Airlines, with a delivery date set for late 2008.
- 2005—The 7E7 was officially renamed the 787 Dreamliner.
- July 2007—The first Dreamliner was unveiled in a rollout ceremony at Boeing's assembly plant in Everett, Washington.
- October 2007—The first six-month delay was announced. The problems identified included supplier delivery delays and problems with the fasteners used to attach composite components of the aircraft together. The program director, Mike Bair, was replaced a week later.
- November 2008—Boeing announced the fifth delay in the schedule, due to continuing coordination problems with global suppliers, repeated failures of fasteners, and the effects of a machinist strike. The first flight was pushed out until the second quarter of 2009.
- June 2009—Boeing announced that the first flight was postponed "due to a need to reinforce an area within the side-of-body section of the aircraft." They further delayed the first test flight until late 2009. At the same time, Boeing wrote off $2.5 billion in costs for the first three 787s built.
- December 7, 2009—First successful test flight of the 787.
- July 2010—Boeing announced that schedule slippages would push first deliveries into 2011. They blamed an engine blowout at a test bed in Rolls-Royce's plant, although Rolls denied that its engines were the cause of schedule delay.
- August 2010—Air India announced a $1 billion compensation claim against Boeing, citing repeated delivery delays for the twenty-seven 787s it had on order.
- November 9, 2010—Fire broke out on Dreamliner #2 on its test flight near Laredo, Texas. The fire was quickly extinguished and the cause was attributed to a fault in the electrical systems. The aircraft were grounded for extensive testing. With that technical mishap, it was feared that the delivery date for the aircraft would be pushed into 2012.
- January 19, 2011—Boeing announced another delay in its 787 delivery schedule. The latest (and seventh official) delay came more than two months after the Dreamliner #2 electrical fire. All Nippon Airways, the jet's first customer, was informed that the earliest it could expect delivery of the first of its 55-airplane order would be the third quarter of 2011, though expectations were high that the airline might not receive any aircraft until early 2012, making final delivery nearly 3½ years late.

There is no question that the Dreamliner is a state-of-the-art aircraft. The 787 is the first commercial aircraft that makes extensive use of composite materials in place of aluminum, both for framing and for the external "skin." In fact, each 787 contains approximately 35 tons of carbon fiber-reinforced plastic. Carbon fiber composites have a higher strength-to-weight ratio than traditional aircraft materials, such as aluminum and steel, and help make the 787 a lighter aircraft. These composites are used on fuselage, wings, tail, doors, and interior sections, and aluminum is used on wing and tail leading edges. The fuselage is assembled in one-piece composite barrel sections instead of the multiple aluminum sheets and some 50,000 fasteners used on existing aircraft. Because of the lighter weight and a new generation of jet engines used to power it, the Dreamliner has lower cost of operations, which makes it especially appealing to airlines. Additionally, the global supply chain that Boeing established to manufacture components for the aircraft reads like a who's who list of international experts. Firms in Sweden, Japan, South Korea, France, England, Italy, and India all have major contracts with Boeing to supply parts of the aircraft, which are shipped to two assembly plants in the United States (one in Washington and the other planned for South Carolina) for final assembly and testing before being sent to customers. In short, the 787 is an incredibly complicated product, both in terms of its physical makeup and the intricate supply chain that Boeing created to produce it.

So complicated is the 787 program, in fact, that it may be the case that in developing the Dreamliner, Boeing has simply tried to do too much at one time. Critics have argued that creating a new generation aircraft with composite materials while routing an entirely new supply chain, maintaining quality control, and debugging a long list of unexpected problems is simply beyond the capability of any organization, no matter how highly skilled in project management they may be. Suppliers have been struggling to meet Boeing's exacting technical standards, with early test versions of the nose section, for example, failing Boeing's testing and being deemed unacceptable. Boeing has undertaken a huge risk with the Dreamliner. In a bid to hold down costs, the company has engaged in extreme outsourcing, leaving it highly dependent on a far-flung supply chain that includes 43 "top-tier" suppliers on three continents. It is the first time Boeing has ever outsourced the most critical areas of the plane, the wing and the fuselage. About 80% of the Dreamliner is being fabricated by outside suppliers, versus 51% for existing Boeing planes.

Jim McNerney, chief executive of Boeing, has admitted that the 787 development plans, involving significant outsourcing, were "overly ambitious": "While game-changing innovation of this magnitude is never easy, we've seen more of the bleeding edge of innovation than we'd ever care to see again. So we are adjusting our approach for future programs." McNerney continued, "We are disappointed over the schedule changes. Notwithstanding the challenges that we are experiencing in bringing forward this game-changing product, we remain confident in the design of the 787."[1]

INTRODUCTION

The previous chapter introduced the challenge of project scheduling, its important terminology, network logic, activity duration estimation, and constructing the critical path. In this chapter, we apply these concepts in order to explore other scheduling techniques, including the use of lag relationships among project activities, Gantt charts, crashing project activities, and comparing the use of Activity-on-Arrow (AOA) versus Activity-on-Node (AON) processes to construct networks. In the last chapter, we used the analogy of the jigsaw puzzle, in which the act of constructing a schedule required a series of steps all building toward the conclusion. With the basics covered, we are now ready to consider some of the additional important elements in project scheduling, all aimed at the construction of a meaningful project plan.

10.1 LAGS IN PRECEDENCE RELATIONSHIPS

The term **lag** refers to the logical relationship between the start and finish of one activity and the start and finish of another. In practice, lags are sometimes incorporated into networks to allow for greater flexibility in network construction. Suppose we wished to expedite a schedule and determined that it was not necessary for a preceding task to be completely finished before starting its **successor**. We determine that once the first activity has been initiated, a two-day lag is all that is necessary before starting the next activity. Lags demonstrate this relationship between the tasks in question. They commonly occur under four logical relationships between tasks:

1. Finish to Start
2. Finish to Finish
3. Start to Start
4. Start to Finish

Finish to Start

The most common type of logical sequencing between tasks is referred to as the Finish to Start relationship. Suppose three tasks are linked in a **serial** path, similar to that shown in Figure 10.2. Activity C cannot begin until the project receives a delivery from an external supplier that is scheduled to occur four days after the completion of activity B. Figure 10.2 visually represents this Finish to Start lag of 4 days between the completion of activity B and the start of activity C.

Note in Figure 10.2 that the early start (ES) date for activity C has now been delayed for the 4 days of the lag. A Finish to Start lag delay is usually shown on the line joining the nodes; it should be added in forward pass calculations and subtracted in backward pass calculations. Finish to Start lags are *not* the same as additional activity slack and should not be handled in the same way.

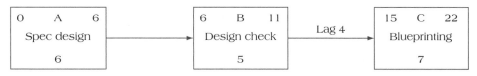

FIGURE 10.2   Network Incorporating Finish to Start Lag of 4 Days

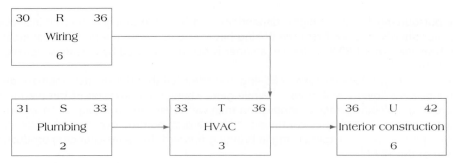

FIGURE 10.3 **Finish to Finish Network Relationship**

Finish to Finish

Finish to Finish relationships require that two linked activities share a similar completion point. The link between activities R and T in Figure 10.3 shows this relationship. Although activity R begins before activity T, they share the same completion date.

In some situations, it may be appropriate for two or more activities to conclude at the same time. If, for example, a contractor building an office complex cannot begin interior wall construction until all wiring, plumbing, and heating, ventilation, and air conditioning (HVAC) have been installed, she may include a lag to ensure that the completion of the preceding activities all occur at the same time. Figure 10.4 demonstrates an example of a Finish to Finish lag, in which the preceding activities R, S, and T are completed to enable activity U to commence immediately afterward. The lag of 3 days between activities R and T enables the tasks to complete at the same point.

Start to Start

Often two or more activities can start simultaneously or a lag takes place between the start of one activity after an earlier activity has commenced. A company may wish to begin materials procurement while drawings are still being finalized. It has been argued that the Start to Start lag relationship is redundant to a normal activity network in which parallel or concurrent activities are specified as business as usual. In Figure 9.20, we saw that Activity C is a burst point in a network and its successor activities (tasks D and G) are, in effect, operating with Start to Start logic. The subtle difference between this example and a Start to Start specification is that in Figure 9.20 it is not necessary for both activities to begin simultaneously; in a Start to Start relationship the logic must be maintained by both the forward and backward pass through the network and can, therefore, alter the amount of **float** available to activity G.

Start to Start lags are becoming increasingly used as a means to accelerate projects (we will discuss this in greater detail later in the chapter) through a process known as **fast-tracking**. Instead of relying on the more common Finish to Start relationships between activities, organizations are attempting to compress their schedules through adopting parallel task scheduling of the sort that is typified by Start to Start. For example, it may be possible to overlap activities in a variety of different settings. Proofreading a book manuscript need not wait until the entire document is completed; a copy editor can begin working on chapter one while the author is still writing the drafts. Further, in software development projects, it is common to begin coding various sequences while the overall design of the software's functions is still being laid out. It is not

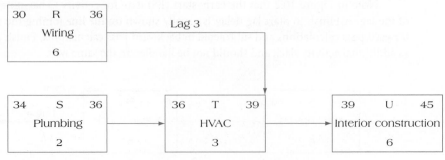

FIGURE 10.4 **Finish to Finish Relationship with Lag Incorporated**

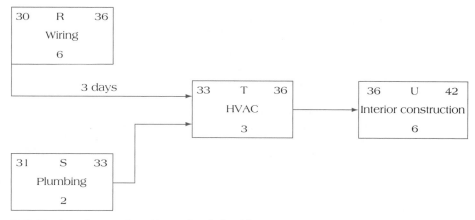

FIGURE 10.5 Start to Start Network Relationship

always possible to reconfigure predecessor/successor relationships into a Start to Start schedule, but where it is possible to do so, the result is to create a more fast-paced and compressed schedule.

Figure 10.5 demonstrates an example of a Start to Start network, in which the lag of 3 days has been incorporated into the network logic for the relationship between activities R, S, and T.

Start to Finish

Perhaps the least common type of lag relationship occurs when a successor's finish is dependent upon a predecessor's start (Start to Finish). An example of such a situation is construction in an area with poor groundwater drainage. Figure 10.6 shows this relationship. The completion of the concrete pouring activity, Y, is dependent upon the start of site water drainage, W. Although an uncommon occurrence, the Start to Finish option cannot be automatically rejected. As with the other types of predecessor/successor relationships, we must examine our network logic to ascertain the most appropriate manner for linking networked activities with each other.

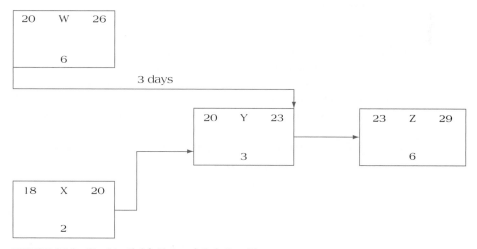

FIGURE 10.6 Start to Finish Network Relationship

10.2 GANTT CHARTS

Developed by Harvey Gantt in 1917, Gantt charts are another extremely useful tool for creating a project network. **Gantt charts** establish a time-phased network, which links project activities to a project schedule baseline. They can also be used as a project tracking tool to assess the difference between planned and actual performance. A sample of a basic Gantt chart is shown in Figure 10.7. Activities are ordered from first to last along a column on the left side of the chart with their ES and EF durations drawn horizontally. The ES and EF dates correspond to the baseline calendar drawn at the top of the figure. Gantt charts represent

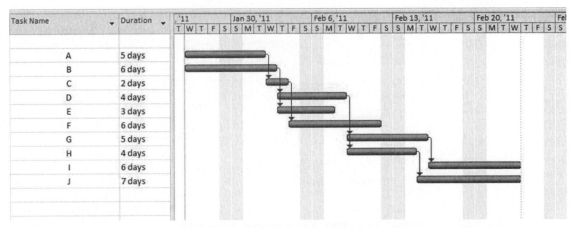

FIGURE 10.7 Sample Gantt Chart using Microsoft Project 2010 "[Note that weekend days are not counted for activity duration times]."

one of the first attempts to develop a network diagram that specifically orders project activities by baseline calendar dates, allowing the project team to be able to focus on project status at any date during the project's development.

Some benefits of Gantt charts are (1) they are very easy to read and comprehend, (2) they identify the project network coupled with its schedule baseline, (3) they allow for updating and project control, (4) they are useful for identifying resource needs and assigning resources to tasks, and (5) they are easy to create.

1. *Comprehension*—Gantt charts work as a precedence diagram for the overall project by linking together all activities. The Gantt chart is laid out along a horizontal time line so that viewers can quickly identify the current date and see what activities should have been completed, which should be in progress, and which are scheduled for the future. Further, because these activities are linking in the network, it is possible to identify predecessor and successor activities.

2. *Schedule baseline network*—The Gantt chart is linked to real-time information, so that all project activities have more than just ES, EF, LS, LF, and float attached to them. They also have the dates when they are expected to be started and completed, just as they can be laid out in conjunction with the overall project schedule.

3. *Updating and control*—Gantt charts allow project teams to readily access project information activity by activity. Suppose, for example, that a project activity is late by 4 days. It is possible on a Gantt chart to update the overall network by factoring in the new time and seeing a revised project status. Many firms use Gantt charts to continually update the status of ongoing activities. Gantt charts allow managers to assess current activity status, making it possible to begin planning for remedial steps in cases where an activity's completion is lagging behind expectations.

4. *Identifying resource needs*—Laying the whole project out on a schedule baseline permits the project team to begin scheduling resources well before they are needed, and resource planning becomes easier.

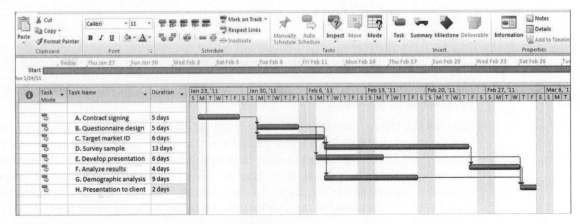

FIGURE 10.8 Completed Gantt Chart for Project Delta

5. *Easy to create*—Gantt charts, because they are intuitive, are among the easiest scheduling devices for project teams to develop. The key is having a clear understanding of the length of activities (their duration), the overall precedence network, the date the project is expected to begin, and any other information needed to construct the schedule baseline, such as whether **overtime** will be needed.

Figure 10.8 uses the information contained in the Project Delta example from the previous chapter to construct a Gantt chart using MS Project 2010 (see Figure 9.11). The start and finish dates and length are ascribed to each activity and represented by the horizontal bar drawn from left to right through the network. The chart lists the early activities in order from top to bottom. The overall "flow" of the chart moves from the top left corner down to the bottom right. The baseline schedule is shown horizontally across the top of the page. Each activity is linked to indicate precedence logic through the network. All activities are entered based on their early start (ES) times. We can adjust the network to change the logic underlying the sequencing of the tasks. For example, the activities can be adjusted based on the **late start (LS) date** or some other convention.

As we continue to fill out the Gantt chart with the complete Project Delta (see Figure 10.8), it is possible to determine additional information from the network. First, activity slack is represented by the long arrows that link activities to their successors. For example, activity E, with its 60 days (12 weeks) of slack, is represented by the solid bar showing the activity's duration and the lengthy arrow that connects the activity to the next task in the network sequence (activity H). Finally, a number of software-generated Gantt charts will also automatically calculate the critical path, identifying the critical activities as the chart is constructed. Figure 10.9 shows the critical path as it is highlighted on the schedule baseline.

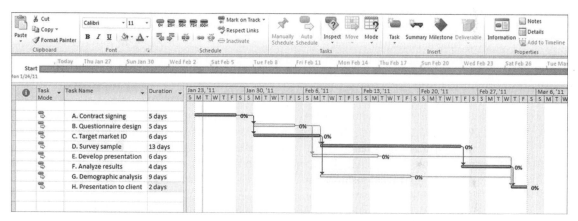

FIGURE 10.9   Gantt Chart for Project Delta with Critical Path Highlighted

Adding Resources to Gantt Charts

Adding resources to the Gantt chart is very straightforward, consisting of supplying the name or names of the resources that are assigned to perform the various activities. Figure 10.10 gives an MS Project output showing the inclusion of a set of project team resources assigned to the various tasks. It is also possible, to

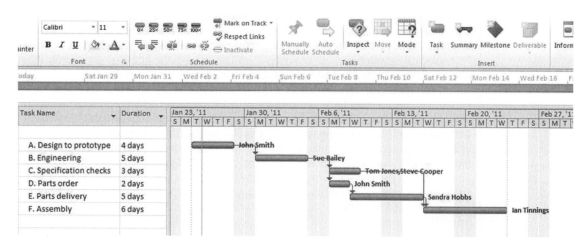

FIGURE 10.10   Gantt Chart with Resources Specified

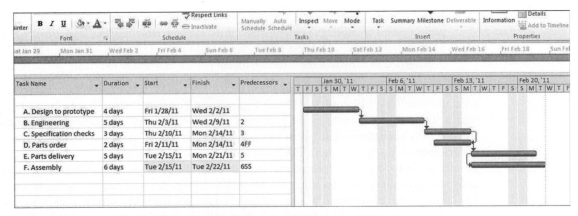

FIGURE 10.11 Gantt Chart with Lag Relationships

assign the percentage of time each resource is assigned to each activity. This feature is important because, as we will see in later chapters, it forms the basis for tracking and control of the project, particularly in terms of cost control.

Figure 10.10 shows six project team members assigned across the six tasks of another project example. Remember that the Gantt chart is based on activity durations calculated with full commitment of resources. Suppose, however, that we were only able to assign resources to the tasks at a lesser figure (say 50%) because we do not have sufficient resources available when they are needed. The result will be to increase the length of time necessary to complete the project activities. The challenge of resource management as it applies to network scheduling is important and will be covered in detail in Chapter 12.

Incorporating Lags in Gantt Charts

Gantt charts can be adjusted when it is necessary to show lags, creating a visual image of the project schedule. Figure 10.11 is a Gantt chart with some alternative lag relationships specified. In this network, activities C (specification check) and D (parts order) are linked with a Finish to Finish relationship that has both ending on the same date. Activity E is a successor to activity D, and the final two activities, E and F, are linked with a Start to Start relationship. Similar to lag relationships in network construction, the key lies in developing a reasonable logic for the relationship between tasks. Once the various types of lags are included, the actual process of identifying the network's critical path and other pertinent information should be straightforward.

BOX 10.1

PROJECT MANAGERS IN PRACTICE

Nilay Yuce, Lamagama

Nilay Yuce is the director and founding partner of Lamagama located in Ankara, the capital of Turkey. She earned her undergraduate and graduate degrees in Economics from the Bilkent University of Ankara. Her involvement in projects dates back to her graduate studies, when she participated in various research projects as a research assistant. After her graduation, she served as a researcher and project manager at Scientific and Technological Research Council of Turkey (TUBITAK) where she got acquainted with 3D animation and the game industry, which would be her next career passion.

After earning a degree in animation from Animator Mentor, Yuce worked for several animation studios in Turkey and later founded Lamagama in 2009 with her business partner Gokhan Ertem in the incubation center of METUTECH Technopolis. The company specializes in mobile and console game development. Yuce serves as a CEO and project manager responsible for the overall success of the development projects from start to finish. For its first R&D project, Lamax motion capture and movement analysis system, Lamagama obtained a grant from the Ministry of Science, Industry and Technology. During this project Yuce not only honed her project management skills, but also obtained invaluable experience in acquiring external financing, communicating with public institutions, executing joint projects, and dealing with technical details of development projects.

Yuce notes that the infrastructure of the Lamax system was reused in another Lamagama project named PARS, a military simulator, and with this project she succeeded in obtaining financial support from the

© Nilay Yuce

FIGURE 10.12 Nilay Yuce, Lamagama

Turkish Small and Medium Industry Development Organization (KOSGEB). She states that after a year-long preparation process to ensure alignment with the PlayStation platform, Lamagama became an official content developer for Sony Entertainment's PS3 in 2010.

In addition to PARS, Yuce has been managing four other game development projects, three online games and a console game. As these projects have grown, so have their teams. People from various disciplines and backgrounds have joined Lamagama, which has necessitated the adoption of a new management approach. As Yuce notes, managing game development projects is a high-pressure job because the gaming industry is a very dynamic and highly competitive industry characterized by fast development, short product life cycles, and ever increasing expectations of global consumers that require maintaining high quality standards. She adds that other challenges in game development projects include creating cohesive and effective project teams comprised of diverse skill sets, perspectives, and personalities, as well as maintaining high integrity in teams and promoting effective communication among team members.

When selecting team members, Yuce gives preference to individuals who are creative, motivated, consistent, flexible, enthusiastic, and optimistic while avoiding impatient, egocentric, and aggressive personalities. To promote harmony and interaction among team members, she regularly organizes fun activities such as volleyball, ping-pong, darts, and movie nights. Yuce argues that since creativity is vital in game development projects, it is essential that a project manager give some autonomy to developers while maintaining a well-balanced control over the team. She adds that to foster creativity, the company has created a comfortable and stimulating work environment with flexible work hours.

At Lamagama, a game development plan is created undergoing the following stages: (1) creation of a one-page proposal after a brainstorming session, which is sent to the publisher for feedback; (2) creation of a detailed proposal and formation of the project team; and (3) development of game design documents, including the work breakdown structure (WBS), the resource-loading form, and the project budget. Yuce supervises the plan development process and makes resource allocation decisions. As creating an efficient and realistic project schedule is essential for project success, before preparing the final project schedule, she talks to project members to get their activity estimates and negotiate when necessary. Further, she ensures that the project plan is carried out smoothly and controls every aspect of the project until its completion.

Since project management is a very dynamic job, despite all planning efforts, a project manager can face unanticipated events; therefore, Yuce argues, flexibility and patience are crucial in project management. For example, Yuce notes that online and console game projects usually last 3 to 4 and 18 to 24 months, respectively; in order to be able to participate in an important event such as an upcoming fair or exhibition, the project team ssometimes needs to deliver the completed game in a shorter time frame by working overtime. After project completion, team members are compensated for overtime work in paid time off.[2]

10.3 CRASHING PROJECTS

At times it is necessary to expedite the project, accelerating development to reach an earlier completion date. The process of accelerating a project is referred to as **crashing**. Crashing a project directly relates to resource commitment. The more resources we are willing to expend, the faster we can push the project to its finish. There can be good reasons to crash a project, including:[3]

1. The initial schedule may be too aggressive. Under this circumstance, we may schedule the project with a series of activity durations so condensed they make the crashing process inevitable.
2. Market needs change and the project is in demand earlier than anticipated. Suppose, for example, your company discovered that the secret project you were working on was also being developed by a rival firm. Because market share and strategic benefits will come to the first firm to introduce the product, you have a huge incentive to do whatever is necessary to ensure that you are first to market.
3. The project has slipped considerably behind schedule. You may determine that the only way to regain the original milestones is to crash all remaining activities.
4. The contractual situation provides even more incentive to avoid schedule slippage. The company may realize that it will be responsible for paying more in late delivery penalties than the cost of crashing the activities.

Options for Accelerating Projects

A number of methods are available for accelerating or crashing projects. One key determinant of which method to use is how "resource-constrained" the project is; that is, whether there is additional budget or extra resources available to devote to the project. The issue of whether the project manager (and organization) is willing to devote additional resources to the project is a primary concern that will weigh in their choices. Depending on the level of resource constraint, certain options will be more attractive than others. Among the primary methods for accelerating a project are the following:

1. *Improve the productivity of existing project resources*—Improving the productivity of existing project resources means finding efficient ways to do more work with the currently available pool of personnel and other material resources. Some ways to achieve these goals include improving the planning and organization of the project, eliminating any barriers to productivity such as excessive bureaucratic interference or physical constraints, and improving the motivation and productivity of project team members. Efforts should always be made to find ways to improve the productivity of project resources; however, these efforts are almost always better achieved during the down time *between* projects rather than in the midst of one.
2. *Change the working method employed for the activity, usually by altering the technology and types of resources employed*—Another option for accelerating project activities is to promote methods intended to change the working method employed for the activity, usually by altering the technology and types of resources employed. For example, many firms have switched to computer-based project scheduling techniques and saved considerable time in the process. Changing working methods can also include assignment of senior personnel, or hiring contract personnel or subcontractors to perform specific project functions.
3. *Compromise quality and/or reduce project scope*—These two options refer to conscious decisions made within the organization to sacrifice some of the original project specifications due to schedule pressure or a need to speed a project to completion. Compromising quality may involve a relatively simple decision to accept the use of cheaper materials or fewer oversight steps as the project moves forward. Rarely are decisions to lower quality beneficial for the project; in fact, the decision usually involves a sense of trying to limit or control the damage that could potentially occur. In some cases, it is impossible to even consider this as an option; construction firms hold safety (and hence, quality) as one of their highest concerns and would not consider deliberate steps to reduce quality.

    Reducing project scope, on the other hand, is a much more common response to critical pressure on the organization to deliver a project, particularly if it has been experiencing delays or if the benefits of being first to market seriously overshadow concerns about reduced scope. For example, suppose a television manufacturer in South Korea (Samsung) is working to devise a new product that offers 3D viewing, state-of-the-art sound quality, Internet connectivity, and a host of other features. While in the midst of development, the company becomes aware that a direct competitor is due to release its new television with a more modest set of features in time for the Christmas shopping season. Samsung might be tempted to limit work on their model to the advances that currently have been completed, scale back on other upgrades for a later model, and deliver their television with this reduced scope in order to maintain their market share.

The decision to limit project scope is not one to be taken lightly, but in many cases, it may be possible to do so with limited negative impact on the company, provided the firm can prioritize and distinguish between the "must-have" features of the project and other add-on functions that may not be critical to the project's mission. Numerous projects have been successfully introduced with reduced scope because the organization approached these reductions in a systematic way, revisiting the work breakdown structure and project schedule and making necessary modifications. Approaching scope reduction in a proactive manner can have the effect of reducing scope while minimizing the negative effects on the final delivered project.

4. *Fast-track the project*—Fast-tracking a project refers to looking for ways to rearrange the project schedule in order to move more of the critical path activities from sequential to parallel (concurrent) relationships. In some cases, the opportunities to fast-track a project only require creativity from the project team. For example, in a simple construction project, it may be possible to begin pouring the concrete foundation while the final interior design work or more detailed drawings are still being completed. That is, the design of cabinetry or the placement or doors and windows in the house will not be affected by the decision to start work on the foundation, and the net effect will be to shorten the project's duration. In Chapter 9, we discussed options to reduce the critical path. Fast-tracking can employ some of those methods as well as other approaches, including:

   a. Shorten the longest critical activities—Identify those critical activities with the longest durations and reduce them by some percentage. Shortening longer activities typically offers the most opportunity to affect the length of the overall project without incurring severe additional risks.

   b. Partially overlap activities—Start the successor task before its predecessor is fully completed. We can use "negative lags" between activities to reschedule our critical activities and allow for one task to overlap another. For example, suppose we had two activities in sequence: (1) program function code, and (2) debug code. In many cases, it is possible to begin debugging code before the programmer has fully completed the assignment. We might indicate, for example, that the debugging activity has a negative lag of two weeks to allow the debugger to begin her task two weeks before the programming activity is scheduled to finish.

   c. Employ Start to Start lag relationships—Standard predecessor/successor task relationships are characterized by finish-to-start relationships, suggesting that the successor cannot begin until its predecessor is fully completed. In start-to-start relationships, the assumption is that both activities can be undertaken at the same time; for example, instead of waiting for a city to issue a building permit approval, a local contractor may begin clearing the site for new construction or contacting other city departments to begin road and sewer applications. Not every set of activities can be redefined from a finish-to-start to a start-to-start lag relationship, but often there are places within the project schedule where it is possible to employ this fast-tracking technique.

5. *Use overtime*—A common response to the decision to accelerate a project is to make team members work longer hours through scheduling overtime. On one level, the decision is an attractive one: If our workers are currently devoting 40 hours a week to the project, by adding another 10 hours of overtime, we have increased productivity by 20%. Further, for salaried employees, we can institute overtime regulations without the additional costs that would accrue from using hourly workers. Thus, the use of overtime appears on the surface to be an option with much to recommend it.

The decision to use overtime, however, comes with some important drawbacks that should be considered. The first is cost: For hourly workers, overtime rates can quickly become prohibitively expensive. The result is to seriously affect the project budget in order to gain time (part of what are referred to as "dollar-day" trade-offs). Another problem with overtime is possible effects on project team member productivity. Work by Ken Cooper offers some important points for project managers to consider when tempted to accelerate their projects through the use of overtime. Figure 10.13 shows the results of his research examining the effects of sustained overtime on project team members for two classes of employee: engineers and production staff. When real productivity and rework penalties (having to fix work incorrectly done the first time) are taken into account, the impact of overtime is worrisome: For only four hours of overtime worked each week, the project can expect to receive less than two hours of actual productivity from both engineers and production staff. The more overtime

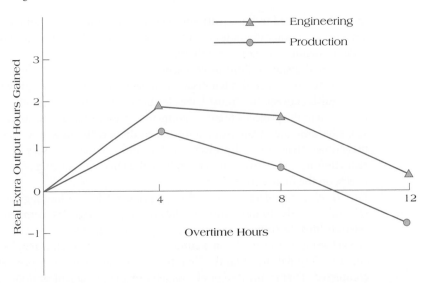

FIGURE 10.13 **Real Output Gained from Different Levels of Sustained Overtime**

is used, the more this problem is exacerbated. Indeed, at 12 hours of sustained weekly overtime, the net output effect is negligible for engineering personnel and actually becomes negative for production resources! In effect, requiring additional overtime work in the hopes of accelerating the project's schedule often has the actual effect of increasing overtime-induced fatigue, adding to our budget while providing almost no real additional productivity.

6. *Add resources to the project team*—Expected activity durations are based on using a set number of individuals to accomplish the task; however, when additional resources become available, they have the net effect of reducing the amount of time to complete the task. For example, suppose we originally assigned one programmer to complete a specific coding operation and determined that the task would take 40 hours. Now, we decide to shorten that task by adding two additional programmers. What is the new expected time to complete the activity? Certainly, we would anticipate it to be less than the original 40 hours, but how much less is not always clear, since the result may not be a simple linear function (e.g., 40/3 = 13.33 hours). Other variables can affect the completion time (e.g., communication delays or difficulty in coordinating the three programmers). In general, however, adding resources to activities can lead to a significant reduction in the expected duration of the programming activity.

   As with overtime, we need to carefully consider the impact of adding resources to a project, especially when some activities are already underway. In adding people to activities, for example, we need to consider "learning curve" effects. Suppose that our programmer has already begun working on the task when we decide to add two additional resources to help him. The effect of adding two programmers to this ongoing activity may actually backfire on the project manager, as was originally suggested by a former IBM executive named Fred Brooks. He suggested, in his famous **Brook's Law**, that adding resources to ongoing activities only delays them further. His point was that the additional time and training needed to bring these extra resources up to speed on the task negates the positive impact of actually adding staff. It is much better, he suggested, to add extra resources to activities that have not yet started, where they can truly shorten the overall task durations. Although research has tended to confirm Brook's Law in most situations, it is possible to realize schedule shrinkage provided sufficient time and current resources are available to train additional staff or they are added early enough into the activity to minimize the negative effects of Brook's Law.[4]

Although the above discussion demonstrates that there are some important issues to consider when adding resources to a project, this alternative remains by far the most common method for shortening activity durations, and it is often useful as long as the link between cost and schedule is respected.

   To determine the usefulness of crashing project activities, we must first be able to determine the actual cost associated with each activity in the project, both in terms of project fixed costs and variable costs. These concepts are discussed in greater detail in Chapter 8 on project budgeting. Let us assume that we have a reasonable method for estimating the total cost of project activities, both in terms of their normal development time and

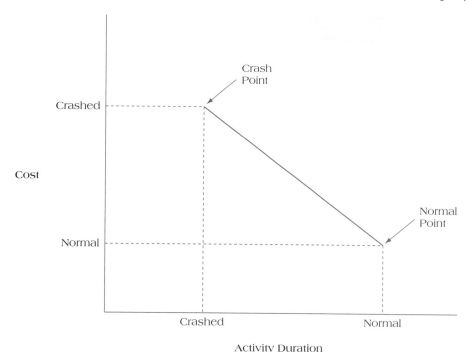

FIGURE 10.14 **Time/Cost Trade-Offs for Crashing Activities**

under a crashed alternative. Figure 10.14 illustrates the relationship between activity costs and duration. Note that the normal length of the duration for an activity reflects a calculated resource cost in order to accomplish that task. As we seek to crash activities, the costs associated with these activities increase sharply. The crash point on the diagram represents the fully expedited project activity, in which no expense is spared to complete the task. Because the line shows the slope between the normal and crash points, it is also understood that a project activity can be speeded up to some degree less than the complete crash point, relative to the slope of the crash line.

In analyzing crash options for project activities, the goal is to find the point at which time and cost trade-offs are optimized. We can calculate various combinations of time/cost trade-offs for a project's crash options by determining the slope for each activity using the following formula:

$$\text{Slope} = \frac{\text{crash cost} - \text{normal cost}}{\text{normal time} - \text{crash time}}$$

EXAMPLE 10.1 **Calculating the Cost of Crashing**

To calculate the cost of crashing project activities, suppose that for activity X, the normal activity duration is 5 weeks and the budgeted cost is $12,000. The crash time for this activity is 3 weeks and the expected cost is $32,000. Using the above formula, we can calculate the cost slope for activity X as:

$$\frac{32,000 - 12,000}{5 - 3} \quad \text{or} \quad \frac{\$20,000}{2} = \$10,000 \text{ per week}$$

In this example, activity X is calculated to cost $10,000 for each week's acceleration to its original schedule. Is this a reasonable price? In order to answer that question, we need to consider:

a. *What costs are associated with accelerating other project activities?* It may be that activity X's unit cost of $10,000 per week is a genuine bargain. Suppose, for example, that an alternative activity would cost the project $25,000 for each week's acceleration.

b. *What are the gains versus the losses in accelerating this activity?* For example, does the project have excessive late penalties that would make crashing cheaper relative to late delivery? Alternatively, is there a huge potential payoff in being first to market with the project?

| EXAMPLE 10.2 | Crashing a Project |

Suppose we have a project with only eight activities, as illustrated in Table 10.1. The table also shows our calculated normal activity durations and costs and crashed durations and their costs. We wish to determine which activities are the optimal candidates for crashing. Assume that the project costs listed include both fixed and variable costs for each activity. Use the formula provided earlier to calculate the per-unit costs (in this case, costs per day) for each activity. These costs are shown in Table 10.2.

TABLE 10.1 Project Activities and Costs (Normal vs. Crashed)

| Activity | Normal | | Crashed | |
	Duration	Cost	Duration	Cost
A	5 days	$ 1,000	3 days	$ 1,500
B	7 days	700	6 days	1,000
C	3 days	2,500	2 days	4,000
D	5 days	1,500	5 days	1,500
E	9 days	3,750	6 days	9,000
F	4 days	1,600	3 days	2,500
G	6 days	2,400	4 days	3,000
H	8 days	9,000	5 days	15,000
Total costs =		$22,450		$37,500

The calculations suggest that the least expensive activities to crash would be first, activity A ($250/day), followed by activities B and G ($300/day). On the other hand, the project would incur the greatest cost increases through crashing activities H, E, and C ($2,000/day, $1,750/day, and $1,500/day, respectively). Note that in this example, we are assuming that activity D cannot be shortened, so no crashing cost can be calculated for it.

Now let's transfer these crashing costs to a network that shows the precedence logic of each activity. We can form a trade-off between shortening the project and increasing its total costs by analyzing each alternative. Figure 10.15 shows the project network as a simplified AON example with only activity identification and crashed duration values included. The network also shows the critical path as A − D − E − H or 19 days. We determined that the initial project cost, using normal activity durations, is $22,450. Crashing activity A (lowest at $250) by 1 day will increase the project budget from $22,450 to $22,700. Fully crashing activity A will shorten the project duration to 25 days while increasing the cost to $22,950. Activities B and G are the next candidates for crashing at $300 per day each. Neither activity is on the project's critical path, however, so the overall benefit to the project from shortening these activities may be minimal. Activity D cannot be shortened. The per unit cost to crash E is $1,750, and the cost to crash H is higher ($2,000). Thus, crashing activity E by 1 day will increase the project budget from $22,950 to $24,700. The total costs for each day the project is crashed are shown in Table 10.3.

TABLE 10.2 Costs of Crashing Each Activity

Activity	Crashing Costs (per day)	On Critical Path?
A	$ 250	Yes
B	300	No
C	1,500	No
D	—	Yes
E	1,750	Yes
F	900	No
G	300	No
H	2,000	Yes

TABLE 10.3 Project Costs by Duration

Duration	Total Costs
27 days	$22,450
26 days	22,700
25 days	22,950
24 days	24,700
23 days	26,450
22 days	28,200
21 days	30,200
20 days	32,200
19 days	34,200

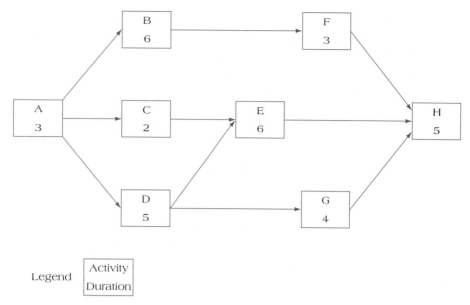

FIGURE 10.15   Fully Crashed Project Activity Network

Note that in the fully crashed project network shown in Figure 10.15, the critical path is unchanged when all activities are fully crashed. The association of costs to project duration is graphed in Figure 10.16. As each project activity has been crashed in order, the overall project budget increases. Figure 10.16 demonstrates, however, that beyond crashing activities A, E, and H, there is little incentive to crash any of the other project tasks. The overall length of the project cannot shrink below 19 days, and additional crashing merely adds costs to the budget. Therefore, the optimal crash strategy for this project is to crash only activities A, E, and H for a total cost of $11,750 and a revised project cost of $34,200.

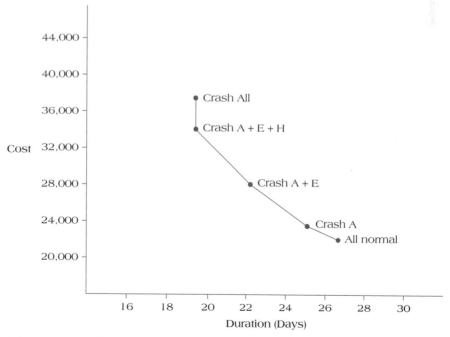

FIGURE 10.16   Relationship Between Cost and Days Saved in a Crashed Project

The decision to crash a project should be carefully considered for its benefits and drawbacks. Considering the relationship between activity duration and increased project costs is never a "painless" operation; there is always a significant cost associated with activity acceleration. However, if the reasons for crashing are sufficiently compelling, the overall project duration can often be shortened significantly.

Crashing the Project: Budget Effects

As we have seen, crashing is the decision to shorten activity duration times through adding resources and paying additional direct costs. There is a clear relationship between the decision to crash project activities and the effect of the crashing on the budget. As Figure 10.16 showed, the cost of crashing is always to be weighed against the time saved in expediting the activity's schedule.

To highlight this problem, consider the crashing table shown in Table 10.4. Let us assume that activities A, C, D, and H are on the critical path; therefore, the first decision relates to which of the critical activities we should crash. A simple side-by-side comparison of the activities and their crash costs reveals the following:

Activity	Crash Cost
A	$2,000
C	$1,500
D	$3,000
H	$3,000

Using Table 10.4, we find that in crashing activity C, the least expensive to crash, we save 3 days at a cost of $1,500 in extra expenses. The other candidates for crashing (A, D, and H) can also be evaluated individually in terms of schedule time gained versus cost to the project budget (assume all other paths are ≤48 days). Crashing Activity A saves the project 3 days at an additional cost of $2,000, raising the total cost of A to $4,000. Crashing Activities D and H represent a time savings of 5 and 3 days respectively at additional costs of $3,000 for each.

Indirect costs are affected by crashing as well. Table 10.5 illustrates the choices the project team is faced with as they continually adjust the cost of crashing the schedule against other project costs. Suppose the project is being charged overhead at a fixed rate, say, $200 per day. Also assume that a series of late penalties is due to kick in if the project is not completed within 50 days. The original 57-day schedule clearly leaves us at risk for penalties, and although we have improved the delivery date, we are still 4 days past the deadline. Now we discover that iterating the crashed schedule three times will take us from our original 57-day schedule to a new schedule of 48 days (crashing first activity C, then A, and then H). The schedule has shortened 9 days against a budget increase of $6,500.

We could make Table 10.5 more complete by following the costs for each successive crashed activity and linking them to total project costs. Intuitively, however, we can see that direct costs would continue to increase as we included the extra costs of more crashed activities. On the other hand, overhead charges and

TABLE 10.4 Project Activities, Durations, and Direct Costs

Activity	Normal		Crashed		Crash Cost
	Cost	Duration	Extra Cost	Duration	
A	$2,000	10 days	$2,000	7 days	$ 667/day
B	1,500	5 days	3,000	3 days	1,500/day
C	3,000	12 days	1,500	9 days	500/day
D	5,000	20 days	3,000	15 days	600/day
E	2,500	8 days	2,500	6 days	1,250/day
F	3,000	14 days	2,500	10 days	625/day
G	6,000	12 days	5,000	10 days	2,500/day
H	9,000	15 days	3,000	12 days	1,000/day

TABLE 10.5 Project Costs over Duration

Project Duration (in days)	Direct Costs	Liquidated Damages Penalty	Overhead Costs	Total Costs
57	$32,000	$5,000	$11,400	$48,400
54	33,500	3,000	10,800	47,300
51	35,500	1,000	10,200	46,700
48	38,500	-0-	9,600	48,100

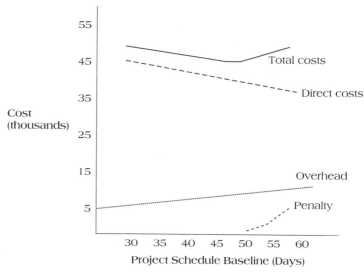

FIGURE 10.17   Project Costs over the Life Cycle

Source: A. Shtub, J. F. Bard, and S. Globerson. (1994). *Project Management: Processes, Methodologies, and Economics,* Second Edition. Copyright © 2005. Adapted by permission of Pearson Education, Inc., Upper Saddle River, NJ.

liquidated damages costs would decrease; in fact, at the 48-day mark, liquidated damages no longer factor into the cost structure. Hence, the challenge becomes deciding at what point it is *no longer* economically viable to continue crashing project activities.

Figure 10.17 depicts the choices the project team faces in balancing the competing demands of schedule and cost, with other intervening factors such as penalties for late delivery included. Direct costs are shown with a downward slope, reflecting the fact that the costs will rapidly ramp up as the schedule shrinks (the time-cost trade-off effect). With liquidated damage penalties emerging after the 50-day schedule deadline, we see that the project team is facing a choice of paying extra money for a crashed schedule at the front end versus paying out penalties upon project delivery for being late. The process the project team faces is a balancing act between competing costs—crashing costs and late completion costs.

10.4 ACTIVITY-ON-ARROW NETWORKS

So far this text has focused exclusively on the use of the **Activity-on-Node (AON)** convention for representing activity network diagrams. Among the reasons for this system's popularity is that it mirrors the standard employed in almost all project management scheduling software, it is visually easier to comprehend, and it simplifies many past standards and conventions in network diagrams. Nevertheless, **Activity-on-Arrow (AOA)** techniques are an alternative to AON methodology. Although no longer as popular as it once was, AOA is still used to some degree in various project management situations. Some AOA conventions are unique to its use and do not directly translate or integrate with AON approaches.

Events shown in node   Activity shown on arrow

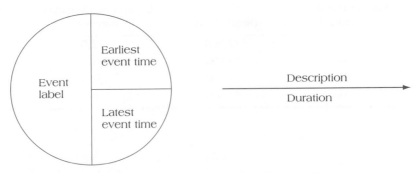

FIGURE 10.18 Notation for Activity-on-Arrow (AOA) Networks

How Are They Different?

Both AON and AOA methods are used to create a project activity network. They simply differ in the means they employ and the graphical manner in which the network, once completed, is represented. AOA networks also employ arrows and nodes to build the activity network; however, with AOA, the arrow represents the activity with its duration time estimate, while the node is used only as an **event** marker, usually representing the completion of a task.

Consider the activity node shown in Figure 10.18. The AOA node is similar to AON nodes in that there is no set standard for the types of information that the node should contain; however, it should be sufficiently clear to convey understanding to the users. The convention in Figure 10.18 offers the major placement of network information for each activity arrow and node:

Arrow includes a short task description and the expected duration for the activity.

Node includes an event label, such as a number, letter, or code, and earliest and latest event times. These values correspond to early start and late finish times for the activity.

EXAMPLE 10.3   **Activity-on-Arrow Network Development**

The development of an AOA network follows a similar process to the one we apply to AON methodology, with some important distinctions. In order to make clear the differences, let us return to the sample network problem from earlier in this chapter: Project Delta. Table 10.6 gives us the relevant precedence information that we need to construct the AOA network.

TABLE 10.6 Project Information

	Project Delta		
Activity	**Description**	**Predecessors**	**Estimated Duration**
A	Contract signing	None	5
B	Questionnaire design	A	5
C	Target market ID	A	6
D	Survey sample	B, C	13
E	Develop presentation	B	6
F	Analyze results	D	4
G	Demographic analysis	C	9
H	Presentation to client	E, F, G	2

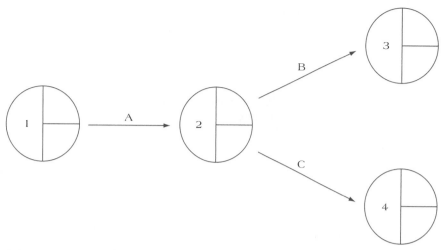

FIGURE 10.19 Sample Network Diagram Using AOA Approach

We begin building a network in the same manner as with AON developed in Chapter 9. First, we can start with activity A and its immediate successors, activities B and C. Because the convention now is to indicate the activity on the arrow, it is common for AOA networks to have an initial "Start" event node that precedes the insertion of the activities. Figure 10.19 shows the process of beginning to add the project information to the network diagram. Note that activities B and C directly succeed activity A. The convention would be to draw two arrows, representing these activities, directly off event node 2.

The first problem with AOA networking becomes apparent once we have to enter activity D into the network. Note that both activities B and C are immediate predecessors for activity D. Representing this relationship with an AON network is easy; we simply draw two arrows connecting nodes B and C to the node for activity D (see Figure 9.10). However, with AOA networks we cannot employ the same process. Why not? Because each arrow is used not just to connect the nodes, but also to represent a separate task in the activity network. How can we show this precedence relationship in the network? Figure 10.20 offers several options, two of which are incorrect. The first option (Figure 10.20a) is to assign two arrows representing activity D and link activities B and C through their respective nodes (3 and 4) with node 5. This would be wrong because the AOA convention is to assign only one activity to each arrow. Alternatively, we could try to represent this precedence relationship by using the second option (Figure 10.20b), in which a double set of activity arrows for activities B and C jointly link node 2 to node 3. Again, this approach is incorrect because it violates the rule that each node represents a unique event, such as the completion of an individual activity. It can also become confusing when the convention is to employ multiple arrows between event nodes. It was in order to resolve just such a circumstance that the use of dummy activities was created.

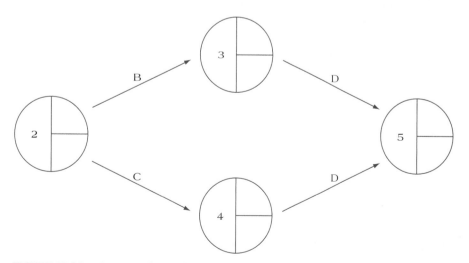

FIGURE 10.20a Representing Activities with Two or More Immediate Successors (Wrong)

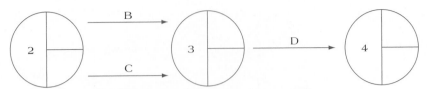

FIGURE 10.20b Alternative Way to Represent Activities with Two or More Immediate Successors (Wrong)

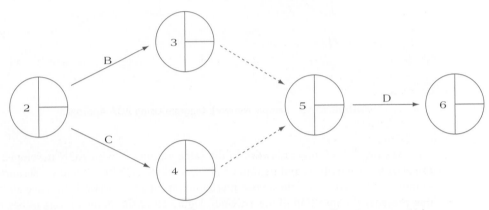

FIGURE 10.20c Representing Activities with Two or More Immediate Successors Using Dummy Activities (Better)

Dummy Activities

Dummy activities are used in AOA networks to indicate the existence of precedent relationships between activities and their event nodes. They do not have any work or time values assigned to them. They are employed when we wish to indicate a logical dependency such that one activity cannot start before another has been completed, but the activities do not lie on the same path through the network. Dummy activities are usually represented as dashed or dotted lines and may or may not be assigned their own identifier.

Figure 10.20c shows the proper method for linking activities B and C with their successor, activity D, through the use of dummy activities. In this case, the dummy activities merely demonstrate that both activities B and C must be completed prior to the start of activity D. When using dummy activities in network diagramming, one good rule for their use is to try to apply them sparingly. The excessive use of dummy activities can add confusion to the network, particularly when it is often possible to represent precedence logic without employing the maximum possible number of dummy activities. To illustrate this point, consider Figure 10.21, in which we have reconfigured the partial activity

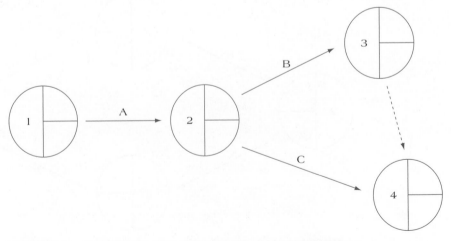

FIGURE 10.21 Partial Project Delta Network Using AOA Notation

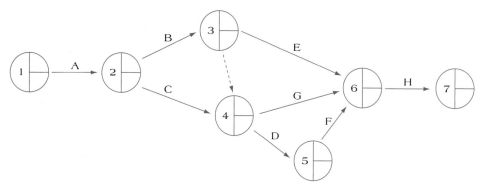

FIGURE 10.22 **Completed Project Delta AOA Network**

network for Project Delta slightly. Note that this diagram has simply eliminated one of the dummy activities about to enter node 5 without changing the network logic.

Now that we have a sense of the use of dummy activities, we can construct the full AOA network for Project Delta. Activity E succeeds B and is entered on the network with its endpoint at node 6. Likewise, activity F, following D, is entered into the network with endpoint at node 6. Activity G can also be entered following the completion of C, and its endpoint node is also 6. Finally, activity H, which has activities E, F, and G as predecessors, is entered and completes the basic AOA network (see Figure 10.22).

Forward and Backward Passes with AOA Networks

The actual information we seek to collect for these processes that determines early and late start dates is slightly different from that used in AON, as we are concerned with the early start (ES) values for each activity node in the forward pass. The decision rules still apply: Where we have nodes that serve as **merge** points for multiple predecessor activities, we select the largest ES. The only other point to remember is that dummy activities do not have any duration value attached to them.

Figure 10.23 shows the forward pass results for Project Delta. The nodes display the information concerning ES in the upper right quadrant. As with the AON forward pass, the process consists simply of adding duration estimates for each activity moving from left to right through the network. The only places in the network that require some deliberation regarding the ES value to apply are at the merge points represented by nodes 4 and 6. Node 4 is the merge point for activity C and the dummy activity represented by the dotted line. Because dummy activities do not have any value themselves, the ES for node 4 is the largest of the additive paths for activities A − C = 11 versus activities A − B = 10. Therefore, we find that the ES at node 4 should be 11. The other merge point, node 6, uses the same selection process. Because the path A − C − D − F = 28, which is the largest of the paths entering the node, we use 28 as the ES for node 6. Finally, after adding the duration for activity H, the overall length of the network is 30 weeks, just as it was in the AON network shown in the previous chapter (see Figure 9.18).

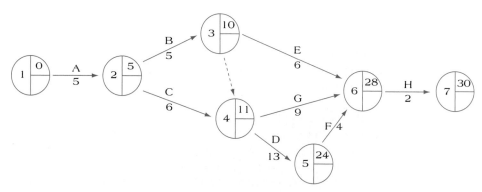

FIGURE 10.23 **Project Delta Forward Pass Using AOA Network**

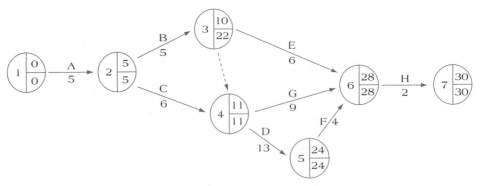

FIGURE 10.24 **Project Delta Backward Pass Using AOA Network**

The backward pass is also similar in procedure to the earlier AON process. The backward pass starts at the far right or completion of the network at node 7 and, using the 30-week duration as its starting point, subtracts activity times along each path (LF − Dur = LS). When we reach a burst event, such as node 2 or 4, we select the smallest LS from the choice of activities. Thus, using Figure 10.24 as our reference, we can begin subtracting duration values as we move from right to left in the network. The LS values are included in the node in the bottom right-hand quadrant, right underneath the ES values.

The forward pass allowed us to determine that the expected duration for the project is 30 weeks. Using the backward pass, we can determine the individual activity slacks as well as the critical path, similar to the AON process. The difference is that the labeling of ES and LS values lies within the event nodes; therefore, it is necessary to examine each activity path to determine the slack associated with it. We know, for example, that the ES for activity E is 10 weeks and the duration of the activity is 6 weeks. Therefore, when comparing the EF for activity E of 16 weeks with the ES value in node 6 of 28 weeks, we can see that the difference, 12 weeks, is the amount of slack for the activity. Likewise, activity G's ES is 11 weeks and its duration is 9. This EF value of 20 weeks is 8 weeks less than the ES for node 6, indicating that activity G's slack is 8. The same logic can be applied to each activity in the network to determine the critical path and the activities with slack time.

AOA Versus AON

Activity-on-Arrow and Activity-on-Node network diagramming are intended to do the same thing: create a sequential logic for all activities with a project and, once they are linked, determine the project's duration, critical path, and slack activities. One common question has to do with the efficacy of one network approach over the other; that is, what are the benefits and drawbacks of selecting either the AON format or the AOA approach? Consequently, in choosing to use either AOA or AON network methods, it is important to consider some of the strengths and weaknesses of each of these techniques.[5]

AON STRENGTHS AND WEAKNESSES   The benefits of AON are centered primarily in the fact that it has become the most popular format for computer software packages, such as MS Project. Hence, as more and more companies use software-based project scheduling software, they are increasingly using the AON method for network diagrams. Another benefit of AON is that we place the activity within a node and use arrows merely as connection devices, thereby simplifying the network labeling. This convention makes AON networks very easy to read and comprehend, even for novice project managers. The primary drawback with AON networks occurs when the project is very complex with numerous paths through the model. The sheer number of arrows and node connections when multiple project activities are merging or bursting can make AON networks difficult to read.

AOA STRENGTHS AND WEAKNESSES   The greatest benefit of AOA modeling lies in its accepted use in certain business fields, such as construction, where AON networks may be less widely used. Also, in the case of large, complex projects, it is often easier to employ the path process used in AOA. Finally, because the activity and node system is used for projects that have many significant milestones, such as supplier deliveries, AOA event nodes are very easy to identify and flag. On the other hand, there is no question that some conventions in AOA diagramming are awkward, particularly the use of dummy activities. The concept of dummy activities is not simple to master, and thus more training is required on the part of novice project managers to be able to use the concept easily. In addition, AOA networks can be "information-intensive" in that both arrows and nodes contain some important project information. Rather than centralizing all data into a node, as in the AON convention, AOA networks use both arrows and nodes to label the network.

Ultimately, the choice to employ AON or AOA network methodology comes down to individual preferences and the external pressures faced in work situations. For example, if the organization I work for has decided to adopt AON modeling because of the commonly used scheduling software, in all likelihood I will concentrate exclusively on AON network diagramming approaches. Regardless of the decision each of us makes regarding the use of AOA or AON methodology, it is extremely important that we all become comfortable with the basic theory and operation of both types of network models.

10.5 CONTROVERSIES IN THE USE OF NETWORKS

The **Program Evaluation and Review Technique**/Critical Path Method (PERT/CPM) is a well understood and much employed system for project planning and scheduling. Nevertheless, networks are abstract representations of events in which time is reduced to a numerical value. They may or may not be drawn to a scale that has a relationship to the ongoing pattern of events. Sometimes this abstraction can be misleading. In fact, there are several criticisms and caveats we need to bear in mind as we develop project activity networks, including:[6]

1. *Networks can become too large and complex to be meaningful.* Many projects are large and hugely complex. For example, the creation of an operating system for personal computers, construction of a sports arena, or development of a drug are all projects that can easily contain thousands of steps or individual activities. Many projects extend over years, and estimation of activity duration can become general guesses at best. As a result, when working with networks for large-scale or long-term projects, it is necessary to find ways to simplify the activity network calculations. One rule of thumb for large projects is to try to simplify network logic and reduce it to the most obvious or meaningful relationships. Rather than showing every possible path through the network and every activity sequence, a "meta-network" that shows only the key subroutines or network paths can be created. These subroutines can be further broken down by the project manager or administrator responsible for their completion, but the overall project network is streamlined to include only the most general or relevant project activities.

    A variably scaled time frame is another option for long-term projects. For example, activities scheduled to occur within the first nine months may be listed with durations scaled to the number of days necessary to complete them. Activities scheduled between the first and second year may be listed on the network with a scaling of weeks or even months, and activities included in the network beyond the second year may only be listed with durations indicated by months.

2. *Faulty reasoning in network construction can sometimes lead to oversimplification or incorrect representations.* Problems frequently occur when organizations attempt to manage their projects on the basis of these multiple layers of activity networks. Information going to different levels in the organization is often not easily understood or translatable between levels because they do not share a common project schedule. Hence, it is important that when simplifying a project network, steps must be taken to ensure that information is not lost through oversimplification or the creation of multiple networks with no integration processes.

    Complex schedules often require a combination "top-down, bottom-up" approach to controlling project activities. Top-down control means that there is a tiered system for project schedules. At the top is the most basic summary information, as in the case of simply listing work packages or summary "roll-ups" of numerous individual tasks. Top management then deals with top-tier summary information that aggregates and simplifies the schedule. Although it is much easier to understand, this top-tier summary network does not give top management a basis for understanding the actual development of the project because they are not privy to the status of individual tasks. On the other hand, those responsible for portions of the project, as well as project managers, need more "bottom-up" information to allow them to maintain hands-on control of the portion of the project network for which they are responsible. Project personnel need specific, lower-tier activity network information to allow for optimal scheduling and control.

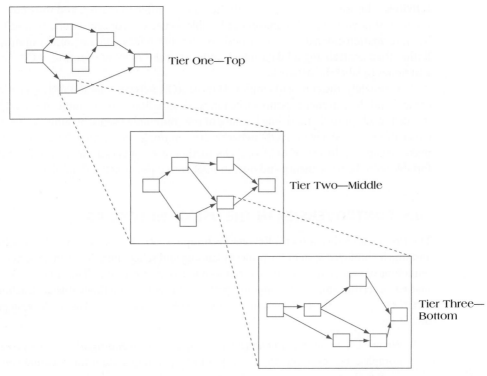

FIGURE 10.25 **Tiered System of Project Schedules**

Figure 10.25 provides an example of a simplified tiered system for schedules. Top management would receive aggregated information from the top tier, middle-level management (e.g., department heads) would get slightly more detailed information based on activities relevant to their departments or functions, and both the project manager and the project team would employ the full, detailed, and specific project schedule in the bottom tier.

3. ***Networks are sometimes used for tasks for which they are not well suited.*** Companies sometimes try to adopt project network scheduling to other scheduling activities in their organizations, but network activities are not useful for all scheduling challenges. Suppose, for example, that a manufacturing organization was having problems with its production scheduling. Under the mistaken notion that PERT can work just as well for manufacturing operations as it does for project planning, managers might mistakenly decide to employ PERT in situations for which it is not suited. In fact, project network scheduling methodologies are an important technique in project management; they do not represent a panacea for all scheduling problems that organizations face.

4. ***Networks used to control the behavior of subcontractors have special dangers.*** Many projects involve the use of subcontractors. When the "prime contracting" organization employs multiple subcontractors, a common mistake is requiring them to develop independent activity plans without reference to or understanding the planning of other subcontractors with whom they may need to interface. If a firm is using multiple subcontractors, two important principles are needed to guide their use of networks: (1) All subcontractors must be privy to the prime contractor's overall network, which includes the schedules for each "sub," so that subcontractors can make scheduling decisions based not on assumptions, but rather on clear knowledge of the plans of other subcontractors; and (2) the networks of all subcontractors need to be merged—using a common set of network techniques, time-frame scaling, and so forth—and the network document must be mutually accessible, which is most likely to occur if all subcontractors are equally aware of the rules governing network creation.

5. ***There is a strong potential for positive bias in PERT estimations used in network construction.*** Research has demonstrated that most activity estimations using PERT methods lead to overly optimistic activity duration estimates. PERT analysis is based on probabilistic time estimates that, if unreasonably determined, can lead to inaccurate and misleading project schedules. The logic that drives duration estimates and the development of the PERT network must be demonstrated as reasonable for PERT scheduling to be meaningful.

Conclusions

Activity network development is the heart of the project management planning process. It requires us to make reasonable estimates of activity durations, and it expects us to develop the logic for activity sequencing and use this information to create meaningful project schedules. Only through the careful analysis of the steps in project scheduling can we turn project concepts into working realities. Scheduling allows us to determine the answers to the truly significant questions of project management: What needs to be accomplished? When does it need to be accomplished? How can it be accomplished? The scheduling techniques you select are not nearly as important to the final success of your projects as is your commitment to performing these operations carefully, methodically, and honestly. The schedule is our road map showing the route we must take to complete the project successfully. The care with which we create that map and the manner in which we follow it will go far to determining whether or not we will be successful in running our projects.

Summary

1. **Apply lag relationships to project activities.** Examples of developing network logic include determining how precedence relationships apply to each project activity; that is, do activities follow one another in a common manner in which the predecessor's early finish becomes the successor activity's early start, or are other relationships specified? Among these alternative relationships, referred to as lag relationships, are finish to start, finish to finish, start to start, and start to finish.

2. **Construct and comprehend Gantt charts.** An alternative method for developing the project network other than the use of PERT diagrams is Gantt charts. Gantt charts offer an important advantage over the early PERT diagrams in that they link the activities to a project schedule baseline based on actual calendar dates. Thus, we can see not only which activities have to occur in what order, but also when they are scheduled to begin and end. In recent years, Gantt charts have been used in conjunction with PERT charts, particularly with most project scheduling software.

3. **Recognize alternative means to accelerate projects, including their benefits and drawbacks.** The project schedule can be accelerated by a number of alternative means, including adding resources to the project team, fast-tracking, compromising quality, reducing the project's scope, and using overtime. Each of these options offers the means to accelerate a project, but not all are appropriate in every circumstance; for example, it may not be useful or helpful to deliberately compromise a project's quality. Some of these options can improve productivity in theory, but may not work as well in reality; for example, research suggests that use of sustained overtime for extended periods can actually have a detrimental effect on a project due to the effects of employee fatigue and rework costs. Finally, the choice of alternatives requires us to understand the resource constraints of the organization.

4. **Understand the trade-offs required in the decision to crash project activities.** When it has been determined that the project must be accelerated, due to either changes in the external environment or pressures from top management or customers, a method known as project crashing is employed. Crashing directly links all activities to their respective costs and allows us to calculate the cost for each day we choose to accelerate the project. The decision of whether or not to crash can therefore be directly linked to the cost implications for crashing, allowing project managers to make an informed decision on time/cost trade-offs.

5. **Develop activity networks using Activity-on-Arrow techniques.** Although AON network diagramming has become the more popular method, for many years AOA network diagramming was the technique of choice, and it is still widely applied in several project settings, such as construction. This chapter discusses in detail AOA networks and their unique properties, including the creation and use of dummy variables, and examines the steps necessary to construct an AOA network, as well as its advantages and disadvantages compared to AON notation.

6. **Understand the differences in AON and AOA and recognize the advantages and disadvantages of each technique.** The chapter concludes with a critical review of some of the controversies found in the development and use of network diagrams for project scheduling. Several drawbacks or concerns in diagramming are listed, including (1) networks can become too large and complex to be meaningful, (2) faulty reasoning can lead to oversimplification or incorrect representations, (3) networks can be used for tasks for which they are not well suited, and (4) network diagramming has special dangers when used to control subcontractor behavior.

Key Terms

Activity-on-Arrow (AOA) (p. 349)

Activity-on-Node (AON) (p. 349)

Arrow (p. 350)

Brook's Law (p. 344)

Crashing (p. 342)

Dummy activities (p. 352)

Event (p. 350)

Fast-tracking (p. 336)

Gantt chart (p. 337)

Lag (p. 335)

Merge (p. 353)

Node (p. 350)

Overtime (p. 339)

Program Evaluation and Review Technique (PERT) (p. 355)

Serial activities (p. 335)

Solved Problems

10.1 Crashing Project Activities

Suppose you are considering whether or not to crash project activities in order to expedite your project. You have calculated the costs per activity for both normal and crashed options. These are shown in the table below:

Activity	Normal Duration	Normal Cost	Crashed Duration	Crashed Cost
A	6 days	$ 2,400	4 days	$ 3,600
B	7 days	3,500	5 days	5,000
C	5 days	3,000	4 days	3,800
D	3 days	2,700	2 days	4,500
E	4 days	800	3 days	1,500
F	5 days	1,200	3 days	2,100
G	8 days	2,400	5 days	4,200
H	3 days	4,500	2 days	7,000
Total costs	=	$20,500		$31,700

a. Which activities are the most likely candidates for crashing (i.e., which are the most cost-effective to crash)?

b. Refer back to Figure 10.24. Using the critical path from this activity network, consider A – C – D – F – H as the critical path and assume all other paths are less than a fully crashed A – C – D – F – H. Prioritize the candidates for crashing. How does the activity network change the decision rule?

SOLUTION

Remember that the formula to calculate crashing costs is based on the slope between the normal and crashed costs of each activity:

$$\text{Slope} = \frac{\text{crash cost} - \text{normal cost}}{\text{normal time} - \text{crash time}}$$

Using this equation, we can create a table showing the crashing costs per day:

Activity	Crashing Costs (per day)
A	$ 600
B	750
C	800
D	1,800
E	700
F	450
G	600
H	2,500

a. Prioritizing crashing choices, the most cost-effective activities to crash are (1) activity F, (2) activities A and G, and (3) activity E.

b. The choices for crashing should be prioritized first by those that are on the critical path. In this example, the critical path is made up of activities A – C – D – F – H. Therefore, the first activity to be crashed would be activity F, followed by activity A. Because neither activity G nor E is on the critical path, crashing them will not reduce the project length but will add to the overall costs.

10.2 Cost of Crashing a Project

Consider the following project activity table, identifying each activity, its normal duration and cost, and expedited durations and costs:

Activity	Normal Duration	Normal Cost	Crashed Duration	Crashed Cost
A	3 days	$1,500	2 days	$2,000
B	5 days	3,500	4 days	5,000
C	4 days	6,800	3 days	7,500
D	5 days	2,500	3 days	6,000
E	7 days	4,200	6 days	5,400
F	4 days	2,000	3 days	2,700

a. What is the cost per day to crash each of the activities?

b. Assuming they are all part of the critical path, which activities should be crashed first?

SOLUTION

a. The formula for calculating crash costs is:

$$\text{Slope} = \frac{\text{crash cost} - \text{normal cost}}{\text{normal time} - \text{crash time}}$$

The crashed costs for each activity are:

Activity A = $500
Activity B = $1,500
Activity C = $700

Activity D = $1,750
Activity E = $1,200
Activity F = $700

b. Assuming the activities are all part of the critical path, we would crash in order from the least expensive activity to the most expensive. In this case, the first choice for crashing is activity A ($500), followed by activities C and F ($700). The last activity we would consider crashing is activity D ($1,750). The total time we can save in crashing all activities is 7 days at a total additional cost of $8,100.

Discussion Questions

1. Give examples of circumstances in which a project would employ lag relationships between activities using:
   a. Finish to start
   b. Finish to finish
   c. Start to start
   d. Start to finish
2. The advantage of Gantt charts lies in their linkage to the project schedule baseline. Explain this concept.
3. What are the advantages in the use of Gantt charts over PERT diagrams? In what ways might PERT diagrams be advantageous?
4. How do concepts such as Brook's Law and the effects of sustained overtime cause us to rethink the best ways to accelerate a project? Is it particularly ironic that these "acceleration" efforts can actually lead to serious delays?

5. Under what circumstances might you wish to crash a project?
6. In crashing a project, we routinely focus on those activities that lie on the critical path, not activities with slack time. Explain why this is the case.
7. What are some of the advantages in the use of AOA notation as opposed to AON? Under what circumstances does it seem better to apply AON methodology in network development?
8. Explain the concept of a dummy variable. Why is this concept employed in AOA notation? Why is there no need to use dummy variables in an AON network?
9. Identify and discuss some of the problems or dangers in using project networks. Under what circumstances can they be beneficial, and when can they be dangerous?

Problems

1. Develop the network activity chart and identify the critical path for a project based on the following information. Draw the activity network as a Gantt chart. What is the expected duration of the project?

Activity	Expected Duration	Predecessors
A	5 days	—
B	6 days	A
C	2 days	A
D	4 days	A
E	6 days	B, C
F	6 days	D, E
G	12 days	F
H	4 days	G
I	6 days	F
J	7 days	H, I

2. Consider a project with the following information. Construct the project activity network using AOA methodology and label each node and arrow appropriately. Identify all dummy activities required to complete the network.

Activity	Duration	Predecessors
A	3	—
B	5	A
C	7	A
D	3	B, C
E	5	B
F	4	D
G	2	C
H	5	E, F, G

Activity	Duration	ES	EF	LS	LF	Slack
A	3	0	3	0	3	—
B	5	3	8	5	10	2
C	7	3	10	3	10	—
D	3	10	13	10	13	—
E	5	8	13	12	17	4
F	4	13	17	13	17	—
G	2	10	12	15	17	5
H	5	17	22	17	22	—

3. You are considering the decision of whether or not to crash your project. After asking your operations manager to conduct an analysis, you have determined the "precrash" and "postcrash" activity durations and costs, shown in the table below (assume *all* activities are on the critical path):

Activity	Normal		Crashed	
	Duration	Cost	Duration	Cost
A	4 days	$1,000	3 days	$2,000
B	5 days	2,500	3 days	5,000
C	3 days	750	2 days	1,200
D	7 days	3,500	5 days	5,000
E	2 days	500	1 day	2,000
F	5 days	2,000	4 days	3,000
G	9 days	4,500	7 days	6,300

a. Calculate the per day costs for crashing each activity.
b. Which are the most attractive candidates for crashing? Why?

4. When deciding on whether or not to crash project activities, a project manager was faced with the following information. Activities on the critical path are highlighted with an asterisk:

Activity	Normal		Crashed	
	Cost	Duration	Extra Cost	Duration
A	$ 5,000	4 weeks	$4,000	3 weeks
B*	10,000	5 weeks	3,000	4 weeks
C	3,500	2 weeks	3,500	1 week
D*	4,500	6 weeks	4,000	4 weeks
E*	1,500	3 weeks	2,500	2 weeks
F	7,500	8 weeks	5,000	7 weeks
G*	3,000	7 weeks	2,500	6 weeks
H	2,500	6 weeks	3,000	5 weeks

a. Identify the sequencing of the activities to be crashed in the first four steps. Which of the critical activities should be crashed first? Why?
b. What is the project's critical path? After four iterations involving crashing project activities, what has the critical path shrunk to? (Assume all noncritical paths are ≤ a fully crashed critical path.)
c. Suppose project overhead costs accrued at a fixed rate of $500 per week. Chart the decline in direct costs over the project life relative to the increase in overhead expenses.
d. Assume that a project penalty clause kicks in after 19 weeks. The penalty charged is $5,000 per week. When the penalty charges are added, what does the total project cost curve look like? Develop a table listing the costs accruing on a per-week basis.
e. If there were no penalty payments accruing to the project, would it make sense to crash any project activities? Show your work.

Case Study 10.1

Project Scheduling at Blanque Cheque Construction (A)

Joe has worked for Blanque Cheque Construction (BCC) for five years, mainly in administrative positions. Three months ago, he was informed that he was being transferred to the firm's project management group. Joe was excited because he realized that project management was typically the career path to the top in BCC, and everyone had to demonstrate the ability to "get their feet wet" by successfully running projects.

Joe has just left a meeting with his superior, Jill, who has assigned him project management responsibilities for a new construction project the company has successfully bid. The project consists of developing a small commercial property that the owners hope to turn into

a strip mall, directly across the street from a suburban college campus. The size of the property and building costs make it prudent to develop the property for four stores of roughly equal size. Beyond that desire, the owners have made it clear to BCC that all project management associated with developing the site is BCC's responsibility.

Joe is sitting in his office at BCC trying to develop a reasonable project plan, including laying out some of the important project activities. At this point, he is content to stick with general levels of activities; that is, he does not want to get too specific yet regarding the various construction steps for developing the site.

Questions

1. Develop a project network consisting of at least 20 steps that should be done to complete the project. As the case suggests, keep the level of detail for these activities general, rather than specific. Be sure to indicate some degree of precedence relationship among the activities.

2. Suppose you now wanted to calculate duration estimates for these activities. How would you make use of the following approaches? Are some more useful than others?

   a. Expert opinion
   b. Past history
   c. Mathematical derivation

3. Joe is trying to decide which scheduling format to employ for his planning: AON or AOA. What are some of the issues that Joe should first consider prior to choosing between these methods?

Case Study 10.2

Project Scheduling at Blanque Cheque Construction (B)

Joe has been managing his project now for more than 12 months and is becoming concerned with how far behind the schedule it is slipping. Through a series of mishaps, late supplier deliveries, bad weather, and other unforeseen circumstances, the project has experienced one delay after another. Although the original plan called for the project to be completed within the next four months, Joe's site supervisor is confident that BCC cannot possibly make that completion date. Late completion of the project has some severe consequences, both for BCC and for Joe. For the company, a series of penalty clauses kicks in for every week the project is late past the contracted completion date. For Joe personally, a late completion to his first project assignment can be very damaging to his career.

Joe has just finished a meeting with his direct supervisor to determine what options he has at this point. The good news is that the BCC bid for the construction project came with some additional profit margin above what is common in the industry, so Joe's boss has given him some "wiggle room" in the form of $30,000 in discretionary budget money if needed. The bad news is that the delivery date for the project is fixed and cannot be altered without incurring substantial penalties, something BCC is not prepared to accept. The message to Joe is clear: You can spend some additional money but you cannot have any extra time.

Joe has just called a meeting with the site supervisor and other key project team members to discuss the possibility of crashing the remaining project activities. He calculates that crashing most of the final activities will bring them in close to the original contracted completion date but at a substantial cost. He needs to weigh these options carefully with his team members to determine if crashing makes sense.

Questions

1. What are some of the issues that weigh in favor of and against crashing the project?

2. Suppose you were the site supervisor for this project. How would you advise Joe to proceed? Before deciding whether or not to crash the project, what questions should you consider and how should you evaluate your options?

MS Project Exercises

Exercise 10.1

Suppose we have a complete activity predecessor table (shown on the next page) and we wish to create a network diagram highlighting the activity sequence for this project. Using MS Project, enter activities A through E, their durations, and their predecessors. Note that all duration times are in days.

Project: Remodeling an Appliance

Activity		Duration	Predecessors
A	Conduct competitive analysis	3	—
B	Review field sales reports	2	—
C	Conduct tech capabilities assessment	5	—
D	Develop focus group data	2	A, B, C
E	Conduct telephone surveys	3	D
F	Identify relevant specification improvements	3	E
G	Interface with marketing staff	1	F
H	Develop engineering specifications	5	G
I	Check and debug designs	4	H
J	Develop testing protocol	3	G
K	Identify critical performance levels	2	J
L	Assess and modify product components	6	I, K
M	Conduct capabilities assessment	12	L
N	Identify selection criteria	3	M
O	Develop RFQ	4	M
P	Develop production master schedule	5	N, O
Q	Liaise with sales staff	1	P
R	Prepare product launch	3	Q

Exercise 10.2

Now, continue developing your Gantt chart with the rest of the information contained in the table in Exercise 10.1, and create a complete activity network diagram for this project.

Exercise 10.3

Identify the critical path for the project shown in Exercise 10.1. How can you identify the critical path? (Hint: Click on the "Tracking Gantt" option.)

Exercise 10.4

Suppose that we wish to incorporate lag relationships into our Remodeling an Appliance activity network. Consider the table shown below and the lag relationships noted. Develop an MS Project Gantt chart that demonstrates these lags.

Activity	Duration	Lag Relationship
A Wiring	6	None
B Plumbing	2	None
C HVAC	3	Wiring (Finish to Start), Plumbing (Finish to Finish)
D Interior construction	6	HVAC (Start to Start)

PMP Certification Sample Questions

1. The IT implementation project is bogging down and falling behind schedule. The department heads are complaining that the project cannot help them if it is not implemented in a reasonable time frame. Your project manager is considering putting extra resources to work on activities along the critical path to accelerate the schedule. This is an example of what?
   a. Rebaselining
   b. Crashing
   c. Fast-tracking the project
   d. Identifying critical dependencies

2. Dummy variables are used in what kind of network diagramming method?
   a. AON
   b. Gantt charts
   c. AOA
   d. OBS

3. Suppose you evaluated the best-case, most likely, and worst-case duration estimates for an activity and determined that they were 3 days, 4 days, and 8 days, respectively. Using PERT estimation techniques, what would be the expected duration for the activity?
   a. 4 days
   b. 8 days
   c. 5 days
   d. 4.5 days

4. Suppose you created your activity network and discovered that you had two critical paths in your project. You share this information with another project manager, who strongly argues that a project can have only one critical path; therefore, your calculations are incorrect. What is the correct response to his assertion?
   a. A project can have more than one critical path, although having multiple critical paths is also likely to increase the risk of the project falling behind.

b. Your coworker is correct: A project can have only one critical path. You need to return to the network and determine where you erred in developing the network logic and diagram.

c. The critical path is the shortest path through the network, so having more than one is not a significant problem.

d. A project can have more than one critical path, although having multiple critical paths is actually likely to decrease the overall risk of the project.

5. Which of the following circumstances would require the creation of a lag relationship in a network diagram?

a. The critical path

b. The insertion of a dummy variable into a network diagram

c. A delay after painting a room to allow for the paint to dry before beginning to carpet the room's floor

d. An early finish relationship between two activities

Answers: 1. b—Accelerating the project through adding resources to critical activities is referred to as "crashing" the project; **2. c**—Dummy variables are employed in Activity-on-Arrow (AOA) network diagrams; **3. d**—PERT estimation would lead to the calculation $(3 + (4 \times 4) + 8)/6 = 27/6$ or 4.5 days; **4. a**—Having more than one critical path is possible; however, the more activities that exist on the critical path(s), the greater the risk to the project's schedule because delays in any critical activities will delay the completion of the project; **5. c**—Allowing for paint to dry before beginning the next activity is an example of a lag relationship occurring between activities.

INTEGRATED PROJECT

Developing the Project Schedule

Develop an in-depth schedule for your initial project based on the Work Breakdown Structure you have completed. You will need to complete several activities at this stage: (1) create an activity precedence diagram showing the network logic for each project activity you have identified; (2) prepare an activity duration table showing optimistic, likely, and pessimistic activity times for each task; and (3) create both the network diagram and Gantt charts for your project, indicating the critical path and all critical activities, total project duration, and all activities with float.

As you prepare the activity precedence diagram, consider:

1. Have we identified opportunities to create parallel paths or are we placing too many activities directly in a serial path?
2. Is our logic correct for identifying preceding and subsequent activities?
3. Are there some clear milestones we can identify along the precedence diagram?

As you prepare the activity duration table, you might wish to set it up along the following lines:

	Duration			
Activity	**Optimistic**	**Likely**	**Pessimistic**	**Est. Duration**
A	6	9	18	10
B	3	8	13	8

Finally, in creating the network diagram and Gantt charts, use MS Project or a comparable scheduling software package (see examples in Figures 10.26, 10.27, and 10.28a, b, and c).

Sample Project Schedule, ABCups, Inc.

Tasks	Duration (in days)
Plant manager feasibility request	1
Get technical approval	5
Determine if additional labor needed	4
Research equipment	26
Determine best suppliers	21
Meet with vendors	21
Obtain quotations from vendors	21
Pick equipment vendor	14
Negotiate price and terms	7
Obtain financing for equipment	3
Calculate ROI	3
Obtain required signatures	3
Capital approved	10
Issue purchase order	1
Equipment being built	40
Marketing new process	21
Create mailer	15
Design new brochure	9
Update Web site	9
Lay out plant for new equipment	15

Note: This is a partial activity network and schedule.

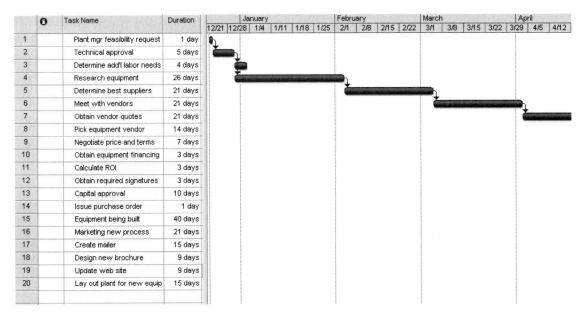

	❶	Task Name	Duration
1		Plant mgr feasibility request	1 day
2		Technical approval	5 days
3		Determine add'l labor needs	4 days
4		Research equipment	26 days
5		Determine best suppliers	21 days
6		Meet with vendors	21 days
7		Obtain vendor quotes	21 days
8		Pick equipment vendor	14 days
9		Negotiate price and terms	7 days
10		Obtain equipment financing	3 days
11		Calculate ROI	3 days
12		Obtain required signatures	3 days
13		Capital approval	10 days
14		Issue purchase order	1 day
15		Equipment being built	40 days
16		Marketing new process	21 days
17		Create mailer	15 days
18		Design new brochure	9 days
19		Update web site	9 days
20		Lay out plant for new equip	15 days

FIGURE 10.26 Partial Gantt Chart for ABCups, Inc. Project (Left Side)

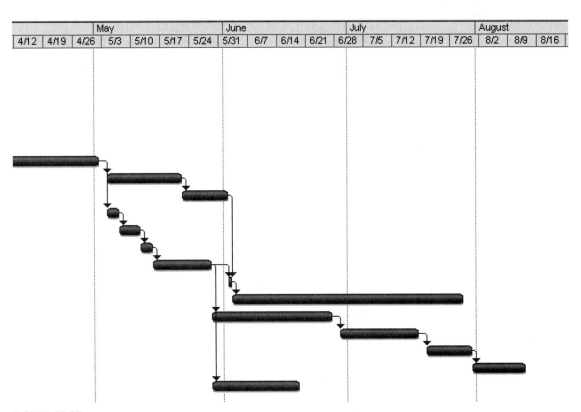

FIGURE 10.27 Partial Gantt Chart for ABCups, Inc. Project (Right Side)

FIGURE 10.28a Network Diagram for ABCups, Inc. Project (Left Side)

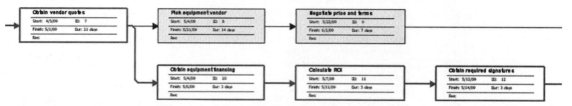

FIGURE 10.28b Network Diagram for ABCups, Inc. Project (Middle)

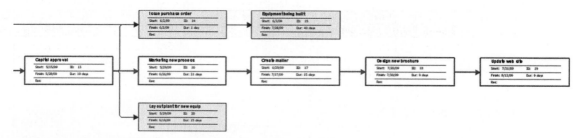

FIGURE 10.28c Network Diagram for ABCups, Inc. Project (Right Side)

Notes

1. Blass, G. (2008). "Boeing's 787 Dreamliner has a composite problem," www.zimbio.com/Boeing+787+Dreamliner/articles/18/Boeing+787+Dreamliner+composite+problem; Cohan, P. (2010). "Yet another problem for Boeing's 787 Dreamliner," www.dailyfinance.com/story/company-news/yet-another-problem-for-boeings-787-dreamliner/19734254/; Done, K. (2007, October 10). "Boeing 787 Dreamliner hit by delays," *Financial Times,* www.ft.com/cms/s/0/d42602de-774c-11dc-9de8-0000779fd2ac.html#axzz17R08yXyV; "The 787 encounters turbulence." (2006, June 19). www.businessweek.com/magazine/content/06_25/b3989049.htm; Johnsson, J. (2010, December 4). "787 Dreamliner proving bedeviling for Boeing," *Chicago Tribune,* http://articles.chicagotribune.com/2010-12-04/business/ct-biz-1205-787-delay-20101204_1_dreamliner-teal-group-richard-aboulafia; Lemer, J. (2010, November 12). "Boeing 787 risks further delays," *Financial Times,* www.ft.com/cms/s/0/941df738-ee8a-11df-9db0-00144feab49a.html#axzz17QyTnbm0; Norris, G. (2010, November 15). "787 schedule hinges on fire investigation," *Aviation Week,* www.aviationweek.com/aw/generic/story.jsp?id=news/avd/2010/11/15/09.xml&channel=comm; Norris, G. (2010, November 26). "787 design and software changes follow fire," *Aviation Week,* www.aviationweek.com/aw/generic/story.jsp?id=news/awx/2010/11/24/awx_11_24_2010_p0-272395.xml&channel=comm; Sanders, P., and Cameron, D. (2011, January 19). "Boeing again delays 787 delivery," *Wall Street Journal,* p. B3.

2. Based on information from an interview with Nilay Yuce, Lamagama, May 16, 2012.

3. Nicholas, J. M. (1990). *Managing Business & Engineering Projects.* Englewood Cliffs, NJ: Prentice-Hall; Hulett, D. (1995). "Project schedule risk assessment," *Project Management Journal,* 26(1): 23–44; Lock, D. (2000). *Project Management,* 7th ed. Aldershot: Gower; Oglesby, P., Parker, H., and Howell, G. (1989). *Productivity Improvement in Construction.* New York: McGraw-Hill.

4. Brooks, F. P., Jr. (1994). *The Mythical Man-Month: Essays on Software Engineering,* Anniversary Edition. Reading, MA: Addison-Wesley; Cooper, K. G. (1998). "Four failures in project management," in Pinto, J. K. (Ed.), *The Project Management Institute Project Management Handbook.* San Francisco, CA: Jossey-Bass, pp. 396-424; Ibbs, C. W., Lee, S. A., and Li, M. I. (1998). "Fast-tracking's impact on project change," *Project Management Journal,* 29(4): 35-42.

5. Gray, C. F., and Larson, E. W. (2003). *Project Management.* Burr Ridge, IL: McGraw-Hill.

6. Shtub, A., Bard, J. F., and Globerson, S. (1994). *Project Management: Engineering, Technology, and Implementation.* Englewood Cliffs, NJ: Prentice-Hall; Navarre, C., and Schaan, J. (1990). "Design of project management systems from top management's perspective," *Project Management Journal,* 21(2), pp. 19–27.

Critical Chain Project Scheduling

Chapter Outline

Chapter Objectives

After completing this chapter, you should be able to:

1. Understand the difference between common cause and special cause variation in organizations.

2. Recognize the three ways in which project teams inflate the amount of safety for all project tasks.

3. Understand the four ways in which additional project task safety can be wasted.

4. Distinguish between critical path and critical chain project scheduling techniques.

5. Understand how critical chain methodology resolves project resource conflicts.

6. Apply critical chain project management to project portfolios.

PROJECT MANAGEMENT BODY OF KNOWLEDGE CORE CONCEPTS COVERED IN THIS CHAPTER

1. Sequence Activities (PMBoK sec. 6.2)
2. Estimate Activity Resources (PMBoK sec. 6.3)
3. Estimate Activity Durations (PMBoK sec. 6.4)
4. Develop Schedule (PMBoK sec. 6.5)
5. Control Schedule (PMBoK sec. 6.6)
6. Develop Schedule (tools and techniques) (PMBoK sec. 6.5.2)
7. Critical Chain Method (PMBoK sec. 6.5.2.3)
8. Resource Leveling (PMBoK sec. 6.5.2.4)

PROJECT PROFILE

Switzerland Celebrates Completion of World's Longest Tunnel

On Friday, October 15, 2010, workers gathered to witness the final completion of the world longest tunnel, drilled through the base of the Swiss Alps, as the country celebrated the completion of the first critical step in a project that has taken nearly 20 years to achieve. The Gotthard Base Tunnel, as the project is known, is the result of a nearly 70-year-old plan formulated to try to find a more economical and efficient means to transport goods through the rugged geography of the Swiss Alps. When the drillers broke through the final yards of earth, they completed a 35.4-mile tunnel that will serve as a major means of transportation in the mountainous country. Because the project is actually a pair of 10-meter-diameter tunnels, laid out side by side, the total excavations for the project have included additional shafts, tunnels, and passages for a total length of 94.3 miles. The current plan is to begin laying railroad tracks in the tunnel to accommodate high-speed trains. The tunnel is due to open for travel in 2017.

The original plan for creating a tunnel under the Alps was based on a need to transport goods from one end of the country to the other. Unfortunately, traveling mountainous roads causes tremendous wear and tear on vehicles, to say nothing of the congestion that builds through hundreds of trucks laboring slowly up steep grades on a daily basis. A combination of concern for the environment, frustration with the delays and constant eyesore

FIGURE 11.1 Workers Celebrate the Drilling Bit Breaking Through the Final Section of the Tunnel

CHRISTIAN HARTMANN/REUTERS/Newscom

(continued)

of truck traffic, and the steadily degrading roads and bridges prompted the Swiss government to initiate the tunneling project. Another objective in developing the tunnel was to encourage further improvement of Europe's high-speed rail network. A currently used shorter tunnel, much higher up, can handle only three truck freight trains of up to 2,000 tons. The new tunnel will take 4,000-ton freight trains—carrying entire trucks on board—through the heart of the mountains. Passenger trains will be able to travel at speeds of up to 250 kph, resulting in a train journey time between Zurich and Milan of just 2 hours and 40 minutes—a third less than at present.

Tunneling is a dangerous procedure. In drilling the tunnel, workers have removed more than 23 million tons of rock. As many as 2,600 people have worked concurrently on the project, battling with the dust, noise, humidity, and temperatures of 30 degrees Celsius (almost 90 degrees Fahrenheit). Eight workers have lost their lives so far in the construction of the Gotthard Base Tunnel. During the construction of the old Gotthard Tunnel in the nineteenth century, the total was close to 300.

One of the most pressing problems was the basic instability of the deep rock formations, which caused unforeseen risks to emerge. For example, in drilling the tunnels, workers relied on the work of eight gigantic, 3,000-ton tunnel boring machines simultaneously. An 800-meter-long shaft was drilled vertically into the mountain, so that workers could begin working in the middle of the tunnel. Often, though, the huge drilling machines could not get the job done on their own. In areas where the rock was particularly brittle, workers were forced to use more traditional methods, such as explosives. Geological layers of stone that had been crushed to bits as the Alps formed proved to be particularly problematic.

Another problem was that it was often impossible to predict what workers would find when they began working. For example, in one stretch of the tunnel, on March 31, 1996, drilling experts were carrying out geologic tests when they suddenly struck a layer known as the Piora Mulde. A huge quantity of water and sand suddenly shot out of the drill shaft with unimaginable force. The Piora Mulde is a narrow, vertical band in the heart of the Alps made up of finely ground Dolomite—a white, often crystalline mineral sediment that settled on the bottom of a sea 230 million years ago. Mixed with water, the substance becomes unpredictable—and presented a difficult challenge for the tunnel engineers to overcome. On that day in March more than 10 years ago, thousands of cubic meters of the stuff flooded into the drill shaft. It was a miracle that none of the workers present were injured.

"Nobody has ever worked in such material at such a depth," says geo-technician Georgios Anagnostou, from the Swiss Federal Institute of Technology in Zurich. In such areas, tunnel engineers were forced into something of a gamble. They allowed for enormous pressure to push softer material into the tunnel (called "distortions") and installed thick tubes in those segments. Computer models had forecast distortions of up to one meter. In the end, the deformations were around 80 centimeters. Workers were ultimately successful in stabilizing the unstable. "There are no longer any parts of the tunnel where there are any distortions worth mentioning," says Anagnostou.

But other problems were uncovered. At the spot where one of the emergency stops was to be built, engineers discovered another area of instability, increasing the possibility of cave-in. The large cavern that was to house the subterranean emergency station had to be built at a different site, farther to the south. Just as one problem would be corrected, another would arise; for example, in the same tunnel segment, one of the drilling machines got stuck and was buried by debris falling from the tunnel roof. Workers had to grind up and remove the stone that had filled the tunnel—the roof was then stabilized using steel and concrete. Similar incidents occurred in several other parts of the tunnel. At one point, one of the drilling machines was unusable for a full six months—while just 40 meters away in the parallel tunnel, workers encountered no trouble at all.

In the effort to create the world's longest tunnel, the Swiss-led consortium has encountered all manner of problems, many of which could not have been fully anticipated in advance. The successful efforts to finish the first and most critical step—the drilling phase—have been a testimony to engineering skills, creative problem solving, and a resolute commitment to succeed in a venture that it is hoped will bring advantages to travelers, the Swiss government, and the country's population as a whole. Although still under construction, the Gotthard Base Tunnel project is a fascinating example of an inventive solution to long-term, pressing national needs.[1]

INTRODUCTION

Scheduling approaches that rely on CPM/PERT are generally accepted as standard operating procedure by most project-based organizations. Complications often occur, however, when we begin linking resource requirements to our developed schedules. As we will see in Chapter 12, the problem of constrained resources often reduces the flexibility we may have to create an optimal project schedule. In recent years, however, an alternative scheduling approach by the name of **Critical Chain Project Management (CCPM)** has become increasingly popular. This alternative approach was developed in the mid-1990s by Dr. Eli Goldratt. CCPM offers some important differences and advantages over more commonly used critical path methodologies. Lucent Technologies, Texas Instruments, Honeywell, and the Israeli aircraft industry are among a diverse group of major organizations that have found the underlying premises of CCPM intriguing enough to begin disseminating the process throughout their project operations.[2]

This chapter will explore in detail some of the important components of Critical Chain Project Management. We will see how, as supporters contend, this alternative scheduling mechanism promises to speed up project delivery, make better use of project resources, and more efficiently allocate and discipline the process of implementing projects. The model is based on Goldratt's **theory of constraints (TOC)** methodology, which was originally proposed as a process for removing bottlenecks from production processes. In its current configuration, TOC also offers some important guidelines for project management. One key feature of CCPM is that it represents both a cultural shift and a change in scheduling processes. In practice, if CCPM theory is to be correctly applied, important technical and behavioral elements must be understood in relation to each other. The chapter will focus on these aspects of the process.

11.1 THE THEORY OF CONSTRAINTS AND CRITICAL CHAIN PROJECT SCHEDULING

In practice, the network schedules we constructed in the previous two chapters, using PERT and probabilistic time estimates, are extremely resource dependent. That is, the accuracy of these estimates and our project schedules are sensitive to resource availability—critical project resources must be available to the degree they are needed at precisely the right time in order for the schedule to work as it is intended. One result of using "early-start" schedules is to make project managers very aware of the importance of protecting their schedule slack throughout the project. The more we can conserve this slack, the better "buffer" we maintain against any unforeseen problems or resource insufficiency later in the project. Thus, project managers are often locked into a defensive mode, preparing for problems, while they carefully monitor resource availability and guard their project slack time. The concept of theory of constraints as it is applied to Critical Chain Project Management represents an alternative method for managing slack time and more efficiently employing project resources.

Theory of Constraints

Goldratt originally developed the theory of constraints (TOC), first described in his book *The Goal* (1984), for applications within the production environment.[3] Among the more important points this author raised was the idea that, typically, the majority of poor effects within business operations stem from a very small number of causes; that is, when traced back to their origins, many of the problems we deal with are the result of a few core problems. The main idea behind TOC is the notion that any "system must have a constraint. Otherwise, its output would increase without bound, or go to zero."[4] The key lies in identifying the most central constraint within the system. Five distinct steps make up the primary message behind TOC methodology (see Figure 11.2):

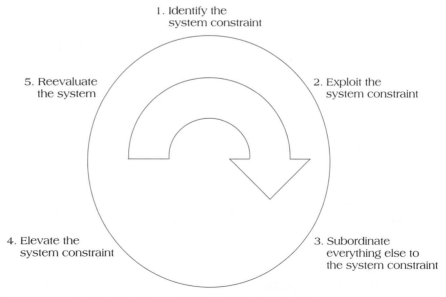

1. Identify the system constraint
2. Exploit the system constraint
3. Subordinate everything else to the system constraint
4. Elevate the system constraint
5. Reevaluate the system

FIGURE 11.2 Five Key Steps in Theory of Constraint Methodology

1. *Identify the system constraint.* First, an intensive search must be made to uncover the principal constraint, the root cause, that limits the output of any system. It is important to not get bogged down in identifying numerous secondary causes or "little problems."

2. *Exploit the system constraint.* Once the constraint is identified, a strategy for focusing and viewing all activities in terms of this constraint is necessary. For example, if the constraint within a software development firm is having only one advanced application programmer, the sequence of all project work to be done by the programmer has to be first scheduled across the organization's entire portfolio of active projects.

3. *Subordinate everything else to the system constraint.* Make resource commitment or scheduling decisions after handling the needs of the root constraint. Using the above example, once the "critical resource constraint" of one programmer has been identified and the programmer's time has been scheduled across multiple projects, the rest of the project activities can be scheduled.

4. *Elevate the system constraint.* The first three steps acknowledge that the system constraint limits an organization's operations. According to Goldratt, the fourth step addresses improvement of the system by *elevating the constraint,* or seeking to solve the constraint problem by eliminating the bottleneck effect. In our software-programming example, this may mean hiring an additional advanced applications programmer. For many project-based examples, "elevating the system constraint" may be as simple as acquiring additional resources at opportune times.

5. *Determine if a new constraint has been uncovered, and then repeat the process.* Clearly, the removal of the key system constraint will lead to positive advantages for a time. Since there is *always* a system constraint, however, removing one constraint is only likely to identify a new source of constraint for the operation. TOC argues for the need to always prepare for the next potential problem before it becomes too serious, so this final step is really only one step in a continuous improvement cycle.

When examining a project schedule from the perspective of TOC methodology, we focus on the key system constraint, that is, the one root cause from which all other scheduling problems evolve. The system constraint for projects is initially thought to be the *critical path.* Remember, the critical path is defined as the earliest possible time on the activity network it can take to complete a project. If activities on the critical path are delayed, the effect is to cause delays in the overall project. Critical path is determined by the series of activities whose durations define the longest path through the network and therefore identify the project's earliest possible completion. Goldratt notes that all scheduling and resource problems associated with projects typically occur due to problems with trying to maintain the critical path, and hence its oft-made identification as the chief system constraint.[5]

Common Cause and Special Cause Variation

A common mistake made in many organizations is to routinely assume that every event (mistake, accident, or defect) is attributable to some direct source or person. It is more typical, in fact, that errors are indicative of general problems within the organization and its operations.[6] We routinely err by assuming that variation (faults in the system) represents special causes rather than common ones. One of the foremost industrial authors of the latter part of the twentieth century, Dr. J. Edwards Deming, suggested that an "understanding of variation" is one of the principal sources of profound knowledge to be acquired from studying organizational activity. He identified two types of variation:[7]

1. **Common cause variation** is inherent in the system; that is, a chance error exists because of flaws in how the system was originally created.

2. **Special cause variation** is attributable to a special circumstance. For example, it may be specific to some set of workers, piece of machinery, or local condition.

The concepts of variation highlight how important it is to identify a system's chief constraint. All projects contain common cause variation in terms of how long it takes to complete project activities. This variation refers to the normal range of uncertainty in any activity's performance time. Because the most common sequencing approach for scheduling is the finish-to-start connection, it follows that projects will contain a degree of statistical variation based on the chain of dependent events. According to Deming, assuming that this statistical, common cause variation is in fact a special cause variation is a common mistake. This happens because along with defining projects as "one of a kind" comes a tendency to also define all project activities as unique, or rooted in special cause variation and not subject to statistical control. Therefore, when problems occur, we react to them individually rather than looking at the system for the source of the underlying cause.

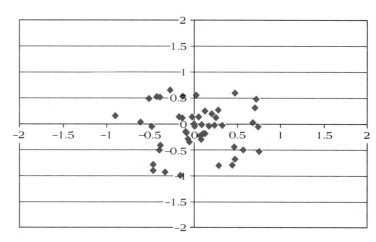

FIGURE 11.3 **Distribution Based on Common Cause Variation**

Source: L. P. Leach. (1999). "Critical chain project management improves project performance," *Project Management Journal, 30*(2), 39–51, figure on page 42. Copyright © 1999 by Project Management Institute Publications. Copyright and all rights reserved. Material from this publication has been reproduced with the permission of PMI.

This type of response to variation can lead management to overreact, to mistake the correct response for the immediate one, or to attempt to correct systemic problems (common cause variation) because they are perceived as unique (special cause variation).[8]

An example of the problems firms have when they mistake difficulties arising from common cause variation for special cause is illustrated by the case where top management at a company demanded a detailed exception report every two weeks from the project manager on project status. Suppose that at one such exception report meeting, the senior executives noted a 5% divergence from the project's planned schedule. Rather than treating this occurrence as a simple case of common cause variation, which might very likely be corrected in the natural course of project development over the coming weeks, the top management group overreacted, ordering detailed (and expensive) project assessment to "correct" the problem. In this case, management chose to treat the variance result as a special cause variation, assuming a unique problem had surfaced. The ultimate result of situations such as this, in which common cause variation is treated as a special cause, is to lead the organization to search for the specific "problem," while wasting considerable time and money on the task, when it may not be necessary.

Deming illustrates his distinction between common cause and special cause risk with a funnel exercise. The funnel drops a marble onto a sheet of paper below that has been quartered, with a midpoint indicating the origin of the problem (see Figure 11.3). The object is to drop the marble directly onto the origin point, indicating no variance. As the figure demonstrates, in a sample exercise where the funnel remained fixed in place, the pattern of marbles that fell onto the paper was clustered around the midpoint. This pattern would represent an example of common cause variation.

Now, assume that the person dropping the marble reacts to each strike on the paper by repositioning the funnel to compensate for the error (distance from the origin at which the marble landed). He moves the funnel the same amount, but in the opposite direction, from the point where the marble struck the target. This is the sort of reaction a manager may make to respond to the variance and correct for it. For example, if a project activity is projected as coming in 10% over schedule, the project manager may redirect resources to respond to the problem. Note the result, as Deming pointed out, when the manager makes a series of discrete, reactive moves in response to each case of variance. Figure 11.4 shows the new marble pattern based on movements made to compensate for suboptimal (not centered on the origin) responses. Variation has increased because, as Deming notes, the manager is misinterpreting common cause variation (inherent in the system) to be special cause variation (unique to the activity).

On the other hand, treating special cause variation as if it were common cause variation can lead to its own form of trouble. Mistaking discrete forms of project risk for overall common cause variation in the system makes it nearly impossible to conduct adequate risk analysis and response exercises. Any identifiable risk is, by definition, a source of special cause variation.

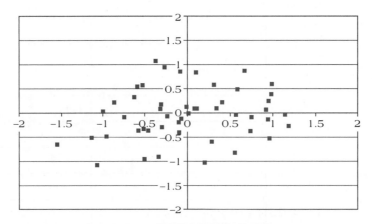

FIGURE 11.4 **Distribution Based on Misinterpretation of Variance**

Source: L. P. Leach. (1999). "Critical chain project management improves project performance," *Project Management Journal, 30*(2), 39–51, figure on page 42. Copyright © 1999 by Project Management Institute Publications. Copyright and all rights reserved. Material from this publication has been reproduced with the permission of PMI.

In applying the principle of common cause variation to the theory of CCPM, writers have offered the following recommendations, based on Deming's analysis.

1. Understand the difference between common and special cause variation.
2. Do not make adjustments to projects when the variation in project performance (or activity durations) lies within the range of common cause variance.
3. Do not include special cause variation in project risk simulation. This causes the project team to overestimate project schedule contingency.
4. Perform project risk management on discrete project risks; do not aggregate the risks.

Even when using Monte Carlo simulation models, it is possible to widely misestimate the time necessary to complete activity tasks. Statistical controls of project scheduling imply that managers must take a realistic view when allocating contingency time. One reason for errors in estimation is based on the concept of common versus special cause variation. Other reasons, as Goldratt and others have pointed out, are more behavioral in nature.[9]

11.2 CCPM AND THE CAUSES OF PROJECT DELAY

CCPM has much to say about the nature of the causes of inaccurate project activity duration estimation. First, the real world is one of statistical fluctuations, so according to CCPM using a point estimate does not make sense and renders most duration values meaningless. Deming would argue that this process is another example of project teams' inability to understand variation. However, even providing for the fallacy of misguided single-point duration estimates, a number of issues can distort accurate duration estimation. Many of these causes, Goldratt contends, are behavioral in nature, rather than technical (related to poor estimation metrics). Specifically, CCPM suggests that there are a number of ways project members can routinely add safety (project slack or buffer) to the estimated length of project activities.

Method One: Overestimation of Individual Activity Durations

When estimating the amount of time needed to complete an activity, it is common for team members to build in, or pad, their estimates with enough safety to feel confident that they will be able to complete the project within their estimated time. For example, when someone traveling to a meeting asks how long it will take to drive from Washington, DC, to Baltimore, Maryland, the reasonable answer might be 45 minutes. If penalties are associated with being late to the meeting, however, it is more likely that the answer will include allowing extra time for unforeseen events disrupting the trip (detours, flat tire, speeding ticket, or heavy traffic). With these contingencies in mind, a new, reasonable guess might be one, two, or even more hours just to travel a route that we normally could drive in 45 minutes. The same principles apply when we change

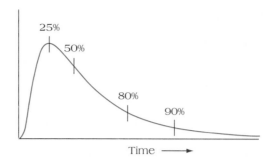

FIGURE 11.5 Gaussian (Lognormal) Distribution

the example to a project case. A member of the project team charged with a task is likely to factor in sufficient extra slack time (safety) to feel reasonably confident that it can be done when promised.

Figure 11.5 shows an example of a Gaussian or lognormal distribution for estimated activity time needed to complete a work package. Note the probabilities for the task's completion as a function of time. The more time allocated to the task, the higher the probability it will be finished within the designated time. Unfortunately, as the distribution suggests, in order to estimate completion of an activity with a 90% or higher degree of confidence, the time may be overestimated by as much as 200%. A project activity we could reasonably expect to be completed by day 6 (based on a mean estimate)* may not be promised until day 18. This overpadding of individual tasks adds an enormous amount of additional time to the project estimate.

Method Two: Project Manager Safety Margin

Once each team member has made his own estimates of activity duration (factoring in padding for each task), the project manager aggregates these estimates into an overall project estimate. However, project managers tend to protect their safety just as their team members do. They typically add to their own margins at the aggregate project level. Consider a case in which three team members each provide their manager with estimates of 2 weeks each per activity. A normal aggregation of these individual estimates would be $2 + 2 + 2 = 6$ weeks. However, because project managers are themselves fearful of the impact of missing deadlines, they often factor in some margin for additional project-level safety. Thus, $2 + 2 + 2$ may equal 8, 9, or even 10 weeks, rather than 6. The project manager has added the additional time after the fact to build in some personal protection for the overall project schedule.

Method Three: Anticipating Expected Cuts from Top Management

The third manner in which additional safety is routinely added to project activities is based on the fact that an organization's top management typically endorses aggressive schedules. Often, members of the top management team will examine a schedule, decide it is too long, and mandate significant cuts. In one case, a firm's top management was noted for their insistence on cutting duration estimates by a minimum of 20%. Eventually, project teams began to recognize this process and simply added an extra 25% to the initial plan in order to protect their "real" time frame.

When combined, these three practices can lead to grossly overinflated duration times, but more importantly, they speak to a central lack of trust within the organization. When an organization's culture does not encourage authentic behavior, it sends the signal that what is "really" rewarded are acts aimed less at project delivery and customer satisfaction than at self-protection and deception. All in all, these practices speak to a lack of organizational discipline in running projects.[10]

11.3 HOW PROJECT TEAMS WASTE THE EXTRA SAFETY THEY ACQUIRE

Some of the ways projects lose time are institutional; they result from cultural attitudes propagated by the firm or are caused more directly by policies the organization promotes. Other reasons for such delays are behavioral in nature, stemming from individual work habits and poor self-discipline.

---

*The idea of mean estimation with the Gaussian distribution is necessary in order to distinguish it from the 50% likelihood estimate based on median. Means are added linearly regardless of distribution, whereas a 50% likelihood refers to the median, which in a skewed distribution such as that shown in Figure 11.5 can be significantly different from the distribution mean.

Method One: The Student Syndrome

The first analysis of why team members waste project activity time is called the **student syndrome** or the term-paper model. Basically it involves procrastination, the tendency to put off maximum effort until the last possible moment. We see this effect occurring in our illustration (see Figure 11.6), which links the percentage of time elapsed on an activity with the percentage of the work completed. This figure represents the type of progress often found in the completion of a project activity. Although an idealized process line would show steadily increasing progress from the starting date to final project completion, many individuals tend to delay the start of the activity as long as possible, concentrating on more immediately visible or critical tasks. Eventually, however, as Figure 11.6 notes, project team members begin to realize the milestone date is approaching, and their effort starts ramping up dramatically. The student syndrome is a useful model for highlighting common project effort because:

1. People have a tendency to minimize responsibilities with long end-date completions in favor of more immediate or critical deadlines.
2. If people believe that they have built extra time into their initial estimates, it further demotivates them from addressing these commitments early.
3. Project resource personnel in "high demand" must routinely juggle their schedules to accommodate multiple commitments, precluding them from addressing tasks with long deadlines in a timely fashion.

Parkinson's Law states that work expands to fill the time available. Rarely do team members finish in less than the amount of time initially projected to accomplish a task. The reason for this phenomenon lies, in part, with the second method for squandering safety time.

Method Two: Failure to Pass Along Positive Variation

When multiple activities are linked in a finish-to-start format, as in the case of most standard activity networks, each subsequent activity is at the mercy of its predecessors in terms of when it can begin. Delays in a project activity (**negative variation**) lead to additional delays downstream, as subsequent activities must be started later, path slack is used up, and so forth. When a preceding activity is actually completed early, it would be natural to expect that the early completion (**positive variation**) would also be passed along and that the network path in which this activity lies would gain additional time downstream. However, one of the arguments underlying the behavioral consequences of project management suggests that the

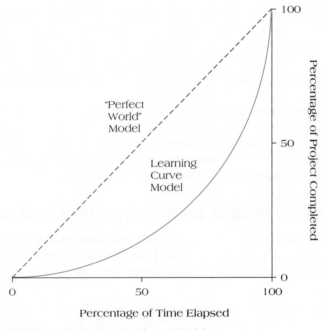

FIGURE 11.6   Student Syndrome Model

opposite case occurs more often; positive variation is not passed along. Why not? There are a number of reasons:

1. Finishing a task early gives project team members the opportunity to work on other projects or work assignments that have backlogged on their desks. In effect, early completions represent an opportunity to put a project on hold for some period of time in order to reduce other commitments.
2. Team members may fear that their future work time estimations will no longer be taken seriously if they deliver early. When asking team members to estimate the amount of time necessary to complete a task, the project manager trusts their technical judgment. If a team member estimates that a task will require 6 days and delivers it in 4, the next time she is asked for an estimate, her project manager may want to trim the estimate based on past performance.
3. Some individuals feel the need to continually tinker with their task assignments, so they may use the extra time to further refine or modify the output. Positive variation for these team members is treated as an opportunity to improve their initial efforts.

Method Three: Negative Consequences of Multitasking

We may use the word **multitasking** to describe how we commonly become involved in multiple efforts or tasks simultaneously. Project personnel for most organizations are routinely expected to be active in several projects, activities, or assignments at the same time and must use time management and prioritization skills to effectively balance their workloads. When project team members are expected to devote their time to, say, 10 projects instead of focusing exclusively on one at a time, time management can be a tremendous challenge. The nature of multitasking also lengthens the time necessary to complete individual project assignments, as Figure 11.7 illustrates. Let us assume that a project team member has three tasks to perform, each with an expected duration of 10 days. The top line shows the activities laid out end to end. In this scenario, because the individual's efforts are fully devoted to only one activity at a time, the total time necessary to complete all three assignments is given as 30 days.

If the individual is expected to work on all three project assignments simultaneously, devoting five days to one project before moving on to the next, and so on, note the effect as shown in the second, or bottom, line. Expected duration for each project activity has just grown dramatically, from the original 10 days to something approaching 20 days for each activity. Through the effects of working in a multitasked environment, the actual expected duration needed to complete each project assignment has doubled. The problem is further compounded by the effects of transition time, or the extra time required to move between tasks. It is usually a mistake to assume that a multitasked individual can move seamlessly from one assignment to the next. In delaying or leaving unfinished project work for an extended time, we must account for some additional wasted start-up time between assignments. As a result, multitasking is likely to not just double the real activity duration; it may increase it even beyond that level.

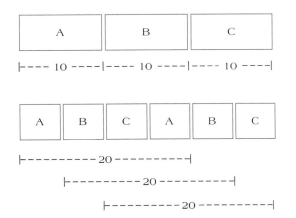

FIGURE 11.7 **Effects of Multitasking on Activity Durations**

Source: E. M. Goldratt, © 1997, "The Critical Chain." Reproduced by permission of The North River Press Publishing Corporation.

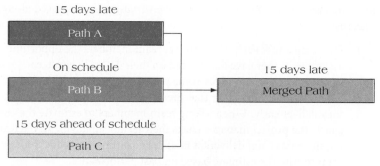

FIGURE 11.8 The Effect of Merging Multiple Activity Paths

Source: L. P. Leach. (1999). "Critical chain project management improves project performance," *Project Management Journal, 30*(2), 39–51, figure on page 44. Copyright © 1999 by Project Management Institute Publications. Copyright and all rights reserved. Material from this publication has been reproduced with the permission of PMI.

Method Four: Delay Caused by Activity Path Merging

The majority of projects have multiple activity paths. For example, a simple PERT chart, shown in Figure 11.8, shows three distinct paths, the critical path and two additional feeder or noncritical paths. At the merge point, near the end of the project's activity network, three paths merge into the final, critical path just prior to project completion. Activity path merging has the effect of creating a filter to eliminate any positive slack. All merging activity paths are held captive to that path with the longest delay. Figure 11.8 illustrates this phenomenon. Assume that paths A, B, and C have schedule status associated with them of 15 days late, on time, and 15 days early, respectively. The problem is that in moving downstream from the merge point, the earliest the subsequent activity can begin is determined by the completion of the latest preceding activity, in this case, path A, which is 15 days late. As a result, paths C and B, which are either early or on time, lose their positive slack due to the delays associated with the other merging path.

The Project Management Institute's Body of Knowledge (PMBoK) identifies this particular problem when it notes, "traditional mathematical analysis techniques such as the Critical Path Method ... do not account for path convergence ... and thus tend to underestimate project durations."[11]

The impact of these two sets of behavior processes—behavior designed to increase project activity safety and behavior resulting in loss of safety—illustrates the challenge faced by teams in attempting to more efficiently schedule and manage their projects.

11.4 THE CRITICAL CHAIN SOLUTION TO PROJECT SCHEDULING

Goldratt's solution to the variables involved in project scheduling involves the aggregation, or collectivizing, of all project risk in the form of uncertain duration estimates and completion times. The aggregation of risk is a well-known phenomenon in the insurance business.[12] The **central limit theorem** states that if a number of probability distributions are summed, the variance of the sum equals the sum of the variances of individual distributions. This formula is given, where there are n independent distributions of equal variance V, as:

$$V_\Sigma = n \times V$$

where V_Σ is the variance of the sum.

The standard deviation σ can be used as a surrogate for risk, and since $\sigma^2 = V$, we find:

$$\sigma_\Sigma = (n)^{1/2} \times \sigma$$

where σ_Σ is the standard deviation of the sum. Therefore:

$$\sigma_\Sigma < n \times \sigma$$

Mathematically, the above formula illustrates the point that aggregating risks leads to a reduction in overall risks.

This same principle of aggregation of risks can be applied in a slightly different manner to the **critical chain** methodology. We have used the term *safety* or *project buffer* to refer to the contingency reserve for individual activities that project managers like to maintain. When we aggregate risk, this reserve is dramatically reduced so that all activity durations are realistic but challenging. That is, rather than establish duration estimates based on a 90% likelihood of successful completion, all activity durations are estimated at the 50% level. The provision for contingency, in the form of project safety, is removed from the individual activities and applied at the project level. Because of the aggregation concept, this total buffer is smaller than the sum of the individual project activity buffers. Thus project duration is reduced.

Apple Computer Corporation's recent success story with its iPad tablet illustrates some of the advantages to be found in aggregating risks. Apple made a conscious decision with the iPad to subcontract most of the components of the product to a variety of suppliers. The company determined that to engineer the entire product would have been a complex and risky alternative. Instead, it contracted with a number of suppliers who had produced proven technology. The decision to combine these product components from other sources, rather than manufacture them in-house, led to a much faster development cycle and greatly increased profitability.[13]

Two fundamental questions to be answered at this point are: Exactly how much is the project's duration reduced? How much aggregated buffer is sufficient? Goldratt and his adherents do not advocate the removal of all project buffer, but merely the reapplication of that buffer to a project level (as shown in Figure 11.9). The determination of the appropriate amount of buffer to be maintained can be derived in one of two ways: (1) a "rule of thumb" approach that Goldratt suggests, namely, retain 50% of total project buffer; and (2) a more mathematically derived model suggested by Newbold (1998):[14]

$$\text{Buffer} = \sigma = [((w_1 - a_1)/2)^2 + ((w_2 - a_2)/2)^2 + \ldots + ((w_i - a_i)/2)^2]^{1/2}$$

where w_i is the worst-case duration and a_i is the average duration for each task that provides part of the aggregated buffer value. The presumed standard deviation would be $(w_i - a_i)/2$. Suppose, for example, that the project team sought a buffer that is 2 standard deviations long. The formula for calculating an appropriate buffer length is:

$$\text{Buffer} = 2 \times \sigma = 2 \times [((w_1 - a_1)/2)^2 + ((w_2 - a_2)/2)^2 + \ldots + ((w_i - a_i)/2)^2]^{1/2}$$

Let us assume, for example, that we have three tasks linked together, each of 20 days in length. Thus, the worst case (w_i) for these durations is the original 20 days. Further, by aggregating the buffer based on a 50% solution, our a_i value is 10 days for each activity. We can solve for the appropriate buffer size (two standard deviations) by:

$$\begin{aligned} \text{Buffer} &= \sqrt{((20_1 - 10_1)^2 + (20_2 - 10_2)^2 + (20_3 - 10_3)^2)} \\ &= \sqrt{300}, \text{ or } 17.32 \text{ days} \end{aligned}$$

Visually, we can understand the application of CCPM in three distinct phases. First, all relevant project tasks are laid in a simplified precedence diagram (shown on line 1 in Figure 11.9), with anticipated durations specified. Remember that the original duration estimates have most likely been based on high probability of completion estimates and therefore require a reexamination based on a more realistic appraisal of their "true" duration. The second step consists of shrinking these duration estimates to the 50% likelihood level. All individual task safety, or buffer, has been aggregated and now is given as the project-level buffer.

At this stage, the overall length of the project has not changed because the individual task buffer is simply aggregated and added to the end of the project schedule. However, line 3 illustrates the final step in the reconfiguration, the point where the project buffer shrinks by some identifiable amount. Using the rule of thumb of 50% shrinkage, we end up with a project schedule that is still significantly shorter than the original. This modified, shortened schedule includes some minor slack for each activity. As a result, CCPM leads to shortened project schedules.

Suppose that a project activity network diagram yielded the initial values given in Table 11.1. Note that the modified network shortens the overall project duration by 22 days, from the original 40 to 18. Because all risk is now aggregated at the project level, there are a total of 22 days of potential slack in the schedule resulting from shrinking activity estimates at each project step. A CCPM-modified project schedule would reapply 11 days of the acquired schedule shrinkage to serve as overall project buffer. Therefore, the new project schedule will anticipate a duration estimated to require 29 days to completion.

What are the implications of this reapplication of project slack to the aggregated level? First, all due dates for individual activities and subactivities have been eliminated. Milestones are not used in the CCPM

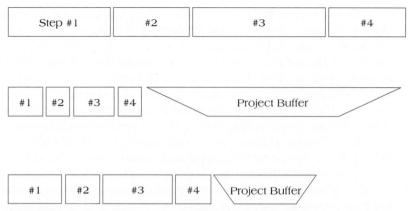

FIGURE 11.9 **Reduction in Project Duration After Aggregation**

Source: L. P. Leach. (1999). "Critical chain project management improves project performance," *Project Management Journal, 30*(2), 39–51, figure on page 44. Copyright © 1999 by Project Management Institute Publications. Copyright and all rights reserved. Material from this publication has been reproduced with the permission of PMI.

TABLE 11.1 Critical Chain Activities Time Reductions

Activity	Original Estimated Duration	Duration Based on 50% Probability
A	10 days	5 days
B	6 days	2 days
C	14 days	7 days
D	2 days	1 day
E	8 days	3 days
Total	40 days	18 days

activity network. The only firm commitment remains to the project delivery date, not to the completion of individual tasks. Project team members are encouraged to make realistic estimates and continually communicate their expectations. Clearly, in order for CCPM to work, a corporate culture that supports a policy of "no blame" is vital. Remember, the nature of requiring 50% likelihood estimates for individual activity durations implies that workers are just as likely to *miss* a commitment date as to achieve it. Under a culture that routinely punishes late performance, workers will quickly reacquire the habits that had once protected them—inflated estimates, wasting safety, and so forth.

A second implication may be more significant, particularly when dealing with external subcontractors. Because individual activity dates have been eliminated and milestones are scrapped, it becomes problematic to effectively schedule subcontractor deliveries. When subcontractors agree to furnish materials for the project, they routinely operate according to milestone (calendar) delivery dates. CCPM, with its philosophy that deemphasizes target dates for individual tasks, creates a complicated environment for scheduling necessary supplier or subcontractor deliveries. Writers on CCPM suggest that one method for alleviating this concern is to work with contractors to negotiate the early completion and delivery of components needed for critical activities.[15]

Developing the Critical Chain Activity Network

Recall from earlier chapters that with traditional CPM/PERT networks, individual activity slack is an artifact of the overall network. Activity start time is usually dictated by resource availability. For example, although an activity could start as early as May 15, we may put it off for three days because the individual responsible for its completion is not available until that date. In this way, float is used as a resource-leveling device.

With CCPM, resource leveling is not required because resources are leveled within the project in the process of identifying the critical chain. For scheduling, therefore, CCPM advocates putting off all

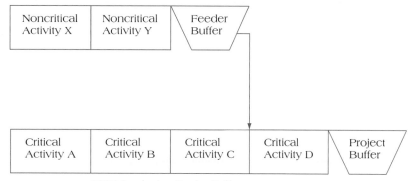

FIGURE 11.10 CCPM Employing Feeder Buffers

Note: Feeder buffers are intended to prevent delays on critical activities.

noncritical activities as late as possible, while providing each noncritical path in the network with its own buffer (see Figure 11.10). These noncritical buffers are referred to as *feeder buffers* because they are placed where noncritical paths feed into the critical path. As Figure 11.10 demonstrates, a portion of the critical path and one of the noncritical feeder paths join just past the point of activity C. Feeding buffer duration is calculated similarly to the process used to create the overall project buffer, attached to the end of the critical chain.

To understand how the logic of the critical chain is constructed, note that the first steps lie in making some important adjustments to traditional scheduling approaches, such as:

1. Adjusting expected activity durations to reflect a 50% probability of completion on time (shrinking the schedule)
2. Changing from an early-start process to a late-finish approach
3. Factoring in the effects of resource contention if necessary

Figures 11.11a, b, and c present a simplified series of examples that follow these steps. Figure 11.11a shows a standard activity network based on a PERT approach. A total of five activities are identified (A, B, C, D, and E) along two separate paths feeding into activity E at the project's conclusion. All activities are scheduled to begin as early as possible (early start) and are based on a standard method for estimating durations. Table 11.2 lists these expected durations.

Figure 11.11a demonstrates an expected overall project duration of 90 days, based on the longest set of linked activities (path A – B – E). The second path, C – D – E, has an overall duration of 60 days and hence, has 30 days of slack built into it. In order to adjust this network, the first step involves changing to a late-start schedule. Second, CCPM challenges the original activity duration estimates and substitutes ones based on the mean point of the distribution. The modified activity network makes the assumption of shrinking these estimates by 50%. Therefore, the new network has an overall duration of 45 days, rather than the original 90-day estimate (Figure 11.11b).

The next step in the conversion to a critical chain schedule involves the inclusion of project and feeder buffers for all network paths. Recall that these buffers are calculated based on applying 50% of the overall schedule savings. The feeder buffer for the path C − D is calculated as $(.50)(10 + 5)$, or 7.5 days. The project buffer, found from the values for path A − B − E, is calculated as $(.50)(5 + 25 + 15)$, or 22.5 days. Hence, once buffers are added to the modified activity network, the original PERT chart showing duration of 90 days with 30 days of slack, the new critical chain network has an overall duration of 67.5 days, or a

TABLE 11.2 Activity Durations

Activity	Duration
A	10 days
B	50 days
C	20 days
D	10 days
E	30 days

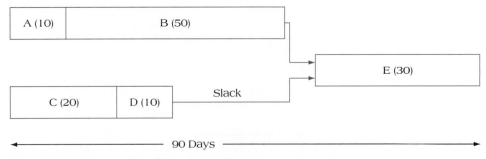

FIGURE 11.11a   Project Schedule Using Early Start

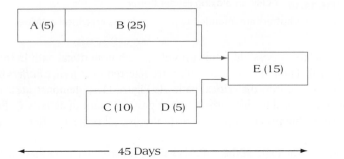

FIGURE 11.11b   Reduced Schedule Using Late Start

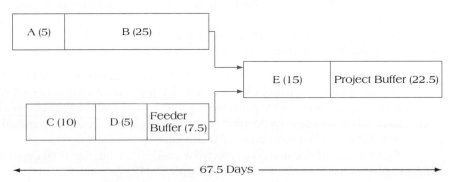

FIGURE 11.11c   Critical Chain Schedule with Buffers Added

savings of 22.5 days (Figure 11.11c). Through three steps, therefore, we move from an early-start to late-start schedule, identify the critical path (sequence of longest linked activities), and then apply feeder and project buffers. The result is a modified project schedule, which, even with buffers inserted, significantly reduces scheduled completion time for the project.[16]

Critical Chain Solutions Versus Critical Path Solutions

So what is the real difference between the critical path method and Critical Chain Project Management? Critical chain is usually not the same path as the critical path within an activity network. The critical path depends only on task dependency, that is, the linkage of tasks with their predecessors. In this process, activity slack is discovered after the fact; once the network is laid out and the critical path identified, all other paths and activities may contain some level of slack. On the other hand, the critical chain usually jumps task dependency links. Again, this effect occurs because critical chain requires that all resource leveling be done before the critical chain can be identified, not afterward as in the case of PERT and CPM networks.

To illustrate this distinction, consider the differences when the activity network in Figure 11.12a is compared with the modified solution in Figure 11.12b. Figure 11.12a shows a simplified PERT network that identifies three paths. The central path is the critical path. The difficulty occurs when we require the same resource (Bob) to complete activities that are scheduled simultaneously. Clearly, Bob cannot perform

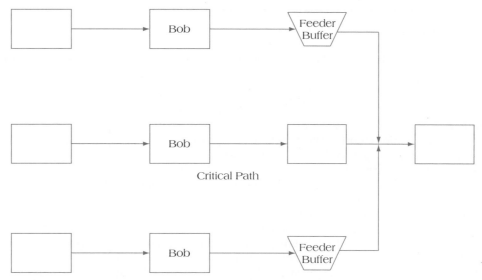

FIGURE 11.12a   Critical Path Network with Resource Conflicts

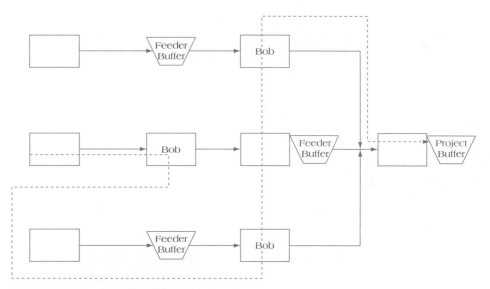

FIGURE 11.12b   The Critical Chain Solution

Note: The critical chain is shown as a dashed line.

the three tasks at the same time without significantly lengthening the overall critical path. The alternative, shown in Figure 11.12b, is to first resource-level the activities that Bob must perform. The project's schedule must take into account the resource conflict and demonstrate a new network logic that allows the project to proceed.

Bob, our resource constraint (Figure 11.12b), forces the schedule to be redrawn in order to reflect his work assignments. Note that with the critical chain schedule (shown with the dashed line), Bob first completes his task on the central path. The other two paths require Bob as well, and so he is first assigned to the task on the lower path and he then accounts for his final assignment, along the top path. Also note how the various feeder buffers must be redrawn in the new critical chain schedule. Because Bob's work on the first task is the predecessor for his subsequent activities, the feeder buffers on the top and bottom schedules are moved forward, or earlier, in the network to account for his resource availability (if he is delayed). Hence, because Bob is the critical resource in the network, it is imperative to first level him across the tasks he is responsible for and then redraw the network to create a new critical chain, which is distinct from the original critical path. Once the critical chain is identified, feeder buffers are added to support the critical activities while providing a margin of safety for the noncritical paths.

PROJECT PROFILE

Eli Lilly Pharmaceuticals and Its Commitment to Critical Chain Project Management

Eli Lilly Corporation is one of the giants in the pharmaceutical industry, but in the drug-manufacturing industry, size is no guarantee of future success. All pharmaceutical firms in the United States are facing increasing pressure from a variety of sources: (1) the federal government, which has just enacted elements of "Obamacare" with strict guidelines for drug cost control; (2) the loss of patents as key drugs become generic; and (3) the need to maintain leadership in a highly competitive industry. Lilly is beginning to feel this sting personally; starting in 2011, several of its top-selling drugs will go off patent, leaving the company scrambling to bring new drugs into the marketplace quickly. Unfortunately, their "late-stage" pipeline is thin; there are few drugs waiting in the wings to be commercialized.

In its efforts to stay out in front, Lilly has announced a series of strategic moves in recent years. First, the firm has instituted a cost-cutting initiative across the organization in hopes of trimming more than $1 billion from operations. Second, Lilly has reorganized into four divisions in order to streamline and consolidate operations to become more market-driven and responsive. Finally, the firm has announced the formation of a Development Center of Excellence in R&D, to be sited at corporate headquarters in Indianapolis, Indiana. The Center will be responsible for accelerating the completion of late-stage trials and release of new drugs. What does Lilly see as being key to the success of its Center of Excellence? One important element is the widespread use of Critical Chain Project Management (CCPM).

Lilly has been championing CCPM in its R&D units since 2007 and is committed to instituting the process throughout its entire R&D organization. The company's support for CCPM is based on the results of hard evidence: "It has now been implemented on 40 of our new product pipeline and our projects are 100 percent on time delivery compared to about 60 percent for the other 60 percent of the [drugs] in the more traditional development programs," according to Steven Paul, President of Lilly Research Labs.

Lilly has found that CCPM gives the company multiple advantages, starting with re-creating a cooperative internal environment based on shared commitment of various departments to the drug development process. Further, CCPM offers a method for maximizing the efficiency of the firm's resources, avoiding common bottlenecks in the development cycle, and moving drugs through the trial stages much more rapidly. Finally, it encourages an internal atmosphere of authenticity in estimating, scheduling, and controlling projects.

The move to CCPM did not come easily. Some managers have noted that it requires a different mind-set on the part of employees, who have to see their projects from an "organizational" point of view rather than from a strictly departmental perspective. Nevertheless, Lilly's public commitment to CCPM has paid off and continues to serve as a catalyst for the company's competitive success.[17]

Blend Images / Alamy

FIGURE 11.13 **Drug Discovery Research Lab**

11.5 CRITICAL CHAIN SOLUTIONS TO RESOURCE CONFLICTS

Suppose that after laying out the revised schedule (refer back to Figure 11.11c), we discover a resource contention point. Let us assume that activities B and D require the same person, resulting in an overloaded resource. How would we resolve the difficulty? Because the start dates of all activities are pushed off as late as possible, the steps to take are as follows:

1. The preceding task for activity D is activity C. Therefore, the first step lies in assigning a start-as-late-as-possible constraint to activity C.
2. To remove the resource conflict, work backward from the end of the project, eliminating the sources of conflict.

Figure 11.14 presents an MS Project file that illustrates the steps in adjusting the critical chain schedule to remove resource conflicts. Note that the original figure (Figure 11.11c) highlights a standard problem when developing a typical early-start schedule, namely, the need to evaluate the schedule against possible resource overload. Suppose, for example, that the Gantt chart (Figure 11.14) indicates a resource conflict in the form of Joe, who is assigned both activities B and D during the week of March 6. Since this person cannot perform both activities simultaneously, we must reconfigure the schedule to allow for this constraint.

Figure 11.15 shows the next step in the process of resolving the resource conflict. While maintaining a late-start format, activity D is pushed back to occur after activity B, thereby allowing Joe to first perform B

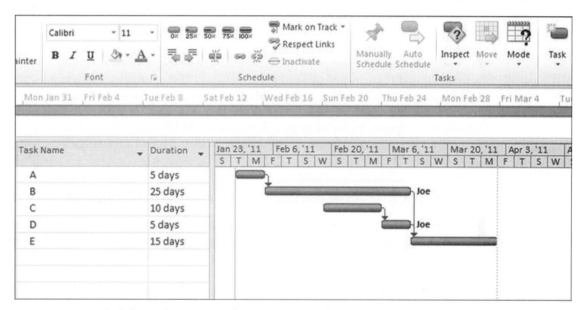

FIGURE 11.14 Scheduling Using Late Start for Project Activities

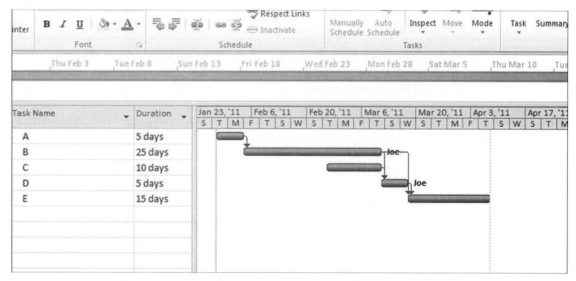

FIGURE 11.15 Reconfiguring the Schedule to Resolve Resource Conflicts

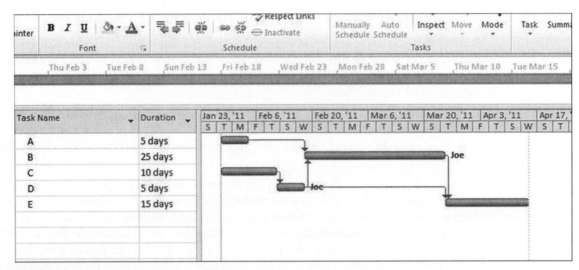

FIGURE 11.16 Alternative Solution to Resource Conflict Problem

before moving to his next assignment. The total schedule delay amounts to approximately one week with the reconfigured schedule.

Alternatively, this resource conflict problem can be rescheduled according to Figure 11.16, in which activities C and D are moved forward in the network. This alternative solution does add additional time to the network path, moving the projected completion date to the second week in April. When choosing the most viable solution to resource conflict issues, you want the option that minimizes total network schedule disruption. In the examples shown, it might be preferable to adopt the schedule shown in Figure 11.15 because it addresses the resource conflict and offers a reconfigured schedule that loses only one week overall.

11.6 CRITICAL CHAIN PROJECT PORTFOLIO MANAGEMENT

Critical Chain Project Management can also be applied to managing a firm's portfolio of projects. Basic TOC logic can be applied to the portfolio of company projects to identify the key systemwide constraint. Recall that in the single-project example, the key constraint is found to be the critical chain. At the organization-wide level, the chief constraint is commonly seen as the company's resource capacity. In balancing the portfolio of projects in process, we must first evaluate the company's chief resource constraints to determine available capacity. The resource constraint may be a person or department; it may be a companywide operating policy, or even a physical resource. In a production capacity, Goldratt has used the term **drum** in reference to a systemwide constraint, because this limiting resource becomes the drum that sets the beat for the rest of the firm's throughput.[18]

In order to apply CCPM to a multiproject environment, we must first identify the current portfolio of projects. Next, the chief resource constraint, or drum, is identified and, following TOC methodology, that system constraint is exploited. With project portfolio scheduling, this step usually consists of pulling projects forward in time because the drum schedule determines the subsequent sequencing of the firm's project portfolio. If the drum resource is early, some projects can be pulled forward to take advantage of the early start. If the drum is late, projects may need to be pushed off into the future. We also need to employ buffers in portfolio scheduling, much as we did for feeder paths and overall project buffering in individual project cases. The term **capacity constraint buffer (CCB)** refers to a safety margin separating different projects scheduled to use the same resource. Applying a CCB prior to sequencing to the next project ensures that the critical resource is protected. For example, if Julia is the quality assessment expert and must inspect all beta software projects prior to their release for full development, we need to apply a CCB between her transition from one project to the next. Finally, we can also use **drum buffers** in portfolio scheduling. Drum buffers are extra safety that is applied to a project immediately before the use of the constrained resource to ensure that the resource will not be starved for work. In effect, they ensure that the drum resource (our constraint) has input to work on when it is needed in the project.[19]

The formal steps necessary to apply CCPM to multiple project portfolios include:[20]

1. Identify the company resource constraint or the drum, the driving force behind multiple project schedules. Determine which resource constraint most directly affects the performance of the overall system or which is typically in short supply and most often requires overtime. Such physical evidence is the best indicator of the company's central constraint.
2. Exploit the resource constraint by—
   a. Preparing a critical chain schedule for each project independently.
   b. Determining the priority among the projects for access to the drum, or constraining resource.
   c. Creating the multiproject resource constraint, or drum, schedule. The resource demands for each project are collected and conflicts are resolved based on priority and the desire to maximize project development performance.
3. Subordinate the individual project schedules by—
   a. Scheduling each project to start based on the drum schedule.
   b. Designating the critical chain as the chain from the first use of the constraining resource to the end of the project.
   c. Inserting capacity constraint buffers (CCBs) between the individual project schedules, ahead of the scheduled use of the constraint resource. This action protects the drum schedule by ensuring the input is ready for it.
   d. Resolving any conflicts if the creation of CCBs adversely affects the drum schedule.
   e. Inserting drum buffers in each project to ensure that the constraint resource will not be starved for work. The buffers should be sited immediately before the use of the constraint resource in the project.
4. Elevate the capacity of the constraint resource; that is, increase the drum capacity for future iterations of the cycle.
5. Go back to step 2 and reiterate the sequence, improving operating flow and resource constraint levels each time.

As an example, consider Figure 11.17. We have identified a drum resource constraint, suggesting that the resource supply is not sufficient to accommodate all three projects (A, B, and C) that are queued to be

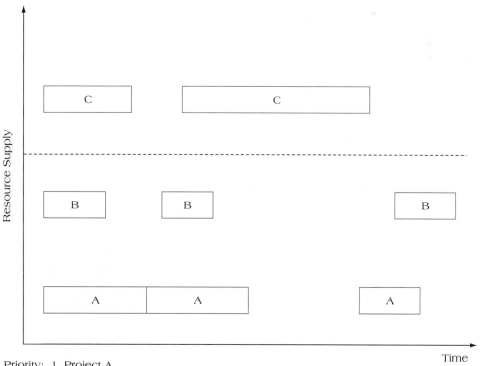

Priority: 1. Project A
           2. Project B
           3. Project C

FIGURE 11.17   Three Projects Stacked for Access to a Drum Resource

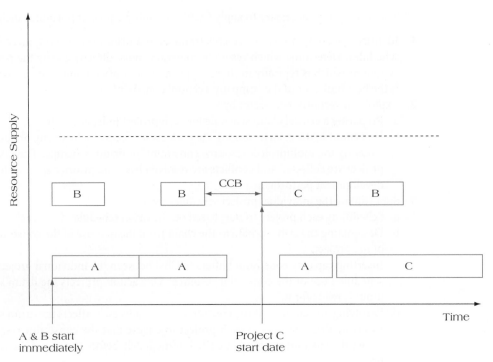

FIGURE 11.18 **Applying CCBs to Drum Schedules**

completed. This point is illustrated by the dashed line running horizontally across the figure. One option, of course, is to drop the project with the lowest priority, in essence allowing the drum resource to dictate the number of projects that can be accomplished. Alternatively, we can consider methods for exploiting the system constraint through the use of capacity constraint buffers to accomplish all three projects, on their priority basis. Figure 11.17 shows the nature of the problem, with project A having the highest priority, B the next highest, and C the lowest priority. Resources exist to handle only two projects simultaneously, but the resources are not needed continuously, as the figure shows. As a result, the resource constraint problem really becomes one of scheduling, similar to the single-project case.

Once we have identified the resource constraint and prioritized the projects for access to the drum resource, we can reschedule the projects in a manner similar to that shown in Figure 11.18.[21] The problem is one of constrained capacity, so the task consists of pushing the additional project C off until such time as it can be included in the drum schedule. A capacity constraint buffer (CCB) is placed in front of the start date to begin work on project C. This buffer ensures that the critical resource is available when needed by the next project in the pipeline and defines the start date for the new project.

This same procedure can be used as we add a fourth, fifth, or sixth project to the portfolio. Each project is constrained by access to the drum resource and must, therefore, be scheduled to take into consideration the system constraint. By so doing, we are able to create a master project schedule that employs Goldratt's theory of constraints philosophy within a multiproject environment.

BOX 11.1

PROJECT MANAGEMENT RESEARCH IN BRIEF

Advantages of Critical Chain Scheduling

Does CCPM really work? Although a number of recent books and articles have appeared championing the methodology, little empirical evidence exists to date to either confirm or disconfirm the viability of the critical chain approach to scheduling. Evidence tends to be primarily anecdotal in nature, as CCPM advocates point to a number of firms that have realized significant savings in time and positive attitudinal changes on the part of project team members following the adoption of critical chain scheduling.

A recent study by Budd and Cooper[22] sought to test the efficacy of CCPM against traditional critical path scheduling in a simulation environment. Using three long projects and more than 1,000 iterations with both a critical chain and a critical path schedule, the authors projected completion times for the projects under study and determined that total activity durations for the critical chain schedules were shorter than durations using the critical path method. For their simulation models, the long projects under a CPM schedule were projected to take from 291 to 312 days to completion, with a mean finish time of 293 days. Critical chain projects were projected to take from 164 to 181 days, with a mean value of 170 days to completion. In fact, in multiple iterations involving different length projects, critical chain scheduling reduced the mean duration time to complete projects anywhere from 18% to 42%. The only caveat the authors noted was their inability to reflect the negative effects of multitasking on either schedule. Nevertheless, their findings offer some evidence in support of critical chain project management as a viable alternative to critical path scheduling.

Additional research evidence is also suggesting that CCPM does have a positive impact on project outcomes. In IT project management, reported results suggest that successfully adopting CCPM shows reductions in project durations of about 25%, increased throughput (the number of projects finished per unit of time) of 25%, and the number of projects completed on time rose to 90%. Finally, a compilation of recent results from different project settings offers some encouraging evidence (see Table 11.3).[23]

TABLE 11.3 Company Project Performance Improvements Using Critical Chain Project Management

CCPM Implementation	Before	After
New Product Development for Home Appliances (Hamilton Beach/Proctor-Silex)	34 new products per year. 74% of projects on time.	Increased to 52 new products in first year and to 70+ in second year. 88% of projects on time.
Telecommunications Network Design and Installation (eircom, Ireland)	On-time delivery less than 75%. Average cycle time of 70 days.	Increased on-time delivery to 98+%. Average cycle time dropped to 30 days.
Helicopter Manufacturing and Maintenance (Erickson Air-Crane)	Only 33% of projects completed on time.	Projects completed on time increased to 83%.
Oil & Gas Platform Design & Manufacturing (LeTourneau Technologies, Inc.)	Design engineering took 15 months. Production engineering took 9 months. Fabrication and assembly took 8 months.	Design engineering takes 9 months. Production engineering takes 5 months. Fabrication and assembly takes 5 months with 22% improvement in labor productivity.
High Tech Medical Development (Medtronic Europe)	Device projects took 18 months on average and were unpredictable.	Development cycle time reduced to 9 months. On-time delivery increased to 90%.
Transformer Repair and Overhaul (ABB, Halle)	42 projects completed January–December 2007. On-time delivery of 68%.	54 projects completed January–December 2008. On-time delivery of 83%.

11.7 CRITIQUES OF CCPM

Critical Chain Project Management is not without its critics. Several arguments against the process include the following charges and perceived weaknesses in the methodology:

1. Lack of project milestones make coordinated scheduling, particularly with external suppliers, highly problematic. Critics contend that the lack of in-process project milestones adversely affects the ability to coordinate schedule dates with suppliers that provide the external delivery of critical components.[24]
2. The "newness" of CCPM is a point refuted by some who see the technique as either ill-suited to many types of projects or simply a reconceptualization of well-understood scheduling methodologies (such as PERT), provided special care has been taken to resource-level the network.[25]
3. Although it may be true that CCPM brings increased discipline to project scheduling, efficient methods for the application of this technique to a firm's portfolio of projects are unclear. The method seems to offer benefits on a project-by-project basis, but its usefulness at the program level has not

been proven.[26] Also, because CCPM argues for dedicated resources, in a multiproject environment where resources are shared, it is impossible to avoid multitasking, which diminishes the power of CCPM.

4. Evidence of success with CCPM is still almost exclusively anecdotal and based on single-case studies. Debating the merits and pitfalls of CCPM has remained largely an intellectual exercise among academics and writers of project management theory. With the exception of Budd and Cooper's modeling work, no large-scale empirical research exists to either confirm or disconfirm its efficacy.

5. A recent review of CCPM contended that although it does offer a number of valuable concepts, it is not a complete solution to current project management scheduling needs. The authors contended that organizations should be extremely careful in excluding conventional project management scheduling processes to adopt CCPM as a sole method for planning and scheduling activities.[27]

6. Critics also charge that Goldratt's evaluation of duration estimation is overly negative and critical, suggesting that his contention that project personnel routinely add huge levels of activity duration estimation "padding" is exaggerated.

7. Finally, there is a concern that Goldratt seriously underestimates the difficulties associated with achieving the type of corporate-wide cultural changes necessary to successfully implement CCPM. In particular, while activity estimate padding may be problematic, it is not clear that team members will be willing to abandon safety at the request of the project manager as long as they perceive the possibility of sanctions for missing deadlines.[28]

Successful implementation and use of CCPM is predicated first on making a commitment to critically examining and changing the culture of project organizations in which many of the problems identified in this chapter are apparent. Truth-in-scheduling, avoiding the student syndrome, transferring project safety to the control of the project manager—these are all examples of the types of actions that bespeak a healthy, authentic culture. Gaining "buy-in" from organizational members for this type of scheduling process is vital to the success of such new and innovative techniques that can dramatically improve time to market and customer satisfaction.[29]

Summary

1. **Understand the difference between common cause and special cause variation in organizations.** Deming identified two main sources of variation (error) in organizations:
   - *Common cause variation*—A cause that is inherent in the system; that is, a chance error exists because of flaws in how the system was originally created.
   - *Special cause variation*—A cause that is attributable to a special circumstance; for example, it may be specific to some set of workers, piece of machinery, or local condition.

   When applying the five steps in theory of constraints, it is necessary to correctly identify the course of bottlenecks or other errors in the activities of an organization. When a common cause variation is mistaken for a special cause variation, there is a potential to misapply corrective actions or waste time and money chasing down the source of problems that are not unique to a project, but inherent in the organization itself. On the other hand, when special cause variation is attributed to common cause, the likelihood exists of missing the true source of error by assuming that the mistakes lie within the system rather than being due to a specific cause.

2. **Recognize the three ways in which project teams inflate the amount of safety for all project tasks.** Goldratt argues that project scheduling is dramatically affected by human behavior. In our desire to "protect" ourselves from negative consequences of missing deadlines, project team members routinely pad their estimates, up to (Goldratt charges) 200%. At the same time, project managers protect themselves by adding their own safety factor to the estimates they receive from subordinates. Finally, they also factor in the expected cuts from top management when they present their schedule estimates. The result is an activity estimating and scheduling process fraught with dishonesty at every stage and padded with excessive safety. Because no one takes estimates seriously, no one gives serious estimates.

3. **Understand the four ways in which additional project task safety can be wasted.** Problems continue once the schedules are set. All project team members are prone to certain behaviors, including the

student "term-paper" model, whereby we put off starting an activity as long as possible. Second, while delays from activity to activity are passed along the schedule, early finishes are never passed along. All team members are loath to admit they finished early for fear that next time, their time estimates will be discounted. Third, Goldratt suggests that we lose time on projects because of the tendency of most organizations to require their project team members to engage in multitasking, in which they work at multiple assignments simultaneously. The more tasks given to team members, the longer it takes them to complete any one task. Finally, activity path merge points represent another manner in which we lose activity safety. At merge points, activities must wait for the slowest of the merging activities to be completed prior to moving to the subsequent task. Activities that finish early waste slack time waiting for the most tardy.

4. **Distinguish between critical path and critical chain project scheduling techniques.** As a result of systematic problems with project scheduling, Goldratt developed the Critical Chain Project Management (CCPM) process. With CCPM, several alterations are made to the traditional PERT scheduling process. First, all individual activity slack, or "buffer," becomes project buffer. Each team member, responsible for her component of the activity network, creates a duration estimate free from any padding, that is, one that is based on a 50% probability of success. All activities on the critical chain and feeder chains (noncritical chains in the network) are then linked with minimal time padding. The project buffer is now aggregated and some proportion of that saved time (Goldratt uses a 50% rule of thumb) is added to the project. Even adding 50% of the saved time significantly reduces the overall project schedule while requiring team members to be less concerned with activity padding and more with task completion.

Second, CCPM applies the same approach for those tasks not on the critical chain. All feeder path activities are reduced by the same order of magnitude and a feeder buffer is constructed for the overall non-critical chain of activities.

Finally, CCPM distinguishes between its use of buffer and the traditional PERT use of project slack. With the PERT approach, project slack is a function of the overall completed activity network. In other words, slack is an outcome of the task dependencies, whereas CCPM's buffer is used as an a priori input to the schedule planning, based on a reasoned cut in each activity and the application of aggregated project buffer at the end.

5. **Understand how critical chain methodology resolves project resource conflicts.** Critical Chain Project Management assumes that the critical chain for a project requires first identifying resource conflicts and then sequencing tasks so as to eliminate these conflicts. Instead of employing early-start methods for networks, the CCPM approach emphasizes using late-start times, adding feeder buffers at the junction of feeder paths to the critical path, and applying an overall project buffer at the project level to be used as needed. All activities are sequenced so as to exploit resource conflicts, ensuring minimal delays between tasks and speeding up the overall project.

6. **Apply critical chain project management to project portfolios.** CCPM can also be applied at the project portfolio level, in which multiple projects are competing for limited project resources. Portfolio management first consists of identifying the maximum resource availability across all projects in a portfolio, prioritizing the projects for access to the constrained resource, and then sequencing other, noncritical project activities around the resources as they are available. The "drum resource" is the critical resource that constrains the whole portfolio. To buffer the projects that are sequenced to use the drum resources, CCPM advises creating capacity constraint buffers (CCBs) to better control the transition between projects as they queue to employ the critical resource.

Key Terms

Capacity constraint buffer (CCB) *(p. 386)*

Central limit theorem *(p. 378)*

Common cause variation *(p. 372)*

Critical chain *(p. 379)*

Critical Chain Project Management (CCPM) *(p. 370)*

Drum *(p. 386)*

Drum buffers *(p. 386)*

Multitasking *(p. 377)*

Negative variation *(p. 376)*

Positive variation *(p. 376)*

Special cause variation *(p. 372)*

Student syndrome *(p. 376)*

Theory of constraints (TOC) *(p. 371)*

Solved Problem

Assume you have the PERT chart shown in Figure 11.19 and you have identified a resource conflict in which Cheryl is scheduled to work on two tasks at the same time. In this case, Cheryl has become the constrained resource for your project. How would you reconfigure this portion of the project's network diagram to better manage your critical resource? What would be the new "critical chain"?

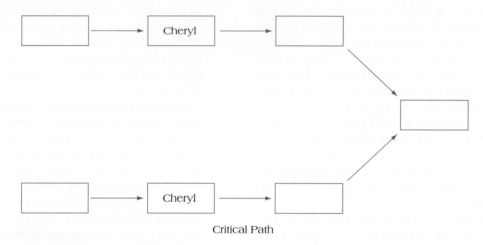

FIGURE 11.19   Current Network

SOLUTION

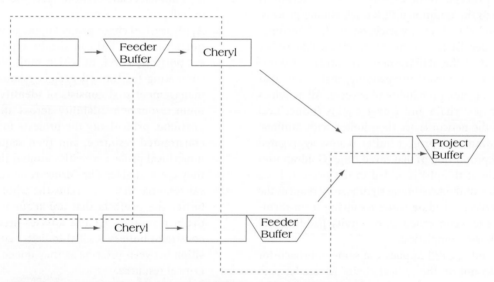

FIGURE 11.20 SOLUTION TO SOLVED PROBLEM   Critical Chain Network

Discussion Questions

1. What are the practical implications internally (in terms of team motivation) and externally (for the customer) of making overly optimistic project delivery promises?
2. In considering how to make a big change in organizational operations (as in the case of switching to CCPM), why might it be necessary to focus on changing the organization's current culture? That is, why does a shift in project scheduling require so many other linked changes to occur?
3. Explain the difference between common cause variation and special cause variation. Why are these concepts critical to understanding successful efforts to improve the quality and reliability of an organizational system?

4. What are the three reasons Goldratt argues are used to justify adding excessive amounts of safety to our project duration estimates? In your project experiences, are these arguments justified?
5. What are the reasons we routinely waste the excessive safety we acquire for our project activities? Are some of these reasons more prevalent in your own experiences than others?
6. How does aggregation of project safety allow the project team to reduce overall safety to a value that is less than the sum of individual task safeties? How does the insurance industry employ this same phenomenon?

7. Distinguish between project buffers and feeder buffers. What is each buffer type used to accomplish?

8. It has been said that a key difference between CCPM safety and ordinary PERT chart activity slack is that activity slack is determined after the network has been created, whereas critical chain path safety is determined in advance. Explain this distinction: How does the project team "find" slack in a PERT chart versus how does the team use the activity buffer in Critical Chain Project Management?

9. What are the steps that CCPM employs to resolve resource conflicts on a project? How does the concept of activity late starts aid this approach?

10. What key steps are necessary to employ CCPM as a method for controlling a firm's portfolio of projects?

11. What is a drum resource? Why is the concept important to understand in order to better control resource requirements for project portfolios?

Problems

1. Assume the network diagram shown in Figure 11.21. Megan is responsible for activities A and C. Use the critical chain methodology to resource-level the network. What are two options for redrawing the network? Which is the most efficient in terms of time to completion for the project? Show your work.

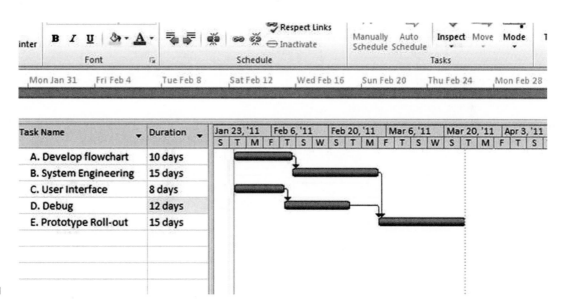

FIGURE 11.21

2. Consider the following activities and their durations. The original project schedule, using early activity starts, is shown in Figure 11.22. Reconfigure the network using critical chain project scheduling.

What is the critical path? How much slack is available in the noncritical path? Reconfigure the network in Figure 11.22 as a critical chain network. What is the new duration of the project? How long are the project and feeder buffers?

Activity	Duration
A	5 days
B	30 days
C	10 days
D	10 days
E	15 days

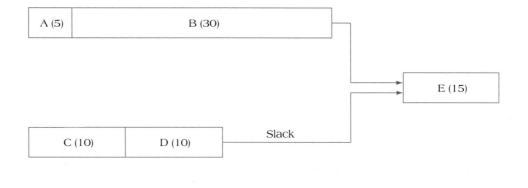

FIGURE 11.22 ◄─────────── 50 Days ───────────►

3. Reconfigure the network in Figure 11.23 using the critical chain approach. Remember to reconfigure the activities to late start where appropriate. What is the original critical path? What is the original project duration? How much feeder buffer should be applied to the noncritical paths? What is the length of the project buffer? Assume the 50% likelihood is exactly half the duration of current project activities.

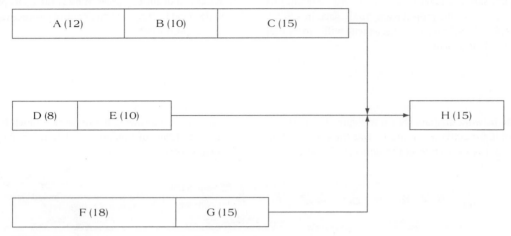

FIGURE 11.23

4. Assume the network in Figure 11.24 with resource conflicts. How would you redraw the network using a critical chain in order to eliminate the resource conflicts? Where should feeder buffers be applied? Why?

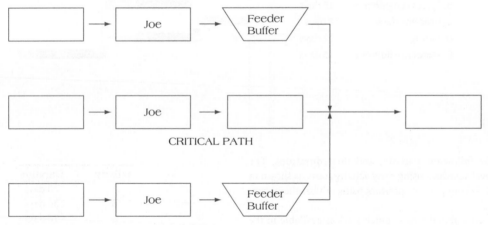

FIGURE 11.24

5. Consider the project portfolio problem shown in Figure 11.25. You are required to manage resources to accommodate the company's current project portfolio. One resource area, comprising Carol, Kathy, and Tom, is responsible for all program debugging as new projects are completed. Four projects have activities that need to be completed. How would you schedule Carol, Kathy, and Tom's time most efficiently? Using buffer drum scheduling, reconfigure the following schedule to allow for optimal use of the resource time:

Priority: 1. Project X
2. Project Y
3. Project Z
4. Project Q

Where would you place capacity constraint buffers? Why?

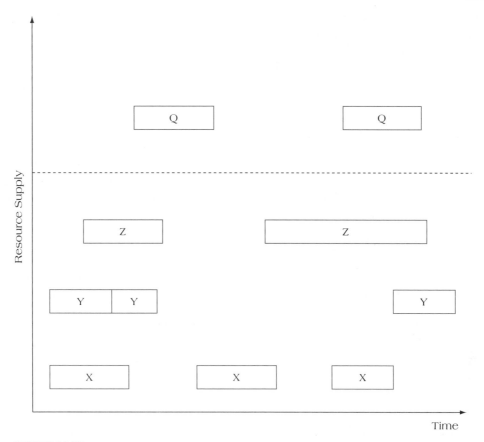

FIGURE 11.25

Case Study 11.1

Judy's Hunt for Authenticity

Judy Thomas barely had time to celebrate her appointment to head her old department at Optimal Logistics before she became embroiled in an ongoing problem with the project management personnel. As part of her new duties, Judy was responsible for heading all new projects at OL, a job that required her to oversee anywhere from 20 to 35 projects at any time. Judy believed in holding detailed project review meetings every two weeks with her immediate subordinates, the six-person senior systems group, to assess the status of ongoing projects, develop resource assignments for new projects, and generally troubleshoot the project development process. One of the senior programmers' responsibilities was to develop a Work Breakdown Structure for new projects and, after consulting with the junior and lead programmers, give a preliminary estimate of the time frame needed to complete the assignment.

Judy soon noticed that her senior programmers had a much more pessimistic assessment of the time needed to complete projects than her own view. In particular, all project assignments seemed to her to be grossly overestimated. As a former programmer herself, with more than 10 years' experience, Judy had a hard time understanding how the programmers and the senior systems managers were coming up with such lengthy estimates.

The problem came to a head one afternoon when she received an assessment for a routine reprogramming job that was estimated to take more than 120 hours of work. Holding the assessment in her hand, she determined to find out how this figure had been derived. Judy first approached the lead programmer, Sid, as he sat at his desk.

"Sid, this estimate from you shows that you requested 32 hours to upgrade an online system that only needs minor tweaks. What gives?"

Sid reacted with a start. "I never put down 32 hours. Randy asked me for my estimate and I told him I thought it would take about 24 hours of work."

(continued)

Judy pursed her lips. "Well, I need to talk about that with Randy. Even allowing for the fact that you requested 24 hours instead of 32, Sid, you and I both know that the work we are estimating should not take anywhere near that much time to finish."

Sid's response did not improve Judy's confidence. "Um, well, Judy, the thing is … I mean, you have to understand that there are a lot of other projects I am working on right now and …"

Judy interrupted, "I'm not concerned with your other assignments right now, Sid. I am trying to get a handle on this estimate. How did you get 24 hours?"

Sid squirmed in his seat. Finally, he cleared his throat and looked Judy in the eye. "Judy, the fact is that I have seven projects going on right now. If you pulled me off the other six, I could get that routine finished in about six hours, but I don't have six uninterrupted hours. Plus, you know how Randy works. If I give him an honest estimate and miss it, even if it isn't my fault, he never lets me

forget it. Put yourself in my position for a moment: How would you handle this job?"

Judy walked back to her desk in a thoughtful mood. "Maybe the problem around here isn't our ability to develop accurate estimates," she thought. "Maybe it's the culture that is pushing us to avoid being authentic with each other."

Questions

1. Identify some of the symptoms in the case that point toward cultural problems in the department.
2. What steps would you take to begin changing the culture in the department? In your answer, consider what changes you would recommend making to the reward systems, methods for estimating activity durations, and task assignments for project personnel.
3. Why do you suppose Randy took Sid's 24-hour activity estimate and increased it to 32 hours when he presented it to Judy?

Case Study 11.2

Ramstein Products, Inc.

Jack Palmer, head of the Special Projects Division for Ramstein Products, had been in his new position for only three months when he ordered an evaluation of project management practices within his division. Ramstein Products is a leading developer of integrated testing equipment for the energy industry, marketing more than 45 product lines to a variety of organizations involved in natural gas and oil exploration, power generation, and utilities. As head of special products, Jack was responsible for an ongoing project portfolio of 50 to 60 new product development projects. Top management at Ramstein estimated that 60% of company revenue came from new products and took a keen interest in the operations of the Special Projects Division.

As part of the evaluation, Jack became aware of the troubling fact that projects were routinely overrunning their budget and schedule targets, often by a significant margin. This fact was particularly troubling because Jack, who had once worked as a project manager within the division, was well aware that project schedules were not terribly aggressive. In fact, he believed that a great deal of padding went into the project schedules as they were initially developed. Why, then, were projects chronically late and over budget?

Although important to Ramstein's future success, the Special Projects Division had long been operating on

a tight resource level. There were seven system integration engineers supporting a portfolio of 55 projects. These engineers were very important to Ramstein's new product development efforts, and their services were often stretched to the breaking point. One of the senior engineers, Mary, recently informed Jack that she was supporting 14 projects, all being developed at the same time!

Jack reflected on some of the information he had received during his evaluation. Clearly, the easiest option would be to approach top management and request more systems integration engineers for his division. He had a hunch, however, that with the current economic conditions, any such request from him would probably be turned down. He needed to get a handle on the problems and apply some solutions now with the resources he had available.

Questions

1. Applying Goldratt's ideas of critical resources, what is the system constraint within the Special Projects Division that is causing bottlenecks and delaying the projects?
2. How is multitasking contributing to systemic delays in project development at Ramstein?
3. How could the drum buffer concepts from Critical Chain Portfolio Management be applied to this problem?

Internet Exercises

1. Go to www.youtube.com/watch?v=BRMDCRPGYBE for a brief overview of Critical Chain Project Management. What does the presenter suggest are the benefits and biggest challenges of implementing CCPM?

2. Go to the Companion Web site and read the article by Frank Patrick (1999), "Critical Chain Scheduling and Buffer Management: Getting Out from between Parkinson's Rock and Murphy's Hard Place," *PMNetwork,* 13(4), pp. 57–62.

3. Visit www.pqa.net/ccpm/W05001001.html and consider some of the key links, including "What's New & Different about Critical Chain (CCPM)?" and "Diagnose Your Project Management Problems." What are the benefits that CCPM offers project organizations?

4. Go to www.focusedperformance.com/articles/multi02.html. In an article entitled "The Sooner You Start, the Later You Finish," a number of points are made about the logic of scheduling and the value of a critical chain solution. What, in your opinion, are the core arguments the author makes in this article?

5. Go to www.goldratt.co.uk/Successes/pm2.html and examine several case stories of firms that implemented CCPM in their project management operations. What underlying characteristics do these firms share that helped enable them to develop CCPM methods for their projects?

Notes

1. www.railway-technology.com/projects/gotthard-base-tunnel/; http://en.wikipedia.org/wiki/Gotthard_Base_Tunnel; www.yourdiscovery.com/machines_and_engineering/megabuilders/gotthardbasetunnel/index.shtml; Seidler, C. (2010). "Miracle under the Alps," www.spiegel.de/international/europe/0,1518,723202,00.html.

2. Leach, L. P. (1999). "Critical chain project management improves project performance," *Project Management Journal,* 30(2): 39–51.

3. Goldratt, E. (1984). *The Goal.* Great Barrington, MA: North River Press; Goldratt, E. (1997). *Critical Chain.* Great Barrington, MA: North River Press.

4. Leach, L. P. (1999). "Critical chain project management improves project performance," *Project Management Journal,* 30(2): 39–51; Leach, L. P., and Leach, S. P. (2010). *Lean Project Leadership.* Boise, ID: Advanced Projects, Inc.

5. Goldratt, E. (1997). *Critical Chain.* Great Barrington, MA: North River Press; Elton, J., and Roe, J. (1998, March–April). "Bringing discipline to project management," *Harvard Business Review,* 76(2): 78–83.

6. Leach, L. P. (2001). "Putting quality in project risk management, part 1: Understanding variation," *PMNetwork,* 15(2): 53–56.

7. Deming, J. E. (1989). *Out of the Crisis.* Cambridge, MA: MIT Press.

8. Leach, L. P. (2001). "Putting quality in project risk management, part 1: Understanding variation," *PMNetwork,* 15(2): 53–56.

9. Goldratt, E. (1997). *Critical Chain.* Great Barrington, MA: North River Press; Herroelen, W., and Leus, R. (2000). "On the merits and pitfalls of critical chain scheduling," *Proceedings of PMI Research Conference 2000.* Newtown Square, PA: Project Management Institute, pp. 283–95; Homer, J. L. (1998). "Applying the theory of constraints to projects," *Proceedings of the 29th Annual Project Management Institute Seminars and Symposium.* CD-ROM. Newtown Square, PA: PMI.

10. Elton, J., and Roe, J. (1998, March–April). "Bringing discipline to project management," *Harvard Business Review,* 76(2): 78–83.

11. Quoted in Leach, L. P. (1999). "Critical chain project management improves project performance," *Project Management Journal,* 30(2): 39–51, p. 43.

12. Steyn, H. (2000). "An investigation into the fundamentals of critical chain project scheduling," *International Journal of Project Management,* 19: 363–69.

13. Sherman, E. (2002). "Inside the iPod design triumph," *Electronics Design Chain Magazine,* www.designchain.com/coverstory.asp?issue=summer02.

14. Newbold, R. C. (1998). *Project Management in the Fast Lane.* Boca Raton, FL: St. Lucie Press; Tukel, O. I., Rom, W. O., and Eksioglu, S. D. (2006). "An investigation of buffer sizing techniques in critical chain scheduling," *European Journal of Operational Research,* 172: 401–16.

15. Steyn, H. (2000). "An investigation into the fundamentals of critical chain project scheduling." *International Journal of Project Management,* 19: 363–69.

16. Hoel, K., and Taylor, S. G. (1999). "Quantifying buffers for project schedules," *Production and Inventory Management Journal,* 40(2): 43–47; Raz, T., and Marshall, B. (1996). "Float calculations in project networks under resource constraints," *International Journal of Project Management,* 14(4): 241–48; Patrick, F. (1999). "Critical chain scheduling and buffer management: Getting out from between Parkinson's rock and Murphy's hard place," *PMNetwork,* 13(4): 57–62; Leach, L. P. (2003). "Schedule and cost buffer sizing: How to account for the bias between project performance and your model," *Project Management Journal,* 34(2): 34–47.

17. Merrill, J. (2009). "Lilly play up R&D productivity with reorganization," www.biopharmatoday.com/2009/09/lilly-plays-up-rd-productivity-with-reorganization-.html.

18. Goldratt, E. (1984). *The Goal.* Great Barrington, MA: North River Press.

19. Gray, V., Felan, J., Umble, E., and Umble, M. (2000). "A comparison of drum-buffer-rope (DBR) and critical chain (CC) buffering techniques," *Proceedings of PMI Research Conference 2000.* Newtown Square, PA: Project Management Institute, pp. 257–64.

20. Leach, L. P. (2000). *Critical Chain Project Management.* Boston: Artech House.

21. Leach, L.P. (1999). "Critical chain project management improves project performance," *Project Management Journal,* 30(2): 39–51, p. 41.

22. Budd, C. S., and Cooper, M. J. (2005). "Improving on-time service delivery: The case of project as product," *Human Systems Management,* 24(1): 67–81.

23. Emam, K. E., and Koru, A. G. (2008). "A replicated survey of IT software project failures," *IEEE Software,* 25(5): 84–90; www.realization.com/customers.html.

24. Zalmenson, E. (2001, January). "PMBoK and the critical chain," *PMNetwork,* 15(1): 4.

25. Duncan, W. (1999, April). "Back to basics: Charters, chains, and challenges," *PMNetwork,* 13(4): 11.

26. Elton, J., and Roe, J. (1998, March–April). "Bringing discipline to project management," *Harvard Business Review,* 76(2): 78–83.

27. Raz, T., Barnes, R., and Dvir, D. (2003). "A critical look at critical chain project management," *Project Management Journal,* 34(4): 24–32.

28. Pinto, J. K. (1999). "Some constraints on the theory of constraints: Taking a critical look at the critical chain," *PMNetwork,* 13(8): 49–51.

29. Piney, C. (2000, December). "Critical path or critical chain. Combining the best of both," *PMNetwork,* 14(12): 51–54; Steyn, H. (2002). "Project management applications of the theory of constraints beyond critical chain scheduling," *International Journal of Project Management,* 20: 75–80.

Resource Management

Chapter Outline

Chapter Objectives

After completing this chapter, you should be able to:

1. Recognize the variety of constraints that can affect a project, making scheduling and planning difficult.

2. Understand how to apply resource-loading techniques to project schedules to identify potential resource overallocation situations.

3. Apply resource-leveling procedures to project activities over the baseline schedule using appropriate prioritization heuristics.

4. Follow the steps necessary to effectively smooth resource requirements across the project life cycle.

5. Apply resource management within a multiproject environment.

PROJECT MANAGEMENT BODY OF KNOWLEDGE CORE CONCEPTS COVERED IN THIS CHAPTER

1. Activity Resource Estimating (PMBoK sec. 6.3)
2. Human Resource Planning (PMBoK sec. 9.1)

PROJECT PROFILE

Nissan LEAF: New Fuel Economy Champ

In this age of heightened environmental awareness, few new products are "greener" than the Nissan LEAF. Hybrid automobiles, employing a combination of gasoline and electric power, have been available for several years now and are becoming ever more mainstream. In fact, *Motor Trend* magazine named the Chevrolet Volt hybrid its 2011 Car of the Year in recognition of the styling, quality, and performance features found in this new venture. Indeed, many have argued that with their ability to use "clean" energy, lower dependence on foreign oil sources, and encourage conservation, the new generation of hybrid automobiles is likely to only gain greater market share and customer acceptance. It is against this backdrop of support for hybrid cars that Nissan's LEAF has made such an impact.

The LEAF is actually an acronym for *Leading, Environmentally friendly, Affordable, Family car*. Nissan developed the LEAF to be different from the current generation of hybrids in one crucial way—it is not, strictly speaking, a hybrid at all because it does not have a gasoline engine. Standard hybrid cars use electricity to run while at relatively low speeds over limited ranges, making them ideal for commuters looking to save money on the daily drive to the office or worksite. However, when traveling at higher speeds on freeways or over longer ranges, the batteries cannot power the car and the gasoline engine automatically engages, while recharging the depleted battery. As a result, hybrids typically average nearly 50 miles per gallon (mpg) for normal commuter driving and somewhat less than that for extended range or highway travel.

Not so with Nissan's LEAF. The LEAF, which uses no gasoline at all, was rated best-in-class for the environment because it emits no greenhouse gases or traditional tailpipe emissions. The EPA has approved a rating of ≈99miles per gallon for the 2011 Nissan LEAF in combined city and highway driving. The agency derived the LEAF's fuel-economy figure using an equivalency formula to give car shoppers a standard by which to judge overall fuel efficiency and environmental impact for a wide range of vehicles using a variety of fuels and power sources.

ZUMA Wire Service / Alamy

FIGURE 12.1   Nissan's LEAF

In recognition of the advances made in its creation, the LEAF earned Green Car Reports' "Best Car to Buy" award in 2010. Their reasons for choosing the LEAF over other hybrids, including the Chevrolet Volt, include:

- **A real electric car:** *"Because it is the sole vehicle offered to U.S. buyers (this model year, by an established global auto maker) that uses absolutely no gasoline. There will be many more coming but this year, the 2011 Leaf is the one and only."*
- **The lowest carbon footprint:** *"[N]o matter how you run the numbers, it is the vehicle with the lowest carbon footprint of any new car sold today."*
- **90% of your needs is enough:** *"Just as General Motors will tell you that more than 70 percent of U.S. vehicles do less than 40 miles a day, Nissan frequently points out that more than 90 percent of U.S. vehicles do less than the Leaf's range of 100 miles per day."*

Green Car sums up the whole thing by concluding that the LEAF is the first practical electric car that one can use, and the fact that no one will ever pump an ounce of gas into it overcomes any shortcomings it may still have over a gas-burning vehicle, hybrid or not.

In going commercial with the LEAF, Nissan is working to minimize all potential risks as they bring the car to America. They recognize that this radical technology will be difficult for dealerships and mechanics to work with initially, and they do not want to sacrifice good will through frustrating technical problems. According to *Automotive News*, the Japanese manufacturer has assembled a rapid-reaction task force to pin down customer complaints before they get out of hand. The team, based in Los Angeles, is led by a group of 10 engineers who have been thoroughly trained on the vehicle's drivetrain, and each engineer will have a squad of around 30 technicians to provide additional assistance as needed. Nissan is currently looking to install similar outfits in both Europe and Japan.

The move is part of an effort to assuage any worries that buyers may have about being among the first to sign on the dotted line for their very own electric vehicle. In Japan, Nissan has even gone so far as to offer a program with free towing, unlimited free charging at dealerships, and a 24-hour hotline for owner questions. It may be that in the near future Nissan USA will do the same. The first of the 2011 electric vehicles arrived in late 2010. By the end of that year, there was a waiting list of more than 20,000 people signed up to purchase one. Nissan's plan is to build them in Japan for the first two years and then shift to a site in Smyrna, Tennessee, to build them in the United States.

Hybrid automobile technology has not been cheap to develop. In fact, Toyota's investments in its hybrid program, which has given it roughly two-thirds of the global market for hybrid-electric cars, are estimated to have cost it upward of $10 billion over 15 years. Critics also charge that automakers use these cars as "loss leaders" for their fleets, noting that the unit cost to manufacture them is higher than their price tag in the marketplace, meaning the more cars sold, the more money automakers lose. Nevertheless, although the technology is still being perfected and the cost of these cars is quite high, a combination of consumer environmental awareness and government incentives is pushing American buyers to consider the electric/hybrid range of vehicles as a serious option. Industry experts suggest that the coming decade will demonstrate cheaper electric cars with enhanced range, cheaper prices, and steadily increasing market share, as consumers in metropolitan areas recognize the advantages of hybrid/electric travel.[1]

INTRODUCTION

As noted in Chapter 1, one of the defining characteristics of projects is the constraints, or limitations, under which they are expected to operate. The number one constraint is the availability of resources, both money and people, at the critical times when they are needed. Initial project cost estimation and budgeting—those activities that nail down resources—are extremely important elements in project management. When these two are performed well, they ensure appropriate resources for the project as it progresses downstream.

In Chapters 9 and 10 on project scheduling, we saw that network diagrams, activity duration estimates, and comprehensive schedules can all be developed without serious discussion of the availability of the resources. It was not until Chapter 11, "Critical Chain Project Scheduling," that resource availability came up as a prerequisite for accurate scheduling. Organizational reality, of course, is very different. If projects are indeed defined by their **resource constraints**, any attempt to create a reasonable project schedule must pass the test of resource availability. So, effective project scheduling is really a multistep process. After the actual network has been constructed, the second stage must always be to check it against the resources that drive each activity. The availability of appropriate resources *always* has a direct bearing on the duration of project activities.

In this chapter, we are going to explore the concept of resource planning and management. Gaining a better understanding of how resource management fits into the overall scheme of project planning and scheduling gives us a prominent advantage when the time comes to take all those carefully laid plans and actually make them work. The chapter will be divided into two principal sections: resource constraints and resource management.

12.1 THE BASICS OF RESOURCE CONSTRAINTS

Probably the most common type of project constraint revolves around the availability of human resources to perform the project. As we have noted, one of the key methods for shortening project durations is to move as many activities as possible out of serial paths and into parallel ones. This approach assumes, of course, that staff is free to support the performance of multiple activities at the same time (the idea behind parallel work). In cases in which we do not have sufficient people or other critical resources, we simply cannot work in a parallel mode. When projects are created without allowing for sufficient human resources, project teams are immediately placed in a difficult, reactive position. Personnel are multitasked with their other assignments, are expected to work long hours, and may not receive adequate training. Trade-offs between the duration of project activities (and usually the project's overall schedule) and resource availability are the natural result.

In some situations, the **physical constraints** surrounding a project may be a source of serious concern for the company attempting to create the deliverable. Environmental or contractual issues can create some truly memorable problems; for example, the Philippine government contracted to develop a nuclear power plant for the city of Manila. Bizarrely, the site selected for its construction was against the backdrop of Mount Natib, a volcano on the outskirts of the city. As construction proceeded, environmentalists rightly condemned the choice, arguing that seismic activity could displace the operating systems of the reactors and lead to catastrophic results. Eventually, a compromise solution was reached, in which the energy source for the power plant was to be converted from nuclear to coal. With the myriad problems the project faced, it became known as the "$2.2 Billion Nuclear Fiasco."[2] This case is an extreme example, but as we will continue to see, many real problems can accrue from taking a difficult project and attempting to develop it in hazardous or difficult physical conditions.

Materials are a common project resource that must be considered in scheduling. This is most obvious in a situation where a physical asset is to be created, such as a bridge, building, or other infrastructure project. Clearly, having a stockpile of a sufficient quantity of the various resources needed to complete the project steps is a key consideration in estimating task duration times.

Most projects are subject to highly constrained (fixed) budgets. Is there sufficient working capital to ensure that the project can be completed in the time frame allowed? It is a safe bet to assume that any project without an adequate budget is doomed.

Many projects require technical or specific types of equipment to make them successful. In developing a new magazine concept, for example, a project team may need leading-edge computers with great graphics software to create glitz and glamour. Equipment scheduling is equally important. When equipment is shared across departments, it should be available at the precise time points in the project when it is needed. In house construction, for example, the cement mixer must be on site within a few days after the ground has been excavated and footers dug.

Time and Resource Scarcity

In the **time-constrained project**, the work must be finished by a certain time or date, as efficiently as possible. If necessary, additional resources will be added to the project to hit the critical "launch window." Obviously, the project should be completed without excessive resource usage, but this concern is clearly secondary to the ultimate objective of completing the project on time. For example, projects aimed at specific commercial launch or those in which late delivery will incur high penalties are often time constrained.

In the **resource-constrained project**, the work must not exceed some predetermined level of resource use within the organization. While the project is to be completed as rapidly as possible, speed is not the ultimate goal. The chief factor driving the project is to minimize resource usage. In this example, project completion delays may be acceptable when balanced against overapplication of resources.

The **mixed-constraint project** is primarily resource constrained but may contain some activities or work package elements that are time constrained to a greater degree. For example, if critical delivery dates must be met for some project subcomponents, they may be viewed as time constrained within the overall, resource-constrained project. In these circumstances, the project team must develop a schedule and resource management plan that works to ensure the minimization of resources overall while allocating levels necessary to achieve deadlines within some project components.

There is, for almost all projects, usually a dominant constraint that serves as the final arbiter of project decisions. Focusing on the critical constraint, whether it is resource-based or time-based, serves as a key starting point to putting together a resource-loaded schedule that is reasonable, mirrors corporate goals and objectives, and is attainable.[3]

The challenge of optimally scheduling resources across the project's network activity diagram quickly becomes highly complex. On the one hand, we are attempting to create an efficient activity network that schedules activities in parallel and ensures the shortest development cycle possible. At the same time, however, we inevitably face the problem of finding and providing the resources necessary to achieve these optimistic and aggressive schedules. We are constantly aware of the need to juggle schedule with resource availability, trying to identify the optimal solution to this combinatorial problem. There are two equally critical challenges to be faced: (1) the identification and acquisition of necessary project resources, and (2) their proper scheduling or sequencing across the project baseline.[4]

EXAMPLE 12.1 Working with Project Constraints

Here is an example that shows what project teams face when they attempt to manage project resources. Suppose we created a simple project activity network based on the information given in Table 12.1. Figure 12.2 demonstrates a partial network diagram, created with Microsoft Project 2010. Note that the first three activities have each been assigned a duration of five days, so activities B and C* are set to begin on the same date, following completion of activity A. Strictly from a schedule-development point of view, there may be nothing wrong with this sequence; unfortunately, the project manager set up the network in such a way that both these activities require the special skills of only one member of the project team. For that person to accomplish both tasks simultaneously, huge amounts of overtime are required or adjustments will need to be made to the estimated time to completion for both tasks. In short, we have a case of misallocated resources within the schedule baseline. The result is to force the project team to make a trade-off decision: either increase budgeted costs for performing these activities or extend the schedule to allow for the extra time needed to do both jobs at the same time. Either option costs the project two things it can least afford: time and money.

TABLE 12.1 Activity Precedence Table

Activity	Description	Duration	Predecessors	Member Assigned
A	Assign Bids	5 days	None	Tom
B	Document Awards	5 days	A	Jeff
C	Calculate Costs	5 days	A	Jeff
D	Select Winning Bid	1 day	B, C	Sue
E	Develop PR Campaign	4 days	D	Carol

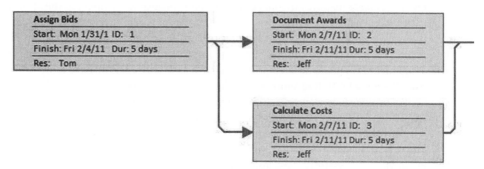

FIGURE 12.2 Sample Activity Network with Conflicts

---

*Microsoft Project 2010 identifies activities B and C as tasks 2 and 3, respectively.

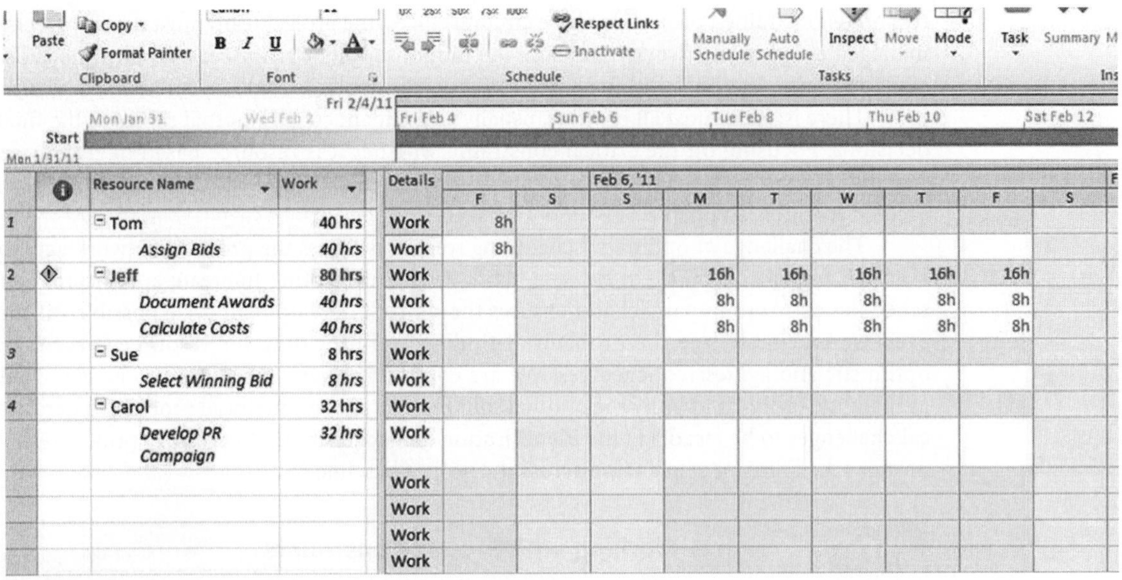

FIGURE 12.3 Resource-Loading Chart Demonstrating Overallocation

	Resource Name	Work	Details	F	S	S	M	T	W	T	F	S
1	Tom	40 hrs	Work	8h								
	Assign Bids	40 hrs	Work	8h								
2	Jeff	80 hrs	Work				16h	16h	16h	16h	16h	
	Document Awards	40 hrs	Work				8h	8h	8h	8h	8h	
	Calculate Costs	40 hrs	Work				8h	8h	8h	8h	8h	
3	Sue	8 hrs	Work									
	Select Winning Bid	8 hrs	Work									
4	Carol	32 hrs	Work									
	Develop PR Campaign	32 hrs	Work									
			Work									
			Work									
			Work									
			Work									

The best method for establishing the existence of resource conflicts across project activities uses *resource-loading charts* (described more fully in the next section) to analyze project resources against scheduled activities over the project's baseline schedule. Resource-loading charts enable the project team, scheduling the work, to check their logic in setting resource requirements for project activities. A simplified MS Project 2010 resource-loading chart highlighting the resource conflict found in Figure 12.2 is shown in Figure 12.3.

Note what has happened to Jeff's resource availability. The MS Project 2010 output file highlights the fact that for a five-day period, Jeff is expected to work 16 hours each day to accomplish activities B and C simultaneously. Because the schedule in Figure 12.2 did not pay sufficient attention to competing demands for his labor when the activity chart was created, the project team is now faced with the problem of having assigned his time on a grossly overallocated basis. Although simplified, this example is just one illustration of the complexity we add to project planning when we begin to couple activity network scheduling with resource allocation.

12.2 RESOURCE LOADING

The concept of **resource loading** refers to the amount of individual resources that a schedule requires during specific time periods.[5] We can *load,* or place on a detailed schedule, resources with regard to specific tasks or the overall project. As a rule of thumb, however, it is generally beneficial to do both: to create an overall project resource-loading table as well as identify the resource needs for each individual task. In practical terms, resource loading attempts to assign the appropriate resource, to the appropriate degree or amount, to each project activity.

If we correlate the simple example, shown in somewhat greater detail in Figure 12.4, with the original project Gantt chart, we can see that these important first steps are incomplete until the subsequent resource assignments are made for each project activity. In Figure 12.4, we have temporarily fixed the problem of Jeff's overallocation by adding another resource, Bob, who has become responsible for activity C, Calculate Costs.

Once we have developed the Work Breakdown Structure and activity networks, the actual mechanics of creating a *resource-loading form* (sometimes referred to as a *resource usage calendar*) is relatively simple. All personnel are identified and their responsibility for each task is assigned. Further, we know how many hours on a per-week basis each person is available. Again, using Microsoft Project's 2010 template, we can create the resource usage table to reflect each of these pieces of information (see Figure 12.5).

Information in the **resource usage table** shown in Figure 12.5 includes the project team members, the tasks to which they have been assigned, and the time each activity is expected to take across the schedule baseline. In this example, we have now reallocated the personnel to cover each task, thereby eliminating the

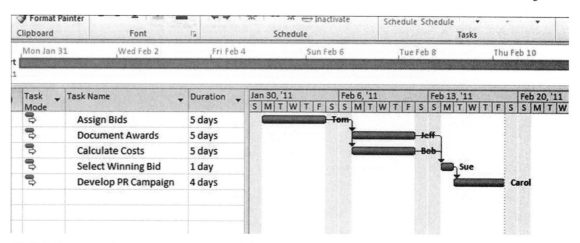

FIGURE 12.4   Sample Project Activity Network and Gantt Charts

Task Mode	Task Name	Duration
	Assign Bids	5 days
	Document Awards	5 days
	Calculate Costs	5 days
	Select Winning Bid	1 day
	Develop PR Campaign	4 days

Resource Name	Work	Details	S	T	T	S	F	W
⊟ Tom	40 hrs	Work	24h	16h				
Assign Bids	*40 hrs*	Work	24h	16h				
⊟ Jeff	40 hrs	Work		8h	32h			
Document Awards	*40 hrs*	Work		8h	32h			
⊟ Sue	8 hrs	Work				8h		
Select Winning Bid	*8 hrs*	Work				8h		
⊟ Carol	32 hrs	Work				24h	8h	
Develop PR Campaign	*32 hrs*	Work				24h	8h	
⊟ Bob	40 hrs	Work		8h	32h			
Calculate Costs	*40 hrs*	Work		8h	32h			
		Work						
		Work						

FIGURE 12.5   Resource Usage Table

overallocation problem originally uncovered in Figure 12.3. Team members are assigned to the project on a full-time (40 hours/week) basis, and the loading of their time commitments across these project activities corresponds to the project activity network, providing, in essence, a time-phased view of the resource-loading table.

The resource usage table also can provide warning signs of overallocation of project resources. For example, suppose that Jeff was again allocated to both activities B and C, as in the example from earlier in this chapter. Simply viewing the original project schedule gives no indication of this resource overallocation. When we generate the resource usage table, however, we discover the truth (see Figure 12.6). In this example, Jeff is currently scheduled to work 64 hours over a one-week period (the week of January 11)—clearly a much-too-optimistic scenario regarding his capacity for work!

The benefit of the resource-loading process is clear; it serves as a "reality check" on the project team's original schedule. When the schedule is subjected to resource loading, the team quickly becomes aware of misallocation of personnel, overallocation of team members, and, in some cases, lack of needed resources. Hence, the resource-loading process may point to obvious flaws in the original project WBS and schedule. How best to respond to resource-loading problems and other project constraints is the next question the project manager and team and need to consider.

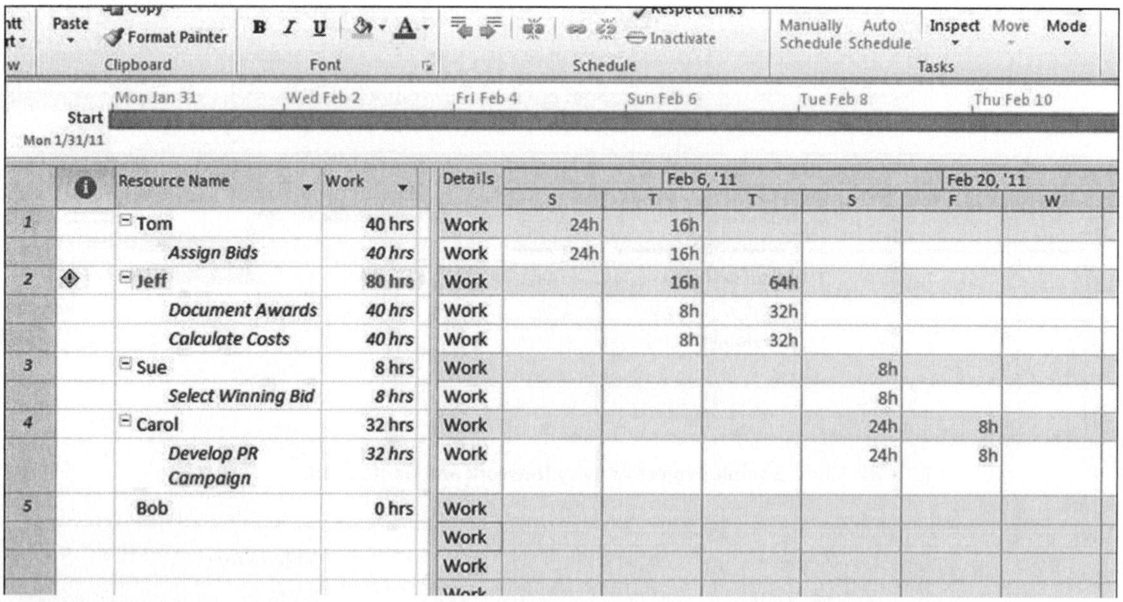

FIGURE 12.6 Example of Resource Usage Table with Overallocation

12.3 RESOURCE LEVELING

Resource leveling is the process that addresses the complex challenges of project constraints. With resource leveling we are required to develop procedures that minimize the effects of resource demands across the project's life cycle. Resource leveling, sometimes referred to as resource **smoothing**, has two objectives:

1. To determine the resource requirements so that they will be available at the right time
2. To allow each activity to be scheduled with the smoothest possible transition across resource usage levels

Resource leveling is useful because it allows us to create a profile of the resource requirements for project activities across the life cycle. Further, we seek to minimize fluctuations from period to period across the project. The farther in advance that we are able to anticipate and plan for resource needs, the easier it becomes to manage the natural flow from activity to activity in the project, with no downtime, while we begin searching for the resources to continue with project tasks. The key challenge consists of making prioritization decisions that assign the right amount of resources to the right activities at the right time.

Because resource management is typically a multivariate, combinatorial problem (i.e., one that is characterized by multiple solutions often involving literally dozens, hundreds, or even thousands of activity variables), the mathematically optimal solution may be difficult or infeasible to find due to the time required to solve all possible equation options. Hence, a more common approach to analyzing resource-leveling problems is to apply some **leveling heuristics**, or simplified rules of thumb, when making decisions among resource-leveling alternatives.[6]

Some simple heuristics for prioritizing resource allocation include applying resources to:

1. *Activities with the smallest amount of slack.* The decision rule is to select for resource priority those activities with the smallest amount of slack time. Some have argued that this decision rule is the best for making priority decisions, resulting in the smallest schedule slippage to the overall project.[7]
2. *Activities with the smallest duration.* Tasks are ordered from smallest duration to largest, and resources are prioritized accordingly.
3. *Activities with the lowest activity identification number.* (e.g., those that start earliest in the WBS). This heuristic suggests that, when in doubt, it is better to apply resources to earlier tasks first.
4. *Activities with the most successor tasks.* We select for resource priority those tasks that have the most tasks following behind them.
5. *Activities requiring the most resources.* It is common to first apply resources to those activities requiring the most support, and then analyze the remaining tasks based on the availability of additional resources.

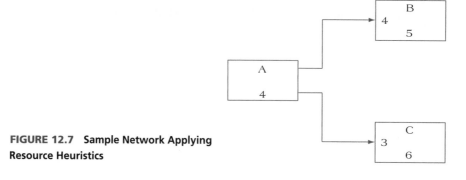

FIGURE 12.7 Sample Network Applying
Resource Heuristics

Using these heuristics, let us consider a simple example and the method we would use to select the activities that get first "rights" to the resource pool. Suppose that a project has two activities (see Figure 12.7) scheduled that require the same resource at the same time. In deciding which activity should receive first priority for available resources, we can follow the heuristic logic used in the first decision rule and examine tasks B and C first in terms of their respective amount of slack time. In this case, activity C, with three days of slack, would be the best choice for prioritizing the resource. However, suppose that activities B and C both had three days of slack. Then, according to the heuristic model, we could move to the second decision rule and award the first priority to activity B. Why? Because activity B has a scheduled duration of five days as opposed to activity C's duration of six days. In the unlikely event that we discovered that a tie remained between activities B and C following the first two heuristics, we could apply the third heuristic and simply assign the resource to the task with the lowest identification number (in this case, activity B). As we will see, the implication of how resources are prioritized is significant, as it has a "ripple effect" on subsequent resource leveling throughout the remainder of the activity network.

EXAMPLE 12.2   An In-Depth Look at Resource Leveling

A more in-depth resource-leveling example illustrates the challenge project teams face when applying resource leveling to a constructed activity network. Suppose we constructed a project network diagram based on the information in Table 12.2. Using the process suggested in Chapter 9, we can also derive the early start (ES), late start (LS), early finish (EF), late finish (LF), and subsequent activity slack for each task in the network. Table 12.3 presents a complete set of data.

TABLE 12.2 Activities, Durations, and Predecessors for Sample Project

Activity	Duration	Predecessors
A	5	—
B	4	A
C	5	A
D	6	A
E	6	B
F	6	C
G	4	D
H	7	E, F
I	5	G
J	3	G
K	5	H, I, J

TABLE 12.3 Fully Developed Task Table for Sample Project

Activity	Duration	ES	EF	LS	LF	Slack
A	5	0	5	0	5	—
B	4	5	9	6	10	1
C	5	5	10	5	10	—
D	6	5	11	8	14	3
E	6	9	15	10	16	1
F	6	10	16	10	16	—
G	4	11	15	14	18	3
H	7	16	23	16	23	—
I	5	15	20	18	23	3
J	3	15	18	20	23	5
K	5	23	28	23	28	—

Table 12.3 identifies the network critical path as A – C – F – H – K. Figure 12.8 presents a simplified project Gantt chart that corresponds to the activities listed in the table, their durations, and their predecessors.

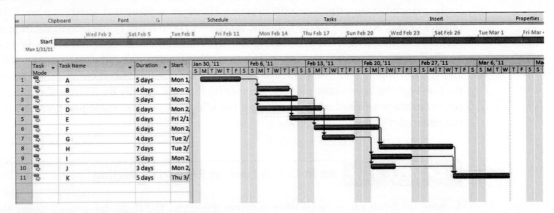

FIGURE 12.8   Gantt Chart for Sample Project

This chart is based on the activity network shown in Figure 12.9. A more completely represented activity network is given in Figure 12.10, listing the ES, LS, EF, and LF for each activity. It is now possible to create a resource-loading table by combining the information we have in Figures 12.8 and 12.10 with one additional factor: the resources required to complete each project activity.

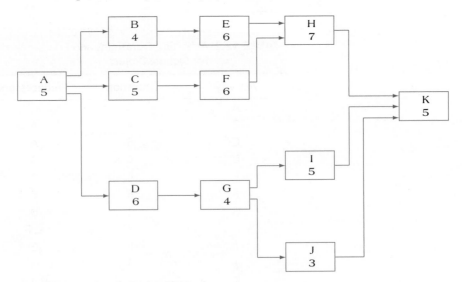

FIGURE 12.9   Sample Project Network

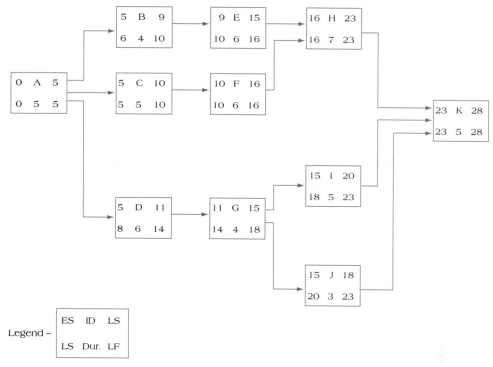

FIGURE 12.10 Sample Project Network with Early and Late Start Indicated

Naturally, there is a direct relationship between the resources we can apply to a task and its expected time to completion. For example, suppose that a task requiring one person working 40 hours per week is estimated to take two weeks (or 80 hours) to complete. Generally, we can modify the duration estimate, given adjustments to the projected resources available to work on the task. For example, if we can now assign two people to work full-time (40 hours) on the task, the new duration for the activity will be one week. Although the task will still require 80 hours of work to complete, with two full-time resources assigned, that 80 hours can actually be finished in one week of the project's scheduled baseline.

Table 12.4 identifies the activities, their durations, total activity float (or slack), and most importantly, the number of hours per week that we can assign resources to the tasks. The time value is less than full-time

TABLE 12.4 Activity Float and Resource Needs for the Sample Network

Activity	Duration	Total Float	Resource Hours Needed per Week	Total Resource Hours Required
A	5	0	6	30
B	4	1	2	8
C	5	0	4	20
D	6	3	3	18
E	6	1	3	18
F	6	0	2	12
G	4	3	4	16
H	7	0	3	21
I	5	3	4	20
J	3	5	2	6
K	5	0	5	25
			Total	194

to illustrate a typical problem: Because of other commitments, project team members may be assigned to the project on a basis that is less than full-time. So, for example, activity A is projected to take five days, given resources assigned to it at six hours per day (or a total estimated task duration of 30 hours). Activity F is projected to take six days to complete with two hours per day assigned to it. The total resources required to complete this project within the projected time frame are 194 hours. Once this information is inserted into the project, it is now possible to follow a series of steps aimed at resource-leveling the activity network. These steps will be considered in turn.

Step One: Develop the Resource-Loading Table

The **resource-loading table** is created through identifying the project activities and their resources required to completion and applying this information to the project schedule baseline. In its simplest form, the resource-loading table can be profiled to resemble a histogram, identifying hours of resource requirements across the project's life (see Figure 12.11). However, a more comprehensive resource-loading table is developed in Figure 12.12. It assumes the project begins on January 1 and the activities follow in the order identified through the project Gantt chart. Note that the resources required per day for each activity are listed against the days of the project baseline schedule when they will be needed. These total resource hours are then summed along the bottom of the table to identify the overall resource profile for the project. Note further that resource requirements tend to move up and down across the baseline, peaking at a total of 10 hours of resources required on day 10 (January 12).

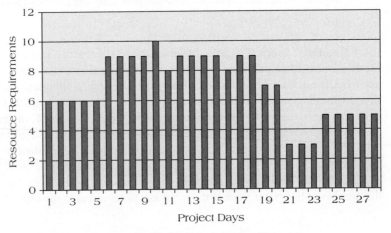

FIGURE 12.11   Resource Profile for Sample Project Network

																								January					February		
Activity	1	2	3	4	5	8	9	10	11	12	15	16	17	18	19	22	23	24	25	26	29	30	31	1	2	5	6	7
A	6	6	6	6	6																							
B						2	2	2	2																			
C						4	4	4	4	4																		
D						3	3	3	3	3	3																	
E										3	3	3	3	3	3													
F											2	2	2	2	2	2												
G												4	4	4	4													
H																	3	3	3	3	3	3	3					
I																4	4	4	4	4								
J																2	2	2										
K																								5	5	5	5	5
Total	6	6	6	6	6	9	9	9	9	10	8	9	9	9	9	8	9	9	7	7	3	3	3	5	5	5	5	5

FIGURE 12.12   Resource-Loading Table for Sample Network

		January				February
Activity	1 2 3 4 5	8 9 10 11 12	15 16 17 18 19	22 23 24 25 26	29 30 31 1 2	5 6 7
A	6 6 6 6 6⌋					
B		2 2 2 2 ⌋				
C		4 4 4 4 4⌋				
D		3 3 3 3 3	3 ⌋			
E		3	3 3 3 3 3	⌋		
F			2 2 2 2 2	2⌋		
G			4 4 4 4	⌋		
H				3 3 3 3	3 3 3⌋	
I				4 4 4 4 4	⌋	
J				2 2 2	⌋	
K					5 5	5 5 5⌋
Total	6 6 6 6	9 9 9 9 10	8 9 9 9 9	8 9 9 7 7	3 3 3 5 5	5 5 5

(⌋ = Late Finish)

FIGURE 12.13 Resource-Loading Table for Sample Network When Activity Float Is Included

The advantage of developing a detailed resource profile is that it provides a useful visual demonstration of the projected resource requirements needed across the entire project baseline. It is possible to use this resource profile in conjunction with the resource-loading table to develop a strategy for optimal resource leveling.

Step Two: Determine Activity Late Finish Dates

The next step in the resource-leveling process consists of applying the additional information regarding activity slack and late finish dates to the resource-loading table (see Table 12.3). This modified table is shown in Figure 12.13. Note that in this figure, we can identify the activities with slack time and those that are critical (no slack time). The late finish dates for those activities with slack are included and are represented as brackets. Hence, activities B, D, E, G, I, and J are shown with late finish dates corresponding to the slack time associated with each task, while the late finish for the activities along the critical path (A – C – F – H – K) is identical to the activities' early finish dates.

Step Three: Identify Resource Overallocation

After the resource-loading table is completed and all activity late finish dates are embedded, the process of actual resource leveling can begin with an examination of the resource profile for the project. What we are looking for here are any points across the project baseline at which resources have been allocated beyond the maximum resource level available. For example, in Figure 12.13, note that the total resources needed (the summation along the bottom row) reveals the maximum needed for any day of the project falls on January 12, when tasks requiring 10 resource units are scheduled. The question project managers need to consider is whether this resource profile is acceptable or if it indicates trouble, due to an allocation of resources that will not be available. If, for example, the project is budgeted for up to 10 resource units per day, then this resource profile is acceptable. On the other hand, if resources are limited to some figure below the maximum found in the project's resource profile, the project has an overallocation problem that must be addressed and corrected.

Certainly, at this point, the best-case scenario is to discover that resources have been allocated at or below the maximum across the project baseline. Given the nature of both time and resource project constraints, however, it is much more common to find situations of resource conflicts that require leveling. Suppose that in our sample project the maximum number of resource units available on any day is nine. We have already determined that on January 12, the project is scheduled to require 10 units, representing an overallocation. The discovery of overallocations triggers the next step in the resource-leveling process, in which we correct the schedule to eliminate resource conflict.

Step Four: Level the Resource-Loading Table

Once a determination has been made that the project baseline includes overallocated resources, an iterative process begins in which the resource-loading table is reconfigured to eliminate the resource contention points. The most important point to remember in resource leveling is that a *ripple effect* commonly occurs when we begin to rework the resource schedule to eliminate the sources of resource conflict. This ripple effect will become evident as we work through the steps necessary to level the sample project.

PHASE ONE Using Figure 12.13, examine the conflict point, January 12, for the tasks that require 10 resource units. Tasks C, D, and E are all scheduled on this day and have resource unit commitments of 4, 3, and 3 hours respectively. Therefore, the first phase in resource leveling consists of identifying the relevant activities to determine which are likely candidates for modification. Next, which activity should be adjusted? Using the priority heuristic mentioned previously, first examine the activities to see which are critical and which have some slack time associated with them. From developing the network, we know that activity C is on the critical path. Therefore, avoid reconfiguring this task if possible because any adjustment of its duration will adversely affect the overall project schedule. Eliminating activity C leaves us the choice of adjusting either activity D or activity E.

PHASE TWO Select the activity to be reconfigured. Both activities D and E have slack time associated with them. Activity D has three days of slack and activity E has one day. According to the rule of thumb, we might decide to leave activity E alone because it has the least amount of slack time. In this example, however, this option would lead to "splitting" activity D; that is, we would begin activity D on January 8, stop on the 12th, and then finish the last two days of work on January 15 and 16. Simply representing this option, we see in Figure 12.14, which shows the Gantt chart for our project, that the splitting process complicates our scheduling process to some degree. Note further that the splitting does not lengthen the overall project baseline, however; with the three days of slack associated with this task, lagging the activity one day through splitting it does not adversely affect the final delivery date.

For simplicity's sake, then, we will avoid the decision to split activity D for the time being, choosing the alternative option of adjusting the schedule for activity E. This option is also viable in that it does not violate the schedule baseline (there is slack time associated with this activity).

Figure 12.15 shows the first adjustment to the original resource-loading table. The three resource units assigned to activity E on January 12 are scratched and added back in at the end of the activity, thereby using up the one day of project slack for that activity. The readjusted resource-loading table now shows that January 12 no longer has a resource conflict, because the baseline date shows a total of seven resource units.

PHASE THREE After making adjustments to smooth out resource conflicts, reexamine the remainder of the resource table for *new* resource conflicts. Remember that adjusting the table can cause ripple effects in that these adjustments may disrupt the table in other places. This exact effect has occurred in this example. Note that under the adjusted table (see Figure 12.15), January 12 no longer shows a resource conflict; however, the act of lagging activity E by one day would create a conflict on January 22, in which 11 resource units would be scheduled. As a result, it is necessary to go through the second-phase process once more to eliminate the latest resource conflict.

Here again, the candidates for adjustment are all project tasks that are active on January 22, including activities E, F, I, and J. Clearly, activities E and F should, if possible, be eliminated as first choices given their

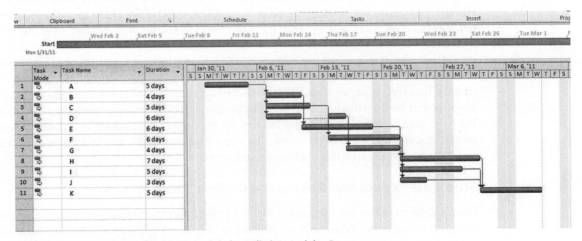

FIGURE 12.14 Reconfiguring the Schedule by Splitting Activity D

Activity	1	2	3	4	5	8	9	10	11	12	15	16	17	18	19	22	23	24	25	26	29	30	31	1	2	5	6	7
																	January								February			
A	6	6	6	6	6⌋																							
B						2	2	2	2	⌋																		
C						4	4	4	4	4⌋																		
D						3	3	3	3	3	3			⌋														
E										3̶	3	3	3	3	3	3⌋												
F											2	2	2	2	2	2⌋												
G												4	4	4	4			⌋										
H																3	3	3	3		3	3	3⌋					
I																4	4	4	4	4				⌋				
J																2̶	2	2	2					⌋				
K																								5	5	5	5	5⌋
Total	6	6	6	6	6	9	9	9	9	7	8	9	9	9	9	9	9	9	9	7	3	3	3	5	5	5	5	5

(⌋ = Late Finish)

FIGURE 12.15 Resource-Leveling the Network Table

lack of any slack time (i.e., they both now reside on a critical path). Adjusting (lagging) one day for either of the alternatives, activities I and J, will reduce the resource requirement to a level below the threshold, suggesting that either of these activities may be used. The earlier heuristic suggested that priority be given to activities with less slack time, so in this example we will leave activity I alone and instead lag the start of activity J by one day. Note that the resource totals summed across the bottom of the table (See Figure 12.15) now show that all activities are set at or below the cutoff level of nine resource hours per day for the project, completing our task. Further, in this example, we were able to resource-level the project without adding additional dates to the project schedule or requiring additional resources; in effect, resource leveling in this example violated neither a resource-constrained nor a time-constrained restriction.

Suppose, however, that our project operated under more stringent resource constraints; for example, instead of a threshold of nine hours per day, what would be the practical effect of resource-leveling the project to conform to a limit of eight hours per day? The challenge to a project manager now is to reconfigure the resource-loading table in such a way that the basic tenet of resource constraint is not violated. In order to demonstrate the complexity of this process, for this example, we will break the decision process down into a series of discrete steps as we load each individual activity into the project baseline schedule (see Table 12.5).

TABLE 12.5 Steps in Resource Leveling

Step	Action
1	Assign Activity A to the resource table.
2	In selecting among Activities B, C, and D, employ the selection heuristic and prioritize C (critical activity) and then B (smallest amount of slack). Load C and B into the resource table. Delay Activity D.
3	On January 12, load Activity D. D had 3 days slack and is loaded four days late. Total delay for Activity D is 1 day.
4	On January 15, load Activities E and F (following completion of B and C). Prioritize F first (critical activity), and then add E. Both activities finish on January 22, so overall critical path schedule is not affected. Total project delay to date = 0.
5	Because of resource constraints, Activity G cannot begin until January 23. G had 3 days slack and is loaded five days late, finishing on January 26. Total delay for Activity G is 2 days.
6	Load Activity H on January 23, following completion of Activities E and F. H is completed on January 31, so overall critical path schedule is not affected. Total project delay to date = 0.
7	Because of resource constraints, Activity I cannot begin until January 29. I is loaded five days late. Total delay for Activity I is 2 days (new finish date = February 2).
8	Because of resource constraints, Activity J cannot begin until February 1. Even with slack time, J is delayed 3 days, completing on February 5.
9	Activity K cannot be loaded until completion of predecessors H, I, and J. K begins on February 6 and completes on February 12. Total project delay = 3 days.

January

Total Slack	Activity	1	2	3	4	5	8	9	10	11	12	15	16	17	18	19	22	23	24	25	26
0	A	[6	6	6	6	6															
1	B						[2	2	2	2	2										
0	C						[4	4	4	4	4										
−1	D						[				3	3	3	3	3	3					
0	E										[	3	3	3	3	3	3				
0	F											[2	2	2	2	2	2				
−2	G															[		4	4	4	4
	H																	[3	3	3	3
	I																	[			
	J																	[			
	K																				
	Total	6	6	6	6	6	6	6	6	6	7	8	8	8	8	8	5	7	7	7	7

February

Total Slack	Activity	29	30	31	1	2	5	6	7	8	9	12	13	14	15	16	17
	A																
	B																
	C																
	D																
	E																
	F																
	G																
0	H	3	3	3													
−2	I	4	4	4	4	4											
−3	J				2	2	2										
−3	K				[			5	5	5	5	5					
	Total	7	7	7	6	6	2	5	5	5	5	5					

[= Original activity early start time

FIGURE 12.16 Resource-Loading Table with Lowered Resource Constraints

Note the need, at times, to make sacrifices to the initial baseline schedule in order to maintain the nonviolation of the resource-loading limit.

Figure 12.16 pictures this resource-leveling example given in Table 12.5 with January and February stacked. As the steps in the table indicate, the determination of total project delay is not evident until all predecessor tasks have been loaded, resources leveled at the point each new activity is added to the table, and the overall project baseline schedule examined. Interestingly, note from this example that the project's schedule did not show a delay through the inclusion of 8 of the 11 activities (through activity H). However, once activity H was included in the resource table, it was necessary to delay the start of activity J in order to account for the project resource constraint. As a result, the project's baseline schedule was delayed through a combination of loss of project slack and the need to reassess the activity network in light of resource constraints. The overall effect of this iterative process was to delay the completion of the project by three days.

The extended example in this section illustrates one of the more difficult challenges that project managers face: *the need to balance concern for resources with concern for schedule.* In conforming to the new, restricted resource budget, which allows us to spend only up to eight resource units per day, the alternatives often revolve around making reasoned schedule trade-offs to account for limited resources. The project's basic schedule dictates that any changes to the availability of sufficient resources to support the activity network are going to involve lengthening the project's duration. Part of the reason for this circumstance, of course, lies in the fact that this example included a simplified project schedule with very little slack built into any of the project activities. As a result, major alterations to the project's resource base were bound to adversely affect the overall schedule.

In summary, the basic steps necessary to produce a resource-leveled project schedule include the following:

1. Create a project activity network diagram (see Figure 12.10).
2. From this diagram, create a table showing the resources required for each activity, the activity durations, and the total float available (see Table 12.4).
3. Develop a time-phased resource-loading table that shows the resources required to complete each activity, the activity early starts, and the late finish times (Figure 12.13).
4. Identify any resource conflicts and begin to "smooth" the loading table using one or more of the heuristics for prioritizing resource assignment across activities (Figure 12.15).
5. Repeat step 4 as often as necessary to eliminate the source of resource conflicts. Use your judgment to interpret and improve the loading features of the table. Consider alternative means to minimize schedule slippage; for example, use overtime during peak periods.

12.4 RESOURCE-LOADING CHARTS

Another way to create a visual diagram of the resource management problem is to employ resource-loading charts. **Resource-loading charts** are used to display the amount of resources required as a function of time on a graph. Typically, each activity's resource requirements are represented as a block (resource requirement over time) in the context of the project baseline schedule. Resource-loading charts have the advantage of offering an immediate visual reference point as we attempt to lay out the resources needed to support our project as well as smooth resource requirements over the project's life.

Here is an example to illustrate how resource-loading charts operate. Suppose our resource profile indicated a number of "highs" and "lows" across the project; that is, although the resource limit is set at eight hourly resource units per day, on a number of days our actual resources employed are far less than the total available. The simplified project network is shown in Figure 12.17 and summarized in Table 12.6, and the corresponding resource-loading chart is shown in Figure 12.18. The network lists the early start and finish dates for each activity, as well as the resources required for each task for each day of work.

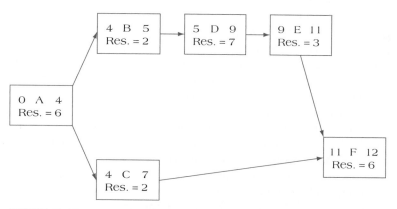

FIGURE 12.17 Sample Project Network

TABLE 12.6 Resource Staffing (Hourly Units) Required for Each Activity

Activity	Resource	Duration	Early Start	Slack	Late Finish
A	6	4	0	0	4
B	2	1	4	0	5
C	2	3	4	4	11
D	7	4	5	0	9
E	3	2	9	0	11
F	6	1	11	0	12

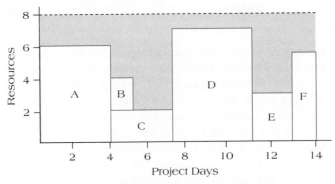

FIGURE 12.18 Resource-Loading Chart for Sample Project

In constructing a resource-loading chart that illustrates the time-limited nature of resource scheduling, there are six main steps to follow:[8]

1. Create the activity network diagram (see Figure 12.17).
2. Produce a table for each activity, the resource requirements, the duration, early start time, slack, and late finish time (see Table 12.6).
3. List the activities in order of increasing slack (or in order of latest finish time for activities with the same slack).
4. Draw an initial resource-loading chart with each activity scheduled at its earliest start time, building it up following the order shown in step 3. This process creates a loading chart with the most critical activities at the bottom and those with the greatest slack on the top.
5. Rearrange the activities within their slack to create a profile that is as level as possible within the guidelines of not changing the duration of activities or their dependence.
6. Use your judgment to interpret and improve activity leveling by moving activities with extra slack in order to "smooth" the resource chart across the project (see Figure 12.18).

Note that the early finish for the project, based on its critical path, is 12 days. However, when we factor in resource constraints, we find that it is impossible to complete all activities within their allocated time, causing the schedule to slip two days to a new early finish date of 14 days. Figure 12.18 illustrates the nature of our problem: Although the project allows for a total of eight hours per day for project activities, in reality, the manner in which the project network is set up relative to the resources needed to complete each task makes it impossible to use resources as efficiently as possible. In fact, during days 5 through 7, a total of only two resource hours is being used for each day.

A common procedure in resolving resource conflicts using resource-loading charts is to consider the possibility of splitting activities. As we noted earlier in the chapter, **splitting** an activity means interrupting the continuous stream of work on an activity at some midpoint in its development process and applying that resource to another activity for some period before returning the resource to complete the original task. Splitting can be a useful alternative technique for resource leveling provided there are no excessive costs associated with splitting the task. For example, large start-up or shutdown costs for some activities make splitting them an unattractive option.

To visually understand the task-splitting option, refer back to the Gantt chart created in Figure 12.14. Note that the decision there was made to split activity D in order to move the start of activity E forward. This decision was undertaken to make best use of constrained resources; in this case, there was sufficient slack in activity D to push off its completion and still not adversely affect the overall project schedule. In many circumstances, project teams seeking to make best use of available resources will willingly split tasks to improve schedule efficiency.

What would happen if we attempted to split activities, where possible, in order to make more efficient use of available resources? To find out, let us return to the activity network in Figure 12.17 and compare it with the resource-loading chart in Figure 12.18. Note that activity C takes three days to complete. Although activity C is not a predecessor for activity D, we cannot start D until C is completed, due to lack of available resources (day 5 would require nine resource hours when only eight are available). However, suppose we were to split activity C so that the task is started on day 4 and the balance is left until activity D is completed.

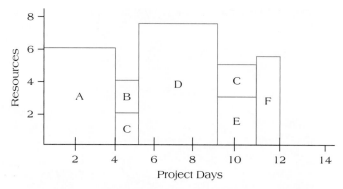

FIGURE 12.19   **Modified Resource-Loading Chart When Splitting Task C**

We can shift part of this activity because it contains 4 days of slack. Figure 12.19 illustrates this alternative. Note that two days of activity C are held until after D is completed, when they are performed at the same time as activity E. Because the final task, F, requires that both C and E be completed, we do not delay the start of activity F by splitting C. In fact, as Figure 12.19 demonstrates, splitting C actually makes more efficient use of available resources and, as a result, moves the completion date for the project two days earlier, from day 14 back to the originally scheduled day 12. This example illustrates the benefit that can sometimes be derived from using creative methods for better utilization of resources. In this case, splitting activity C, given its four days of slack time, enables the project to better employ its resources and regain the original critical path completion date.

BOX 12.1

PROJECT MANAGERS IN PRACTICE

Captain Kevin O'Donnell, U.S. Marine Corps

As a Marine officer, Captain Kevin O'Donnell has been working as a "project manager" for a number of years. As O'Donnell freely admits, at first glance, his duties do not seem to align with the traditional roles of project managers, and yet, the more we consider them, the more we can see that although the circumstances are unique, the principles and practices of project management remain applicable.

O'Donnell received a bachelor's degree in Criminal Justice from The Citadel, The Military College of South Carolina, and was commissioned as a second lieutenant in the U.S. Marine Corps. He is currently posted as a project officer and company executive officer at Marine Barracks, Washington, DC, and also has been posted to the presidential retreat, Camp David, as the guard officer and company executive officer.

As a second and first Lieutenant, O'Donnell served in the Second Battalion, 6th Marine Regiment, as a platoon commander and company executive officer while completing two combat deployments to Fallujah, Iraq. Although his duties have been far-ranging, including leading a number of missions and duty assignments, in O'Donnell's words, he prefers to focus on the way in which he has used project management in his career. Concepts such as a strategic vision, stakeholder management, scope of work, Work Breakdown Structure, tasks, time lines, and risk assessments are common to all projects, and the Marines use them daily during the planning of training, and while deployed and conducting combat operations.

As a platoon commander, O'Donnell was responsible for leading a force of 45 Marines during his first deployment to Iraq. They were tasked with conducting a variety of missions, and routinely engaged in vehicle and foot patrols, convoys, random house searches, and targeted raids on enemy personnel. O'Donnell notes:

> Take, for example, an intelligence-driven targeted raid on a known insurgent. This situation, viewed as a "project," required me as the platoon commander to analyze the area of operations and available intelligence, generate a five-paragraph order that contained a mission statement, tasking statements, scheme of maneuver for the operation, and logistic considerations (very similar to a project vision, scope of work, and Work Breakdown Structure). Additionally, I would need to coordinate with all adjacent and subordinate units that would be affected by the mission, and brief senior members of the chain of command (stakeholder management). I would also conduct

(continued)

FIGURE 12.20   Captain Kevin O'Donnell, USMC

an operational risk assessment, identifying issues that might arise during the execution of the mission, and enemy courses of action that may occur. Risks were prioritized, accepted, planned for, or mitigated. Finally, I would issue the order to my subordinate leaders in the platoon; they would, in turn, generate an order for their squad and issue it to them.

As the project manager for this mission, it was O'Donnell's responsibility to ensure that everyone on his team knew what they were going to do, why they were going to do it, how they were going to get it done, and what the expected outcome was to be.

Moreover, scheduling with important milestones was part of O'Donnell's duties. These time lines would be established during the plan, and more times than not, it was critical that they were met. Precombat checks and inspections would be conducted, along with rehearsals of the raid prior to beginning the mission. As the order to move was given, the platoon would step out of friendly lines and begin to patrol to the objective site. Upon reaching the objective, each subordinate unit (a squad) led by their squad leader would begin to seamlessly perform their portion of the raid. O'Donnell notes that communication, coordination, and control are critical during these types of operations. Many lessons learned come from after-action reviews, and more importantly, others can learn from what they had done well or poorly.

O'Donnell further describes his project management duties:

During my second deployment to Iraq, I was charged with planning and executing a large-scale company operation called Operation Alljah. This operation encompassed a number of smaller missions, such as the raid example above. Additionally, it involved executing a nontraditional plan of action that had not been done before in the city of Fallujah. We partnered with the Iraqi Army and Fallujah Police to re-empower them, provide them with the required training and infrastructure needed to police and secure their own city, and ultimately transition the responsibility of this mission to them in order to provide the citizens of Fallujah with a safe and stable living environment. The mission encompassed just about every principle of project management. In addition to the ones identified above, this mission required stakeholder management and increased stakeholder involvement, building and leading multicultural teams, breaking down language and cultural barriers, change management throughout the organization, command and control, and to a degree, selling the concept, creating ownership, and achieving "buy-in" amongst the team and the citizens. Strategic vision, described through our commander's intent, was critical to this mission's success. Our ability to build, refine, and execute a solid plan of action, while meeting critical milestones and time lines, significantly impacted the successful execution of the mission.

The ability of my subordinate leaders, and adjacent units, to seamlessly integrate and interact with each other and with their Iraqi counterparts played a significant role in the success of the organization as a whole. We were forced to operate in a continually changing external environment, and our ability to effortlessly adapt and adjust our plan accordingly paid dividends to the mission's success. Throughout the execution of this mission, stakeholder requirements changed, mission parameters were adjusted, internal and external environment dynamics shifted, and personnel and team compositions were adjusted. However, at the end of it, through solid leadership at all levels of the chain of command, and fundamental execution of project management skills and principles, the mission was completed and dubbed a huge success. The city of Fallujah is now a self-secured and governed area of Iraq, and my battalion's actions there were utilized as the role model for pacifying and defeating the insurgency in other cities throughout Iraq.

Although O'Donnell's duties may not seem to be those of traditional project management, he is quick to point out that, in fact, the opposite is true. Carefully planned operations, defined objectives, clear strategies, and coordination and scheduling are all hallmarks of project management, and they form the critical processes for O'Donnell's duties commanding Marines in a hostile environment. "At the end of the day, regardless of industry, project management remains the same," O'Donnell concludes. "Understanding the difference between leadership and management is critical. Knowing your internal and external environments, along with how to plan, task and manage personnel, maintain a budget and time lines, have a clear understanding of your objectives, how you must meet customer and stakeholder requirements, and achieving desired results, are critical to any project manager's success."

12.5 MANAGING RESOURCES IN MULTIPROJECT ENVIRONMENTS

Most managers of projects eventually will be confronted with the problem of dealing with resource allocation across multiple projects. The main challenge is one of interdependency: Any resource allocation decisions made in one project are likely to have ramifications in other projects. What are some of the more common problems we find when faced with this sort of interdependency among projects? Some of the better known problems include inefficient use of resources, resource bottlenecks, ripple effects, and the heightened pressure on personnel to multitask.[9]

Any system used to resolve the complex problems with multiproject resource allocation has to consider the need, as much as possible, to minimize the negative effects of three key parameters: (1) schedule slippage, (2) resource utilization, and (3) in-process inventory.[10] Each of these parameters forms an important challenge across multiple projects.

Schedule Slippage

For many projects, schedule slippage can be more than simply the realization that the project will be late; in many industries, it can also result in serious financial penalties. It is not uncommon for companies to be charged thousands of dollars in penalty clauses for each day a project is delayed past the contracted delivery date. As a result, one important issue to consider when making decisions about resource allocation across multiple projects is their priority based on the impact of schedule slippage for each individual project.

Resource Utilization

The goal of all firms is to use their existing pool of resources as efficiently as possible. Adding resources companywide can be expensive and may not be necessary, depending upon the manner in which the present resources are employed. To illustrate this point, let us reconsider the example of a resource-loading chart, shown in Figure 12.21, applied to a firm's portfolio of projects rather than to just one project's activities. In this load chart, top management can assign up to eight resource units for each week of their project portfolio. Even using a splitting methodology to better employ these resources, there are still some clear points at which the portfolio is underutilizing available resources. For example, in week 5, only four resource units have been employed. The shaded area in the load chart (Figure 12.21) shows the additional available resources not employed in the current project. To maximize the resource utilization parameter, we would attempt to assign the available resources on other, concurrent projects, thereby improving the overall efficiency with which we use project resources.

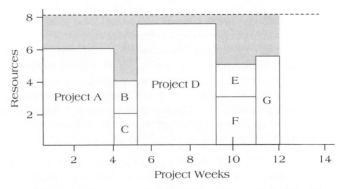

FIGURE 12.21 **Resource-Loading Chart Across Multiple Projects**

In-Process Inventory

The third standard for analyzing the optimal use of multiproject resources is to consider their impact on in-process inventory. **In-process inventory** represents the amount of work waiting to be completed but delayed due to unavailable resources. For example, an architectural firm may find several projects delayed because it only employs one checker responsible for final detailing of all blueprints. The projects stack up behind this resource bottleneck and represent the firm's in-process inventory of projects. Excessive in-process inventory is often caused by a lack of available resources and represents the kinds of trade-off decisions companies have to make in multiproject environments. Should we hire additional resources in order to reduce our in-process inventory? If this problem is only temporary, will hiring additional resources lead to inefficient resource allocation later on?

In effect, project organizations often have to strike an appropriate balance across the three parameters: schedule slippage, resource allocation, and in-process inventory. The steps necessary to improve one measure may have negative effects on one or more of the other standards. For example, steps to maximize resource allocation may provoke schedule slippage or increase in-process inventory. Any strategies we use to find a reasonable balance among these parameters must recognize the need to juggle multiple competing demands.

Resolving Resource Decisions in Multiproject Environments

The challenge of scheduling resources in multiproject environments has to do with the need to work on two levels to achieve maximum efficiency. First, with multiple projects, we have to make considered decisions regarding which projects should be assigned highest priority to resources. However, it is also vital to recognize that we are often required to schedule the activities of multiple projects simultaneously. Consider the resource-loading chart in Figure 12.21. On one level, we can see that this chart has scheduled projects A through G across 12 weeks. Project A will take the majority of resources for the first four weeks. However, during the fourth week, we have scheduled two projects at the same time (B and C). We must now work to balance their individual activity resource requirements so that both projects can be completed during the same time period. This figure illustrates the nature of the problem: On a larger level, resource allocation across multiple projects requires us to schedule projects in order to most efficiently use our resources. However, on another level, when projects compete for resources at the same time, we need to work to ensure that we can prioritize our resources across them to maximize their availability.

There are a number of potential methods for resolving resource allocation challenges in a multiproject setting, ranging from highly simplified heuristics to more complex mathematical programming options. The goal of each technique is to make the most efficient use of resources across multiple projects, often with competing requirements and priorities.

FIRST IN LINE The simplest rule of thumb for allocating resources is to prioritize on the basis of which projects entered the queue first. This "first come, first served" approach is easy to employ, because it simply follows the master project calendar. When resource allocation decisions need to be made, they can be done quickly by comparing the starting dates of the projects in question. Unfortunately, this technique ignores any other important information that may suggest the need to reorder the resource allocation process, such as strategic priorities, emergency or crisis situations, or projects with higher potential for commercial success. The first-in-line option can cause companies to underallocate resources to potentially high-payoff projects purely on the basis of when they were authorized, relative to earlier and less useful projects.

GREATEST RESOURCE DEMAND   This decision rule starts by determining which projects in the company's portfolio will pose the greatest demand on available resources. Those projects that require the most resources are first identified and their resources are set aside. Once they have been prioritized and resources allocated, the company reexamines the remaining pool of projects and selects those with the next highest resource demands until the available pool is exhausted. The logic of the greatest-resource-demand approach is to recognize that resource bottlenecks are likely to spring from unexpected peaks in resource needs relative to the number of projects under development. Consequently, this approach identifies these possible bottlenecks and uses them as the starting point for additional resource allocation.

GREATEST RESOURCE UTILIZATION   A variation of the greatest-resource-demand heuristic is to allocate resources in order to ensure the greatest use of project resources, or in order to minimize resource idle time. For example, an organization may seek to prioritize three projects, A, B, and C, across a resource pool made up of programmers, system analysts, and networking staff. Although project A requires the most resources for completion, it does not require any work from the system analyst resource pool. On the other hand, project B does not require as many total resources for completion, but it does need to utilize members of all three resource pool groups, that is, programmers, system analysts, and network specialists. As a result, the company may elect to prioritize project B first in order to ensure that all resources are being utilized to the greatest possible degree.

MINIMUM LATE FINISH TIME   This rule stipulates that resource priority should be assigned to activities and projects on the basis of activity finish dates. The earliest late finishers are scheduled first. Remember that "late finish" refers to the latest an activity can finish without compromising the overall project network by lengthening the critical path. The goal of this heuristic is to examine those project activities that have extra slack time as a result of later late finish dates and prioritize resources to the activities with minimal slack, that is, early late finish dates.

MATHEMATICAL PROGRAMMING   Math programming can be used to generate optimal solutions to resource-constrained problems in the multiproject setting, just as it can be employed for single projects. The common objectives that such models seek to maximize are:[11]

1. Minimize total development time for all projects
2. Minimize resource utilization across all projects
3. Minimize total lateness across all projects

These goals are subject to the resource constraints that characterize the nature of the problem, including: (1) limited resources, (2) precedence relationships among the activities and projects, (3) project and activity due dates, (4) opportunities for activity splitting, (5) concurrent versus nonconcurrent activity performance requirements, and (6) substitution of resources to assign to activities. Although mathematical programming is a worthy approach to resolving the constrained resource problem in either a single or multiproject setting, its use tends to be limited depending on the complexity of the problem, the large number of computational variables, and the time necessary to generate a sufficiently small set of options.

Resource management in projects is a problem that is frequently overlooked by novice project managers or in firms that have not devoted enough time to understanding the full nature of the project management challenge they face. As noted, it is common to develop project plans and schedules under the assumption of unlimited resources, as if the organization can always find the trained personnel and other resources necessary to support project activities no matter how committed they currently are to project work. This practice inevitably leads to schedule slippages and extra costs as the reality of resource availability overshadows the optimism of initial scheduling. In fact, resource management represents a serious step in creating reasonable and accurate estimates for project activity durations by comparing resources needed to undertake an activity to those available at any point in time. Further, resource management recognizes the nature of time/cost trade-offs that project managers are frequently forced to make. The extra resources necessary to accomplish tasks in a timely fashion do not come cheap, and their expense must be balanced against too aggressive project schedules that put a premium on time without paying attention to the budget impact they are likely to have.

Resource management is an iterative process that can be quite time-consuming. As we balance our activity network and overall schedule against available resources, the inevitable result will be the need to make adjustments to the network plan, rescheduling activities in such a way that they have minimal negative effect on the overall activity network and critical path. Resource leveling, or smoothing, is a procedure that seeks to make resource scheduling easier through minimizing the fluctuations in resource needs across the project by applying resources as uniformly as possible. Thus, resource management can make project schedules more accurate while allowing for optimal scheduling of project resources. Although this process can take time early in the project planning phase, it will pay huge dividends in the long run, as we create and manage project plans based on meaningful resource requirements and duration estimates rather than wishful thinking.

Summary

1. **Recognize the variety of constraints that can affect a project, making scheduling and planning difficult.** Effectively managing the resources for projects is a complex challenge. Managers must first recognize the wide variety of constraints that can adversely affect the efficient planning of scheduling of projects, including technical constraints, resource constraints, and physical constraints. Among the set of significant resource constraints are project personnel, materials, money, and equipment. A reasonable and thorough assessment of both the degree to which each of these resource types will be needed for the project and their availability is critical for supporting project schedules.

2. **Understand how to apply resource-loading techniques to project schedules to identify potential resource overallocation situations.** Resource loading is a process for assigning the resource requirements for each project activity across the baseline schedule. Effective resource loading ensures that the project team is capable of supporting the schedule by ensuring that all activities identified in the schedule have the necessary level of resources assigned to support their completion within the projected time estimates. We can profile the resource requirements for a project across its life cycle to proactively plan for the needed resources (both in terms of type of resource and amount required) at the point in the project when activities are scheduled to be accomplished. One effective, visual method for resource planning utilizes resource-leveling techniques to "block out" the activities, including required resource commitment levels, across the project's baseline schedule. Resource leveling offers a useful heuristic device for recognizing "peaks and valleys" in our resource commitment over time that can make resource scheduling problematic.

3. **Apply resource-leveling procedures to project activities over the baseline schedule using appropriate prioritization heuristics.** We employ "resource-smoothing" techniques in an effort to minimize the

problems associated with excessive fluctuations in the resource-loading diagram. Resource smoothing minimizes these fluctuations by rescheduling activities in order to make it easier to apply resources continuously over time. The first step in resource leveling consists of identifying the relevant activities to determine which are likely candidates for modification. The next question to resolve is: Which activity should be adjusted? Using the priority heuristic mentioned previously, we would first examine the activities to see which are critical and which have some slack time associated with them. The second step is to select the activity to be reconfigured. According to the rule of thumb, we first select the activities with the most slack time for reconfiguration.

4. **Follow the steps necessary to effectively smooth resource requirements across the project life cycle.** In constructing a resource-loading chart that illustrates the time-limited nature of resource scheduling, there are six main steps to follow: (1) Create the activity network diagram for the project; (2) produce a table for each activity that includes the resources required, the duration, and the early start time, slack, and late finish time; (3) list the activities in order of increasing slack (or in order of latest finish time for activities with the same slack); (4) draw an initial resource-loading chart with each activity scheduled at its earliest start time, building it up following the order shown in step 3, to create a loading chart with the most critical activities at the bottom and those with the greatest slack on the top; (5) rearrange the activities within their slack to create a profile that is as level as possible within the guidelines of not changing the duration of activities or their dependence; and (6) use judgment to interpret and improve activity leveling by moving activities with extra slack in order to "smooth" the resource chart across the project.

5. **Apply resource management within a multiproject environment.** Resource management is a far

more complex activity when we consider it within a multiproject environment, that is, when we try to schedule resources among multiple projects that are all competing for a limited supply of resources. In such circumstances, a number of options are available to project managers to find the optimal balance between multiple competing projects and finite resources. Among the decision heuristics we can employ in making the resource allocation decisions are those which choose on the basis of (1) which projects are first in line, (2) which projects have the greatest resource demand, (3) which projects will enable our firm to use the greatest resource utilization, (4) which will enable us to reach the goal of minimizing late finish times, and (5) through the use of mathematical programming.

Key Terms

In-Process Inventory
  (p. 420)
Leveling heuristics
  (p. 406)
Mixed-constraint project
  (p. 402)

Physical constraints
  (p. 402)
Resource-constrained
  project *(p. 402)*
Resource constraints
  (p. 401)

Resource leveling *(p. 406)*
Resource loading *(p. 404)*
Resource-loading charts
  (p. 415)
Resource-loading table
  (p. 410)

Resource usage table
  (p. 404)
Smoothing *(p. 406)*
Splitting activities *(p. 416)*
Time-constrained project
  (p. 402)

Solved Problem

1. Consider the resource-loading table shown here. Assume that we cannot schedule more than eight hours of work during any day of the month.

   a. Can you identify any days that involve resource conflicts?
   b. How would you reconfigure the loading table to resolve these resource conflicts?

June

Activity	1	2	3	4	5	8	9	10	11	12	15	16	17	18	19	22	23	24	25	26
A	4	4	4	4	4⌋															
B						4	4	4		⌋										
C						4	4	4	4	4⌋										
D						3	3	3	3	3	3			⌋						
E											3	3	3	3	3	⌋				
F											2	2	2	2	2	2⌋				
G												4	4	4	4					⌋

SOLUTION

a. According to the resource-loading table, the dates June 8, 9, and 10 are all overallocated (11 hours), as are June 16, 17, 18, and 19 (9 hours).

b. One solution for leveling the resource-loading table is by taking advantage of slack time available in activities D and G and moving these activities later in the schedule to correspond with their late finish dates (see the resource-loading table shown below).

June

Activity	1	2	3	4	5	8	9	10	11	12	15	16	17	18	19	22	23	24	25	26
A	4	4	4	4	4⌋															
B						4	4	4		⌋										
C						4	4	4	4	4⌋										
D						~~3~~	~~3~~	~~3~~	3	3	3	3	3	3	⌋					
E											3	3	3	3	3			⌋		
F											2	2	2	2	2	2⌋				
G												~~4~~	~~4~~	~~4~~	~~4~~	4	4	4	4	⌋
Total	4	4	4	4	4	8	8	8	7	7	8	8	8	8	5	6	4	4	4	

Discussion Questions

1. Consider a project to build a bridge over a river gorge. What are some of the resource constraints that would make this project challenging?
2. For many projects, the key resources to be managed are the project team personnel. Explain in what sense and how project team personnel are often the project's critical resource.
3. What is the philosophy underlying resource loading? What does it do for our project? Why is it a critical element in effectively managing the project plan?
4. It has been argued that a project schedule that has not been resource-leveled is useless. Do you agree or disagree with this statement? Why or why not?
5. Discuss the nature of "time/cost trade-offs" on projects. What does this concept imply for our project management practices?
6. When resource-leveling a project, a number of heuristics can help us prioritize those activities that should receive resources first. Explain how each of the following heuristics works and give an example:

   a. Activities with the smallest slack
   b. Activities with the smallest duration
   c. Activities with the lowest identification number
   d. Activities with the most successor tasks
   e. Activities requiring the most resources
7. Multitasking can have an important negative impact on your ability to resource-level a project. When team members are involved in multiple additional commitments, we must be careful not to assign their time too optimistically. In fact, it has been said: "Remember, 40 hours is not the same as one week's work." Comment on this idea. How does multitasking make it difficult to accurately resource-level a project?
8. Why is resource management significantly more difficult in a multiproject environment? What are some rules of thumb to help project managers better control resources across several simultaneous projects?

Problems

Consider a project with the following information:

Activity	Duration	Predecessors
A	3	—
B	5	A
C	7	A
D	3	B, C
E	5	B
F	4	D
G	2	C
H	5	E, F, G

Activity	Duration	ES	EF	LS	LF	Slack
A	3	0	3	0	3	—
B	5	3	8	5	10	2
C	7	3	10	3	10	—
D	3	10	13	10	13	—
E	5	8	13	12	17	4
F	4	13	17	13	17	—
G	2	10	12	15	17	5
H	5	17	22	17	22	—

Activity	Duration	Total Float	Resource Hours Needed per Week	Total Resources Required
A	3 weeks	—	6	18
B	5 weeks	2	4	20
C	7 weeks	—	4	28
D	3 weeks	—	6	18
E	5 weeks	4	2	10
F	4 weeks	—	4	16
G	2 weeks	5	3	6
H	5 weeks	—	6	30
			Total	146

1. Construct the project activity network using AON methodology.
2. Identify the critical path and other paths through the network.
3. Create a time-phased resource-loading table for this project, identifying the activity early start and late finish points.
4. Assume that there is a maximum of eight resource hours per week available for the project. Can you identify any weeks that have resource overcommitments?
5. Resource-level the loading table. Identify the activity that can be rescheduled and reconfigure the table to show this reallocation.

6. Consider the partial resource-loading chart shown below. Suppose that you can commit a maximum of 8 resource hours per day.
   a. What are the dates on which project resources are overallocated?
   b. How should the resource-loading table be reconfigured to correct for this overallocation?
   c. Now suppose that the maximum number of resource hours per day you can commit is reduced to six. How would you reconfigure the resource-loading table to adjust for this number? What would be the new project completion date?

Project Calendar Dates

June

Activity	1	2	3	4	5	8	9	10	11	12	15	16	17	18	19	22	23	24	25	26
A	6	6	6	6	6]															
B						2	2	2	2						]					
C						4	4	4	4	4]										
D						3	3	3	3	3	]									
E											4	4	4	4	4]					
F											2	2	2	2	2	2				]
G																	4	4	4	]
Total	6	6	6	6	6	9	9	9	9	7	6	6	6	6	6	2	4	4	4	

Case Study 12.1
The Problems of Multitasking

An eastern U.S. financial services company found itself way behind schedule and over budget on an important strategic program. Both the budget and schedule baselines had begun slipping almost from the beginning, and as the project progressed, the lags became severe enough to require the company to call in expert help in the form of a project management consulting firm. After investigating the organization's operations, the consulting firm determined that the primary source of problems both with this project in particular and the company's project management practices in general was a serious failure to accurately forecast resource requirements. In the words of one of the consultants, "Not enough full-time [human] resources had been dedicated to the program."

The biggest problem was the fact that too many of the project team members were working on two or more projects simultaneously—a clear example of multitasking. Unfortunately, the program's leaders developed their ambitious schedule without reflecting on the availability of resources to support the project milestones. With their excessive outside responsibilities, no one was willing to take direct ownership of their work on the program, people were juggling assignments, and everyone was getting farther behind in all the work. Again, in the words of the consultant, "Project issues would come up and there would be nobody there to handle them [in a timely fashion]." Those little issues, left unattended, eventually grew to become big problems. The schedule continued to lag, and employee morale began to bottom out.

Following their recognition of the problem, the first step made by the consultants was to get top management to renegotiate the work assignments with the project team. First, the core team members were freed from other responsibilities so they could devote their full-time attention to the program. Then, other support members of the project were released from multitasking duties and assigned to the project on a full-time or near full-time basis as well. The result, coupled with other suggested

(continued)

changes by the consultants, was to finally match up the project's schedule and activity duration estimates with a realistic understanding of resources needs and availability. In short, the program was put back on track because it was finally resource-leveled, particularly through creating full-time work assignments for the project team that accurately reflected the need to link resource management with scheduling.[12]

Questions

1. How does multitasking confuse the resource availability of project team personnel?

2. "In modern organizations, it is impossible to eliminate multitasking for the average employee." Do you agree or disagree with this statement? Why?

3. Because of the problems of multitasking, project managers must remember that there is a difference between an activity's duration and the project calendar. In other words, 40 hours of work on a project task is *not* the same thing as one week on the baseline schedule. Please comment on this concept. Why does multitasking "decouple" activity duration estimates from the project schedule?

Internet Exercises

1. Access www.fastcompany.com/magazine/87/project-management.html. What suggestions does the author offer for managing the pressures to multitask? The author suggests the need to "multiproject." What is her point about the idea of learning how to multiproject?

2. Search the Web for examples of projects that suffer from each of the following:
   a. Time constraints
   b. Resource constraints
   c. Mixed constraints

For each of these examples, cite evidence of the types of constraints you have identified. Is there evidence of how the project is working to minimize or resolve these constraints?

3. Access Web sites related to the Boston tunnel project known as the "Big Dig." Describe the problems that the project has had. How has resource management played a role in the severe delays and cost overruns associated with the project?

MS Project Exercises

Exercise 12.1

Refer to the activity network table shown below. Enter this information using MS Project to produce a Gantt chart. Assume that each resource has been assigned to the project activity on a full-time (8 hours/day or 40 hours/week) basis.

Activity	Duration	Predecessors	Resource Assigned
A. User survey	4	None	Gail Wilkins
B. Coding	12	A	Tom Hodges
C. Debug	5	B	Wilson Pitts
D. Design interface	6	A, C	Sue Ryan
E. Develop training	5	D	Reed Taylor

Exercise 12.2

sing the information from Exercise 12.1, produce a resource usage sheet that identifies the total number of hours and daily commitments of each project team member.

Exercise 12.3

Refer to the activity network table shown in Exercise 12.1. Suppose that we modified the original table slightly to show the following

predecessor relationships between tasks and resources assigned to perform these activities. Enter this information into MS Project to produce a Gantt chart. Assume that each resource has been assigned to the project activity on a full-time (8 hours/day or 40 hours/week) basis.

Activity	Duration	Predecessors	Resource Assigned
A. User survey	4	None	Gail Wilkins
B. Coding	12	A	Tom Hodges
C. Debug	5	A	Tom Hodges
D. Design interface	6	B, C	Sue Ryan
E. Develop training	5	D	Reed Taylor

a. Using the Resource Usage view, can you determine any warning signs that some member of the project team has been overassigned?

b. Click on the Task Usage view to determine the specific days when there is a conflict in the resource assignment schedule.

Exercise 12.4

Using the information provided in Exercise 12.3, how might you resource-level this network to remove the conflicts? Show how you would resource-level the network. From a schedule perspective, what is the new duration of the project?

PMP Certification Sample Questions

1. The project manager identifies 20 tasks needed to complete her project. She has four project team members available to assign to these activities. The process of assigning personnel to project activities is known as:
   a. Resource leveling
   b. Resource loading
   c. Finding the critical path
   d. Creating a Work Breakdown Structure (WBS)

2. The correct definition of resource leveling is:
   a. A graph that displays the resources used over time on a project
   b. The process of applying resources to a project's activities
   c. The process of creating a consistent (level) workload for the resources on the project, driven by resource constraints
   d. A project schedule whose start and finish dates reflect expected resource availability

3. Project resource constraints can involve any of the following examples:
   a. Poorly trained workers
   b. Lack of available materials for construction
   c. Environmental or physical constraints of the project site itself
   d. All of the above would be considered examples of project resource constraints

4. When adopting resource-leveling heuristics, which of the following are relevant decision rules?
   a. The activities with the least slack time should have resources allocated to them first
   b. The activities with the longest duration are the best candidates for receiving extra resources
   c. Activities with the fewest successor tasks should have resource priority
   d. Activities with the highest WBS identification numbers are the first to receive available resources

5. One of the benefits of resource-loading charts is that they:
   a. Represent a method for finding available activity slack
   b. Graphically display the amount of resources required as a function of time
   c. Help resolve resource conflicts in multiproject settings
   d. All of the above are benefits of using resource-loading charts

Answers: **1.** b—The act of assigning personnel to specific project activities is usually referred to as resource loading; **2.** c—Resource leveling involves smoothing, or creating consistent workloads across the project schedule for the available resources; **3.** d—Project resources can include people, physical conditions, and material resources; therefore, all of the examples cited represent project resource constraints; **4.** a—As a useful resource-leveling heuristic, the activities with the least slack time should have resources allocated to them first; **5.** b—Resource-loading charts are a graphic means of identifying resource requirements as a function of the project's duration; they can help visually identify overloads or inefficient undercommitment of resources.

INTEGRATED PROJECT

Managing Your Project's Resources

You have an important task here. Now that you have created a network plan, including a schedule for your project, it is vital to resource-level the plan. Develop a resource-loading chart for your project. As you do this, keep in mind the budget you created for your plan and the personnel you have selected for the project team. Your resource-leveling procedure must be congruent with the project schedule (as much as possible) while maintaining your commitment to the use of the project resources you are intending to employ.

Remember that the key to doing this task efficiently lies in being able to maximize the use of project resources while having a minimally disruptive effect on your initial project schedule. As a result, it may be necessary to engage in several iterations of the resource-leveling process as you begin to shift noncritical tasks to later dates in order to maximize the use of personnel without disrupting the delivery date for the project. For simplicity's sake, you may assume that your resources for the project are committed to you at 100% of their work time. In other words, each resource is capable of working 40 hours each week on this project.

Create the resource-leveling table. Be sure to include the schedule baseline along the horizontal axis. What was your initial baseline? How did resource-leveling your project affect the baseline? Is the new projected completion date later than the original date? If so, by how much?

Notes

1. Bowman, Z. (2010). "Nissan Leaf owners have rapid response system lying in wait," www.autoblog.com/2010/11/24/nissan-leaf-owners-have-rapid-response-system-lying-in-wait/; Cole, J. (2010). "Best car to buy in 2011? Nissan LEAF according to green car reports," http://nissan-leaf.net/2010/11/20/best-car-to-buy-in-2011-nissan-leaf-according-to-green-car-reports/; Ramsey, M. (2010, November 23). "Nissan Leaf claims 99 MPG," *Wall Street Journal*, p. B8; Voelker, J. (2010). "GM confirms, yes, we're losing money on every Volt we build," www.greencarreports.com/blog/1052107_gm-confirms-yes-were-losing-money-on-every-volt-we-build; Welsh, J. (2010, November 24). "Nissan Leaf gets 99-MPG rating from EPA, Volt still waiting," *Wall Street Journal*, http://blogs.wsj.com/drivers-seat/2010/11/24/nissan-leaf-gets-99-mpg-rating-from-epa-volt-still-waiting/.

2. Dumaine, B. (1986, September 1). "The $2.2 billion nuclear fiasco," *Fortune*, 114: 14–22.

3. Raz, T., and Marshall, B. (1996). "Effect of resource constraints on float calculation in project networks," *International Journal of Project Management*, 14(4): 241–48.

4. Levene, H. (1994, April). "Resource leveling and roulette: Games of chance—Part 1," *PMNetwork*, 7; Levene, H. (1994, July). "Resource leveling and roulette: Games of chance—Part 2," *PMNetwork*, 7; Gordon, J., and Tulip, A. (1997). "Resource scheduling," *International Journal of Project Management*, 15: 359–70; MacLeod, K., and Petersen, P. (1996). "Estimating the tradeoff between resource allocation and probability of on-time completion in project management," *Project Management Journal*, 27(1): 26–33.

5. Meredith, J. R., and Mantel, Jr., S. J. (2003). *Project Management: A Managerial Approach*, 5th ed. New York: Wiley and Sons.

6. Fendley, L. G. (1968, October). "Towards the development of a complete multiproject scheduling system," *Journal of Industrial Engineering*, 19, 505–15; McCray, G. E., Purvis, R. L., and McCray, C. G. (2002). "Project management under uncertainty: The impact of heuristics and biases," *Project Management Journal*, 33(1): 49–57; Morse, L. C., McIntosh, J. O., and Whitehouse, G. E. (1996). "Using combinations of heuristics to schedule activities of constrained multiple resource projects," *Project Management Journal*, 27(1): 34–40; Woodworth, B. M., and Willie, C. J. (1975). "A heuristic algorithm for resource leveling in multiproject, multiresource scheduling," *Decision Sciences*, 6: 525–40; Boctor, F. F. (1990). "Some efficient multi-heuristic procedures for resource-constrained project scheduling," *European Journal of Operations Research*, 49: 3–13.

7. Fendley, L. G. (1968), as cited.

8. Field, M., and Keller, L. (1998). *Project Management*. London: The Open University; Woodworth, B. M., and Shanahan, S. (1988). "Identifying the critical sequence in a resource-constrained project," *International Journal of Project Management*, 6(2): 89–96; Talbot, B. F., and Patterson, J. H. (1979). "Optimal models for scheduling under resource constraints," *Project Management Quarterly*, 10(4), 26–33.

9. Gray, C. F., and Larson, E. W. (2003). *Project Management*, 2nd ed. Burr Ridge, IL: McGraw-Hill.

10. Meredith, J. R., and Mantel, Jr., S. J. (2003), as cited.

11. Meredith, J. R., and Mantel, Jr., S. J. (2003), as cited.

12. Weaver, P. (2002). "Vanquishing PM nightmares," *PMNetwork*, 16(1): 40–44.

Project Evaluation and Control

Chapter Outline

Chapter Objectives

After completing this chapter, you will be able to:

1. Understand the nature of the control cycle and four key steps in a general project control model.

2. Recognize the strengths and weaknesses of common project evaluation and control methods.

3. Understand how Earned Value Management can assist project tracking and evaluation.

4. Use Earned Value Management for project portfolio analysis.

5. Understand behavioral concepts and other human issues in evaluation and control.

6. From Appendix 31.1: Understand the advantages of Earned Schedule methods for determining project schedule variance, schedule performance index, and estimates to completion.

PROJECT MANAGEMENT BODY OF KNOWLEDGE CORE CONCEPTS COVERED
IN THIS CHAPTER

1. Control Schedule (PMBoK sec. 6.6)
2. Control Costs (PMBoK sec. 7.3)
3. Earned Value System (PMBoK sec. 7.3.2)

PROJECT PROFILE

Case: New Zealand's Te Apiti Wind Farm—Success under Pressure

In the modern era's search for alternative energy sources, one of the most popular in recent years is harnessing the use of wind power. Wind energy generation can be an important means for minimizing the use of fossil fuels in generating electricity. The government of New Zealand has been working diligently over the past decade to expand their commitment to wind energy, an obvious source of power in a country with extensive natural beauty but without local sources of more well-known energy sources like coal or oil. Since 2000, New Zealand has developed 12 wind farms with a combined capacity of nearly 500 megawatts and able to generate 4% of the country's current power needs.

Perhaps the most impressive wind farm project was New Zealand's first effort to supply power to the national grid: the Te Apiti wind farm, located in the southern region of the north island. The setting for Te Apiti is in the Manawatu Gorge, an exceptional location in that the gorge acts as a natural wind tunnel, creating consistent high wind speeds. Unfortunately, the advantages of the location were also a major constraint on the project: The site is in a remote location, surrounded by privately held lands and with limited access into the construction zone.

When the project began in November 2003, the first steps involved constructing more than 20 kilometers of roadways into the Manawatu Gorge and laying more than 40 kilometers of underground cabling. The terrain itself is riddled with gullies, streams, steep drop-offs, and unstable soil. All wind farm equipment, including 55 turbines, material to construct the towers, and wind blades, had to be transported along a narrow and difficult track into the interior construction site. Each tower was designed to be about 220 feet high and to house

Picade LLC / Alamy

FIGURE 13.1 Power Generation at the Te Apiti Wind Farm

three turbine blades, each more than 100 feet in length. Additionally, construction of the wind farm required pouring 60,000 cubic meters of concrete and moving 1.2 million cubic meters of soil.

The project got off to a rocky start, through no fault of its own. From the moment the first crews began work at the site, weather conditions were atrocious. More than double the average rainfall inundated the project site in a nearly continuous series of storms. On February 6, 2004, the rainfall peaked at a 50-year storm record, followed ten days later by another storm that set a new 100-year record! The rainfall resulted in the area's highest-ever recorded flooding and led to the declaration of a civil emergency. The main access bridge to the construction site was swept away in the flooding, and the Manawatu Gorge, the main water route, was closed for four months, leaving the project team with a single muddy track for moving all material and equipment into the construction site.

The weather affected the project and led to some major changes to the initial scope, including:

1. Working with local government to restore the destroyed access bridge
2. Revising the work schedule to allow all contractors, facilities, and work crews to assist in flood recovery as part of New Zealand's Civil Emergency Act
3. Stabilizing existing roads to ensure continuous material deliveries
4. Updating the schedules to maintain the wind farm project's completion despite these additional responsibilities

The project constraints forced all members to work together in a collaborative way to address the new construction challenges while maintaining an ambitious schedule for completion of the wind farm. Using effective risk management techniques, the project was able to avoid many of the more common problems that occur on large-scale civil construction projects. For example, there were no lost time incidents in the project's entire 250,000 man hours of work.

Overall, the Te Apiti wind farm project was completed five days ahead of schedule in July 2004, with an excellent safety record, and within the $150 million budget. It is currently the largest wind farm in the southern hemisphere, producing enough energy for 45,000 homes. In spite of having to deal with horrific weather conditions, unremitting rain, and having to be agile enough to expand the original project scope to include assisting in civil emergency measures, the project is an excellent example of working in a difficult environment, applying effective project management techniques, and rigorously enforcing ambitious schedule and budget conditions to complete a project that has had important results for the New Zealand government's energy policy.[1]

INTRODUCTION

One of the most significant challenges with running a project has to do with maintaining an accurate monitoring and control system for its implementation. Because projects are often defined by their constraints (i.e., budget and schedule limitations), it is vital that we ensure they are controlled as carefully as possible. Project monitoring and control are the principal mechanisms that allow the project team to stay on top of a project's evolving status as it moves through the various life cycle stages toward completion. Rather than adopting a "no news is good news" approach to monitoring and control of projects, we need to clearly understand the benefits that can be derived from careful and thorough status assessments as the project moves forward.

In order to best ensure that the project's control will be as optimal as possible, we need to focus our attention on two important aspects of the monitoring process. First, we need to identify the appropriate cues that signal project status as well as understand the best times across the project's life cycle to get accurate assessments of its performance. In other words, we need to be fully aware of the *what* and *when* questions: What information concerning the project should be measured, and when are the best times to measure it? Our goal is to have a sense of how to develop systematic project control that is comprehensive, accurate, and timely. Put another way, when we are responsible for a multimillion-dollar investment in our organization, we want to know the status of the project, we want that information as soon as we can get it, and we want it to be as up-to-date as possible.

13.1 CONTROL CYCLES—A GENERAL MODEL

A general model of organizational control includes four components that can operate in a continuous cycle and can be represented as a wheel. These elements are:

1. ***Setting a goal.*** Project goal setting goes beyond overall scope development to include setting the project baseline plan. The project baseline is predicated on an accurate Work Breakdown Structure (WBS) process. Remember that WBS establishes all the deliverables and work packages associated with the project, assigns the personnel responsible for them, and creates a visual chart of the project from

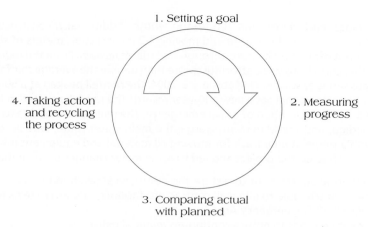

FIGURE 13.2 **The Project Control Cycle**

the highest level down through the deliverable and task levels. The project baseline is created as each task is laid out on a network diagram and resources and time durations are assigned to it.

2. ***Measuring progress.*** Effective control systems require accurate project measurement mechanisms. Project managers must have a system in place that will allow them to measure the ongoing status of various project activities in real time. We need a measurement system that can provide information as quickly as possible. *What to measure* also needs to be clearly defined. Any number of devices will allow us to measure one aspect of the project or another; however, the larger question is whether or not we are getting the type of information we can really use.

3. ***Comparing actual with planned performance.*** When we have some sense of the original baseline (plan) and a method for accurately measuring progress, the next step is to compare the two pieces of information. A gap analysis can be used as a basis for testing the project's status. *Gap analysis* refers to any measurement process that first determines the goals and then the degree to which the actual performance lives up to those goals. The smaller the gaps between planned and actual performance, the better the outcome. In cases where we see obvious differences between what was planned and what was realized, we have a clear-cut warning signal.

4. ***Taking action.*** Once we detect significant deviations from the project plan, it becomes necessary to engage in some form of corrective action to minimize or remove the deviation. The process of taking corrective action is generally straightforward. Corrective action can either be relatively minor or involve significant remedial steps. At its most extreme, corrective action may even involve scuttling a nonperforming project. After corrective action, the monitoring and control cycle begins again.

As Figure 13.2 demonstrates, the **control cycle** is continuous. As we create a plan, we begin measurement efforts to chart progress and compare stages against the baseline plan. Any indications of significant deviations from the plan should immediately trigger an appropriate response, leading to a reconfiguration of the plan, reassessment of progress, and so on. Project monitoring is a continuous, full-time cycle of target setting, measuring, correcting, improving, and remeasuring.

13.2 MONITORING PROJECT PERFORMANCE

As we discovered in the chapters on project budgeting and resource management, once we have established a **project baseline** budget, one of the most important methods for indicating the ongoing status of the project is to evaluate it against the original budget projections. For project monitoring and control, both individual task budgets and the cumulative project budget are relevant. The cumulative budget can be broken down by time over the project's projected duration.

The Project S-Curve: A Basic Tool

As a basis for evaluating **project control** techniques, let us consider a simple example. Assume a project (Project Sierra) with four work packages (Design, Engineering, Installation, and Testing), a budget to completion of $80,000, and an anticipated duration of 45 weeks. Table 13.1 gives a breakdown of the project's cumulative budget in terms of both work packages and time.

TABLE 13.1 Budgeted Costs for Project Sierra (in thousands $)

| | Duration (in weeks) | | | | | | | | | |
	5	10	15	20	25	30	35	40	45	Total
Design	6	2								
Engineer		4	8	8	8					
Install				4	20	6				
Test						2	6	4	2	
Total	6	6	8	12	28	8	6	4	2	
Cumul.	6	12	20	32	60	68	74	78	80	80

To determine project performance and status, a straightforward time/cost analysis is often our first choice. Here the project's status is evaluated as a function of the accumulated costs and labor hours or quantities plotted against time for both budgeted and actual amounts. We can see that time (shown on the *x*, or horizontal, axis) is compared with money expended (shown on the *y*, or vertical, axis). The classic **project S-curve** represents the typical form of such a relationship. Budget expenditures are initially low and ramp up rapidly during the major project execution stage, before starting to level off again as the project gets nearer to its completion (see Figure 13.3). Cumulative budget projections for Project Sierra shown in Table 13.1 have been plotted against the project's schedule. The S-curve figure represents the project budget baseline against which actual budget expenditures are evaluated.

Monitoring the status of a project using S-curves becomes a simple tracking problem. At the conclusion of each given time period (week, month, or quarter), we simply total the cumulative project budget expenditures to date and compare them with the anticipated spending patterns. Any significant deviations between actual and planned budget spending reveal a potential problem area.

Simplicity is the key benefit of S-curve analysis. Because the projected project baseline is established in advance, the only additional data shown are the actual project budget expenditures. The S-curve also provides real-time tracking information in that budget expenditures can be constantly updated and the new values plotted on the graph. Project information can be visualized immediately and updated continuously, so S-curves offer an easy-to-read evaluation of the project's status in a timely manner. (The information is not necessarily easily interpreted, however, as we shall see later.)

Our Project Sierra example (whose budget is shown in Table 13.1) can also be used to illustrate how S-curve analysis is employed. Suppose that by week 21 in the project, the original budget projected

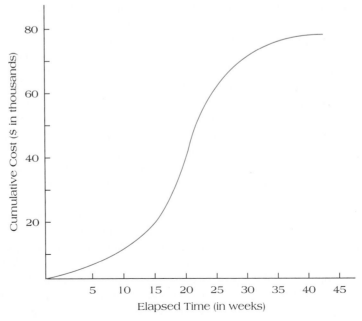

FIGURE 13.3 Project S-Curves

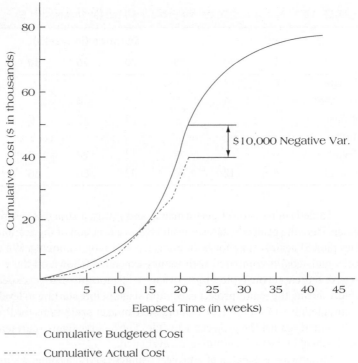

FIGURE 13.4 **Project Sierra's S-Curve Showing Negative Variance**

expenditures of $50,000. However, our actual project expenditures totaled only $40,000. In effect, there is a $10,000 budget shortfall, or negative variance between the cumulative budgeted cost of the project and its cumulative actual cost. Figure 13.4 shows the tracking of budgeted expenditures with actual project costs, including identifying the negative variance shown at week 21. In this illustration, we see the value of S-curve analysis as a good visual method for linking project costs (both budgeted and actual) over the project's schedule.

S-Curve Drawbacks

When project teams consider using S-curves, they need to take the curves' significant drawbacks as well as their strengths into consideration. S-curves can identify positive or negative variance (budget expenditures above or below projections), but they do not allow us to make reasonable interpretations as to the cause of variance. Consider the S-curve shown in Figure 13.4. The actual budget expenditures have been plotted to suggest that the project team has not spent the total planned budget money to date (there is negative variance). However, the question is how to interpret this finding. The link between accumulated project costs and time is not always easily resolved. Is the project team behind schedule (given that they have not spent sufficient budget to date) or might there be alternative reasons for the negative variance?

Assume that your organization tracks project costs employing an S-curve approach and uses that information to assess the status of an ongoing project. Also assume that the project is to be completed in 12 months and has a budget of $150,000. At the six-month checkup, you discover that the project S-curve shows significant shortfall; you have spent far less on the project to date than was originally budgeted. Is this good or bad news?

On the surface, we might suppose that this is a sign of poor performance; we are lagging far behind in bringing the project along and the smaller amount we have spent to date is evidence that our project is behind schedule. On the other hand, there are any number of reasons why this circumstance actually might be positive. For example, suppose that in running the project, you found a cost-effective method for doing some component of the work or came across a new technology that significantly cut down on expenses. In that case, the time/cost metric may not only be misused, but might lead to dramatically inaccurate conclusions. Likewise, positive variance is not always a sign of project progress. In fact, a team may have a serious problem with overexpenditures that could be interpreted as strong progress on the project when in reality it signals nothing more than their inefficient use of project capital resources. The bottom line is this: Simply evaluating a project's status according to its performance on time versus budget expenditures may easily lead us into making inaccurate assumptions about project performance.

Milestone Analysis

Another method for monitoring project progress is *milestone analysis*. A **milestone** is an event or stage of the project that represents a significant accomplishment on the road to the project's completion. Completion of a deliverable (a combination of multiple project tasks), an important activity on the project's critical path, or even a calendar date can all be milestones. In effect, milestones are road markers that we observe on our travels along the project's life cycle. There are several benefits to using milestones as a form of project control.

1. *Milestones signal the completion of important project steps.*   A project's milestones are an important indicator of the current status of the project under development. They give the project team a common language to use in discussing the ongoing status of the project.

2. *Milestones can motivate the project team.*   In large projects lasting several years, motivation can flag as team members begin to have difficulty seeing how the project is proceeding overall, what their specific contribution has been and continues to be, and how much longer the project is likely to take. Focusing attention on milestones helps team members become more aware of the project's successes as well as its status, and they can begin to develop greater task identity regarding their work on the project.

3. *Milestones offer points at which to reevaluate client needs and any potential change requests.*   A common problem with many types of projects is the nature of repetitive and constant change requests from clients. Using project review milestones as formal "stop points," both the project team and the clients are clear on when they will take midcourse reviews of the project and how change requests will be handled. When clients are aware of these formal project review points, they are better able to present reasonable and well-considered feedback (and specification change requests) to the team.

4. *Milestones help coordinate schedules with vendors and suppliers.*   Creating delivery dates that do not delay project activities is a common challenge in scheduling delivery of key project components. From a resource perspective, the project team needs to receive supplies before they are needed but not so far in advance that space limitations, holding and inventory costs, and in some cases spoilage are problems. Hence, to balance delays of late shipments against the costs associated with holding early deliveries, a well-considered system of milestones creates a scheduling and coordinating mechanism that identifies the key dates when supplies will be needed.

5. *Milestones identify key project review gates.*   For many complex projects, a series of midterm project reviews are mandatory. For example, many projects that are developed for the U.S. government require periodic evaluation as a precondition to the project firm receiving some percentage of the contract award. Milestones allow for appropriate points for these reviews. Sometimes the logic behind when to hold such reviews is based on nothing more than the passage of time ("It is time for the July 1 review"). For other projects, the review gates are determined based on completion of a series of key project steps (such as the evaluation of software results from the beta sites).

6. *Milestones signal other team members when their participation is expected to begin.*   Many times projects require contributions from personnel who are not part of the project team. For example, a quality assurance individual may be needed to conduct systems tests or quality inspection and evaluations of work done to date. If the quality supervisor does not know when to assign a person to our project, we may find when we reach that milestone that no one is available to help us. Because the quality assurance person is not part of the project team, we need to coordinate her involvement in order to minimize disruption to the project schedule.

7. *Milestones can delineate the various deliverables developed in the Work Breakdown Structure and thereby enable the project team to develop a better overall view of the project.*   We then are able to refocus efforts and function-specific resources toward the deliverables that show signs of trouble, rather than simply allocating resources in a general manner. For example, indications that the initial project software programming milestone has been missed allows the project manager to specifically request additional programmers downstream, in order to make up time later in the project's development.

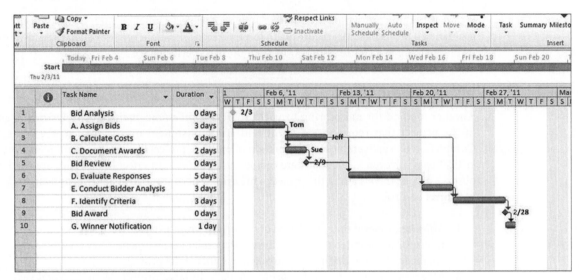

FIGURE 13.5 Gantt Chart with Milestones

Figure 13.5 gives an example of a simple Gantt chart with milestones included. The milestones in this case are simply arbitrary points established on the chart; we could just as easily have placed them after completed work packages or by using some other criteria.

Problems with Milestones

Milestones, in one form or another, are probably the simplest and most widely used of all project control devices. Their benefits lie in their clarity; it is usually easy for all project team members to relate to the idea of milestones as a project performance metric. The problem with them is that they are a reactive control system. You must first engage in project activities and then evaluate them relative to your goal. If you significantly underperform your work to that point, you are faced with having to correct what has already transpired. Imagine, for example, that a project team misses a milestone by a large margin. Not having received any progress reports until the point that the bad news becomes public, the project manager is probably not in a position to craft an immediate remedy for the shortfall. At this point, the problems are compounded. Due to the delay in receiving the bad news, remedial steps are themselves delayed, pushing the project even farther behind.

The Tracking Gantt Chart

One form of the Gantt chart, referred to as a *tracking Gantt chart,* is useful for evaluating project performance at specific points in time. The **tracking Gantt chart** allows the project team to constantly update the project's status by linking task completion to the schedule baseline. Rather than monitor costs and budget expenditures, a tracking Gantt chart identifies the stage of completion each task has attained by a specific date within the project. For example, Figure 13.6 represents Project Blue, involving five activities. As the

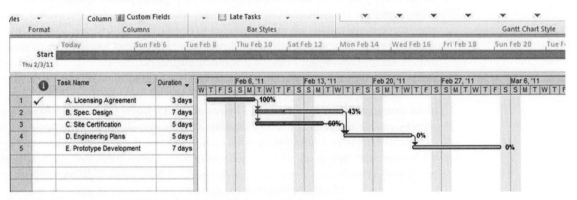

FIGURE 13.6 Assessing Project Blue's Status Using Tracking Gantt Chart

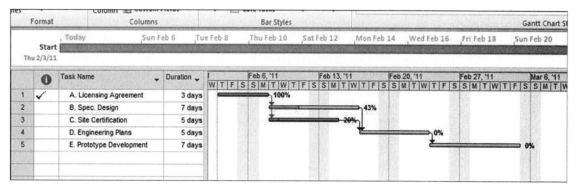

FIGURE 13.7 **Tracking Gantt with Project Activity Deviation**

project progresses, its current status is indicated by the vertical status bar shown for Thursday, February 10. To date, activity A (Licensing Agreement) has been 100% completed, while its two subsequent tasks, Specification Design and Site Certification, are shown as having progressed proportionally by the identified tracking date. That is, activity B (Specification Design) is rated as 43% completed, and activity C (Site Certification) as 60% completed. Activities D and E have not yet begun in this example.

It is also possible to measure both positive and negative deviations from the schedule baseline with the tracking Gantt chart. Let us suppose, using our Project Blue example, that activity B remains approximately 43% completed as of the baseline date indicated. On the other hand, activity C has not progressed as rapidly and is only 20% completed as of the February 10 date. The chart can be configured to identify the variations, either positive or negative, in activity completion against the project baseline. These features are demonstrated in Figure 13.7, showing the current date for the project and the delay in progress on activity C.

Benefits and Drawbacks of Tracking Gantt Charts

A key benefit of tracking Gantt charts is that they are quite easy to understand. The visual nature of the feedback report is easy to assimilate and interpret. This type of control chart can be updated very quickly, providing a sense of real-time project control. On the other hand, tracking Gantt charts have some inherent drawbacks that limit their overall utility. First, although they may show which tasks are ahead of schedule, on schedule, and behind schedule, these charts do not identify the underlying source of problems in the cases of task slippage. Reasons for schedule slippage cannot be inferred from the data presented. Second, tracking control charts do not allow for future projections of the project's status. It is difficult to accurately estimate the time to completion for a project, particularly in the case of significant positive or negative variation from the baseline schedule. Is a series of early finishes for some activities good news? Does that signal that the project is likely to finish earlier than estimated? Because of these drawbacks, tracking charts should be used along with other techniques that offer more prescriptive power.

13.3 EARNED VALUE MANAGEMENT

An increasingly popular method used in project monitoring and control consists of a mechanism that has become known as **Earned Value Management (EVM).*** The origins of EVM date to the 1960s when U.S. government contracting agencies began to question the ability of contractors to accurately track their costs across the life of various projects. As a result, after 1967, the Department of Defense imposed 35 Cost/Schedule Control Systems Criteria that suggested, in effect, that any future projects procured by the U.S. government in which the risk of cost growth was to be retained by the government must satisfy these 35 criteria.[2] In the more than 4 years since its origin, EVM has been practiced in multiple settings, by agencies from governments as diverse as Australia, Canada, and Sweden, as well as by a host of project-based firms in numerous industries.

Unlike previous project tracking approaches, EVM recognizes that it is necessary to jointly consider the impact of time, cost, and *project performance* on any analysis of current project status. Put another

---

*Note that Earned Value Management (EVM) is used interchangeably with Earned Value Analysis (EVA). EVA is an older term, though still widely in use. EVM has become increasingly common and is used within many project firms.

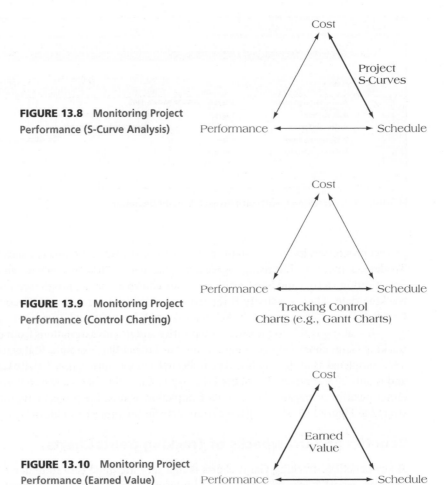

FIGURE 13.8 Monitoring Project Performance (S-Curve Analysis)

FIGURE 13.9 Monitoring Project Performance (Control Charting)

FIGURE 13.10 Monitoring Project Performance (Earned Value)

way: Any monitoring system that only compares actual against budgeted cost numbers ignores the fact that the client is spending that money to accomplish something—to create a project. Therefore, EVM reintroduces and stresses the importance of analyzing the time element in project status updates. Time is important because it becomes the basis for determining how much work should be accomplished at certain milestone points. EVM also allows the project team to make future projections of project status based on its current state. At any point in the project's development, we are able to calculate both schedule and budget efficiency factors (the efficiency with which budget is being used relative to the value that is being created) and use those values to make future projections about the estimated cost and schedule to project completion.

We can illustrate the advance in the project control process that Earned Value Management represents by comparing it to the other project tracking mechanisms. If we consider the key metrics of project performance as those success criteria discussed in Chapter 1 (schedule, budget, and performance), most project evaluation approaches tend to isolate some subset of the overall success measure. For example, project S-curve analysis directly links budget expenditures with the project schedule (see Figure 13.8). Again, the obvious disadvantage to this approach is that it ignores the project performance linkage.

Project control charts such as tracking Gantt charts link project performance with schedule but may give budget expenditures short shrift (see Figure 13.9). The essence of a tracking approach to project status is to emphasize project performance over time. Although the argument could be made that budget is implicitly assumed to be spent in some preconceived fashion, this metric does not directly apply a link between the use of time and performance factors with project cost.

Earned value (EV), on the other hand, directly links all three primary project success metrics (cost, schedule, and performance). This methodology is extremely valuable because it allows for regular updating of a *time-phased* budget to determine schedule and cost variances, as identified by the regular measurement of project performance (see Figure 13.10).

Terminology for Earned Value

Following are some of the key concepts that allow us to calculate earned value and use its figures to make future project performance projections.

PV   **Planned value**. A cost estimate of the budgeted resources scheduled across the project's life cycle (cumulative baseline).

EV   **Earned value**. This is the real budgeted cost, or "value," of the work that has actually been performed to date.

AC   **Actual cost of work performed**. The cumulative total costs incurred in accomplishing the various project work packages.

SPI   **Schedule Performance Index**. The earned value to date divided by the planned value of work scheduled to be performed (EV/PV). This value allows us to calculate the projected schedule of the project to completion.

CPI   **Cost Performance Index**. The earned value divided by the actual, cumulative cost of the work performed to date (EV/AC). This value allows us to calculate the projected budget to completion.

BAC   **Budgeted cost at completion**. This represents the total budget for a project.

Creating Project Baselines

The first step in developing an accurate control process is to create the project baselines against which progress can be measured. Baseline information is critical regardless of the control process we employ, but baselines are elemental when performing EVM. The first piece of information necessary for performing earned value is the planned value, that is, the project baseline. The PV should comprise all relevant project costs, the most important of which are personnel costs, equipment and materials, and project overhead, sometimes referred to as *level of effort*. Overhead costs (level of effort) can include a variety of fixed costs that must be included in the project budget, including administrative or technical support, computer work, and other staff expertise (such as legal advice or marketing). The actual steps in establishing the project baseline are fairly straightforward and require two pieces of data: the Work Breakdown Structure and a time-phased project budget.

1. The Work Breakdown Structure identified the individual work packages and tasks necessary to accomplish the project. As such, the WBS allowed us to first identify the individual tasks that would need to be performed. It also gave us some understanding of the hierarchy of tasks needed to set up work packages and identify personnel needs (human resources) in order to match the task requirements to the correct individuals capable of performing them.

2. The time-phased budget takes the WBS one step further: It allows us to identify the correct sequencing of tasks, but more importantly, it enables the project team to determine the points in the project when budget money is likely to be spent in pursuit of those tasks. Say, for example, that our project team determines that one project activity, Data Entry, will require a budget of $20,000 to be completed, and further, that the task is estimated to require two months to completion, with the majority of the work being done in the first month. A time-phased budget for this activity might resemble the following:

Activity	Jan	Feb	...	Dec	Total
Data Entry	$14,000	$6,000		-0-	$20,000

Once we have collected the WBS and applied a time-phased budget breakdown, we can create the project baseline. The result is an important component of earned value because it represents the standard against which we are going to compare all project performance, cost, and schedule data as we attempt to assess the viability of an ongoing project. This baseline, then, represents our best understanding of how the project *should* progress. How the project is actually doing, however, is another matter.

Why Use Earned Value?

Let us illustrate the relevancy of EVM using our Project Sierra example. Return to the information presented in Table 13.1, as graphically represented on the project S-curve in Figure 13.3. Assume that it is now week 30 of the project and we are attempting to assess the project's status. Also assume that there is no difference

TABLE 13.2 Percentage of Tasks Completed for Project Sierra (in thousands $)

| | Duration (in weeks) | | | | | | | | | |
	5	10	15	20	25	30	35	40	45	% Comp.
Design	6	2								100
Engineer		4	8	8	8					100
Install				4	20	6				50
Test						2	6	4	2	0
Total	6	6	8	12	28	8	6	4	2	
Cumul.	6	12	20	32	60	68	74	78	80	

between the projected project costs and actual expenditures; that is, the project budget is being spent within the correct time frame. However, upon examination, suppose we were to discover that Installation was only half completed and Project Testing had not yet begun. This example illustrates both a problem with S-curve analysis and the strength of EVM. Project status assessment is relevant only when some measure of performance is considered in addition to budget and elapsed schedule.

Consider the revised data for Project Sierra shown in Table 13.2. Note that as of week 30, work packages related to Design and Engineering have been totally completed, whereas the Installation is only 50% done, and Testing has not yet begun. These percentage values are given based on the project team or key individual's assessment of the current status of work package completion. The question now is: What is the earned value of the project work done to date? As of week 30, what is the status of this project in terms of budget, schedule, *and* performance?

Calculating the earned value for these work packages is a relatively straightforward process. As Table 13.3 shows, we can modify the previous table to focus exclusively on the relevant information for determining earned value as of week 30. The planned budget for each work package is multiplied by the percentage completed in order to determine the earned value to date for the work packages, as well as for the overall project. In this case, the earned value at the 30-week point is $51,000.

Now we can compare the planned budget against the actual earned value using the original project budget baseline, shown in Figure 13.11. This process allows us to assess a more realistic determination of the status of the project when the earned value is plotted against the budget baseline. Compare this figure with the alternative method from Figure 13.4, in which a negative variance is calculated, with no supporting explanation as to the cause or any indication about whether this figure is meaningful or not. Recall that by the end of week 30, our original budget projections suggested that $68,000 should have been spent. Instead, we are projecting a shortfall of $17,000. In other words, we are showing a negative variance not only in terms of money spent on the project, but also in terms of value created (performance) of the project to date. Unlike the standard S-curve evaluation, EVM variance is meaningful because it is based not simply on budget spent, but value earned. A negative variance of $10,000 in budget expenditures may or may not signal cause for concern; however, a $17,000 shortfall in value earned on the project to date represents a variance of serious consequences.

TABLE 13.3 Calculating Earned Value (in thousands $)

	Planned	% Comp.	Earned Value
Design	8	100	8
Engineer	28	100	28
Install	30	50	15
Test	14	0	0
Cumul. Earned Value			51

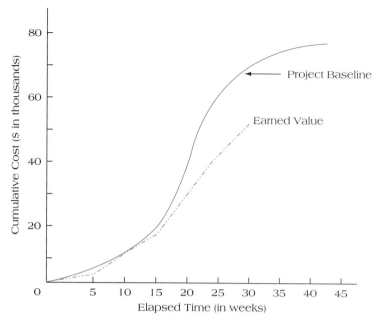

FIGURE 13.11 Project Baseline, Using Earned Value

Steps in Earned Value Management

There are five steps in Earned Value Management (EVM):

1. ***Clearly define each activity or task that will be performed on the project, including its resource needs as well as a detailed budget.***   As we demonstrated earlier, the Work Breakdown Structure allows project teams to identify all necessary project tasks. It further allows for each task to be assigned its own project resources, including equipment and materials costs, as well as personnel assignments. Finally, coupled with the task breakdowns and resource assignments, it is possible to create the budget figure or cost estimate for each project task.

2. ***Create the activity and resource usage schedules.***   These will identify the proportion of the total budget allocated to each task across a project calendar. Determine how much of an activity's budget is to be spent each month (or other appropriate time period) across the project's projected development cycle. Coupled with the development of a project budget should be its direct linkage to the project schedule. The determination of how much budget money is to be allocated to project tasks is important. Equally important is the understanding of when the resources are to be employed across the project's development cycle.

3. ***Develop a "time-phased" budget that shows expenditures across the project's life.***   The total (cumulative) amount of the budget becomes the project baseline and is referred to as the **planned value (PV)**. In real terms, PV just means that we can identify the cumulative budget expenditures planned at any stage in the project's life. The PV, as a cumulative value, is derived from adding the planned budget expenditures for each preceding time period.

4. ***Total the actual costs of doing each task to arrive at the actual cost of work performed (AC).***   We can also compute the budgeted values for the tasks on which work is being performed. This is referred to as the earned value (EV) and is the origin of the term for this control process.

5. ***Calculate both a project's budget variance and schedule variance while it is still in process.***   Once we have collected the three key pieces of data (PV, EV, and AC), it is possible to make these calculations. The **schedule variance** is calculated by the simple equation $SV = EV - PV$, or the difference between the earned value to date minus the planned value of the work scheduled to be performed to date. The budget, or cost, variance is calculated as $CV = EV - AC$, or the earned value minus the actual cost of work performed.

A simplified model that fits the three principal parts of earned value together (PV, EV, and AC) is shown in Figure 13.12. The original baseline data, comprising both schedule and budget for all project tasks,

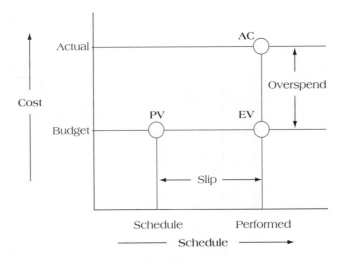

FIGURE 13.12 Earned Value Milestones

is indicated by the circle in the lower left part of the chart as PV. Any schedule slippage from the original PV is attributed to the EV and comprises the project's earned value. Finally, using the earned value figures, which are based on an assessment of the degree to which project tasks are completed, we can create the project's AC. Now we have another direct link to the difference between the budgeted and actual costs of the project's activities.

Assessing a Project's Earned Value

Table 13.4 presents the first components of a calculated earned value analysis on Project Mercury.[3] This project has a planned seven-month duration and a $118,000 budget. The project began in January and we are interested in calculating its earned value as of the end of June. For simplicity's sake, the total work packages for this project are only seven in number. If we know the amount budgeted for each work package and when that work is slated to be done, we can construct a budget table similar to that shown in Table 13.4. Notice that each work package has a fixed budget across a number of time periods (e.g., Staffing is budgeted to cost $15,000 and is to be performed almost equally across the months of January and February, while Blueprinting begins in March, with $4,000 budgeted to be spent, and concludes in April with $6,000).

TABLE 13.4 Earned Value Table (end of June) with $6,000 for Project Mercury (in thousands $)

Activity	Jan	Feb	Mar	Apr	May	June	July	Plan	% Comp.	Value
Staffing	8	7						15	100	15
Blueprinting			4	6				10	80	8
Prototype Development			2	8				10	60	6
Full Design				3	8	10		21	33	7
Construction					2	30		32	25	8
Transfer							10	10	0	0
Punch List						15	5	20	0	0
						Σ =		118		44
Monthly Plan	8	7	6	17	10	55	15			
Cumulative	8	15	21	38	48	103	118			
Monthly Actual	8	11	8	11	10	30	0			
Cumulative Actual	8	19	27	38	48	78				

If we plot the expenses across each month of the project completed to date (January through June), we find that we can determine the amount budgeted and, through gathering some information from the project team and the accountant, the actual amount spent each month. These sets of figures are added to the bottom four rows of the table. For example, note that by March, we had planned to spend $21,000 in project budget on activities to date. Our actual cumulative costs were $27,000. The obvious question is: Is this good news or bad news? On the surface, we might conclude that it is bad news because we have overspent our budget. However, recall that the chief problem with S-curve methodology is that it only considers actual costs versus planned costs. This simply is not sufficient information for us to make any real determination of the status of the project.

The key pieces of information that allow us to identify earned value are included in the right-hand columns. We are very interested in determining the current status of the project based on the number of tasks completed over the time budgeted to them. Therefore, the last columns show the planned expenditures for each task, the percentage of the tasks completed, and the calculated value. *Value* in this sense is simply the product of the planned expenditures and the percentage of these tasks completed. For example, under the work package Blueprinting, we see that this activity was given a planned budget of $10,000 across two months total. To date, 80% of that activity has been completed, resulting in $8,000 in value. If we total the columns for planned expenditures and actual value (EV), we come up with our project's planned budget ($118,000) and the value realized at the end of June ($44,000).

We now have enough information to make a reasonable determination of the project's status using Earned Value Management. The first number we require is the planned value (PV). This value can be found as the cumulative planned costs at the end of the month of June ($103,000). We also have calculated that the earned value for the project to date (EV) totals $44,000. The schedule variances that are of interest to us are the Schedule Performance Index (SPI) and the estimated time to completion. The SPI is determined by dividing the EV by the PV. Table 13.5 shows this calculation ($44,000/103,000 = .43). With the SPI, we can now project the length of time it should take to complete the project. Because the SPI is telling us that we are operating at only 43% efficiency in implementing the project, we take the reciprocal of the SPI multiplied by the original project schedule to determine the projected actual time frame to completion for the project ($1/.43 \times 7 = 16.3$ months). The bad news is: It appears that as of June, we cannot expect to complete this project for an additional 10 months; we are running more than nine months behind schedule.

How about costs? Although we are running more than nine months late, can we make similar projections about the project in terms of how much it is projected to finally cost? The answer, according to EVM, is yes. Just as we can determine schedule variances, we can also compute cost variances, as long as we have two very important pieces of data—the cumulative actual cost of work performed (AC) and the earned value (EV). The earned value figure has already been calculated ($44,000), and now we turn back to Table 13.4 to locate the AC. The cumulative actual cost at the end of June is $78,000. This figure is our AC and is entered into Table 13.6.

TABLE 13.5 Schedule Variances for Project Mercury EVM

Schedule Variances	
Planned Value (PV)	103
Earned Value (EV)	44
Schedule Performance Index	EV/PV = 44/103 = .43
Estimated Time to Completion	$(1/.43 \times 7) = 16.3$ months

TABLE 13.6 Cost Variances for Project Mercury EVM

Cost Variances	
Cumulative Actual Cost of Work Performed (AC)	78
Earned Value (EV)	44
Cost Performance Index	EV/AC = 44/78 = .56
Estimated Cumulative Cost to Completion	$(1/.56 \times \$118,000) = \$210,714$

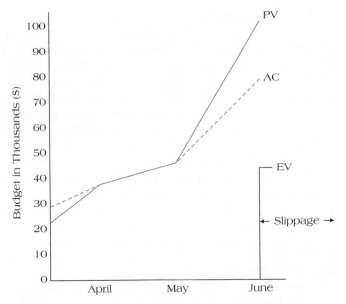

FIGURE 13.13 Earned Value Variances for Project Mercury

As we did in calculating schedule variance, we calculate cost variance by dividing the EV by AC, or $44,000/78,000 = .56. That is the Cost Performance Index (CPI) for this project. Determining the projected cost of the project involves taking the reciprocal of the CPI multiplied by the original project budget ($118,000). The bad news is: Not only is this project well behind schedule, but it also is projected to end up costing more than $210,000, a significant cost overrun.

Finally, we can plot these variance values graphically, showing the difference between EV (earned value) and PV and AC (see Figure 13.13). The intriguing result of this example suggests how misleading simple S-curves can sometimes be. For example, in this case, we have discovered a difference at the end of June of $25,000 between the AC ($78,000) and PV ($103,000). Although the analysis at that point showed that we had underspent our budget slightly, the results were actually more serious when viewed from the perspective of earned value by the end of June ($44,000). In reality, the schedule and cost variances were much more severe due to the lag in earned value on the project, as calculated by the percentage completion of all scheduled tasks. This example clearly shows the advantages of earned value for more accurately determining actual project status as a function of its three component pieces: time, budget, and completion.

We can also perform Earned Value Management using MS Project 2010. Suppose that we wished to track Project Atlas, shown in Figure 13.14. Notice that as of March 7, the project is beginning to show some signs of delay. By this point, we should have completed four of the six work packages, and yet Testing, for which Stewart is responsible, is only now getting under way. From a monitoring and control perspective, the question we want to answer is: How does EVM indicate the potential delays in our project?

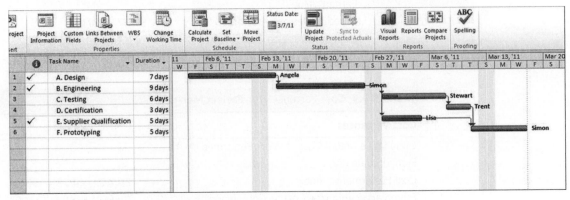

FIGURE 13.14 Sample Gantt Chart for Project Atlas Showing Status on March 7

Task Name	Fixed Cost	Fixed Cost Accrual	Total Cost	Baseline	Variance	Actual	Remaining
A. Design	$0.00	Prorated	$1,960.00	$1,960.00	$0.00	$1,960.00	$0.00
B. Engineering	$0.00	Prorated	$2,880.00	$2,880.00	$0.00	$2,880.00	$0.00
C. Testing	$0.00	Prorated	$1,560.00	$1,560.00	$0.00	$520.00	$1,040.00
D. Certification	$0.00	Prorated	$480.00	$480.00	$0.00	$0.00	$480.00
E. Supplier Qualification	$0.00	Prorated	$1,000.00	$1,000.00	$0.00	$1,000.00	$0.00
F. Prototyping	$0.00	Prorated	$1,600.00	$1,600.00	$0.00	$0.00	$1,600.00

FIGURE 13.15 Sample Cost Report for Project Atlas on March 7

Suppose that, in addition to regularly updating the baseline schedule, we have been tracking the costs associated with each of the work packages and have found, as Figure 13.15 shows, that we have spent all budgeted money allotted to the work packages of Design, Engineering, and Supplier Qualification. We have only spent $520 of our Testing budget. These are the actual cost values (AC) for these activities. We now have sufficient updated information to determine the earned value for Project Atlas as of March 7.

Task Name	Planned Value - PV	Earned Value - EV	AC (ACWP)	SV	CV	EAC	BAC
A. Design	$1,960.00	$1,960.00	$1,960.00	$0.00	$0.00	$1,960.00	$1,960.00
B. Engineering	$2,880.00	$2,880.00	$2,880.00	$0.00	$0.00	$2,880.00	$2,880.00
C. Testing	$1,300.00	$519.95	$520.00	($780.05)	($0.05)	$1,560.16	$1,560.00
D. Certification	$0.00	$0.00	$0.00	$0.00	$0.00	$480.00	$480.00
E. Supplier Qualification	$1,000.00	$1,000.00	$1,000.00	$0.00	$0.00	$1,000.00	$1,000.00
F. Prototyping	$0.00	$0.00	$0.00	$0.00	$0.00	$1,600.00	$1,600.00

FIGURE 13.16 Earned Value Report for Project Atlas on March 7

Figure 13.16 shows an example of an earned value report generated by MS Project 2010 for our Project Atlas.* In addition to providing the key metrics of PV, EV, and AC (see footnote), the report generates both schedule and cost variances. Schedule variance (SV) is simply the difference between earned value and planned value, while cost variance (CV) is the difference between earned value and actual cost. The **Estimate at Completion (EAC)** column shows the expected total cost of the project to completion based on performance across the various tasks up to the status date. Note that for Project Atlas, we are currently projecting schedule and cost variances, suggesting that our project is over budget and behind schedule. In fact, the EAC demonstrates that as of March 7, this project is expected to cost $9,480 to completion.

13.4 USING EARNED VALUE TO MANAGE A PORTFOLIO OF PROJECTS

Earned Value Management can work at the portfolio level as well as with individual projects. The process simply involves the aggregation of all earned value measures across the firm's entire project portfolio in order to give an indication as to the efficiency with which a company is managing its projects. Table 13.7 gives an example of a portfolio-level Earned Value Management control table that identifies both positive and negative cost and schedule variances and, based on these evaluations, projects the cost to completion of each current project.[4]

---

*MS Project 2010 uses the term BCWS (Budgeted Cost of Work Scheduled) for planned value (PV), BCWP (Budgeted Cost of Work Performed) for earned value (EV), and ACWP (Actual Cost of Work Performed) for actual cost (AC). MS Project 2010 employs older terms that have been updated by the Project Management Institute's PMBoK.

TABLE 13.7 Project Portfolio Earned Value (in thousands $)

Project	PV	EV	Time Var ($)	Var	AC	Cost Var ($)	Var +	Plan	Est. at Completion
Alpha	91	73	−18	18	83	−10	10	254	289
Beta	130	135	5	0	125	10	0	302	280
Gamma	65	60	−5	5	75	−15	15	127	159
Delta	25	23	−2	2	27	−4	4	48	56
Epsilon	84	82	−2	2	81	1	0	180	178
	395	373			391				962

Total Schedule Variance 27 Total Cost Variance 29

Relative Schedule Variance 27/395 = 6.84% Relative Cost Variance 29/395 = 7.34%

Other useful information contained in the Portfolio Earned Value Management table includes the total positive variances for both budget and schedule, as well as a determination of the relative schedule and cost variances as a percentage of the total project portfolio. In the example shown in Table 13.7, the company is running average cost and schedule variances on its projects of 7.34% and 6.84%, respectively. The use of Earned Value Management for portfolio tracking and control offers top management an excellent window into the firm's ability to efficiently run projects, allows for comparisons across all projects currently in development, and isolates both the positive and negative variances as they occur. All of this is useful information for top-level management of multiple projects.

PROJECT PROFILE

Earned Value at Northrop Grumman

"There comes a time to shoot the engineers and get on with production." This statement, commonly voiced in defense industry companies, refers to the engineers' tendency to continually improve but never complete a project. The penchant for continual "tinkering" has enormous implications for companies that live or die by their ability to effectively and efficiently implement their projects. The type of work defense contractors perform further complicates the problem. There is a standing requirement that a company must meet the government's stringent cost and quality control tests as it brings projects through the development cycle. In an effort to regain control of the project development process, defense contractor Northrop Grumman has been committed to the use of Earned Value Management for a number of years.

Northrop Grumman, one of the world's leading defense contractors (see Figure 13.17), has been using Earned Value Management as a key component of its approach to better project tracking and control. Because of the numerous projects the company's Defense Systems Division routinely undertakes, its annual operating budget for projects runs into the billions of dollars. With dozens of projects under way at any time and enormous capital commitments supporting these ventures, it is imperative that the corporation develop and maintain the most sophisticated project control system possible.

Northrop Grumman has selected Earned Value Management as its primary project control device for the following reasons:

1. EVM develops a comprehensive baseline plan for the scope of the program's work over its entire duration.
2. The system incorporates tools to measure work performance and accomplishments based on objective criteria.
3. EVM analyzes and forecasts the impact of significant variances from the plan.
4. It produces managerial decision-making information in ascending levels of management.
5. EVM provides action plans for corrective actions when something digresses from the baseline plan.
6. All parties involved in the plan agree to and document all changes.

The company has developed a four-tier approach for project control using EVM. All projects are classified into one of the following categories, requiring an individualized approach to EVM creation:

Tier One is the most stringent because it requires most of the system's features to be identified. This approach is employed when a contract requires that a large amount of detailed information be produced and reported.

PJF News / Alamy

FIGURE 13.17 Northrop Grumman's F-35 Joint Strike Fighter

Tier Two is similar to Tier One except that the contract requires close management oversight because the project is risky, and there is a heavier burden to meet profit margin goals.

Tier Three applies to programs of significant size that are mature and running smoothly.

Tier Four applies the benefits of earned value to projects with low administrative costs.

Once the stringency level (the tier into which the project is classified) is determined, Northrop Grumman applies the EVM framework to its contracts based on six considerations:

1. Requirements of the contract
2. Risk of the program
3. Type of contract incentives
4. Degree of development and production involved in the program
5. The program's visibility
6. The customer's reporting requirements

Depending on how the considerations are applied, a differentially developed EVM is tailored to the type of program on which the company is working.

At Northrop Grumman, EVM is not simply an option, but a corporate mandate. The four-tier approach helps the company tailor the system to each new project in order to apply it correctly for maximum benefit, cost control, and corporate profitability.[5]

13.5 ISSUES IN THE EFFECTIVE USE OF EARNED VALUE MANAGEMENT

As with any other metric that helps us understand the "true" status of an ongoing project, the key to effective use of EVM lies in providing accurate and up-to-date information on the project, particularly in terms of the percentage of work packages completed. Because this information is key to determining the earned value at any point in time, the calculated EV is only as accurate as project team members and managers allow it to be through developing and enforcing an honest reporting system.

In our Project Mercury example shown earlier (Table 13.4), the percentage completion column included values ranging from 100, 80, 60, 33, 25, to zero. In reality, organizations often adopt a simpler decision rule for assigning completion percentages. Among the more common methods for assigning completion values are the following:

1. *0/100 rule*—The simplest and perhaps least effective method requires that a project activity be assigned a value of zero (0) until the point the activity is finished, at which time the value switches to 100%.

This rule works best for work packages with very short durations, such as a day or two, but it is not useful for longer work packages because it provides little real-time information on an ongoing basis. It also makes sense for work packages that require vendor deliveries or that depend upon external stakeholders performing required steps. For example, we count a work package as "complete" when the vendor delivers a needed component.

2. **50/50 rule**—Under this decision rule, an activity that has been started automatically receives a valuation of 50% completed. That value remains attached to the work package until the activity has been completed, at which time it becomes 100% completed. Like the 0/100 rule above, this decision model is used most often for work packages of very short duration.

3. *Percentage complete rule*—Under the percentage complete rule, the project manager and team members mutually agree on a set of completion milestones, whether they are based on quarters (25%, 50%, 75%, 100%), thirds (33%, 67%, 100%), or some other values. Then, on a regular basis, the status of each in-process work package in the project is updated. A new completion value may or may not be assigned to the package, and then the project's EVM is updated based on this new information. As noted earlier, the key to making this process work lies in honest appraisal of the status of ongoing activities, based not on time elapsed or budget spent but on actual percentage of the activity completed.

An important caveat with the percentage complete rule has to do with the controversy surrounding the level of detail to be used in calculating task value. Critics of earned value argue that unless reasonable gradients of completion are acknowledged and used by all parties, there is a high potential to create misleading information through the earned value analysis. For example, one criticism leveled at EVM argues that excessive levels of detail are dangerous and essentially not interpretable. For example, suppose a project uses completion values based on 10% increments (e.g., 10%, 20%, 30%, etc.). As a practical matter, it is fundamentally impossible to successfully delineate between, say, 30% and 40% completion for most project activities; hence, the use of too much detail is more likely to mislead than to clarify the true status of a project.

The chief exception to this difficulty with the project complete rule occurs in projects in which there is a fair degree of prior knowledge of how well delineated the development process is or in situations where it is easier to accurately gauge the amount of work done within any project task. In a simple construction project, for example, where the project steps are well known in advance and rigorously followed, a higher level of detail can be employed. Likewise, in the case of software development where the task consists of writing code, a senior programmer may have an excellent sense of the total number of lines of code needed to complete the task. Therefore, if the total task requires approximately 5,000 lines of code and a programmer completes 500 lines of the program, it would be reasonable to assign a figure of 10% completion of the total task performance requirement.

The importance of establishing a reasonable standard for project performance cannot be overemphasized. In the absence of a clear set of guidelines for identifying cutoff points and the appropriate level of detail, it is possible to derive very different conclusions from the same project information. For example, let us revisit the earlier EVM problem shown in Table 13.4. This time, we will use two decision rules as regards the levels of detail for project activities in calculating value and EV. In the first example, shown in Table 13.8, column 1 gives the original calculations, based on the first set of percentage complete values from Table 13.4. In column 2, I have employed a simple decision rule based on three increments (0, 50%, and 100% complete). Column 3 shows a slightly more precise level of detail, employing levels of 0, 25%, 50%, 75%, and 100% complete. I have rounded the original percentage completion values (shown in column 1) to the closest equivalents in the other two alternatives.

Note what occurs as a result of using alternative levels of detail; rounding the level of completion values to a simplified 0%, 50%, 100% completion scheme results in significantly different results, both for projecting future project schedule and cost deviations. The original schedule overrun that projected a new completion of 16.28 months has been improved to 12.73 months, or a schedule overrun of only 5.73 months. Likewise, the original earned value budget projection for the project ($210,714) has been reduced to $163,889, for a savings of $46,825 due merely to adopting an alternative level of detail for project activity completion. Similarly, using the level of detail with slightly more gradients (0, 25%, 50%, 75%, and 100%), shown in column 3, and rounding the original values to most closely match this alternative, we discover that the future projections for the project, as developed through the SPI and CPI, are more negative than the originals. The new project schedule is forecast to last 17.5 months and the revised project budget has increased to $226,923, or $16,209 more than our first projection. Even more compelling, the absolute difference between the high and low budget projections is more than $63,000, all due to moving from a three-point level of detail (column 2) to one

TABLE 13.8 Calculating Project Mercury Earned Value Based on Alternate Levels of Detail (in thousands $)

Activity	Planned Value	Col. 1 (Original)		Col. 2 (0, 50, 100%)		Col. 3 (0, 25, 50, 75, 100%)	
		% Comp.	Value	% Comp.	Value	% Comp.	Value
Staffing	15	100	15	100	15	100	15
Blueprinting	10	80	8	100	10	75	7.5
Prototype Development	10	60	6	50	5	50	5
Full Design	21	33	7	50	10.5	25	5.25
Construction	32	25	8	50	16	25	8
Transfer	10	0	0	0	0	0	0
Punch List	20	0	0	0	0	0	0
Total EV =			44		56.5		40.75
SPI and Projection to Completion		44/103 = .43 $(1/.43 \times 7) = 16.28$ mos.		56.5/103 = .55 $(1/.55 \times 7) = 12.73$ mos.		40.75/103 = .40 $(1/.40 \times 7) = 17.5$ mos.	
CPI and Project to Completion		44/78 = .56 $210,714		56.5/78 = .72 $163,889		40.75/78 = .52 $226,923	

based on five levels of completion (column 3). Is one approach "more correct" than the other? Absent some decision rule or logic for making these determinations, it is virtually impossible to suggest that one level of detail is more representative of the "true" status of project activity completion.

As this chapter has noted, earned value management is not a flawless methodology for project tracking and control, particularly as it pertains to the problems in accurately determining the percentage of work packages completed at any time point during the project's development. Nevertheless, EVM does represent a significant step forward in allowing project managers and their teams to gain a better perspective on the "true" nature of a project's status midstream, that is, in the middle of the development and implementation process.[6] This sort of real-time information can be invaluable in helping us gain current information and begin to develop realistic plans for correcting any systematic problems with the development process. The more we learn, and the faster we learn it, of a project's status, the better equipped we will be to take measured and effective steps to get a troubled project back on track.

13.6 HUMAN FACTORS IN PROJECT EVALUATION AND CONTROL

Another recurring problem with establishing accurate or meaningful EVM results has to do with the need to recognize the human factor in all project activity completion projections. That is, there is a strong incentive in most organizations for project team members to continuously report stronger results than may be warranted in the interest of looking good for the boss or sending the right signals about the project's status. Worse, many times implicit or even explicit pressure may come from the project managers themselves, as they find themselves under pressure from top management to show steady results. Hence, the level of detail controversy is not simply one of accurately matching technical performance on the project to the best external indicator or number of gradients. Often it is also a problem rooted in human behavior, suggesting that excessively fine levels of detail not only may be inappropriate for the types of project activities we engage in, but also may be prone to misuse by the project team.

The common feature of control approaches is their reliance on measurable data based on project outcomes; that is, the results of project actions taken in any one time period are collected and reported after the fact. Hence, we determine schedule or cost variance after the information has been collected and reported. Some project management writers, however, have suggested that it is equally essential to maintain a clear understanding of the importance of the management of people in the project implementation process. In other words, the data collected from the various evaluation and control techniques represents important *outcome* measures of the project; however, comprehensive project control also requires that the project organization employ sufficient process evaluations to determine how the development is progressing.

A key component of any process evaluation of project performance must include an assessment of its people, their technical skills, management, teamwork, communication processes, motivation, leadership, and so forth.[7] In short, many evaluation and control techniques (such as EVM) will do an excellent job in answering the "what" questions (What is the status of the project? What is our cost efficiency factor? What tasks are currently running late?), but they do not attempt to answer the "why" questions (Why are activities behind schedule? Why is the project team performing at a suboptimal level?). In an effort to provide answers to the "why" questions, work on the human processes in project management has been initiated and continues to be done.

Past research examining the impact of human factors on project success bears out the importance of considering the wider "management" challenge inherent in managing projects. For example, early work of Baker and colleagues[8] identified a variety of factors that directly predict project success. Included in their list were issues such as:

- Project coordination and relations among stakeholders
- Adequacy of project structure and control
- Project uniqueness, importance, and public exposure
- Success criteria salience and consensus
- Lack of budgetary pressure
- Avoidance of initial overoptimism and conceptual difficulties

Their findings bear out the importance of having a clear knowledge of the managerial challenges involved when implementing projects. These findings have been reinforced by other research that has examined a set of both successful and unsuccessful projects across their life cycle.[9]

The findings of such research are intriguing because of the importance they place on the managerial and human behavioral aspects of project management for project success. As Table 13.9 shows, regardless of whether the project studied was a success or failure, the factors that were of highest importance demonstrate some clear similarities. Issues such as leadership, top management support, team and personal motivation, and client support were consistently linked with project success, suggesting once again that an understanding of the project management *process* is keenly important for determining the likelihood of a project's successful outcome.

TABLE 13.9 Key Success Drivers and Inhibitors

Stage	Successful Projects Factors	Stage	Failed Projects Factors
Formation	Personal ambition Top management support Team motivation Clear objectives Technological advantage	Formation	Unmotivated team Poor leadership Technical limitations Funding problems
Buildup	Team motivation Personal motivation Top management support Technical expertise	Buildup	Unmotivated team Conflict in objectives Leadership problems Poor top management support Technical problems
Main Phase	Team motivation Personal motivation Client support Top management support	Main Phase	Unmotivated team Poor top management support Deficient procedures
Closeout	Personal motivation Team motivation Top management support Financial support	Closeout	Poor control Poor financial support Unclear objectives Leadership problems

One of the key recurring problems, however, with making wider use of nontechnical information as a method for controlling projects and assessing their ongoing status lies in the question of measurement. Although financial and schedule data can be easily acquired and are relatively easy to interpret, measuring human processes such as motivation level, leadership, top management support, and so forth is highly problematic. As a result, even though a number of project management theorists have accepted the argument for inclusion of human process factors in assessing the status of ongoing projects, there has been little agreement as to how best to make such assessments, interpret the results, and use the findings in a prescriptive manner to improve the project processes.

The work of Pinto and Slevin[10] addresses the shortcomings with behavioral assessments of project management processes. They formulated the Project Implementation Profile (PIP), a 10-factor instrument that assesses the performance of the project team with respect to 10 critical success factors, that is, those factors they found to be predictive of project success. The advantage of the PIP is that it allows project teams to formally assess their performance on the ongoing project, allowing for midcourse correction and improvement of the management *process* itself. The 10 critical success factors represent an important, supplemental source of information on the project's status. Coupled with other types of evaluation and control information supplied through the tracking of cost and schedule variance against the project baseline, project teams can develop a comprehensive vision of the project's status throughout its development.

Critical Success Factor Definitions

The 10 critical success factors identified by Pinto and Slevin in formulating the Project Implementation Profile (PIP) instrument are (1) project mission, (2) top management support, (3) project plans and schedules, (4) client consultation, (5) personnel, (6) technical tasks, (7) client acceptance, (8) monitoring and feedback, (9) communication, and (10) troubleshooting. Each of these factors is discussed in more detail in the text that follows.

Project mission, the first factor, relates to the underlying purpose for the project. Project success is predicated on the importance of clearly defining objectives as well as ultimate benefits to be derived from the project. Many times, the initial stage of project management consists of a feasibility decision. Are the objectives clear and can they succeed? Project mission refers to a condition in which the objectives of the project are clear and understood, not only by the project team involved, but also by the other departments in the organization. The project manager must be concerned with clarification of objectives as well as achieving broad belief in the congruence of the objectives with overall organizational objectives.

Top management support, the second factor, has long been considered of great importance in distinguishing between ultimate success and failure. Project managers and their teams not only are dependent upon top management for authority, direction, and support, but also are the conduit for implementing top management's plans, or goals, for the organization.[11] Further, if the project is being developed for an internal audience (one within the company), the degree of management support for a project will lead to significant variations in the degree of acceptance or resistance to that project or product. Top management's support of the project may involve aspects such as allocation of sufficient resources (financial, personnel, time, etc.) as well as project management's confidence in support from top management in the event of a crisis.

The third factor, *project plans and schedules,* refers to the importance of developing a detailed plan of the required stages of the implementation process. It is important to remember, however, that the activities associated with project planning and project scheduling are distinct from each other. Planning, which is the first and more general step in developing the project implementation strategy, is composed of scope definition, creation of a Work Breakdown Structure, and resource and activity assignments. Scheduling is the setting of time frames and milestones for each important element in the overall project. The project plans and schedules factor is concerned with the degree to which time schedules, milestones, labor, and equipment requirements are specified. There must be a satisfactory measurement system to judge actual performance against budget allowances and time schedules.

The fourth factor is *client consultation.* The "client" is anyone who ultimately will be using the product of the project, either as a customer outside the company or as a department within the organization. Increasingly, the need for client consultation has been recognized as important in attempting a system implementation; indeed, the degree to which clients are personally involved in the implementation process correlates directly with variations in their support for projects.[12] It is important to identify the clients for the project and accurately determine if their needs are being met.

The fifth factor, *personnel,* includes recruitment, selection, and training of project team members. An important, but often overlooked, aspect of the implementation process concerns the nature of the personnel involved. In many situations, personnel for the project team are chosen with less than full regard for the skills necessary to actively contribute to implementation success. The personnel factor is concerned with developing an implementation team with the ability and commitment to perform their functions.

Technical tasks, the sixth factor, refers to the necessity of having not only the required numbers of personnel for the implementation team but also ensuring that they possess the technical skills and the technology and technical support needed to perform their tasks. It is important that people managing a project understand the technology involved. In addition, adequate technology must exist to support the system. Without the necessary technology and technical skills, projects quickly disintegrate into a series of miscues and technical errors.

The seventh factor, *client acceptance,* refers to the final stage in the project development process, at which time the overall efficacy of the project is to be determined. In addition to client consultation at an earlier stage in the system implementation process, it remains of ultimate importance to determine whether the clients for whom the project has been initiated will accept it. Too often project managers make the mistake of believing that if they handle the other stages of the implementation process well, the client (whether internal or external to the organization) will accept the resulting system. In fact, client acceptance is a stage in the project life cycle process that must be managed like any other.

The eighth factor, *monitoring and feedback,* refers to the project control process by which, at each stage of the project implementation, key personnel receive feedback on how the project is progressing compared to initial projections. Making allowances for adequate monitoring and feedback mechanisms gives the project manager the ability to anticipate problems, to oversee corrective measures, and to ensure that no deficiencies are overlooked. Project managers need to emphasize the importance of constant monitoring and fine-tuning project development; tracking control charts and Earned Value Management are excellent examples of the techniques and types of monitoring and control mechanisms necessary to develop a project.

Communication, the ninth factor, is not only essential within the project team itself, but—as we discussed in regard to stakeholder management—it is also vital between the team and the rest of the organization as well as with clients. Communication refers both to feedback mechanisms and to the necessity of exchanging information with both clients and the rest of the organization concerning the project's capabilities, the goals of the project, changes in policies and procedures, status reports, and so forth. Therefore, channels of communication are extremely important in creating an atmosphere for successful project implementation.

Troubleshooting is the tenth and final factor of the model. Problem areas exist in almost every project development. The measure of a successful project is not the avoidance of problems, but taking the correct steps once problems develop. Regardless of how carefully the implementation effort is initially planned, it is impossible to foresee every trouble area or problem that can possibly arise. As a result, the project manager must include mechanisms in the implementation plan for recognizing problems and for troubleshooting them when they arise. Such mechanisms make it easier not only to react to problems as they arise, but also to foresee and possibly forestall potential problem areas in the implementation process.

Conclusions

This chapter has addressed a variety of approaches to project tracking and control. Although most of the models mentioned have many advantages associated with them, project management professionals should be aware of the concomitant problems and shortcomings with these approaches as well. The key to developing a useful project control process lies in recognizing the strengths and weaknesses of the alternative methods and ultimately developing an approach that best suits the organization, the projects undertaken, and the stakeholders of the project. A project control process should be tailored, to the degree possible, to the specific needs, culture, and uses for which an organization intends it. Thus, under some circumstances, a simplified control system may be sufficient for providing management with the types of information they require. Alternatively, some organizations and/or projects will need to employ highly sophisticated control processes because of either the unique nature of their operating processes or the demands that developing projects place on them (e.g., governmental stipulations and mandates).[13]

The comprehensive and intricate concept of project evaluation and control involves the need to understand alternative evaluation techniques, recognizing their particular usefulness and the types of information they can provide. Ultimately, however, these techniques are merely as good as the project planning process; that is, a good control system cannot make up for inadequate or inaccurate initial plans. Without effective baselines, good project cost estimation and budgeting, and adequate resource commitments, project control simply will not work. However, if the up-front planning has been done effectively, project evaluation and control can work in harmony with the project plans, providing the project team with not only a clear road map to success, but also excellent mileposts along the highway.

Summary

1. **Understand the nature of the control cycle and four key steps in a general project control model.** Accurately evaluating the status of ongoing projects represents a real challenge for project teams and their parent organizations. The process of project control, consisting of a recurring cycle of four steps (setting goals, measuring progress, comparing actual progress with plans, and correcting significant deviations), demonstrates a theoretical framework for understanding the continuous nature of project monitoring and control.

2. **Recognize the strengths and weaknesses of common project evaluation and control methods.** A number of project evaluation and control techniques exist, from the simplistic to the highly sophisticated. The most basic evaluation process, project S-curves, seeks to reconcile the project schedule baseline with planned budget expenditures. The cumulative project budget, resembling the letter *S*, creates a schedule/budget relationship that early project monitoring methods found useful as an indicator of expected progress. Unfortunately, a number of problems with S-curve analysis preclude its use as an accurate evaluation and control technique. Other evaluation methods include milestone analysis and tracking Gantt charts. These approaches link project progress to the schedule baseline, rather than the project budget. As with S-curves, milestones and tracking charts have some advantages, but they all share a common drawback: the inability of these methods to accurately assess the status of ongoing activities, and therefore the "true" status of the project, in a meaningful way. Specifically, because these monitoring and control methods do not link schedule and budget baselines to actual ongoing project performance, they cannot offer a reasonable measure of project status.

3. **Understand how Earned Value Management can assist project tracking and evaluation.** Earned Value Management (EVM) is a powerful tool, developed through a mandate from the federal government, to directly link project progress to schedule and budget baselines. In effect, EVM provides the missing piece of the control puzzle by requiring the reporting of actual project activity status on a real-time basis. Earned Value Management has begun to diffuse more rapidly within ordinary project-based organizations as they increasingly perceive the advantages of its use.

4. **Use Earned Value Management for project portfolio analysis.** The basic principles that govern the use of earned value on a single project can be applied to a portfolio of projects. Each project is evaluated in terms of the basic efficiency indexes for time and cost, and an overall evaluation can be calculated for a firm's project portfolio. This portfolio model allows us to determine the overall efficiency with which we manage projects, to see which are ahead and which are behind the firm's baseline standards.

5. **Understand behavioral concepts and other human issues in evaluation and control.** A final method for tracking and evaluating the status of ongoing projects lies in the use of alternative control methods, aimed at assessing and managing the "human issues" in project management, rather than focusing exclusively on the technical ones. In other words, EVM and other previously discussed tracking and control mechanisms focus on data-driven measures of performance (budget, schedules, and functionality); but other models that address the managerial and behavioral issues in project management argue that unless we merge these data-driven models with those that assess the project in terms of human interactions (leadership, top management support, communication, and so forth), it is possible to generate a great deal of information on the current status of a project without recognizing the primacy of human behavior in determining the success or failure of project activities. To create a well-rounded sense of the project performance, it is necessary to blend purely data-driven monitoring models with managerial-based approaches.

6. **Understand the advantages of Earned Schedule methods for determining project schedule variance, schedule performance index, and estimates to completion.** The accompanying text should be: Earned schedule represents an alternative method for determining the status of a project's schedule to completion by recognizing that standard Earned Value employs budget data to calculate not only estimates of project cost but also time (schedule). Arguing that "schedule is different," earned schedule identifies the possible schedule estimation errors EVM can be prone to and offers some corrective procedures to adjust these calculations.

Key Terms

Actual cost of work performed (AC) (p. 439)

Budgeted cost at completion (BAC) (p. 439)

Control cycle (p. 432)

Cost Performance Index (CPI) (p. 439)

Earned Schedule (ES) (p. 462)

Earned value (EV) (p. 438)

Earned Value Management (EVM) (p. 437)

Estimate at Completion (EAC) (p. 445)

Milestone (p. 435)

Planned value (PV) (p. 441)

Project baseline (p. 432)

Project control (p. 432)

Project S-curve (p. 433)

Schedule Performance Index (SPI) (p. 439)

Schedule variance (p. 441)

Tracking Gantt chart (p. 436)

Solved Problem

Example of Earned Value

The Project Management Institute, the largest professional organization of project management professionals in the world, has developed a simple example of the logic underlying earned value assessment for a project. It demonstrates, in the following steps, the calculation of the more relevant components of earned value and shows how these steps fit together to contribute an overall understanding of earned value.

Earned value is a management technique that relates resource planning to schedules and to technical cost and schedule requirements. All work is planned, budgeted, and scheduled in time-phased planned value increments constituting a cost and schedule measurement baseline. There are two major objectives of an earned value system: to encourage contractors to use effective internal cost and schedule management control systems, and to permit the customer to be able to rely on timely data produced by those systems for determining product-oriented contract status.

Baseline. The baseline plan in Table 13.10 shows that six work units (A–F) would be completed at a cost of $100 for the period covered by this report.

Schedule Variance. As work is performed, it is "earned" on the same basis as it was planned, in dollars or other quantifiable units such as labor hours. Planned value compared with earned value measures the dollar volume of work planned versus the equivalent dollar volume of work accomplished. Any difference is called a schedule variance. In contrast to what was planned, Table 13.11 shows that work unit D was not completed and work unit F was never started, or $35 of the planned work was not accomplished. As a result, the schedule variance shows that 35% of the work planned for this period was not done.

Cost Variance. Earned value compared with the actual cost incurred (from contractor accounting systems) for the work performed provides an objective measure of planned and actual cost. Any difference is called a cost variance. A negative variance means more money was spent for the work accomplished than was planned. Table 13.12 shows the calculation of cost variance. The work performed was planned to cost $65 and actually cost $91. The cost variance is 40%.

Spend Comparison. The typical spend comparison approach, whereby contractors report actual expenditures against planned

TABLE 13.10 Baseline Plan Work Units

	A	B	C	D	E	F	Total
Planned value	10	15	10	25	20	20	100

TABLE 13.11 Schedule Variance Work Units

	A	B	C	D	E	F	Total
Planned value	10	15	10	25	20	20	100
Earned value	10	15	10	10	20	—	65
Schedule variance	0	0	0	−15	0	−20	−35, or −35%

TABLE 13.12 Cost Variance Work Units

	A	B	C	D	E	F	Total
Earned value	10	15	10	10	20	—	65
Actual cost	9	22	8	30	22	—	91
Cost variance	1	−7	2	−20	−2	0	−26, or −40%

expenditures, is not related to the work that was accomplished. Table 13.13 shows a simple comparison of planned and actual spending, which is unrelated to work performed and therefore not a useful comparison. The fact that the total amount spent was $9 less than planned for this period is not useful without the comparisons with work accomplished.

Use of Earned Value Data. The benefits to project management of the earned value approach come from the disciplined planning conducted and the availability of metrics that show real variances from the plan in order to generate necessary corrective actions.[14]

TABLE 13.13 Spend Comparison Approach Work Units

	A	B	C	D	E	F	Total
Planned spend	10	15	10	25	20	20	100
Actual spend	9	22	8	30	22	—	91
Variance	1	−7	2	−5	−2	20	9, or 9%

Discussion Questions

1. Why is the generic four-stage control cycle useful for understanding how to monitor and control projects?
2. Why was one of the earliest project tracking devices referred to as an S-curve? Do you see value in the desire to link budget and schedule to view project performance?
3. What are some of the key drawbacks with S-curve analysis?
4. What are the benefits and drawbacks with the use of milestone analysis as a monitoring device?
5. It has been said that Earned Value Management (EVM) came about because the federal government often used "cost-plus" contractors with project organizations. Cost-plus contracting allows the contractor to recover full project development costs plus accumulate profit from these contracts. Why would requiring contractor firms to employ Earned Value Management help the government hold the line against project cost overruns?
6. What are the major advantages of using EVM as a project control mechanism? What do you perceive as its disadvantages?

7. Consider the major findings of the research on human factors in project implementation. What common themes seem to emerge from the research on behavioral issues as a critical element in determining project status?
8. The 10 critical success factors have been applied in a variety of settings and project types. Consider a project with which you have been involved. Did any of these factors emerge clearly as being the most important for the project's success? Why?
9. Identify the following terms: PV, EV, and AC. Why are these terms important? How do they relate to one another?
10. What do the Schedule Performance Index and the Cost Performance Index demonstrate? How can a project manager use this information to estimate future project performance?
11. Suppose the SPI is calculated as less than 1.0. Is this good news or bad news for the project? Why?

Problems

1. Using the following information, develop a simple S-curve representation of the expected cumulative budget expenditures for this project (figures are in thousands).

Duration (in days)

	10	20	30	40	50	60	70	80
Activities	4	8	12	20	10	8	6	2
Cumulative	4	12	24	44	54	62	68	70

2. Suppose the expenditure figures in Problem 1 were modified as follows (figures are in thousands).

Duration (in days)

	10	20	30	40	50	60	70	80
Activities	4	8	10	14	20	24	28	8
Cumulative	4	12	22	36	56	80	108	116

Draw this S-curve. What does the new S-curve diagram represent? How would you explain the reason for the different, non-S-shape of the curve?

3. Assume the following information (figures are in thousands):

Budgeted Costs for Sample Project

	Duration (in weeks)									
	5	10	15	20	25	30	35	40	45	Total
Design	4	4	2							
Engineer		3	6	12	8					
Install			4	12	24	6				
Test					2	6	6	4	2	
Total Monthly Cumul.										

a. Calculate the monthly budget and the monthly cumulative budgets for the project.

b. Draw a project S-curve identifying the relationship between the project's budget baseline and its schedule.

4. Use the following information to construct a tracking Gantt chart using MS Project.

Activities	Duration	Preceding Activities
A	5 days	none
B	4 days	A
C	3 days	A
D	6 days	B, C
E	4 days	B
F	2 days	D, E

Highlight project status on day 14 using the tracking option and assuming that all tasks to date have been completed on time. Print the output file.

5. Using the information in Problem 4, highlight the project's status on day 14 but assume that activity D has not yet begun. What would the new tracking Gantt chart show? Print the output file.

6. Use the following table to calculate project schedule variance based on the units listed (figures are in thousands).

Schedule Variance Work Units

	A	B	C	D	E	F	Total
Planned Value	20	15	10	25	20	20	110
Earned Value	25	10	10	20	25	15	
Schedule Variance							

7. Using the data in the table below, complete the table by calculating the cumulative planned and cumulative actual monthly budgets through the end of June. Complete the earned value column on the right. Assume the project is planned for a 12-month duration and a $250,000 budget.

8. Using the data from Problem 7, calculate the following values:

Schedule Variances

Planned Value (PV)	_____
Earned Value (EV)	_____
Schedule Performance Index	_____
Estimated Time to Completion	_____

Cost Variances

Actual Cost of Work Performed (AC)	_____
Earned Value (EV)	_____
Cost Performance Index	_____
Estimated Cost to Completion	_____

9. You are calculating the estimated time to completion for a project of 15 months' duration and a budgeted cost of $350,000. Assuming the following information, calculate the Schedule Performance Index and the estimated time to completion (figures are in thousands).

Schedule Variances

Planned Value (PV)	65
Earned Value (EV)	58
Schedule Performance Index	_____
Estimated Time to Completion	_____

10. Suppose, for Problem 9, that your PV was 75 and your EV was 80. Recalculate the SPI and estimated time to completion for the project with this new data.

11. Assume you have collected the following data for your project. Its budget is $75,000 and it is expected to last four months. After two months, you have calculated the following information about the project:

$$PV = \$45,000$$
$$EV = \$38,500$$
$$AC = \$37,000$$

Activity	Jan	Feb	Mar	Apr	May	Jun	Plan	% Comp.	Value
Staffing	8	7					15	100	_____
Blueprinting		4	6				10	100	_____
Prototype Development			2	8			10	70	_____
Full Design				3	8	10	21	67	_____
Construction					2	30	32	25	_____
Transfer						10	10	0	_____
Monthly Plan	___	___	___	___	___	___			___
Cumulative	___	___	___	___	___	___			
Monthly Actual	10	15	6	14	9	40			
Cumul. Actual	___	___	___	___	___	___			

Calculate the SPI and CPI. Based on these values, estimate the time and budget necessary to complete the project. How would you evaluate these findings? Are they good news or bad news?

12. (Optional—Based on Earned Schedule discussion in Appendix 13.1.) Suppose you have a project with a Budget at Completion (BAC) of $250,000 and a projected length of 10 months. After tracking the project for six months, you have collected the information in the table below.

a. Complete the table. How do Earned Value SPI (based on $) and Earned Schedule SPI differ?

b. Calculate the schedule variances for the project for both Earned Value and Earned Schedule. How do the values differ?

	Jan	Feb	Mar	Apr	May	Jun
PV ($)	25,000	40,000	70,000	110,000	150,000	180,000
EV ($)	20,000	32,000	60,000	95,000	123,000	151,000
SV ($)	−5,000					
SPI ($)	0.80					
ES (mo.)	0.80					
SV (t)	−.20					
SPI (t)	0.80					

Case Study 13.1

The IT Department at Kimble College

As part of the effort to upgrade the IT capabilities at Kimble College, the institution initiated a program more than five years ago to dramatically increase the size of the IT department while focusing efforts toward data management and improving administrative functions. As part of the upgrade, Kimble hired a new vice president of information systems, Dan Gray, and gave him wide latitude in identifying problems and initiating projects that would result in improving the IT system campuswide. Dan also was given the final power to determine the development of new projects, which allowed him to field requests from the various college departments, determine which needs were most pressing, and create a portfolio of prioritized projects. Within two years of his arrival at Kimble, Dan was overseeing an IT department of 46 people, divided into four levels: (1) help desk support, (2) junior programmers, (3) senior programmers, and (4) project team leaders. There were only four project team leaders, with the majority of Dan's staff working either at the entry-level help desk or as junior programmers.

In the past three years, the performance of Dan's department has been mixed. Although it has been responsible for taking on a number of new projects, its track record for delivery is shaky; for example, well over half of the new projects have run past their budgets and initial schedules, sometimes by more than 100%. Worse, from the college president's perspective, it does not appear that Dan has a clear sense of the status of the projects in his department. At board meetings, he routinely gives a rosy picture of his performance but seems incapable of answering simple questions about project delivery beyond vague declarations that "things are moving along just fine." In the president's view, Dan's departmental track record is not warranting the additional funding he keeps requesting for new equipment and personnel.

You have been called in, as an independent consultant, to assess the performance of Dan's department and, in particular, the manner in which it runs and monitors the development of its project portfolio. Your initial assessment has confirmed the college president's hunch: The ongoing status of projects in the IT department is not clearly understood. Everyone is working hard, but no one can provide clear answers about how the projects being developed are doing. After asking several project leaders about the status of their projects and repeatedly receiving "Oh, fine" as a response, you realize that they are not being evasive; they simply do not know from day to day how their projects are progressing. When you ask them how they determine project status, the general consensus is that unless the project team leaders hear bad news, they assume everything is going fine. Furthermore, it is clear that even if they wanted to spend more time monitoring their ongoing projects, they are not sure what types of information they should collect to develop better on-time project tracking and control.

Questions

1. As a consultant monitoring this problem, what solutions will you propose? To what degree has Dan's management style contributed to the problems?

2. What are some types of project status information you could suggest the project team leaders begin to collect in order to assess the status of their projects?

3. How would you blend "hard data" and "managerial or behavioral" information to create a comprehensive view of the status of ongoing projects in the IT department at Kimble College?

Case Study 13.2

Hong Kong's Cyberport

Cyberport was conceived as becoming a hub for the information and technology community in the Asia-Pacific region. Cyberport is owned and managed by the Hong Kong government, but is a commercial operation.

In March 1999, the $2 billion project was announced to be located on Telegraph Bay. The Hong Kong government had signed a deal with the Pacific Century Group (PCG) to construct the development. It would be a combination of offices, retail outlets, a residential department, and a five-star hotel. The main purpose of the site was to host IT-related businesses that would help make Hong Kong the main digital player in the region.

It was a classic public-private deal in which the government would provide the land and the private company would take responsibility for the development, construction, and infrastructure. The two parties agreed to a profit-sharing scheme regarding the residential units that would be built.

The CEO of PCG was clear from the outset that the whole purpose of the project was to attract IT companies and that, unless Cyberport succeeded in this mission, the project would fail. Cyberport was designed to provide sufficient office space for 30 medium to large IT companies and up to 100 small companies. It was estimated that there would be around 12,000 people working from the office space. All of the offices were equipped with broadband and optical fiber networks. It was also planned to provide high-quality technical support. Comparatively, the monthly rental costs were considerably lower than other office space in Hong Kong.

However, by the close of 2004, just 42% of the office space had been taken and there were only 33 companies operating out of the site with a workforce of only 2,000. Rather than receiving a share of the profits from Cyberport, the site was actually costing the Hong Kong government money. Total losses for 2004 stood at $11.64 million. Maintenance and administration costs far outweighed the rental income.

Critics were already claiming that Cyberport was a real estate development masquerading as a technology project. When it was announced that the profits from the residential component (Bel-Air) had been substantial, this only seemed to prove the point. By the end of 2004, sales had been brisk for the residential units and profits of $218 million had been shared between PCG and the government. To fill up the office space, Cyberport began to actively seek non-IT and creative companies.

Why Hong Kong Needed Cyberport

In comparison to Beijing, Hong Kong lacked technology talent. Global technology giants like Microsoft and Google had ignored Hong Kong. Shanghai was beating Hong Kong too, attracting overseas interest. What technology talent Hong Kong did have was moving to mainland China. Hong Kong needed to stem the flow of talent out of the city-state and establish itself in the technology market.

These were primary reasons for the development of Cyberport. By 2010, however, Cyberport was full. The years of half-empty office and retail units had passed. The Bel-Air development had proved to be a spectacular success, but its profitability had undermined the whole purpose of Cyberport and the original intent behind its development.

Why Cyberport Finally Succeeded

Compared to mainland China, Hong Kong still offers some considerable advantages to IT development. Many analysts have cited the reasons for the eventual Cyberport turnaround, highlighting the following issues:

- Hong Kong can be seen as an early adopter market compared to mainland China. This is particularly true in terms of the demand for software applications for mobile devices. Developing these applications on sites such as Cyberport need not be expensive.
- Hong Kong has a comparatively high market penetration of newer mobile technologies than mainland China.
- Although salaries in Hong Kong are higher than in the mainland, the less strict currency movement allows IT companies to sell globally and break even more quickly.
- Hong Kong has a very high population density and actually has better broadband coverage than the majority of other cities in the world. This means that high-end telecommunications hardware and software can be developed, sold, and test-marketed in Hong Kong prior to a global roll-out.
- The banking system in Hong Kong is set up to deal with incoming and outgoing transactions in virtually any currency which makes it much easier to set up commercial businesses.
- Unlike mainland China, Hong Kong businesses and residents are not blocked from access to globally used search engines and applications.
- Facebook and Twitter are freely accessible in Hong Kong, and websites are not censored. This means that there is no requirement to install proxy servers.
- In Hong Kong, the mobile phone market is relatively unregulated. In mainland China, there are just three mobile phone operators that must defer to the Chinese government. Mobile phone operators in Hong Kong can make immediate business decisions and are not restricted in their operations, allowing them to introduce new services and applications.

- Hong Kong is not subject to Internet censorship, which allows developers to access material that is not normally available to developers based on the mainland.
- On the mainland, website content is strictly controlled. The Chinese government holds the website owner responsible for all content, and it has been seen to slow down Internet development. This is not the case in Hong Kong.
- Several global brands such as Yahoo and eBay have failed to succeed in mainland China; Hong Kong is now seen by businesses as the logical access point to China.
- Hong Kong has managed to attract some of the largest Internet companies in the world on account of the fact that it is rated as the fourth-largest capital market in the world.

To put the relative failure of Cyberport into perspective and to explain the reasons for the slow take up of office space, there is no better place to look than Silicon Valley in the United States. Cyberport may have had a rocky start, but it has, in 10 years, achieved similar results to what it took Silicon Valley 20 years to accomplish.[15]

Questions

1. Suppose you were a consultant called into the project by the government in 1999, when it was launched. Given the start to the project, what steps would you have taken to ensure there was positive "spin" on Cyberport?
2. What were the warning signs of impending failure as the project progressed? Could these signs have been foreseen and addressed or, in your opinion, was the project simply impossible to achieve? Take a position and argue its merits.
3. Search for Cyberport on the Internet. How do the majority of stories about the project present it? Given the negative perspective, what are the top three lessons to be learned from this project?

Internet Exercises

1. Go to the Companion Web site supporting this text at *www.pearsonglobaleditions.com/pinto* and access the article by Q. W. Fleming and J. M. Koppelman, "Earned value project management …an introduction," *Crosstalk: The Journal of Defense Software Engineering* (July 1999), pp. 10–14. From your reading, summarize the key points or advantages they argue earned value offers for project control and evaluation.
2. Go to www.acq.osd.mil/evm and explore the various links and screens. What does the size and diversity of this site tell you about the acceptance and use of earned value in organizations today?
3. Go to www.erpgenie.com/general/project.htm and access the reading on "Six Steps to Successful Sponsorship." Consider the critical success factors it identifies for managing an IT project implementation. How do these factors map onto the 10-factor model of Pinto and Slevin? How do you account for differences?

4. Type in the address www.massdot.state.ma.us/highway/TheBigDig.aspx and navigate through the Web site supporting the Boston Tunnel project. Evaluate the performance of this project using the model of 10 critical project success factors discussed in this chapter. How does the project rate, in your opinion? Present specific examples and evidence to support your ratings.
5. Go to the Companion Web site supporting this text and access the article by J. K. Pinto and J. G. Covin, "Critical factors in project implementation: A comparison of construction and R&D projects," *Technovation*, 9 (1989), pp. 49–62. What does this research suggest about the nature of critical success factor importance across different types of projects? Across the project life cycle?

MS Project Exercises

Exercise 13.1

Using the following data, enter the various tasks and create a Gantt chart using MS Project. Assign the individuals responsible for each activity, and once you have completed the network, update it with the percentage complete tool. What does the MS Project output file look like?

Activity	Duration	Predecessors	Resource	% Complete
A. Research product	6	—	Tom Allen	100
B. Interview customers	4	A	Liz Watts	75
C. Design survey	5	A	Rich Watkins	50
D. Collect data	4	B, C	Gary Sims	0

Exercise 13.2

Now, suppose we assign costs to each of the resources in the following amounts:

Resource	Cost
Tom Allen	$50/hour
Liz Watts	$55/hour
Rich Watkins	$18/hour
Gary Sims	$12.50/hour

Create the resource usage statement for the project as of the most recent update. What are project expenses per task to date?

Exercise 13.3

Use MS Project to create a Project Summary Report of the most recent project status.

Exercise 13.4

Using the data shown in the network precedence table below, enter the various tasks in MS Project. Then select a date approximately halfway through the overall project duration, and update all tasks in the network to show current status. You may assume that Activities A through I are now 100% completed. What does the tracking Gantt look like?

Project—Remodeling an Appliance

Activity	Duration	Predecessors
A. Conduct competitive analysis	3	—
B. Review field sales reports	2	—
C. Conduct tech capabilities assessment	5	—
D. Develop focus group data	2	A, B, C
E. Conduct telephone surveys	3	D
F. Identify relevant specification improvements	3	E
G. Interface with marketing staff	1	F
H. Develop engineering specifications	5	G
I. Check and debug designs	4	H
J. Develop testing protocol	3	G
K. Identify critical performance levels	2	J
L. Assess and modify product components	6	I, K
M. Conduct capabilities assessment	12	L
N. Identify selection criteria	3	M
O. Develop RFQ	4	M
P. Develop production master schedule	5	N, O
Q. Liaison with sales staff	1	P
R. Prepare product launch	3	Q

PMP Certification Sample Questions

1. Suppose your PV for a project was $100,000 and your EV was $60,000. Your Schedule Performance Index (SPI) for this project would be:
   a. 1.52
   b. .60
   c. You cannot calculate SPI with the information provided
   d. 1.66

2. Activity A is worth $500, is complete, and actually cost $500. Activity B is worth $1,000, is 50% complete, and has actually cost $700 so far. Activity C is worth $100, is 75% complete, and has actually cost $90 so far. What is the total earned value for the project?
   a. $1,600
   b. $1,075
   c. $1,290
   d. −$1,075

3. Using the information in Question 2, calculate the Cost Performance Index (CPI) for the project.
   a. 1.20
   b. −1.20
   c. 0.83
   d. −0.83

4. Which of the following gives the remaining amount to be spent on the project in Questions 2 and 3 based on current spending efficiency?
   a. Budget remaining
   b. Estimate to complete
   c. Cost variance
   d. Cost Performance Index (CPI)

5. Activity A is worth $100, is complete, and actually cost $150. Activity B is worth $500, is 75% complete, and has actually cost $400 so far. Activity C is worth $500, is 25% complete, and has actually cost $200 so far. What is the estimated cost to completion for the project?
   a. $1,100
   b. $750
   c. $880
   d. $1,375

Answers: **1.** b—SPI is calculated by dividing earned value (EV) by planned value (PV); **2.** b—Earned Value is $1,075 to date; **3.** c—CPI is calculated as earned value (EV) divided by actual cost (AC). In this case, that is $1.075/$1,290, or 0.83; **4.** b—Estimate to complete; **5.** d—Estimate to completion is based on the formula (1/.80) × $1,100, or $1,375.

APPENDIX 13.1

Earned Schedule*

Research and practice using Earned Value Management (EVM) has shown that this method for project tracking and forecasting is reliable and offers the project team an accurate snapshot of both the project's current status and a forecast of its completion conditions. However, in recent years, some critics have noted that EVM also has some important limitations. One of the most important of these limitations is the fact that all project status information is derived in terms of the project's budget, including the project Schedule Performance Index (SPI) and schedule variance. A second concern voiced about EVM is that it becomes less precise (unreliable) the farther a project progresses and that by the latter stages of the project, the information derived from EVM may be either unjustifiably positive or negative. Finally, it has been suggested that EVM becomes an imprecise metric for projects that have already overrun, that is, whose duration has exceeded the original baseline end date. In other words, how do we determine the ongoing status of a project once it is officially "late"?

Let us consider these objections to EVM in turn. First, we know that EVM is derived from the project's budget, not its schedule performance, but intuitively, it makes better sense that a project's schedule performance should be in terms of units of time. For example, remember that Schedule Variance (SV) is calculated by Earned Value (EV) minus Planned Value (PV), and the formula for finding the Schedule Performance Index (SPI) is SPI = EV/PV. Thus, we are assessing the project's schedule performance, not as a function of time, but of money. We can see this graphically by considering Figure 13.18, which shows a generic project EVM measure. The vertical axis of the performance chart is in terms of budget dollars, and the resulting schedule variance is also expressed in terms of the project's budget. The EVM metrics for schedule, then, are Earned Value (EV) and Planned Valued (PV).

The second concern suggests that the closer to completion a project gets, the less precise and useful is the information that EVM provides. The significance of cost-based ratios used with planned duration to predict a project's final duration can be illustrated by a simple example. Assume a project with a budget of \$1,000 has completed most of its planned work, with EV = \$990, PV = \$1,000, BAC = \$1,000, and PD (Planned Duration) = 12 weeks. These metrics give an SPI of 0.99, which yields a final duration of 12.12 weeks: Estimate at Completion = 1/.99 × 12. We can see from simple inspection that as EV approaches PV, and ultimately BAC, forecasted project duration decreases, because the upper limit for EV is always BAC. Regardless of whether this calculation is performed during week 10 or week 15, the cost-based ratio yields

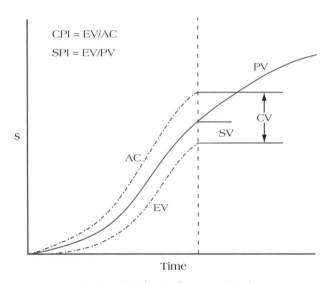

FIGURE 13.18   Earned Value Performance Metrics

Source: Lipke, W. H. (2003, Spring). "Schedule is different," *The Measureable News,* pp. 10–15.

---

*Portions of this appendix were prepared in collaboration with Bill Mowery, MPM, PMP.

the same results and can show that an in-progress project has a forecasted completion date in the past. This issue suggests that EVM becomes less precise the closer a project is to its completion. Where early indicators are reasonably accurate, by the final stages of the project's life cycle, the project schedule metric (remember, it is based on monetary units) is likely to show encouraging evidence of completion. However, it is during the final stages of the project that Cost Variance and Schedule Variance data begin to diverge.

Critics of EVM have pointed out this quirk in the system; as a project moves closer to its supposed completion date, its planned value converges on the project's planned cost—that is, PV = BAC (Budgeted at Completion). However, with late projects, the project's planned value has usually already converged on the project's overall budget (i.e., PV = BAC), while EV is still incrementally achieving this value. Once PV = BAC at the project's planned completion date, the project cannot be measured as being "later." In effect, there are measurement errors that do not become apparent until a project is already late.

The solution that researchers have adopted is to introduce the concept of **Earned Schedule (ES)** project management. Earned Schedule recognizes, first, that for accurate forecasts of project schedule, some unit of time must be the metric to consider, rather than EVM's cost-based approach. Earned Schedule uses a relatively simple formulation to achieve its purpose, which is to derive a time-based measurement of schedule performance by comparing a project's EV today (actual time) to a point on the performance measurement baseline (the Planned Value curve) where it should have been earned. The difference in the two times represents a true time-based Schedule Variance, or, in Earned Schedule notation, SV_t. The derivation of Earned Schedule metrics is shown in Figure 13.19. As the figure demonstrates, the Schedule Performance Index for any project can be reconfigured from the original, SPI($) = EV/PV, to the alternative: SPI(t) = ES/AT. In the second equation, the Schedule Performance Index for an Earned Schedule calculation divides the Earned Schedule value by Actual Time. Likewise, in this second configuration, Earned Schedule variance equals Earned Schedule minus Actual Time (ES – AT).

To calculate Earned Schedule, we use the project's current earned value (EV) to identify in which time increment of PV the cost value occurs. The value of ES is then equal to the cumulative time to the beginning of that increment plus some portion of it. For example, suppose we wished, at the end of June, to calculate the ES of a project that began January 1 (see Figure 13.19). We use monthly increments in our calculation; thus, because we are at the end of June, AT = 6. We can see visually that by the end of June, the project's schedule has slipped some degree; in fact, we see that we have completed all of April and some portion of May's work by the end of June. We can use the following formula to determine the project's ES:

$$ES = C + (EV - PV_c)/(PV_{c+1} - PV_c)$$

where C is the number of time increments on the project schedule baseline where EV ≥ PV. In our specific example above, with monthly time increments, the formula becomes:

$$ES = 4 + [EV(\$) - PV \, (April)]/[PV \, (May) - PV \, (April)]$$

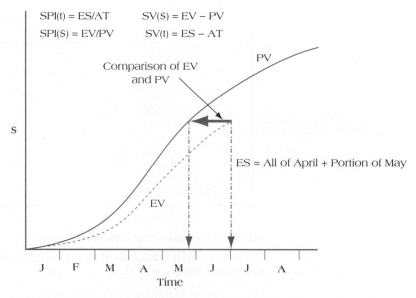

FIGURE 13.19 Earned Schedule Example (end of June)

TABLE 13.14 Earned Schedule Table

	Jan	Feb	Mar	Apr	May	Jun	Jul
PV ($)	105	200	515	845	1175	1475	1805
EV ($)	95	180	470	770	1065	1315	
SV ($)	−10	−20	−45	−75	−110	−160	
SPI ($)	0.91	0.90	0.91	0.91	0.90	0.89	
Month Count	1	2	3	4	5	6	7
ES (mo)							
SV (t)							
SPI (t)							

We can see an example of a complete Earned Schedule calculation in the following case. Suppose we have been collecting data on the status of our project for the past six months, using the standard EVM method. Table 13.14 gives this information.

Calculating the ES for January, we have the values:

EV (Jan) = 95
PV (Jan) = 105

We can use this information to calculate ES, SV, and SPI for the project, using the formulas we found previously:

ES = 0 + (95 − 0) / (105 − 0) = 0.90
SV (t) = ES − AT, or 0.90 − 1.0 = −0.10
SPI (t) = ES / C, or 0.90 / 1 = 0.90

Using this information, let's complete the ES table to the end of June (see Table 13.15). The table now aligns with Figure 13.19.

We can see from the information we have calculated in Table 13.15 coupled with Figure 13.19 that by the end of June, a comparison of the project's PV with actual ES shows a serious slippage. Specifically, by the end of June, we have only completed the project's schedule to approximately halfway through the May period. Furthermore, the schedule variance and SPI values have been worsening over the past four months, suggesting that the slippage is accelerating. This information is not necessarily obvious from the standard earned value table, which uses project budget dollars. Finally, research demonstrates that the SPI based on dollars versus the SPI using time can become very different as the project moves toward completion. Thus, as noted earlier, real data confirm one of the central concerns about EVM, namely, that its estimates for schedule become increasingly imprecise the later into the project we move.

The relative accuracy of Earned Schedule versus EVM can be further illustrated when we use it to anticipate schedule variances and possible project delays. Let's use the following example to compare the results we might find when using EVM versus Earned Schedule. Suppose we have a project planned for 18 months' duration (PD) and a total budget of $231,280 (BAC). At the end of 16 months, $234,080 has been spent (AC)

TABLE 13.15 Completed Earned Value/Schedule Table

	Jan	Feb	Mar	Apr	May	Jun	Jul
PV ($)	105	200	515	845	1175	1475	1805
EV ($)	95	180	470	770	1065	1315	
SV ($)	−10	−20	−45	−75	−110	−160	
SPI ($)	0.91	0.90	0.91	0.91	0.90	0.89	
Month Count	1	2	3	4	5	6	7
ES (mo)	0.90	1.79	2.86	3.77	4.66	5.47	
SV (t)	−0.10	−0.21	−0.14	−0.23	−0.33	−0.53	
SPI (t)	0.90	0.90	0.95	0.94	0.93	0.91	

while we only have achieved an EV of $207,470. We first calculate budget performance, or Cost Variance (CV), as $CV = EV - AC$, or:

$$CV = \$207,470 - \$234,080, \text{ or } -\$26,610$$

Schedule Variance (SV), for our example, also can be calculated based on this information. Recall that $SV = EV - PV$, or:

$$SV = \$207,470 - \$220,490, \text{ or } -\$13,020$$

The above figures show that the project is over budget and behind schedule, but to what degree over the life of the project? We can also use this information to calculate Schedule Performance Index (SPI) and Cost Performance Index (CPI) for the project. Respectively, these values are found as:

$$CPI = EV/AC, \text{ or } \$207,470/\$234,080 = .89$$
$$SPI = EV/PC, \text{ or } \$207,470/\$220,490 = .94$$

We know from earlier in this chapter that the simple interpretation of these values suggests that each dollar spent on the project is only producing 89 cents' worth of work, and each 8-hour day is producing only 7.5 hours of effective work. What would the long-term effects of these values be on the project? One way to determine that is estimate the final schedule duration, the Estimate at Completion for Time (EAC_t), found through the following formula:

$$EAC_t = \frac{\dfrac{BAC}{SPI}}{\dfrac{BAC}{PD}}$$

where

BAC = Budget at Completion ($231,280)
PD = Planned Duration (18 months)
SPI = Schedule Performance Index (0.94)

Solving for EAC_t in our example, we find:

$$\frac{\dfrac{231,280}{0.94}}{\dfrac{231,280}{18}} = 19.15 \text{ months}$$

We can solve a similar equation to find the Estimate at Completion (EAC) for the project's budget. Dividing the BAC of $231,280 by the CPI (0.89) yields an estimated cost at completion for the project of $259,870.

To see how Earned Value and Earned Schedule calculations can lead to important divergence, let's use the same information from the above example, shown in Table 13.16, with ES formulas to determine the project's schedule status when we use *time metrics, not budget data.*

Recall that at the end of month 16, we are interested in determining the status of the schedule. Our formula to calculate Earned Schedule (ES) is given as:

$$ES = C + (EV - PV_c)/(PV_{c+1} - PV_c)$$

where

C = the number of time months on the schedule baseline where $EV \geq PV$, or 14 months
EV = $207,470
PV_{14} = $198,720
PV_{15} = $211,490
ES = 14 + (207,470 − 198,720) / (211,490 − 198,720) = 14.69 months

Applying our Schedule Variance equation, $SV_t = ES -$ Actual Time (AT), we find that the project is 1.31 months behind schedule ($SV_t = 16 - 14.69$). We can now apply this information to the Earned Schedule's Schedule Performance Index (SPI_t) formula, given as:

$$SPI_t = ES/AT = 14.69/16 = 0.92$$

TABLE 13.16 Sample Performance Data (in thousands $)

	Dec	Jan	Feb	Mar
Month	13	14	15	16
Planned Value	184.47	198.72	211.49	220.49
Earned Value	173.51	186.71	198.74	207.47
Cumul Actual Cost	196.76	211.25	224.80	234.08

TABLE 13.17 Comparison of EVM and Earned Schedule Metrics for Sample Project

Metric	Earned Value	Earned Schedule
Schedule Variance (SV)	−$13,020	−1.31 months
Schedule Performance Index (SPI)	0.94	0.92
Forecast Duration (IEAC)	19.15 months	19.61 months

Lastly, we can derive our projection for the project's final duration, using the Independent Estimate at Completion for time ($IEAC_t$), and come up with the duration forecast, as shown:

$$IEAC_t = PD/SPI_t$$

where

PD (Planned Duration) = 18 months

$IEAC_t = 18/0.92 = 19.51$ months

Consider the results condensed into Table 13.17. When we compare the variances, performance indexes, and projections to completion for the project using EVM versus Earned Schedule, we can see some important discrepancies. First, note the obvious point that for schedule variance, Earned Schedule provides an actual duration estimate based on time, not dollars. Thus, we can relate to the information more easily. However, it is more intriguing to see the differences when Earned Schedule is applied to the SPI in order to determine the likely overall project duration. In this case, the Earned Schedule value suggests final project duration of 19.51 months, or about a half a month later than a similar calculation using EVM.

Earned Schedule is a relatively new concept that has sparked debate within the project management community. To date, most research supporting Earned Schedule has come either from small samples in field tests or through computer models. Nevertheless, the underlying arguments supporting Earned Schedule do bear careful consideration. Research suggests that EVM has a tendency to become unreliable as a project moves to completion, and thus it is important to understand to what degree that is the case. It has been demonstrated, on the other hand, that as a project progresses, the accuracy of the ES approach actually improves. Another advantage of Earned Schedule is that the calculations are relatively straightforward and the data can be manipulated from the same information obtained for EVM calculations. Thus, at a minimum, Earned Schedule offers an important "check" to verify the accuracy of EVM for project monitoring, particularly as the project begins to overrun its baseline or move toward completion.[16]

Notes

1. www.windenergy.org.nz/; www.windenergy.org.nz/nz-wind-farms/operating-wind-farms/te-apiti; "New Zealand wind farm: Completed on-time and within budget despite record storms," PMI case study, www.pmi.org/Business-Solutions/OPM3-Case-Study-Library.aspx.
2. Departments of the Air Force, the Army, the Navy, and the Defense Logistics Agency. (1987). *Cost/Schedule Control Systems Criteria: Joint Implementation Guide.* Washington, DC: U.S. Department of Defense; Fleming, Q., and Koppelman, J. (1994). "The essence of evolution of earned value," *Cost Engineering,* 36(11): 21–27; Fleming, Q., and Koppelman, J. (1996). *Earned Value Project Management.* Upper Darby, PA: Project Management Institute; Fleming, Q., and Koppelman, J. (1998, July). "Earned value project management: A powerful tool for software projects," *Crosstalk: The Journal of Defense Software Engineering,* pp. 19–23; Hatfield, M. A. (1996). "The case for earned value," *PMNetwork,* 10(12): 25–27; Robinson, P. B. (1997). "The performance measurement baseline—A statistical view," *Project Management Journal,* 28(2): 47–52; Singletary, N. (1996).

"What's the value of earned value?" *PMNetwork,* 10(12): 28–30.

3. Brandon, Jr., D. M. (1998). "Implementing earned value easily and effectively," *Project Management Journal,* 29(2): 11–18.

4. Brandon, Jr., D. M. (1998), ibid.

5. Petro, T., and Milani, K. (2000). "Northrop Grumman's four-tier approach to earning value," *Management Accounting Quarterly,* 1(4): 40–48.

6. Christensen, D. S., McKinney, J., and Antonini, R. (1995). "A review of estimate at completion research," *Journal of Cost Analysis,* pp. 41–62; Christensen, D. S. (1998). "The costs and benefits of the earned valued management process," *Acquisition Review Quarterly,* 5, pp. 373–86; Marshall, R. A., Ruiz, P., and Bredillet, C. N. (2008). "Earned value management insights using inferential statistics," *International Journal of Managing Projects in Business,* 1: 288–94.

7. Morris, P. W. G. (1988). "Managing project interfaces—Key points for project success," in Cleland, D. I., and King, W. R. (Eds.), *Project Management Handbook,* 2nd ed. New York: Van Nostrand Reinhold, pp. 16–55.

8. Baker, B. N., Murphy, D. C., and Fisher, D. (1988). "Factors affecting project success," in Cleland, D. I., and King, W. R. (Eds.), *Project Management Handbook,* 2nd ed. New York: Van Nostrand Reinhold, pp. 902–19.

9. Morris, P. W. G. (1988), as cited.

10. Slevin, D. P., and Pinto, J. K. (1987). "Balancing strategy and tactics in project implementation," *Sloan Management Review,* 29(1): 33–41; Pinto, J. K. (1998). "Critical success factors," in Pinto, J. K. (Ed.), *Project Management Handbook.* San Francisco, CA: Jossey-Bass, pp. 379–95; Slevin, D. P., and Pinto, J. K. (1986). "The project implementation profile: New tool for project managers," *Project Management Journal,* 17(3): 57–70; Belout, A., and Gauvreau, C. (2004). "Factors affecting project success: The impact of human resource management," *International Journal of Project Management,* 22: 1–11; Belout, A. (1998). "Effect of human resource management on project effectiveness and success: Toward a new conceptual framework," *International Journal of Project Management,* 16: 21–26.

11. Beck, D. R. (1983). "Implementing top management plans through project management," in Cleland, D. I., and King, W. R. (Eds.), *Project Management Handbook.* New York: Van Nostrand Reinhold, pp. 166–84.

12. Manley, J. H. (1975). "Implementation attitudes: A model and a measurement methodology," in Schultz, R. L., and Slevin, D. P. (Eds.), *Implementing Operations Research/ Management Science.* New York: Elsevier, pp. 183–202.

13. Lock, D. (2000). "Managing cost," in Turner, J. R., and Simister, S. J. (Eds.), *Gower Handbook of Project Management,* 3rd ed. Aldershot, UK: Gower, pp. 293–321.

14. www.acq.osd.mil/pm/evbasics.htm.

15. "Cyberport: Realisation of an IT park through a public-private partnership," www.acrc.org.hk/promotional/promotional_shownote.asp?caseref=849&page=1; "Cyperport," www.cyberport.hk; "Why not give Cyberport a chance?" www.legco.gov.hk/yr04-05/english/panels/itb/papers/itb0202cb1-814-2e.pdf; "Why Hong Kong is China's new tech hub," www.forbes.com/sites/china/2010/05/11/why-hong-kong-is-chinas-new-tech-hub/.

16. Lipke, W. H. (2003, Spring). "Schedule is different," *The Measureable News,* pp. 10–15; Lipke, W. H. (2009). *Earned Schedule.* Lulu Publishing; Book, S. A. (2006, Spring). "Earned schedule and its possible unreliability as an indicator," *The Measureable News,* pp. 24–30; Lipke, W. H. (2006, Fall). "Applying earned schedule to critical path analysis and more," *The Measureable News,* pp. 26–30; Book, Stephen A. (2003, Fall). "Issues associated with basing decisions on schedule variance in an earned-value management system," *National Estimator,* Society of Cost Estimating and Analysis, pp. 11–15; www.earnedschedule.com; Vanhouckel, M., and Vandevoorde, S. (2007). "A simulation and evaluation of earned value metrics to forecast the project duration," *Journal of the Operational Research Society,* 58(10): 1361–74.

Project Closeout and Termination

Chapter Outline

Chapter Objectives

After completing this chapter, you will be able to:

1. Distinguish among the four main forms of project termination.
2. Recognize the seven key steps in formal project closeout.
3. Understand key reasons for early termination of projects.
4. Know the challenges and components of a final project report.

PROJECT MANAGEMENT BODY OF KNOWLEDGE CORE CONCEPTS COVERED IN THIS CHAPTER

1. Close Project (PMBoK sec. 4.6)
2. Report Performance (PMBoK sec. 10.5)
3. Close Procurements (PMBoK sec. 12.4)

PROJECT PROFILE

Case—New Jersey Kills Hudson River Tunnel Project

When dignitaries broke ground on the Access to the Region's Core (ARC) project in northern New Jersey in 2009, it was supposed to be a celebration to signal the start of a bright new future. Creating a commuter rail tunnel under the Hudson River was not a particularly new or difficult idea, but it was viewed as a critical need. The project was first proposed in 1995, and every New Jersey governor after that time had publicly supported the need for the tunnel. The reasons were compelling: The entire commuter rail system connecting New York and New Jersey was supported by only one congested 100-year-old, two-track railroad tunnel into an overcrowded Penn Station in midtown Manhattan; both tracks had reached capacity and could no longer accommodate growth. Passengers were making more than 500,000 trips through Penn Station every day, with station congestion and overcrowding the norm. The project was especially critical for New Jersey residents because their commuter ridership to New York had more than quadrupled in the past 20 years from 10 million annual trips to more than 46 million annual passenger trips. In the peak hours, the New Jersey Transit Authority operated 20 of the 23 trains heading into or out of New York. Building the ARC would double the number of New Jersey Transit commuter trains, from 45 to about 90, that could come into Manhattan every morning at rush hour.

In the face of such congestion and perceived need, the ARC project was conceived to include the following elements:

- Two new tracks under the Hudson River and the New Jersey Palisades
- A new six-track passenger station, to be known as "New York Pennsylvania Station Extension" (NYPSE) under 34th Street, with passenger connection to Penn Station
- A new rail loop near the Lautenberg Secaucus Junction station to allow two northern New Jersey line trains access to New York City
- A midday rail storage yard in Kearny, New Jersey

Proponents also argued the environmental advantages of the project, noting that the ARC project would eliminate 30,000 daily personal automobile trips, taking 22,000 cars off the roads and resulting in 600,000 fewer daily vehicle miles traveled. The project was expected to thus reduce greenhouse gas emissions by nearly 66,000 tons each year.

The ARC project was anticipated to take eight years to complete, coming into service in 2017. The cost of the project was significant, as the Federal Transit Administration (FTA) reported the project cost as $8.7 billion in their *Annual Report*. In order to share the burden of the project costs, the funding as originally proposed included the following sources:

- Federal government: $4.5 billion
- Port Authority of New York and New Jersey: $3.0 billion
- New Jersey Turnpike Authority: $1.25 billion

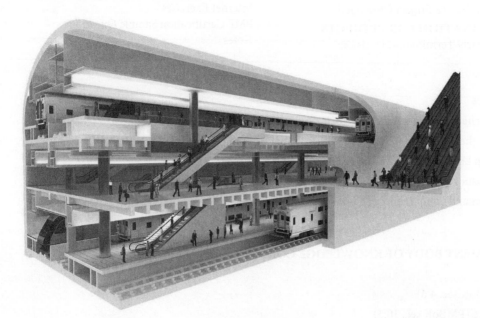

FIGURE 14.1   Artist's Rendition of Underground Train Platform at Penn Station for ARC Project

A final important feature of the funding plan limited the exposure of the federal government for any project overruns, meaning that the government was locked into its original commitment amount only. Any cost overruns or project slippages would have to be covered exclusively by the state of New Jersey.

The contracts for various parts of the project began to be awarded following competitive bidding in June 2009, and the first tunneling contract was awarded in May 2010. Within little more than three months, rumbles began being heard from the New Jersey governor's office on the viability of the project. Governor Chris Christie ran and was elected on the promise of reining in what many viewed as out-of-control spending by the state's legislature, coupled with some of the highest property and business taxes in the country. As a self-described "budget hawk," Christie was increasingly troubled by rumors of cost overruns in the ARC project. Worse, all projections for completion of the project pointed to a much higher final price tag than the original $8.7 billion estimate.

In early September 2010, Governor Christie ordered a temporary halt in awarding new contracts for the project until his office had a chance to study project cost projections more thoroughly. This issue was highlighted when U.S. Transportation Secretary Ray LaHood, though a supporter of the tunnel, publicly admitted that federal estimates showed the project could go between $1 billion and $4 billion over budget. Christie suspected that even those estimates might be low, putting his state on the hook for a potentially huge new debt, at a time when the economy was sour and the state was already desperately seeking means to trim runaway spending. As additional evidence of highly suspect initial cost estimates, Christie's supporters pointed to the recently completed "Big Dig" project in Boston, which started with an initial price tag of $2.5 billion and ultimately ended up costing well over $14 billion to complete.

Governor Christie first canceled the contract on October 7, 2010, citing cost overruns for which he said the state had no way to pay. The following day, he agreed to temporarily suspend his cancellation order so that he could try to resolve the funding dilemma with federal transportation officials and other project stakeholders. After a two-week period to analyze all their options, the governor made the cancellation official. Christie said that given the impact of the recession and the probability of continuing cost overruns, the state could no longer afford the tunnel's escalating costs. More than a half-billion dollars had already been spent on construction, engineering, and land acquisition for a project that was budgeted at $8.7 billion, but which the governor said could go as high as $14 billion. "The only prudent move is to end this project," Governor Christie said at a Trenton news conference. "I can't put taxpayers on a never-ending hook."[1]

INTRODUCTION

One of the unique characteristics of projects, as opposed to other ongoing organizational activities or processes, is that they are created with a finite life; in effect, when we are planning the project, we are also planning for its extinction. The project life cycle shown in Chapter 1 illustrates this phenomenon; the fourth and final stage of the project is defined as its termination. **Project termination** consists of all activities consistent with closing out the project. It is a process that provides for acceptance of the project by the project's sponsor, completion of various project records, final revision and issue of documentation to reflect its final condition, and the retention of essential project documentation.

In this chapter, we will explore the process of project termination and address the steps necessary to effectively conclude a project. Projects may be terminated for a variety of reasons. The best circumstance is the case where a project has been successfully completed and all project closeout activities are conducted to reflect a job well done. On the other hand, a project may conclude prematurely for any number of reasons. It may become irrelevant over time and be quietly shut down. It may become technologically obsolete due to a significant breakthrough by the competition. It may fail through a lack of top management support, organizational changes, or strategic priority shifts. It may be terminated due to catastrophic failure.

In short, although the best alternative is to be able to approach project termination as the culmination of a task well done, in reality many projects end up being terminated short of realizing their goals. These two alternatives are sometimes referred to as **natural termination**, in which the project has achieved its goals and is moving toward its logical conclusion, and **unnatural termination**, in which a shift in political, economic, customer, or technological conditions has rendered the project without purpose.[2] In this chapter, we will explore both types of termination in detail as we examine the steps we need to take to effectively close out a project during termination.

14.1 TYPES OF PROJECT TERMINATION

Although "project closeout" might imply that we are referring to a project that has been successfully completed and requires a systematic closeout methodology, as stated previously, projects can be terminated for a variety of reasons. The four main reasons for project termination are:[3]

1. **Termination by extinction.** This process occurs when the project is stopped due to either a successful or an unsuccessful conclusion. In the successful case, the project has been transferred to its intended users and all final phase-out activities are conducted. Whether successful or not, however, during termination the project's final budget is audited, team members receive new work assignments, and any material assets the project employed are dispersed or transferred according to company policies or contractual terms.

2. **Termination by addition.** This approach concludes a project by institutionalizing it as a formal part of the parent organization. For example, suppose a new hardware design at Apple Computer has been so successful that the company, rather than disband the project team, turns the project organization into a new operating group. In effect, the project has been "promoted" to a formal, hierarchical status within the organization. The project has indeed been terminated, but its success has led to its addition to the organizational structure.

3. **Termination by integration.** Integration represents a common, but exceedingly complicated, method for dealing with successful projects. The project's resources, including the project team, are reintegrated within the organization's existing structure following the conclusion of the project. In both matrix and project organizations, personnel released from project assignments are reabsorbed within their functional departments to perform other duties or simply wait for new project assignments. In many organizations, it is not uncommon to lose key organizational members at this point. They may have so relished the atmosphere and performance within the project team that the idea of reintegration within the old organization holds no appeal for them, and they leave the company for fresh project challenges. For example, the project manager who spearheaded the development and introduction of a geographic information system (GIS) for the city of Portland, Maine, left soon after the project was completed rather than accept a functional job serving as the system administrator. He found the challenge of managing the project much more to his liking than maintaining it.

4. **Termination by starvation.** Termination by starvation can happen for a number of reasons. There may be political reasons for keeping a project officially "on the books," even though the organization does not intend it to succeed or anticipate it will ever be finished. The project may have a powerful sponsor who must be placated with the maintenance of his "pet project." Sometimes projects cannot be continued because of general budget cuts, but an organization may keep a number of them on file so that when the economic situation improves, the projects can be reactivated. Meredith and Mantel[4] argue that termination by starvation is not an outright act of termination at all, but rather a willful form of neglect in which the project budget is slowly decreased to the point at which the project cannot possibly remain viable.

BOX 14.1

PROJECT MANAGERS IN PRACTICE

Mike Brown, Rolls-Royce Plc

With a 40-year career in project management, Mike Brown (see Figure 14.2) can safely claim that he has seen and done pretty much everything when it comes to running projects. With a background that includes degrees in industrial chemistry and engineering construction project management, Brown has worked on major construction projects around the world. His resume, which makes for fascinating reading, includes (1) running pharmaceutical research and development projects, (2) building refineries and petrochemical plants, (3) spearheading power and infrastructure projects, and (4) managing a variety of aeronautical development programs. Among his largest projects were a $500 million liquid natural gas tank farm project and a $500 million power plant construction project in India. Brown has worked in a number of exotic locations, including Sri Lanka, India, Africa, and the Pacific Rim.

It is in his current job with Rolls-Royce Corporation, however, that Brown has found the greatest opportunities to pass along the wealth of knowledge he has amassed. As Brown describes it:

My title is Head of the Center for Project Management, which is the Rolls-Royce Center of Excellence for Project Management. The Center is tasked with driving improvement in Project,

Program, and Portfolio Management across the entire company under the sponsorship of the Project Management Council, which is the senior management group that owns project management in Rolls-Royce.

At a personal level I coach, mentor, run seminars, and give presentations across the company to individuals and groups of practitioners. Having developed the University of Manchester and Penn State Masters programs eight years ago, there are now some 125 UK Masters graduates and 50 in North America. This network is now able to support improvement activities alongside me and is becoming a powerful driver for change.

In addition to my internal role, I represent Rolls-Royce in terms of project management to the outside world. This includes representing the company in various forums, as well as chairing the British Standards Committee responsible for the Project Management Standard.

When asked what has kept him so committed to the project management profession, Brown provided these reflections:

In my younger days it was the challenge of carrying on three conversations at the same time, solving problems, firefighting, and the general buzz of working with a great team, all driving towards the same goal. As I matured, it became clear to me that you solved problems on projects before you "started" them, through strategic thinking and actions in areas like requirements management, stakeholder management, value management, and solid business case development. In addition there are not many "professions" in which you can touch, feel, or experience the fruits of your labor. In project management you can.

When asked about the most memorable experiences of his career, Brown replied:

Every project is unique and so, in many ways, every project has offered its own memorable experiences. One that stands out for me, however, was a construction project in India that involved the development of a fertilizer complex. For the heavy lifting, we used everything from standard cranes to my favorite piece of heavy equipment—an elephant! Someone (probably the site safety officer) had even painted a Safe Working Load number on the elephant's back!

I guess one of the reasons that I relish the job is because it is a great developmental role for anyone in business. As a project manager you have all the responsibilities of a CEO. You deal with your own people, budgets, customers, and technical issues. You make critical decisions daily and you run your own operation. Really, with the exception of a company's CEO, a project manager has the most autonomy and responsibility within the firm. But it also takes a kind of magic to make it work. You don't have a lot of formal authority so you have to understand how to influence, lead your team, and gain respect—all based on your drive and setting a personal example.

FIGURE 14.2 Mike Brown of Rolls-Royce Plc.

14.2 NATURAL TERMINATION—THE CLOSEOUT PROCESS

When a project is moving toward its natural conclusion, a number of activities are necessary to close it out. Figure 14.3 provides a simple model that identifies the final duties and responsibilities of the project manager and team.[5] If the horizontal dimension is represented as a time line, we can view the activities as occurring both sequentially and concurrently. For example, some of the activities identified, such as finishing the work, handing over the project, and gaining acceptance for the project, are intended to occur in a serial path, from one set of activities to the next. At the same time that these tasks are being done, however, other activities occur concurrently, such as completing documentation, archiving records, and disbanding the team.

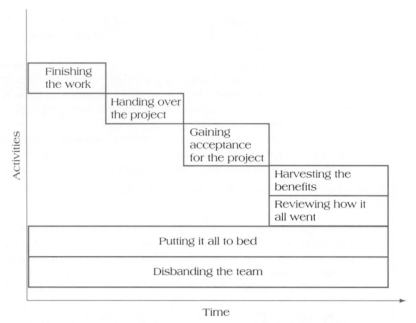

FIGURE 14.3 The Seven Elements of Project Closeout Management

Thus, the process of closing out a project is complex, involving multiple activities that must occur across a defined period. Let us consider these activities and the steps necessary to complete them in order.

Finishing the Work

As a project moves toward its conclusion, a number of tasks still need to be completed or polished, such as a final debug on a software package. At the same time, people working on the project naturally tend to lose focus—to begin thinking of new project assignments or their pending release from the team. The challenge for the project manager is to keep the team zeroed in on the final activities, particularly as the main elements of the project dramatically wind down. An orderly process for completing final assignments usually requires the use of a checklist as a control device.[6] For example, in building a house, the contractor will walk through the almost completed house with the new owner, identifying a *punch list* of final tasks or modifications that are needed prior to project completion.

Completing the final project activities is often as much a motivational challenge as a technical or administrative process for the project manager. Checklists and other simple control devices provide an important element of structure to the final tasks, reminding the project team that although the majority of the work has been finished, the project is not yet done. Using punch lists also demonstrates that even in the best projects, modifications or adjustments may be necessary before the project will be acceptable to the client.[7]

Handing Over the Project

Transferring the project to its intended user can be either a straightforward or a highly complex process, depending on the contractual terms, the client (either in-house or external), environmental conditions, and other mediating factors. The process itself usually involves a formal transfer of ownership of the project to the customer, including any terms and conditions for the transfer. This transfer may require careful planning and specific steps and processes. Transfer does not just involve shifting ownership; it also requires establishing training programs for users, transferring and sharing technical designs and features, making all drawings and engineering specifications available, and so on. Thus, depending on the complexity of the transfer process, the handing-over steps can require meticulous planning in their own right.

As a form of risk management in large industrial projects, it has become popular for customers such as foreign countries to refuse initial acceptance of a project until after a transition period in which the project contractor must first demonstrate the viability of the project. In the United Kingdom, these arrangements are often referred to as **Private Finance Initiatives (PFIs)** and are used to protect the excessive financial exposure of a contracting agency to a project being developed.[8] For example, suppose your company has just built a large iron-ore smelting plant for Botswana at a cost to the country of $1.5 billion. Under these circumstances, Botswana, for which such an investment is very risky, would first require your firm to operate the plant for some period to ensure that all technical features check out. This is the **Build, Operate, and Transfer (BOT)** option for large projects, which is a method for allowing the eventual owner of the project to mitigate risk in the short run. A modification on this BOT alternative is the **Build, Own, Operate, and Transfer (BOOT)** option. Under a BOOT contract, the project contractor takes initial ownership of the plant for a specified period to limit the client's financial exposure until all problems have been contractually resolved. The disadvantage to project organizations of BOT and BOOT contracts is that they require the contractor to take on high financial risk through operation or ownership of the project for some specified period. Hence, although they serve to protect the client, they expose the contractor to serious potential damages in the event of project failure.

Gaining Acceptance for the Project

A research study conducted on the critical success factors for projects found that client acceptance represents an important determination of whether the project is successful.[9] "Client acceptance" represents the recognition that simply transferring the project to the customer is not sufficient to ensure the customer's happiness with it, use of it, and recognition of its benefits. Many of us know, from our own experience, that gaining customer acceptance can be tricky and complex. Customers may be nervous about their capabilities or level of technical know-how. For example, in transferring IT projects to customers, it is common for them to experience initial confusion or miscomprehension regarding features in the final product. Some customers will purposely withhold unconditional acceptance of a project because they fear that after granting it, they will lose the ability to ask for modifications or corrections for obvious errors. Finally, depending on how closely our project team has maintained communication ties with the customer during the project's development, the final product may or may not be what the customer actually desires.

Because the process of gaining customer acceptance can be complicated, it is necessary to begin planning well in advance for both the transfer of the final product to the client and the creation, if necessary, of a program to ease the client's transition to ownership. In other words, when we start planning for the project's development, we need to also start planning for the project's transfer and use. The project team should begin by asking the hard questions, such as "What objections could the client make to this project, when it is completed?" and "How can we remove the client's concerns regarding the project's commercial or technical value?"

Harvesting the Benefits

Projects are initiated to solve problems, capitalize on opportunities, or serve some specific goal or set of goals. The benefits behind the completion of a project should be easy to determine; in fact, we could argue that projects are created for the purpose of attaining some benefit to their parent organizations. As a result, the idea of harvesting these benefits suggests that we be in a position to assess the value the project adds, either to an external customer or to our own firm, or both.

Benefits come in many forms and relate to the project being created. For example, in a construction project, the benefits may accrue as the result of public acclamation for the project on aesthetic or functional grounds. For a software project, benefits may include enhanced operating efficiency and, if designed for the commercial market, high profits and market share. The bottom line for harvesting the benefits suggests that the project organization should begin to realize a positive outcome from the completion of the project.

In practical terms, however, it may be difficult to accurately assess the benefits from a project, particularly in the short run. For instance, in a project that is created to install and modify an Enterprise Resource Planning (ERP) package, the benefits may be discovered over a period of time as the package allows the company to save money on the planning, acquisition, storage, and use of production materials for operations. The true benefits of the ERP system may not become apparent for several years, until all the bugs have been chased out of the software. Alternatively, a project that has been well run and is cost-effective may fail in the marketplace because of a competitor's unexpected technological leap forward that renders the project, no matter how well done, obsolete. For example, some have argued that Toyota's commitment to launching six new hybrid cars in 2011–2012 may not have been a well-reasoned strategy, given the new "all-electric" vehicle being offered by Nissan and U.S. automakers' move into more efficient hybrid vehicles. The concern of industry watchers was that the hybrid, in its current form, is a "bridge product" that may be supplanted by newer and even more efficient technologies (e.g., next-generation gas or ethanol-powered engines) during the same time window in which Toyota hoped to introduce their new products.

The key to begin harvesting the benefits of a project is to first develop an effective and meaningful measurement system that identifies the goals, time frame, and responsibilities involved in project use and value assessment. For example, at a minimum, a project assessment system should measure the following:[10]

1. The criteria by which benefits of the product or service will be measured
2. The points in time at which the measurement or assessment will be carried out
3. The individual who has accepted responsibility for carrying out the measurement or assessment in the agreed-upon way at the agreed-upon points in time

All of these issues must be worked out in advance, either as part of the project scope statement or during project development.

Reviewing How It All Went

One of the most important elements in the project closeout involves conducting an in-depth **lessons learned** analysis based on a realistic and critical review of the project—its high and low points, unanticipated difficulties, and elements that provide suggestions for future projects. Even among firms that conduct lessons learned reviews, a number of errors can occur at this stage, including:

- *Misidentifying systematic errors.*   It is human nature to attribute failures or mistakes to external causes, rather than internal reasons. For example, "The client changed the specifications" is easier to accept than the frank admission, "We didn't do enough to determine the customer's needs for the project." Closely related to this error is the desire to perceive mistakes as one-time or nonrecurring events. Rather than looking at our project management systems to see if the mistakes could be the result of underlying problems with them, many of us prefer the easier solution of believing that these results were unpredictable, that they were a one-time occurrence and not likely to recur, and that therefore we could not have prepared for them and do not need to prepare for them in the future.
- *Misapplying or misinterpreting appropriate lessons based on events.*   A related error of misinterpretation occurs when project team members or those reviewing the project wrongfully perceive the source of an encountered problem. Sometimes the correct lessons from a terminated project are either ignored or altered to reflect a prevailing viewpoint. For example, a computer manufacturer became so convinced that the technology its team was developing was superior to the competition's that the manager routinely ignored or misinterpreted any counteropinions, both within her own company and during focus group sessions with potential customers. When the project failed in the marketplace, the common belief within the company was that marketing had failed to adequately support the product, regardless of the data that marketing had been presenting for months suggesting that the project was misguided.
- *Failing to pass along lessons learned conclusions.*   Although it is true that an organization's projects are characterized as discrete, one-time processes, they do retain enough areas of overlap, particularly within a single firm's sphere, to make the application of lessons learned programs extremely useful. These **lessons learned** serve as a valuable form of organizational learning whereby novice project managers can access and learn from information provided by other project managers reporting on past projects. The success of a lessons learned process is highly dependent upon senior managers enforcing the archiving of critical historical information. Although all projects are, to a degree, unique, that uniqueness should never be an excuse to avoid passing along lessons learned to the rest of the organization. In the U.S. Army, for example, past project lessons learned are electronically filed and stored. All program managers are required to access these previous records based on the type of project they are managing and to develop a detailed response in advance that addresses likely problems as the project moves forward.

To gain the maximum benefit from lessons learned meetings, project teams should follow three important guidelines:

1. *Establish clear rules of behavior for all parties to the meeting.*   Everyone must understand that effective communication is the key to deriving lasting benefits from a lessons learned meeting. The atmosphere must be such that it promotes interaction, rather than stifling it.
2. *Describe, as objectively as possible, what occurred.*   People commonly attempt to put a particular "spin" on events, especially when actions might reflect badly on themselves. The goal of the lessons learned meeting is to recapitulate the series of events as objectively as possible, from as many viewpoints as possible, in order to reconstruct sequences of events, triggers for problems, places for miscommunication or misinterpretation, and so forth.

3. *Fix the problem, not the blame.* Lessons learned sessions work only when the focus is on problem solving, not on attaching blame for mistakes. Once the message is out that these sessions are ways for top management to find scapegoats for failed projects, they are valueless. On the other hand, when personnel discover that lessons learned meetings are opportunities for everyone to reflect on key events and ways to promote successful practices, defensiveness will evaporate in favor of meetings to resolve project problems.

Putting It All to Bed

The conclusion of a project involves a tremendous amount of paperwork needed to document and record processes, close out resource accounts, and, when necessary, track contractual agreements and the completed legal terms and conditions. Some of the more important elements in this phase are:

1. *Documentation.* All pertinent records of the project must be archived in a central repository to make them easy for others to access. These records include all schedule and planning documents, all monitoring and control materials, any records of materials or other resource usage, customer change order requests, specification change approvals, and so forth.
2. *Legal.* All contractual documents must be recorded and archived. These include any terms and conditions, legal recourse, penalties, incentive clauses, and other legal records.
3. *Cost.* All accounting records must be carefully closed out, including cost accounting records, lists of materials or other resources used, and any major purchases, rebates, or other budgetary items. All cost accounts related to the project must be closed at this time, and any unused funds or budget resources that are still in the project account must be reverted back to the general company budget.
4. *Personnel.* The costs and other charges for all project team personnel must be accounted for, their time charged against project accounts, and any company overhead in the form of benefits identified. Further, any nonemployees involved in the project, such as contractors or consultants, must be contractually released and these accounts paid off and closed.

Figure 14.4 shows some sample pages of a detailed project sign-off document. Among the important elements in the full document are a series of required reviews, including:

- *General program and project management confidence*—assessing the overall project specifications, plans, resources, costs, and risk assessment
- *Commercial confidence*—determining that the "business case" driving the project is still valid
- *Market and sales confidence*—based on pricing policies, sales forecasting, and customer feedback
- *Product quality confidence*—verifying all design reviews and relevant change requests
- *Manufacturing confidence*—manufacturing quality, production capability, and production confidence in creating the project
- *Supply chain logistics confidence*—ensuring that the project supply chain, delivery performance, and supplier quality are up to acceptable standards
- *Aftermarket confidence*—analyzing issues of delivery, customer expectations, and project support during the transfer stage
- *Health, safety, and environment confidence*—verifying that all HS&E impacts have been identified and documented

Disbanding the Team

The close of a project represents the ending of the project team's relationship, originally founded on their shared duties to support the project. Disbanding the project team can be either a highly informal process (holding a final party) or one that is very structured (conducting detailed performance reviews and work evaluations for all team members). The formality of the disbanding process depends, to a great degree, on the size of the project, the authority granted the project manager, the organization's commitment to the project, and other factors.

We noted in Chapter 2 that, in some project organizations, a certain degree of stress accompanies the disbanding of the team, due to the uncertainty of many members about their future status with the firm. In most cases, however, project team members are simply transferred back to departmental or functional duties to await their appointment to future projects. Research clearly demonstrates that when team

Chair: The meeting chair is either the Project Manager or some other person instructed by the project manager.

Discipline	Attendee	Comment/Approval Signature
Engineering		
Manufacturing		
Product & Tech Develop.		
Quality & Safety		
Finance		
Marketing		
Additional Attendees		
Procurement		
Legal		

Review Decision

The Chair is to sign appropriate box and insert expenditure limit.

APPROVAL LEVEL	
a. Proceed to next phase	
b. Proceed with actions to next phase	
c. Stop until designated actions have been completed	
d. No further work	
FINANCIAL LIMITS	
Approved expenditure limit for next phase	$

Additional Notes/Comments/Summary

Actions Arising

This action sheet should be used to document actions required by the review and conditions of approval. The project team is responsible for completing all actions by the due date. The named individual will be responsible for the review on or before the due date if the action has been completed. The project will proceed at risk until all actions are completed and accepted.

FIGURE 14.4   Sample Pages from Project Sign-Off Document

Action No.	Action Description	Date Due	Person Responsible	Accepted/ Signature

FIGURE 14.4 Continued

Project Management Confidence	Yes	No	Comments/Reference
Required Reviews			
Have all actions from the project review been cleared?			
Has an implementation sign-off review been held?			**Ref:**
Have all actions from the implementation sign-off review been cleared?			
Lessons Learned			
Have lessons learned from project been recorded and archived? (Indicate storage locations and who may access these records.)			
Have action plans been prepared for follow-up on projects?			
Project Specifications			
Have project specifications been collected and reported since the last review?			
Project Plan			
Has the Project Plan been updated and issued?			**Ref:**
Have all planned key customer milestones been achieved since the last review?			
Have all planned key internal milestones been achieved since the last review?			
Project Resources			
Have all planned resources been released into and out of the project on schedule?			
Have all comparisons of planned versus actual resource usage been carried out and relevant departmental metrics updated?			
Project Costs			
Has the project met its cost targets?			
Project Risk Assessment			
Is an updated risk assessment available?			
Project General			
Has the team carried out a review of the entire project?			**Ref:**
Has it been confirmed that the customer has received all agreed-upon deliverables, including documents, mock-ups, etc.?			
Has the project closure report been prepared?			
Are there any follow-up projects that need to be initiated?			
Have all project accounts been closed?			

FIGURE 14.4 Continued

Business Confidence	Yes	No	Comments/Reference
Business Case			
Is the current product cost acceptable?			**Ref:**
Are the assumptions of the product life cycle and their effect on product cost still valid?			
Have customer schedule adherence targets been met?			
Has the commercial performance matched the financial criteria in the initial business case?			**Ref:**
Has the business model been updated?			
Are the other financial measures (including IRR and NPV) still acceptable?			
Are follow-up projects still viable under this business case model?			

Market and Sales Confidence	Yes	No	Comments/Reference
Pricing Policy			
Is the pricing policy for original equipment and spares still valid?			
Sales Forecast—Confidence			
Have all sales schedules, including customer support group schedules, been agreed on?			
Customer Feedback			
Has customer feedback been received on project performance?			
Have action plans been created to identify opportunities for improvement based on customer feedback?			

Product Quality Confidence	Yes	No	Comments/Reference
Design			
Have the design changes since previous reviews been listed?			
Have all design change requests (DCRs) been implemented?			
Are all engineering design review actions complete?			**Ref:**
Is the certification of project performance up-to-date and approved?			**Ref:**
Has the design process been reviewed and any lessons learned been highlighted?			
Have the lessons learned been summarized and entered in the database?			

FIGURE 14.4   Continued

members have experienced positive "psychosocial" outcomes from the project, they are more inclined to work collaboratively in the future, have more positive feelings toward future projects, and enter them with greater enthusiasm.[11] Thus, ending project team relationships should never be handled in an offhand or haphazard manner. True, these team members can no longer positively affect the just-completed project, but their accomplishments, depending upon how they are celebrated, can be a strong force of positive motivation for future projects.

What Prevents Effective Project Closeouts?

The creation of a system for capturing the knowledge from completed projects is so important that it seems the need for such a practice would be obvious. Yet, research suggests that many organizations do not engage in effective project closeouts, systematically gathering, storing, and making available for future dissemination the lessons they have learned from projects.[12] Why is project closeout handled haphazardly or ineffectively in many companies? Some of the common reasons are:

- *Getting the project signed off discourages other closeout activities.* Once the project is paid for or has been accepted by the client, the prevailing attitude seems to be that this signals that no further action is necessary. Rather than addressing important issues, the final "stamp of approval," if applied too early, has the strong effect of discouraging any additional actions on the project. Final activities drag on or get ignored in the hope that they are no longer necessary.
- *The assumed urgency of all projects pressures us to take shortcuts on the back end.* When a company runs multiple projects at the same time, its project management resources are often stretched to the hilt. An attitude sometimes emerges suggesting that it is impossible to delay the start of new projects simply to complete all closeout activities on ones that are essentially finished. In effect, these companies argue that they are too busy to adequately finish their projects.
- *Closeout activities are given a low priority and are easily ignored.* Sometimes, firms assign final closeout activities to people who were not part of the project team, such as junior managers or accountants with little actual knowledge of the project. Hence, their analysis is often cursory or based on a limited understanding of the project and its goals, problems, and solutions.
- *Lessons learned analysis is viewed simply as a bookkeeping process.* Many organizations require lessons learned analyses only to quickly file them away and forget they ever occurred. Organization members learn that these analyses are not intended for wider dissemination and, consequently, do not take them seriously, do not bother reading past reports, and do a poor job of preparing their own.
- *People may assume that because all projects are unique, the actual carryover from project to project is minimal.* This myth ignores the fact that although projects may be unique, they may have several common points. For example, if projects have the same client, employ similar technologies, enlist similar contractors or consultants, or employ similar personnel over an extended period, they may have many more commonalties than are acknowledged. Although it is true that each project is unique, that does not imply that all project management circumstances are equally unique and that knowledge cannot be transferred.

Developing a natural process for project closeout offers the project organization a number of advantages. First, it allows managers to create a database of lessons learned analyses that can be extremely beneficial for running future projects more effectively. Second, it provides a structure to the closeout that turns it from a slipshod process into a series of identifiable steps for more systematic and complete project shutdown. Third, when handled correctly, project closeout can serve as an important source of information and motivation for project team members. They discover, through lessons learned analysis, both good and bad practices and how to anticipate problems in the future. Further, when the team is disbanded in the proper manner, the psychological benefits are likely to lead to greater motivation for future projects. Thus, systematic project closeout usually results in effective project closeout.

14.3 EARLY TERMINATION FOR PROJECTS

Under what circumstances can a project organization reasonably conclude that a project is a candidate for **early termination**? Although a variety of factors can influence this decision, Meredith identifies six categories of dynamic project factors and suggests that it is necessary to conduct periodic monitoring of these factors to determine if they have changed significantly.[13] In the event that answer is "yes," follow-up questions should seek to determine the magnitude of the shift as a basis for considering if the project should be continued or terminated. Table 14.1 shows these dynamic project factors and some of the subjects within them about which pertinent questions should be asked.

As shown in Table 14.1, static project factors, relating to the characteristics of the project itself and any significant changes it has undergone, are the first source of information about potential early termination. Factors associated with the task itself or with the composition of the project team are another important

---

TABLE 14.1 Dynamic Project Factors to Review

1. **Static Factors**
   a. Prior experience
   b. Company image
   c. Political forces
   d. High sunk costs
   e. Intermittent rewards
   f. Salvage and closing costs
   g. Benefits at end
2. **Task-Team Factors**
   a. Difficulty achieving technical performance
   b. Difficulty solving technological/manufacturing problems
   c. Time to completion lengthening
   d. Missing project time or performance milestones
   e. Lowered team innovativeness
   f. Loss of team or project manager enthusiasm
3. **Sponsorship Factors**
   a. Project less consistent with organizational goals
   b. Weaker linkage with other projects
   c. Lower impact on the company
   d. Less important to the firm
   e. Reduced problem or opportunity
   f. Less top management commitment to project
   g. Loss of project champion
4. **Economic Factors**
   a. Lower projected ROI, market share, or profit
   b. Higher cost to complete project
   c. Less capital availability
   d. Longer time to project returns
   e. Missing project cost milestones
   f. Reduced match of project financial scope to firm's budget
5. **Environmental Factors**
   a. Better alternatives available
   b. Increased competition
   c. Less able to protect results
   d. Increased government restrictions
6. **User Factors**
   a. Market need obviated
   b. Market factors changed
   c. Reduced market receptiveness
   d. Decreased number of end-use alternatives
   e. Reduced likelihood of successful commercialization
   f. Less chance of extended or continuing success

---

source of information about whether a project should be terminated. Other important cues include changes to project sponsorship, changes in economic conditions or the organization's operating environment that may negate the value of continuing to pursue the project, and user-initiated changes. For example, the client's original need for a project may be obviated due to changes in the external environment, such as when Goodrich Corporation's acquisition of TRW Corporation allowed it to cancel several of its own aeronautics projects because the purchase supplied it with the technologies it had been pursuing.

A great deal of research has been conducted on the decision to cancel projects in order to identify the key decision rules by which organizations determine that they no longer need to pursue a project opportunity. An analysis of 36 companies terminating R&D projects identified low probabilities of achieving technical or commercial success as the number one cause for terminating R&D projects.[14] Other important factors in the termination decision included low probability of return on investment, low market potential, prohibitive costs for continuing with the project, and insurmountable technical problems. Other authors have highlighted additional critical factors that can influence the decision of whether to terminate projects, including (1) project management effectiveness, (2) top management support, (3) worker commitment, and (4) project leader championship of the project.[15]

One study has attempted to determine warning signs of possible early project termination that can be identified before a termination decision has, in fact, been made.[16] The authors examined 82 projects over four years. Their findings suggest that for projects that were eventually terminated, within the first six months of their existence, project team members already recognized these projects as having a low probability of achieving commercial objectives, as not being managed by team members with sufficient decision authority, as being targeted for launch into relatively stable markets, and as being given low priority by the R&D top management. In spite of the fact that these projects were being managed effectively and given valuable sponsorship by top management, these factors allowed project team members to determine after very little time had been spent on the project that it was likely to fail or suffer from early termination by the organization.

Making the Early Termination Decision

When a project is being considered as a candidate for early termination, the decision to pull the plug is usually not clear-cut. There may be competing information sources, with some suggesting the project can succeed and others arguing that the project is no longer viable. Often the first challenge in project termination is sorting among these viewpoints to determine which views of the project are the most accurate and objective ones. Remember, typically a project's viability is not a purely internal issue; that is, just because the project is being well developed does not mean that it should continue to be supported. A significant shift in external forces can render any project pointless long before it has been completed.[17] For example, if the project's technology has been superseded or market forces have made the project's goals moot, the project should be shut down. Alternatively, a project that can fulfill a useful purpose in the marketplace may still be terminated if the project organization has begun to view its development as excessively long and costly. Another common internal reason for ending a project in midstream is the recognition that the project does not meet issues of strategic fit within the company's portfolio of products. For example, a major strategic shift in product offerings within a firm can make several ongoing projects no longer viable because they do not meet new requirements for product development. In other words, projects may be terminated for either external reasons (e.g., changes in the operating environment) or internal reasons (e.g., projects that are no longer cost-effective or that do not fit with the company's strategic direction).

Some important decision rules that are used in deciding whether to terminate an ongoing project include the following:[18]

1. **When costs exceed business benefits.** Many projects must first clear return on investment (ROI) hurdles as a criterion for their selection and start-up. Periodic analysis of the expected cost for the project versus the expected benefits may highlight the fact that the project is no longer financially viable. This may be due either to higher costs than anticipated in completing the project or a lower market opportunity than the company had originally hoped for. If the net present value of an ongoing project dips seriously into financial losses, the decision to terminate the project may make sound business sense.

2. **When the project no longer meets strategic fit criteria.** Firms often reevaluate their strategic product portfolios to determine whether the products they offer are complementary and their portfolio is balanced. When a new strategic vision is adopted, it is common to make significant changes to the product mix, eliminating product lines that do not fit the new goals. For example, when Jack Welch, former CEO at General Electric, issued his famous "One or two or out" dictate, he meant that GE

PROJECT PROFILE

Case—The Zion Nuclear Plant Tear-Down

At a time when the search for alternative energy sources is prompting state and federal agencies to take another look at nuclear power, the industry faces a separate, but no less important, challenge: the safe tear-down of aging nuclear power plants and disposal of waste and contaminated material. The U.S. Nuclear Regulatory Commission (NRC) is currently reviewing 22 applications for construction of nuclear power plants at 13 sites nationwide. At the same time, they have recently approved the demolition and haul-away of at least eight other aging power plants that are shut down and inactive. In many ways, decommissioning and dismantling nuclear plants is just as challenging as building them and requires the expertise that only a few companies possess.

One upcoming example is the Zion nuclear power plant, sitting on 257 acres on a site 40 miles north of Chicago on the shores of Lake Michigan. When it was first powered up in 1973, the Zion plant was the largest nuclear power plant in the world, with a new generation of reactors designed for safety. Run by Commonwealth Edison (ComEd), the plant was a major source of power for the Chicago metropolitan area. Although it had permits that allowed the plant to continue operating well into the 21st century, by the late 1990s, the owners of the plant decided that the economics of keeping the reactors online simply did not add up anymore. Too many problems with structural and procedural safety had made the plant uneconomical, and in late 1997, they decided to pull the plug.

Unfortunately, taking a nuclear power plant off-line is only part of the problem; the bigger issue is: what to do with it? Exelon Corporation, the sister company to ComEd and the owners of the plant, let the plant sit idle for 12 years, paying more than $132 million to mothball the site, seal all hazardous materials, and pay for site upkeep and security. Exelon, however, had a plan in place for the final removal of the plant, having collected more than $1 billion during its operating life from ComEd customers who began paying into that fund in the late 1970s, a fee not removed from their bills until 2006.

Exelon contracted with EnergySolutions, Inc., of Salt Lake City, to dismantle the Zion nuclear power plant. The project, anticipated to begin in 2012, should take up to 10 years to complete—seven years to dismantle the plant and safely remove all materials, and another three years to restore the area to a green zone. The projected cost will be approximately $1.1 billion when completed.

The process for dismantling old nuclear plants requires careful planning and execution. In addition to removing all spent nuclear rods and other radioactive materials, many of the containment domes and other plant surfaces that are also impregnated with radioactivity must be carefully dismantled, packaged, and shipped. EnergySolutions CEO Val Christensen notes, "It's much harder to take these plants apart than put them together."

The spent nuclear fuel will be put into giant concrete storage "casks" that look like small farm silos, storing about 2.2 million pounds of spent nuclear fuel and another 80,000 pounds of highly radioactive material from the

FIGURE 14.5 Zion Nuclear Power Plant

(continued)

two reactors. These will remain indefinitely at the site, under secure guard, until EnergySolutions and the federal government can locate a permanent storage option for them. Meanwhile, Christensen suggests, his company will employ a "rip and ship" approach to the other parts of the power plant, dismantling and removing large sections of the plant in careful sequence. Although the timetable has not been set, more than 500,000 cubic feet of material will be moved, including everything from concrete walls, pipes, wiring, and machinery to desks and chairs. Much of this material (enough to fill roughly 80 rail cars) is contaminated with low-level radiation; it will be transported to an EnergySolutions site 80 miles west of Salt Lake City, where it will be crushed and compacted.

Meanwhile, both companies are planning well into the future for their next initiatives. Exelon has already determined that two of its facilities, in Illinois and Pennsylvania, will be shuttered and dismantled within the next 20 years. EnergySolutions, with solid successes in demolishing plants in New England and the Midwest, is looking for future decommissioning projects. The challenges of building safe and reliable nuclear power plants are considerable. Just as important, however, is good project management in dismantling and removing them.[19]

would no longer support business units unless they were either first or second in their industry. The result was a weeding out of several business lines that did not meet the new strategic vision.

3. ***When deadlines continue to be missed.***   Continually missed key milestones or deadlines are a signal that a project is in trouble. Even when there are some good reasons for initially missing these milestones, the cumulative effect of continuing to miss deadlines will, at a minimum, cause the project organization to analyze the causes of these lags. Are they due to poor project management, unrealistic initial goals, or simply the fact that the technology is not being developed fast enough? During President Reagan's first term in office, the Strategic Defense Initiative (SDI) was started. More than 25 years later, many of the technical problems with creating a viable missile defense are still being addressed. Most experts readily admit that they do not have a good idea when the system will be sufficiently robust to be deployed with confidence.

4. ***When technology evolves beyond the project's scope.***   In many industries, such as the IT arena, technological changes are rapid and often hugely significant. Thus, IT professionals always face the challenge of completing projects while the technology is in flux. Their natural fear is that by the time the project is introduced, the technology will have advanced so far beyond where the project is that the project will no longer be useful. The basic challenge for any IT project is trying to find a reasonable compromise between freezing the project's scope and allowing for ongoing spec changes that reflect new technology. Obviously, at some point the scope must be frozen or the project could never be completed. On the other hand, freezing the scope too early may lead to a project that is already obsolete before it has been launched.

Shutting Down the Project

Let us assume that following an analysis of a troubled project and its ongoing viability, the decision has been reached to terminate it. The next steps involved in the termination process can be difficult and very complex. Particularly, there are likely to be a number of issues that must be resolved both prior to and following the project's early termination. These termination decisions are sometimes divided into two classes: emotional and intellectual.[21] Further, under each heading, additional concerns are listed. Figure 14.6 shows the framework that employs a modified Work Breakdown Structure to identify the key decisions in a project termination.

The decision to terminate a project will give rise to a variety of responses and new duties for the project manager and team (see Table 14.2). Pulling the plug on a project usually leads to serious emotional responses from stakeholders. Within the project team itself, it is natural to expect a dramatic loss in motivation, loss of team identity, fear of no future work among team members, and a general weakening and diversion of their efforts. The project's intended clients also begin disassociating themselves from the project, in effect, distancing themselves from the project team and the terminated project.

In addition to the expected emotional reactions to the termination decision, there are a number of administrative, or intellectual, matters to which the project team must attend. For example, internal to the project organization, closing down a project requires a detailed audit of all project deliverables, closure of work packages, disposal of unused equipment or materials, and so forth. In relation to the client, the termination decision requires closure of any agreements regarding deliverables, termination of outstanding contracts or commitments with suppliers, and the mothballing of facilities, if necessary. The important point is that a systematic process needs to be established for terminating a project, in terms of both the steps used to decide if the project should be terminated and, once the decision has been made, the manner in which the project can be shut down most efficiently.

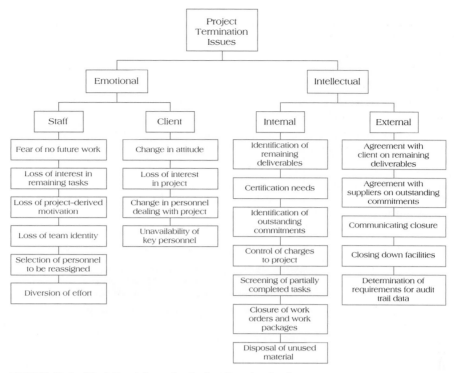

FIGURE 14.6 **Work Breakdown for Project Termination Issues**

TABLE 14.2 Concerns When Shutting Down a Project

Emotional Issues of the Project Team

1. Fear of no future work—The concern that once the project is shut down, there is no avenue for future work for team members.
2. Loss of interest in remaining tasks—The perception that a terminated project requires no additional performance.
3. Loss of project-derived motivation—All motivation to perform well on the project or to create a successful project is lost.
4. Loss of team identity—The project is being disbanded; so is the team.
5. Selection of personnel to be reassigned—Team members already begin jockeying for reassignment to better project alternatives.
6. Diversion of effort—With the project winding down, other jobs take greater priority.

Emotional Issues of the Clients

1. Changes in attitude—Now that the project has been canceled or concluded, client attitude may become hostile or indifferent
2. Loss of interest in the project—As the project team loses interest, so does the client.
3. Change in personnel dealing with the project—Many times, as they move their key people to new challenges, clients will shift new people into the project who have no experience with it.
4. Unavailability of key personnel—Resources at the client organization with needed skills are no longer available or interested in contributing their input to the project that is being terminated.

Intellectual Issues—Internal

1. Identification of the remaining deliverables—The project team must distinguish between what has been accomplished and what has not been completed.
2. Certification needs—It may be necessary to provide certification of compliance with environmental or regulatory standards as part of the project closeout.
3. Identification of outstanding commitments—The project team must identify any outstanding supply deliveries, milestones that will not be met, and so forth.
4. Control of charges to the project—By the closeout, a number of people and departments are aware of project account numbers. It is necessary to quickly close out these accounts to prevent other groups from hiding their expenses in the project.
5. Screening of partially completed tasks—It is necessary to begin eliminating the work being done on final tasks, particularly when they no longer support the project's development.
6. Closure of work orders and work packages—Formal authorization to cancel work orders and project work packages is necessary once ongoing tasks have been identified.
7. Disposal of unused material—Projects accumulate quantities of unused supplies and materials. A method must be developed for disposing of or transferring these materials to other locations.

(continued)

TABLE 14.2 Continued

Intellectual Issues—External

1. Agreement with the client on remaining deliverables—When a project is being canceled, the project organization and the client must jointly agree on what final deliverables will be supplied and when they will be scheduled.
2. Agreement with suppliers on outstanding commitments—Suppliers who are scheduled to continue delivering materials to the project must be contacted and contracts canceled.
3. Communicating closure—The project team must ensure that all relevant stakeholders are clearly aware of the project shutdown, including the date by which all activities will cease.
4. Closing down facilities—When necessary, a schedule for facilities shutdown is needed.
5. Determination of requirements for audit trail data—Different customers and stakeholders have different requirements for record retention used in postproject audits. The project team needs to conduct an assessment of the records required from each stakeholder in order to close out the project.

BOX 14.2

PROJECT MANAGEMENT RESEARCH IN BRIEF

Project Termination in the IT Industry

In mid-2010, a lawsuit was settled between Waste Management and SAP Corporation. The original lawsuit arose from a failed implementation effort to install and make usable SAP's Enterprise Resource Planning (ERP) software throughout Waste Management's organization. Waste Management is a giant company that has been built through acquisition. As a result, legacy systems were everywhere, and many of them were outdated. In 2005, Waste Management was looking to overhaul its order-to-cash process—billing, collections, pricing, and customer setup. It was at this point that SAP stepped in, promising that its out-of-the-box ERP system would be capable of handling all Waste Management's needs with minimal tweaking. It wasn't. The trash-disposal conglomerate claimed it suffered significant damages, including more than $100 million, which is the amount it spent on the project (dubbed by Waste Management as "a complete and utter failure") and more than $350 million for benefits it would have realized if the software had been successful.

As part of its complaint in the lawsuit, Waste Management argued that they wanted an ERP package that could meet their business requirements without large amounts of custom development, but instead, SAP used a "fake" product demonstration to trick Waste Management officials into believing its software fit the bill. Although SAP did not accept guilt in the case, Waste Management received "a one-time cash payment" in accordance with the settlement.

Some of the most difficult challenges faced in effectively running and completing projects are those presented in the information technology (IT) industry. Research investigating project management in IT has not been reassuring. The Standish Group of Dennis, Massachusetts, conducted a lengthy and thorough study of IT projects and determined that:

- 40% of IT application development projects are canceled before completion.
- 33% of the remaining projects face significant cost and/or schedule overruns or changes in scope.
- IT projects failures cost U.S. companies and governmental agencies an estimated $145 billion each year.

Given all the examples of projects at risk, what are some of the warning signs that signal a project may become a candidate for cancellation? The 10 signs of pending IT project failure are:

1. Project managers do not understand users' needs.
2. Scope is ill defined.
3. Project changes are poorly managed.
4. Chosen technology changes.
5. Business needs change.
6. Deadlines are unrealistic.
7. Users are resistant.
8. Sponsorship is lost.
9. Project lacks people with appropriate skills.
10. Best practices and lessons learned are ignored.

In order to avoid the inevitability of project failure, it is critical to recognize the warning signs, including the inability to hit benchmark goals, the piling up of unresolved problems, communication breakdowns among the key project stakeholders, and escalating costs. Such red flags are sure signals that an IT project may be a candidate for termination.[20]

Allowing for Claims and Disputes

For some types of projects, the termination decision itself can initiate a host of legal issues with the client. The most common types of problems revolve around outstanding or unresolved claims that the customer or any project suppliers may hold against the project organization for early termination. Although the legal ramifications of early termination decisions cannot be explored in great detail here, it is important to recognize that the termination of a project can itself generate a number of contractual disagreements and settlements. This potential for dealing with claims or **disputes** should be factored into the decision on terminating a project. For example, a company could discover that because of severe penalties for nondelivery, it actually would be less expensive to complete a failing project than to shut it down.

Two common types of claims that can arise in the event of project closure are:

1. *Ex-gratia claims.* These are claims that a client can make when there is no contractual basis for the claim but when the client thinks the project organization has a moral or commercial obligation to compensate it for some unexpected event (such as premature termination). Suppose, for example, that a client was promoting a new line of products that was to use a technology the project organization had been contracted to develop. Should the project firm cancel the project, the client might decide to make an ex-gratia claim based on its charge that it had planned its new product line around this advanced technology.

2. *Default claims by the project company in its obligations under the contract.* When contractual claims are defaulted due to the failure of a project to be completed and delivered, the client firm may have some legal claim to cost recovery or punitive damages. For example, liquidated damages claims may be incurred when a contractor awards a project to a supplier and uses financial penalties as an inducement for on-time delivery of the project. In the event of noncompliance or early project termination, the client can invoke the liquidated damages clause to recoup its financial investment at the expense of the project organization.

In addition to claims from interested stakeholders, the project organization also may face legal disputes over contractual terms, prepurchased materials or supplies, long-term agreements with suppliers or customers, and so forth.

Project organizations can protect themselves from problems with claims during project termination by the following means:[22]

- Consider the possible areas of claims at the start of the contract and plan accordingly. Do not wait until they happen.
- Make sure that the project stakeholders know their particular areas of risk under the contract to help prevent baseless claims after the fact.
- Keep accurate and up-to-date records from the start of the contract. A good factual diary can help answer questions if the project develops fatal flaws downstream.
- Keep clear details of customer change requests or other departures from the original contracted terms.
- Ensure that all correspondence between you and clients is retained and archived.

When disputes are encountered, they are typically handled through legal recourse, often in the form of arbitration.

Arbitration refers to the formalized system for dealing with grievances and administering corrective justice to parties in a bargaining situation. It is used to obtain a fair settlement or resolution of disputes through an impartial third party. For projects, arbitration may be used as a legal recourse if parties who disagree on the nature of contractual terms and conditions require a third party, usually a court-appointed arbitrator, to facilitate the settlement of disputed terms. Provided that all parties agree to the use of arbitration, it can serve as a binding settlement to all outstanding claims or disputes arising from a contract that was not adequately completed. Alternatively, the parties may opt for nonbinding arbitration, in which the judge can offer suggestions or avenues for settlement but cannot enforce these opinions. Although arbitration has the advantage of being faster than pursuing claims through standard litigation, in practice, it is risky: The judge or arbitrator can side with the other party in the dispute and make a decision that is potentially very expensive to the project organization; and when nonbinding, arbitration can be considered "advisory." If the parties wish to adopt the award as their settlement, they may do so. On the other hand, if they decide against adopting the award, they may be forced to repeat the entire process at a subsequent administrative hearing, court trial, or binding arbitration. Any of these choices can lengthen the dispute even further.[23]

Not all claims against a project are baseless. Many times the decision to terminate a project will be made with the understanding that it is going to open the company to litigation or claims from external parties, such as the client firm. In these cases, the termination decision must be carefully weighed before being enacted. If a project is failing and termination is the only realistic option, the resulting claims the company is likely to face must be factored into the decision process and then addressed in full after the fact.

14.4 PREPARING THE FINAL PROJECT REPORT

The final project report is the administrative record of the completed project, identifying all its functional and technical components, as well as other important project history. A final project report is valuable to the organization precisely to the degree that the project team and key organizational members take the time to conduct it in a systematic fashion, identify all relevant areas of concern, and enact processes to ensure that relevant lessons have been identified, learned, and passed on. The important point to remember is that a final project report is more than a simple recitation of the history of the project; it is also an evaluative document that highlights both the strengths and weaknesses of the project's development. As such, the final project report should offer a candid assessment of what went right and what went wrong for the project over its life cycle.

The elements of the final project report include an evaluation of a number of project and organizational factors, including:[24]

1. *Project performance.*   The project performance should involve a candid assessment of the project's achievements relative to its plan. How did the project fare in terms of standard metrics such as baseline schedule and budget? Did the project achieve the technical goals that it set out to accomplish? How did the project perform in terms of stakeholder satisfaction, particularly customer satisfaction? Are there any hard data to support the assessments? The final project report is an evaluative document that should offer candid criticisms, where appropriate, of the project's performance and, if performance was deemed substandard, the most likely causes of that performance and recommended remedial steps to ensure that similar results do not occur in the future.

2. *Administrative performance.*   The project's administrative performance evaluation refers to the evaluation of any standard administrative practices that occur within the organization, and their benefits or drawbacks in developing the just-completed project. For example, in one organization, it was found that all project change order requests had to be endorsed by five layers of management before they could be addressed, leading to a long lag between the time a customer asked for a change and when the decision was made to either accept or reject the change request. The result of this analysis led to a streamlined change order process that made the organization much faster at responding to clients' change order requests.

3. *Organizational structure.*   The final report should offer some comments on how the organization's operating structure either helped or hindered the project team and their efforts. It may be found, for example, that the standard functional structure is a continual problem when trying to respond quickly to opportunities in the marketplace or that it represents a problem in communicating between groups involved in the project. Although it is unlikely that one bad project experience will trigger an immediate demand to change the company's structure, repeated project failures that point squarely to problems with the organizational structure can eventually create the impetus to make changes that will better align the structure with project activities.

4. *Team performance.*   The final report should also reflect on the effectiveness of the project team, not only in terms of their actual performance on the project, but also with regard to team-building and staffing policies, training or coaching, and performance evaluations for all project team members. In short, the team performance assessment should address the efficacy of the company's staffing of its project teams ("Did we find the best people within the organization to serve on the project?"), its team-building and training activities ("How are we ensuring that team members are adequately trained?" "If team members need training, do we have programs to provide it?"), and postproject evaluation policies ("Does the project manager have the ability to evaluate the performance of project team members?" "Does the project manager's evaluation carry weight in the subordinate's annual review?").

5. *Techniques of project management.*   In the final report, it is useful to consider the methods used by the organization for estimating activity duration and cost, as well as any scheduling processes or

techniques used. It may be found, for example, that the organization consistently underestimates the duration time necessary to complete tasks or underestimates the resource costs associated with these tasks. This information can be extremely helpful for future project estimation. Further, other techniques that are used for project management (e.g., scheduling software, rules and procedures, etc.) should be critically reviewed in order to suggest ways to improve the process for future projects.

6. ***Benefits to the organization and the customer.***   All projects are guided by a goal or series of discrete goals that have, as their bottom line, the assumption of providing benefits to the sponsoring organization and the project's clients. A final analysis in the final project report should consider the degree to which the project has succeeded in accomplishing its goals and providing the anticipated benefits. One important proviso, however: Remember that in some cases, the benefits that are anticipated from a completed project may not occur immediately, but over time. For example, if our goal in constructing a housing development is to return a high profit to our company, it may be necessary to wait several months or even years, until all lots and houses have been sold, before evaluating whether the goal has been achieved. Thus, we have to always try to maintain a balance between assessments of immediate benefits and those that may accrue over time.

The goal in requiring a final project report is to lay the groundwork for successful future projects. Although the final report is used to reflect on what went right and what went wrong with the current project, it is fundamentally a forward-looking document used to improve organizational processes in order to make future projects more effective, project activities more productive, and project personnel more knowledgeable.

Learning organizations are keen to apply the important lessons learned from experience. As one senior project manager has explained, "It is the difference between a manager with 10 years' experience, and one with one year's experience 10 times!" The more we can apply the important lessons from past projects through activities such as final reports, the greater the likelihood that our project managers will evolve into knowledgeable professionals, as opposed to simply repeating the same mistakes over and over—the classic definition of a manager with "one year's experience 10 times."

CONCLUSION

"The termination of a project is a project."[25] This statement suggests that the degree to which a project team makes a systematic and planned effort to close out a project affects whether the termination will be done efficiently and with minimal wasted effort or loss of time. In the case of projects that are naturally terminated through being completed, the steps in termination can be thought out in advance and pursued in an orderly manner. On the other hand, in circumstances where the project suffers early termination, the closeout process may be shorter and more ad hoc, that is, it may be done in a less-than-systematic manner.

This chapter has highlighted the processes of both natural and unnatural project terminations. One of the greatest challenges facing project teams during termination is maintaining the energy and motivation to make the final "kick to the finish line." It is natural to start looking around for the next project challenge once a project is moving toward its inevitable conclusion. Our challenge as project managers is, first, to recognize that it is natural for team members to lose their enthusiasm and, second, to plan the steps needed to close out the project in the most effective way. When the project's termination is treated as a project, it signals that we are intent on having our projects end not with a negative whimper, but with a positive bang.

Summary

1. **Distinguish among the four main forms of project termination.**   We identified four ways in which projects get terminated; they are termination by (a) extinction, (b) addition, (c) integration, and (d) starvation. Termination by extinction refers to projects in which all activity ends without extending the project in any way, usually as the result of a successful completion or decision to end the project early.

Termination by addition implies bringing the project into the organization as a separate, ongoing entity. Termination by integration is the process of bringing the project activities into the organization and distributing them among existing functions. Finally, termination by starvation involves cutting a project's budget sufficiently to stop progress without actually killing the project.

2. **Recognize the seven key steps in formal project closeout.** The seven steps of the formal project closeout are:
   - Finishing the work
   - Handing over the project
   - Gaining acceptance for the project
   - Harvesting the benefits
   - Reviewing how it all went
   - Putting it all to bed
   - Disbanding the team

3. **Understand key reasons for early termination of projects.** A project may become a candidate for early termination for a number of reasons, including the recognition of significant changes in the following critical factors: (a) static factors, (b) task-team factors, (c) sponsorship, (d) economics, (e) environment, and (f) user requirements. Research has determined a number of early warning signs of pending problems with projects that can signal fatal errors or irrecoverable problems. This chapter also examined some of the decision rules that allow us to make reasonable choices about whether to cancel an ongoing project. Specifically, we may choose to terminate ongoing projects when:

- Costs exceed business benefits.
- The project no longer meets strategic fit criteria.
- Deadlines continue to be missed.
- Technology evolves beyond the project's scope.

4. **Know the challenges and components of a final project report.** The components of the final project report include evaluations of project performance, administrative performance, organizational structure, team performance, techniques of project management, and benefits of the project to the organization and the customer. Two challenges are involved in developing effective final reports: first, being willing to take a candid and honest look at how the project progressed, highlighting both its strengths and weaknesses; and second, developing reports in such a manner that they contain a combination of descriptive analysis and prescriptive material for future projects. The goal in requiring a final project report is to lay the groundwork for successful future projects. Although the final report is used to reflect on what went right and wrong with the current project, it is fundamentally a forward-looking document used to improve organizational processes in order to make future projects more effective, project activities more productive, and project personnel more knowledgeable.

Key Terms

Arbitration (p. 487)
Build, Operate, Transfer (BOT) (p. 473)
Build, Own, Operate, Transfer (BOOT) (p. 473)
Default claims (p. 487)
Disputes (p. 487)

Early termination (p. 480)
Ex-gratia claims (p. 487)
Lessons learned (p. 474)
Natural termination (p. 469)
Private Finance Initiatives (PFIs) (p. 472)
Project termination (p. 469)

Termination by addition (p. 470)
Termination by extinction (p. 470)
Termination by integration (p. 470)

Termination by starvation (p. 470)
Unnatural termination (p. 469)

Discussion Questions

1. Why is the decision to terminate a project often as much an emotional one as an intellectual one?
2. Comment on the different methods for project termination. How have you seen an example of one of these methods, through either your school or work experience?
3. Why do so many projects end up terminated as a result of termination through starvation? Discuss the role of ego, power, and politics in this form of project termination.
4. Refer back to Chapter 2. How does the concept of escalation of commitment factor into decisions of whether to terminate projects?
5. Of the seven elements in project closeout management, which do you view as being most important? Why?
6. Why do lessons learned programs often fail to capture meaningful information that could help guide future projects?
7. Comment on the following statement: "In deciding on whether or not to kill a project, it is critical to continually monitor the environment for signs it may no longer be viable."
8. Refer to the Project Management Research in Brief box in this chapter. In your opinion, why is it so difficult to bring IT projects to successful completion? In other words, identify some reasons why the cancellation rate for IT projects is 40%.
9. Imagine you are a team member on a project that has missed deadlines, has not produced the hoped-for technological results, and has been a source of problems between your team and the customer. You have just been informed that the project is being canceled. In what ways is this good news? How would you view it as bad news?

Case Study 14.1

Project Libra: To Terminate or Not to Terminate

The headline in an issue of *ITWeek* e-magazine confirmed what many people had known for a long time about the status of a high-profile IT project initiated by the British government: "Government Refuses to Bail Out Libra—Troubled Project Still Delayed." After significant delays of more than two years, the UK government finally determined that it would spend no more money on the troubled Libra project at the Lord Chancellor's department.

Libra combined office infrastructure and a new casework system linking magistrates' courts, but the software application was not delivered in July 2001 as planned and continued to be delayed. A spokesperson for the Lord Chancellor's office claimed that the project was in place at 70% of the magistrates' courts. However, he explained that the contract with Fujitsu Services (formerly ICL) was currently under renegotiation and that "it is not yet possible to indicate the outcome."

The department said that it had so far paid £33m to Fujitsu Services. The cost of the contract had already increased from £183m to £319m due to additional work that the Lord Chancellor's department requested. Fujitsu had been under heavy pressure from both the government and opposition parties, but by then it had been recognized that the project's final costs and completion date could not be reasonably determined, suggesting that Project Libra could continue well into the future.

Unfortunately, Libra continues a long tradition of poorly managed government IT projects within the United Kingdom. Recently it was estimated that the cost of canceled or overbudget government IT projects had topped £1.5bn in the past six years. The latest *Computing* survey into government IT spending showed a 50% increase in the amount of money squandered on mismanaged projects since its previous study nearly two years before that.

Treasury minister Paul Boateng recently admitted that his department does not know how much has been wasted since the Labour government came to power. High-profile disasters taken into account in *Computing*'s research include the £698m wasted on the canceled Pathway project to develop smart cards for benefits payments, and the £260m overspent on the magistrates' courts Libra system identified by the National Audit Office in 2008.

"In business no group of shareholders would stomach the losses, overruns, and even pretty poor software that successive governments have made," said Derek Wyatt, a Member of Parliament. "The opportunity cost value is hundreds of small new hospitals and schools. Perhaps civil servants who fail frequently should lose their jobs."[26]

Questions

1. Do a Google search for "UK's Project Libra" to see the string of news stories related to Project Libra. Identify some of the sources of the problems the project faced.
2. If you were the one to decide whether to terminate this project, what would your decision have been? Justify your position.

Case Study 14.2

The Project That Wouldn't Die

Ben walked into his boss's office Tuesday morning in a foul mood. Without wasting any time on pleasantries, he confronted Alice. "How on earth did I get roped into working on the Regency Project?" he asked, holding the memo that announced his immediate transfer. Alice had been expecting such a reaction and sat back a moment to collect her thoughts on how to proceed.

The Regency Project was a minor legend around the office. Begun as an internal audit of business practices 20 months earlier, the project never seemed to get anything accomplished, was not taken seriously within the company, and had yet to make one concrete proposal for improving working practices. In fact, as far as Ben and many other members of the company were concerned, it appeared to be a complete waste of time. And now here Ben was, assigned to join the project!

Ben continued, "Alice, you know this assignment is misusing my abilities. Nothing has come from Regency; in fact, I'd love to know how top management, who are usually so cost conscious, have allowed this project to continue. I mean, the thing just won't die!"

Alice laughed. "Ben, the answer to your question can be easily found. Have you bothered taking a look at any of the early work coming out of Regency during its first three months?" When Ben shook his head, she continued, "The early Statement of Work and other scope development was overseen by Harry Shapiro. He was the original project manager for Regency."

(continued)

All of a sudden, light dawned on Ben. "Harry Shapiro? You mean Vice President Harry Shapiro?"

"That's right. Harry was promoted to the VP job just over a year ago. Prior to that, he was responsible for getting Regency off the ground. Think about it—do you really expect Harry to kill his brainchild? Useless or not, Regency will be around longer than any of us."

Ben groaned, "Great, so I'm getting roped into serving on Harry's pet project! What am I supposed to do?"

Alice offered him a sympathetic look. "Look, my best advice is to go into it with good intentions and try to do your best. I've seen the budget for Regency, and top management has been trimming their support for it. That means they must recognize the project isn't going well. They just don't want to kill it outright."

"Remember," Alice continued, "the project may not die because Harry's so committed to it, but that also means it has high visibility for him. Do a good job and you may get noticed. Then your next assignment is bound to be better." Alice laughed. "Heck, it can't be much worse!"

Questions

1. What termination method does it appear the company is using with the Regency Project?
2. What are the problems with motivation when project team members perceive that a project is earmarked for termination?
3. Why would you suspect Harry Shapiro has a role in keeping the project alive?

Case Study 14.3

Eight Years in the Making

In February 2012, the Danish Minister of Justice announced to the Danish parliament that the long-running development of a police IT system had been canceled. The system was being developed by the multinational, U.S.-listed IT company Computer Sciences Corporation (CSC).

The project had begun in 2004, and in the following year, the Danish parliament had approved the deal. By late 2006, the Danish police signed the contract for the final development of the system that would be called Polsag, which was originally designed as a complete system that would manage case files, records, and incorporate e-mailing systems. At this stage, the system was quoted as costing $153 million. However, four years later this figure had risen to a massive $425.2 million.

Also in Denmark, CSC was facing another challenge from the Danish Tax and Customs Administration, which was a major client for them. Things had gone wrong on an IT project with delays and spiralling costs being the main concerns; and this led to the resignation of CSC's Danish manager Carsten Lind.

Denmark was by no means the only country in which CSC was facing problems with canceled projects. In February 2012, CSC announced that it was shedding 500 employees. This was just a week after the UK government announced a $1.5 billion write-down for them after the cancellation of the $20 billion National Health Service Programme for IT (NPfIT), a system that had been designed to revolutionize patient administration and health records. CSC had a $4.7 billion contract as part of the overall scheme.

CSC had been aggressively expanding its health care systems across the world; however, the company had consistently missed deadlines, and in the space of nine years' involvement with the NHS, it had delivered only three acute hospital systems. The UK's Department of Health was convinced that it might actually cost more to cancel CSC's contract than see it through to the end.

Clearly, canceling an IT project at such a late stage in the process is fraught with danger, particularly for the client. The UK's Department of Health outlined the key costs that are common in all cases, including the canceled Polsag project:

- Contractual costs: these involve the minimum amounts payable to the supplier under the terms of the contract
- Damages: this would have to cover some of the supplier's unrecoverable costs to date
- Other costs: the supplier would expect to recover any accrued costs prior to the date of the cancelation
- Ongoing costs: once the supplier is aware of the fact that the contract is being terminated, there is an expectation that any ongoing service costs would be charged to the client in an attempt to recoup some of the losses from the contract cancellation
- Post-termination costs: whatever replacement systems, support, and development would have to be sourced by the client from another supplier
- Legal fees: the client would have to pay any legal fees related to the termination of the contract, and in addition, consultants might be needed to organize the transfer of work and investigate the problems (and propose solutions) that gave rise to the termination of the contract

CSC had become involved in Denmark in 1996 when they had bought the state-owned company Datacentralen. This company had developed and maintained the data systems for much of the public sector in Denmark. Initially, CSC had hired Danish consultants and programmers, but this changed in 2007 when CSC acquired several contracts to maintain the IT systems of some Danish businesses. CSC hired several hundred Indian IT specialists from its sister company in India. Problems arose when it was discovered that CSC was paying the Indian workers far less than their Danish counterparts, which was in contravention of Danish law. CSC acceded to demands to equalize pay, but then in 2010 the situation re-emerged. This time, they wanted to increase the working hours of Danish employees and bring in a 10% pay cut.

Relations between the Danish employees and CSC were acrimonious, and it would take nearly two years before there would be a settlement. In the meantime, 120 employees had been locked out of work and 330 employees had been on strike. The conflict, according to CSC, was instrumental in causing the many problems behind the Polsag project and the work with the Danish Tax and Customs Administration. To put the dispute and project issues into perspective, during the period 2008–2009, the Danish IT sector lost around 5,400 jobs. In the previous four years, the sector had seen a rise of 80% in terms of employment. Post 2009, Denmark has continued to lose IT jobs rapidly, many of them permanently moving to India and other outsource locations around the world.[27]

Questions

1. Government departments in many countries have had major problems with IT projects. If you were assigned as a member of a project review team for a governmental IT project, what criteria would you insist on the project having in order to be supported? In other words, what are the bare essentials needed to support such a project?
2. Why, in your opinion, is there such a long history of IT projects overshooting their budgets or failing some critical performance metrics?
3. The cancelation of the Polsag contract should have taken place long before it did. Do you agree with this assessment? Why or why not?

Internet Exercises

1. Search the Internet for links to the Boston Tunnel, "The Big Dig"; the Channel Tunnel, "The Chunnel"; and London's Millennium Dome. Why do you think these projects were supported to their conclusion in spite of their poor cost performance? What would it take to kill a high-visibility project such as these?
2. Go to http://blog.projectconnections.com/project_practitioners/2009/04/why-bad-projects-are-so-hard-to-kill.html and read the executive blog on killing bad projects. What are some of the critical stories or pieces of advice offered by the blog writer and those commenting on his suggestions? How do corporate politics play a role in the continuation of poorly conceived projects? Which of these arguments makes the most sense to you? Why?
3. Go to http://cs.unc.edu/~welch/class/comp145/media/docs/Boehm_Term_NE_Fail.pdf and read the article "Project Termination Doesn't Equal Project Failure" by Barry Boehm. Summarize his main arguments. What does he cite as the top 10 reasons for project failure?
4. Go to www.pmhut.com/wp-content/uploads/2008/03/project-closeout-document.pdf. Critique the content of this closeout form. What information would you suggest adding to the form to make it a more comprehensive closeout document?
5. Go to a search engine (Google, Yahoo!, Ask, etc.) and enter the term "project failure" or "project disaster." Select one example and develop an analysis of the project. Was the project terminated or not? If not, why, in your opinion, was it allowed to continue?

PMP Certification Sample Questions

1. When does a project close?
   a. When a project is canceled
   b. When a project runs out of money
   c. When a project is successfully completed
   d. All of the above are correct answers

2. You have just completed your project and have to confront the final activities your company requires when putting a project to bed. Which of the following activities is *not* expected to be part of the project closeout?
   a. Lessons learned
   b. Project archives
   c. Release of resources
   d. Supplier verification

3. Your project is nearing completion. At your request, members of your project team are grouping together critical project documentation, including contracts and financial records, change orders, scope and configuration management materials, and supplier delivery records. This process involves the creation of which of the following?
   a. Archives
   b. Lessons learned
   c. Contract and legal files
   d. Scope document

4. The execution phase of the IT project has just finished. The goals of this project were to update order-entry systems for your company's shipping department. Which of the following is the next step in the process of completing the project?
   a. Gaining acceptance or the project by your shipping department
   b. Finishing the work
   c. Closing the contract
   d. Releasing the resources

5. The team has just completed work on the project. By all accounts, this was a difficult project from the beginning and the results bear this out. You were over budget by 20% and significantly behind your schedule. Morale became progressively worse in the face of the numerous challenges. At the close of the project, you decide to hold an informal meeting with the team to discuss the problems and identify their sources, all with the goal of trying to prevent something like this from happening again. This process is known as what?

    a. Closing the project
    b. Procurement audit
    c. Lessons learned
    d. Early termination

Answers: 1. d—All are reasons why a project will close; **2.** d—Supplier verification is a process that must occur early in the project to ensure that deliveries will arrive when needed and are of sufficient quality; **3.** a—The collection of relevant project documentation is known as archiving; **4.** b—The start of the final phase of a project usually involves completing all final tasks; **5.** c—A lessons learned meeting is intended to critically evaluate what went well and what went poorly on a project to promote good practices and prevent poor ones on future projects.

Notes

1. Malanga, S. (2010, October 16–17). "Christie is right about the Hudson River big dig," *Wall Street Journal*, p. A15; Schuerman, M. (2010). "New Jersey Governor Chris Christie kills Hudson River train tunnel for second time," www.wnyc.org/articles/wnyc-news/2010/oct/26/new-jersey-governor-chris-christie-kills-hudson-river-train-tunnel-second-time/; "N.J. Gov. Christie kills Hudson River tunnel project, citing taxpayers woes." (2010, October 7). www.nj.com/news/index.ssf/2010/10/gov_christie_kills_hudson_rive.html; http://en.wikipedia.org/wiki/Access_to_the_Region%27s_Core; www.arctunnel.com/pdf/news/Tunnel%20Info%20Kit_Dec2009_single%20page%20layout.pdf; http://blog.nj.com/njv_editorial_page/2009/06/arc_transhudson_rail_tunnel_co.html; Smart, M. (2009). "Digging deep," *PMNetwork*, 23(10): 40–45.

2. Spirer, H. F., and Hamburger, D. (1983). "Phasing out the project," in Cleland, D. I., and King, W. R. (Eds.), *Project Management Handbook*. New York: Van Nostrand Reinhold, pp. 231–50.

3. Meredith, J. R., and Mantel, Jr., S. J. (2003). *Project Management*, 5th ed. New York: Wiley.

4. Meredith, J. R., and Mantel, Jr., S. J. (2011). *Project Management*, 8th ed. New York: Wiley.

5. Cooke-Davies, T. (2001). "Project closeout management: More than simply saying good-bye and moving on," in Knutson, J. (Ed.), *Project Management for Business Professionals*. New York: Wiley, pp. 200–14.

6. Cooke-Davies, T. (2001), ibid.

7. Turner, J. R. (1993). *Handbook of Project-Based Work*. London: McGraw-Hill.

8. Ive, G. (2004). "Private finance initiatives and the management of projects," in Morris, P. W. G., and Pinto, J. K. (Eds.), *The Wiley Guide to Managing Projects*. New York: Wiley.

9. Pinto, J. K., and Slevin, D. P. (1987). "Critical factors in successful project implementation," *IEEE Transactions on Engineering Management*, EM-34: 22–27.

10. Cooke-Davies, T. (2001), as cited.

11. Pinto, M. B., Pinto, J. K., and Prescott, J. E. (1993). "Antecedents and consequences of project team cross-functional cooperation," *Management Science*, 39: 1281–97.

12. Cooke-Davies, T. (2001), as cited; Dinsmore, P. C. (1998). "You get what you pay for," *PMNetwork*, 12(2): 21–22.

13. Meredith, J. R. (1988). "Project monitoring and early termination," *Project Management Journal*, 19(5): 31–38.

14. Dean, B. V. (1968). *Evaluating, Selecting and Controlling R&D Projects*. New York: American Management Association.

15. Balachandra, R. (1989). *Early Warning Signals for R&D Projects*. Boston: Lexington Books; Balachandra, R., and Raelin, J. A. (1980). "How to decide when to abandon a project," *Research Management*, 23(4): 24–29; Balachandra, R., and Raelin, J. A. (1984). "When to kill that R&D project," *Research Management*, 27: 30–33; Balachandra, R., and Raelin, J. A. (1985). "R&D project termination in high-tech industries," *IEEE Transactions on Engineering Management*, EM-32: 16–23.

16. Green, S. G., Welsh, M. A., and Dehler, G. E. (1993). "Red flags at dawn or predicting project termination at start-up," *Research Technology Management*, 36(3): 10–12.

17. Meredith, J. R. (1988), as cited; Cleland, D. I., and Ireland, L. R. (2002). *Project Management: Strategic Design and Implementation*, 4th ed. New York: McGraw-Hill; Staw, B. M., and Ross, J. (1987, March–April). "Knowing when to pull the plug," *Harvard Business Review*, 65: 68–74; Shafer, S. M., and Mantel, Jr., S. J. (1989). "A decision support system for the project termination decision," *Project Management Journal*, 20(2): 23–28; Tadasina, S. K. (1986). "Support system for the termination decision in R&D management," *Project Management Journal*, 17(5): 97–104; Cooper, R. G., and Kleinschmidt, E. J. (1990). "New product success: A comparison of 'kills' versus successes and failures," *Research and Development Management*, 20(1): 47–63; Royer, I. (2003). "Why bad projects are so hard to kill," *Harvard Business Review*, 81(2): 48–56; Spiller, P. T., and Teubal, M. (1977). "Analysis of R&D failure," *Research Policy*, 6: 254–75; Charvat, J. P. (2002). "How to identify a failing project," articles.techrepublic.com.com/5100-10878_11-1061879.html; Mersino, A. (2001). "Three warning signs that your project is doomed," articles.techrepublic.com.com/5100-10878_11-1046522.html?tag=rbxccnbtr1; Mersino, A. (2001). "Four more warning signs that your project is doomed," articles.techrepublic.com.com/5100-10878_11-1046005.html?tag=rbxccnbtr1.

18. Frame, J. D. (1998). "Closing out the project," in Pinto, J. K. (Ed.), *The Project Management Institute Project Management Handbook*. San Francisco, CA: Jossey-Bass, pp. 237–46; Kumar, V., Sersaud, A. N. S., and Kumar, U. (1996). "To terminate or not an ongoing R&D project: A managerial dilemma," *IEEE Transactions on Engineering Management*,

43(3): 273–84; Pritchard, C. L. (1998). "Project termination: The good, the bad, the ugly," in Cleland, D. I. (Ed.), *Field Guide to Project Management.* New York: Van Nostrand Reinhold, pp. 377–93.

19. Smith, R. (2010, September 1). "Nuclear plant's tear-down is template," *Wall Street Journal,* p. B10; Long, J. (2010). http://articles.chicagotribune.com/2010-06-10/news/ct-met-zion-nuke-plant-0610-20100610_1_ion-plant-exelon-nuclear-exelon-officials; www.chicagobreakingnews.com/2010/06/zion-nuclear-plant-powers-up-for-teardown.html.

20. Field, T. (1997, October 15). "When bad things happen to good projects," *CIO Magazine*; Dignan, L. (2008). "Promises, promises: A look at Waste Management's case against SAP," www.zdnet.com/blog/btl/promises-promises-a-look-at-waste-managements-case-against-sap/833; Kanaracus, C. (2010, May 3). "SAP, Waste Management settle lawsuit," www.computerworld.com/s/article/9176259/SAP_Waste_Management_settle_lawsuit.

21. Spirer, H. F., and Hamburger, D. (1983), as cited.

22. Marsh, P. (2000). "Managing variation, claims, and disputes," in Turner, J. R., and Simister, S. J. (Eds.), *Gower Handbook of Project Management,* 3rd ed. Aldershot, UK: Gower.

23. Bennett, S. C. (2006). "Non-binding arbitration: An introduction," *Dispute Resolution Journal*, 61(2), 22–27.

24. Frame, J. D. (1998), as cited.

25. Spirer, H. F., and Hamburger, D. (1983), as cited.

26. Ranger, S. (2002, May 28). "Government refuses to bail out Libra," *ITWeek,* itweek.co.uk/News/1132159; Arnott, S. (2003, March 13). "Government IT projects squander £1.5bn," *ITWeek,* itweek.co.uk/News/1139438.

27. "Major CSC project cancelled due to delay and cost over-run," www.publictechnology.net/sector/defence-fire-police/major-csc-project-cancelled-due-delay-and-cost-over-run; "Disastrous performance of project leads to big financial hit," www.cfoworld.co.uk/news/financial-planning/3336236/csc-books-943m-it-charge/; "CSC wounded as it books £943m NHS IT charge," www.computerworlduk.com/news/public-sector/3336065/csc-wounded-as-it-books-943m-nhs-it-charge/.

APPENDIX A

The Cumulative Standard Normal Distribution

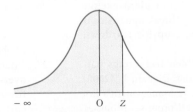

Z	.00	.01	.02	.03	.04	.05	.06	.07	.08	.09
0.0	.5000	.5040	.5080	.5120	.5160	.5199	.5239	.5279	.5319	.5359
0.1	.5398	.5438	.5478	.5517	.5557	.5596	.5636	.5675	.5714	.5753
0.2	.5793	.5832	.5871	.5910	.5948	.5987	.6026	.6064	.6103	.6141
0.3	.6179	.6217	.6255	.6293	.6331	.6368	.6406	.6443	.6480	.6517
0.4	.6554	.6591	.6628	.6664	.6700	.6736	.6772	.6808	.6844	.6879
0.5	.6915	.6950	.6985	.7019	.7054	.7088	.7123	.7157	.7190	.7224
0.6	.7257	.7291	.7324	.7357	.7389	.7422	.7454	.7486	.7518	.7549
0.7	.7580	.7612	.7642	.7673	.7704	.7734	.7764	.7794	.7823	.7852
0.8	.7881	.7910	.7939	.7967	.7995	.8023	.8051	.8078	.8106	.8133
0.9	.8159	.8186	.8212	.8238	.8264	.8289	.8315	.8340	.8365	.8389
1.0	.8413	.8438	.8461	.8485	.8508	.8531	.8554	.8577	.8599	.8621
1.1	.8643	.8665	.8686	.8708	.8729	.8749	.8770	.8790	.8810	.8830
1.2	.8849	.8869	.8888	.8907	.8925	.8944	.8962	.8980	.8997	.9015
1.3	.9032	.9089	.9066	.9082	.9099	.9115	.9131	.9147	.9162	.9177
1.4	.9192	.9207	.9222	.9236	.9251	.9265	.9279	.9292	.9306	.9319
1.5	.9332	.9345	.9357	.9370	.9382	.9394	.9406	.9418	.9429	.9441
1.6	.9452	.9463	.9474	.9484	.9495	.9505	.9515	.9525	.9535	.9545
1.7	.9554	.9564	.9573	.9582	.9591	.9599	.9608	.9616	.9625	.9633
1.8	.9641	.9649	.9656	.9664	.9671	.9678	.9686	.9693	.9699	.9706
1.9	.9713	.9719	.9726	.9732	.9738	.9744	.9750	.9756	.9761	.9767
2.0	.9772	.9778	.9783	.9788	.9793	.9798	.9803	.9808	.9812	.9817
2.1	.9821	.9826	.9830	.9834	.9838	.9842	.9846	.9850	.9854	.9857
2.2	.9861	.9864	.9868	.9871	.9875	.9878	.9881	.9884	.9887	.9890
2.3	.9893	.9896	.9898	.9901	.9904	.9906	.9909	.9911	.9913	.9916
2.4	.9918	.9920	.9922	.9925	.9927	.9929	.9931	.9932	.9934	.9936
2.5	.9938	.9940	.9941	.9943	.9945	.9946	.9948	.9949	.9951	.9952
2.6	.9953	.9955	.9956	.9957	.9959	.9960	.9961	.9962	.9963	.9964
2.7	.9965	.9966	.9967	.9968	.9969	.9970	.9971	.9972	.9973	.9974
2.8	.9974	.9975	.9976	.9977	.9977	.9978	.9979	.9979	.9980	.9981
2.9	.9981	.9982	.9982	.9983	.9984	.9984	.9985	.9985	.9986	.9986
3.0	.99865	.99869	.99874	.99878	.99882	.99886	.99889	.99893	.99897	.99900
3.1	.99903	.99906	.99910	.99913	.99916	.99918	.99921	.99924	.99926	.99929
3.2	.99931	.99934	.99936	.99938	.99940	.99942	.99944	.99946	.99948	.99950
3.3	.99952	.99953	.99955	.99957	.99958	.99960	.99961	.99962	.99964	.99965
3.4	.99966	.99968	.99969	.99970	.99971	.99972	.99973	.99974	.99975	.99976
3.5	.99977	.99978	.99978	.99979	.99980	.99981	.99981	.99982	.99983	.99983
3.6	.99984	.99985	.99985	.99986	.99986	.99987	.99987	.99988	.99988	.99989
3.7	.99989	.99990	.99990	.99990	.99991	.99991	.99992	.99992	.99992	.99992
3.8	.99993	.99993	.99993	.99994	.99994	.99994	.99994	.99995	.99995	.99995
3.9	.99995	.99995	.99996	.99996	.99996	.99996	.99996	.99996	.99997	.99997

Entry represents area under the cumulative standardized normal distribution from $-\infty$ to z.

APPENDIX B

Tutorial for MS Project 2010

EXERCISE A: CONSTRUCTING THE NETWORK: SITE PREPARATION PROJECT

Task	Title	Predecessors	Duration
A	Contract Approval	-	5
B	Site Survey	A	5
C	Permit Application	A	4
D	Grading	B, C	5
E	Sewer Lines	B	7
F	Base Paving	D	3
G	City Approval	C, F	6
H	Final Paving	E, G	8

Using the above information, complete the following tasks:

1. Construct this network using MS Project 2010.
2. Identify the critical path. How long will this project take?
3. Assign and level resources.
4. Suppose Rose is responsible for Activities B and C. Are there any resource conflicts? How do we know?
5. Show the same project with a Gantt chart and a network diagram.

1. CONSTRUCT THIS NETWORK USING MS PROJECT 2010

To create an MS Project 2010 file, the first step is to enter the information on the Project screen. Under "Task Name," list the different tasks and their expected durations. Figure A.1 shows a partially completed network with task names and their respective durations. Note that not all durations have been completed. Further, note that at this point all the activities are shown as starting immediately. In other words, precedence has not yet been assigned to order the activities.

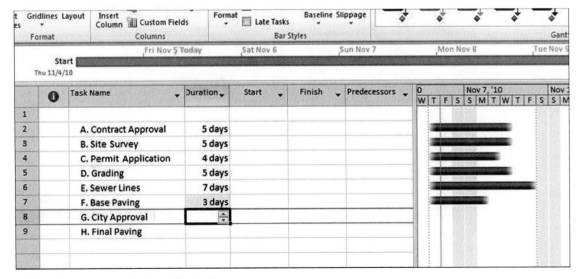

FIGURE A.1   Entering Project Information

The second step is to assign the predecessor relationships to each of the activities. Double-click on Task B, Site Survey. This will open a new dialogue box in the window, as seen in Figure A.2.

Note that one of the tabs in this dialogue box is labeled "Predecessors." Click on this tab to open a second dialogue box. Then click on Task Name, and the list of all activities will come up. Click on the "Contract Approval," activity, as shown in Figure A.3.

Finally, click out of the dialogue box and observe what has happened to the Gantt chart: A precedence arrow has been added from Activity A to Activity B (see Figure A.4). "Start" and "Finish" dates have been automatically created, based on the date the chart was created.

To complete the chart, double-click on each activity and assign its predecessors in the dialogue window. When you have finished, the Gantt chart should look like that shown in Figure A.5.

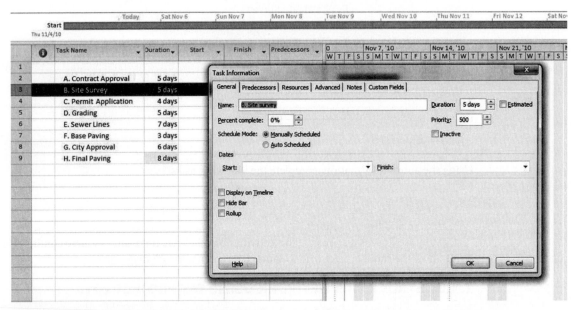

FIGURE A.2 Assigning Predecessor Relationships

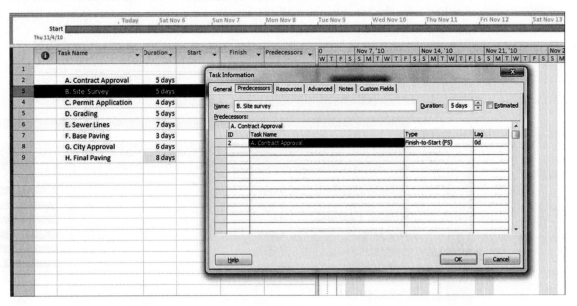

FIGURE A.3 Selecting Predecessors

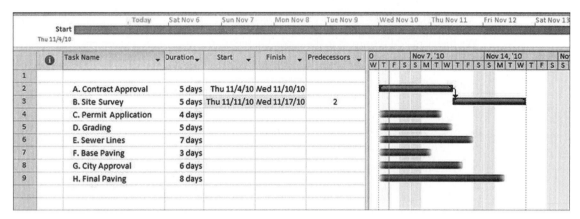

FIGURE A.4   Predecessor Arrow Added

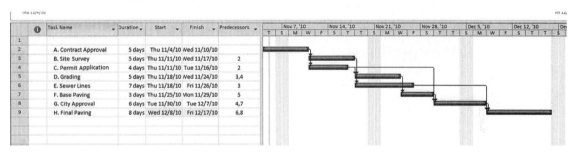

FIGURE A.5   Predecessor Arrows Completed

2. IDENTIFY THE CRITICAL PATH. HOW LONG WILL THIS PROJECT TAKE?

How do you determine which are the critical tasks; that is, what does the project's critical path look like? In order to find this information, click on the "Format" tab at the top of the screen and then check the box that says "Critical Tasks" beneath it. Immediately, on a computer monitor, all the critical activities will be highlighted in red (see Figure A.6). The critical path follows the activity path A – B – D – F – G – H and results in a duration of 32 days (or November 4 through December 17, using the calendar and allowing for weekends off).

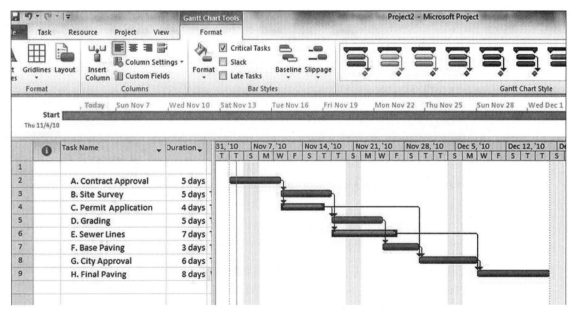

FIGURE A.6   Critical Path and Project Duration Identified

Note: In predecessor column, all activities are assigned a number corresponding to their row in the left-most column. Thus, 'Contract Approval' is assigned the number '2'

3. ASSIGN AND LEVEL RESOURCES

We then can add resources to the project based on the information given below:

Activity	Resource Responsible
A	Todd
B	Rose
C	Rose
D	Mike
E	Josh
F	Todd
G	Mary
H	Todd

Click on the "Resource" tab and then click on "Assign Resources." This will open up a new window for entering all the resource names for the project. Once the name "Todd" has been assigned to Activity A, the screen should look like Figure A.7.

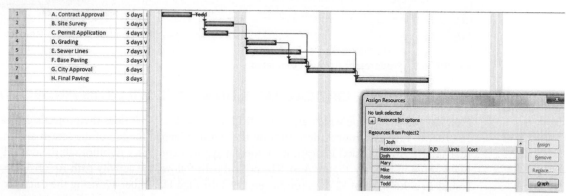

FIGURE A.7   Assigning Resources

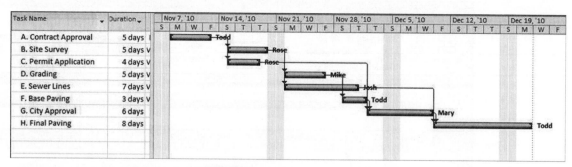

FIGURE A.8   Resource Assignment Completed

Continue assigning resources to the project activities from the people identified in the "Assign Resources" box. The completed resource assignment will look like Figure A.8.

4. SUPPOSE ROSE IS RESPONSIBLE FOR ACTIVITIES B AND C. ARE THERE ANY RESOURCE CONFLICTS? HOW DO WE KNOW?

Will assigning Rose to Activities B and C cause a resource conflict? To determine this information, take a look at the Gantt chart constructed in Figure A.9 and note the human figures in the information column at the left. This is a warning of resource conflict. Just by looking at the Gantt chart, you can see that assigning

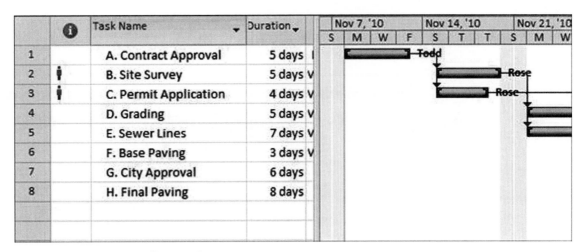

FIGURE A.9   **Resource Conflict Warning**

Rose to Activities B and C will be a problem because both activities are scheduled to begin at the same time. How do you resolve this conflict?

One option is to click on the "Resource" tab and highlight the two activities that are in conflict (B and C). Then, click the "Level Resource" option and a dialogue box will appear in which you can highlight the name of the resource conflict (Rose). Figure A.10 shows the screen with Rose's name highlighted. Click "Level Now" in the box.

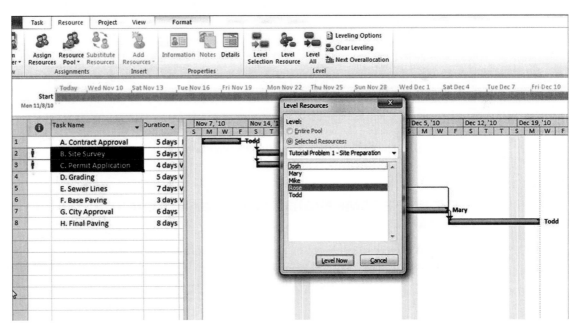

FIGURE A.10   **Leveling Resources**

Notice that the project schedule (Gantt chart shown in Figure A.11) has been modified as a result of the decision to level the resource. As the figure shows, the new precedence ordering for the activities moves Activity C into a sequential relationship with Activity D. The important question is, "What happens to the project's duration as a result of leveling the resources?" Figure A.11 shows that it does not change the expected completion date for this project because there were several days of slack built into Activity C. In this example, delaying the start of Activity C does not affect the project's critical path, as Figure A.12 shows.

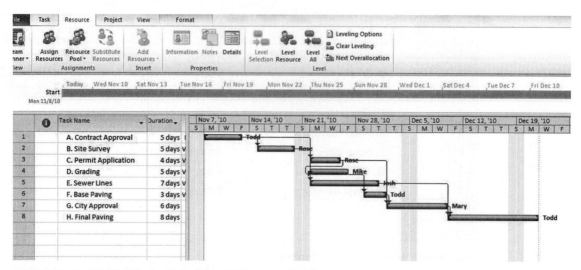

FIGURE A.11 Modified Project Schedule with Resource Leveling

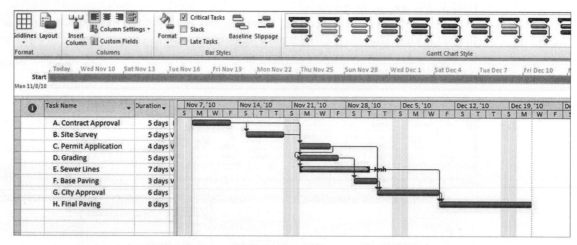

FIGURE A.12 New Project Critical Path After Resource Leveling

5. SHOW THE SAME PROJECT WITH A GANTT CHART AND A NETWORK DIAGRAM

Finally, this project schedule can be shown as a network diagram rather than in Gantt chart format. To do this, click on the "Task" tab on the far left and click on the "Gantt Chart View" option. From the pull-down menu, click on "Network Diagram" and the view shown in Figure A.13 will appear.

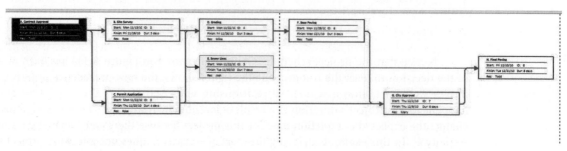

FIGURE A.13 Network Diagram

EXERCISE B: ADDING DETAILS AND UPDATING THE NETWORK FOR AN ONGOING PROJECT

It is important to be able to make mid-project adjustments to a project schedule to reflect the latest information and update the schedule accordingly. Maintaining up-to-date MS Project plans allows you to generate the latest cost information, earned value or other status updates, and any additional reports that will help keep track of the ongoing project.

Consider the Site Preparation Project plan from Exercise A. We have created a resource-leveled schedule that will take 32 days to complete. For simplicity's sake, Mary has replaced Rose for Activity C (Permit Application) to omit the resource conflict from the first exercise (see Figure B.1). This reassignment does not change the network logic or the expected duration of the project; it merely removes the potential resource conflict from the first tutorial exercise.

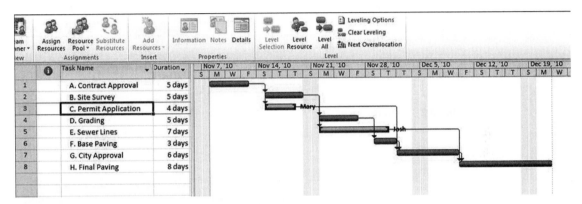

FIGURE B.1   Starting Conditions for Site Preparation Project

More detailed information can be added to this project plan, including details about each activity (lag relationships, priority, activity hours, etc.), assignable costs of materials and equipment, and the hourly cost of each of the assigned resources. In the View tab, select "Resource Sheet" to see the current list of resources for the project, including spaces for their standard and overtime rates, and other pertinent information. Assign the hourly costs for the resources at the following example rates:

Resource	Hourly Cost
Todd	$22/hour
Rose	$30/hour
Mike	$14/hour
Josh	$18/hour
Mary	$10/hour

Fill these values in on the resource sheet shown in Figure B.2.

The next step is to update the actual performance of the project. Suppose that we decide to update the project to the date November 30 on our schedule. The simplest way to do this is to click on the Project tab and the "Update Project" option. This will open a dialogue box requesting the date you wish to update the project to. Once we have set the date to November 30, you will see that several events occur (see Figure B.3). First, the program assumes that all tasks have been successfully completed to that point in time. In the far left column, check marks appear to indicate the completion of the first five activities (A–E). Furthermore, a solid bar is drawn through the middle of the activities completed, while a partial bar appears in Activity F (Base Paving) because this task is only 67% finished.

We can also update the project on a task-by-task basis by clicking on the Task tab and then highlighting each task in order. We have the option of marking each as "Mark on Track," or we can manually click on the options to the left of "Mark on Track" and assign project completion rates of 0%, 25%, 50%, 75%, or 100% complete for each activity. Finally, we can click on the activities themselves on the Gantt chart and, holding

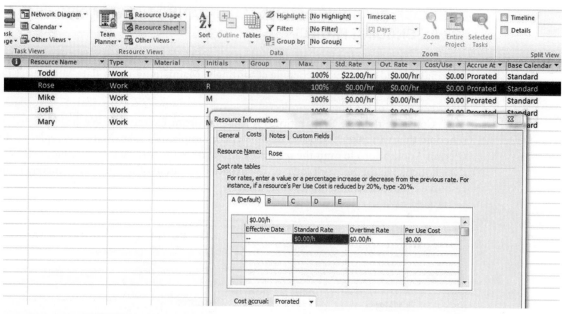

FIGURE B.2   Resource Sheet

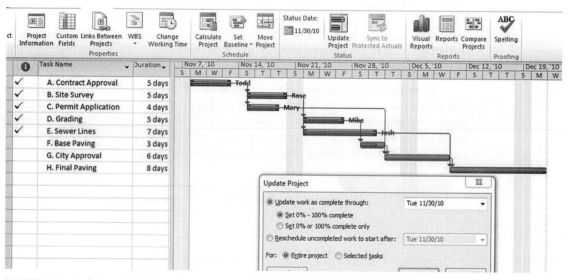

FIGURE B.3   Updating the Project to November 30

down the left mouse button, drag the cursor to the right, over the activity bar, to highlight the amount of work completed on the task. Doing so will identify the task as being complete through a specific date in the schedule.

In addition, we can generate other useful information about the current status of the project. For example, suppose we would like to know about resource usage and project costs to date (remember that for this example, all project costs are understood to be resource costs; no additional costs of materials or machinery are included). We can access this information by clicking on the Project tab and the "Reports" option. In the opened box, click on the "Overview" to pull up a "Project Summary." Figure B.4 shows the summary, which lists the major details of the project as of November 30.

The project summary table highlights all the most important project information, including the scheduled project duration, the amount of scheduled work (in hours) both completed and remaining, and so forth.

Dates			
Start:	Mon 11/8/10	Finish:	Tue 12/21/10
Baseline Start:	NA	Baseline Finish:	NA
Actual Start:	Mon 11/8/10	Actual Finish:	NA
Start Variance:	0 days	Finish Variance:	0 days

Duration			
Scheduled:	32 days	Remaining:	11.16 days
Baseline:	0 days	Actual:	20.84 days
Variance:	32 days	Percent Complete:	65%

Work			
Scheduled:	344 hrs	Remaining:	120 hrs
Baseline:	0 hrs	Actual:	224 hrs
Variance:	344 hrs	Percent Complete:	65%

Costs			
Scheduled:	$6,384.00	Remaining:	$2,064.00
Baseline:	$0.00	Actual:	$4,320.00
Variance:	$6,384.00		

Task Status		Resource Status	
Tasks not yet started:	2	Work Resources:	5
Tasks in progress:	1	Overallocated Work Resources:	0
Tasks completed:	5	Material Resources:	0
Total Tasks:	8	Total Resources:	5

FIGURE B.4   Project Summary

Let us return to our example of the project's status on November 30, but with some different parameters this time. For example, suppose that the actual performance of the project tasks by November 30 were as follows:

Activity	Percentage Completed
A	100
B	100
C	75
D	40
E	40
F	0
G	0
H	0

We can update the progress of our project by taking the following steps: First, on the View tab, click the arrow on "Other Views" and then select "Task Sheet." This will show each activity, the amount of work assigned to complete it, and the amount that has actually been done to date. In the View tab in the "Data" group, click on "Tables" and then click on "Work." It is possible to update all project information, one task at a time, using the information shown in the preceding table. The reconfigured Task Sheet is shown in Figure B.5.

The Task Sheet corresponds to an updated Gantt chart shown in Figure B.6. Note that because we specified the actual work completed, only Activities A and B are shown as having been completed. For the other ongoing activities, the task bars now show only partial completion.

As a last exercise, suppose we wished to determine the earned value for this project as of November 30 with the updated activity status information. There are some steps to create the necessary information for an earned value table. First, it is necessary to set the project baseline. This can be done by clicking the Project tab. In the Schedule group, point to "Set Baseline" and click on this option. This establishes the overall project baseline. Then, in the View tab, in the Data group, click "Tables," and then click on "More Tables" for the Earned Value option. Apply this option and the information becomes available in the earned value table shown in Figure B.7.

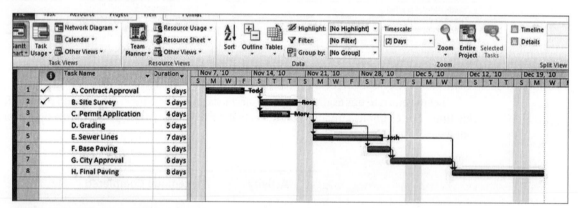

FIGURE B.5 Reconfigured Task Sheet for November 30

	Task Name	Work	Baseline	Variance	Actual	Remaining	% W. Comp.	Add New Colu
1	A. Contract Approval	40 hrs	0 hrs	40 hrs	40 hrs	0 hrs	100%	
2	B. Site Survey	40 hrs	0 hrs	40 hrs	40 hrs	0 hrs	100%	
3	C. Permit Application	32 hrs	0 hrs	32 hrs	24 hrs	8 hrs	75%	
4	D. Grading	40 hrs	0 hrs	40 hrs	16 hrs	24 hrs	40%	
5	E. Sewer Lines	56 hrs	0 hrs	56 hrs	22.4 hrs	33.6 hrs	40%	
6	F. Base Paving	24 hrs	0 hrs	24 hrs	0 hrs	24 hrs	0%	
7	G. City Approval	48 hrs	0 hrs	48 hrs	0 hrs	48 hrs	0%	
8	H. Final Paving	64 hrs	0 hrs	64 hrs	0 hrs	64 hrs	0%	

FIGURE B.6 Reconfigured Gantt Chart

		Task Name	Duration
1	✓	A. Contract Approval	5 days
2	✓	B. Site Survey	5 days
3		C. Permit Application	4 days
4		D. Grading	5 days
5		E. Sewer Lines	7 days
6		F. Base Paving	3 days
7		G. City Approval	6 days
8		H. Final Paving	8 days

FIGURE B.7 Earned Value Table

	Task Name	Planned Value - PV (BCWS)	Earned Value - EV (BCWP)	AC (ACWP)	SV	CV	EAC	BAC	VAC	Add New
1	A. Contract Approval	$880.00	$880.00	$880.00	$0.00	$0.00	$880.00	$880.00	$0.00	
2	B. Site Survey	$1,200.00	$1,200.00	$1,200.00	$0.00	$0.00	$1,200.00	$1,200.00	$0.00	
3	C. Permit Application	$320.00	$240.00	$240.00	($80.00)	$0.00	$320.00	$320.00	$0.00	
4	D. Grading	$560.00	$224.00	$224.00	($336.00)	$0.00	$560.00	$560.00	$0.00	
5	E. Sewer Lines	$1,008.00	$403.20	$403.20	($604.80)	$0.00	$1,008.00	$1,008.00	$0.00	
6	F. Base Paving	$352.00	$0.00	$0.00	($352.00)	$0.00	$528.00	$528.00	$0.00	
7	G. City Approval	$0.00	$0.00	$0.00	$0.00	$0.00	$480.00	$480.00	$0.00	
8	H. Final Paving	$0.00	$0.00	$0.00	$0.00	$0.00	$1,408.00	$1,408.00	$0.00	

The table in Figure B.7 also contains the Planned Value (PV, also referred to as BCWS), Earned Value (EV or BCWP), Actual Cost (ACWP), and schedule and cost variances for each task. In addition, the table calculates the Budget at Completion (BAC) value for each activity to project the likeliest cost to completion, given the current delays in completing several activities. As with the other tables and charts, this information can be continuously updated by adding more information on actual task performance throughout the life of the project.

GLOSSARY

1. Inclusions and Exclusions

This glossary includes terms that are

- Unique or nearly unique to project management (e.g., project scope statement, work package, work breakdown structure, critical path method).
- Not unique to project management, but used differently or with a narrower meaning in project management than in general everyday usage (e.g., early start date, schedule activity).

This glossary generally does not include:

- Application area-specific terms (e.g., project prospectus as a legal document—unique to real estate development).
- Terms used in project management which do not differ in any material way from everyday use (e.g., calendar day, delay).
- Compound terms whose meaning is clear from the combined meanings of the component parts.
- Variants when the meaning of the variant is clear from the base term (e.g., exception report is included, exception reporting is not).

As a result of the above inclusions and exclusions, this glossary includes:

- A preponderance of terms related to Project Scope Management, Project Time Management, and Project Risk Management, since many of the terms used in these Knowledge Areas are unique or nearly unique to project management.
- Many terms from Project Quality Management, since these terms are used more narrowly than in their everyday usage.
- Relatively few terms related to Project Human Resource Management and Project Communications Management, since most of the terms used in these Knowledge Areas do not differ significantly from everyday usage.
- Relatively few terms related to Project Cost Management, Project Integration Management, and Project Procurement Management, since many of the terms used in these Knowledge Areas have narrow meanings that are unique to a particular application area.

2. Common Acronyms

AC	actual cost
ACWP	actual cost of work performed
BAC	budget at completion
BCWP	budgeted cost of work performed
BCWS	budgeted cost of work scheduled
CCB	change control board
COQ	cost of quality
CPAF	cost plus award fee
CPF	cost plus fee
CPFF	cost plus fixed fee
CPI	cost performance index
CPIF	cost plus incentive fee
CPM	critical path methodology
CV	cost variance
EAC	estimate at completion
EF	early finish date
EMV	expected monetary value
ES	early start date
ETC	estimate to complete
EV	earned value
EVM	earned value management
FF	finish-to-finish
FFP	firm fixed price
FMEA	failure mode and effect analysis
FP-EPA	fixed price with economic price adjustment
FPIF	fixed price incentive fee
FS	finish to start
IFB	invitation for bid
LF	late finish date
LOE	level of effort
LS	late start date
OBS	organizational breakdown structure
PDM	precedence diagramming method
PMBOK®	Project Management Body of Knowledge
PMIS	project management information system
PMP®	Project Management Professional
PV	planned value
QA	quality assurance
QC	quality control
RACI	responsible, accountable, consult, and inform
RAM	responsibility assignment matrix
RBS	risk breakdown structure
RFI	request for information
RFP	request for proposal
RFQ	request for quotation
SF	start-to-finish
SOW	statement of work
SPI	schedule performance index
SS	start-to-start
SV	schedule variance
SWOT	strengths, weaknesses, opportunities, and threats
T&M	time and material
TQM	Total Quality Management
WBS	work breakdown structure

3. Definitions

Many of the words defined here have broader, and in some cases different, dictionary definitions.

The definitions use the following conventions:

- In some cases, a single glossary term consists of multiple words (e.g., risk response planning).
- When synonyms are included, no definition is given and the reader is directed to the preferred term (i.e., see preferred term).
- Related terms that are not synonyms are cross-referenced at the end of the definition (i.e., see also related term).

Acceptance Criteria. Those criteria, including performance requirements and essential conditions, which must be met before project deliverables are accepted.

Acquire Project Team [Process]. The process of confirming human resource availability and obtaining the team necessary to complete project assignments.

Activity. A component of work performed during the course of a project.

Activity Attributes [Output/Input]. Multiple attributes associated with each schedule activity that can be included within the activity list. Activity attributes include activity codes, predecessor activities, successor activities, logical relationships, leads and lags, resource requirements, imposed dates, constraints, and assumptions.

Activity Code. One or more numerical or text values that identify characteristics of the work or in some way categorize the schedule activity that allows filtering and ordering of activities within reports.

Activity Duration. The time in calendar units between the start and finish of a schedule activity. See also *duration*.

Activity Identifier. A short unique numeric or text identification assigned to each schedule activity to differentiate that project activity from other activities. Typically unique within any one project schedule network diagram.

Activity List [Output/Input]. A documented tabulation of schedule activities that shows the activity description, activity identifier, and a sufficiently detailed scope of work description so project team members understand what work is to be performed.

Actual Cost (AC). Total costs actually incurred and recorded in accomplishing work performed during a given time period for a schedule activity or work breakdown structure component. Actual cost can sometimes be direct labor hours alone, direct costs alone, or all costs including indirect costs. Also referred to as the actual cost of work performed (ACWP). See also *earned value management* and *earned value technique*.

Actual Cost of Work Performed (ACWP). See *actual cost* (AC).

Actual Duration. The time in calendar units between the actual start date of the schedule activity and either the data date of the project schedule if the schedule activity is in progress or the actual finish date if the schedule activity is complete.

Administer Procurements [Process]. The process of managing procurement relationships, monitoring contract performance, and making changes and corrections as needed.

Analogous Estimating [Technique]. An estimating technique that uses the values of parameters, such as scope, cost, budget, and duration or measures of scale such as size, weight, and complexity from a previous, similar activity as the basis for estimating the same parameter or measure for a future activity.

Application Area. A category of projects that have common components significant in such projects, but are not needed or present in all projects. Application areas are usually defined in terms of either the product (i.e., by similar technologies or production methods) or the type of customer (i.e., internal versus external, government versus commercial) or industry sector (i.e., utilities, automotive, aerospace, information technologies, etc.). Application areas can overlap.

Approved Change Request [Output/Input]. A change request that has been processed through the integrated change control process and approved.

Assumptions. Assumptions are factors that, for planning purposes, are considered to be true, real, or certain without proof or demonstration.

Assumptions Analysis [Technique]. A technique that explores the accuracy of assumptions and identifies risks to the project from inaccuracy, inconsistency, or incompleteness of assumptions.

Authority. The right to apply project resources, expend funds, make decisions, or give approvals.

Backward Pass. The calculation of late finish dates and late start dates for the uncompleted portions of all schedule activities. Determined by working backwards through the schedule network logic from the project's end date. See also *schedule network analysis*.

Baseline. An approved plan for a project, plus or minus approved changes. It is compared to actual performance to determine if performance is within acceptable variance thresholds. Generally refers to the current baseline, but may refer to the original or some other baseline. Usually used with a modifier (e.g., cost performance baseline, schedule baseline, performance measurement baseline, technical baseline).

Bottom-up Estimating [Technique]. A method of estimating a component of work. The work is decomposed into more detail. An estimate is prepared of what is needed to meet the requirements of each of the lower, more detailed pieces of work, and these estimates are then aggregated into a total quantity for the component of work. The accuracy of bottom-up estimating is driven by the size and complexity of the work identified at the lower levels.

Brainstorming [Technique]. A general data gathering and creativity technique that can be used to identify risks, ideas, or solutions to issues by using a group of team members or subject-matter experts.

Budget. The approved estimate for the project or any work breakdown structure component or any schedule activity. See also *estimate*.

Budget at Completion (BAC). The sum of all the budgets established for the work to be performed on a project or a work breakdown structure component or a schedule activity. The total planned value for the project.

Budgeted Cost of Work Performed (BCWP). See *earned value* (EV).

Budgeted Cost of Work Scheduled (BCWS). See *planned value* (PV).

Buffer. See *reserve*.

Buyer. The acquirer of products, services, or results for an organization.

Calendar Unit. The smallest unit of time used in scheduling a project. Calendar units are generally in hours, days, or weeks, but can also be in quarter years, months, shifts, or even in minutes.

Change Control. Identifying, documenting, approving or rejecting, and controlling changes to the project baselines.

Change Control Board (CCB). A formally constituted group of stakeholders responsible for reviewing, evaluating, approving, delaying, or rejecting changes to a project, with all decisions and recommendations being recorded.

Change Control System [Tool]. A collection of formal documented procedures that define how project deliverables and documentation will be controlled, changed, and approved. In most application areas, the change control system is a subset of the configuration management system.

Change Request. Requests to expand or reduce the project scope, modify policies, processes, plans, or procedures, modify costs or budgets, or revise schedules.

Charter. See *project charter*.

Claim. A request, demand, or assertion of rights by a seller against a buyer, or vice versa, for consideration, compensation, or payment under the terms of a legally binding contract, such as for a disputed change.

Close Procurements [Process]. The process of completing each project procurement.

Close Project or Phase [Process]. The process of finalizing all activities across all of the Project Management Process Groups to formally complete the project or phase.

Closing Processes [Process Group]. Those processes performed to finalize all activities across all Project Management Process Groups to formally close the project or phase.

Code of Accounts [Tool]. Any numbering system used to uniquely identify each component of the work breakdown structure.

Collect Requirements [Process]. Collect Requirements is the process of defining and documenting stakeholders' needs to meet the project objectives.

Co-location [Technique]. An organizational placement strategy where the project team members are physically located close to one another in order to improve communication, working relationships, and productivity.

Common Cause. A source of variation that is inherent in the system and predictable. On a control chart, it appears as part of the random process variation (i.e., variation from a process that would be considered normal or not unusual), and is indicated by a random pattern of points within the control limits. Also referred to as random cause. Contrast with *special cause*.

Communication Management Plan [Output/Input]. The document that describes the communications needs and expectations for the project, how and in what format information will be communicated, when and where each communication will be made, and who is responsible for providing each type of communication. The communication management plan is contained in, or is a subsidiary plan of, the project management plan.

Conduct Procurements [Process]. The process of obtaining seller responses, selecting a seller, and awarding a contract.

Configuration Management System [Tool]. A subsystem of the overall project management system. It is a collection of formal documented procedures used to apply technical and administrative direction and surveillance to identify and document the functional and physical characteristics of a product, result, service, or component; control any changes to such characteristics; record and report each change and its implementation status; and support the audit of the products, results, or components to verify conformance to requirements. It includes the documentation, tracking systems, and defined approval levels necessary for authorizing and controlling changes.

Constraint [Input]. The state, quality, or sense of being restricted to a given course of action or inaction. An applicable restriction or limitation, either internal or external to a project, which will affect the performance of the project or a process. For example, a schedule constraint is any limitation or restraint placed on the project schedule that affects when a schedule activity can be scheduled and is usually in the form of fixed imposed dates.

Contingency. See *reserve*.

Contingency Allowance. See *reserve*.

Contingency Reserve [Output/Input]. The amount of funds, budget, or time needed above the estimate to reduce the risk of overruns of project objectives to a level acceptable to the organization.

Contract [Output/Input]. A contract is a mutually binding agreement that obligates the seller to provide the specified product or service or result and obligates the buyer to pay for it.

Control. Comparing actual performance with planned performance, analyzing variances, assessing trends to effect process improvements, evaluating possible alternatives, and recommending appropriate corrective action as needed.

Control Account [Tool]. A management control point where scope, budget (resource plans), actual cost, and schedule are integrated and compared to earned value for performance measurement. See also *work package*.

Control Chart [Tool]. A graphic display of process data over time and against established control limits, and that has a centerline that assists in detecting a trend of plotted values toward either control limit.

Control Costs [Process]. The process of monitoring the status of the project to update the project budget and managing changes to the cost baseline.

Control Limits. The area composed of three standard deviations on either side of the centerline, or mean, of a normal distribution of data plotted on a control chart that reflects the expected variation in the data. See also *specification limits*.

Control Schedule [Process]. The process of monitoring the status of the project to update project progress and managing changes to the schedule baseline.

Control Scope [Process]. The process of monitoring the status of the project and product scope and managing changes to the scope baseline.

Controlling. See *control*.

Corrective Action. Documented direction for executing the project work to bring expected future performance of the project work in line with the project management plan.

Cost Management Plan [Output/Input]. The document that sets out the format and establishes the activities and criteria for planning, structuring, and controlling the project costs. The cost management plan is contained in, or is a subsidiary plan of, the project management plan.

Cost of Quality (COQ) [Technique]. A method of determining the costs incurred to ensure quality. Prevention and appraisal costs (cost of conformance) include costs for quality planning, quality control (QC), and quality assurance to ensure compliance to requirements (i.e., training, QC systems, etc.). Failure costs (cost of non-conformance) include costs to rework products, components, or processes that are non-compliant, costs of warranty work and waste, and loss of reputation.

Cost Performance Baseline. A specific version of the time-phased budget used to compare actual expenditures to planned expenditures to determine if preventive or corrective action is needed to meet the project objectives.

Cost Performance Index (CPI). A measure of cost efficiency on a project. It is the ratio of earned value (EV) to actual costs (AC). CPI = EV divided by AC.

Cost-Plus-Fixed-Fee (CPFF) Contract. A type of cost-reimbursable contract where the buyer reimburses the seller for the seller's allowable costs (allowable costs are defined by the contract) plus a fixed amount of profit (fee).

Cost-Plus-Incentive-Fee (CPIF) Contract. A type of cost-reimbursable contract where the buyer reimburses the seller for the seller's allowable costs (allowable costs are defined by the contract), and the seller earns its profit if it meets defined performance criteria.

Cost-Reimbursable Contract. A type of contract involving payment to the seller for the seller's actual costs, plus a fee typically representing seller's profit. Cost-reimbursable contracts often include incentive clauses where, if the seller meets or exceeds selected project objectives, such as schedule targets or total cost, then the seller receives from the buyer an incentive or bonus payment.

Cost Variance (CV). A measure of cost performance on a project. It is the difference between earned value (EV) and actual cost (AC). CV = EV minus AC.

Crashing [Technique]. A specific type of project schedule compression technique performed by taking action to decrease the total project schedule duration after analyzing a number of alternatives to determine how to get the maximum schedule duration compression for the least additional cost. Typical approaches for crashing a schedule include reducing schedule activity durations and increasing the assignment of resources on schedule activities. See also *fast tracking* and *schedule compression*.

Create WBS (Work Breakdown Structure) [Process]. The process of subdividing project deliverables and project work into smaller, more manageable components.

Criteria. Standards, rules, or tests on which a judgment or decision can be based, or by which a product, service, result, or process can be evaluated.

Critical Activity. Any schedule activity on a critical path in a project schedule. Most commonly determined by using the critical path method. Although some activities are "critical," in the dictionary sense, without being on the critical path, this meaning is seldom used in the project context.

Critical Chain Method [Technique]. A schedule network analysis technique that modifies the project schedule to account for limited resources.

Critical Path. Generally, but not always, the sequence of schedule activities that determines the duration of the project. It is the longest path through the project. See also *critical path methodology*.

Critical Path Methodology (CPM) [Technique]. A schedule network analysis technique used to determine the amount of scheduling flexibility (the amount of float) on various logical network paths in the project schedule network, and to determine the minimum total project duration. Early start and finish dates are calculated by means of a forward pass, using a specified start date. Late finish and start dates are calculated by means of a backward pass, starting from a specified completion date, which sometimes is the project early finish date determined during the forward pass calculation. See also *critical path*.

Data Date. The date up to or through which the project's reporting system has provided actual status and accomplishments. Also called as-of date and time-now date.

Decision Tree Analysis [Technique]. The decision tree is a diagram that describes a decision under consideration and the implications of choosing one or another of the available alternatives. It is used when some future scenarios or outcomes of actions are uncertain. It incorporates probabilities and the costs or rewards of each logical path of events and future decisions, and uses expected monetary value analysis to help the organization identify the relative values of alternate actions. See also *expected monetary value*.

Decomposition [Technique]. A planning technique that subdivides the project scope and project deliverables into smaller, more manageable components, until the project work associated with accomplishing the project scope and providing the deliverables is defined in sufficient detail to support executing, monitoring, and controlling the work.

Defect. An imperfection or deficiency in a project component where that component does not meet its requirements or specifications and needs to be either repaired or replaced.

Defect Repair. The formally documented identification of a defect in a project component with a recommendation to either repair the defect or completely replace the component.

Define Activities [Process]. The process of identifying the specific actions to be performed to produce the project deliverables.

Define Scope [Process]. The process of developing a detailed description of the project and product.

Deliverable [Output/Input]. Any unique and verifiable product, result, or capability to perform a service that must be produced to complete a process, phase, or project. Often used more narrowly in reference to an external deliverable, which is a deliverable that is subject to approval by the project sponsor or customer. See also *product* and *result*.

Delphi Technique [Technique]. An information gathering technique used as a way to reach a consensus of experts on a subject. Experts on the subject participate in this technique anonymously. A facilitator uses a questionnaire to solicit ideas about the important project points related to the subject. The responses are summarized and are then recirculated to the experts for further comment. Consensus may be reached in a few rounds of this process. The Delphi technique helps reduce bias in the data and keeps any one person from having undue influence on the outcome.

Dependency. See *logical relationship*.

Determine Budget [Process]. The process of aggregating the estimated costs of individual activities or work packages to establish an authorized cost baseline.

Develop Human Resource Plan [Process]. The process of identifying and documenting project roles, responsibilities, and required skills, reporting relationships, and creating a staffing management plan.

Develop Project Charter [Process]. The process of developing a document that formally authorizes a project or a phase and documenting initial requirements that satisfy the stakeholder's needs and expectations.

Develop Project Management Plan [Process]. The process of documenting the actions necessary to define, prepare, integrate, and coordinate all subsidiary plans.

Develop Project Team [Process]. The process of improving the competencies, team interaction, and the overall team environment to enhance project performance.

Develop Schedule [Process]. The process of analyzing activity sequences, durations, resource requirements, and schedule constraints to create the project schedule.

Direct and Manage Project Execution [Process]. The process of performing the work defined in the project management plan to achieve the project's objectives.

Distribute Information [Process]. The process of making relevant information available to project stakeholders as planned.

Duration (DU or DUR). The total number of work periods (not including holidays or other nonworking periods) required to complete a schedule activity or work breakdown structure component. Usually expressed as workdays or workweeks. Sometimes incorrectly equated with elapsed time. Contrast with *effort*.

Early Finish Date (EF). In the critical path method, the earliest possible point in time on which the uncompleted portions of a schedule activity (or the project) can finish, based on the schedule network logic, the data date, and any schedule constraints. Early finish dates can change as the project progresses and as changes are made to the project management plan.

Early Start Date (ES). In the critical path method, the earliest possible point in time on which the uncompleted portions of a schedule activity (or the project) can start, based on the schedule network logic, the data date, and any schedule constraints. Early start dates can change as the project progresses and as changes are made to the project management plan.

Earned Value (EV). The value of work performed expressed in terms of the approved budget assigned to that work for a schedule activity or work breakdown structure component. Also referred to as the budgeted cost of work performed (BCWP).

Earned Value Management (EVM). A management methodology for integrating scope, schedule, and resources, and for objectively measuring project performance and progress. Performance is measured by determining the budgeted cost of work performed (i.e., earned value) and comparing it to the actual cost of work performed (i.e., actual cost).

Earned Value Technique (EVT) [Technique]. A specific technique for measuring the performance of work and used to establish the performance measurement baseline (PMB).

Effort The number of labor units required to complete a schedule activity or work breakdown structure component. Usually expressed as staff hours, staff days, or staff weeks. Contrast with *duration*.

Enterprise Environmental Factors [Output/Input]. Any or all external environmental factors and internal organizational environmental factors that surround or influence the project's success. These factors are from any or all of the enterprises involved in the project, and include organizational culture and structure, infrastructure, existing resources, commercial databases, market conditions, and project management software.

Estimate [Output/Input]. A quantitative assessment of the likely amount or outcome. Usually applied to project costs, resources, effort, and durations and is usually preceded by a modifier (i.e., preliminary, conceptual, feasibility, order-of-magnitude, definitive). It should always include some indication of accuracy (e.g., ±*x* percent). See also *budget*.

Estimate Activity Durations [Process]. The process of approximating the number of work periods needed to complete individual activities with estimated resources.

Estimate Activity Resources [Process]. The process of estimating the type and quantities of material, people, equipment, or supplies required to perform each activity.

Estimate at Completion (EAC) [Output/Input]. The expected total cost of a schedule activity, a work breakdown structure component, or the project when the defined scope of work will be completed. The EAC may be calculated based on performance to date or estimated by the project team based on other factors, in which case it is often referred to as the latest revised estimate. See also *earned value technique* and *estimate to complete*.

Estimate Costs [Process]. The process of developing an approximation of the monetary resources needed to complete project activities.

Estimate to Complete (ETC) [Output/Input]. The expected cost needed to complete all the remaining work for a schedule activity, work breakdown structure component, or the project. See also *earned value technique* and *estimate at completion*.

Execute. Directing, managing, performing, and accomplishing the project work, providing the deliverables, and providing work performance information.

Executing Processes [Process Group]. Those processes performed to complete the work defined in the project management plan to satisfy the project objectives.

Expected Monetary Value (EMV) [Analysis]. A statistical technique that calculates the average outcome when the future includes scenarios that may or may not happen. A common use of this technique is within decision tree analysis.

Expert Judgment [Technique]. Judgment provided based upon expertise in an application area, knowledge area, discipline, industry, etc. as appropriate for the activity being performed. Such expertise may be provided by any group or person with specialized education, knowledge, skill, experience, or training.

Failure Mode and Effect Analysis (FMEA) [Technique]. An analytical procedure in which each potential failure mode in every component of a product is analyzed to determine its effect on the reliability of that component and, by itself or in combination with other possible failure modes, on the reliability of the product or system and on the required function of the component; or the examination of a product (at the system and/or lower levels) for all ways that a failure may occur. For each potential failure, an estimate is made of its effect on the total system and of its impact. In addition, a review is undertaken of the action planned to minimize the probability of failure and to minimize its effects.

Fast Tracking [Technique]. A specific project schedule compression technique that changes network logic to overlap phases that would normally be done in sequence, such as the design phase and construction phase, or to perform schedule activities in parallel. See also *crashing* and *schedule compression*.

Finish Date. A point in time associated with a schedule activity's completion. Usually qualified by one of the following: actual, planned, estimated, scheduled, early, late, baseline, target, or current.

Finish-to-Finish (FF). The logical relationship where completion of work of the successor activity cannot finish until the completion of work of the predecessor activity. See also *logical relationship*.

Finish-to-Start (FS). The logical relationship where initiation of work of the successor activity depends upon the completion of work of the predecessor activity. See also *logical relationship*.

Firm-Fixed-Price (FFP) Contract. A type of fixed price contract where the buyer pays the seller a set amount (as defined by the contract), regardless of the seller's costs.

Fixed-Price-Incentive-Fee (FPIF) Contract. A type of contract where the buyer pays the seller a set amount (as defined by the contract), and the seller can earn an additional amount if the seller meets defined performance criteria.

Float. Also called slack. See *total float* and *free float*.

Flowcharting [Technique]. The depiction in a diagram format of the inputs, process actions, and outputs of one or more processes within a system.

Forecast. An estimate or prediction of conditions and events in the project's future based on information and knowledge available at the time of the forecast. The information is based on the project's past performance and expected future performance, and includes information that could impact the project in the future, such as estimate at completion and estimate to complete.

Forward Pass. The calculation of the early start and early finish dates for the uncompleted portions of all network activities. See also *schedule network analysis* and *backward pass*.

Free Float. The amount of time that a schedule activity can be delayed without delaying the early start date of any immediately following schedule activities. See also *total float*.

Functional Manager. Someone with management authority over an organizational unit within a functional organization. The manager of any group that actually makes a product or performs a service. Sometimes called a line manager.

Functional Organization. A hierarchical organization where each employee has one clear superior, and staff are grouped by areas of specialization and managed by a person with expertise in that area.

Gantt Chart [Tool]. A graphic display of schedule-related information. In the typical bar chart, schedule activities or work breakdown structure components are listed down the left side of the chart, dates are shown across the top, and activity durations are shown as date-placed horizontal bars.

Grade. A category or rank used to distinguish items that have the same functional use (e.g., "hammer"), but do not share the same requirements for quality (e.g., different hammers may need to withstand different amounts of force).

Hammock Activity. See *summary activity*.

Historical Information. Documents and data on prior projects including project files, records, correspondence, closed contracts, and closed projects.

Human Resource Plan. A document describing how roles and responsibilities, reporting relationships, and staffing management will be addressed and structured for the project. It is contained in or is a subsidiary plan of the project.

Identify Risks [Process]. The process of determining which risks may affect the project and documenting their characteristics.

Identify Stakeholders [Process]. The process of identifying all people or organizations impacted by the project, and documenting relevant information regarding their interests, involvement, and impact on project success.

Imposed Date. A fixed date imposed on a schedule activity or schedule milestone, usually in the form of a "start no earlier than" and "finish no later than" date.

Influence Diagram [Tool]. A graphical representation of situations showing causal influences, time ordering of events, and other relationships among variables and outcomes.

Initiating Processes [Process Group]. Those processes performed to define a new project or a new phase of an existing project by obtaining authorization to start the project or phase.

Input [Process Input]. Any item, whether internal or external to the project, that is required by a process before that process proceeds. May be an output from a predecessor process.

Inspection [Technique]. Examining or measuring to verify whether an activity, component, product, result, or service conforms to specified requirements.

Invitation for Bid (IFB). Generally, this term is equivalent to request for proposal. However, in some application areas, it may have a narrower or more specific meaning.

Issue. A point or matter in question or in dispute, or a point or matter that is not settled and is under discussion or over which there are opposing views or disagreements.

Lag [Technique]. A modification of a logical relationship that directs a delay in the successor activity. For example, in a finish-to-start dependency with a ten-day lag, the successor activity cannot start until ten days after the predecessor activity has finished. See also *lead*.

Late Finish Date (LF). In the critical path method, the latest possible point in time that a schedule activity may be completed based upon the schedule network logic, the project completion date, and any constraints assigned to the schedule activities without violating a schedule constraint or delaying the project completion date. The late finish dates are determined during the backward pass calculation of the project schedule network.

Late Start Date (LS). In the critical path method, the latest possible point in time that a schedule activity may begin based upon the schedule network logic, the project completion date, and any constraints assigned to the schedule activities without violating a schedule constraint or delaying the project completion date. The late start dates are determined during the backward pass calculation of the project schedule network.

Lead [Technique]. A modification of a logical relationship that allows an acceleration of the successor activity. For example, in a finish-to-start dependency with a ten-day lead, the successor activity can start ten days before the predecessor activity has finished. A negative lead is equivalent to a positive lag. See also *lag*.

Lessons Learned [Output/Input]. The learning gained from the process of performing the project. Lessons learned may be identified